CATION
Omay, Adrienne and Nenita

...uthern Africa (Pty) Ltd
...en Eiland, Cape Town
... Ltd

...branches and representatives

...uthern Africa (Pty) Ltd 1979

...ed)
...er)

The Shaping of South African Society, 1652–1820

EDITED BY
Richard Elphick and Hermann Giliomee

Longman Penguin So
Marine Drive, Paarde
And Longman Group
London

Associated companies.
throughout the world

First published 1979

ISBN 0 582 64644 8 (cas
0 582 64687 1 (pap

Printed in South Africa by
Printpak (Cape) Ltd
Cape Town

Longman

Contents

Figures

Tables

Contributors

James C. Armstrong is writing a doctoral dissertation on Cape slavery during the Company period. He is Field Director of the Library of Congress in Nairobi, Kenya.

Richard Elphick studied at the University of Toronto, University of California at Los Angeles and Yale University. His Yale Ph.D. thesis has been published as *Kraal and Castle: Khoikhoi and the Founding of White South Africa* (New Haven and London, 1977). He is Associate Professor of History at Wesleyan University, Middletown, Connecticut, U.S.A.

William M. Freund obtained his doctorate from Yale University in 1971 with a thesis on the Batavian Period at the Cape. He was formerly Senior Lecturer in History at Ahmadu Bello University, Zaria, Nigeria. His publications include 'Race in the Social Structure of South Africa, 1652—1836' in *Race and Class*, XVIII, (1976).

Hermann Giliomee is a graduate of the University of Stellenbosch where he is at present Senior Lecturer. A revision of his doctoral dissertation on the British occupation of the Cape from 1795—1803 was published as *Die Kaap tydens die Eerste Britse Bewind* (Cape Town, 1975).

Leonard Guelke studied at the University of Cape Town, York University and the University of Toronto, where he completed his doctoral dissertation on the early European settlement of South Africa. He is Associate Professor of Geography at the University of Waterloo, Ontario, Canada and the author of many scholarly articles.

Martin Legassick studied at the Universities of Cape Town, Oxford, Ghana and California (Los Angeles), and received a Ph.D. degree from U.C.L.A. in 1969 for a thesis entitled 'The Griqua, the Sotho-Tswana, and the missionaries, 1780—1840: the politics of a frontier zone'. He has published extensively on South African history in articles dealing with periods from the pre-colonial to the contemporary. He is lecturing in Sociology at the University of Warwick, Coventry, in the U.K.

Gerrit Schutte studied history at Utrecht University, where he received a doctorate in 1974. His thesis on the Patriots in the Netherlands and the Dutch colonies was published as *De Nederlandse Patriotten en de Koloniën: Een onderzoek naar hun denkbeelden en optreden, 1770—1800* (Groningen, 1974). He teaches in the Department of History at the Free University, Amsterdam.

Robert Shell was an undergraduate student at the University of Cape Town and did his M.A. at the University of Rochester. He is now a graduate student at Yale University where he is doing doctoral research on the slaves and free blacks at the Cape.

Acknowledgements

We are grateful to the Southern African Research Program (SARP), whose award of a fellowship to Hermann Giliomee in 1977—78 made possible the final editing of this book and the redrafting of the last chapter. SARP is funded by the National Endowment for the Humanities and the Ford Foundation, and is located at Yale University.

Hermann Giliomee wishes to thank Leonard Thompson and Yale University for a post-doctoral research fellowship in 1973, when this project was conceived and planned; and the University of Stellenbosch for leave of absence for three visits to the United States, during which much of the editorial work was done. Richard Elphick is grateful to the National Endowment for the Humanities and the Meigs fund of Wesleyan University for making possible his visit to South Africa in 1976; he also wishes to thank Nico and Ellen Smith for gracious hospitality, and the Department of Entomology, University of Stellenbosch, for providing office space. Both of us are indebted to Robin Winks for much encouragement and advice; to Edna Haran, Jane Tosto, and June Urquhart for expert typing; and to Betty Barton of Wesleyan University and Niklaas Plaatjes of the University of Stellenbosch, for help in many concrete ways.

We wish especially to thank Gerrit Schutte, who completed the first draft of his chapter in accordance with our original request and then readily consented to make extensive cuts, alterations and additions to fit the evolving structure of the book.

We are grateful to Christina Millar of the Longman staff, whose tolerance as deadlines were missed and assistance in the preparation of the book made the publication an agreeable venture.

We and other contributors received much help in our research and writing; this is acknowledged at appropriate places throughout the book.

RICHARD ELPHICK
HERMANN GILIOMEE

Abbreviations

Archives

Unless otherwise indicated, all documentary series are in the Cape Town depot of the South African State Archives. KA denotes the Koloniaal Archief, and KZ the Kamer Zeeland, series in the Algemeen Rijksarchief, The Hague. Other series in the Algemeen Rijksarchief are prefaced by AR.

DO   Deeds Office, Cape Town
LM   Leibbrandt's manuscripts
LMS   Archives of the London Missionary Society, School of Oriental and African Studies, London
MMS   Archives of the Methodist Missionary Society, London
PEMS Archives of the Paris Evangelical Missionary Society, Paris
PRO   Public Record Office, London
Staf Staffordshire County Record Office, Stafford, England

Other abbreviations

AYB   *Archives Yearbook for South African History*
DR   Dagregister
JAH   *Journal of African History*
KP   *Kaapse Plakkaatboek,* ed M.K. Jeffreys, *et al*
RCC   *Records of the Cape Colony,* ed. G.M. Theal
Res   *Resolusies van die Politieke Raad* (Suid-Afrikaanse Argiefstukke)
Res   Resolution
RZA   *Reizen in Zuid-Afrika in de Hollandse Tijd,* ed. E.C. Godée Molsbergen
VOC   Dutch East India Company
VRJ   *Journal of Jan van Riebeeck,* ed. H.B. Thom
VRS   Van Riebeeck Society
XVII Heren XVII

Conventions, terminology and units of currency

Foreign words are italicised when they first appear. Unless defined in the text or self-explanatory, these words are briefly explained in the glossary at the end of the book.

In this work the terms 'white' and 'European' are used interchangeably. The editors use the term 'European' in their own chapters for reasons explained in fn. †, p. 359. Those peoples whom modern scholars usually call 'San' are denoted in this book as '(Khoisan) hunter-gatherers' or '(Khoisan) hunters'. In a few instances where the text focuses on colonists' perceptions of these peoples, the term 'Bushmen' is used in quotation marks. Some of the reasons for avoiding the name 'San' are explained in fn. ‡, p. 4.

Almost all prices in this book are cited in guilders (florins) or rixdollars (in Dutch, *rijksdaalders*). In the VOC period a rixdollar was worth approximately 2½ guilders. Readers who wish to explore the intricacies of Cape currency should begin with C.R. Boxer, *The Dutch Seaborne Empire* (London, 1965), pp. 304–05. Some idea of the value of the guilder and rixdollar can be found on pp. 55, 57–58, 64, 66, 89–90, 100–01 and 184 of this book.

Introduction

Three hundred years ago the Cape Colony was a poor, underpopulated territory of interest to no one but its inhabitants, its neighbours and a few inquisitive travellers. Yet in this colony there developed a complex society which in part prefigured that of modern South Africa. And South Africa is much that the early Cape Colony was not — rich, populous and of intense interest to the whole world.

This book is about the Cape Colony in its formative early years — 1652 to c. 1820. During this period began the integration of southern Africa into a world economy, and the dominance of Europeans over blacks, which have since been the main themes of South African history. Not of course that every feature of modern South Africa can be traced to this era. The Great Trek, the conquest of most Bantu-speaking chiefdoms, the mineral revolution, urbanisation, the rise of Afrikaner nationalism — all followed this era and all were important. But each intensified, modified or extended patterns of social and economic organisation established in the early Cape Colony. This book attempts to analyse the development of these early patterns.

The historiography of the early Cape is, with two or three outstanding exceptions, undistinguished. Many studies are very narrow in compass; others are based not on systematic documentary research, but on the published compilations of Moodie and Leibbrandt, or on no primary research at all. Important categories of primary documentation are only now being exploited. For this reason the editors of this book sought contributions only from scholars who had recently done prolonged research in archives in South Africa, the Netherlands or Great Britain.

The editors were concerned not only about the comparative neglect of the documents, but about the limited questions thus far asked of them. For example, most historians of the Cape, like those of many regions of European colonisation, have given inadequate attention to non-Europeans: in this case the slaves, Khoikhoi, Khoisan hunter-gatherers, Bantu-speakers, free blacks and persons of mixed descent. This book attempts to redress the balance. Its focus, however, is the Cape Colony, not southern Africa as a whole. Thus contributors deal with groups who lived in colonial society or, like the Griqua, emanated from it. Communities indigenous to southern Africa — the Khoikhoi, hunter-gatherers and Bantu-speakers — are studied only in so far as they interacted with the colony.

Moreover, traditional historiography has tended to treat the early Cape in isolation from the rest of the world. Recently, it is true, the developing field of African history has helped historians to see the Cape as part of the African continent, a viewpoint reflected in several chapters of this book. However, there are other contexts in which the colony can be placed. It was, for example, a slave society; it bears comparison with many New World colonies and can be enlightened by insights emerging from the fertile historiography of comparative slavery. It was also a frontier society, and questions raised by the study of frontiers in America and elsewhere can appropriately be asked about the Cape. And, of course, the Cape Colony was by definition a colonial society, part of the vast empires of the Dutch East India Company and, latterly, of the British and Batavian governments — a relationship which has been curiously under-researched in Cape historiography. The contributors to this book are aware of these perspectives and have read extensively in the comparative literature appropriate to their chapters. This reading is reflected in the questions they ask and the insights they offer: they have not tried to write systematic comparative history.

The editors did not wish to impose a uniform tone or conceptual scheme on the contributors. Thus there are considerable differences of opinion between some chapters; for example, on the relative importance assigned to race and class in social stratification. Nonetheless, one perspective did emerge spontaneously in all parts of the book. Much previous writing on Cape history has dealt with the activities of individuals — governors, commissioners, explorers or chiefs — and central government policies. This book, by contrast, tends to emphasise groups over individuals, process over episode, structure over policy. For some contributors these emphases reflect only a desire to explore previously neglected themes; for others they are rooted in convictions about the nature of history. But all would probably agree that, in the early Cape Colony, individuals and their policies rarely changed the direction of social development. This was true even of the highest officials who, generally speaking, could not or would not control those developments which interest modern readers most: the incorporation of native peoples, the formation of classes, the development of 'racial' attitudes. The comparative weakness of government in social matters is a major theme of the period 1652–1820, one which justifies treating it as a unit, as we have done in this work.

The book ends at around 1820. A number of very different events occurred between 1810 and 1820 which, we feel, together formed a watershed dividing our era from its successor. In 1811 the colonial government effectively separated European settlement from Xhosa chiefdoms at the Fish River, thus ending the first phase of European-Xhosa conflict on the Eastern Frontier. In 1815, by the Treaty of Vienna, the Cape Colony was formally turned over to Britain: this transfer ended the transitional era in Cape governance, and facilitated more active intervention of the imperial factor in South African affairs. In 1815 the last of a long series of rebellions of European farmers against colonial governments occurred; the next response of the farmers would be not rebellion but the decisive withdrawal from the colony known as the Great Trek. And, finally, in this decade the Griqua consolidated a polity beyond the Northern Frontier, thus creating a temporary order in that troubled region.

This volume consists of four parts. Part one deals with the major population groups in the colony: chapter one with the Khoisan indigenes, chapter two with the free European agriculturalists (freeburghers), and chapter three with the Asian and African slaves. The final chapter of part one describes several processes of interaction among these three groups and introduces a fourth group, the free blacks.

Part two concerns a more traditional topic — relations between rulers and their subjects at the Cape. The authors deal with this theme by offering a synthetic and structural analysis of long periods which historians have normally fragmented: the era of the Dutch East India Company (1652—1795) in chapter five, and of the transitional British and Batavian regimes (1795—1820) in chapter six.

Part three examines the expansion of the Cape Colony and the formation and development of the two most important Cape frontiers — the Northern Frontier (chapter seven) and the Eastern Frontier (chapter eight). Chapter nine offers a reinterpretation of the freeburgher rebellions on the Eastern Frontier.

In the final chapter the editors review the development of social stratification over the whole period. This review is based not only on their own research but also on the preceding chapters of the book.

These ten chapters do not cover all the important topics of this period nor, taken together, do they form a thorough or definitive history of the Cape Colony. There is, for example, too little on European settlement in the seventeenth century, too little on Cape Town throughout. Large areas of the frontier are passed over, particularly in the northeast and northwest. Moreover, social history is stressed far more than cultural or economic history. Yet, despite its gaps and other imperfections, this volume is fairly reflective of the present state of research. The authors and editors hope that it will stimulate further enquiry into the fascinating and complex processes which first shaped South African society.

The major population groups

PART I

The major population groups

The Khoisan to c. 1770[*]

Richard Elphick

Jan van Riebeeck did not found the Cape Colony in an empty land. In 1652, when he set foot on the shores of Table Bay, the territories to the north and east had been occupied for centuries by the Khoikhoi ('Hottentots') and for millenia by hunter-gatherers ('Bushmen'). For the next 150 years the colony's expansion would be both hindered and assisted by these peoples. Yet until recently many writers on Cape history have dismissed them with a paragraph or even a sentence.[1] C.W. de Kiewiet's summary of Khoikhoi decline is typical:

> The Hottentots broke down undramatically and simply. Their end had little of the tragedy which lies in the last struggles of a dying race.[2]

The collapse of Khoikhoi in the face of colonial expansion was indeed 'undramatic' in that there were few decisive wars and few heroic personalities in the story. But it was scarcely 'simple'. It consisted of a complex web of social and economic processes which is difficult to reconstruct given the scantiness of our data.

The major questions facing the historian are why Khoikhoi society and economy disintegrated so rapidly, and why Khoikhoi were incorporated so easily into colonial society as an inferior caste. By contrast the so-called 'Bushmen' seem to have put up more ferocious and protracted resistance. How is this difference to be explained?

It is often assumed that the failure of the Khoikhoi was due to their small numbers[3] — perhaps about 50,000 in the whole of the southwestern Cape.†

---

* The first four sections of this chapter are based on research done for my Ph.D. thesis, now published as *Kraal and Castle: Khoikhoi and the Founding of White South Africa* (New Haven and London, 1977). The remaining sections are based on less systematic archival research and should therefore be regarded as presenting more tentative conclusions. I am grateful to Jeffrey Butler, Hermann Giliomee, Leonard Guelke, Adrian Leftwich and Leonard Thompson for generous and helpful advice on this chapter.

† The term 'southwestern Cape' is used in this chapter and in chapters 4 and 10 to denote lands south and west of a line running from the Oliphants River mouth to modern Tulbagh, and thence to the mouth of the Breede River.

However, the population of the colony itself was also very small (only 394 Europeans and slaves in 1662, and 3,878 in 1714).[4] Population figures, though not irrelevant, do not tell the whole story. Neither does the catastrophic smallpox epidemic of 1713, which is often used to explain Khoikhoi decline. True, this disaster apparently swept away the majority of Khoikhoi in the southwestern Cape, but it merely consummated a long process of breakdown among Khoikhoi which was already far advanced by 1713. The first part of this chapter will be devoted to a description and explanation of that breakdown.

The Khoisan: Khoikhoi and hunters

The Khoisan were brown-skinned, usually rather short, and had 'peppercorn' rather than frizzy hair. Their languages were all characterised by the use of implosive consonants ('clicks') and were not related to the Bantu languages now prevalent in most of sub-equatorial Africa. The term 'Khoisan' is an amalgam, coined by scholars, of names for the two groups into which Khoisan are conventionally divided: the Khoikhoi ('Hottentots') who kept cattle and sheep, and the San ('Bushmen') hunter-gatherers who did not. The two groups are in fact far harder to distinguish than historians have usually assumed, and the relationships between them are complex.

The hunter-gatherers were scattered throughout much of sub-equatorial Africa long before the Christian era. Their economies varied with the terrain in which they lived, though they always consisted of some combination of hunting, fishing or gathering. These economies forced them into constant movement, but within very circumscribed areas. Over the many centuries that they occupied southern Africa, the languages of hunter-gatherers and some aspects of their material and intellectual culture diversified enormously. Because of this diversity, and for other reasons,‡ I have avoided giving them the quasi-ethnic name 'San' and refer to them simply as 'hunter-gatherers' or (more simply but less accurately) as 'hunters'.

In contrast to the hunters, the Khoikhoi were remarkably homogeneous. Though scattered over much of southern Africa, they all spoke closely related dialects of the same language and practised roughly the same culture.

‡ My main reasons for not using the terms 'Bushmen' or 'San' are (1) that they have been used in so many ways in scholarly and non-scholarly literature that they convey very different meanings to different people; (2) that they imply that the hunters were a culturally cohesive group like Khoikhoi — which they were not; and   (3) that 'San' was a pejorative term used by Khoikhoi.

Unlike the hunters, who rarely belonged to a unit larger than a small hunting band, the Khoikhoi were aware of their cultural and historic bonds with other Khoikhoi, often hundreds of miles away. Apparently all Khoikhoi called themselves 'Khoikhoi' (or a dialectical variant thereof);[5] this term means 'men of men', and they used it to distinguish themselves both from Bantu-speaking negroes and from hunters.

The Khoikhoi originated not (as has long been supposed) in northern or eastern Africa, but in or near northern Botswana, where one still finds hunters whose language and kinship structure closely approximate those of Khoikhoi. The Khoikhoi were originally a hunter community who stole or otherwise acquired livestock from early agricultural migrants into the region, probably speakers of Bantu or Central Sudanic languages.[6] The date of this 'pastoral revolution' cannot yet be established, though it was probably in the first millenium A.D. The pastoral revolution forced the Khoikhoi to move into new pastures to support their growing herds and flocks. The needs of their new economy, aided by a social structure which permitted easy fission of clans and tribes, was the mainspring of their extraordinary expansion over southern Africa.

The main directions of this expansion can only be speculatively reconstructed. Most likely the Khoikhoi first moved into the grasslands of Matabeleland and the Transvaal (where they came into contact with Bantu-speaking cultivators) and hence to the tributaries of the Orange River. Here a split occurred: one group (consisting of the ancestors of the Cape Khoikhoi) passed down to the southern coast and then westward along the coastal plains to the Cape of Good Hope; the other group (ancestors of the Nama) pushed westward along the Orange until they neared the Atlantic coast, and then split into two groups, one moving north into Namibia, the other south towards the Cape. The Cape Khoikhoi and the southern wing of the Nama met again in the region 100 to 200 km north of Cape Town.[7]

Those Khoikhoi who finally reached the southwestern Cape were pure pastoralists and planted no crops except *dagga*. This was so even though their ancestors had been in close contact with Bantu-speaking cultivators at different stages of their expansion — particularly, it seems, in the high grasslands of the Transvaal.

The pastoralism of these Khoikhoi influenced their social and political structure in several ways. Since Khoikhoi herders had to move constantly and disperse widely in search of fresh pasture, their society was based not on the possession of land, but on small kin groups whose members were related to each other through the male line. Several of these patrilineal clans were often loosely organised together in a 'tribe'¶, whose chief could overrule the clan heads only if he was extraordinarily wealthy or talented. Political power at both tribe and clan level was weak and a function more of individual merit and achievement than of the legitimacy of the office or the command of force. Only rarely did a strong chief pass his rule on to an equally strong successor. Frequently one clan under a resourceful or resentful leader hived off into new pastures and soon ceased to pay any but ritual allegiance to the tribal chief. This tradition of fission favoured the rapid expansion of Khoikhoi, but also hindered their consolidation into large and stable political units.

Because they were based on pastoralism, the economies of the Khoikhoi tribes were extremely fragile. Most wealth consisted of livestock, and livestock was a vulnerable possession. It could be stolen by neighbouring Khoikhoi or hunters, killed by many kinds of wild animals, or slowly consumed by disease and drought. Such disasters were frequent, and wealthy individuals and tribes were often impoverished overnight. Since livestock was owned by families and individuals rather than by clans or tribes, resources were not easily pooled in rebuilding herds after a disaster. The only obvious hope for the newly poor was to capture livestock from their neighbours, and thus to perpetuate the endemic (though not very sanguinary) warfare characteristic of the Khoikhoi. Thus the economic position of the wealthy was perpetually insecure, as was the political authority of rulers to the degree that such authority was tied to wealth.

Individuals and groups who had suddenly lost their livestock had two options other than going to war. They could hire themselves out as herders for wealthy Khoikhoi, who would pay them in animals suitable for rebuilding their herds. Or, if the disaster had affected their neighbours as well, they could fall back on hunting and gathering. Even in times of prosperity the Khoikhoi continued to hunt and gather, and in times of distress they could rely on these as their sole means of subsistence.

Of course such former pastoralists might try to recover their stock by robbery and, if successful, return to their preferred economy of herding. In many areas of Khoikhoi habitation there thus recurred an 'ecological cycle' from pastoralism to hunting and back to pastoralism. The downward phase of the cycle was marked by a decline in the number of Khoikhoi engaged in pastoralism and by an increase of hunter-robbers; the upward phase was the exact reverse. This cycle was both a cause and an effect of the economic

¶ Since we lack information on the lineage structure of most Khoikhoi communities, it is impossible to give a structural definition of the term 'tribe'. By this term I simply mean a group larger than a clan which regularly called itself, or was called by others, by a specific name.

instability of the Khoikhoi regions.[8]

Despite their intermittent poverty, some Khoikhoi lived in a most favoured region of Africa, namely the southwestern Cape. Here the heavy rainfall and excellent pastures supported a population which was rather high by Khoikhoi standards. All the tribes of this area spoke approximately the same dialect of Khoikhoi and practised the same culture. Their chiefly lineages were related to each other and to other chiefs further east.[9] I call this cluster of tribes the Western Cape Khoikhoi. The main groups of the cluster were the 'Peninsular'** clans and tribes near Table Bay, the Cochoqua just to the north of the bay, the Guriqua to the north of the Cochoqua, and the Chainouqua and Hessequa, whose pastures stretched from Hottentots-Holland to near modern Swellendam (see Fig. 1.1, p. 8).

The lands of the Western Cape Khoikhoi were suitable for cultivation as well as for pastoralism, but before 1652 these Khoikhoi, unlike most pastoralists throughout the world, did not have to compete with cultivators for its use. Whenever they attained a measure of political and economic stability, their luxuriant pastures could support immense herds and flocks. These pastures, and the animals on them, were to make the Khoikhoi objects of envy when a new force arrived in the southwestern Cape, not from the interior of Africa, but from over the sea.

Frontiers of trade and agrarian settlement, c. 1590—1672

The European thrust into the lands of the Khoikhoi consisted of three distinct, though overlapping, phases. Each phase is identified by the European agents who were most prominent in relations with Khoikhoi — the traders, the cultivators and the pastoral farmers (or *trekboers*). Each group of Europeans had a different impact on Khoikhoi and elicited from them a different response.

The first phase was a frontier†† of trade and the political initiatives associated with trade. The European agents were 'servants' (employees) of trading companies of various European nations. From 1652, when Dutch traders founded a permanent colony, until about 1700, this frontier expanded from Table Bay throughout the southwestern Cape and bore

---

** A term which I have coined to refer to the Goringhaiqua, Gorachouqua, Goringhaicona and other scattered groups, all of which acknowledged the authority of a single overlord.
†† By a 'frontier' I mean a region where regular contact takes place between two or more culturally distinct communities, and where at least one of the communities is attempting to control the others but has not yet completely succeeded in doing so. This definition is substantially based on those of Martin Legassick and Hermann Giliomee.

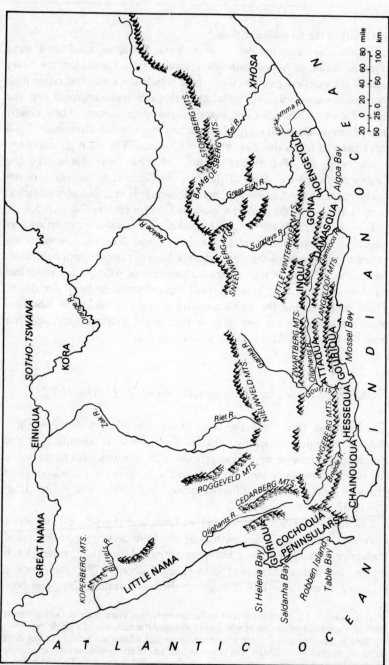

Figure 1.1 Approximate locations of Khoikhoi before contact with Europeans
Source: Richard Elphick, *Kraal and Castle: Khoikhoi and the Founding of White South Africa* (New Haven & London, 1977).
Reproduced by kind permission of Yale University Press

initial responsibility for the decline of Khoikhoi in that region; in the eighteenth century it moved hesitantly further into the interior. The agrarian frontier began in 1657, when the first free farmers were settled behind Table Mountain, and expanded outward well behind the first frontier, very rarely being the cutting edge of European advance. The third frontier, that of the semi-nomadic European pastoralists, did not greatly affect the southwestern Cape; it originated on the fringes of the colony in the 1690s and moved inland into the drier regions to the north and east, gradually superseding the Company's frontier of trade as the chief threat to Khoikhoi in these regions.

The trading frontier was founded in the 1590s, when Dutch and English ships began to put in regularly at Table Bay en route between Europe and the Indies. The land near Table Bay was an ideal stop-over for the tired and sick crews of these ships, for it offered a benign climate, excellent soil for growing vegetables, and a regular supply of fresh water. Moreover, local Khoikhoi were willing to supply large quantities of beef and mutton to the ships. Fresh meat was a boon to sailors who had been eating salty or rancid pork for months, and it helped restore them to health for their onward voyage.

In the pre-colonial period, Khoikhoi were willing to barter sheep and cattle in surprising numbers, given the high position these animals occupied in their economic and aesthetic value systems. This was because the Europeans from the ships offered Khoikhoi three products — tobacco, copper and iron — which satisfied a demand for narcotics and metals previously only incompletely met by trade with interior peoples. Thus Khoikhoi took to smoking tobacco as a substitute for the mild form of dagga which they used as a narcotic. They also bought copper beads and flat copper discs from the Europeans, using the metal for fashioning jewellery, just as they had done when it had reached them from distant peoples in modern Namibia and Botswana. There was a continuous market for copper among Khoikhoi both before and after 1652, and trade networks in copper sprang up between tribes near Table Bay and other Khoikhoi tribes in the interior.[10]

The Khoikhoi used iron chiefly for making spear- and arrow-points. The market for iron was enormous from the early 1590s to 1610, by which time the tribes near Table Bay had a surplus of it. No inland trade network developed for iron as it had for copper, perhaps because Khoikhoi were unwilling to pass it on to potential enemies. From 1610 the demand for iron became spasmodic, and after 1652 the Dutch government of the colony, realising the folly of improving the weapons of Khoikhoi who might become their enemies, embargoed further trade in the metal.[11]

Before 1652 the European traders were sailors from sundry nations, often sick and hungry, and uninhibited by long-range considerations in their treatment of Khoikhoi. In consequence the trade frequently degenerated into theft, which in turn led to reprisals from Khoikhoi. Moreover, because they lacked continuity of leadership, the Europeans were unable to impose a uniform price policy on the Khoikhoi: during the early seventeenth century the price for livestock continuously rose.

When in 1652 the Netherlands East India Company (*VOC*) founded a post at Table Bay, its goals were simply to regularise the benefits which sailors had long derived from the Cape stopover. Trade with Khoikhoi was thus a major concern of the early Dutch commanders. Copper and tobacco continued to be traded against sheep and cattle, but under different circumstances. The new Cape authorities were able largely to eliminate the violence of the early years and to impose controls which slowed the rise of prices.

The volume of the livestock trade grew slowly but steadily in response to a growing Dutch demand. Now that there was a permanent establishment at Table Bay, more ships called there than formerly, and their numbers continued to increase during the seventeenth century. An additional market for meat was created among the permanent population of soldiers and administrators; moreover, the hospital for ailing sailors needed a constant supply of mutton, and the Company wanted Khoikhoi oxen for hauling building materials.

The Khoikhoi always sold fewer livestock than the Dutch required, since for their highly valued animals they received only luxuries (and, in tobacco, a rapidly consumable luxury). They were particularly reluctant to part with beef cattle and tried to promote trade in sheep instead. To assure the future growth of their beef herds, they generally refused to sell young, fecund cows and urged the Dutch to accept sickly cows or oxen instead. Consequently the supply of beef cattle in Cape Town was inadequate. The Company was constantly forced to seek new trading partners, and the Dutch commanders had to lure distant tribes to the fort for barter.[12]

Dependent on the Khoikhoi for the colony's supplies and anxious to avoid costly wars at the Cape, the directors of the Company (*Heren XVII*) made it a cardinal policy that the Khoikhoi were a free people; thus they were to be neither conquered nor enslaved, but were to be treated with respect and consideration. The first commander, Jan van Riebeeck (1652–62), was anxious to please the Heren XVII and to repair his career in the Company, which had been damaged by earlier indiscretions. Thus he conscientiously pursued the Company's mild policy (in which he himself did not always concur), regularly entertaining Khoikhoi delegates at the fort, controlling his subordinates who wished to plunder or punish the Khoikhoi, and offering gifts and services to Khoikhoi camped nearby.[13]

Nonetheless, several problems tried Van Riebeeck's forbearance. Chief among these were petty thievery by Khoikhoi, mainly of metal items, but also sometimes of the Company's livestock; the unwillingness of the Peninsulars (the tribes and clans closest to the fort) to part with enough stock to feed the ships; and the belief, perhaps ill-founded, that Khoikhoi gave sanctuary to slaves fleeing the colony. All this was aggravated by the complex manoeuvres of the Khoikhoi interpreter, Harry, who used his knowledge of Dutch and his friendship with Van Riebeeck to enrich himself and gain political influence with the Peninsulars. Van Riebeeck repeatedly appealed to the directors to let him enslave the Peninsulars and confiscate their cattle. The directors never consented to such a drastic step, and toward the middle of his term at the Cape Van Riebeeck was reduced to seizing individual Khoikhoi chiefs and holding them until he gained satisfaction for his grievances. Such hostage-taking was generally successful in Van Riebeeck's time, but it naturally undermined much of the goodwill which the commander had so diligently nurtured by his other policies.[14]

Good relations were further strained when Khoikhoi discovered that the frontier was changing and that they were facing not only a trading post but also a growing agricultural community. The second frontier between Khoikhoi and Europeans, the frontier of agrarian settlement, was established in 1657 when the Company released some of its employees from their contracts and set them up as independent farmers (see ch. 2, p. 45 ff.). These *freeburghers* were to sell grain and meat to the Company at fixed prices, thus easing the colony's dependence on East Indian imports and on trade with Khoikhoi. The Company was determined that the European farmers should be subject to all its laws — commercial as well as criminal — but it had nonetheless created a community whose members would eventually become much more numerous and scattered than the Company's own employees, and who would less easily submit to its dictation.

Friction between Khoikhoi and freeburghers was almost inevitable. Even in the early years, when all farmers were in Table Valley or just behind Table Mountain, they were annoyed by Khoikhoi stealing their stock and trampling their crops. Similarly, the vast herds and flocks of the Khoikhoi were a temptation to the farmers, who needed livestock to start or expand their own holdings. Because of the proximity of the government, thefts by Europeans were probably rare in the early decades of settlement, but they were still numerous enough to create a grievance among Khoikhoi.

As soon as the freeburghers first put their land to the plough the

Peninsular Khoikhoi realised that the European presence at the Cape would be permanent and most probably expansive. Khoikhoi resented not only the loss of exceptional pastures near Table Mountain, but also the way the new farms blocked their access to watering areas on the Cape Peninsula.[15] However, Gogosoa, the nominal head of all the Peninsulars, was too cautious and the other chiefs too divided to transform this widespread resentment into active resistance. This task was left to Doman, a man of common origin but uncommon skill, who had been an interpreter for the Company and had visited the Dutch holdings in Java. Armed with an understanding of Dutch intentions and a clear apprehension of the Europeans' strengths and weaknesses, Doman gradually convinced the Peninsular leaders to unite in an attack on the colony. In May 1659 the Khoikhoi, under Doman's leadership, attacked suddenly and in force, jumping about erratically to present moving targets to the Dutch marksmen, and taking advantage of rainstorms to frustrate the operation of the colonists' matchlocks. They concentrated on the Europeans' food supply and in time destroyed most of the colonists' farms and stole the bulk of their cattle and sheep.

The early Khoikhoi successes forced Van Riebeeck to withdraw Company servants, freeburghers and their remaining livestock to a defensive position at the fort. The war soon drifted into a stalemate: the Khoikhoi were unwilling or unable to storm the well-gunned stockade and the Dutch lacked the information and mobility to locate and force into decisive battle the fast-moving Peninsulars. During this period of inaction Doman's coalition of Peninsulars began to disintegrate, especially after Doman himself was seriously injured in a skirmish on 19 July 1659. With the Khoikhoi divided and dispirited, peace was only a matter of time; neither side found it easy to harm the other further. In April and May of 1660 the two leading Peninsular tribes, the Goringhaiqua and Gorachouqua, made peace with the Company. The terms of the treaties reflected the ambiguous outcome of the war. The Khoikhoi kept the livestock they had seized and paid no reparations for the damage they had inflicted; but they recognised the sovereignty of the Company over the land where freeburghers had settled — a concession with ominous implications for the future.[16]

The First Khoikhoi-Dutch War had led only to the discomfiture, not the total defeat, of a comparatively poor group of clans. The powerful Cochoqua, who lived just to the north of the Peninsulars, had been urged by both sides to enter the war but had remained resolutely neutral. Other wealthy tribes of this region were untouched by the war which, though it was a crucial test for the young colony, was far from decisive in the decline of the Khoikhoi in the southwestern Cape.

Frontiers of trade and agrarian settlement, 1672—1701

In the decades after the First Khoikhoi-Dutch War the Company's frontier of trade expanded much more rapidly than agrarian settlement, which remained very much under the supervision of the colonial government. Thus in 1679 and 1687, when Europeans under Company direction settled in Stellenbosch and Drakenstein, they came into contact with Khoikhoi who had long participated in the Company's trade and had long felt its political influence.

The Company's impact on Khoikhoi was gradual and cumulative rather than cataclysmic. Nonetheless, there was a decisive turning point in the mid-1670s when its determination to recognise Khoikhoi independence waned and it began to impinge on Khoikhoi sovereignty in many ways — military, diplomatic, economic and judicial. The comprehensiveness of the Company's threat was not entirely coincidental. In part it resulted from a growing confidence among Europeans that they could easily bend Khoikhoi to their wills if necessary. In Van Riebeeck's day the tribes had been perceived as a threat to the colony's existence; but by the early 1670s the increasing numbers of Europeans and a series of defensive measures (watchhouses, mounted patrols and the famous almond hedge) had given the colony a new sense of security. It had also become obvious that firearms provided even isolated European farmers with an extremely effective defense against Khoikhoi attack.

In part because of this new security, the directors of the East India Company were losing interest in the Khoikhoi. The Cape government no longer fed them long reports on the colony's relations with the Khoikhoi, and the Heren XVII were rarely moved to comment on, much less overrule, the actions of Cape officials. Consequently the Cape government became progressively bolder in dealing with Khoikhoi, a tendency which was to be greatly strengthened by the arrival in 1679 of the brilliant and domineering commander, Simon van der Stel.

Of the various prongs of the Company's assault on Khoikhoi independence the most dramatic was the military. The Second Khoikhoi-Dutch War (1673—77) in varying ways affected most Khoikhoi of the southwestern Cape. Unlike the First Khoikhoi-Dutch War, it did not result from agricultural expansion of the colony; Khoikhoi were defending neither their pastures nor their water supplies. The Europeans' main opponent was Gonnema, the influential chief of a sub-group of the Cochoqua, whose people normally pastured their stock in a zone considerably to the north of European settlement. Gonnema had visited the colony very early in its history[17] but had apparently seen little advantage in further contacts; thus unlike his fellow Cochoqua chief, Oedosoa, he avoided Europeans as much as possible.

In the early 1670s the colonial government became convinced that Gonnema was instigating a series of attacks on Europeans. In some of these incidents his people (or people in clans subject to him) assaulted farmers, and in others 'Bushman' hunters, supposedly under his protection, ambushed and killed European hunters penetrating their territories. Only in one case did the Company's evidence clearly prove Gonnema's personal involvement; in most cases the government obtained its information from accusations made by Gonnema's Khoikhoi enemies, and it assumed that he had greater control over his subordinates than was probably the case. It is certain that Gonnema detested the colony, but it is virtually impossible to assess his responsibility for the various individual incidents. Later, in the final stages of the war, the Dutch governor collected evidence that some of these incidents had in fact been provoked by Europeans.[18]

The war consisted chiefly of four punitive expeditions which the Company sent out against Gonnema: one in 1673, one in 1674 and two in 1676. In the first of these the Dutch gained an effortless and spectacular victory. This encouraged most tribes and clans of the southwestern Cape to ally with the Company in the expectation of booty. Surrounded by covetous enemies, Gonnema adopted a defensive strategy — he apparently attacked the Company only once — and ordered his people to disperse their livestock and melt into the bush when a European expedition approached. After initial heavy losses the Cochoqua so perfected this technique that the frustrated expedition leaders took to attacking other Khoikhoi who had only tenuous connections with Gonnema's alleged crimes. They thus spread the destructive impact of the war even further. By 1677 it was clear that the war would yield little further booty to the Europeans and their allies, and the colonial government (now under Joan Bax, a governor more sympathetic than his predecessors to Khoikhoi), concluded peace with Gonnema, who had long sought relief from the unequal conflict.[19]

In the peace treaty Gonnema promised to bring an annual 'tribute' of thirty cattle to the colony. Though the Company did not always insist on his strict compliance, Gonnema was sufficiently cooperative for the rest of his life (he died in 1685 or 1686) for both Europeans and Khoikhoi to realise that the strongest and most anti-Dutch of the Khoikhoi chiefs had been humiliated.

The war accomplished more for the Dutch than merely the defeat of the Cochoqua. It also accelerated the Company's control over its Khoikhoi allies. During the conflict the government had forced various tribes to stop communicating and trading with Gonnema. After the war it tightened its control over them by insisting on regular payments from the cattle booty it had given them from Gonnema's captured herds. Most importantly, however, in 1676 and 1677 the Company had first asserted its right to adjudicate disputes among Khoikhoi clans or tribes and to impose its decision by force.[20] On the arrival of Simon van der Stel in 1679 these interventions became more frequent and more blunt. The pretence that chiefs were respected allies was gradually dropped. Van der Stel also developed the practice of approving the installation of each new Khoikhoi chief: he ceremonially presented the new ruler with a cane of office with an engraved copper handle and bestowed on him a classical name like Hercules or Hannibal. These canes gave the chiefs a certain prestige as clients of the great Company, but also made manifest their loss of independence and perhaps compromised them in the eyes of their followers.[21]

During the 1670s trading relations between the colony and the Khoikhoi also changed as the long-established barter at the fort was replaced by other forms of exchange. The main participants in the older barter had been the Peninsulars, whose strength had begun to decline in the First Khoikhoi-Dutch War and continued to decline thereafter. Among the reasons for their decline were an increasing fragmentation among their political leaders after the death of Gogosoa (between 1663 and 1667), an increasing drift of Peninsulars into the colony as cattleless labourers, and several bouts with deadly diseases.[22] The ensuing breakdown in the Peninsulars' social and political structure made it quite impossible for them to satisfy the growing livestock demands of the colony.

The government thus relied more and more on sending bartering expeditions to more distant tribes. These expeditions were usually led by officers who had some knowledge of Khoikhoi culture and politics. They travelled inland for a month or more, bartering with many different clans and tribes. The new system progressively displaced barter at the fort as the main source of the colony's supply. This change was important to the Khoikhoi not only because the trading expeditions brought all of the Western Cape Khoikhoi into contact with the Company's trading network, but also because the repeated visits of armed soldiers strengthened the Company's capacity to interfere in Khoikhoi affairs.

Not all long-distance trade was conducted by European officers. Since the 1650s several enterprising Khoikhoi had enriched themselves by acting as middlemen in the trade between the colony and inland tribes. At times these traders even blocked or disrupted trade into the colony in order to make their services indispensable.[23] Company officials almost always opposed them because they drove prices higher and, contrary to Company policy, traded with freeburghers. However, in the mid-1670s the government relaxed its hostility in one particular case and contracted the most vigorous of the Khoikhoi entrepreneurs to be its agent.

Dorha (or Klaas as the Dutch called him) was a captain of one of the westernmost Chainouqua clans. He first gained prominence in the Second Khoikhoi-Dutch War and became the most eager and useful of the Company's Khoikhoi allies. Even before the war he had conceived the idea of bartering on behalf of the Dutch. By repeatedly proving his loyalty to the Company he induced the government to entrust him with increasing quantities of trade goods. Klaas traded these goods to inland tribes in return for livestock, of which he kept the cows (normally a small minority of the cattle obtained) and gave the Company the oxen, calves and sheep. Even the cows were to be returned to the Company at a rate of 20 per cent each year, though Klaas could keep all calves born to them in the mean time.

Klaas used his position to become a wealthy and influential chief, attracting many followers and concluding prestigious alliances with chiefs greater than he. The Company was delighted by this system which brought in livestock much more cheaply than the barter expeditions; and it also valued Klaas's endless supply of information and advice on Khoikhoi affairs.[24] It appeared that one Khoikhoi at least had learned to use the Dutch to enrich himself and his followers and to reverse the disintegration of traditional society which the colony's presence had encouraged.

Nevertheless this promising experiment failed. In 1693 Governor van der Stel, possibly anxious to seize Klaas's herds, suddenly abandoned the twenty-year alliance and ordered his soldiers, in company with Klaas's enemy Koopman, to attack Klaas's kraal. The latter was arrested and imprisoned on Robben Island; though Van der Stel later released him, he recovered only part of his former wealth and influence and was murdered in 1701 by Koopman. Van der Stel claimed that he had attacked Klaas to punish him for disloyalty to the Company. He provided only the slightest evidence to substantiate his charges and failed to convince either the Heren XVII or a number of observers at the Cape.[25] Nevertheless the damage had been done. All responses to the Dutch had seemingly failed: the open resistance of Doman, the cautious withdrawal of Gonnema, the eager cooperation of Klaas.

The fall of Klaas forced the Company to rely exclusively on its own trading expeditions to acquire Khoikhoi stock. These expeditions were organised as in the past, but by the 1690s they had been transformed into collections of tribute. Most Khoikhoi were now so alarmed by the decline of their herds and flocks (a process described on pp. 18—21) that they did all they could to avoid the European traders; they tried to camouflage their true wealth and, failing all else, parted with only their sickliest animals. The

Dutch officers now spent long hours convincing Khoikhoi chiefs to trade, first with arguments, then with threats. Prices were not allowed to rise; they were in fact lower after 1700 (when Khoikhoi sold under some duress) than in the 1660s (when they had sold willingly though cautiously). The trade was now enmeshed with the progressing subordination of Khoikhoi chiefs. In effect the government was inducing chiefs to sell part of their herds to avoid retaliation from the Company. More positively from the Khoikhoi point of view, the Company also offered such tribes protection from their enemies, particularly hunters.[26]

The decline of Khoikhoi chiefs and the increasingly coercive nature of the trade occurred concurrently with another major development — the intensification of labour relations between Khoikhoi and the colony. Ever since Van Riebeeck's time some Khoikhoi had worked in the colony as cook's aids, domestics, building labourers and dispatch runners. Because they feared thefts of livestock, Europeans did not hire Khoikhoi as herders or shepherds before the 1670s, and even then under close European super-vision. However, the rapid expansion of the colony into Stellenbosch (1679) and Drakenstein (1687) greatly intensified the need for Khoikhoi labour.

Most farmers in these new settlements had fewer slaves than the farmers who remained in the older Cape district. According to the census of 1690 there was one slave in the Cape district for every nine cattle tended and for every *muid* of seed sown; in Drakenstein there was one slave for every sixty-three cattle and twenty muiden of seed.[27] Naturally, then, the new settlers turned to Khoikhoi to augment their slave force. The Khoikhoi, who were experiencing a rapid decline in their wealth and security, responded in large numbers. Most came to work on the farms though a few also made a meagre living in Cape Town, acting as porters for sailors and as errand boys for innkeepers and restaurateurs.[28]

Little is known about the conditions of employment on the farms. It seems that at first the Khoikhoi took employment for a season and left their families at home in the *kraal*. By the mid-1690s some Khoikhoi were in permanent employment and lived with their families and livestock on the farmers' land, but in their own huts. At a third stage — most characteristic of the eighteenth century but probably beginning earlier — some Khoikhoi moved into one of the masters' main buildings. At first they served only as herders and shepherds, but by the turn of the eighteenth century they had learned how to cultivate, harvest, prune vines and drive wagons: in short, they did almost anything a slave could do. In 1695 Johannes Willem de Grevenbroek enthusiastically described the skills of Khoikhoi:

They are apt in applying their hands to unfamiliar tasks. Thus they readily acquire the veterinary skill to cure scab in sheep, and they make faithful and efficient herds. They train oxen for use in ploughing . . . and are found exceedingly quick at inspanning or outspanning or guiding a team. Some of them are very accomplished riders, and have learned to break horses and master them . . . They make trusty bearers, porters, carriers, postboys and couriers. They chop wood, mind the fire, work in the kitchen, prune vines, gather grapes, or work in the wine press industriously . . . Without relaxation they plough, sow and harrow.[29]

The wages of these Khoikhoi were neither uniform nor regulated by government. The main attraction of life on a farm was a regular supply of tobacco, alcohol, bread, milk and vegetables, as well as increased security from the ravages of drought, wild animals and war. In addition some Khoikhoi were paid with a small number of calves or lambs.

As more and more Khoikhoi participated in the colonial economy the government deemed it necessary to assimilate them into the colony's legal system. The most decisive steps in this process were taken in 1671—72. Before that time virtually all Khoikhoi had been regarded as members of independent tribes, and if the Dutch interfered in their tribal affairs (as they rarely did) they did so as an act of 'foreign policy', without appeal to the laws of the Cape settlement. But in 1672 the Council of Justice passed judgement in two cases involving Khoikhoi, thus establishing their jurisdiction (1) over Khoikhoi who by culture, domicile and associations could be regarded as subjects of the colony rather than of a traditional chief, and (2) over independent Khoikhoi involved in disputes with a European or slave.[30] In coming decades Khoikhoi normally appeared in cases of the second category — almost always robberies, assaults or murders of Khoikhoi by Europeans, or of Europeans by Khoikhoi.

In general the Khoikhoi were treated fairly by the courts. They were allowed to initiate proceedings and to testify against Europeans, and the judges often decided in their favour. However, in one respect they did experience blatant discrimination: European murderers of Khoikhoi typically suffered confiscation of their goods and a period of banishment whereas Khoikhoi who had murdered Europeans were routinely executed. It must, however, be remembered that only a minority of disputes between Khoikhoi and Europeans actually reached the courts. Most were settled informally by executive action: in such cases the documentary evidence is inadequate for us to assess the quality of justice.[31]

The breakdown of Khoikhoi society, 1672—1701

Between 1672 and 1701 many (but not all) Western Cape Khoikhoi became partially or totally dependent on the colony for their livelihood and security. The Company, not the settlers, had triggered the processes leading to this new dependence. It was the Company which consumed large numbers of Khoikhoi cattle, subordinated and humiliated the Khoikhoi chiefs, assimilated Khoikhoi into its legal systems, and instigated the expansion of the colony into Khoikhoi pastures. Only at the last stage did the freeburghers' role become decisive — in providing employment for impoverished Khoikhoi.

To say that the Company's operations were chiefly responsible for Khoikhoi collapse is not to imply that they were always intentionally so. It is true that from time to time the Company acted aggressively (e.g., against Gonnema and Klaas) but such acts were intermittent and only partially explain Khoikhoi decline. The Company did not have to be consistently aggressive; to some degree at least Khoikhoi society simply fell apart as its age-old weaknesses were exacerbated by interaction with an alien society.

This proposition can be illustrated by posing and answering a difficult question. Why did Khoikhoi enter the colonial economy? Was it because the settlers under Company direction had displaced them from their pastures and springs or because they had attracted them to their farms with various inducements? An accurate answer must accommodate both 'push' and 'pull' processes but with the emphasis on the latter. In the first years of their settlement in a new region, European farmers doubtless deprived some Khoikhoi of good pastures, which they then used for cultivation or for grazing their own livestock; but the Khoikhoi, being transhument pastoralists, were not ruined as long as some good land between the farms remained unsown and accessible. Only after a generation of European settlement do we hear of Khoikhoi cattle trampling down farmers' crops, and we can suppose that by then pasture land was becoming more scarce.[32] However, the influx of Khoikhoi into the colonial labour force partly antedated this period and must have been largely due to the attractions of farm employment. Farm life would only be deemed attractive in comparison with life in the kraals, and the crucial stimulant to the labour influx was that conditions of traditional life were deteriorating alarmingly; indeed, that the traditional society itself was in jeopardy. The squeeze on land was a part of this threat, but only a part.

Two facets of the Khoikhoi economy — land and cattle — were obviously interdependent: for pastoralists one without the other was useless. In later eras of South African history Europeans and Africans would clash mainly over land, but in this early period the bone of contention was mainly livestock, the retention of which was essential not only for the nourishment of Khoikhoi but also for their continuing independence and self-esteem.

From the mid-1660s their herds and flocks began a steady decline, first among the Peninsulars, later among the more wealthy tribes inland.

Obviously the Company's trade contributed greatly to this loss. Between 1652 and 1699 its official papers record the purchase of 15,999 cattle and 36,636 sheep from Khoikhoi, and the actual figures were somewhat higher.[33] However, the original herds and flocks of the Western Cape Khoikhoi must have numbered well into the hundreds of thousands, and the Company's purchases were spread more or less evenly over half a century. Furthermore, as we noted, Khoikhoi were shrewd traders, reluctant to sell the healthy cows and ewes on which further growth of their livestock holdings depended. Thus the Company's trade accounts for only part of the decline.

It has sometimes been suggested that the freeburghers greatly contributed to Khoikhoi losses, both through robbery and illegal trade. However, the Company, in order to protect its monopoly, conducted a zealous campaign to protect the Khoikhoi from these dangers, and until about 1690 its control over the farmers was sufficiently tight that only miniscule numbers were traded or stolen.[34] We must note that the Company itself seized livestock in war, directing well-placed blows at the very wealthy Gonnema and at the rising entrepeneurs, Harry (in the 1650s) and Klaas (in the 1690s). But even when livestock thus obtained are added to all the others, the phenomenal decline of Khoikhoi herds and flocks is only partly explained.

We must remember that violent fluctuations between wealth and poverty had always been common among Khoikhoi. This resulted from their penchant for prolonged vendettas and stop-start wars, their fluid political structure, and the menace of hunter-robbers. The depredations by hunters increased as Khoikhoi tribes disintegrated, thus intensifying each downward phase of the 'ecological cycle'. It is not known to what degree the long decline after the 1650s was a normal phase in this recurring cycle of Khoikhoi history, and to what degree a product of European presence. But it is certain that the decline was prolonged and intensified by all the European demands on Khoikhoi livestock which we have enumerated. This was the case particularly after 1690, when the demands of both Company and freeburghers became increasingly peremptory.

Moreover, the colony's presence frustrated the normal mechanism whereby Khoikhoi society recovered from economic decline, namely the emergence of a military leader who captured sufficient livestock and recruited sufficient followers to create a growing economy and a secure society. The colony's demand for Khoikhoi labour deprived potential leaders of the impoverished individuals who would have been their most natural recruits. The periodic visitations of disease, almost certainly of European origin, also cut into the Khoikhoi population. But even more fundamentally, the colony made military aggrandisement impossible by suppressing wars in its hinterland and by quashing leaders like Klaas and Harry who made a successful start at recovery.

Faced with reduced security and a disintegrating economy, Khoikhoi naturally gravitated to the colonists' farms. This response was not alien to their traditions: it had long been customary for Khoikhoi who had lost stock to herd for wealthy kinsmen or neighbours and thus re-start their herds. But there was an important difference between the two cases. Khoikhoi who entered the colonial economy normally remained there since few were paid in livestock, the normal wages being food, lodging, and luxuries like tobacco. Most colonial Khoikhoi in the service of colonists were thus permanently lost to independent Khoikhoi society. So, too, were those Khoikhoi who chose to trek inland from the southwestern Cape and thus delay for at least a century their showdown with the growing European power in southern Africa.

In the face of all these adverse developments the leaders of Khoikhoi tribes — who were weak at the best of times — failed to rally their followers to effective resistance or response. Indeed, by the turn of the eighteenth century all of the still independent Khoikhoi near the colony — the Peninsulars, Chariguriqua, Cochoqua and Chainouqua — had no visible leadership at all above the clan level. All groups were much less numerous than formerly (the overwhelming majority of some clans being on European farms) and owned small flocks and even smaller herds. In the southwestern Cape the demographic and economic base of Khoikhoi society was so small, and the political superstructure so feeble, that by the first decade of the eighteenth century the traditional order had disintegrated beyond recall.[35]

Advance of the trekboer frontier, c. 1700—c. 1770

The Western Cape Khoikhoi received three final blows from the colony in the early eighteenth century. First came the rapid northward expansion of settlement into the Land of Waveren (Tulbagh basin) in 1700. This was the first region of settlement whose climate, terrain, and distance from markets favoured a chiefly pastoral rather than a mixed agricultural economy. Shortly thereafter, from 1701—03, farmers along the whole northern edge of the colony suffered from massive attacks on their livestock. Historians have usually called the attackers 'Bushmen' (meaning hunters who were not Khoikhoi), but many of them were in fact Khoikhoi who had lost livestock in the general decline and had seen in the colonial herds, particularly those in newly occupied Waveren, an opportunity to regain their wealth.[36] The Company and its Khoikhoi allies eventually learned how to contain these attacks, and in 1703 they fizzled out. But during the course of these hostilities the Khoikhoi allies of the Dutch, who had been safeguarding their dwindling livestock under Company protection, suffered severe losses.

The second blow to the Khoikhoi was the relaxation of the Company's control over freeburghers. The colony was now too big for officials to monitor its borders readily, and the Heren XVII made matters worse by vastly increasing the rights of freeburghers. From February 1700 to October 1702, and again after July 1704, the freeburghers were permitted to go inland and barter with Khoikhoi — a freedom that easily led to abuse. During the decade many cases of plunder came to light, the most notorious being an expedition in 1702 which ranged as far as the Xhosa and stole almost 2,000 cattle and 2,500 sheep from the Inqua (the largest Khoikhoi tribe between the Hessequa and the Xhosa).[37] The livestock holdings of the colonists jumped dramatically, in part at least because of trade and theft. During the eight years before the opening of the trade in 1700 their (probably under-reported) herds had grown by 3,712, their flocks by 5,449; in the first eight years of free trade the corresponding figures for growth were 8,871 and 35,562.[38]

However, the third and final blow made the others insignificant by comparison. In February 1713 a visiting fleet sent its linen ashore to be washed by the Company slaves in Cape Town. The laundry bore a smallpox virus which was to rage throughout the year, killing hundreds of Europeans and slaves. Its impact was even more severe on the Khoikhoi who apparently had almost no immunity to it. Beginning with the Khoikhoi in Cape Town, it spread relentlessly to those on the farms and hence outward to the independent tribes, who vainly tried to protect themselves by shooting down infected Khoikhoi that approached their kraals.[39]

We have only one contemporary estimate of the extent of Khoikhoi fatalities — namely that scarcely one in ten in the southwestern Cape survived. Since Khoikhoi virtually disappeared from the records of subsequent years, this assessment is probably not greatly overdrawn.[40] The smallpox came close to annihilating the largest cluster of Khoikhoi in southern Africa, and wrote *finis* to a long process of disintegration.

The near disappearance of Khoikhoi in the southwestern Cape, along with the emergence of an expanding frontier of European pastoralists in regions to its north and east, meant that the main zone of European-Khoikhoi interaction shifted to these latter regions. Here rainfall levels and conditions of pasture were much less favourable than in the southwestern Cape. For these reasons the Khoikhoi of the new regions were poorer, less numerous and less organised — in short, even less able to resist encroachment than the Khoikhoi who had encountered the Dutch in the earlier period. At the same time the nature of the European challenge altered as settlers in the new regions abandoned cultivation for a ranching economy and as initiative passed from the Company to the European migrant farmers (trekboers).

Smallpox continued its destructive course after 1713. From the southwestern Cape it spread north to the Tswana and hence back to the Little Nama (around 1722—24), among whom it caused great disruption of social and economic life. In 1755 another smallpox epidemic broke out at the Cape and eventually spread at least to the Great Nama far to the north and probably to the Xhosa far to the east. Both peoples, as well as the Tswana, were frequently hit in the latter half of the eighteenth century, though they often regarded the immediate source of the plague as 'inland peoples' and not the southwestern Cape. It is likely that Khoikhoi suffered greatly in these later outbreaks. For example, in the 1780s the traveller François le Vaillant learned that more than half of the Gona (the largest independent tribe besides the Nama) had been killed in a single outbreak of the pox.[41]

In the decades after 1713 the colony continued its demands on Khoikhoi livestock. However, the rapid increase of the freeburghers' herds and the corresponding decrease in those of Khoikhoi made the latter much less important to the colony than they had been. In the 1720s and 1730s the Company still sent out bartering expeditions every year or so, mainly to the Nama, for pack oxen and (after 1729) for goats: the officers in charge often bartered sheep on their own account. Various freeburgher expeditions were also mounted, though after 9 April 1729 these were again made illegal. There is evidence that both Company servants and freeburghers cajoled Khoikhoi into overselling and plundered them if they refused. The Khoikhoi responded with grim defiance, slaughtering their cattle rather than paying what they regarded as tribute.[42]

The crucial feature of the new frontier region was the rapid extension, after 1700, of the trekboer economy which had originated in the southwestern Cape in the late 1680s and the 1690s (see ch. 2, pp. 58—59). Opposition to this eighteenth-century expansion seemed to come less from 'Hottentots', as in the seventeenth century, than from 'Bushmen'. This was partly because trekboers found relatively few Khoikhoi settled in the regions they occupied. Rainfall levels were less favourable here than in the southwestern Cape, and Khoikhoi tended to pasture over greater distances and had thus formed less populous and cohesive units than the Western Cape Khoikhoi. Apart from the Gona (discussed in ch. 8) we know of only one large inland tribe, the Inqua (or Heykon) — and they had been battered by the freeburgher expedition of 1702. Indeed, some Khoikhoi whom trekboers encountered had previously worked for colonists; they seem to have pioneered the advance of the colony, only later to be dispossessed by Europeans.[43]

A less obvious cause of feeble Khoikhoi resistance was the traditional cycle of decline which overtook Khoikhoi groups. While the harsh environment of these regions doubtless made a downturn in the cycle easier than in the southwestern Cape, it was in some cases at least triggered by diseases and by unscrupulous European traders who arrived before the first trekboers. All eighteenth-century descriptions of the areas north and east of the colony show Khoikhoi in a lamentable condition: poor, disunited, and in perpetual fear of hunter-robbers. Many poor Khoikhoi were forced to become hunters and robbers themselves. In 1752 one Dutch observer noted of a group of Khoikhoi near the Gona:

> All these Hottentots, who formerly were rich in cattle are now, through the thefts of the Bushmen, entirely destitute of them. Some have been killed and some are scattered through wars with each other and with the Caffers. Those who are still found here and there consist of various groups which have united together. *They live like Bushmen* from stealing, hunting and eating anything eatable which they find in the field or along the shore. [Italics mine][44]

In such conditions the few Khoikhoi with livestock may well have looked to the trekboer as the lesser of two evils. The trekboer was after all a defender of the pastoral way of life which Khoikhoi wished to preserve. He offered his Khoikhoi labourers security from hunger and robbery while allowing them to keep their own herds and flocks with them on the farm. Thus, instead of resisting the newcomers, many Khoikhoi took employment with them; for example, scarcely a decade after the opening up of the Camdebo region, virtually all Khoikhoi there were in European service.[45]

However, the Dutch did face some resistance. A number of Khoikhoi protested the loss of their pastures, usually after a generation or so of trekboer occupation. In the 1770s a disgruntled Khoikhoi captain informed Anders Sparrman that Khoikhoi in his area were forced to move almost daily when Europeans demanded their pastures. Formerly, he said, Khoikhoi chiefs had been left on their land; but now, as the European population expanded, chiefs too were being removed from good pasture and soon, he feared, from bad pasture as well. Attempts to displace Khoikhoi often led to brawls, retaliatory robberies by Khoikhoi, and even loss of life. These episodes occasionally appear in the court records but were usually no more than local disturbances.[46]

By contrast the disruptions caused by cattleless marauders were both widespread and effective. The Dutch and their Khoikhoi allies sometimes referred to these attackers as 'Hottentots' but more often as 'Bushmen'. Confusion of terminology reflected confusion in reality. In some cases the 'Bushmen' were aborigines, i.e., speakers of non-Khoikhoi languages and descendants of hunters who had inhabited the area before Khoikhoi first arrived. In others they were merely Khoikhoi without cattle. In yet other cases 'Bushman' raiding parties consisted of persons of both categories. [47]

Clearly the term 'Bushman' had no simple definition. In this period 'Bushmen' were sometimes defined by their non-Khoikhoi culture or ancestry, sometimes by their hunting economy, and sometimes by their penchant for robbery. Also to many Europeans 'Bushmen' were any Khoisan who resisted trekboer expansion. Of course robbery and resistance closely overlapped. Thus one can loosely define 'Bushmen' as brownskinned people who lived from hunting, gathering and robbery and posed a threat to the security of pastoralists, both Khoikhoi and European. A concise descriptive term would be 'hunter-robber'.

'Bushmen', in this sense, had little in common with the 'harmless' hunter-gatherers described by modern anthropologists. Though they probably did not breed livestock themselves, they had professional expertise in dealing with their stolen animals. They knew how to drive, corral and feed hundreds of sheep and cattle. They sold animals (particularly cows, whose productive capacity they did not value) to farmers in return for tobacco, dagga and other animals. They understood much of the technology and economic mores of their European enemies, and fought not only with poisoned arrows and *assegais* but increasingly with stolen or bartered guns: European commandos often found large caches of gunpowder and lead in their kraals. When they attacked European farms the 'Bushmen' did more than steal livestock: they kidnapped slaves, burned standing crops, and scattered harvested grains. Sometimes they even hauled away the grain in wagons or on pack oxen. At other times they rode on horseback. These skills are in part explained when we remember that some 'Bushmen' were Khoikhoi, many of whom had once been in European service. [48]

Between 1701 and 1754 most 'Bushman' disturbances occurred in the colony's northernmost regions in the district of Stellenbosch, though some incidents are also recorded from Swellendam district. As we noted, Europeans on the northern fringes of the settlement were first attacked in 1701—03 in the wake of the colony's expansion into the Land of Waveren. Waveren and the area of the Berg River experienced further robberies in 1715—16, and a commando was formed which made peace with the robbers. Minor outbreaks occurred in subsequent years, the most important being in 1738—39 when large numbers of aboriginal hunters and Little

Nama harrassed Europeans in the Piketberg and Bokkeveld regions. These attacks led to the formation of three punitive expeditions which recovered much livestock, killed many Khoikhoi, and pacified the area. Again in 1754 the northern regions were disrupted on a wide front. In these last two cases many Europeans were forced to leave their homes, but colonial expansion was not permanently blocked.[49]

The Company responded to these attacks in several ways. Its initial impulse was to protect the threatened regions with small outpost garrisons and then to attempt to make peace with the attackers. This last policy was occasionally successful, but more often officials and settlers favoured retaliation, and the institution of the commando was born.

The commando,[50] which was later to become a symbol of the trekboer's considerable self-sufficiency, was called into being by the Company. Between 1700 and 1715 punitive expeditions consisted mainly of Company employees with only a smattering of freeburghers. In 1715 the first purely civilian commando was formed under freeburgher officers, but it and its successors continued to be subject to the Company's regulations and dependent on it for ammunition. In 1739 a new stage was reached when commando service became compulsory for freeburghers in threatened regions:[51] in many cases the freeburghers brought Khoikhoi dependants with them on commando. The three commandos which responded to the disorders of 1738—39 were probably more violent than their predecessors. They systematically attacked the kraals of the region, sequestering livestock and weapons and killing or wounding many Khoisan. In one case a commander calmly ordered the massacre of thirty or forty Khoisan with whom he was conversing: he did so, he said, because he knew they planned to attack him later.[52]

In many respects these events presaged the much bigger 'Bushman' wars in the Sneeuwberg after 1770 (ch. 8, pp. 339—40 and pp. 342—43), when for more than a generation Europeans would suffer serious losses and see their century-long expansion checked.[53] However, in view of what we know of the cultural identity of the Sneeuwberg Khoisan[54] it seems that theirs was a straightforward resistance of hunter-gatherers to foreign intrusion rather than resistance intertwined with the breakdown of a partially pastoral society — a pattern which seems to have been common on the trekboer frontier before 1770.

Khoisan and the trekboer frontier

By the middle of the eighteenth century few Khoikhoi except the Gona and

Nama were members of tribes, much less of large tribes. In the southwestern Cape there were hardly any Khoikhoi at all. In 1726 only a few scattered families could be found within 100 kilometres of Cape Town — a situation substantially unchanged in the 1770s.[55] As travellers proceeded further north and east into the Stellenbosch and Swellendam districts, they encountered larger numbers of Khoikhoi on farms, but usually no independent groups before they reached the Little Nama in the north or the Hessequa in the east. The Little Nama, who mainly lived south of the Orange River near the Atlantic coast, were impoverished and harrassed when visited by Hop in 1761, and were reduced to about 400 people under five captains by 1779. Beyond them along the Orange River were the Great Nama and Einiqua, who were not to be threatened by the colony until the end of the century. To the east the major group described by travellers between the 1730s and 1770s was the once populous Hessequa, now scattered around the Company's cattle posts near modern Swellendam on the Rivier Zondereind. East of this region travellers found only tiny, impoverished groups until they reached the Gona.[56]

In addition to members of these tribes, there were a few independent Khoikhoi who wandered peacefully within the colonial boundaries, supporting themselves by gathering: many of these had once worked for Europeans and were now seeking a new job, or were elderly runaways whose masters had no interest in recapturing them.[57]

Moreover, some Khoikhoi who did have intimate economic contacts with Europeans still preferred to live in small groups away from the farms. Some such Khoikhoi were led by chiefs or clan captains who carried a cane of office granted by the Company or (apparently) by nearby farmers. These rulers appear to have enjoyed little respect from either Europeans or Khoikhoi.

Another group of partially independent Khoikhoi lived at or near the Company's posts in Groene Kloof and on the Rivier Zondereind. In 1768 J.W. Cloppenberg observed that Khoikhoi preferred to 'serve us [the Company] . . . for very little rather than the boers for much.' He also noted that Khoikhoi had abandoned their circular camping formation because of decreasing danger from wild animals, and now formed their kraals on the basis of friendship rather than kinship ties. Such Khoikhoi periodically served the Company as herders, wagon drivers and guides and were paid in tobacco, arak (an East Indian liquor) and sheep. A similar type of semi-independent Khoikhoi were those who, in partially arable regions like those near the Xhosa frontier, hired themselves to farmers for the harvest and threshing season and were paid an amount fixed in advance.[58]

However, most Khoikhoi seem to have lived on European farms, either in their own huts or in the farmers' main buildings. So, too, did a large number of people conventionally denoted 'Bushmen' (i.e., former robbers). Both groups performed agrarian and pastoral tasks differing only in scale from those of their seventeenth-century Khoikhoi counterparts. Single Khoikhoi men (and occasionally women) were sometimes left in control of enormous herds and even of whole farms when the farmers were away in Cape Town. In addition, Khoikhoi women often acted as cooks, domestics and nannies when slaves were unavailable. Khoikhoi were also employed in hunting wild animals and capturing 'Bushman' children to become labourers for the farmers.[59]

The wages of Khoikhoi differed greatly from region to region. In the 1770s farmers near Tijgerhoek on the Rivier Zondereind paid their Khoikhoi rations of food and tobacco as well as an annual wage of one or two sheep and their lambs, *or* one cow and calf, *or* the equivalent in money. Mentzel said that farmers needed 50 to 100 pounds of tobacco annually for their slaves and Khoikhoi, and Lichtenstein visited a farmer in Bruintjes Hoogte who slaughtered 600 sheep a year to feed his family, slaves and Khoikhoi. Khoikhoi were allowed to keep their own stock on farms: in 1731 one group of Khoikhoi on a farm near Saldanha Bay had at least 50 cattle. Even as late as 1798 Khoikhoi on farms in the Graaff-Reinet district owned an average of 5 beef cattle and 23 sheep per capita.[60]

As Khoikhoi became poorer and less able to find alternative subsistence, some farmers probably cut back on payments in meat. Thus in the 1770s Thunberg found farmers who made their Khoikhoi hunt for their meat (the farmers supplied the ammunition and insisted on receiving the skins) and in 1798 Lady Anne Barnard found that the Khoikhoi nearest the Cape were normally fed only on bread and melons.[61]

Labour contracts between Europeans and Khoikhoi were not written and could easily be broken by either side. Travellers are sharply divided on how well the farmers treated their Khoikhoi. There is considerable evidence that they could be brutal and serenely indifferent to sufferings and death among their servants, whom they apparently thrashed often. But we also have vignettes of happy farms where Khoikhoi received generous and considerate treatment and looked to their masters with evident affection.[62] By their very nature, isolated farms do not lend themselves to generalisation.

In this period farmers were not organised in asking the government to control their labour force. They seem to have relied on their own methods, often chasing Khoikhoi who ran away from the farm[63] or holding children hostage to force the return of their parents (see also ch. 8, pp. 317–19). Further research is needed to determine how widely these customs were practised. It is, however, clear that the government neither countenanced them nor took active measures to suppress them — unless a Khoikhoi had been murdered in the process.

The farmers, however, did ask the government's aid in gaining control of children born on their farms of slave males and Khoikhoi females. The Europeans objected to feeding these children who, having a Khoikhoi mother, were technically free and could not be forced to labour for their benefactor when they reached maturity. In 1721 a group of farmers petitioned the Council of Policy to declare that such children could be indentured for a fixed number of years. The Council did not act on the request. It was not until 1775 that the governor approved a regulation in Stellenbosch which would legally deprive Khoikhoi of some of their rights as free persons by allowing a *Bastaard* child (of Khoikhoi mother and slave father) to be indentured to age twenty-five: this procedure was, however, subject to several conditions designed to protect the child. The history of this *inboek* system — its extension to other regions and to children other than those of Khoikhoi mother and slave father — lies beyond the scope of this chapter.[64]

Thus before the 1770s the Company's theoretical policy to Khoikhoi was roughly as it had always been: the Khoikhoi, whether farm labourers or not, were free persons, entitled to own property (though not to hold loan farms), move about freely, and seek justice in the courts as the legal equals of Europeans. In general, colonial laws and regulations did not infringe on these rights (despite ephemeral statutes such as one in 1755 which discriminated against 'Bastaard Hottentot' women who wished to live in Cape Town other than with burghers).[65] However, the central government was much less energetic in enforcing its policy than it had been in the seventeenth century.[66] As its controls over the trekboers weakened, so did its capacity, and perhaps its will, to check the inevitable abuses of a labour system in which employees were impoverished, unorganised, and largely ignorant of the laws of the society in which they lived.

Normally Khoikhoi appeared before the Council of Justice in Cape Town only in serious cases referred to that body by the *landdrosts*. Only rarely did these cases involve Khoikhoi alone. For example, in 1732 and 1736 Khoikhoi men were sentenced to be drowned for buggery with sheep; and in 1746 a Khoikhoi woman who had failed to cut the umbilical cord of her new-born baby, thus allegedly causing its death, was sentenced to be whipped, branded, and banished for life on Robben Island.[67] Bizarre as these sentences are to modern readers, they probably reflect the era's conceptions of crime and punishment rather than judicial discrimination against Khoikhoi.

Most cases involving Khoikhoi concerned murders of slaves by Khoikhoi or vice versa (these will be discussed shortly), and murders of Khoikhoi by Europeans. In this latter category the punishment was usually as it had been before 1700 — banishment overseas of the convicted European.[68] However, in one such case in 1744 the governor, Hendrik Swellengrebel, personally intervened to raise a sentence from banishment to death; in his decision he reiterated the traditional policy of the government:

> Such atrocities were, and perhaps still are, committed in this farflung land . . . that these natives are barbarously treated and murdered for slight reasons as if they were wild beasts rather than men fashioned by the same Creator: thus God's chastizing hand was made heavy on this land and many calamities were caused . . . [Those who harm Khoikhoi should] be punished as if the deed were done to a Christian.[69]

It was unfortunate for the Khoikhoi that Swellengrebel's ideals could not be implemented without a well-funded administrative structure; and for the protection of Khoikhoi the Company was not likely to spare either its funds or its employees.

Khoikhoi and slaves

During the first century of European settlement the Khoikhoi were drawn progressively closer to the slaves in culture, status and economic function. Nevertheless the relations between Khoikhoi and slaves were marked by an extreme hostility, only rarely relieved by brief suggestions of union against a common enemy. The deeper aspects of Khoikhoi-slave antagonism lie beyond the ken of our documents and can only be speculatively reconstructed. Possibly the slaves, many of whom came from the complex civilisations of India and Indonesia, had a contempt for Khoikhoi culture and for some of the customs which Europeans also found revolting — the use of body grease, the eating of lice, etc. Similarly the Khoikhoi, who enjoyed the freedom of a nomadic and largely egalitarian society, may well have despised the constrained and subordinate slaves, perhaps even comparing them to the lowly servile class in their own society, the former hunters whom they called by the derogatory term 'San'.[70]

This is, however, conjecture. The means whereby this antagonism was perpetuated — namely, the repeated cycle of violence caused by slaves escaping from the colony — are better documented. In the early decades of European settlement the Khoikhoi feared not so much the Cape government (which encouraged only the slowest expansion), but fugitives from the colony. These were often company servants, less frequently freeburghers, who wanted to escape the Company's discipline, taxes or justice. In Van

Riebeeck's time Khoikhoi returned a cabin boy and gardener who had absconded from the colony: periodically in the seventeenth century they dragged back deserters from Company ships.[71] But the most threatening refugees were slaves, whose escapes were a frequent preoccupation of the government (see ch. 3, pp. 104—07).

The slaves often escaped in groups of five or more. Many had stolen guns; all were tired, angry, hunted men or women. Sometimes they tried to barter food from Khoikhoi in return for tobacco. But more often they simply attacked kraals, killing and dispersing the Khoikhoi and stealing their stock. At other times they forced Khoikhoi to be their guides. It sometimes took weeks or even years before slaves were apprehended by the authorities: consequently they often had the opportunity to attack many Khoikhoi kraals. This repeated violence hardened Khoikhoi attitudes against the slaves. For example, in 1674 an escaped Javanese convict ripped open the stomach of a Khokhoi (or 'San') who was trying to capture him. Even though the convict was subsequently shot by a European party, members of the victim's tribe volunteered to aid the Europeans in capturing other slaves, provided they had the right to take vengeance on the escapees by 'similar means'.[72] In such an atmosphere escaped slaves had little chance and little inclination to win the cooperation of the Khoikhoi.

This hostility was intensified by the consistent help which the Khoikhoi gave the Dutch in capturing slaves. Cooperation was first instituted by Van Riebeeck who for each captured slave offered Khoikhoi a bounty in copper equal to the price of a head of cattle. In coming decades many such agreements were made, and at many rates. In 1677, for example, the rate was three 'fathoms' of tobacco per slave; in 1680 again the price of one head of cattle; but by 1713, confronted with a large number of escaped slaves, the Company began to pay cash at the rate of 3 rixdollars per slave.[73]

Khoikhoi aided the colony's campaign against slave escapes in several ways. In some cases they simply attacked the escapees and inflicted so much damage on them that they deemed it best to return to the colony; in others they welcomed the slaves temporarily into their kraal and later killed them. Quite often Khoikhoi would come to the colony volunteering to catch slaves for bounty — either alone or as members of an expedition led by Europeans. Or, if a few forlorn slaves arrived in the territory of a remote tribe, the Dutch would urge its chief to organise a chase; if the slaves had firearms the Khoikhoi party might simply surround them and send to the colony for a Dutch party to effect the capture. Alternatively, the Khoikhoi might meekly approach the slaves with an offer of food at their kraal and then lead them into a Dutch ambush.[74]

Although the Khoikhoi-slave vendetta continued throughout the late seventeenth century, the Europeans were constantly afraid that the two groups would ally against the colony. For example, in the First Khoikhoi-Dutch War (1659) Van Riebeeck at first armed the slaves, confident that their hatred of Khoikhoi would keep them loyal; but being informed that the slaves intended to escape and make common cause with the Khoikhoi, he returned them to their chains.[75] Though such fears often cropped up, there are only a few definite indications of Khoikhoi-slave cooperation. In one isolated case of 1692 a Khoikhoi named Frans seems to have induced two slaves to abscond by promising to bring them to a 'better land'. In 1747 a Khoikhoi joined a party of escaped slaves in terrorising the countryside in Stellenbosch district.[76] Finally, there is considerable evidence that in the late seventeenth century the Guriqua and Nama (somewhat to the north of the colony) repeatedly gave succour to escaped slaves. At the very least their hospitality gave slaves another hope alongside the belief that they could escape overland to Madagascar. As a result many escapees headed north, and in the 1720s escaped slaves still regarded Nama country as their promised land.[77]

One might suspect that as the Khoikhoi drifted into colonial employment after the 1670s they would draw closer to the slaves with whom they now shared the same occupations, if not the same legal status. Though they were still subject to attacks from escaped slaves, they now shared this danger with the Europeans — and even with the slaves — on their farms. The social distance between Khoikhoi and slaves decreased: if the two groups did not always live together, they did perform the same tasks and usually ate a common meal.[78] Khoikhoi learned the slaves' languages, and by the mid-eighteenth century sexual unions between them became common (see ch. 4, pp. 132—33).

Moreover, there was an increasing tendency among Europeans to disregard the legal distinctions between the two groups and to bracket the slaves and Khoikhoi together in their minds. In the eighteenth century there were separate places of execution for Europeans on the one hand and for Khoikhoi and slaves on the other. By the 1740s *meid*, the term for slave women, was being used to refer to Khoikhoi. Most important, however, were the informal attempts, already discussed, of European farmers to deprive Khoikhoi of their liberties and to make them immobile labourers on their farms. The combined effect of these developments was such that even a precise observer like Sparrman could conclude in the 1770s that 'the majority [of Khoikhoi] are slaves'. [79]

The two oppressed groups had abundant opportunities to cooperate with each other. On big farms the slaves and Khoikhoi had to deal with the large family of the European owner; but on the numerous cattle posts the only resident European was usually a hired man (*knecht*) surrounded by many

Khoikhoi and slaves, some of whom knew how to use firearms. Thus in 1746 a group of Khoikhoi and slaves were convicted of combining to beat up a knecht.[80] However, incidents of slave-Khoikhoi cooperation are rare in the court records before 1750, even though Europeans could be expected to prosecute such cases with vigour.

There is much evidence that the tradition of Khoikhoi-slave hostility persevered on some farms at least. Starting in 1675 with a case of a slave who killed a Khoikhoi, allegedly in sport, we have a fairly steady stream of murders of slaves by Khoikhoi or of Khoikhoi by slaves. By the 1730s and 1740s several such homicides were often tried in a year. These cases are more numerous than murder cases involving Khoikhoi and Europeans. Since the Company's justice was not systematic, and since these cases often represented the last phase of protracted feuds, it may be that they are only the visible tip of much undocumented hostility and related violence. The usual penalty for convicted killers of either group was to be hanged, crucified or beaten to death.

Some of these cases involved cultural differences between the two groups. For example, some slaves assumed that Khoikhoi had special magical powers as the ancient occupants of the land: thus on 16 November 1696 Anthony of Bengal severely beat Thore, a Khoikhoi woman whom he accused of bewitching him with a steady stomach pain. In 1745 Alexander of Malabar murdered a Khoikhoi woman who had long before arranged to have him beaten up by a male Khoikhoi: though this past insult was the source of Alexander's grievance against her, his violent assault was triggered when she spoke to him in a language he could not understand. Another group of murders were explicable simply in terms of the victims' employment: often indigent Khoikhoi wanted to steal a European farmer's sheep, but had first to eliminate the slave shepherd.[81]

Obviously these specific sources of irritation only partly explain why the hostility between Khoikhoi and slaves lasted far into the eighteenth century. There are clearly deeper reasons. One of these is the natural desire of Khoikhoi to avoid identification with slaves, whose legal status and living conditions they did not wish to share. Another is that both oppressed groups seem to have displaced their aggression from their European masters to another group of aliens whom for various reasons they despised, and whom they could attack (though not murder) without fear of serious punishment.

Conclusion

The Cape colonists dispossessed and subjugated the Khoikhoi with comparative ease. It was not smallpox which was primary in this success, but the broad array of demands which the colony made on the Khoikhoi, and their weakness in resisting them.

Prior to 1700 the Khoikhoi of the southwestern Cape were challenged first by the Company's traders and later by agrarian settlers. The traders did not integrate the Khoikhoi into the global economy as providers of exportable raw materials; but they did associate them indirectly with intercontinental commerce by obtaining from them, under monopoly conditions, essential foodstuffs for the sailors and merchants who conducted the trade, and the Cape Town garrison and community which supported it. Throughout the seventeenth century the Company's goals in relation to Khoikhoi were predominantly commercial. After the 1660s, when Khoikhoi ceased to be a serious threat to the colony, the Company interfered in their politics mainly because it wanted to monopolise the cattle trade and keep prices low. As we saw, these political initiatives were as influential as the trade itself in causing the decline of the Khoikhoi herds.

Despite determined efforts the Khoikhoi could not resist the pressures which the trading frontier placed on their livestock economy. This very economy was in fact largely responsible for their weakness. Firstly, their constant transhumance and periodic dispersal in search of pasture and waterholes had inhibited the development of a strong, central leadership among them; thus they repeatedly failed to unite against the colonists at crucial junctures. Secondly, their pastoral economy had limited them to a much smaller, hence more readily displaceable, population than the southwestern Cape could have supported under cultivation. Thirdly, the extreme vulnerability of livestock wealth added greatly to the instability of Khoikhoi polities, making Khoikhoi easy targets for settlers and Company officials with horses and firearms. Khoikhoi resisted Europeans more effectively *after* they had lost their livestock and had adopted the 'guerilla' techniques of 'Bushman' hunter-robbers.

It was crucial to the failure of Khoikhoi resistance that only a few Khoikhoi in the southwestern Cape opted to become hunter-robbers. A number of others trekked away from the advancing colony, but most came to terms with the agrarian frontier. The European cultivators following in the wake of the trading frontier had two main needs — land and labour — both of which the Khoikhoi could supply. Again the Khoikhoi proved weak in the face of colonial demands. Except in the First Khoikhoi-Dutch War they mounted no concerted resistance to the cultivators' occupation of their pastures. When Europeans settled in Stellenbosch and Drakenstein, the Khoikhoi leadership had already been discredited by its failure to cope with the trading frontier. Moreover, the settlers only gradually excluded Khoikhoi from the pastures of the new districts, thus making it easy for Khoikhoi to temporise with the new frontier until it was too late. But most important, the farmers offered Khoikhoi employment under terms which would include security from hunger and protection of their livestock from hunter-robbers. The increasingly impoverished and demoralised Khoikhoi could not refuse these terms.

The trekboer frontier of the eighteenth century was much like its agrarian predecessor in its impact on Khoikhoi. The trekboers, like the earlier settlers of Stellenbosch and Drakenstein, needed many labourers to perpetuate (and expand to proportions appropriate to pastoralism) their traditions of extensive settlement. Also, like their earlier counterparts, they could not, on their first arrival in a new area, afford many slaves. The Khoikhoi responded as before by providing essential labour for the trekboers' economy. Thus they entrenched the settlers' assumption that Europeans should not perform physical labour for one another, and that native peoples were destined first to lose their land and then to work for European masters. The Europeans would cling to these convictions when they began more demanding and dangerous struggles with hunters and Bantu-speakers after 1770.

The Khoikhoi were to be affected for far longer by the colony's demand for labour than by its demand for cattle or land. In the earliest days of settlement the Company had regarded Khoikhoi as independent peoples who could not be enslaved. As some Khoikhoi were absorbed into the colony the officials' attitude, especially to Eva (ch. 4, p. 118), made it seem possible that Khoikhoi would eventually become free citizens of the colony. But it soon became clear that colonial Khoikhoi were settling into an intermediate status: they were free men who could not be enslaved or (in theory) coerced to labour, but they held no land from the Company and had neither the duties nor the obligations of freeburghers. Throughout its rule at the Cape the VOC officially maintained that Khoikhoi were free men, as did the Khoikhoi themselves, who were often at pains to distance themselves from slaves. But eventually the colony's desire for labour triumphed over these obstacles and Khoikhoi gradually and informally lost much of their freedom — losses which, after 1795, the transitional regimes would write into law (ch. 8, p. 319). Furthermore, the unbalanced sex ratios among slaves encouraged miscegenation between slaves and Khoikhoi; this miscegenation, when combined with the increasing correspondence in the socio-economic position of the two groups, eventually caused the merger of Khoikhoi and slaves into a labouring class which South Africans of the nineteenth century would call the Cape Coloured people.

Chapter One   Notes

1. Important exceptions are: Shula Marks, 'Khoisan Resistance to the Dutch in the Seventeenth and Eighteenth Centuries', *JAH*, XIII (1972), pp 55—80; H.J. le Roux, 'Die Toestand, Verspreiding en Verbrokkeling van die Hottentotstamme in Suid-Afrika 1653—1713' (M.A. thesis, University of Stellenbosch, 1945).

2. C.W. de Kiewiet, *A History of South Africa, Social and Economic* (Oxford, 1957), p. 20.

3. For a discussion of Khoikhoi population see Richard Elphick, *Kraal and Castle: Khoikhoi and the Founding of White South Africa* (New Haven and London, 1977), p. 23, n. 1.

4. KA 3974, 1 April 1662, n.p.; KA 4051, Opgaaf, 15 April 1714, p. 509. The former figure includes the garrison, the latter does not.

5. This assertion has been challenged by A.J. Böeseken. See her 'The meaning, origin, and use of the terms Khoikhoi, San and Khoisan', *Cabo* I (1972), pp. 5—10; *Cabo*, II (1974), pp. 8—10; *Cabo*, II (1975), pp. 16—18; and my replies to her under the same title in *Cabo*, II (1974), pp. 3—7; *Cabo*, II (1975), pp. 12—15.

6. On the latter suggestion see Christopher Ehret, 'Patterns of Bantu and Central Sudanic Settlement in Central and Southern Africa', *Transafrican Journal of History*, III (1973), pp. 13, 64.

7. The arguments behind this reconstruction are found in Elphick, *Kraal and Castle,* pp. 14—21.

8. The model of the 'ecological cycle' is defended in Elphick, *Kraal and Castle,* pp. 30—42. For evidence of Khoikhoi communities becoming totally reliant on hunting, gathering and robbery, see KA 4031, Dag Verhaal . . . Starrenburgh, 26 Oct. and 4 Nov. 1705, pp. 743v.—44; *RZA*, III, 280; *The Journal of Hendrik Jacob Wikar (1779) and the Journals of Jacobus Coetsé Jansz (1760) and Willem van Reenen (1791),* ed. E.E. Mossop and A.W. van der Horst (Cape Town, 1935), p. 315; George W. Stow, *The Native Races of South Africa* (London, 1905), pp. 276, 336.

9. Elphick, *Kraal and Castle*, pp. 49—53.

10. On pre-colonial Khoikhoi trade see Richard Hall Elphick, 'The Cape Khoi and the First Phase of South African Race Relations' (Ph.D. dissertation, Yale University, 1972), pp. 115—19. On trade networks from Table Bay see *VRJ*, I, 128 (14 Jan. 1653).

11. R. Raven-Hart, *Before Van Riebeeck: Callers at South Africa from 1488 to 1652* (Cape Town, 1967), pp. 15, 19, 20, 47, 48; Elphick, *Kraal and Castle*, p. 165, n. 33. The Company occasionally gave small amounts of iron as gifts to chiefs.

12. E.g., for the time of Van Riebeeck, *VRJ*, II, 370 (7 Nov. 1658); 378 (16 Nov. 1658); III, 5 (20 Jan. 1659); KA 3972, Van Riebeeck — XVII, 19 March 1660, p. 15.

13. *VRJ*, I, xxiv; 39 (11 May 1652); 270 (3 Nov. 1654).

14. KA 3967, Van Riebeeck — XVII, 22 April 1654, pp. 13—14; *VRJ* II, 288—342 (22 June — 21 Sept. 1658).

15. *Ibid.*, III, 176 (18 Jan. 1660); KA 3972, Van Riebeeck — Batavia, 29 July 1659, pp. 46—46v.

16. On the war see *VRJ*, III, 45—205 (19 May 1659 to 27 April 1660); Elphick,

Kraal and Castle, pp. 110—15.

17. E.g., *VRJ*, I, 371 (27 Nov. 1655).

18. Gonnema's responsibility is assessed in Elphick, *Kraal and Castle,* pp. 127—30.

19. The main sources on the war are KA 3987, Dagelyckse aantekening . . ., 12—25 July, 1673, pp. 213—16v; KA 3988, DR, 24 March and 7—15 April 1674, pp. 103v—10; KA 3989, Dagelyckse aanteyckening . . ., 27 March — 17 April 1676, pp. 217v—24; KA 3989, DR, 1—19 Nov. 1676, pp. 334—39v.

20. KA 3989, DR, 23 and 25 Dec. 1676, pp. 367, 370v; KA 3990, DR, 17 and 19 Jan. 1677, pp. 245, 251v—52.

21. For examples of difficulties caused by the possession of the Company's canes, see KZ 3193, Dag Verhaal . . . Slotsbo, 18 and 24 Oct. 1712, n.p. Some Small Nama chiefs were apparently attacked because of their possession of the canes; others who had canes burned them as a sign of their unwillingness to trade further with the Dutch. These acts of defiance, it should be emphasised, took place at the fringes of the Company's sphere of influence, and were not duplicated among the Western Cape Khoikhoi.

22. *VRJ*, III, 420—21 (25 Sept. 1661); 437 (21 Nov. 1661); KA 3975, DR, 26—27 May 1662, pp. 173—73v; KA 3976, DR, 29 Nov. 1663, n.p.; Donald Moodie, *The Record . . .* (Cape Town, 1838—42), p. 291.

23. For examples of informal blockades see *VRJ*, I, 273 (23 Nov. 1654); II, 36 (22 May, 1656).

24. For the life of Klaas see Elphick, *Kraal and Castle*, pp. 141—48. A good survey of the advantages of Klaas's barter to the Company is found in KA 3977, S. van der Stel — XVII, 30 April 1684, pp. 416v—17v.

25. Van der Stel made his case in KA 4011, S. van der Stel — XVII, 9 May 1695, pp. 11—13. The Heren XVII rebuked him for his action and ordered Klaas released. This order reached the Cape after Van der Stel had already freed Klaas on his own initiative. The real reasons behind Van der Stel's actions have not been authoritatively determined, but for speculation on this subject see Elphick, *Kraal and Castle*, p. 146.

26. KA 4017, Declaration of Ambrosius Zassé and Jacob Leven, 23 Jan. 1699, pp. 350—55v; KA 4031, Dag Verhaal . . . Starrenburgh, 16 Oct. — 8 Dec. 1705, pp. 740—55; KZ 3193, Dag Verhaal . . . Slotsbo, 13 Oct. — 22 Nov. 1712, n.p.

27. KA 4005, Opgaaf of 1690, p. 82.

28. Charles Lockyer, *An Account of the Trade in India* (London, 1711), p. 298; *Collectanea* (Cape Town, 1924), pp. 114—17, 126.

29. *The Early Cape Hottentots*, ed. I. Schapera (Cape Town, 1933), pp. 271—73. I am grateful to Leonard Guelke for this reference.

30. KA 3984, Prosecution of Sara, 18 Dec. 1671, pp. 222v—24; Prosecution of Five Hottentots, n.d. [1672], pp. 382—87v.

31. For an extended discussion of Khoikhoi under Dutch justice see Elphick, *Kraal and Castle*, pp. 181—88.

32. For evidence of early displacement of Khoikhoi from pastures in Stellenbosch see A. Hulshof, 'H.A. van Reede tot Drakenstein, Journaal van zijn verblijf aan de Kaap', *Bijdragen en mededeelingen van het Historisch Genootschap*, LXII (1941), pp. 128—29. I am grateful to Leonard Guelke for this reference. For early complaints that crops are trampled by Khoikhoi see Stel. 20/1, Landdrost and Heemraden — Simon van der Stel, n.d., n.p.; KA 4034, Request of Jan van Bevernasie, n.d. (1706), p. 536—37.

33. I compiled sales figures from the dagregisters of the period, and tested them against the more reliable data in the Company's ledgers when such ledgers are available (1652–53; 1655–63; 1665–67).

34. Before 1690 all the illegal traders apprehended by the Company were convicted of trading fewer than ten animals, many of them only one or two.

35. For overviews of the state of Western Cape Khoikhoi in the early eighteenth century see KA 3031, Dag Verhaal . . . Starrenburgh, (1705), *passim*; KZ 3193, Dagh Verhaal . . . Slotsbo, (1712), *passim*; KA 4037, Dagverhaal . . . Hartogh, (1707), *passim*.

36. KA 4024, DR, 13 March 1701, p. 125; DR, 16 June 1701, p. 145.

37. KA 4027, Interrogations of Willem van Sijburg, Lambert Symonsz, Jacob Holland, David Pannesmit, and the Khoikhoi Soetekoek *et al.*, Oct. and Nov. 1702, pp. 442–56, 469–71.

38. A.J.H. van der Walt, *Die Ausdehnung der Kolonie am Kap der Guten Hoffnung (1700–1779)* (Berlin, 1928), p. 15.

39. KA 4048, DR, 1713, *passim*.

40. KA 4050, DR, 13 Feb. 1714, p. 274v. For a review of the records after 1713 see Elphick, *Kraal and Castle*, p. 234.

41. *The Journals of Brink and Rhenius*, ed. E.E. Mossop (Cape Town, 1947), 'Dagh Register . . .Rhenius', 9, 14, 20 Oct. 1724, pp. 134, 140, 142; *ibid.*, 'Dag Register . . . Hop', (Brink), 6 Dec. 1761, p. 56; *Journal of Wikar*, 'Report to his Excellency Joachim van Plettenbergh', (by Wikar), 4 Sept. 1779, p. 25; Staf D 593 /U/4/1/3, Journal van de vierde reyse van Capptein R.J. Gordon, 26 July 1779, n.p.; François le Vaillant, *Voyage de Monsieur le Vaillant dans l'intérieur de l'Afrique* (Paris, 1790), II, 95; *RZA*, IV, 'Journaal en verbaal eener landreyse . . . Janssens', 4 June 1803, p. 157; Henry Lichtenstein, *Travels in Southern Africa in the Years 1803, 1804, 1805, and 1806* (Cape Town, 1928, 1930), I, 110, 310–11; II, 311–12.

42. Rhenius, *passim; Res*, V, 329 (31 Jan. 1719); VI, 288 (9 March 1723); *KP*, II, 129–30, 167–69 (4/9 April 1727 and 8 Dec. 1739); O.F. Mentzel, *A Complete and Authentic . . . Description of the . . . Cape of Good Hope* (Cape Town, 1921, 1925, 1944), III, 123; KA 4093, Interrogation of Dragonder, 5 July 1729, p. 625v.

43. Mentzel, *Description*, I, 36.

44. *RZA*, III, 'Journaal . . . Beutler', 5 June 1752, p. 292. See also KA 4031, Dag verhaal . . . Starrenburgh, 4 Nov. 1705, p. 749v; and Rhenius, *passim*.

45. *RZA*, II, 'Dagverhaal . . . Plettenberg . . .' 27 Sept. 1778, p. 73.

46. André Sparrman, *Voyage au Cap de Bonne-Espérance et autour du monde . . .* (Paris, 1787), I, 259; KA 4116, Prosecution of Harmen Cloppenburg, 2 Jan. 1738, pp. 862v–68v.

47. This is seen most clearly in connection with the 1739 disturbances; the insurgent leaders were brought to the Cape for interrogation and gave their tribal affiliations variously as Nama (i.e. Khoikhoi) and 'Bushman'. See KA 4119, Res 13 March 1739, p. 240v.

48. KA 4093, Declaration of the Hottentot Schagger Jantje, 8 March 1729, p. 630; KA 4119, Report of Johannes Kruywagen, pp. 281v–82, 293; KA 4119, Aangenoomene Togt of Dagregister . . . Theunis Botha, pp. 357, 360–65, and *passim*.

49. Marks, 'Khoisan Resistance', p. 72, n. 76; *Res*, IV, 461–63 (15 Oct. 1715);

477—78 (20 Nov. 1715); *Res*, V, 1—2 (7 Jan. 1716); 42—43 (10 March 1716); p. 168 (11 May 1717); KA 4115, Res 23 Oct. 1738, pp. 195v—96; KA 4119, Res 13 March, 28 April, 2 June, 7 and 21 July, 31 Oct., 8 Dec. 1739, pp. 240v—45v, 262—65, 274v—97, 305v—08v, 313—14v, 356v—70, 394—401v.

50. On the evolution of the commando, see Petrus Johannes van der Merwe, *Die Noordwaartse Beweging van die Boere voor die Groot Trek (1770—1842)* (The Hague, n.d.), pp. 25—27 and ch. 7, pp. 247—50 in this volume.

51. The level of compliance was, however, not high.

52. KA 4119, Res 8 Dec. 1739, pp. 395v—96.

53. Van der Merwe, *Noordwaartse Beweging*, p. 10.

54. Eighteenth-century travellers emphasised that the Sneeuwberg hunters spoke a language not mutually intelligible with Khoikhoi: this language is probably a member of Dorothea Bleek's 'Southern Bush' family. They were also the only hunter group among whom eighteenth-century observers found rock paintings. These facts together indicate that theirs was an aboriginal rather than a Khoikhoi culture. The main references on these people are cited in Elphick, *Kraal and Castle*, p. 28, n. 19, and p. 30, ns. 25, 26.

55. Van der Walt, *Ausdehnung*, p. 45; John Splinter Stavorinus, *Voyages to the East Indies . . .* (London, 1798), I, 547—48; C.P. Thunberg, *Voyages de C.P. Thunberg . . .* (Paris, 1796), I, 223.

56. *Brink*, p. 29; Staf D 593 /U/4/1/3, Vierde reyse . . . Gordon, 28 July 1779, n.p.; KZ 3947/8302, Dag register . . . Jan de la Fontaine, 16 July 1734, n.p.; KA, Aanwinsten 1881, A viii, Kol. Aanw. 242, Journal van mijn Reÿs (J.W. Cloppenburg), 26 Sept. 1768, p. 1; Sparrman, *Voyage*, I, 191; William Paterson, *A Narrative of Four Journeys . . .* (London, 1790), I, 13.

57. Sparrman, *Voyage*, I, 330—32.

58. Le Vaillant, *Voyage*, I, 253—58; Sparrman, *Voyage*, I, 257—59; KA, Aanwinsten 1881, A viii, Kol. Aanw. 242, Journaal (Cloppenburg), 29 Sept., 14 Nov. 1768, pp. 4, 20.

59. Lichtenstein, *Travels*, I, 67; *Travels*, II, 102; Sparrman, *Voyage*, I, 196, 327—28; II, 343; KA 4143, Prosecution of Alexander of Malabar, 25 March 1745, p. 624; KA 4146, Prosecution of Hottentot Frederick, 15 Sept. 1746, pp. 1113v—14; Thunberg, *Voyages*, I, 141.

60. Sparrman, *Voyage*, I, 192; Mentzel, *Description*, I, 84; Lichtenstein, *Travels*, I, 446; KA 4094, Res 31 May 1731, p. 222v. The figures on Graaff-Reinet were kindly supplied by Hermann Giliomee.

61. Thunberg, *Voyages*, I, 144; Lady Anne Barnard, *South Africa a Century Ago (1797—1801)*, ed. H.J. Anderson (Cape Town, n.d.), pp. 211—12.

62. Lichtenstein, *Travels*, I, 272; *RZA*, IV, Journaal . . . Janssens, 13 and 19 April 1803, pp. 110, 115; KA 4146, Prosecution of Hendrick Tessenaar and Anthony Minie, 3 Nov. 1746, pp. 1233v—36.

63. E.g., KA 4140, Interrogation of Martinus Spangenbergh, 18 March 1744, p. 1636.

64. *Res*, VI, 128 (2 Sept. 1721); P.J. Venter, 'Die Inboekstelsel', *Die Huisgenoot*, (1 June 1934).

65. *KP*, III, 15 (n.d., 1755). See also a proclamation of 1741 which forbade Khoikhoi and slaves to burn the veld: but this applied to Khoikhoi in their role as servants of European farmers and it was against these, in a sense, that the

regulation was directed: KA 4122, Res 19 Jan. 1741, pp. 392—94.
66. Further research must be done on the role of landdrosts and other local officials.
67. KA 4098, Criminal Rolls, Case of Hottentot Kluijtje, 30 May 1732, pp. 942v—43v; KA 4109, Prosecution of Hottentot Arnoldus, 29 March 1736, pp. 685—86; KA 4146, Landdrost vs. Hottentot Juliana, 22 Dec. 1746, pp. 1307—07v.
68. E.g., KA 4059, Sentence of Fredrick van Eeden, 5 May 1718, pp. 547—48; KA 4116, Fiscal vs. Harmen Cloppenburg, 16 Jan. 1738, pp. 795v—96.
69. KA 4140, Statement of Governor Hendrik Swellengrebel, 4 April 1744, pp. 1649—50v. The quotation is on pp. 1649v—50.
70. Hermann Giliomee, *Die Kaap tydens die Eerste Britse Bewind* (Cape Town and Pretoria, 1975), p. 261.
71. *VRJ*, II, 14, 52 (19 Feb. and 22 July 1656); KA 3999, DR, 8 Nov. 1685, p. 307v.
72. KA 4033, DR, 5 Oct. 1706, pp. 373v—75v; KA 3988, DR, 15 and 21 Nov. 1674, pp. 168, 170v—71.
73. *VRJ*, II, 301 (5 July 1658); KA 3990, DR, 19 Jan. 1677, p. 252; KA 3993, DR, 22 Jan. 1680, p. 71v; KA 4046, Helot—XVII, 4 April 1713, p. 36.
74. KA 4013, DR, 8 Aug. 1695, p. 776; KA 4015, DR, 11 Feb. 1697, pp. 481v—82; KA 4000, DR, 28 Oct. 1686, pp. 395v—96v; KA 3988, DR, 15 Nov. 1674, p. 168; KA 4002, DR, 18 March 1687, p. 207v; KA 3992, DR, 26 Jan. 1679, pp. 228—28v; KA 3993, DR, 24 and 27 Jan. 1680, pp. 72—73; KA 4013, DR, 2 Feb. 1695, pp. 706v—09.
75. *VRJ*, III, 121 (18 Aug. 1659). For another possible example see KA 7571/KZ 3179, DR, 27 Jan. 1688, n.p.
76. KA 4008, DR, 9 Nov. 1692, p. 333v; KA 4150, Interrogation of Hottentot Jantje Wemmershoek, 28 Sept. 1747, p. 1191.
77. KA 3987, DR, 24 May 1673, p. 196v; KA 3993, DR, 27 Jan. 1680, 72v—73; Moodie, *The Record*, p. 374, n. 2; KA 3996, DR, 16 Nov. 1683, pp. 343v—44; KA 4013, S. van der Stel—XVII, 30 June 1697, pp. 167—69; KA 4066, Interrogation of Scipio of Batavia, 28 Nov. 1720, p. 706v.
78. KA 4140, Testimony of Pilatus of Bengal, 29 Jan. 1744, p. 1642.
79. Thunberg, *Voyages*, I, 223; Paterson, *Narrative*, p. 12; KA 4113, Prosecution of Claas of Bengal, 6 June 1737, p. 1200v; KA 4136, Testimony of Fortuijn of Bengal, 16 Jan. 1743, p. 843; Sparrman, *Voyage*, I, 149. The quotation is in *ibid.*, I, 387.
80. KA 4146, Prosecution of Jephta of Sumbawa *et al.*, 5 May 1746, p. 963v—65.
81. KA 4014, DR, 29 Dec. 1696, pp. 1026v—28; KA 4143, Confession of Alexander of Malabar, 11 Feb. 1745, p. 646; KA 4109, Prosecution of Hottentots Ruijter and Jantje, 1 March 1736, pp. 640—42v; KA 4109, Prosecution of Hottentot Dirk, 29 March 1736, pp. 676—77v.

The white settlers, 1652—1780*

Leonard Guelke

In 1652 the Dutch East India Company (*VOC*) founded a refreshment station on the shores of Table Bay for the scurvy-ridden crews of its fleets plying between Europe and Asia. A few years later, in 1657, the Company gave out land at Rondebosch to former employees and encouraged them to settle. These settlers formed the nucleus of a permanent white population which grew slowly during the next two decades. In 1679 there were only 259 free people, of whom 55 were women and 117 were children,[1] and permanent settlement remained confined to the Cape Peninsula. From 1679 to 1717 the VOC attempted to stimulate agricultural production by granting land to settlers in fertile areas beyond the Cape Flats. When in 1717 this land-granting policy was terminated, the free population numbered just about 2,000, including about 350 women.[2] This population was largely engaged in cultivation of wheat and grapes and in the raising of sheep and cattle.

After 1717 a growing number of settlers moved inland to join the few *freeburghers* who, since 1703, had established themselves as pastoralists or *trekboers* on land leased from the Company. From 1703—80 the trekboers increased the area of white occupation almost tenfold as the Cape Colony grew from a compact settlement in the southwestern Cape to a vast, ill-defined area stretching almost to the Orange River in the north and to the Great Fish River in the east (Fig. 2.1, p. 42). During the same period there was a steady increase in the free population, which numbered 5,000 in 1751 and 10,500 in 1780.[3] In this population men consistently outnumbered women in a ratio of about 3:2 and children composed just over half the total. Most settlers lived on the land, and by 1780 a large majority of them were pastoralists. Cape Town was the only town of significance and accounted for about one fifth of the free population, which included a number of free blacks.

The Cape settlers were drawn from many sources. In the early years most of them were former VOC employees of Dutch or German origin. In the

---

* This chapter includes material from the author's 'Frontier Settlement in Early Dutch South Africa', reproduced with permission from the *Annals of the Association of American Geographers*, LXVI (1976).

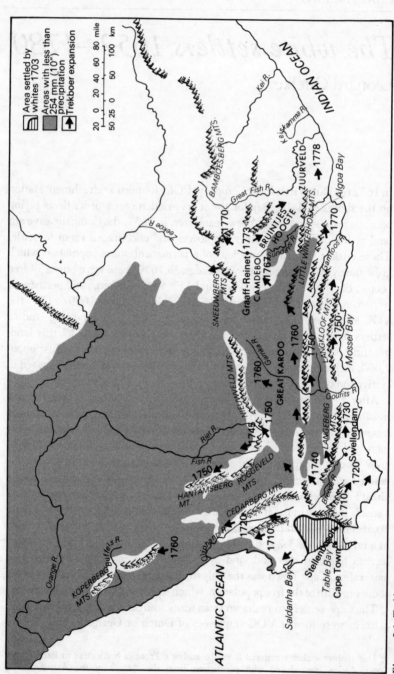

Figure 2.1 Trekboer expansion, 1703–1780

Area settled by whites 1703

Areas with less than 254 mm (10") precipitation

Trekboer expansion

ATLANTIC OCEAN

INDIAN OCEAN

Orange R.

Koperberg 1760

KOPERBERG MTS.

Buffels R.

Olifants R.

1720

1710

CEDARBERG MTS.

ROGGEVELD MTS.

HANTAMSBERG MT.

1750

Fish R.

Riet R.

1745

1750

NIEUWVELD MTS.

1760

1760

Gamka R.

1750

GREAT KAROO

1750

1750

SNEEUWBERG MTS.

1767

1760

1773

Graaff-Reinet

CAMDEBO

Sundays R.

BRUINTJES HOOGTE

LITTLE WINTERHOEK MTS.

ZUURVELD

1778

1770

Keiskamma R.

Kei R.

Great Fish R.

Zeekoe R.

1770

BAMBOES BERG MTS.

1770

Kamtoos R.

1750

LANGKLOOF MTS.

1750

Algoa Bay

Mossel Bay

Gourits R.

LANGEBERG MTS.

1730

Swellendam

1720

Breede R.

1740

1710

Table Bay

Cape Town

Stellenbosch

Saldanha Bay

50   25   0   50   100 km

20   0   20   40   60   80 mile

1680s the original settlers were joined by more Company employees, including a number on their way home after working in the East.[4] Also among the settlers of this time were a number of former African and Asian slaves, some of whom became landholders. A few white colonists married former slave women, and their children were assimilated into the otherwise white community (see ch. 4, pp. 129—31). In 1685 the VOC offered free passages to intending immigrants from Europe, but few availed themselves of the offer.[5] The Company did, however, send a handful of women from Dutch orphanages as wives for established bachelor settlers.[6] It also arranged for 156 Huguenot refugees to be settled in South Africa, most of whom arrived in 1688.[7] A few immigrants intending to become freeburghers continued to arrive directly from Europe until 1707, when the scheme of free passages was terminated. Thereafter the growth in the free population was largely due to natural increase; but many Company employees, who had often worked for freeburghers, continued to take their discharges at the Cape and reinforced the rapidly growing white population.[8] The settler population was largely of Dutch, German and, to a lesser degree, French extraction.[9]

The Cape settlers came from widely different social and economic backgrounds. Most of them came as individuals or families, not in groups. Among each of the major national groups (Dutch, German and French) were farmers, skilled artisans and labourers. Some were reasonably affluent, but many more were poverty-stricken immigrants from the lower rungs of European society. The VOC — with its low pay and high death rate — employed many down-at-heel adventurers, some of whom eventually became freeburghers.[10] There were also some well-educated and many talented individuals, especially among the Huguenots and the German-speakers. Many of the latter had been unable to get ahead in the rigidly stratified and economically depressed societies of Central Europe recovering from the devastation of the Thirty Years War.[11]

However, regardless of the specific circumstances of individual colonists — and detailed research on the social and occupational make-up of the immigrants to the Cape has yet to be done — almost all of them had been exposed to the individualistic and commercial values which were gradually spreading through Europe with the decline of feudalism. Moreover, as individual colonists faced the common tasks of making a living in a new environment, their social and occupational diversity was quickly reduced. The free society of the Cape was surprisingly homogeneous in view of the cultural variety of its founding settlers.†

† For a comparative analysis of early white society at the Cape, see Cole Harris and Leonard Guelke, 'Land and Society in Early Canada and South Africa', *Journal of Historical Geography*, III (1977), pp. 135—53.

The rapid spread of white settlement in eighteenth-century South Africa has attracted considerable scholarly attention. In seeking to explain it, scholars have drawn attention to insecurity of land tenure, overpopulation, political oppression, and a variety of economic factors.[12] The most detailed and thorough study is by P. J. van der Merwe, who emphasised the crucial role of population pressure.[13] However, this conclusion was challenged by S.D. Neumark who, in the best known study in English of the early South Africa frontier, argued that the economic attractiveness of inland areas constituted the primary factor encouraging the dispersal of settlement away from the Cape. Neumark was particularly critical of the notion that the South African trekboer was largely a self-sufficient subsistence farmer who settled on the frontier for political or social rather than commercial reasons.[14]

In this chapter I shall re-examine early European settlement in South Africa, briefly reviewing seventeenth-century developments which set the stage for later expansion. But my main concern is with trekboer expansion in the eighteenth century. My conclusions differ substantially from those of Neumark, whose arguments are critically reviewed in the final section.

The failure of intensive agriculture, 1652–1679

The directors of the VOC, the *Heren XVII*, were unprepared for the many difficulties encountered by the first Cape commander, Jan van Riebeeck, in establishing agriculture at the Cape. The memorandum of Janssen and Proot, which had prompted them to establish a settlement on the African mainland, maintained that the agricultural potential of the Cape, with its fresh water, fertile soil and temperate climate, was outstanding.[15] Van Riebeeck, who had spent a few weeks at the Cape in 1648, concurred with this appraisal and suggested that there was nothing to prevent the Cape from rivalling Japan and northern China in the variety and abundance of its produce.[16] This view was reinforced when, shortly after his arrival at the Cape, Van Riebeeck inspected the lands on the eastern side of Table Mountain. This land, he wrote, was so extensive that

> it would take a whole day to cover it by foot. According to our estimate it is a good 10 miles wide, traversed by the loveliest fresh rivers one could desire; even if there were thousands of Chinese or other tillers they could not take up or cultivate a tenth part of this land. It is moreover so fertile and rich that neither Formosa, which I have seen, nor New Netherlands, which I have heard of, can be compared with it.[17]

These appraisals of the resources of the Cape were clearly based on the assumption that intensive forms of agriculture would be adopted.

The first attempts to cultivate the Cape soil fell short of expectations.

Unacclimatised wheat seed, poor tools, a shortage of draft animals, severe south-east winds and unenthusiastic labour were all problems in the early years.[18] Some of these difficulties were due to bad luck, others to lack of foresight and a general unawareness that a considerable investment of capital and labour was needed to develop profitable agriculture on new land. As a result of this initial failure, Van Riebeeck suggested to the Heren XVII that they place agricultural operations in the hands of freemen or freeburghers who would, he felt, be inclined to work harder on their own than they had as Company employees.

Van Riebeeck received prompt authorisation from the Heren XVII to settle freeburghers, but he considered it advisable in the light of previous experience to make some preliminary trials on the land designated for their use east of Table Mountain (Fig. 2.2, p. 46).[19] Early in May 1656 Van Riebeeck had five fields prepared at Rondebosch on which rice, oats, tobacco, beans and clover were sown.[20] All these crops, with the exception of rice, did well. Van Riebeeck was well satisfied when he visited Rondebosch in October:

> The haymakers . . . had gathered a large quantity of hay into heaps and were still busy mowing. The clover was especially fine, being knee high and standing very thick. It will be very useful for the horses during the dry season when there is hardly any grazing for them. As in the fatherland, hay will be collected annually for that purpose.[21]

The importance Van Riebeeck attached to clover is noteworthy. Clover was a key crop in Dutch rotation systems because it restored worked-out land and provided feed for additional livestock. The extra manure obtained from the livestock in turn permitted the intensive cultivation of land from which high crop yields were obtained.

In February 1657 Van Riebeeck allocated land near the trial fields to the first freeburghers.[22] A freeburgher remained a subject, though not an employee, of the VOC; he acquired certain economic freedoms of which the most important was the right to own land.[23] The early freeburghers received land grants of only 11.3 ha (28 acres) each; Van Riebeeck obviously expected the Cape farmers to employ intensive Dutch agricultural methods. He recognised that freeburghers would need financial assistance, but did not succeed in convincing the Heren XVII, who placed tight restrictions on the amount of credit that could be extended to them. Moreover, the Heren XVII set prices at which the Company would purchase their wheat, and these were low in accordance with prices then prevailing in Europe.[24] Van Riebeeck sought to alleviate the labour shortage by importing slaves, who were made available to the freeburghers on credit. The early slaves were not efficient

Figure 2.2 The southwestern Cape, c.1710

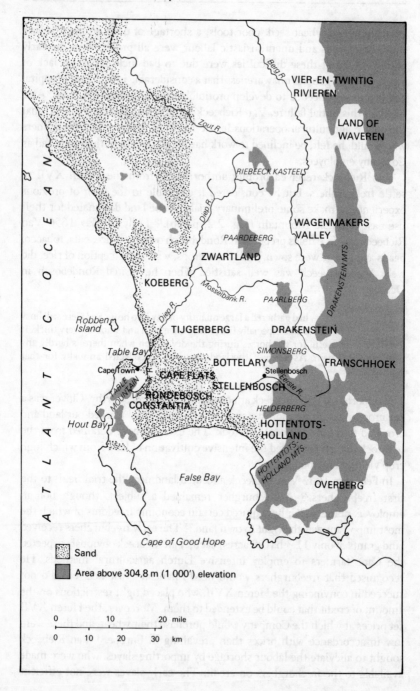

workers; many deserted while others were so intractable that their owners returned them to the Company.

Economic conditions at the Cape were not conducive to the system of intensive mixed farming on which Van Riebeeck had based his plans. Both the capital and labour for such a system were lacking. The freeburghers concentrated on reducing the investment of capital and labour to a minimum. As a result they did not take up the cultivation of clover or other fodder crops, and pastured their livestock on the veld near their freehold land. The pure-bred Dutch sheep, which did not do well on the natural pasture, were allowed to mingle with stock obtained from the Khoikhoi, and disappeared as a distinctive breed.[25] Oxen, which could fend for themselves, replaced more efficient horses as plough animals, although most farmers retained a few horses for riding.

The freeburghers — even when using extensive methods of farming which dispensed with such labour-intensive practices as crop rotation, fallows, careful weeding and manuring — found the cultivation of wheat barely profitable, and turned elsewhere to make a living for themselves. The raising of livestock, which were purchased from the VOC and bartered or robbed from the Khoikhoi, became a mainstay of most farming operations. The reliance the freeburghers placed on the open veld for pasture weakened the link between cultivation and livestock farming. Although sheep and cattle were able to survive in the open throughout the year, large areas of land were needed for each animal, especially in the dry summer months. This dispersal of livestock made the collection of manure impractical and longer fallow periods were required for the rejuvenation of soils. Freeburghers also took every opportunity to obtain extra income from non-farming activities. In 1660 a *plakkaat* prohibited freeburghers from collecting wood for foreign ships instead of using their oxen to plough their fields.[26]

When Van Riebeeck left the Cape in 1662 he clearly recognised the extent to which his plans for the settlement had failed. In a memorandum to his successor he maintained that no more land for cultivation could be provided west of the Liesbeek River without reducing the already inadequate amounts of pasture available for livestock.[27] A large portion of an area which Van Riebeeck had expected to support thousands of families was now considered to be fully occupied with only about fifteen operating farms. This re-evaluation of the Cape's resources clearly stemmed from Van Riebeeck's recognition that intensive mixed farming had failed and that future development would have to be based on extensive methods.

For many years after Van Riebeeck's departure little was done to reinvigorate Cape agriculture, and the settlement remained dependent on imported rice to meet its cereal needs. The adoption of extensive methods of wheat farming on small farms made it imperative that the area under cultivation be expanded if the colony was ever to become self-sufficient in grain. Those freeburghers who survived on the land (and many did not) did so on the basis of extensive livestock farming and by taking advantage of non-farming opportunities such as wood hauling, hunting and fishing.[28] The Heren XVII, however, were loath to expend additional funds on the Cape, which had already proved to be something of a financial burden.

The occupation of Hottentots-Holland by Company soldiers in 1672 would probably have been followed by the permanent settlement of freeburghers beyond the Cape Flats had not the Second Khoikhoi-Dutch war (1673—77) put an end to any ideas of expansion; in the event the settlement remained confined to the Cape Peninsula for another seven years. When in 1679 the VOC finally adopted a policy of expansion, fewer than half the 142 adult freeburghers had a stake in farming; the rest made a living as artisans and traders near the small town growing up on the shores of Table Bay.[29]

A development of major significance during the first twenty-seven years of European colonisation was the adoption of extensive agriculture — a reversal of the agricultural intensification process of Western Europe. Extensive methods had been adopted before the freeburghers had enough arable land either to keep themselves or to meet the cereal requirements of the VOC. Had the Heren XVII been prepared to invest the capital needed to get intensive agriculture firmly established, or set wheat prices at levels which would have encouraged the freeburghers themselves to make these investments, expansion beyond the Cape Peninsula would not have been necessary. And a settlement more in keeping with the initial intentions of the Heren XVII, who had planned to confine settlement to a small easily defensible portion of the Cape Peninsula, might have emerged.

The southwestern Cape, 1679—1780

In 1679 Simon van der Stel arrived at the Cape with orders from the Heren XVII to begin new expansion; Van der Stel's land policy was to have important implications for the development of extensive agriculture. Under this policy, land at Stellenbosch was made available for settlement on a first come, first served basis.[30] No limits were placed on the quantity of land an individual might claim, but all claimed land had to be cultivated within three years or be forfeited. The freehold land grants which were finally authorised at Stellenbosch were usually smaller than initial claims, but they were three to six times larger than those of earlier times, ranging in size from 32 to 64 ha (80 to 160 acres).[31] Only between a fifth and a tenth of the land suitable for cultivation had been given out by 1687 when Simon van der Stel closed the Stellenbosch area to further settlement, although a few grants were made thereafter on an individual basis. The decision to limit the growth of settlement at Stellenbosch was probably taken on the urging of established farmers, who needed large areas of unallocated land as rough grazing for their livestock.[32]

In allowing settlers to claim their own land, Van der Stel avoided the mistake of imposing an unsuitable framework of landholding in advance of settlement. However, for Commissioner Hendrik Adriaan van Reede, who visited Stellenbosch in 1685, the disadvantages of Van der Stel's policy were more apparent than the advantages. Van Reede complained that future settlers would be cut off from water because all the good arable land next to rivers and streams had been given out (Fig. 2.3, p. 50), a situation which he predicted would give rise to many 'disputes, quarrels and unpleasantness.'[33] In Van Reede's eyes the problem could have been avoided had land grants been rectangular and aligned at right angles to the streams. The disputes anticipated by Van Reede did not arise, however, because the land beyond the rivers was not allocated to settlers and remained in VOC hands. It would not have occured to Van Reede, who assessed the situation in European terms, that Stellenbosch was close to being considered fully settled with about sixty land grants comprising only about 5 per cent of the total area, including mountainous and other areas unsuitable for cultivation.[34]

As new lands were given out in Drakenstein, Paarl, Franschhoek, Tijgerberg, Wagenmakers Valley, Land of Waveren and the Paardeberg, the general land policy adopted in Stellenbosch remained in force. Large areas of potentially cultivable land were not allocated and became available to freeburghers as rough grazing for their livestock. In the upper Berg River Valley, however, the policy of allowing freeburghers to stake out the

Table 2.1   Freehold land grants, 1657—1717

District	Number of grants	Area of grants km² (square miles)	Total area settled* km² (square miles
Cape	107	45.6 (17.6)	1,300 (500)
Stellenbosch	108	53.3 (20.6)	1,300 (500)
Drakenstein	189	94.0 (36.3)	3,900 (1,500)
Total	404	192.9 (74.5)	6,500 (2,500)

Source: DO, Old Cape Freeholds Vols. 1 and 2; Old Stellenbosch Freeholds Vols. 1 and 2.

* Approximate total of areas of more or less continuous settlement.

Figure 2.3 Patterns of landholdings in Stellenbosch and Drakenstein, 1680–1700

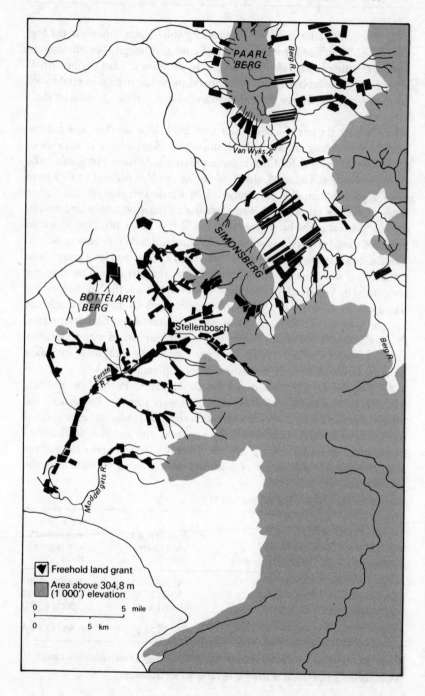

PAARL BERG

Berg R.

Van Wyks R.

SIMONSBERG

BOTTELARY BERG

Stellenbosch

Berg R.

Eerste R.

Moddergats R.

▼ Freehold land grant

Area above 304,8 m (1 000') elevation

0   5   mile

0   5   km

boundaries of their own farms was replaced by one in which authorities allocated standard rectangular grants of 50.5 ha (125 acres),[35] a policy modification almost certainly stemming from Van Reede's criticism of Stellenbosch landholding (Fig. 2.3). When in 1717 the granting of new land ceased, there were about 400 freehold farms in the colony, covering in all 194 km² (75 square miles) (Table 2.1, p. 49).[36] This figure was remarkably low — even when one takes account of the extensive areas unsuitable for cultivation — and represented only a small fraction of the area exploited by the colonists.

The land policy of Simon van der Stel helped early settlers to establish viable farming operations without much capital. In economic terms, land, a factor in abundant supply, was substituted for capital and labour. Although capital requirements were low, most colonists were not in a position to meet them. Van der Stel described the measures he adopted to encourage agriculture in a letter to the Heren XVII:

> The poor and needy farmers who are in distressing circumstances were provided with enough land, animals and wheat seed to be repaid to the Company after the harvest; as without this measure the projected goal [of colonial self-sufficiency] could never have been reached; . . . it would be an absolutely impossible thing for a poor destitute people to have accomplished anything with empty hands, except with our encouragement.[37]

These measures would not have succeeded if settlers had not been able to use extensive methods of agriculture, which permitted a quick return on small amounts of invested capital.

The extensive methods of farming, under which each settler received a *de facto* land allocation equivalent to about 8 km² (3 square miles) (including both an individual's freehold land and his 'share' of VOC pasture land), and the nature of the country with its large areas of mountains and sand flats, combined to scatter the population over a considerable area (Fig. 2.2, p. 46 and Table 2.1, p. 49). In the more closely settled areas of Stellenbosch and Drakenstein there were about two free people per 2.6 km² (1 square mile), and in the Tijgerberg and Zwartland even lower population densities were found. Sparse settlement, in the absence of good natural transportation routes, meant that there were relatively few people among whom the costs of providing transportation and other common facilities could be shared. These facilities were supposed to be provided by local authorities (*landdrost* and *heemraden*) and supported by taxes and labour provided by settlers.[38] But the freeburghers evaded local taxes and delegated inept slaves to acquit their corvée. In consequence Cape farmers were obliged to put up with rough tracks instead of roads, and the oxwagon became the most popular vehicle for transporting farm produce and supplies. Although oxen are slow-moving and cumbersome animals, they were well suited to haul heavy wagons over the Cape's sandy tracks and were able to thrive on rough forage along the route.

The poor transportation system worked against the exchange of goods and services between farm and village. In the vast area beyond the Cape Flats there was only one village, Stellenbosch, although a few artisans were scattered throughout the countryside (see ch. 5, p. 189). The lack of service centres meant that most Cape farmers had to be much more self-reliant than their European counterparts, and lost some of the advantages associated with specialisation and the division of labour. Yet, in spite of its drawbacks, dispersed settlement had obvious short-term economic advantages for settlers without capital. These advantages were most attractive in the early days of settlement. The first freeburghers benefited from game and timber on or near their farms, and from nearby Khoikhoi labour. But as the game was destroyed and the timber used up, the disadvantages of dispersed settlement became more severe. However, despite its disadvantages, an extensive agricultural system is not easily given up, once adopted. The problem is that the substantial benefits of close settlement are realised only gradually. Its disadvantages, however, appear immediately in the form of the longer and harder working hours necessary to maintain or increase the productivity of a fixed quantity of land.[39]

The expansion of the settlement created a demand for more labourers. This demand was largely met by importing African and Asian slaves, who were sold to settlers on credit by the Company. More affluent settlers employed white servants in supervisory positions. The less affluent settlers could not afford slaves and for the most part worked their own land, employing extra workers when they were needed.[40] The Khoikhoi, whose traditional communities slowly disintegrated under the impact of European settlement, were particularly useful as a source of casual labour for those settlers who had no slaves. But they also found employment on large estates, especially at harvest time (see ch. 1, p. 17). In 1713 the Khoikhoi near the Cape were decimated by a smallpox epidemic, and their importance as a source of labour in the arable areas declined sharply.

The Cape administration found it increasingly difficult to control the freeburghers who sought opportunities on the wider frontier created by the expansion of the settlement. In the 1690s the illicit livestock trade with Khoikhoi of the interior was lucrative enough to spawn a group of frontier traders who acted as middlemen for the Khoikhoi and the farmers of Stellenbosch and Drakenstein.[41] Although freeburghers were occasionally apprehended while engaged in illicit trading, the frontier was by this time too wide and the number of Company officials too few to stop it. The decrees or plakkaten issued and reissued against trade with the Khoikhoi bear testimony to the inability of the Company to control frontier activity.[42] The situation demanded more effective policing of the frontier rather than the promulgation of plakkaten with heavy sentences for the contravention of laws every trader was confident he could avoid.

As their flocks and herds increased, the freeburghers did not hesitate to use the pasture lands beyond the settled areas. In the dry summer months it became common for farmers to send their livestock inland under the care of a son, trusted slave, or Khoikhoi. This incipient system of transhumance received a setback when Simon van der Stel, anxious to reassert Company control on the frontier, ordered freeburghers to keep their livestock within a day's journey of their freehold properties.[43] This measure appears to have been reasonably effective, perhaps because freeburghers were unwilling to risk heavy sentences merely for seeking good pasture for their stock.

In 1703, however, the administration of Willem Adriaan van der Stel reversed this policy and began issuing free grazing permits to all applicants. The holder of one of these early grazing permits was entitled to the exclusive use of a designated area for a period of three to four months. The standard period of a permit's validity was soon extended to six months, and general criteria were gradually established to define its limits. The basic rule was that no grazing permit would be issued to a new applicant if his grazing area would be within an hour's walking distance of the centre of an existing one. In practice this meant that each permit holder had exclusive control of a minimum of 2,420 ha (6,000 acres). Although in theory these holdings were circular, this theory meant little to the trekboer of the eighteenth century. As long as he did not infringe on his neighbours, a trekboer had *de facto* control of all the land he could use, often twice or four times the theoretical minimum. In 1714 a small fee was charged for a grazing permit or loan farm (*leningplaats*) as these permits came to be known.[44] In the same year, permission to cultivate wheat on loan farms, which up to that time had been granted only on an individual basis, was made a standard concession.[45]

In addition to trade and pasture, the remote regions of the colony offered incomparable hunting opportunities of which freeburghers had availed themselves from the earliest times. Small hunting parties were constantly setting out in search of game, particularly hippopotamus and eland. Such expeditions might last a week or more. A few freeburghers made careers for themselves as professional elephant hunters and penetrated deep into the country.[46] Hunting expeditions provided colonists with cheap meat for themselves and their slaves. More important, these expeditions permitted freeburghers to become acquainted with the resources of the interior. This knowledge was to be of value to many colonists who decided to set up as stock farmers in the interior as agricultural opportunities in the settled areas declined.

In 1717 the Heren XVII decided not to encourage further European migration to the Cape and to continue to rely on slave labour for the future development of the colony. Consequently they ordered the local authorities not to give out any more land in freehold.[47] This decision, however, was not as important for settlement as it might otherwise have been, because land was still available on loan. Many cultivators had in earlier times commenced farming on a loan farm, a portion of which was later converted into a freehold farm. The latter possibility was now closed, but was reintroduced in 1743, when the holder of a loan farm was given the option of converting a portion of it (50.6 ha or 125 acres) into freehold tenure on payment of a lump sum based on the value of the property. The occupant of such a property still had to pay the annual rent he had formerly paid on his loan farm. Only a handful of cultivators took advantage of this option. After 1717 an individual could acquire land for his own use through inheritance, by purchase, or by leasing a loan farm. In practice there was little distinction between freehold land and loan farms, whose leases became so secure that the fixed improvements (which could be sold) came to include the value of the land on which they stood.[48]

The VOC no longer desired a growing freeburgher population, largely because it was experiencing difficulty in marketing their produce. Overproduction, which was already a serious problem before 1717, continued to plague the Cape farmer throughout the eighteenth century. In the absence of a large home population, Cape farmers were chiefly dependent on passing ships for a market. The business generated by ships calling at Table Bay included sales to free-spending crews on shore leave and delivery of supplies directly to the ships. In times of war, troops were frequently stationed at the Cape and provided an additional market for Cape produce. From 1717 to 1780, except in the final decade, the number of ships calling at the Cape did not increase. The stagnation of this vitally important market had a detrimental effect on demand for arable produce, and freeburghers generally had to be content with selling to the VOC at low official prices. The VOC tried to get rid of some of the surplus wheat that was piling up at the Cape by exporting about 5,000 muiden (15,500 bushels) annually to the East.[49] However, this was not nearly enough to deal with the problem of overproduction. Wine farmers fared even worse as Cape wine travelled badly and acquired a poor reputation abroad. Nonetheless, after 1743 some wine was exported annually to Batavia.[50]

The markets for meat and other pastoral products were also largely tied to the volume of shipping in Table Bay. The Company did not control the market for livestock as tightly as it controlled that for wheat and wine, and the price of meat and live animals tended to reflect supply and demand. Demand for livestock was reasonably stable, but drought and diseases occasionally reduced the supply, and prices were forced up. A particularly serious rash of diseases decimated Cape flocks and herds in the period 1714—18.[51] Meat prices were high for a few years thereafter, but began a steady decline in the mid-1720s as the supply of animals increased. Live sheep, which fetched over 7 guilders in the early 1720s, usually sold for from 2 to 3 guilders after 1730.[52]

The weak demand for Cape wine and wheat put arable farming at the Cape into the doldrums. The effects of the slack market, however, were not felt evenly by all cultivators, but varied according to the size of their operations. In general, large estates were more efficient than small ones, whose production costs tended to increase with time. The lack of a reliable and inexpensive group of artisans to serve them was one barrier to efficient production that was keenly felt by small and medium producers. Baron van Imhoff, who inspected the Cape in 1743, remarked:

> It seems incredible that a mason and a carpenter each earns from eight to nine schellingen [twenty schellingen equalled one guilder] a day and in addition receives food and drink and withal does not do as much as a half trained artisan in Europe. It is a burden this colony cannot bear and it certainly has a prejudicial effect on agriculture.[53]

The larger producers avoided the cost of hiring independent artisans by establishing their own specialised estate workshops which were manned by skilled slaves.[54]

The small cultivator was also hard hit by the catastrophic decline in the number of Khoikhoi workers. Expensive slave help had to be hired from other freeburghers at busy times in the agricultural year, because marginal farmers could not afford more than a few costly slaves of their own.[55] More affluent farmers, although they, too, were affected by increased dependence on slave labour (Table 2.2, p. 56), were able to achieve some economies by dividing farm tasks among a dozen or so slaves, each of whom might have a special skill.

In addition to gaining economic advantages from the size of their operations, wealthy farmers were often able to procure monopoly leases from the VOC. The holders of such leases, which were regularly auctioned by the Company, obtained the sole right of supplying the VOC or Cape public with a specific commodity such as meat, wine or beer. A monopoly lease provided an

Table 2.2 Distribution of cultivators‡

| | Number of slaves held (adult males) | | | | | | | | | |
| | 0 | | 1–5 | | 6–10 | | Over 10 | | |
Year	No. of cultivators	% of all cultivators	No. of cultivators	% of all cultivators	No. of cultivators	% of all cultivators	No. of cultivators	% of all cultivators	Total No. of cultivators
1716	40	17.7	90	39.8	53	23.5	43	19.0	226
1746	19	6.6	108	37.8	85	29.7	74	25.9	286
1770	11	3.6	108	35.1	98	31.8	91	29.5	308

Source: KA 4053, 4144 and 4240 (Opgaaf Rolls).

‡ This table is concerned with adult male slaves held by cultivators. Table 3.7 in the next chapter includes all slaves — men, women and children — and is not restricted to slave holders involved in arable farming.

Table 2.3 Estates of cultivators: Debts as a proportion of all assets, 1731–1780

| | Average gross value of estate (Cape guilders) | | | | | | | | |
| | Under 10,000 | | | 10,000 to 20,000 | | | Over 20,000 | | |
Period	No. of estates	Avg. debt	Avg. debt as a per cent of avg. assets	No. of estates	Avg. debt	Avg. debt as a per cent of avg. assets	No. of estates	Avg. debt	Avg. debt as a per cent of avg. assets
1731–1742	14	4,170	78.6	12	7,620	53.2	7	11,000	26.7
1751–1762	8	3,120	52.8	6	3,530	21.3	4	10,450	38.2
1770–1780	5	3,850	64.1	6	7,680	54.4	9	27,450	36.2

Source: Inventarissen, MOOC (Weeskamer), vols. 8/5–8/17 and Stel., vols. 18/30–18/34.

attractive investment opportunity for well-established freeburghers, and assured them a market for their own produce covered by the lease.

The poor markets for arable produce and the high production costs were reflected in a general tendency for land prices to remain static or to decline from 1720 to 1770.[56] This tendency, however, did not make it much easier for a newcomer to get started in arable farming. In the seventeenth and early eighteenth centuries a new settler was able to commence farming on unimproved land which he obtained for nothing from the VOC. After 1717 a new cultivator was obliged to purchase a farm with its improvements, which often added little to the productive potential of the land. Indeed, there is considerable evidence to suggest that the productivity of cultivated land generally declined with use.[57] In addition to having to purchase land, which in spite of the trends referred to above still demanded a substantial capital outlay, a new arable farmer had also to acquire slaves, stock and equipment. The average cost of a working farm before 1770 was about 15,000 guilders, comprising 6,000 guilders for land, 2,000 guilders for slaves, and the rest for stock and equipment.[58] A prospective new cultivator would have needed minimum capital of 5,000 to 10,000 guilders for the purchase of such a working farm, depending on how much additional capital was available on loan.

The ability of a young person to take up arable farming was largely determined by the amount of capital he or she was able to command. A number of sources of capital, both public and private, were available to freeburghers in the eighteenth century, but by far the most important was inheritance. Under the Cape system of partible inheritance the estate of a freeburgher was normally divided equally between the children and the surviving spouse.[59] Each child, regardless of sex, was entitled to an equal portion of the children's half of the estate. Inheritance portions could be altered if a will were made, but no spouse or child could be disinherited of more than one half of his or her standard portion. The standard inheritance portions, however, were seldom much altered even when a will was prepared.

At the close of the VOC-supervised phase of settlement (1717), wealth was unevenly distributed among the farming population. The young adult children of the established freeburghers were in a good position to establish careers for themselves, but there were also a large number of young people who were destined to inherit virtually nothing, and who consequently had limited access to loans. Mentzel noted that the difficulty of obtaining a loan was a major grievance of colonists.[60] The amount of capital an individual might assemble could also be affected by marriage, by the extent of the financial support of parents before their deaths, by the number of brothers and sisters with whom an inheritance had to be shared, and by many other factors.

Poor but enterprising colonists were able to put capital together through their own efforts. Elephant hunting offered good returns for a small investment. Nevertheless, only the children of the more affluent families were generally in a position to assemble the considerable amount of capital needed to become successful cultivators.

The operation of the demand and supply factors of arable farming was reflected in a general tendency for the size and gross value of working arable farms to increase. This tendency was clearly revealed in the increasing number and the changing distribution of slaves employed by arable farmers (Table 2.2, p. 56). The number of male slaves in arable farming increased from 1,500 in 1716 to 2,800 in 1770; the number of cultivators who owned one or two slaves declined, but an increasing number of farmers owned ten or more.[61] Additional evidence of trends in arable farming is to be found in the estate records which reveal that many small farmers were deeply in debt and left no assets at all.[62] In the period 1731—42 the average debt of estates with a gross value of less than 10,000 guilders was 4,170 guilders, which comprised fully 78.6 per cent of the average gross assets of these estates (Table 2.3, p. 56). While small cultivators found it increasingly difficult to secure a reasonable return on their invested capital, many large producers became exceptionally wealthy. In the period 1771—80 several colonists left estates with a net value of over 30,000 guilders; the largest, that of Martin Melck in 1776, was valued at 225,000 guilders.[63]

The trekboer economy, 1703—1780

As the number of stock farmers increased, more and more loan farms were taken out at ever-increasing distances from Cape Town. The number of independent stockholders, ¶ who comprised about one tenth of the 260 agricultural producers in 1716, increased to 225 in 1746 and to 600 in 1770.[64] In 1770 they represented two thirds of all independent farmers. In other words, a rapid increase in the number of pastoralists took place while the number of arable farmers grew very slowly.

The direction of trekboer expansion was largely a function of the nature of the terrain, the availability of permanent surface water, and the quality of

¶ I define an independent stockholder as someone who is not engaged in commercial arable farming and who owns at least fifty sheep and twenty cattle. Almost all cultivators also possessed stock. Some of these took out loan farms on which their animals could graze during the dry summer months, but usually they pastured their sheep and cattle on the open veld near their cultivated lands.

pasture. The main areas settled before 1720 included the country to the north of the Berg River (Piketberg) and to the east of the Hottentots-Holland Mountains. In the 1720s the trekboers settled the Oliphants River Valley, the upper Breede River Valley and adjacent valleys and basins, and pushed eastwards in the coastal area to the south of the Langeberg Mountains. The 1730s saw them entering the Little Karoo which, with the expanding area of settlement south of the Langeberg Mountains, became the district of Swellendam in 1745. In the north a group of trekboers crossed the arid plain between the Cape mountains and the Roggeveld escarpment in 1745 and occupied the most accessible portions of the interior plateau. The initial settlement expanded northwards and eastwards; the Hantamsberg was occupied in the 1750s and the Nieuwveld in the 1760s. Settlement spread into the summer rainfall area in the late 1760s, and the leading colonists occupied good sites in the Camdebo (Graaff-Reinet area) and the Sneeuwberg Mountains. In the 1770s trekboers occupied the areas to the north and east of the Sneeuwberg Mountains, and to the southeast the country behind Bruintjes Hoogte was taken up. Meanwhile, in the south, Swellendam colonists pushed eastwards in the Little Karoo and the Langkloof. When in 1770 the administration made an abortive attempt to check further expansion at the Gamtoos River, a number of trekboers had already taken out loan farms beyond it. The eastward expansion continued, and by the late 1770s settlers had occupied the Zuurveld (see Fig. 2.1, p. 42).

Population densities in stock farming areas were extraordinarily low everywhere. The extremely dispersed settlement pattern was fostered in part by the nature of the country with its large areas of arid and mountainous land; more important, however, was the system of land granting, which entitled each landholder to at least 2,420 ha (6,000 acres). Although large areas of arid or semi-arid land were incapable of supporting high population densities, even the better endowed areas were sparsely inhabited. The country almost certainly supported more nomadic Khoikhoi per km^2 in the seventeenth century than trekboers in the eighteenth. A well-endowed portion of the south coast, for instance, had 142 loan farms in an area of about 11,500 km^2 (4,450 square miles) (Fig. 2.4, p. 60). Assuming an average household of seven people, the mean population density of the region was approximately one free person per 10 km^2 (four square miles). In the arid regions much lower densities were typical — anything from one free person per 13 km^2 (five square miles) to one free person per 26 km^2 (ten or more square miles).

The dispersal of settlement away from Cape Town created even more serious transportation problems for the inhabitants of the inland regions than those experienced by the arable farmers. The routes that connected the frontier areas with Cape Town were little more than rough tracks. The

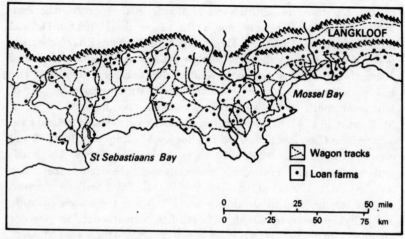

Figure 2.4 Distribution of loan farms: Southcentral Swellendam
After map A231, Van de Graaff collection

number of people available for construction and maintenance of transportation facilities in any given area was too small for anything else. Indeed, had it not been possible to extend unbeaten tracks over large areas of the country, the stock farmers' rapid expansion inland would not have been possible. The only noteworthy improvement in transportation facilities for the entire stock farming area was the establishment of a ferry (the colony's second) on the Breede River near Swellendam in 1757.[65] Even this ferry was so small that heavily laden wagons had to be taken across the river in two loads.[66]

All trekboers in the more remote sections of the colony were obliged to put up with excessively high transportation costs. True, slaughter stock could walk to market, but driving them hundreds of miles added considerably to their cost. The trekboers themselves did not normally accompany their animals to market. This task was usually in the hands of the employees of the meat contractors, who travelled the country districts buying up stock. Many inland farmers also produced butter, tallow, gum aloe and other produce on which heavy transportation costs could not be avoided. The difficulty a trekboer encountered in transporting his produce to Cape Town is clearly described in the following account of Anders Sparrman, a Swedish scientist who visited the Cape in the 1770s.

Every peasant for such a journey as this [from just east of Mossel Bay to Cape Town] has two or three Hottentots, one to lead the oxen, and either one or two to drive the spare team; besides which his wife often goes with him, either for the purpose of having her children baptized at the Cape, or else for fear of being attacked by the Hottentots in her husband's absence. Thus, taking it at the lowest, and reckoning only three persons and twenty oxen for thirty days, it stands a great many farmers in ninety days of work of themselves and men, and six hundred of their cattle, in order to make one turn with their butter to the market, and so in proportion for such as are less distant. Hence it is evident, that many thousand days work are unnecessarily lost and thrown away every year.[67]

Sparrman was of the opinion that the days 'unnecessarily lost and thrown away' in transporting goods could be overcome if ships called at Mossel Bay or elsewhere along the eastern coast. The VOC, however, did not consider that the volume of trade merited the construction of the harbour and storage facilities, and the trekboers remained dependent on overland routes to Cape Town.

For the remoter inhabitants of the colony, such as those in the Sneeuwberg Mts., Agter Bruintjes Hoogte or the Zuurveld, the journey to Cape Town and back might take three months or more. Travel was always demanding and often dangerous. The English plant collector, Francis Masson, described the descent from the Roggeveld:

We were furnished with fresh oxen, and several Hottentots, who, with long thongs of leather fixed to the upper part of our wagons, kept them from overturning, while we were obliged to make both the hind wheels fast with an iron chain to retard their motion. After two hours and a half employed in hard labour, sometimes pulling on one side, sometimes on the other, and sometimes all obliged to hang on with our whole strength behind the wagon, to keep it from running over the oxen, we arrived at the foot of the mountain, where we found the heat more troublesome than the cold had been at the top.[68]

The improvements made to a few of the passes closest to Cape Town barely shortened the already enormous time many trekboers were obliged to spend on the road.

The high cost of transportation was also reflected in the prices of all items imported to the interior. The trekboers were under enormous economic pressure to reduce such items to a bare minimum. Imported items generally considered essential were guns, gunpowder, coffee, tea, tobacco, sugar, and (in the early days) soap. Guns and gunpowder were absolutely indispensable, but the teeming herds of game provided the trekboers with raw materials to make local substitutes for a number of manufactured items. For instance, the Swedish botanist, Carl Peter Thunberg, who visited the frontier in the 1770s, noted that 'thongs made of the hides of animals were everywhere used by the farmers instead of cords and ropes, both for the tackling of wagons and other purposes.'[69] Skins were also used for making saddle blankets, sacks, and even, among the poorest, for clothes.[70] Trekboers in remote areas appeared poverty-stricken to Europeans. Hendrick Swellengrebel Jr, a VOC official who made an inspection of the stock farming areas in 1776, attributed the appalling conditions in the Camdebo to the distance separating that region from Cape Town.[71] Thunberg observed that 'the farmers who live up-country, have generally the misfortune to be poorer, and to be subjected to greater expenses than others.'[72]

The poorly developed transportation system and low population densities also combined to prevent any significant labour specialisation. This situation was reflected in the complete absence of any urban development. The administrative centre of Swellendam illustrates the point nicely. In 1745 a *drostdy* was established for the new district of Swellendam on the site of the present village of that name.[73] In 1750 the landdrost and heemraden of the new district discussed plans for controlling the growth of the village as artisans and others set up businesses to serve the inhabitants of the district.[74] The expected development never occurred. In 1774 no artisans were available to repair official buildings.[75] In 1777, over thirty years after the founding of the drostdy, Swellendam comprised but four houses, one of them used by the landdrost.[76]

In the absence of artisans and other specialists, the inhabitants of the frontier forfeited many of the economic advantages and social amenities derived from the division of labour. For the most part they did without physicians, blacksmiths, carpenters, wagonmakers, masons, teachers and the like. The early trekboers and their descendants had to be far more self-reliant than had hitherto been necessary for anyone at the Cape. In fact, the trekboers had no choice but to become jacks-of-all-trades and, it might be added, masters of none. A trekboer would make use of artisans if his business took him to Cape Town, but for everyday construction and maintenance work he was entirely dependent on his own resources. In the absence of frontier churches, religious services were often conducted on the loan farm by the trekboer himself, occasionally by a visiting preacher. Wealthier trekboers hired ill-qualified itinerant teachers, usually ex-Company servants, to look after the education of their children. Children of poorer people grew up without formal education.[77]

The gradual disintegration of the Khoikhoi communities in the interior provided trekboers with cheap labour. The Khoikhoi were excellent stockmen who were intimately acquainted with the local grazing and water resources. Khoikhoi workers were particularly valuable to trekboers (often hard pressed for cash) as they were paid in kind — usually their keep and sometimes a small proportion of the increase of the stock they tended (see ch. 1, p. 28). More importantly, the availability of Khoikhoi made it unnecessary for a trekboer to invest much capital in slaves.[78] Occasionally Khoikhoi who were still adherents of existing tribes would work for a trekboer for a year or two before returning to their people. In the 1760s and 1770s the Khoikhoi workers were joined by 'Bushman' women and children (see ch. 1, p. 25) who had been captured in the various campaigns waged against their bands.

In addition to certain economic hardships, the frontier trekboers had to put up with severe social isolation. The day-to-day life on a loan farm was often monotonous and dull, and was probably harder on women than on men. Men spent much time in the saddle supervising their workers or hunting with their sons. The sporting life, however, was not a substitute for a fuller social life, and isolation from the outside world tended to blunt the trekboers' intellectual development. The wives of the trekboers were responsible for running the home and rearing their numerous children. Much of the actual work about the house was done by Khoikhoi servants and slaves, and frontier women found themselves with time on their hands but little to do with it. But although frontier life was generally rather dull, there were times of excitement and even danger. The excitement, however, did not make frontier life more appealing, because it often involved violent clashes with the 'Bushmen', who became increasingly hostile as their hunting grounds were taken over by the trekboers.

Europeans were impressed by the egalitarianism and independent spirit of the trekboers. These characteristics were undoubtedly related to their economic circumstances. On their isolated farms each trekboer produced almost everything he needed and acquired other items directly from Cape Town. A trekboer was, therefore, largely independent of his neighbours for his economic well-being. If neighbouring trekboers quarrelled — and in an unsurveyed land there was much to quarrel about — there was little economic incentive for them to patch things up, neither being likely to need the other's cooperation to maintain his economic position. Extreme individualism was further fostered by the absence of a non-farm rural population dependent on the farming community. Because artisans, retailers and innkeepers in rural areas are dependent for their economic survival on the goodwill of the entire farming community, people in such occupations tend to be tolerant and flexible in their attitudes, and actively promote these values within the whole society. Trekboer society lacked the cement that a community-minded non-farm rural population could have provided and became, in consequence, even more atomised.[79]

The trekboers did, however, set some limits to their independent behaviour. They were noted for their hospitality to travellers. In a country without any stores, inns or guest houses, all travellers were dependent on farmers living along the road for refreshments and supplies. As all inland farmers were obliged to make occasional journeys to the Cape, everyone stood to benefit from an informal system of reciprocal help to travellers.[80] Another area in which inland inhabitants cooperated with each other was in the defence of their property against the 'Bushmen'. The need for such cooperation is obvious, the very existence of the settler community depending on it.

Trekboer life had its hardships, but it did not demand the capital needed by a new cultivator. Land was available on the edge of the settled areas for a small annual rent, and elsewhere in the frontier regions by purchase of the *opstal* (fixed improvements) of an existing loan farm plus the standard rent. The cost of an opstal in areas suitable for stock farming was usually considerably lower than the cost of an arable freehold farm. The average value of an opstal ranged from 300 to 500 guilders compared with 6,000 to 10,000 guilders for a freehold farm.[81] In some areas an opstal could be purchased for as little as 100 guilders while a good arable farm could cost as much as 20,000 guilders. Moreover, the stock farmer did not have to purchase many slaves or expensive equipment. His heaviest investment was for the purchase of stock. Assuming a pastoralist could get started with one horse, twenty cattle, fifty sheep, a wagon and a little equipment, his capital needs amounted to about 1,000 guilders.** Those lacking any capital resources whatsoever could become *bijwoners* (tenant farmers) on the properties of established settlers. A bijwoner with no resources of his own might look after his patron's stock on a system of shares. Many young men began their farming careers this way.

In addition to being financially qualified to become pastoralists, many settlers possessed other necessary qualities to make successes of such careers. On the farms and cattle posts of the interior. African-born colonists and also European immigrants learned to know and like the African veld. They became inured to the hardships of an isolated but independent way of life and mastered the skills and techniques necessary to survive in it. In the process sons lost the skills of their fathers, many of whom had been skilled artisans.

The fact that colonists were well prepared for farming careers meant that they were ill prepared for other kinds of work. More important, there was little non-farm employment in the arable farming areas and virtually none in the stock farming areas. The very name 'boer' that came into use to denote this new African people reflected this aspect of the economic situation. There were a few opportunities for artisans near Cape Town, but they were not sufficiently attractive to encourage young colonists to become apprenticed in blacksmithing, carpentry or some other trade. The low level of business activity and the prospects of slave competition were the two main negative

---

** This amount would have been close to the minimum needed. It would have been broken down as follows: horses, 50; cattle, 150; sheep, 350; wagon, 300; rent on loan farm, 72; other equipment, 78. All figures are in Cape guilders.

factors. When a need arose for more artisans, the positions were filled by ex-VOC employees born in Europe.

The prospect for a poor man to become a labourer was ruled out by the use of slaves. The disdain with which labouring jobs were regarded by the European community was enough to prevent any self-respecting member of it from contemplating such employment. Manual work, when it involved serving others (an important qualification), was 'slave work' and beneath the dignity of a white freeburgher.[82] The social attitudes adopted toward this type of work by the Cape freeburgher community probably reflected the economic reality that free manual work could not compete with slave labour.

The prospect of enlisting as a soldier or sailor in the VOC was somewhat more attractive than that of becoming a labourer, but rarely received serious consideration from young men brought up in the relatively free environment of the Cape. Pay in the VOC was low and the discipline harsh. Chances of promotion for someone with a poor education were slight. The fact that forced enlistment (and deportation) was a procedure for dealing with less serious crimes can have done little to popularise VOC careers.[83]

Moreover, the opportunities seized by the colonists of Van Riebeeck's day to become townsmen (tavern keepers, retailers and the like) were no longer available. Trading activities were dominated by a small, entrenched merchant class with which a poor country boy could not compete. Other less glamorous occupations, such as fishing, were dominated by free blacks. An additional factor that may have deterred poor colonists from seeking their fortunes at the Cape between 1724 and 1727 was the 72 guilder tax assessed on anyone who changed his district of residence. In brief, there were exceedingly few opportunities outside stock farming (or elephant hunting) for the growing number of colonists of moderate or poor circumstances who sought to make a living at the Cape after 1717.

Although a pastoralist could get started with little capital, further investment brought limited returns. The isolation of the individual farm was so severe, and transportation costs were so high, that the investment of large amounts of capital was seldom justified. Unimproved pasture was the basic resource of the frontier regions, and it could be exploited directly by the farmer's stock without much investment of capital. The expansion of stock farming involved enlarging the area of activity rather than using the area already occupied in a more intensive manner. This kind of expansion, however, was not conducive to dynamic regional development.

In fact the trekboers, far from improving the resource base, generally over-used the resources that were available. There are numerous references to declining resources from the second half of the eighteenth century. In a petition to the Cape authorities in 1758, Swellendam officials partly blamed the deterioration of the veld for the poverty-stricken condition of the inhabitants of their district, and asked that rents on loan farms be lowered.[84] Similar complaints were made by officials of Swellendam and Stellenbosch in later decades.[85]

Freeburgher officials no doubt exaggerated the extent of resource deterioration to bolster claims for low rents or more land, but the basic truth of their contentions was confirmed by independent observers. In 1776 Hendrick Swellengrebel Jr was appalled at the extent to which the pasture of the newly settled Camdebo had been destroyed, and anticipated that the region would have to be abandoned in a few years.[86] Robert Gordon reported that areas of Swellendam, which had once been rich in grasses, were covered with bushes which cattle refused to eat.[87] In the Bokkeveld Gordon noted that the spread of the unpalatable *renosterbos* troubled the farmers of the area.[88]

Unlike their arable counterparts the value of stock farms, including the opstal, slaves, stock and equipment, tended to decline in the course of time. In the period 1731–42 the average value of estates left by trekboers was 3,760 guilders; this figure had declined to 2,850 guilders in the period 1770–80.[89] The position of stock farming relative to arable farming was much less favourable toward the end of the period than it had been at the beginning (Table 2.4). Wealth was fairly evenly distributed among stock farmers and tended to become even more so. Few of them were wealthy. In the final period (1771–80) over two thirds of the stock farmers left estates worth less than 2,500 guilders.

Table 2.4 Cultivators and pastoralists: Net value of estates* (Cape guilders), 1731–1780

Period		1731–1742	1751–1762	1771–1780
Estates of cultivators	No.	33	18	20
	Total value	307,650	187,700	486,640
	Average value	9,300	10,430	24,330
Estates of pastoralists	No.	24	36	27
	Total value	90,220	126,230	77,000
	Average value	3,760	3,500	2,850
Average value of a pastoral estate as a per cent of arable estate		40.4	33.6	11.7

Source: Inventarissen, MOOC (Weeskamer), vols. 8/5–8/17 and Stel., vols. 18/30–18/34.
* An estate inventory included stock, slaves, land, equipment, and all monetary assets and liabilities.

These figures suggest that the conditions which had allowed a small number of trekboers to obtain a modest livelihood as quasi-subsistence pastoralists were already beginning to break down before 1780. The trekboer economy was based upon the ultra-extensive use of the resources of the country. The disadvantages of not being an integral part of an exchange economy were largely compensated for by the ease with which these resources could be exploited. However, the advantages of a quasi-subsistence economy based upon extensive exploitation of resources began to disappear as soon as the population increased. The decline in the average value of trekboer estates from 1731 to 1780 suggests that, even before 1780, the number of people that could comfortably be supported on a quasi-subsistence basis had been exceeded. The general economic rule that exchange economies are more efficient than subsistence ones was beginning to catch up with the trekboers as their numbers grew, as the resource value of the land declined, and as the average distance separating them from essential supplies and services increased.

The following observations about arable and stock farming can now be made. There is no question that a large, well-financed arable farm, particularly if it was combined with the holding of a monopoly lease, could be extremely profitable. Arable farming on a small scale, however, was often a marginal economic activity, and small cultivators were often heavily in debt. Stock farming brought good returns on the investment of small amounts of capital, but further investments produced rapidly diminishing returns. In the arable areas wealth became ever more unevenly distributed with the emergence of a small, very rich group, but in the stock farming regions of the open frontier (see ch. 8, pp. 296 ff.) most people were rather poor, although they lived in rough comfort and were free of large debts.[90]

Critical review and conclusions

In his account of the expansion of European settlement in South Africa, Neumark clearly established that the trekboer was not a subsistence farmer (as had sometimes been argued), but that throughout the years of colonial expansion he maintained economic links with the Cape, where there was a reasonably good demand for inland produce. Neumark, however, went further and argued that the profits from such activities were sufficiently large to attract a large number of settlers inland.[91] In Neumark's view the trekboer was a profit-seeker who invested his capital in the interior because it offered him a better return on his money than was available elsewhere.

In developing his thesis Neumark drew a distinction between factors which, he argued, made the expansion of settlement technically feasible and those that made it desirable.[92] In the former category Neumark included Khoikhoi labour and fat-tailed sheep; in the latter he placed the demand for frontier and pastoral produce, especially meat. In other words, Neumark argued that the inland movement of trekboers was causally connected to the demand for produce of the interior. But trekboer expansion could not have taken place without guns, gunpowder, wagons and other manufactured items, which the trekboer could only obtain by exchanging the produce of the interior for them. Apart from essential goods and commodities, the trekboers also needed some cash to pay district taxes and rents on their loan farms, although these could be paid in kind. Hence there is no reason why the demand for frontier and pastoral produce should not itself (in the absence of further evidence) be considered as yet another factor making the expansion technically feasible.

The case in favour of Neumark's interpretation would be strengthened (but not proven) if it could be shown that there was in fact a close connection between the rate at which new loan farms were issued and variations in the demand for inland produce.†† Neumark himself suggested that there ought to be a good correlation between the rate of new settlement and the increase in the number of foreign ships calling at the Cape, but no strong correlation between these two elements is discernible (Fig. 2.5). The marked increase in the number of loan farms in the early 1760s preceded by a decade the rapid build-up in the number of foreign ships calling at the Cape. One cannot argue that the trekboers moved inland in anticipation of the improved conditions of the 1770s, because this development was the result of complex international events beyond their competence to forecast.

The picture is the same when settlement expansion is compared with meat prices. In the early 1740s, for instance, applications for loan farms continued to be received by the Cape authorities when the meat market was flooded and prices were exceptionally low. Had commercial considerations been foremost in the trekboer's mind, a marked decline in the number of new loan farms issued would have been expected. Neumark, who noted this period of low prices for meat, contended that it was 'reasonable' to assume that the outlet for meat was large though the prices were relatively low. However, contemporary records reveal that stock farmers were complaining to the local authorities that they were unable to get rid of their produce at

†† Neumark was not correct in stating that 'we have no exact data for correlating the rate of expansion with increase in foreign shipping or with the expansion of the market for pastoral products'. These data are in fact reasonably exact and readily available.

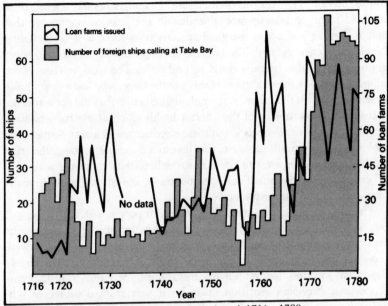

Figure 2.5 Foreign ships calling and loan farms issued, 1716—1780
Source: Coenraad Beyers, *Die Kaapse Patriotte,* 2nd ed. (Pretoria, 1967), pp. 333—35,
and Oude Wildschutteboeken, R.L.R., vols 3—26

any price.[93] The movement of settlers inland continued.

The fact that the expansion of settlement was apparently not sensitive to
fluctuations in the demand for inland produce supports the view that the
trekboers were moved by prospects other than those of commercial gain in
settling the interior. The alternatives open to a colonist who might consider
becoming a trekboer must be taken into account if the expansion movement
is to be understood. The high threshold capital demanded of anyone wishing
to purchase a viable arable farm effectively excluded a large number of
moderately well-off to poor persons. When such a person (worth, perhaps,
1,000 guilders) decided to put his capital into a stock farm, he was taking
the only action that offered him a reasonable chance of earning a living
while preserving his independence. The applications for loan farms
continued at all times, partly because there were no viable alternatives.

In support of his economic interpretation of inland settlement, Neumark
maintained that the frontier offered 'good opportunities for people with
some capital.'[94] If 'some capital' was an amount below the threshold
demanded of an arable farming operation, the statement is well supported by
the evidence, but if 'some capital' was the amount required to purchase a
viable arable farm, there is little evidence that much of it ever found its way

to the interior. The fact that well-established cultivators did not sell their freehold farms to take up stock farming in the interior is evidence that arable farming was not as marginal an activity as some writers, including Neumark, have suggested. The impressive estates of some of the cultivators confirm that arable farming could be profitable. The weak interest in the interior shown by the wealthier colonists of the Cape, who had a clear choice of where to invest their money, strongly suggests that they did not assess the investment opportunities of the interior highly. Rich arable farmers often held loan farms for their stock, but these were not major assets. Rather than looking to the north or east for investment opportunities, the rich freeburghers looked west to Cape Town, where they competed with each other and with townsmen for the monopoly leases that were annually auctioned by the administration.

The interior provided a reasonable outlet for people with a little capital; but, as I have shown, it offered few prospects for sustained growth. Its economy was primitive, and a large proportion of its goods and services were produced and consumed at the same point. The trekboer was largely dependent on the natural environment with, perhaps, a little home processing. Economic isolation made for a very marked degree of self-sufficiency on all frontier farms. Farm improvements waited on better transportation; improvements in transportation waited on an increase in population density; an increase in population density waited on farm improvements. As land was abundant on the open frontier, here was a vicious circle from which there was no escape. Lacking the basic requirements for sustained economic growth, the Cape interior remained economically stagnant for the greater part of the eighteenth century.

The inland movement of trekboers, if not geared to market conditions, was economic in the sense that abundant land and resources provided the wherewithal for white settlers to live in rough comfort despite their isolation. The general rule that a subsistence economy is undesirable because it inhibits effective deployment of human resources or regional specialisation broke down under the special conditions of Cape frontier settlement. Here a few settlers amidst abundant resources managed to achieve a modest standard of living with scarcely any participation in the exchange economy. In the final analysis Neumark's interpretation of frontier settlement in South Africa is a defence of conventional economic theory, which maintains that subsistence economies are less efficient than exchange ones. On this assumption the trekboer expansion was 'irrational' unless it could be related to the exchange economy. An implicit acceptance of this view probably lay behind Neumark's overemphasis on the few commercial ties the trekboers did maintain with the outside world, and his failure to appreciate the considerable economic benefits that were to be obtained from the direct exploitation of resources on an extensive scale.

Chapter Two   Notes

1. C 499, Uitgaande Brieven, H. Crudop — XVII, 18 April 1679, p. 119.
2. KA 4053, Opgaaf Roll (1716); C. Beyers, *Die Kaapse Patriotte gedurende die Laaste Kwart van die Agtiende Eeu en die Voortlewing van hul Denkbeelde,* 2nd edn (Pretoria, 1967), p. 341. The figure includes free blacks.
3. KA 4161, Opgaaf Roll (1751); *Kaapse Archiefstukken, 1778—1783,* ed. K.M. Jeffreys (Cape Town, 1926—38), IV, 1 May 1780, pp. 355—57.
4. G.M. Theal, *History of South Africa before 1795* (London, 1927), II, 325.
5. C 416, Inkomende Brieven, XVII — Simon van der Stel, 8 Oct. 1685, p. 213.
6. Theal, *History of South Africa,* II, 316.
7. C.G. Botha, *The French Refugees at the Cape,* 3rd edn (Cape Town, 1970), p. 100.
8. Robert Ross, 'The "White" Population of the Cape Colony in the Eighteenth Century', *Population Studies,* XXIX (1975), pp. 217—30.
9. According to the research of J.A. Heese, the Afrikaner people (of 1807) were derived from the following ethnic groups: Dutch, 36.8 per cent; German, 35.0 per cent; French, 14.6 per cent; 'non-white', 7.2 per cent; other and indeterminable, 6.4 per cent: J.A. Heese, *Die Herkoms van die Afrikaner* (Cape Town, 1971), p. 21.
10. O.F. Mentzel, *A Geographical-Topographical Description of the Cape of Good Hope* (Cape Town, 1924), II, 21.
11. G. Barraclough, *The Origins of Modern Germany,* 2nd edn (Oxford, 1947), pp. 391—96.
12. The important studies of frontier expansion in eighteenth-century South Africa are: A.J.H. van der Walt, *Die Ausdehnung der Kolonie am Kap der Guten Hoffnung (1700—1779)* (Berlin, 1928); P.J. van der Merwe, *Die Trekboer in die Geskiedenis van die Kaapkolonie (1657—1842)* (Cape Town, 1938); P.J. van der Merwe, *Trek: Studies oor die Mobiliteit van die Pioniersbevolking aan die Kaap* (Cape Town, 1945); S.D. Neumark, *Economic Influences on the South African Frontier: 1652—1836* (Stanford, 1957).
13. Van der Merwe, *Trek,* pp. 43—61.
14. Neumark, *South African Frontier,* p. 5.
15. H.C.V. Leibbrandt, *Précis of the Archives of the Cape of Good Hope: Letters and Documents Received, 1649—1662* (Cape Town, 1896—99), I, 26 July 1649, p. 12.
16. *Ibid.,* I, June 1651, pp. 18—29.
17. *Journal of Jan van Riebeeck, 1651—1662,* ed. H.B. Thom (Cape Town, 1954), 28 April 1652, pp. 35—36. This is hereafter cited as *VRJ.*
18. A.J. du Plessis, 'Die Geskiedenis van die Graankultuur in Suid-Afrika, 1652—1752', *Annals of the University of Stellenbosch,* Series B1, II, (1933) pp. 2—5 and 113.
19. H.M. Robertson, 'The Economic Development of the Cape under Jan van Riebeeck', *South African Journal of Economics,* XIII (1945), p. 77.
20. *VRJ,* II, 6 May 1656, pp. 32—33.
21. *Ibid.,* 24 Oct. 1656, p. 69.

22. *Suid-Afrikaanse Argiefstukke; Kaap: Resolusies van die Politieke Raad*, ed. A.J. Böeseken (Cape Town, 1957—62), I, 21 Feb. 1657, pp. 90—93.
23. *Ibid.*
24. C 409, Inkomende Brieven, XVII—Council of Policy, 16 April 1658, p. 1036.
25. H.B. Thom, *Die Geskiedenis van die Skaapboerdery in Suid-Afrika* (Amsterdam, 1936), p. 246.
26. *Kaapse Argiefstukke: Kaapse Plakkaatboek, 1652—1795*, ed. K.M. Jeffreys and S.D. Naudé (Cape Town, 1944—49), I, 26 Sept. 1660, p. 61.
27. *Belangrike Kaapse Dokumente: Memoriën en Instructiën 1657—1699*, ed. A.J. Böeseken (Cape Town, 1966), 5 May 1662, p. 39.
28. C 499, Uitgaande Brieven, H. Crudop—XVII, 18 April 1679, p. 119.
29. C 499, Uitgaande Brieven, Simon van der Stel—XVII, 27 March 1680, p. 477.
30. *Ibid.*, p. 514.
31. DO, Old Stellenbosch Freeholds, I.
32. L.T. Guelke, 'The Early European Settlement of South Africa' (Ph.D. diss., University of Toronto, 1974), p. 123.
33. H.A. van Reede, 'Joernaal van zijn Verblijf aan de Kaap', *Bijdragen en Mededelingen van het Historisch Genootschap*, LXII, 20 May 1685, pp. 122—23.
34. Guelke, 'European Settlement', pp. 119—23.
35. DO, Old Stellenbosch Freeholds, I and II.
36. Guelke, 'European Settlement', p. 179.
37. C 500, Uitgaande Brieven, Simon van der Stel—XVII, 23 April 1682, p. 39.
38. *Memoriën en Instructiën,* 16 July 1685, pp. 223—26; *Resolusies,* III, 5 August 1686, pp. 140—42.
39. E. Boserup, *The Conditions of Agricultural Growth* (Chicago, 1965), p. 73.
40. Guelke, 'European Settlement', p. 160.
41. *Kaapse Plakkaatboek*, I, 22 Jan. 1692, p. 282.
42. *Ibid.*, I, 8 Sept. 1693, p. 263.
43. *Ibid.*, I, 22 Jan. 1692, p. 263.
44. *Resolusies*, IV, 3 July 1714, p. 412.
45. See Van der Merwe, *Trekboer,* pp. 63—132 for a detailed analysis of the origins and administration of the loan farm system.
46. The best account of hunting expeditions at the Cape is Mentzel, *Description of the Cape*, III, 125—26. Mentzel lived at the Cape in the early part of the eighteenth century.
47. C 436, Inkomende Brieven, 15 July 1717, p. 604. The views of the members of the Cape Council of Policy, whose advice was sought before the Heren XVII's decision on slavery was announced, are in *Reports of Chavonnes and his Council and of Van Imhoff, on the Cape* (Cape Town, 1918). All but one councillor argued in favour of the retention of slavery.
48. This statement is based on an examination of the prices paid at public auctions for the fixed improvements or *opstal* of loan farms. MOOC Series 10, Vendu-Rollen, Vols. 6—14.
49. Du Plessis, 'Geskiedenis van die Graankultuur', p. 67.
50. J.I.J. van Rensburg, 'Die Geskiedenis van die Wingerdkultuur in Suid-Afrika tydens die Eerste Eeu, 1652—1752', *Archives Yearbook of South African History*, II (1954), pp. 1—96.

51. Thom, *Skaapboerdery*, pp. 47—48.
52. *Ibid.*, p. 50.
53. *Reports of Chavonnes et al.*, p. 137.
54. Items of equipment are listed under workshop headings in inventories of the larger estates; MOOC series 8, Inventarissen, Vols. 1—17.
55. Van der Walt, *Ausdehnung*, p. 40.
56. Guelke, 'European Settlement', p. 274. Data on land prices are in DO, *Transporten en Schepenenkennis* volumes, which are complete except for one year for the eighteenth century.
57. A. Sparrman, *A Voyage to the Cape of Good Hope, 1772—1776,* 2nd edn (London, 1786), I, 250—52.
58. Guelke, 'European Settlement', p. 277.
59. Theal, *History of South Africa*, III, 360.
60. Mentzel, *Description of the Cape*, II, 148—49.
61. Guelke 'European Settlement', pp. 293—97.
62. Data from MOOC series 8, Inventarissen, Vols. 5—8.
63. St 18/31, Inventarissen, 24—26 June 1776, no. 17.
64. KA 4053, 4144, and 4240, Opgaaf Rolls (1716, 1746, and 1770).
65. SWM 1/1, Notule van Landdrost en Heemraden, 10 Jan. 1757, p. 390.
66. C 655, DR (Stellenbosch, Drakenstein en Swellendam), 11 Jan. 1774, p. 357.
67. Sparrman, *Voyage to the Cape,* I, 264.
68. F. Masson, 'An Account of three Journeys from Cape Town into the Southern Parts of Africa', *Philosophical Transactions of the Royal Society*, LXVI (1776), p. 315.
69. C.P. Thunberg, *Travels in Europe, Africa and Asia made between the Years 1770 and 1779,* 3rd edn (London, 1795), II, 52.
70. VC 595, Gordon Journals, p. 47; J. Barrow, *An account of Travels into the Interior of Southern Africa in the Years 1797 and 1798* (London, 1801), I, 105.
71. ACC 477, Swellengrebel Papers, p. 22.
72. Thunberg, *Travels*, II, 173.
73. Theal, *History of South Africa*, III, 71.
74. C 653, DR (Stellenbosch, Drakenstein en Swellendam), 18 March 1750, p. 815.
75. C 655, DR (Stellenbosch, Drakenstein en Swellendam), 11 Jan. 1774, pp. 344—45.
76. VC 592, Gordon Journals, p. 32.
77. C 311, *Memoriën en Rapporten*, 24 March 1778, p. 429.
78. Jacob Koch of the Langekloof, an exceptional case, was reported to have employed as many as 100 Khoikhoi. See Masson 'Southern Parts of Africa', p. 291.
79. Guelke, 'European Settlement', pp. 255—56.
80. Mentzel, *Description of the Cape*, III, 119.
81. These data were obtained from estate inventories covering the period 1731—80: MOOC series 8, Vols. 5—17 and Stel. series 18, Vols. 30—34.
82. Van der Merwe, *Trek,* pp. 6—7.
83. Between 1738 and 1778 thirty-three persons were deported; Theal, *History of South Africa*, III, 177.
84. SWM 1/1, Notule van Landdrost en Heemraden, 24 Jan. 1758, pp. 424—27.
85. C 655, DR (Stellenbosch, Drakenstein en Swellendam), 15 June 1771, p.

65; C 310, *Memoriën en Rapporten*, 7 May 1776, p. 78.
86. ACC 447, Swellengrebel Papers, 31 Oct. 1776, p. 24.
87. VC 592, Gordon Journals, Oct. 1777, p. 34.
88. VC 593, Gordon Journals, 4 Dec. 1778, p. 163.
89. These data were obtained from estate inventories covering the period 1731—80: MOOC series 8, Inventarissen, Vols. 5—17 and Stel. series 18, Vols. 30—34. Estate inventories included the value of a deceased person's stockholdings.
90. Guelke, 'European Settlement', p. 327.
91. Neumark, *South African Frontier*, pp. 5, 17, 79.
92. *Ibid.*, pp. 74, 79.
93. *Ibid.*, p. 45; Leibbrandt MSS, Resolutions of the Council of Policy, 17 April 1742, p. 126.
94. Neumark, *South African Frontier*, p. 38.

The slaves, 1652—1795

James C. Armstrong

The growth of the slave society at the Cape in the seventeenth and eighteenth centuries is one of the most neglected themes of South African history and in the history of slavery.[1] Starting from zero in 1652, the slave population had risen to at least 25,754 in 1798 and exceeded the free population, excluding Khoikhoi, of 21,746. It has long been appreciated that the presence of slaves in such numbers must have had profound effects on the Cape Colony's social and economic development, but they have received little detailed study.

Domestic slavery had disappeared in the Netherlands by the turn of the seventeenth century. However, in the following decades the Dutch gained experience of slavery as their commerce expanded into the West and East Indies.[2] From the 1620s onwards the Dutch were involved in the slave trade from West Africa to the Americas, and their participation grew rapidly after they conquered northeastern Brazil in 1634—38.[3] In Asia, Dutch commerce did not centre on the slave trade, and the degree of Dutch involvement never matched that in West Africa. However, slavery flourished in varying degrees in all their Asian possessions, and slave trading figured in their activities throughout the seventeenth and eighteenth centuries.

The Netherlanders came into contact with indigenous Asian slave-owning societies in the East Indies, India and Ceylon. Here the institution of slavery had been long established even before the arrival of the Portuguese in the early sixteenth century. Forms of slavery throughout this vast region varied greatly, though in many cases slavery was based on debt-bondage or upon the capture of prisoners of war.[4] The Portuguese had introduced to their Asian possessions concepts of servitude ultimately derived from the Roman law of slavery. When the Dutch arrived, they did the same.

Thus from the beginning of the Dutch East India Company's activities in the Indies, slavery played an accepted and important part.[5] Under the governor-generalship of Laurens Real (1615—19) it became the basis of nutmeg cultivation on Amboina. Real's capable and ruthless successor, Jan

Pieterzoon Coen (1619−23; 1627−29), encouraged its spread throughout the Company's territories. In time, large-scale Company enterprises such as gold mining at Salida on Sumatra (1670s−1739) and the construction of forts, as at the Cape (1665−79) and Ceylon (in the 1690s), relied heavily on slave labour.[6]

Origins of the Cape slaves

As may be seen from the above, the Dutch were well acquainted with slavery by the year 1652 when the Company established a refreshment station at the Cape. The introduction of slavery to the new colony came as a virtually foreordained, although incidental, consequence of its settlement. For the Company, a commercial enterprise whose resources were much over-extended even in its periods of prosperity, and which was always short of manpower, slavery solved otherwise intractable problems of labour supply. The East Indian experience of the Dutch meant that slavery came to the Cape fully developed, governed by laws already in force (the Statutes of India, 1642, and their amendments),[7] and overseen by Company officials with experience of the institution in the East Indies. The forms which slavery assumed at the Cape could not be influenced by pre-existent forms of bondage in indigenous society, for there were none.

However, it took some months for the extent of the labour needs of the Cape to become apparent, and even longer before an initial supply of slaves was forthcoming.[8] Labour was needed for the cutting and hauling of timber and firewood; for the construction of the first fort and buildings (storerooms, dwellings, a barn, a hospital); for fishing, sealing and whaling; for saltworks, brickmaking, cultivation, livestock herding and exploration; and for the primary task of the refreshment post: the servicing of the visiting Dutch East India Company vessels and their crews. For these tasks the garrison, which numbered only about 100 to 200 during the first decade, was wholly insufficient. The other immediate source of labour was the transient personnel of the Company's fleets. Available only irregularly, these men were often too few and too sickly for the tasks at hand, and they sometimes lacked the necessary skills. Alternative sources of labour − convicts, and the indigenous Khoikhoi population − were also unsuitable for the immediate needs of the Company's settlement; the convicts were too few, and the Khoikhoi proved unwilling.

Van Riebeeck very soon concluded that slaves were essential. In May 1652, not two months after the establishment of the Dutch post at the Cape, he wrote to Batavia that slaves would be useful for the dirtiest and heaviest work.[9] Thereafter he frequently pleaded for slaves as well as for free Chinese and *Mardijkers*, emphasising the savings that their introduction might effect. The Council of India at Batavia was not able to send slaves, Chinese or Mardijkers to the Cape, however, and Van Riebeeck sought other means of supplying his settlement's needs. He hoped to supply both Batavia and the Cape with slaves from Antongil Bay in Madagascar where the Dutch, from their initial settlement at Mauritius, had formerly obtained slaves between 1641 and 1647.[10] To these proposals he added that of supplying Mauritius with slave-grown provisions from the Cape, thereby saving Batavia the trouble. The first slaving voyage was attempted in 1654 by the *Roode Vos*, which was to proceed to Mauritius and thence to Antongil Bay, where it was ordered to buy thirty or forty slaves, including ten girls twelve to fifteen years of age.[11] This effort failed. The *Tulp* was dispatched in the same year from the Cape to Antongil, but obtained only two slaves.[12]

Prior to 1658, then, there were only a handful of personal slaves at the Cape, including a few in Van Riebeeck's household.[13] The first significant numbers were imported that year in two shiploads.[14] One, consisting of 228 slaves, was the result of a Dutch East India Company expedition sent (with secret instructions from the *Heren XVII*) to Dahomey, which lay within the official monopoly area of the Dutch West India Company. Another shipload of 174 slaves, chiefly children, was the result of a chance capture by the Dutch of a Portuguese slaver bound for Brazil with Angolan slaves. Of these initial slaves some were sent on to Batavia, some retained by the Company, and some assigned to the first *freeburghers*. These two shiploads of Angolan and Dahomean slaves were, excepting a few individuals, the only West African slaves brought to the Cape during the Company period.

Slaves were thereafter mainly brought to the Cape in three ways. Firstly, Company-sponsored voyages from the Cape visited slave outlets in Madagascar and elsewhere. Secondly, the Company 'return' fleets, sailing each year from the East Indies and Ceylon to Europe, usually brought a few slaves to the Cape, occasionally for the Company's own use, but more often to be sold to individual burghers. Thirdly, foreign slavers en route to the Americas from Madagascar, Mozambique and East Africa sometimes sold slaves in Cape Town. It will be useful to examine each of these categories in turn.

Company-sponsored slaving voyages, which are well documented, are summarised in Table 3.1 (p. 78). The predominance of Malagasy slaves, 66 per cent of the total, is apparent. Madagascar was a logical source of slaves for the Cape. It was relatively close, the navigational problems in reaching it were not great, and the Dutch had had some prior experience with slave trading there. However, their experience was limited to Antongil Bay and, in the 1660s, to St Augustine Bay.

Table 3.1 Company-sponsored slaving voyages, 1652—1795[15]
(Number of slaves delivered to Cape in italics)

Region	1652—1699	1700—1749	1750—1795	Totals
Madagascar	12 (*1,064*)	9 (*779*)	12 (*977*)	33 (*2,820*)
Mozambique, East African coast, and Zanzibar	—	—	5 (*974*)	5 (*974*)
Delagoa Bay	—	several (*c. 280*)	—	several (*c. 280*)
Dahomey	1 (*226*)	—	—	1 (*226*)
Totals	13 (*1,290*)	9+ (*c. 1,059*)	17 (*1,951*)	39+ (*c. 4,300*)

Until 1672 the Dutch at the Cape were ignorant of the main outlet for Malagasy slaves, which lay on the northwest coast at Boina Bay.[16] There, in the early decades of the seventeenth century, the trade had been in Portuguese and Arab hands. In the 1660s English slave traders began to appear, seeking slaves for the West Indies. In 1673 the Dutch captured one of these English vessels and brought its cargo of 184 Malagasy slaves to the Cape. The first significant Cape trade at Boina occurred in 1676 (the *Voorhout*: 279 slaves).[17] For a century thereafter slaving voyages from the Cape were made fairly regularly to Massailly at Boina as well as to other Madagascar ports: St Augustine, Tulear, Maningaar, Morondava, Foulpointe, and Ft Dauphin.

Malagasy slaves of the Company were taken on these voyages as interpreters. Slaves were traded primarily for firearms, brandy and Spanish reals of eight, a medium of exchange widely used in Asian trade. Trading conditions varied greatly, depending on local circumstances and the presence or absence of competing slave traders. Prices also varied but averaged under 20 rixdollars per slave in the seventeenth century, and in the eighteenth century ranged from 20 to 30 rixdollars; higher prices were exceptional. During the years that the Company maintained its outpost at Delagoa Bay (1724—32) the trade with Madagascar was interrupted. Delagoa Bay produced few slaves while causing much sickness among Company employees, and the post was abandoned.[18] In 1740 the Madagascar trade was resumed.

The Company's attempts to obtain slaves from the East African coast north of Delagoa Bay were limited to the decade 1776—86 and were successful although attended by heavy slave mortality. Slaves were traded at Zanzibar, the offshore island Oibo (Ibo) and Mozambique. The Company organised no slaving voyages at all after 1786.[19]

Virtually all the slaves obtained on these Company-sponsored voyages were destined for use by the Company at the Cape. In addition to those traded on Company account, however, some slaves were obtained by Company personnel in private trading. From scattered evidence it seems likely that roughly 10 per cent should be added to the official figures to include slaves obtained in this manner. This private trade was conducted without the knowledge or approval of the Heren XVII or the Council of India. It was not mentioned in official correspondence, nor were the numbers of slaves acquired privately included in the official reports on these voyages. Indeed, it was only after the Company ceased making slaving voyages, near the end of its administration, that the Heren XVII took any official cognisance of this individual trading by its Cape officials. It was defended as a customary usage, without any specific known authorisation, which compensated the ships' officers and supercargoes for the dangers and discomforts they underwent in the trade, and as an encouragement for them to go on future voyages.[20]

The volume of the Cape-based slave trade was affected by many factors, only one of which was the immediate labour needs of the Company at the Cape. The outbreak or anticipated outbreak of European wars, the wishes of the Heren XVII and the Batavian authorities, the lack of ships and specie, the activity of pirates, and reports of poor trading conditions at the slaving ports, could all thwart a projected voyage.

The number of slaves which were brought to the Cape by the annual return fleets is not easily determined. There were a few occasions, usually following wars or famines, when the Batavia or Colombo authorities dispatched on the home fleets considerable numbers of slaves for the Company's use at the Cape. In 1677 ninety-three 'Tutucorin' slaves were sent from Southern India; in 1712 thirty-six slaves arrived from Jaffnapatnam on Ceylon; in 1719 another eighty arrived from Jaffnapatnam, and there was a further shipment in 1754.[21] The overall contribution of these shipments to the Cape's slave population was small.

On the return fleets there was also a steady private trade in slaves from India and the East Indies conducted by Company officials for their own profit. Usually these officials were returning home themselves, but sometimes they remained in the Indies and entrusted their slaves to others for sale at the Cape. In conducting this trade the officials were taking advantage of (and stretching) a Company rule which allowed them to be accompanied by personal slaves as far as the Cape. There was no similar encouragement to bring slaves to the Netherlands where indeed they were legally free on arrival.[22]

The practice of bringing East Indian and Indian slaves on the homeward bound fleets was sporadic at first but became more frequent in the late 1680s. The Council at Batavia attempted to regulate the passage of slaves to the Cape by requiring each owner to obtain its permission for each slave sent. By 1713 the Heren XVII had become so concerned by the growth in this traffic, and by the smaller flow of slaves accompanying their masters to the Netherlands, that it required return passages for all slaves exported from the Indies to be paid in advance.[23] This requirement was plainly intended as a disincentive to the trade, to which the Company objected not on humanitarian grounds, but because it represented an unwelcome utilisation for private profit of the carrying capacity of the Company's ships. In 1716 Batavia issued a *plakkaat* against the clandestine transport of slaves, on pain of confiscation.[24] Nevertheless the traffic, both open and covert, continued, although on a smaller scale. C.P. Thunberg, writing in 1772, observed: 'The company brings the greatest part of its slaves from Madagascar, whereas private persons buy their's [sic] of the officers belonging to the ships, as well Dutch as French, that are on their return home from the East Indies, seldom of the English and never of the Swedish.'[25]

The numbers involved in this traffic were never large, as space on the return fleets was usually at a premium.[26] The documentable numbers on Company vessels appear to have been about twelve to thirty a year, with the average being about twenty, exclusive of clandestine trade. However, the importance of these slaves in the Cape slave community was out of proportion to their numbers. They were in many instances skilled domestics or artisans, of high value to their owners. Hence their chances of mild treatment and of longevity were probably better than those of most unskilled slaves.

In early 1767 the Council of Policy, reacting to a series of violent crimes by Indonesian slaves, resolved to ask Batavia to forbid the export of Buginese and other Eastern slaves to the Cape.[27] Batavia promptly complied, and the export to the Cape of oriental slave men was prohibited, such slaves to be confiscated if found.[28] The trade in women slaves was not affected, nor was the practice, which continued to the end of the Company period, of permitting slaves to accompany their masters to the Netherlands. It is even doubtful that the export of slave men ceased, but it is difficult to document until the 1780s. In 1784 the earlier prohibition was repeated and a penalty of 300 rixdollars was added to that of confiscation.[29] However, the confiscation of slaves occurred very rarely, suggesting that the practice of sending slaves to the Cape was winked at by officials both at Batavia and the Cape.[30] In 1787 the prohibition was again promulgated, and the following year the Heren XVII urged that Cape authorities keep each newly arrived ship under the closest scrutiny, the better to enforce the ban.[31]

Foreign slave traders also played a significant role in bringing slaves to the Cape. From 1664 to the 1720s these were chiefly Englishmen transporting slaves from Madagascar to Barbados and later to Virginia and Buenos Aires. Initially they were interlopers seeking to avoid the Royal African Company's monopoly of the English West African slave trade. In Madagascar they traded at 'Lightfoot's River' (Lahefoutsy's River) and Massailly. From the 1720s the English were joined by merchants of other nationalities.

En route to the New World foreign slavers frequently stopped for refreshment at the Cape, and their willingness to sell slaves there depended on several factors. They had to balance the advantage of immediate sale at the Cape against an anticipated higher price in the New World, should their cargoes survive the risky middle passage across the Atlantic. If their slave cargoes were in ill health, or if prices were thought to be relatively low in the Americas (e.g., because of a depression in the plantation economy or because competitors were likely to beat them to their favoured ports), slaves might then be traded at the Cape. In practice, foreigners frequently sold only part of their cargo as a hedge against losses in transit and unpredictable market conditions in the Americas.

The Company rarely purchased slaves from transient slavers for its own use; hence most of these sales were to burghers or to Company officials. The Company's permission was required for such sales. Even where it was granted, records were not always kept.[32] Where it was not granted, the possibility of illicit trade arose. Partly for these reasons it is difficult to ascertain the total number of slaves imported to the Cape by foreign slavers. Nonetheless, it is clear that for much of the period prior to the 1780s the numbers of slaves purchased annually from individual transient slavers were small relative both to the Cape slave population and to the numbers carried to the New World past the Cape. In the 1780s, however, boom conditions at the Cape made it a profitable market for the slavers, who by this time were mainly French and Portuguese, and a few large shiploads were sold. For example, in 1782 *L'Union* sold 279 slaves; in 1785 *L'Estrelle d'Afrique* sold 194 and *Le Télémacque* 75 slaves.[33] These three shiploads were purchased by the Company for resale to the burghers, the last two at the initiative of Governor van de Graaff.[34] In 1786 Van de Graaff and his Council estimated the burghers' annual import needs at 200 to 300.[35] This was a level which foreign slavers were plainly able to supply.

From time to time Cape residents sought the Company's permission to engage in private trade to include slaving at Madagascar and along the East African coast. Such a request was made in 1687 following English reports that cheap slaves were obtainable at 'Lightfoot's River'. Governor Simon van der Stel forwarded the request to the Heren XVII, noting that free traders might prosecute the trade more zealously, but nothing came of this request.[36] In 1719 there were some persons residing in the colony with experience in trade and piracy at Madagascar, and they persuaded the Council of Policy to forward to the Heren XVII their request for a vessel to trade there.[37] There was no positive response, the Company being jealous of its trading monopoly. Some years later, in 1731, the Heren XVII, perhaps prompted by the failure of the Delagoa Bay outpost, disinterred this request and indeed sought to encourage a free trading venture from the Cape to Madagascar; but by this time the earlier enthusiasm for such voyages had died at the Cape.[38] Free trade was again sought in 1745—46, in 1779 (in the petition of the burgher 'Patriots') and in 1784; it was finally permitted in 1791, too late to have any impact on the slave population of the Cape.[39]

These requests were fuelled by the apparent profitability of trading in slaves. Adult slaves were generally obtainable at Madagascar at prices ranging from 20 to 30 rixdollars, and were saleable at the Cape for three to four times these figures. But the overheads were large and the risks considerable, as the Company's experience showed. The Company's own bookkeeping practices tended to conceal the true costs of its expeditions, however. Vessel and crew overheads were not taken into account in calculating the real costs of these voyages; they were absorbed in the general expenses of the Company while only the purchase prices and rations of the slaves were reckoned. The risks were also real, chiefly loss of slaves and seamen through illness and death, or escape. Shipwreck was always a possibility, as was at times attack by pirates or rival traders.

The closing years of the Company's administration, a period of economic decline, saw few slaves imported by any legal means into the Cape. Some were doubtless smuggled, but few or no shiploads were landed. After 1793 no slaves were imported until the government of the first British occupation, under pressure from the Burgher Senate, permitted slaves to be brought in. In the first thirty-three months of British rule 605 slaves were imported, followed by an additional 400 in March 1799.[40]

The data are not sufficiently complete or sufficiently comparable to permit an analysis of the origins of Cape slaves analogous to that of Heese on the freeburghers. However, it is plain that the major single geographical source for Cape slaves was Madagascar. No fewer than 66 per cent of the Company's direct imports came from there, and the burghers also acquired many Malagasy slaves from transient merchants. Clearly Malagasy slaves predominated among the Company slaves for most of the Company period. For example, on one detailed listing of Company slaves and convicts (1693) 21 were Asian convicts, 85 were mixed-bloods and hence almost all Cape-born, and of the remaining 169 slaves the majority of those with identifiable names were Malagasy.[41]

Asian slaves were drawn chiefly from Ceylon, India and the outer islands of Indonesia, though scattered names appear from Siam, the Philippines, Java, Japan, and so on. These slaves formed a heterogeneous group in which no single geographic source predominated. During the Company's administration, slaves from continental Africa were relatively few, being imported only at the very beginning from West Africa, from Angola during the brief period of slaving at Delagoa Bay (1724—32), and after 1776 when significant numbers came from Mozambique and East Africa.

Given the varied origins of Cape slaves, it is not surprising that freeburghers developed stereotypes of individual ethnic groups, particularly regarding their capacity for different types of labour. Malagasy slaves, at first only a handful, had a poor reputation initially, but by the 1670s it was appreciated that they were skilled and industrious agriculturalists. Thereafter references to them were usually very favourable.[42] Malagasy slaves were used to pioneer the Company farmland in Hottentots-Holland in 1677. In subsequent lists of Company slaves, Malagasy are typically found to have been assigned to the outposts and to the Company's garden.[43]

The Delagoa Bay slaves were held in very low esteem, and are characterised in the documents as murderous and thievish.[44] Mentzel records that these were 'a foul evil-smelling race, with villainous slits in their faces which have been cut into all sorts of patterns.'[45] They were housed in the basement of the Company lodge, away from the other slaves, and were given the dirtiest jobs to do. Even their deaths were recorded separately from those of the other slaves.

Other ethnic groups were also characterised variously. The few early Angola slaves were thought to be suited for heavy work.[46] The Mozambique slaves acquired in the late eighteenth century appear to have been well-regarded, especially for the purposes of agriculture. Although the Buginese were usually seen as cruel and dangerous as well as stoical under punishment, other slaves from India and Indonesia were too diverse to permit ready stereotyping.[47]

The ethnic diversity of the Cape slaves meant linguistic diversity as well. Slaves from Angola, Dahomey, Madagascar, various Indonesian islands, South India and the East African coast and its hinterland, would bring their own languages with them, consequently having difficulty communicating among themselves and with their masters. Not surprisingly a lingua franca emerged; in fact there were two. Some slaves used a form of creolised Portuguese, which persisted throughout the Company period; its prevalence has long been a matter of scholarly contention.[48] But it is clear that most masters and slaves conversed in an evolving form of Dutch which developed into Afrikaans. Again, the extent of the slave contribution to this development has been hotly contested by Afrikaans linguists.[49] The details of this controversy need not detain us here. What is significant from the standpoint of the imported slaves is that their native languages were of only limited utility and survival value to them in their new home. A communal identity based on their traditional languages and cultures was rapidly eroded away, even in the case of the relatively numerous Malagasy. Like the slaves who went to the American South, the slaves at the Cape appear to have quickly learned the language of their masters.[50]

As in other slave societies, the names given to slaves were often those assigned by their masters, and the original names of the imported slaves have usually been lost. The names chosen were frequently identical to those used by Europeans: Andries, Anna, Catharina, David, Job, etc. Others were distinctively slavish, and are rarely found among whites: Augustyn, Fortuyn, Coridon, Cupido, Scipio, Titus, Octavia, etc. Such names were used repeatedly, a practice which vexes the researcher attempting to identify individual slaves.

An exception to the pattern of renaming of slaves is found with the Company's slaves. The Company tended to preserve the original names of its slaves, especially when they were acquired from Madagascar. Hence lists of Company slaves abound with such Malagasy names as Leidzare, Lambo, Ratzi, Calle Mironde, Ingore, etc. This conservatism was doubtless not due to any preference for the original names as such. But as the Company recorded the purchase of traded slaves under their original names, any change in those names might have suggested to the minds of' visiting commissioners or other Company officials the substitution of slaves as well as names.

It is noteworthy that the Cape, unlike Latin America, did not adopt or evolve a complicated system of socio-racial terminology to distinguish between persons of various racial backgrounds. Slaves at the Cape, as in Indonesia, were *slaaven* (singular *slaaf*) or *lijfeigenen*. These words were used interchangeably without distinctive connotations. Persons, whether slave or free, of African, Malagasy, Indian or Indonesian origin were all *zwarten*. The terms *heelslag* (full-breed) and *halfslag* (half-breed) were but rarely used. Even rarer was *mesties* (half-breed), a word of Portuguese usage. A person of colour who had been a free man in Indonesia was known there, and at the Cape, as a Mardijker. Slaves freed at the Cape became *vrijzwarten* (free blacks). Further definition in racial terms was not needed. The term *kleurling* (coloured) did not emerge until the nineteenth century. It is possible that this lack of elaboration stems from the Dutch custom of referring to individuals by their place of origin (e.g. Jan van Ceylon), which may have made an additional scheme of social classification redundant.

The Company slaves

The Company's labour force consisted primarily of slaves, but it also included Asian and Indonesian convicts (*bandieten*) sent by the Batavian and Ceylon authorities to serve out their sentences at the Cape. This latter group was distinct from that of the much smaller number of political exiles. The convicts lived in the slave lodge and on the outposts, and were generally treated like slaves. The more dangerous were kept in chains, as were unruly slaves. In theory convicts were free after completing their sentences, but they usually did not live to enjoy their freedom; in addition, the records of their cases were sometimes lost and they remained in captivity. The number of convicts fluctuated, but during much of the eighteenth century they were a significant part of the Company's adult labour force.

The Company's slaves are far better documented than the numerically more important slaves of the burghers. Relatively good information is available on their origins, living conditions, genealogies, deaths and manumissions. Population statistics are also fairly good, because the *VOC* as a business enterprise had both the motive and the means to keep an accurate check on its labour force. Very detailed figures are found in its *negotie-boeken* (trade ledgers) which, however, are not available for much of the eighteenth century, and in other Company documents. The size of the Company's slave force can be seen in Table 3.2 (p. 86), compiled from scattered but usually trustworthy sources.*

Moderate fluctuations in the Company's slave population took place from year to year. However, no dramatic growth is discernible in the totals which, having passed 300 in the late 1670s, rose only slowly into the eighteenth century and remained well below 1,000 during the whole of the VOC period. The very circumscribed nature of the Company's slave population was due to the Company's realistic calculation of its labour needs. Moreover, its economic needs were fairly constant, being linked mainly to activity in the port (which expanded slowly) and to occasional construction projects in Cape Town. The Company played only the slightest role in enterprises in the interior. It did not participate as a producer in the expanding agricultural

---

* The Company sometimes reckoned its convicts as slaves, and in sources which give a single figure for slaves it is not always clear whether bandieten are included. Where possible a distinction between the two has been made in the table.

The figures also include slaves who had escaped and not been recovered, for no regular bookkeeping procedures existed for writing off successful escapees. For example, in 1753 there were no fewer than fifty such escaped slaves among the roughly six hundred slaves the Company then 'held'. (KA 4169, Res 24 July 1753, pp. 470—72).

Bookkeeping inconsistencies explain some of the seemingly rapid fluctuations of less than a hundred in totals from year to year, though a good part of the fluctuation is doubtless due to the arrival of new cargoes and to mortality from epidemics.

sector of the economy, which had a growing need of slaves, since it had handed over to the burghers most of its arable farming in 1657 and its pastoral activities in the 1690s. Before the settlement of Stellenbosch in 1679 the Company's slave force exceeded that of the burghers; in that year the Company had 310 slaves, the burghers 191. But thereafter the burghers' totals rose rapidly, surpassing those of the Company in 1692. In 1750 burgher slaves exceeded Company slaves by more than ten to one; in 1793 by almost thirty to one.

Table 3.2   Company slaves and convicts (*bandieten*) 1661–1793[51]

	Men	Women	Children	Total slaves	Convicts	Total forced labour
1661	22	34	11	67	—	—
1669	23	32	46	101	—	—
1679	67	121	122	310	—	—
1685	53	194	90	337	51	388
1693	152	170	●	322	49	371
1714	224	129	92	445	22	467
1727	266	228	103	597	104	701
1742	—	—	—	605	—	—
1752	253	179	74	506	138	644
1764	198	159	77	434	—	—
1777	281	166	112	559	122	681
1784	360	176	89	625	112	737
1789	—	—	—	—	—	946
1793	325	123	61	509	73	582

●Children included with adults

The very limited expansion of the Company slave population through most of the eighteenth century, despite continued infusions from outside, clearly suggests that mortality rates must have surpassed fertility rates among Company slaves. Low fertility cannot be attributed simply to a low ratio of women to men. In fact, as Table 3.2 indicates, the Company's slave women actually outnumbered the men in the seventeenth century. In the eighteenth century, however, Company slave men outnumbered the women, but never at ratios as disproportionate as among burgher slaves. The relatively balanced sex ratios among Company slaves may be due more to the working of various chance factors than to Company policy. Indeed, the Company consistently instructed its slavers to obtain male slaves whenever possible.

Moreover, the impact of sexual imbalance on fertility was offset by the frequent contacts which female Company slaves had with other slaves as well as with Europeans. In 1665 cash payment was given to slave women for bearing children, but this was soon dispensed with as unnecessary.[52] Many travellers observed that the Company's slave lodge served as a house of prostitution for visiting sailors and residents, and there is ample evidence that the children of Company slave women frequently had white fathers (see ch. 4, p. 127).[53] Evidence regarding the attitude of the women to sexual exploitation is fragmentary and contradictory. On the one hand there are scattered references throughout the period to abortions and (rarely) to infanticides.[54] On the other hand there is the evidence of Peter Kolbe and others, who noted that Company slave women welcomed pregnancies, which freed them from work for six weeks before and after delivery.[55]

Some stable unions were formed between slaves in the lodge. Lasting attachments also occurred between European men and Company slave women. In a few cases the man purchased the freedom of his partner and subsequently married her.[56] More frequent, however, was the manumission of Company slave children by European men resident at the Cape, with the clear implication that the child's benefactor was his father.[57] However, the rate of both types of manumission was lower at the Cape than in many slave societies.[58] Company slave manumissions in the period 1715—92 totalled only eighty-six, an average of about one slave per year. Thus the average annual manumission rate for Company slaves was about 0.17 per cent.

A crude measure of the fertility of the Company's slave women can be derived from the Company's ledgers, where annual totals of births are available for some years. It can be seen from Table 3.3 that roughly one in ten of the Company's woman slaves gave birth annually. When we recall that some of them were old it is clear that this fertility rate was very high. We do not know how many women were of childbearing age; probably a high percentage were so, in part because of the short life span of slaves and in part because of the Company's occasional manumission of its older slaves.

Table 3.3 Annual incidence of births among Company slave women[59]

	Number of Company slave women	Number of births	Ratio of women to births
1665	c. 30	9	3.3 : 1
1690	c. 120	13 (+?)	9.2 : 1
1691	c. 120	12 (+?)	10.0 : 1
1692	122	10	12.2 : 1
1769—70	c. 120	10	12.0 : 1
1777—78	166	17	9.8 : 1
1778—79	212	20	10.6 : 1

The number of Company slave children per slave woman varied from 0.4

to 1.4, the average being 0.64.[60] This ratio was comparable to but somewhat lower than that for burgher slaves, and much lower than the equivalent ratio among white freeburghers. (See Figures 3.1 and 3.2, pages 91 and 94.) For both Company and burgher slaves the ratio was affected by many factors other than birth and death rates, e.g. new imports of either women or children, escapes and manumissions.

Mortality rates among Company slaves were high, as can be seen from Table 3.4 below. The concentration of Company slaves in the lodge made them particularly liable to contagious diseases. Smallpox epidemics killed many: in 1713 about 200; in 1753 and 1754 about 300; in 1767, 67. Dysentery, measles and unnamed infectious diseases killed many more. The figures also include accidental deaths, suicides, murders and executions. However, the greatest threat was disease.

Table 3.4 Deaths among Company slaves[61]
(Mortality rates in parentheses)

1661	11 (16%)	1753/54	146 (25%)
1677/78	125 (39%)	1754/55	176 (40%)
1687	many	1755/56	58
1700/01	220 in six months	1756/57	21
1713	200 in six months	1767	67 (12%)
1715/16	56	1771	99
1716/17	15?	1774/75	98
1717/18	19	1777/78	154 (18%)
1718/19	122	1778/79	32
1719/20	96	1779/80	152
1731	55	1780/81	143
1741/42	48+	1781/82	60
1742/43	53	1782/83	46

New arrivals were particularly susceptible to mortal illnesses, although their deaths are often concealed in the overall mortality figures for a given year. For example, of the 221 Malagasy slaves of the *Joanna Catherina*, 129 died within fourteen months of their arrival in 1673. Of the *Voorhout's* 257 slaves (mostly children) landed in 1676, 92 were dead in three and a half months. Of the *Soldaat's* 119 slaves, the largest part were dead within a year of their arrival in 1697.[62]

A comparison of birth and death statistics shows that deaths far exceeded births, and confirms the observation made above that the Company's slave force was not self-reproducing, but relied for its survival on replenishments from imports. In this respect it was similar not only to the British West Indies and South America, but also in all probability to the burghers' slave force at the Cape, which resembled it in woman-child ratios and possibly also

— though this needs further confirmation — in fertility and death rates.

The slaves, excepting those who worked on outposts or for Company officials, were housed in the Company's slave lodge, a brick structure built in 1679.[63] This large building measured 86 by 42 metres; it had a central court where roll-call was taken and food prepared.[64] Men, women and children, as well as convicts, were kept in the lodge. On occasion, when the hospital was full, the lodge was also used to house the sick from the VOC fleets.[65] In Kolbe's time, pigs were kept in the courtyard.[66] Within the lodge there was no privacy, although in 1685 Van Reede ruled that men be separated from women and children from adults. However, this regulation was subsequently ignored.[67]

Daily control over the work of Company slaves was exercised by overseers (*mandoors*) who were slaves themselves. There were also paid overseers, either Europeans or free blacks. Responsibility for the slaves in the lodge was that of the European *opziender* (also called *oppermandoor*, *oppermeester*, or *opzichter*) who dwelt in a separate building adjoining the lodge. His duties included counting the slaves each day and locking them up at night. This was probably a brutalising job and it conferred only low status. The salary was initially meagre but rose to 30 Cape guilders a month, plus rations, by the end of the VOC period.[68]

A large number of the Company slaves were general labourers, available for a variety of tasks as needed. Others were stevedores, gardeners, domestics, masons, carpenters, coopers, smiths, nurses, herdsmen, chalk burners and so on. As noted above, some served as overseers of their fellow slaves. Some favoured slaves worked as domestics for the governor and other high officials, including the Dutch Reformed ministers (*predikanten*). A few were assigned to each of the outposts of the Company; for example, in 1793 slaves were located at Riet Valley, the Rivier Zondereind, Klapmuts, Mossel Bay and False Bay.[69]

One special group were the so-called *Kaffirs*, eastern slaves or convicts who functioned as auxiliary police to apprehend escaped slaves and to act as disciplinarians. Punishments, whether judicial or not, were usually administered to slaves and sometimes to Europeans by these 'servants of justice'. On this account the Kaffirs were hated and feared by the slaves, and indeed by some whites. It is noteworthy that at the Cape this function was performed by Asians; at Batavia the Kaffirs were African slaves.[70]

The Company occasionally granted its slaves small rewards in return for meritorious work. For example, in the seventeenth century extra tobacco was passed out at the New Year, skilful brick-makers were given small cash payments, and slave children in school were eligible for prizes.[71] Malagasy slaves who served as interpreters on slave voyages were treated with special caution, and given special rewards, because of their critical role in the trade.[72]

The Company's outlay for its slaves' food and clothing naturally varied with the size of its slave force. The average cost of feeding and clothing a Company slave per year was in the eighteenth century only about 45 to 48 Cape guilders (15 to 16 rixdollars), a very low figure.[73] During the eighteenth century total expenditure for slave maintenance ranged from 20,000 to 30,000 Cape guilders per annum until the 1780s, when it rose rapidly to a high of 68,365 guilders in 1786—87.[74] These figures represented only about 4 to 7 per cent of the cost of administering the Cape. Although the actual amounts spent on the slaves increased, they formed a diminishing percentage of the Company's overall expenses at the Cape. The Company clearly paid very little for the indispensable labour which its slaves performed.

The burghers' slaves

All but a few privately owned slaves belonged to freeburghers, the remainder being held by Company officials. After 1692 burgher slaves were the most numerous group of slaves at the Cape and soon far exceeded in numbers those of the Company. By 1795 the Cape's reported slave population of 16,839 consisted almost entirely of burgher slaves, the Company possessing only about 3 per cent of this figure.

Despite their larger numbers, the burghers' slaves are less well documented than Company slaves. The burghers kept few records on their slaves, and of those, fewer have survived. Plantation records do not exist. No *opgaaf* roll or other document gives an overall listing of the burghers' slaves by name. A good deal of information is available from sales records, wills, judicial records and travellers' accounts. Nevertheless, there are many details about diet, clothing, working conditions, incentives and so on which are available for Company slaves but are typically lacking for burgher slaves.

The burghers' slaves were employed in many roles, the most important being domestic service and agricultural labour. Some slaves were also employed as shepherds and herders, although here the employment of Khoikhoi was far more usual. Some, especially in Cape Town, worked as artisans.

Field labourers were responsible for a wide range of agricultural tasks which were performed, except on the largest farms, under the direct supervision of the slave-holder or a member of his family. There were few slave overseers on the Cape farms, although *knechts* (hired whites or sometimes free blacks) occasionally performed this task. A basic limiting factor on the use of knechts was their cost; in the 1717 slavery 'debate' at the Cape it was reckoned that four slaves could be maintained for the cost of one knecht and that, furthermore, Europeans required periodic rises.[75] These knechts were always a very small group; in 1760 they numbered only 128 in the entire colony, and 67 of these were in the Cape district.[76] It is true that the wealthy Henning Husing employed 24 knechts in 1701, but this was an extraordinary number.[77]

Some burgher slaves, particularly in Cape Town, engaged in specialised trades: among others carpentry, smithing and masonry. There are also several accounts of skilled slave musicians on white farms.[78] The handsome eighteenth-century domestic architecture of the southwestern Cape is traditionally credited to the skills of slave masons and craftsmen, although there is little documentary evidence to identify the individuals responsible for particular buildings. Some slaves, for example street vendors, were

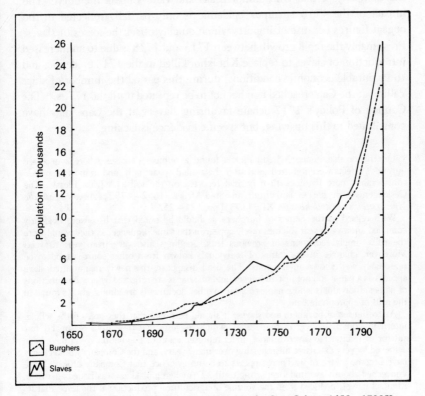

Figure 3.1 Freeburghers and freeburghers' slaves in the Cape Colony, 1658—1798[79]

allowed to work quasi-independently, bringing home to their masters a daily minimum sum, the so-called *koeliegeld* (coolie-money), and keeping the rest.[80]

Systematic statistics are available on the burgher slaves from the opgaaf rolls — annual tallies of the freeburghers and their property made by Company officials for purposes of taxation. Although slaves were not taxable property, the rolls record the number held by each slave-holder (Company officials excepted) as well as their geographical distribution by district. An almost complete series of the opgaaf rolls from 1670 to 1773 is housed at the Rijksarchief at The Hague. The question must be asked: how reliable are these rolls? No simple and comprehensive answer can be given. Obviously figures on harvest and livestock given by burghers for purposes of taxation will reflect rather less than the truth. On the other hand, for information on burghers' names and on the number of their slaves (which were not taxed), the opgaafs seem surprisingly consistent.†

Figure 3.1 (p. 91) shows a very steady increase in the slave population over the Company period. Only minor peaks and valleys break the curve. The impact of the 1713 smallpox epidemic is only partially reflected in the opgaaf figures because of imports which quickly offset the losses of slaves. Presumably the rapid growth between 1713 and 1738 is due to an increased introduction of slaves to replace Khoikhoi killed in the 1713 epidemic, and to favourable economic conditions; during this period the number of ships calling at the Cape reached heights not to be repeated until the 1770s.[81] The Council of Policy's 1717 debate favouring slavery at the Cape may have contributed to this upswing, but specific evidence is lacking.

† On the taxable items, A.J. du Plessis found a number of cases where a deceased burgher's effects were itemized soon after the annual opgaaf tally, and in most he owned considerably more livestock than he had reported on the rolls. (A.J. du Plessis, 'Die Geskiedenis van die Graankultuur in Suid-Afrika, 1652—1752', *Annale van die Universiteit van Stellenbosch,* XI B [1933] pp. 124—25.)

With regard to the names of burghers it should be noted that lists were evidently compiled anew each year. Names rarely appear in the same sequence, as they would were the rolls simply redactions of previous lists. Spellings also vary from year to year. Moreover, changes in the status of individuals known from other sources tend to be reasonably well shown in the rolls. The dead disappear, the newly manumitted slave appears as a name and not just an integer, and marriages are reflected by new conjunctions of names. Individuals whose names appear in other documents are almost always found in the rolls of appropriate date.

As to figures of burghers and slaves, it should be noted that they are, on the whole, internally consistent over many decades, which suggests that they are a reasonably fair mirror of reality. However, a large under-representation of population could have been achieved by very extensive misreporting over many years, and the Company would clearly have become aware of it. There appears to be no evidence that Company officials were concerned about slave under-reporting until 1776 when a plakkaat was issued against it. Mentzel naively deduced from the volume of agricultural production at the Cape that its real population was two and a half times that reported on the rolls.

A short-term drop in the importation of slaves, which coincided with a decrease in shipping in Table Bay, partially accounts for the major decline between 1738 and 1748. The second smallpox epidemic (1755) is reflected in declining figures of slaves, the more minor epidemic of 1767 less so. Major imports in 1772–73 may have been responsible for the major rise in that year. The steep rise in the 1780s reflects the short-lived era of great prosperity which the Cape then enjoyed.

Opgaaf returns of the 1790s show some fluctuations too small to be plotted on the scale of the graph in Figure 3.1. The reforms of Commissioners Nederburgh and Frykenius (1791) brought a halt to the rate of increase of previous years. However, a fall-off in the returns of 1791–93 is to be explained not so much by the outbreak of war in 1792 and subsequent economic distress as by faulty returns made by burghers fearing further taxation. There was a dramatic rise in the reported slave population between 1795 (16,389 slaves) and 1798 (25,754) despite only minor slave imports during this period. This increase was due to strict British instructions that the opgaaf be administered under oath and that tough punishment be meted out to those who evaded the opgaaf or gave false returns.[82] In 1795 returns were also low because of administrative disruptions caused by the arrival of the British. A conclusion to be drawn from the substantial increase in the 1798 slave figures is, of course, that the slave population in the final decades of the Company's rule may indeed have been significantly larger than the reported figures.

A noteworthy feature of Figure 3.1 is that after 1710 the growth of the slave population almost exactly matched that of the burgher population, except for the prosperous 1720s and 1730s when the number of slaves briefly surged ahead. However, despite the similarities in their totals, the make-up of each group was very different. The male adult component of the burgher population was much smaller than that of the slaves, with the result that there were many more adult slave men than adult burgher men at the Cape; the former outnumbered the latter by four to one in 1738 and by almost three to one in 1768. These striking ratios may partly account for the burghers' fear of the slave population, a fear which would presumably have been less had the male populations of the two groups been more nearly equal. On the other hand, the number of adult female slaves was almost the same as the number of adult female burghers from 1710 to 1770, and these ratios deviated by no more than 33 per cent between 1770 and 1790.

In short, the two population groups were roughly similar in their total size and the size of the female component, but dissimilar in the size of the adult male component. The free population consisted of a far greater percentage of children than did the slave population, as shown by Figure 3.2 (p. 94).

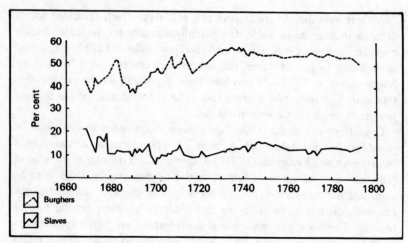

Figure 3.2 Percentage of children in slave and freeburgher populations, 1668–1793[83]

It can be inferred from Figure 3.2 that the continued growth of the slave population depended more on continued infusions from outside and far less on internal generation than that of the burgher population. This pattern parallels what we have already noted about Company slaves, and is probably due to the same factors: high mortality which offset high fertility rates among the slaves, and relative availability of replacements from outside. However, it is likely that there were some minor differences between the two cases. Mortality rates were possibly lower among burgher slaves, who did not live in the close and filthy quarters of the slave lodge and who represented a far larger component of their masters' invested capital, hence presumably commanding better treatment. On the other hand, fertility among burgher slave women may have been slightly lower since few of them were prostitutes. That fertility rates among them were indeed very low — as compared to those of free women — is shown by Figure 3.3.‡

The steady growth of the slave population was linked to an ongoing expansion of the agricultural economy of the southwestern Cape, where the bulk of the slaves resided. The almost certainly under-reported figures for wheat and wine harvests from 1701 to 1795 show a gradual rate of increase.

‡ In the absence of figures relating to family size, number of childbearing women, etc., this graph gives only a rough indication of fertility levels. It is based on the total reported adult female population which of course included childless women and those past childbearing age. The figures may also be slightly distorted if, as seems likely, slave children were reckoned adults at an earlier age (12–13?) than burgher children (15–16?).

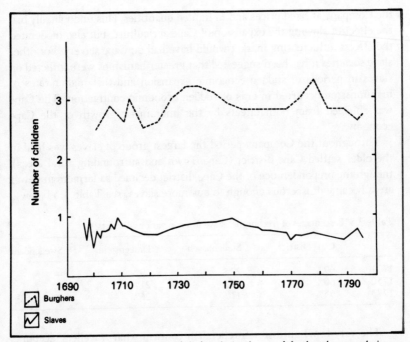

Figure 3.3 Number of children per adult female in slave and freeburgher populations, 1695–1795[84]

It was of great significance that there was no sudden spurt in the Cape economy, no discovery of a miracle crop such as sugar in the Caribbean.

Cape agriculture resembled Caribbean plantation agriculture only in that some farmers had very large farms, particularly vineyards, on which they employed scores of field hands. But among Cape agricultural products only wines had access to a free market overseas, and even for wines, which were generally of inferior quality, such opportunities were limited. The growth of viticulture at the Cape shows a gradual rise throughout the eighteenth century. Wine was produced for the local market, for the provision of ships, and a small amount for export. The latter went chiefly to the Indies, although Constantia wines found increasing favour with the Heren XVII. But these were not major export markets, and the ships' market fluctuated, depending on the numbers of ships visiting the Cape. There is a six-fold increase in the number of vines reported in the opgaaf rolls for the period 1701–95; reported wine production was more variable but, bad years aside, kept pace with the increase in vines.

All other Cape products were bulky staple crops and were purchased by the Company at fixed prices and in limited quantities. This undoubtedly had the effect of slowing the expansion of Cape agriculture, but also moderated the effects a fluctuating market would have had on Cape slavery. For other slave societies it has been suggested that greater hardships were inflicted on slaves in periods of sudden economic expansion and that higher rates of manumission occurred in eras of sudden economic contraction. The Cape was shielded from both effects by the undramatic growth of the Cape economy.

Throughout the Company period the largest group of slaves was held in the older settled Cape district (Cape Town and surrounding rural areas), though the preponderance of the Cape district declined as farmers in newer areas became prosperous enough to buy more slaves (see Table 3.5 below).

Table 3.5 Percentages of freeburgher slave force in various districts[85]

	Cape District	Stellenbosch	Drakenstein	Swellendam
1701	69%	22%	9%	—
1750	60%	14%	21%	5%
1773	55%	11%	26%	7%

The very low figures for Swellendam confirm what travellers' accounts suggest, namely that slaves were found in far fewer numbers on pastoral than on arable farms. Swellendam district, unlike Stellenbosch and Drakenstein, had no sizeable region of cultivation. On the other hand, the higher figures for Drakenstein than for Stellenbosch can be somewhat misleading, for Drakenstein had a much larger white population. A complementary view of slave densities by district can be obtained by comparing ratios of freeburghers to slaves (Table 3.6 below). It is plain from this Table that the proportion of slaves declined markedly as one went from the settled to the frontier districts.

Table 3.6 Ratios of freeburghers to slave population by district[86]

	Cape District	Stellenbosch	Drakenstein	Swellendam	Total
1701	1 : 1	1.7 : 1	4.6 : 1	—	1.5 : 1
1750	0.7 : 1	0.7 : 1	0.8 : 1	2.4 : 1	0.9 : 1
1773	0.5 : 1	0.8 : 1	1.1 : 1	2.5 : 1	0.9 : 1

Some idea of the distribution of slaves among burgher owners can be obtained from the opgaaf rolls. Table 3.7 shows the pattern in 1750. From this Table it is clear that the number of large owners was fairly circumscribed. Indeed only 4.7 per cent of all slave-owners possessed more than twenty-five slaves, and most of these were in the Cape district. None of these owners had enormous slave forces — the largest had ninety-four, the next largest sixty-nine — but together they accounted for 24 per cent of all the colony's slaves.

Table 3.7 Numbers of slave-owners grouped according to number of slaves owned (1750)[87]

Slaves	Cape District	Stellenbosch	Drakenstein	Swellendam	Total Owners
1—5	171	39	109	66	385
6—10	74	22	43	8	147
11—25	71	16	29	1	117
26—50	19	5	0	1	25
51+	6	1	0	0	7
Total owners	341	83	181	76	681

Large slave-holders at the Cape thus formed a small class, but one of particular interest. Their emergence in the 1690s is partly attributable to the Company's continuing use of the *pacht* system, whereby it let out to the highest bidder supply contracts for the colony's basic commodities, especially meat and wine. The successful bidder contracted to supply the Company's needs at a fixed price and, moreover, enjoyed monopoly privileges in the buying and selling of these commodities. This system encouraged the concentration of agricultural enterprises in the hands of a few successful *pachters*, who thus had the strongest financial incentives to maximise production and hence the size of their slave forces. Not all succeeded, and indeed failures to meet the terms of the contract were not uncommon. The most conspicuous success was that of the meat-contractor Henning Husing who by 1701 had seventy-two slaves (all men) and of course numerous livestock, vines, and so on.[88] During the administration of Governor Willem Adriaan van der Stel the pachts were subject to considerable manipulation, and Van der Stel became a very substantial slave-holder himself, although the exact size of his slave force is uncertain because of his use of Company slaves.

It is clear that small slave-owners predominated. In 1750, 57 per cent of owners had only one to five slaves, 22 per cent had six to ten. Analysis of the slave-holding patterns for other years reveals similar figures. For example, in 1701, 64 per cent of Cape district slave-owners were small slave-owners with five slaves or less; in 1716, 57 per cent. This pattern resulted in a very great spread of slave-holding throughout the society. The overwhelming majority of slave-owners were men, either single or heads of households, although widows and single women also had slaves. In the adult male free population one finds an astonishingly high incidence of slave-holding. In 1750 almost exactly half the male freeburghers in the colony held at least one slave.

The slave as property and person

Slave-owning was thus a widespread characteristic of Cape society in the eighteenth century, where slaves were held not only by prosperous larger farmers but also by persons of much more modest means, including free blacks. There are many reasons why this pattern emerged.

Most obviously, slaves were useful and sometimes profitable. For the large-scale wheat and wine farmers, slaves might contribute directly to a successful harvest with consequent profits for their masters. But even for the small farmer or householder there were time-consuming and laborious tasks which could be performed by slaves — the hauling of firewood and water, cooking, gardening, child care, and so on — in which there might be no direct advantage except, of course, in the increase of the slave-owner's leisure-time. Owning slaves was also a hedge against inflation.

Moreover, the ownership of slaves enhanced an individual's status. Company officials and wealthy burghers alike owned slaves, and it was natural that less wealthy inhabitants should seek to acquire them as well. Supporting this ambition was a growing belief, found also in other slave societies, that manual labour for others should be done by slaves, and that the proper role for the white inhabitants was to be a land-owning and slave-owning elite. The Cape thus illustrates Fernando Cardoso's point that freedom in a slave society is defined by slavery; therefore everyone aspired to have slaves and, having them, not to work. For these reasons, economic and non-economic alike, slaves were in demand at the Cape, and there was always a ready market for them. In a labour-intensive economy they were a particularly good investment.

Entrepreneurial speculation in slaves was an option for those with the necessary capital in a colony where such investment opportunities were few. The role of Company officials in bringing slaves from the Indies to the Cape has already been mentioned, as has the private trading done by officials on the Company's own ventures to Madagascar. But there was also room for the Cape buyer who hoped for a quick profit on an early resale. For example, on 6 September 1697 Henricus Muncerus bought Susanna of Bengal, aged twenty, from Governor Simon van der Stel for 65 rixdollars, and on 13 November 1697 resold her to Geertruyd Lubberinck for 75 rixdollars.[89]

Given the Company's jealous exploitation of its prerogatives, it is at first glance surprising that it did not attempt to monopolise the importing of slaves at the Cape. Indeed, had its own experience of slave-trading at Madagascar and elsewhere been more successful, this might have occurred. But the Company's own efforts were costly and risky, facts that were appreciated by the Heren XVII. As slaves were always in demand at the Cape, foreign slavers represented a welcome source of supply to Cape officials and burghers, although under normal circumstances the Cape trade was only of marginal interest to slavers bound for the New World. They did not represent a competitive threat to the Company's own weak efforts, but were an essential factor in supplying the labour needs of the Cape. Any initiative for the control of these imports would have had to come either from the officials at the Cape or Batavia, or from the Heren XVII. But the Cape officials themselves, and to a lesser degree those of Batavia, were directly and individually involved in the buying, selling and owning of slaves, and it was not in their interest to advocate greater Company control of the traffic. Whether the Heren XVII were aware of the extent of foreign slave imports at the Cape is a moot point. References to imports of private slaves rarely appear in the outgoing correspondence of the Cape officials, except during the 1780s.

The Heren XVII's lack of enthusiasm for slaving voyages was based not only on their experience of the voyages but also on the lack of any reasonable way of assessing the return on their investment. Nowhere in the Company's own records do we find figures on what slavery earned for the Company, nothing which resembles the ruthless calculations that were made by Jamaican sugar planters. The Company's slaves were seen simply as units of labour who were plainly cheaper than the European and Asian Company employees, and whose upkeep cost little.

Ironically it was only in 1782, towards the end of the Company period when slave prices were rising rapidly, that the Cape government decided it would be in the best interests of the Company to regulate the traffic and, moreover, to act as middleman between the foreign slavers and the burghers.[90] However, prior to this decade the level of the Cape trade had been relatively low, and the cupidity of the Company had not been excited.

Prices for slaves at any one time varied considerably according to the sex, age and condition of the slave. Male slaves were preferred to female, and young adults to children and the aged. Experienced, seasoned slaves brought more than new arrivals; locally born slaves — those with the toponym 'van de Kaap' — were often valued more highly than imported slaves.

Slaves were sometimes sold for reasons other than the economic gain of their masters. On the death of their owners, slaves were disposed of as part of the estate.[91] Unruly slaves were also sold, or sometimes given to the Company.[92] Others were sold when their masters were convicted of crimes.[93] And an Eastern slave woman, who had presumably been her late master's mistress, would sometimes be sent by the master's widow to be sold at the Cape.[94]

A legal *transport* or deed was required for the sale of each slave, a copy of which was to be registered with the secretary of the Council of Policy (or in country districts, with the *landdrost*).[95] A small revenue fee of 12 stuivers ($^{12}/_{16}$ of a Cape guilder) was charged for each deed of sale.[96] Transporten were also required for the manumission of slaves. However, these documents were sometimes omitted, and sales and manumissions occasionally occurred without official knowledge or legal validity.[97] There was no tax on the ownership of slaves and no import duties were imposed on them until 1790, when an impost of 10 rixdollars was levied on each slave imported by a private person.[98]

Table 3.8 Sale prices of adult male slaves at the Cape[99]

1658	Rxd. 25—33.3		
1662	Rxd. 100		
1674	Rxd. 100		
1677	Rxd. 30 (concessionary price)		
1697	Rxd. 50—133	*Average price*	Rxd. 82
1712	Rxd. 60—190	*Average price*	Rxd. 114
1768	Rxd. 60—333	*Average price*	Rxd. 149
1782	—	*Average price*	Rxd. 220
1783	Rxd. 100—730	*Average price*	Rxd. 379

A few illustrations from the thousands of recorded transactions will indicate the range and trend of slave prices at the Cape (Table 3.8). The Table clearly indicates the upward trend of slave prices over time, a trend also confirmed by contemporary observers. The inflation in prices in the 1780s was particularly notable; prices more than doubled between 1778 and 1792.[100]

Privately owned slaves were hired out to the Company when it needed additional labour. In Governor van de Graaff's time (1785—91) such slaves were used for quarrying and work on fortifications; in 1787—88 no less than 67,145 guilders was spent on the hiring of slaves for the Company's projects.[101] In the early years of the settlement the slave-owners involved were usually Company officials, and the practice was lucrative, the monthly rate (*slavengeld*) per slave being 8 or 10 guilders.[102] The cost of a slave could be covered in two or three years at this rate, a fact which doubtless encouraged slave-holding among the high officials. By the mid- and late eighteenth century the rate had risen to 5 rixdollars per month.[103] It should be remembered that the salaries of Company officials were, with the exception of the governor's, not high. In the late seventeenth century a captain received 13 rixdollars per month, as did a minister, but the range of salaries for lesser officials was from 4 to 8 rixdollars. Even Governor Simon van der Stel received only 66 rixdollars per month. Hence the opportunity to lease slaves to the Company was a valuable perquisite for Cape officialdom.

In addition, the Company sometimes requisitioned privately owned slaves to work for brief periods on community projects. For example, the square (*plein*) separating the castle from the houses of Cape Town occasionally needed levelling and filling after rains.[104] The owners were not compensated for this labour.

We have seen that slaves at the Cape were regarded as property — property which not only produced goods and services but which was also a fruitful form of investment. But David Brion Davis, Eugene Genovese and others have noted that a basic tension arose in slave societies from defining as property a being who was, in ways which the most brutal masters and officials could not ignore, a person. At the Cape, as in most slave societies, this tension was observable not only in the practice of slave-holding but in the law itself. It is true that slaves had few rights, but they did have some.

The laws governing slavery at the Cape were included in the Statutes of India *(Statuten van Indië)* of 1642 and their amendments, recodified in the New Statutes of 1766.[105] In addition, the Cape government itself issued numerous ordinances (plakkaten) to remedy specific problems. These were collected and repromulgated in 1754 during the governorship of Rijk Tulbagh.[106] It is questionable how widely the various provisions of these codes were known and observed. Some of the Statutes were relevant only to the Indies and were a dead letter at the Cape. As for the Cape ordinances, they were frequently reissued, which suggests that observance of them tended to wane.[107]

A few examples of these codes will indicate something of the legal constraints under which slaves lived. Slaves on errands, such as carrying messages, were required to carry a signed and dated letter from their masters. Similarly, slave shepherds and cowherds had to carry a lead medal with their master's name on it. The law also required slaves to carry lighted torches at night and to observe certain curfews. It forbade slaves from carrying firearms and from gathering together in groups of more than three.

Slaves who stole or committed other crimes were subject to fearsome punishments. Any slave who raised his hand against his master was to be punished with death. A Malagasy slave who in 1689 stole some vegetables from a garden was comparatively fortunate; he was thoroughly scourged and forced to stand with a noose around his neck beneath two cabbages.[108] In 1698 an Indian slave who had stolen some silver buttons from the four-year-old son of a burgher was sentenced to be hanged and his body left to the birds.[109] To discourage robbery a plakkaat of 1700 forbade anyone to purchase clothing, household articles and so on from slaves.[110]

Escapees were severely punished, usually by whipping, mutilation and branding. By a resolution of 1711, runaway Company slaves were to be whipped and branded on one cheek for the first offence, whipped and branded on the other cheek for the second. At the third offense they were to be whipped and have their noses and ears cut off.[111] From 1715 such slaves were also to be chained in pairs while working.[112] By 1727 there were so many mutilated and disfigured slaves that the law was changed out of consideration for the feelings of Europeans, particularly pregnant women, who might encounter them; thereafter escaped slaves were to be branded on the back.[113] By a plakkaat of 1714, slaves who had been at large for three or more days and who resisted capture could be shot on sight by the settlers.[114] In 1715 the *landdrost* and *heemraden* of Stellenbosch sought permission to cut the Achilles tendon of runaways.[115]

Gruesome tortures were a routine punishment. In addition, the bodies of executed slaves were, depending on their crime, defiled in various ways: suspended from gibbets, quartered, dragged through the streets, and displayed in various public places.[116]

These laws and punishments are important not only for the light they shed on the lives of slaves, but also for what they reveal about the attitudes and conceptions of the slave-holders. It is true that the punishments of Europeans, both freeburghers and Company servants, were also severe in this period. But a comparison of sentences passed on slaves and on whites shows that the former were far more severely punished than the latter. Europeans were sometimes given partially suspended sentences and could be released early from terms of banishment on Robben Island. This was not true of slaves. Moreover, slave-owners could beat their slaves with virtual impunity, whereas the slaves' assaults on their masters could result in execution.[117] Occasionally whites were punished for assaults on slaves, as in 1685 when a sailor from the *Moercappel* was sentenced to walk three times from the mainyard of his ship and to be beaten, for attacking a Company slave with a knife.[118] In 1693 the Company's butcher was sentenced to be beaten for violently hitting and ill-treating Anna van de Kaap, a Company slave.[119] Such instances usually involved sailors or other Company employees, and not burgher slave-owners.

The slave was subject not only to the legal controls found in the Statutes of India and the Cape plakkaten, but also to the daily control exercised over him by his owner. The master had the legal right to punish his slaves for failure to obey orders or perform according to his wishes. Slave-owners were rarely punished for maltreating their slaves. Only particularly flagrant or notorious cases appear to have been tried.

It is true that slaves could complain of maltreatment to the fiscal (prosecutor) or landdrost, but their complaints were often not taken seriously and they were returned to the power of their masters.[120] However, where the master had a reputation for severity or cruelty, the slaves had a better chance of being believed, as in 1767 when four slaves of the Stellenbosch burgher Arnold Heering complained that they had been ill-treated.[121] In one case a slave brought along the ear of a dead fellow slave to prove the brutality of his master.[122] In other cases the heemraden would exhume a slave's body to determine if he had died from beating.[123] Such exhumations usually ended with no charges being laid. It is a moot point whether these verdicts were valid or merely a result of inadequate medical knowledge or a reluctance to prosecute slave-holders.

A few cases of the many in which maltreatment of slaves by owners was involved will indicate the range of reported incidents:

1695 — Simon of Batavia, a slave of the burgher Jacobus de Wilde, was taken over by the Company because of the 'undue punishments' he had suffered.[124]

1697 — Gottfried Meyhuysen, a freeburgher of Drakenstein, unmercifully beat his slave, Bastiaan of the Kanara Coast, and caused him to be further whipped by his family and other slaves to whom he offered wine. Before dying, Bastiaan cried out 'o, mijn gemagtstucken!' Meyhuysen was sentenced to be blinded, deprived of all his goods, and banished for life to Robben Island.[125]

1702 — A burgher, Jan Schepping of Drakenstein, was accused of illtreating his slave Jan by rubbing his back with a currycomb, thus removing his skin. Part of Schepping's defense was that other freeburghers did the same. He was fined 25 rixdollars, and the slave was confiscated by the Company.[126]

1711 — Christoffel Groenwalt of Stellenbosch was accused by another burgher of beating to death a slave, Leendert of Madagascar, this being the second of Groenwalt's slaves to die thus. The authorities investigated the case and cleared the accused.[127]

1725 — Jan Steenkamp, a burgher at Paarl, beat the slave Domingo to death. His slaves complained to the fiscal, but Steenkamp was acquitted and the slaves punished.[128] In 1729 another of his slaves, Hector, was brutally beaten and died; on this occasion Steenkamp was convicted, but his sentence was light.[129]

Isolation of the farms was doubtless a factor in the harshness of the treatment of slaves, as has been noted in other slave societies.[130] Yet of the deeper motives for these beatings, mutilations and deaths we must remain ignorant. The reasons stated — for 'stealing mutton' and so on — may reveal much or little. They do not usually tell the history of that particular master-slave relationship: whether the slave was defiant or the master sadistic.

In law a slave's property belonged to his master, and in practice this may have been the rule, but there were exceptions. Domestic slaves, particularly in Cape Town, were sometimes permitted to have small gardens and to sell produce.[131] In some periods Company slaves also kept gardens. Moreover, slave artisans retained some of their earnings. Some slaves purchased their manumissions, clearly having obtained their master's consent to accumulate the necessary sum.[132] There are even instances of slaves being given bequests in wills, as in 1726 when two Company slaves inherited about 535 guilders left to them by their brother, a Company soldier.[133] (Slaves themselves could not make wills, though free blacks could and did.) Of course slaves also acquired property by various illegal means, including theft, prostitution, and occasionally selling information to foreigners on visiting ships.[134] Gambling, prohibited repeatedly, was also popular.[135]

The slave's response: Resistance and accommodation

The commonest form of slave resistance was escape. The first recorded slave escape at the Cape was in March 1655, when Anthony of Madagascar ran away and was not seen again.[136] In 1658, soon after the Angolan and Guinean slaves arrived, slave escapes began in earnest and continued frequently for several months despite all measures that were taken to stop them.[137] So dangerous was the situation in 1658 that the freeburghers returned about half of their own slaves to the Company, regarding them as more trouble than they were worth.[138]

Thereafter slave escapes were a regular feature of life at the Cape. Comprehensive statistics are lacking, but the records of the Company and the Council of Justice report many hundreds of escapes throughout the VOC period. Most often the escapees were individuals or small groups of two or three, but instances of larger escapes of ten to twenty slaves were not uncommon. Large groups were less likely than individuals to evade pursuers but had a better chance of avoiding capture if overtaken. The most common group escapes occurred among newly-arrived 'salt-water' slaves. Malagasy slaves were particularly prone to escape as they are reported to have believed that they could reach Madagascar by travelling overland.[139] During 1715—16 no fewer than thirty-five Company slaves fled, apparently with that goal in mind.[140] But from time to time new arrivals of other nationalities also fled in groups.

Both Company and burgher slaves escaped, sometimes in concert.[141] On the whole the burgher slaves probably had more chance of successful escape, as many lived on isolated farms and were probably less effectively confined than the Company's slaves. Moreover, if they had served their masters as herders or wagon-drivers, they probably had a good knowledge of the terrain and some experience in the use of firearms. As usual we have our best information on Company slaves.

The motivations for escape varied. Overwork and harsh treatment are the most frequently cited reasons for escape.[142] For many escapees it was a specific incident — a beating or other punishment — which triggered their decision to go. At times, especially in the 1670s, it is clear that poor living conditions such as inadequate food and clothing were factors as well.[143] But for many the records cite no reason, and their flight was seen by their masters as 'heel frivool', completely frivolous, a phrase which recurs monotonously.

The pattern of escapes in the southwestern Cape was strongly affected by topography. Table Mountain, other mountains on the Cape Peninsula, the Hottentots-Holland Mountains and the Drakenstein Mountains all offered an immediate refuge, a safe 'overnight' if not a hospitable home. All were within a few hours' journey for many slaves, and all provided good visibility of pursuers and were free of dangerous wild animals.

Successful escapes usually entailed careful preparation. In particular food and weapons, especially guns, were essential. Indeed, the want of food curtailed many escapes as escapees were forced to steal supplies from farm gardens and buildings and were thus detected and caught. Many escapes occurred at harvest time when food was plentiful. Sometimes escapees could count on being given food by friends, but this was risky for both parties. Mentzel records a 'troop' of escaped slaves on Table Mountain in the 1770s who had worked out a silent barter system, exchanging firewood for food with slave woodcutters.[144]

As for firearms, they were widespread in the burgher community — the opgaaf rolls list at least one per household — and their presence was always a temptation for slaves who contemplated escape. A plakkaat of 1688 endeavoured to thwart such slaves by ordering all slave-holders' guns to be partially dismantled when not in use.[145] This had little effect. Trusted slaves, particularly herders, were sometimes given the use of firearms.[146] This was risky for them, however; they might be mistaken for escaped slaves and shot, as happened in 1690 when an armed slave of a free black was killed in error while pursuing some escaped slaves.[147]

We know rather little about the leaders of large slave escapes. They came from different backgrounds but were most frequently from Asia, particularly Indonesia, and led parties whose ethnic make-up was often extremely varied. One notable escape in 1688 was led by a free black, Sante of Sant Jago (Cape Verdes).[148] In 1712 another of about thirty slaves was led by a Javanese exile.[149]

Some slaves escaped by sea, either as stowaways or by enlisting as sailors on visiting ships, Company and foreign, which were desperately short of hands because of the ravages of illness among their crews.[150] Sometimes these ships returned to the Cape months or years later and the slaves were recognised and arrested.

In their campaign against escapes the Dutch developed an alarm system in which tolling bells and a blue signal flag at the Castle and on the hilltops warned the public of an escape.[151] Slave-owners were required to report runaways immediately to the fiscal, landdrost or heemraden. Horseback parties of soldiers and farmers were quickly organised and pursued the fugitives into the interior, receiving hospitality at burghers' farms. The Company offered bounties of 3 to 10 rixdollars for the return of captured slaves and enlisted Khoikhoi as informers and trackers (see ch. 1, p. 31). Slaves who informed on runaways were rewarded, in some cases with manumission.[152]

Although it is clear that most slave escapees were eventually apprehended it is difficult to give precise figures. From 1720 to 1747 only fifty-six Company slaves (including six women and six convicts) evaded capture — an average of about two per year. In this period the number of Company slave escapes was several times larger.[153]

Some slaves returned to their masters of their own accord, apparently preferring bondage to freedom with the prospect of starvation and unending harassment from Khoikhoi and search parties.[154] These were heavily punished, but less so than captured slaves. In some instances escapees found employment as slaves with unscrupulous frontier farmers who were willing to conceal their presence from the authorities — a very serious crime.[155] Those slaves who refused to surrender were usually tracked down by Khoikhoi or parties of Europeans, and their escapes often ended in gunfights and death.[156] Those captured alive were tried and convicted by the Council of Justice and suffered the kind of punishments already described. Accounts of trials of escaped slaves form a major portion of the judicial records for the entire period. Occasionally a captured escapee would manage to commit suicide, providing a sequel to his escape that was infuriating to his owner.[157]

Some slaves escaped for good, although the chances of their long-term survival were slim. The countryside was too open to permit concealment of major communities of escapees like the *quilombos* of Portuguese Brazil, and successful escapees necessarily lived alone or in very small groups. One such group was discovered along a remote beach in 1730; here eight men and a woman had been living for months in a house with several rooms and an adjoining garden.[158]

The escaped slave was a dangerous and desperate man (or woman), frequently armed. At large in the countryside, he presented a potential threat to the lives and property of the inhabitants, and was often forced by hunger to remain on the fringe of settled areas; slave campfires on Table Mountain were sometimes seen from Cape Town. He was thus near at hand to those who might well have reason to fear his revenge. Uncaught, he was a symbol of defiance to the existing order and a potential model for other slaves to follow. Hence the escapee was feared and hated by slave-owners and others. The vigorous efforts at pursuit and the vindictive punishments inflicted are therefore to be understood in psychological as well as instrumental terms. Sparrman and others noted that tensions in Cape society were greatly increased by the chronic presence of escaped slaves.[159]

In the Company period there are no instances of slave uprisings or revolts at the Cape. This is not surprising, given the ready avenues of escape offered by the topography of the southwestern Cape. But other factors made large-scale uprisings impossible. One was the dispersed settlement pattern, which separated farms (and slaves) and made communication among plotters difficult. Another was the great ethnic heterogeneity of the slave population, which militated against easy cooperation among slaves and deprived them of the use of a common language unknown to whites. The numbers of slaves and freeburghers were virtually equal at the Cape; in the Americas slave revolts tended to occur in slave societies where the odds heavily favoured the slaves.

In addition to absconding, slaves offered other forms of resistance to their masters. They sometimes burned houses, which were usually thatched, and grain crops.[160] Sometimes, too, they assaulted whites, either with premeditation or in spontaneous response to punishment. Murders were also committed, although not often, and were always a potential threat. It seems clear that the presence of slavery added markedly to the level of violence in Cape colonial society.

But while many slaves resisted their servitude in various ways, many others accommodated themselves, willingly or unwillingly, to their station in Cape society. There were many reasons why this was so, chief of which was probably the lack of viable alternatives. To refuse to be a slave, to refuse to carry out a master's bidding, meant punishment and perhaps even death. The alternative of escape was equally dangerous and the uncertainty of its outcome too great to offer a temptation to most slaves. The weak, the timid, the aged, could not choose escape. The safest course — except perhaps in time of epidemic — was to remain within the system and obey orders. That many did so is clear. Manumissions were awarded for different reasons, but in some cases in recognition of years of faithful service.[161]

The ratio of masters to slaves meant that for most slaves the master was not a distant figure, but a close one, a situation which had its disadvantages but which meant that close bonds could develop between slave and master. Where conditions were favourable the relationship might not preclude affectionate paternalism on the part of the master. The slave who did not opt to defy his master, to sabotage his property or to escape, became in effect an accomplice in maintaining his slavery. Defiance and flight might be in his heart, but his (or her) body and labour belonged to the master. The slave shepherd with his musket offered a symbol of a man who had accepted his condition.

Chapter Three   Notes

1. The most extensive account of slavery at the Cape in the seventeenth and eighteenth centuries is Victor de Kock's *Those in Bondage* (Cape Town, 1950). De Kock's book is based on archival research, but is uncritical and anecdotal in its treatment. W. Blommaert's 'Het Invoeren van de Slavernij aan de Kaap', *AYB*, I, i, 1938, pp. 1—29 is a meticulous chronicle of the introduction of the first individual slaves and of the arrival of the first two shiploads. Slavery finds occasional mention in the works of other historians, most notably in those of Anna Böeseken. Lewis J. Greenstein's 'Slave and Citizen: the South African Case', *Race,* XV, 1 (1973) pp. 25–46 is a useful recent survey of Cape slavery based on published sources. The one aspect of Cape slavery which has been the focus of considerable scholarly attention and lively debate is that of the language of the slaves and its impact on the evolution of Afrikaans. Two studies appeared after this chapter was written: Anna J. Böeseken, *Slaves and Free Blacks at the Cape 1658—1700* (Cape Town, 1977) and F. Bradlow and M. Cairns, *The Early Cape Muslims* (Cape Town, 1978).
2. Albert van Dantzig's *Het Nederlandse Aandeel in de Slavenhandel* (Bussum, 1968) is a convenient survey.
3. The major study of this traffic is Johannes Postma's unpublished Ph.D. dissertation 'The Dutch participation in the African slave trade: slaving on the Guinea Coast, 1695—1795' (Michigan State University, 1969/70).
4. The major study remains Bruno Lasker's *Human Bondage in Southeast Asia* (Chapel Hill, c. 1950).

5. There is no comprehensive study of the Dutch experience with slavery in the East Indies.

6. On the use of slaves at Ceylon, see KA 4009, Thomas van Rhee (Colombo) — Simon van der Stel (Cape), 13 Jan. 1694, p. 449v.

7. This is discussed in more detail on pp. 101—04.

8. J.C.H. Grobler's unpublished master's thesis 'Die Arbeidvraagstuk aan die Kaap, 1652—1662' (University of Stellenbosch, 1968) contains a detailed discussion of Van Riebeeck's attempts to ensure an adequate labour supply for the Cape.

9. Van Riebeeck's views on the need for slaves may be seen in his official correspondence with the Heren XVII and the Raad van Indië, and in his journal: C 493, J. van Riebeeck — Raad van Indië, 25 May 1652, p. 25; C 493, J. van Riebeeck — XVII, 14 April 1653, p. 70, and C 493, 16 April 1655, p. 384; C 493, J. van Riebeeck — Raad van Indië, 24 July 1655, p. 435; J. van Riebeeck, *Daghregister*, ed. H.B. Thom (Cape Town, 1952), I, 2 April 1654, p. 212; 8 Aug. 1655, p. 334; 4 Oct. 1655, p. 352.

10. The Dutch settlement on Mauritius (1638—58) and its modest slave trading with Madagascar are described in K. Heeringa, 'De Nederlanders op Mauritius en Madagascar', *De Indische Gids* (1895), I, 864–92; (1895), II, 1005–36.

11. Van Riebeeck, *Daghregister*, I, 222—23, 225, 248, 446. Also 'Instructie voor d'Opperhoofden van 't Galijot de Rode Vos . . . ' (8 May 1654) in *Precis of the Archives of the Cape of Good Hope, Letters Despatched 1652—1662*, ed. H.C.V. Leibbrandt (Cape Town, 1900), I, 300—05.

12. Van Riebeeck, *Daghregister*, I, 235, 268—70.

13. Blommaert, 'Het Invoeren', pp. 5—7.

14. *Ibid.*, pp. 24—27.

15. The data summarised from over forty specific sources in this tabulation are primarily drawn from the trade journals of the individual voyages as well as from relevant correspondence from the Cape to the Heren XVII found in the Cape Archives and in the Algemeen Rijksarchief.

16. For a history of the Malagasy slave trade, see 'Madagascar and the slave trade in the seventeenth century' by J.C. Armstrong (forthcoming).

17. KA 3989, Joan Bax — XVII, 14 March 1677, p. 7.

18. For the VOC's brief occupation of Delagoa Bay and the slave trade there, see C.G. Coetzee, 'Die Stryd om Delagoabaai en die Suidooskus, 1600—1800' (Ph.D. thesis, Stellenbosch University, 1954), especially pp. 195—99.

19. The final Company voyage was that of the *Meermin* under captain Duminy which returned to the Cape on 28 Feb. 1786 with 295 slaves from Mozambique, having lost a further 50 en route. KA 4293, Van de Graaff — XVII, 4 March 1786, pp. 587v—88. A final Council of Policy resolution to abandon the slave trade came only in 1792. C 99, Res 26 Nov. 1792, p. 672.

20. C 472, XVII — Governor and Council, 8 Jan. 1788, pp. 217 ff; C 83, Res 13 June 1788, pp. 690—94.

21. Tutucorin slaves: KA 3990, P. de Graeuwe — Joan Bax, 25 Jan. 1677, p. 283; KA 3989, Joan Bax — XVII, 22 May 1677, p. 863v; Jaffnapatnam: C 443, II, Hendrik Becker — Pol. Raad, 14 Dec. 1712; C 510, III, W. Helot — Abraham van Riebeeck, 13 March 1713, pp. 999–1000; Jaffnapatnam: C 338, Attestatien, 17 March 1719, pp. 165—68. An additional twenty-one died en route from Ceylon.

22. Simon van Leeuwen, *Het Rooms-Hollands-Regt*, 10th edn (1732), p. 2. Nevertheless, domestic slaves were brought to the Netherlands repeatedly in the seventeenth and early eighteenth centuries. Batavian plakkaats during the period 1637—57 repeatedly but ineffectually prohibited the bringing of slaves to the Netherlands. The *Nederlandsch-Indisch Plakkaatboek 1602—1811*, ed. J.A. van der Chijs (The Hague, 1885—91), vols. I and II.

23. C 717, XVII — Generaal en Raaden, 30 Oct. 1713, p. 409.

24. C 120, Plakkaat of 5 Sept. 1716, p. 463. Also *Nederlandsch-Indisch Plakkaatboek*, IV, 84—85.

25. Charles Peter Thunberg, *Travels in Europe, Africa, and Asia performed between the years 1770 and 1779* (London, n.d.), I, 113.

26. In 1735 the Heren XVII, noting that each slave brought to the Netherlands was also accompanied by a sea-chest, limited to four the number of slaves that repatriating officials could bring home. C 445, Extract uyt de Generale Brief, 3 Sept. 1735, p. 503.

27. C 59, Res 10 March 1767, pp. 143—45.

28. C 168, Bylagen, Ordonnantie, 28 Sept. 1767, p. 477. Batavia had previously, in 1757, prohibited the import into Batavia of 'Oostersche' slaves over the age of fourteen. Batavian Res 25 Feb. 1757, in *Realia* III (The Hague, 1886), p. 209.

29. C 186, Bylagen, 2 Sept. 1784, p. 477. See also Plakkaat of 13 Jan. 1785, in *KP* I—IV (1652—1795) (Cape Town, 1944—49), III, 164.

30. One instance of a confiscation of three oriental slaves did occur in 1784, but this was because of their apparent attempt to incite a mutiny on the ship *Java* en route to the Cape. In early 1787 a ship's captain was arrested for slave smuggling and the two slaves were returned to Batavia. C 76, Res 14 April 1784, pp. 217—19; C 81, Res 17 Jan. 1787, pp. 62—63.

31. C 82, Res 19 Dec. 1787, p. 963. C 472, XVII — Cape, 8 Jan. 1788, pp. 252—53. See also A.L. Geyer, *Das wirtschaftliche System der niederländischen ostindischen Kompanie am Kap der guten Hoffnung 1785—95* (Munich, 1923), p. 40.

32. Though these individual private transactions rarely figure in the official correspondence of the Company, many of them do appear in the 'Transporten' in the Deeds Office, Cape Town.

33. *Kaapse Archiefstukken 1782*, I (Cape Town, 1931), Res 21 May 1782, p. 172; Res 18 June 1782, p. 207. DR, 3 June 1782, p. 338. Also C 78, Res 11 Oct. 1785, pp. 642—45; C 78, Res 17 Nov. 1785, p. 765.

34. The slaves of *L'Union* were purchased by the Company for 39,532.4 rixdollars and sold for 49,250.4 rixdollars, a profit of 24.6%.

    Of *L 'Estrelle d'Afrique's* 194 slaves, 177 were sold by the Company at a profit of 69%. The remaining 17 were taken over by the Company.

    Le Télémacque's slaves were bought for 9,000 Spanish realen (10,125 rixdollars) and sold for 15,455 rixdollars, a profit for the Company of 53%. KA 4292, Inkoop en verkoop rekening van sodanige lading slaven als in den Maand October 1785 Ten behoeven de E. Comp. zyn gekogt en wederom vercogt . . ., p. 260. These were in part fictitious profits, as some slaves were purchased on credit and the buyers subsequently defaulted. See C 218, Dec. 1794, p. 959.

35. C 79, Res 19 April 1786, p. 434; KA 4293, Van de Graaff — XVII, 19 April 1786, p. 433.

36. KA 4001, Simon van der Stel — XVII, 20 May 1687, p. 703.
37. C 512, M.P. Chavonnes — XVII, 31 July 1719, pp. 519—21.
38. C 443, XVII — J. de la Fontaine, 14 Sept. 1731, pp. 524—25.
39. KA 318, s.d. 14 July citing a request of 23 March 1745; C 450, XVII — H. Swellengrebel, 10 Sept. 1746, p. 451; KA 4464, DD, J. van Plettenburg — XVII, 20 March 1781, Bylaag 8, Litt. A., p. 37. Eduard Moritz, *Die Deutschen am Kap unter der holländischen Herrschaft 1652—1806* (Weimar, 1938), p. 181.
40. BO 50, Ross — Burgher Senate, 2 Dec. 1797, p. 355; BO 32, Memorial, 25 Feb. 1799, pp. 54—55; BO 52, Dundas — Burgher Senate, 4 March 1799, n.p.; VC 104, General Description of Cape of Good Hope, I, pp. 30—31.
41. KA 4007, 'Generale opneming en monster rolle van s'Comps. soo Slaven als banditen . . . primo Jan'y 1693', pp. 359—68.
42. KA 3978, Isbrant Goske — XVII, 31 Aug. 1665, pp. 776v—77; C 412, I, XVII — Joan Bax, 21 Oct. 1676, p. 1260; KA 3998, R. van Goens — XVII, 24 March, 1685, p. 985v; C 83, Res 14 Feb. 1788, pp. 216—17.
43. KA 3990, DR, 30 Aug. 1677, pp. 369v—70; KA 3990, DR, 19 Dec. 1677, pp. 414—14v.
44. C 524, Hendrik Swellengrebel — XVII, 6 May 1739, pp. 309—10.
45. O.F. Mentzel, *A Geographical-Topographical Description of the Cape of Good Hope* (Cape Town, 1925), II, 125.
46. KA 3983, P. Hackius — XVII, 22 Feb. 1671, p. 21; *Suid-Afrikaanse Argiefstukke, Belangrike Kaapse Dokumente, Memoriën en Instructiën 1657—1699*, ed A.J. Böeseken (Cape Town, 1966), Memorie van Matthias van den Brouch, 14 March 1670, p. 93.
47. Anders Sparrman, *A Voyage to the Cape of Good Hope,* ed. V.S. Forbes (Cape Town, 1977), II, 258.
48. J.L.M. Franken's *Taalhistoriese Bydraes* (Amsterdam, 1953) cites many of the typically fragmentary archival traces of spoken Portuguese found in the Cape judicial records. M.F. Valkhoff in his *Studies in Creole and Portuguese* (Johannesburg, 1966) offers a spirited but tendentious review of the arguments for Portuguese at the Cape.
49. M.F. Valkhoff's *New Light on Afrikaans and 'Malayo-Portuguese'* (Louvain, 1972) is a summary of the recent debate by one of the debaters.
50. Eugene Genovese, *Roll, Jordan, Roll* (New York, 1974), p. 432.
51. Figures taken from twenty Company documents in the Cape Archives and the Rijksarchief.
52. KA 3978, 'Extraordinaire Oncosten', 1665, p. 502.
53. KA 3991, DR, 9 Dec. 1678, pp. 481v—82v; *Res*, II, 270 (30 Nov. 1978); KA 3994, DR, 27 Nov. 1681, pp. 218—19; *Res*, III, 28 (26 Nov. 1681); Charles Lockyer, *An Account of the Trade in India* . . . (London, 1711), p. 297; Nicolas Louis de la Caille, *Journal Historique du Voyage fait au Cap de Bonne-Espérance* (Paris, 1763), pp. 309—12; J. Hoge, 'Rassenmischung in Südafrika im 17. und 18. Jahrhundert', *Zeitschrift für Rassenkunde*, VIII (1938), pp. 138—51.
54. For an early instance of infanticide, see the sentence of Susanna of Bengal, who strangled her *'misties'* (mestizo) daughter, C J 780, Sententiën, 1652—97, no. 112, pp. 333—36. Her punishment was to be drowned in Table Bay, in view of the other slaves.

55. Peter Kolbe, *Naaukeurige en Uitvoerige Beschryving van de Kaap de Goede Hoop* (Amsterdam, 1727), I, 389.
56. J. Hoge's 'Personalia of the Germans at the Cape, 1652—1804', *AYB*, IX (1946), *passim*, documents some of these relationships.
57. H.P. Cruse identified nineteen instances of Company slave children manumitted through purchase by whites in the period 1715—92, *Die Opheffing van die Kleurling-bevolking* (Stellenbosch, 1947), p. 253. The actual number may have been somewhat higher and may have included some of those twenty-nine children whose freedom was nominally purchased by their (slave) mothers.
58. On manumissions, see ch. 4, pp. 135—45.
59. Data from Company records in Cape Archives and Rijksarchief.
60. See Fig. 3.2, p. 94.
61. Data from various Company records.
62. KA 3987, Isbrant Goske — XVII, 20 May 1674, p. 23; KA 3989, Joan Bax — XVII, 14 March 1677, pp. 25v—26; KA 4015, Simon van der Stel — XVII, 8 March 1698, p. 79.
63. Its predecessor had been burnt down through the carelessness of a slave; KA 3992, Simon van der Stel — XVII, 23 Dec. 1679, p. 18. The new lodge was repaired and enlarged several times. In 1729 it was so dilapidated that there were many places in it where the slaves could not escape the wind and rain; C 519, I, P.G. Noodt — XVII, 15 March 1729, p. 301.
64. O. Geyer, *Die Ouhooggeregshofgebou* (Cape Town, 1958), pp. 7—8.
65. KA 4015, Regelement... voor het Hospitaal..., 3 May 1697, p. 508v.
66. Kolbe, *Beschryving*, I, 397.
67. KA 3999, DR, 9 July 1685, pp. 277—77v.
68. C 800, Burger Besware en kommissies van ondersoek, 1742—96, [Item 5] No. 30, 'Antwoord... nopens de slaven de E. Compagnie...', 16 Aug. 1789.
69. C 214, Generale lyst van alle 's Compagnies Slaven... 31 Dec. 1793, pp. 151—53.
70. C 72, Res, 1780, pp. 245—47; C 80, Res 1 Nov. 1786, pp. 1112—14; KA 4331, Van de Graaff —Willem Arnold Alting (Batavia), 29 Feb. 1790, n.p.
71. KA 3978, Extraordinaire Oncosten, 1664, p. 501; KA 3985, Extraordinaire Oncosten, 1670, p. 433; KA 4001, Cassa Boeck, 30 Nov. 1686, p. 1156. *Res,* III, 179 (22 Dec. 1687).
72. KA 4014, Instructie voor de opperhoffden van het freguat de Soldaat, 31 Oct. 1696, pp. 1070—82.
73. Average cost obtained by dividing figures for Company slave expenses by reported number of slaves for selected years. For example, in 1784/85, 856 slaves and convicts cost the Company 41,536.7.8 guilders, or an average of 44 guilders per slave. The Company's slave expenses were 3.2% of the overall Cape expense of 1,284,912.3.8 guilders. KA 4298, Van de Graaff — XVII, 24 April 1787, p. 654; C 402, Attestatien, 1785, p. 483.
74. Company slave expenses were reported annually in the Cape outgoing correspondence. C 83, Res 4 April 1788, p. 423.
75. VC 59, Materie van rescriptie volgens resolutie van der 20 Jan. 1717..., p. 3, fol. 651.
76. KA 4198, Opgaaf, 1760, n.p.
77. KA 4022, Opneem van vryluyden (1701), p. 972.
78. AR, Collectie Van Hoorn-Riebeeck, No. 15, Aanteekeningen rakende Cabo de

Boa Esperança zedert 17ᵉ November tot den 9 December 1676, pp. 24, 30; Johannes Prinz, *Das Württembergische Kapregiment 1786—1808* (Stuttgart, 1932), p. 322, n. 61.

79. Compiled from original opgaaf returns and also those reproduced in Coenraad Beyers, *Die Kaapse Patriotte gedurende die laaste kwart van die Agtiende Eeu* (Pretoria, 1967).
80. CJ 331, Verklaring van de slaaf Cupido van Bengalen, 30 Nov. 1726, pp. 31—33.
81. See Fig. 2.5, p. 69.
82. I am indebted to Hermann Giliomee for this point.
83. Derived from population data given in the opgaaf rolls. The large fluctuations in the early decades reflect the impact of mortality and new slave arrivals on a relatively small population rather than changes in fertility levels.
84. From opgaaf rolls and Beyers, *Die Kaapse Patriotte*.
85. From opgaaf rolls and Beyers, *Die Kaapse Patriotte*.
86. From opgaaf rolls and Beyers, *Die Kaapse Patriotte*.
87. Analysis based on opgaaf returns for 1750, KA 4158. See also Table 2.2 (p. 56) for figures of other years.
88. KA 4022, Opneem van vryluyden (1701), p. 972.
89. DO, Transporten, 1697, pp. 257—58, 264—65.
90. *Kaapse Archiefstukken 1782*, I, Res 21 May 1782, p. 172. See also notes 33 and 34 above.
91. MOOC 10/1, Vendu Rollen 1691—1717, *passim*.
92. KA 4135, Res 23 July 1743, pp. 244v—46.
93. CJ 2915, Sale of effects of Abraham van de Velden, 2 March 1697, p. 12.
94. KA 3994, DR, 21 March 1681, p. 151.
95. Most slave 'Transporten' are located in the Cape Town Deeds Office. Others are in the Cape Archives.
96. *KP*, II, 29 (9 July 1714).
97. *Res*, VI, 208 (22 Sept. 1722).
98. C 88, Res 9 July 1790, pp. 125—27.
99. Prices from transporten and various VOC records. The 'concessionary' price in 1677 was given to ten able but needy farmers; all the slaves were 'Tutucorin' slaves; *Res*, II, pp. 180—81, 26 March 1677.
100. A.L. Geyer, *Das wirtschaftliche System*, p. 75.
101. AR, Aanwinsten, No. LX¹¹⁷, Memorie van Consideratie over het beloop der lasten van het Gouvernement van de Kaap de Goede Hoop en aanwijzing van middelen tot dezelver vermindering (by O.W. Falck *et al.*), 3 May 1790, n.p.
102. In the account books in which these transactions are recorded the payees are anonymous, in contrast with the Company's usual bookkeeping practice.
103. KA 4138, Res 29 Oct. 1744, pp. 661v—62v. See also Res 20 Jan. 1778 in *Kaapse Argiefstukken*, 1778, p. 4.
104. KA 4015, DR, 1 Oct. 1697, p. 573; KA 4019, DR, 28 Sept. 1699, p. 603.
105. For the text of the Statuten van Indië (1642) and that of the New Statutes of 1766 as they pertain to slavery, see *Nederlandsch-Indisch Plakkaatboek*, I, 572—76; IX, 572—92.
106. *KP*, I—IV. Tulbagh's codification is in III, 1—6.
107. *Ibid.*, I—IV, *passim*.
108. KA 4004, Criminele rolle, 19 April 1689, pp. 696-96v.

109. KA 4017, DR, 4 Jan. 1698, p. 402.
110. A plakkaat of 1700 forbade the purchase of clothing, household untensils, weapons, gold, silver, cattle, grain or any merchandise from Company or private slaves, unless the slaves had special consent to act as vendors. *Res,* III, 327–73 (28 June 1700) (Plakkaat 5 July 1700).
111. *Res*, IV, 227 (1 June 1711).
112. *Res*, IV, 452 (16 July 1715).
113. C 22, Res 4 March 1727, pp. 101–02.
114. *KP*, II, 298f.
115. A. Nachtigal, *De oudere Zending in Zuid-Afrika* (Amsterdam, 1893) p. 81.
116. For an occasion which combined all of these methods, see C 629, DR, 27 July 1760, pp. 636–39.
117. The Statutes of India stipulated the death penalty for a slave who struck his master; *Nederlandsch-Indisch Plakkaatboek*, I, 575.
118. KA 3999, DR, 10 Oct. 1685, p. 302.
119. KA 4010, Criminele Rolle, 16 June 1693, p. 247.
120. This right was included in the original Statutes of India; *Nederlandsch-Indisch Plakkaatboek*, I, 375.
121. C 460, II, J.J. de Sueur (Stellenbosch) – Rijk Tulbagh, 10 June 1767, pp. 679–81.
122. CJ 329, Criminele Process Stukken, 1725 (Testimony of Pieter of Bengal, 4 Dec. 1725), pp. 421–23.
123. C 452, Letter of J.A. Horak (landdrost, Swellendam), 11 Oct. 1750, pp. 377–79.
124. KA 4014, Criminele Rolle, 1695, p. 1222v.
125. KA 4015, DR, 27 April 1697, pp. 501–06.
126. KA 4026, Criminele Rolle, 12 Jan. 1702, pp. 404–04v.
127. C 335, Attestatien, 9 Feb. 1711, p. 279–81.
128. CJ 329, Criminele Process Stukken, 1725, pp. 411–60.
129. CJ 333, Criminele Process Stukken, 1729, pp. 275–77; C 24, Res 23 June 1729, pp. 162–63.
130. H. Hoetinck, 'Surinam and Curaçao', *Neither Slave Nor Free,* ed. David W. Cohen and Jack P. Greene (Baltimore, 1972), p. 62.
131. KA 3989, Cassa Boeck, 18 May 1676, p. 544.
132. Some of the Company's manumissions, in which a new slave was substituted for the freed slave by the latter, fell into this category.
133. C 21, Res 26 March 1726, pp. 45–47.
134. For slaves as possible sources of information, see KA 3983, Pieter Hackius – (Batavia), 25 Sept. 1670, p. 80.
135. *KP*, I–IV, *passim*.
136. Van Riebeeck, *Daghregister* II, 294, 295, 370.
137. *Ibid.*, II, 1 June 1658, p. 281 ff.
138. *Ibid.*, II, 8 Sept. 1658, p. 371.
139. KA 3990, DR, 8 Feb. 1677, p. 256.
140. C 511, II, M.P. de Chavonnes – XVII, 3 April 1717, p. 1137.
141. One group escape of Company and burgher slaves occurred in 1674. KA 3988, DR, 14 Nov. 1674, pp. 167–68v.
142. See for example: KA 3996, DR, 3 March 1683, p. 201; KA 4000, DR, 19 Dec. 1686, p. 449; KA 4017, DR, 4 Jan. 1698, p. 397v.

143. KA 3988, DR, 14 Nov. 1674, p. 168v.
144. Sparrman, *Voyage*, I, 73.
145. *Res*, III, 184 (14 Jan. 1688); *KP*, I, 246—47.
146. This was forbidden by various plakkaats, as in 1687: KA 4002, DR, 2 Jan. 1687, p. 138v; KA 3991, Criminele Rolle, 1 Sept. 1678, p. 537v.
147. *Res*, III, 239 (11 April 1691).
148. *Res*, III, 188—89 (16 March 1688).
149. C 510, W Helot — XVII, 4 April 1713, pp. 1059—63.
150. KA 4127, Res 14 March 1741, p. 486v.
151. *Res*, III, 224 (29 July 1690).
152. C 52, Res 19 Aug. 1760, pp. 383—86.
153. KA 4169, Res 24 July 1753, pp. 470—72.
154. For an early instance of hunger forcing slaves to return, KA 3990, DR, 15 July 1677, p. 341.
155. CJ 333, Criminele Process Stukken, 1729, Case of Jan Bronkhorst, p. 5, 19b 25—29.
156. A notable instance occurred in 1688: KA 4002, Simon van der Stel — XVII, 26 April 1688, pp. 26v—28.
157. A typical example is recounted in C 442, P. Lourens (Stellenbosch landdrost) — P.G. Noodt, 12 Feb. 1729, pp. 61—62.
158. C 442, C. van Roeje *et al.* — (P. Lourens?), 25 Sept. 1730, pp. 1029—30.
159. Sparrman, *Voyage*, I, 101—02.
160. Arson, like escapes, is difficult to quantify. Instances are reported throughout the Company period.
161. This would appear to be particularly true of testamentary manumissions.

Intergroup relations: Khoikhoi, settlers, slaves and free blacks, 1652–1795*

Richard Elphick and Robert Shell

In the first decades of the colony's history, Khoikhoi, European settlers and slaves were quite distinct from one another in religion, culture and physical appearance. Moreover, they differed in legal status. The slaves were unlike the European settlers and Khoikhoi in that they were the property of others; the Khoikhoi differed from both Europeans and slaves in being subject to their traditional authorities rather than to the laws and government of the Dutch East India Company.[1] But by 1795 a number of processes had eroded these boundaries. The most important of these were: (1) the incorporation of the Khoikhoi into the European-dominated society as wage-labourers subject to Dutch law, (2) the conversion of slaves and free blacks to Christianity or Islam, (3) miscegenation and intermarriage among groups, (4) the manumission of slaves and the consequent emergence of an important new group — the free blacks,† (5) cultural exchanges among groups. The first chapter dealt with the incorporation of Khoikhoi. The present chapter covers the remaining four processes.

We shall try to determine how far these processes increased or decreased the access of Khoikhoi, slaves and free blacks to the legal and socio-economic benefits which the colonial system granted to European settlers

---

* We are grateful to James Armstrong, Stanley Engerman, Anna Böeseken, Hermann Giliomee, Keith Gottshalk, Martin Legassick, Robert Ross, Kenneth Hughes and Michael Whisson whose comments on earlier drafts have greatly improved this chapter. We are also indebted to J.A. Heese for his careful critique of parts of the chapter and his generosity in sharing his data with us.

† By 'free blacks' we mean all free persons wholly or partially of African (but not Khoikhoi) or Asian descent. This was roughly what the term meant in the Company period, though its boundaries were shifting and imprecise. Apparently the VOC never applied the term 'free black' to either the Khoikhoi or the Bastaards, the other major category of free people of colour. It was, however, applied to Chinese. A.J. Böeseken has found the first usage of the term 'free black' at the Cape in 1671, though the status which it denoted existed much earlier: 'The Free Blacks during the 17th Century' (unpublished paper), p. 9.

and Company officials. In short, we shall attempt to measure the 'openness'‡ or fluidity of early Cape society. In this inquiry we shall be concerned not only with significant changes that occurred in the course of time, but also with geographical variations. We shall develop the notion, by no means original, that there were three increasingly distinct regions within the Cape Colony. These were the port city of Cape Town, tied to the vicissitudes of international trade and the fortunes of the *VOC*; the settled, arable, slave-owning area of the southwestern Cape; and the pastoral *trekboer* region. These regions with their distinctive, although interconnected, economies developed substantially different social structures and cultures.

Religion

Until recently, I.D. MacCrone's *Race Attitudes in South Africa*, which first appeared in 1937, has dominated the interpretation of intergroup relations in the VOC period. Most writers on this period repeat MacCrone's views (often in misleadingly simple form), and through textbooks and popular histories his views have molded the impressions many South Africans have of their country's early history. Among MacCrone's most influential propositions was that, at first, Cape society was divided along religious lines (i.e., Christian vs non-Christian, either Muslim or 'heathen') and that in the eighteenth century this cleavage was increasingly associated in the colonists' minds with a cleavage by race (i.e., 'whites' vs 'non-whites'). In time the racial cleavage overshadowed its religious counterpart, largely because of the experience of colonists on the frontier.

MacCrone, unlike some more recent authors, was not denying that seventeenth-century Europeans at the Cape had various prejudices against other groups. Rather he was asserting that legal disabilities were not imposed on people because of their race, but because of their religion. This proposition led naturally to the corollary that if one changed one's religion one could change one's legal and social position in society. As MacCrone put it: 'a non-European at the Cape, once he had been baptized, was immediately accepted as a member of the Christian community and, as such, was entitled to his

‡ Frank Tannenbaum's pioneering comparative work, *Slave and Citizen* (New York, 1947) was the first attempt to apply the sociological concept of 'openness' to slave societies. Comparing Brazilian and North American slavery, Tannenbaum concluded that Brazilian slaves had much greater opportunities for legal freedom and upward mobility than their counterparts in the American South. We have combined Tannenbaum's concept of 'openness' with I.D. MacCrone's observations about the extent of fluidity or 'flux' in early Cape society. See his *Race Attitudes in South Africa: Historical, Experimental and Psychological Studies* (Johannesburg, 1937), pp. 70 and 73.

freedom, if a slave.'² This naturally is a crucial characterisation of Cape society, one which suggests that it was a comparatively 'open' one in the earlier decades. This would especially be the case if, as G.M. Theal (but not MacCrone) asserted, 'in those days [i.e. the seventeenth century] nearly every one believed it his duty to have his slave children baptized, and hence those who were born in this colony usually became free.'³

Our first task, then, is to assess how easy it was for a slave or Khoikhoi to receive the rites of baptism. Adult candidates for baptism had to show some formal knowledge of the doctrines of the Christian faith. Knowledge sufficient to satisfy the clergy would not be likely to spread spontaneously. Hence the speed with which Christianity would grow at the Cape was largely a function of the determination of Europeans that it should spread. However, other than the Moravian Georg Schmidt, who won a few converts in the interior at Genadendal between 1737 and 1744,⁴ there were no fulltime missionaries independent of the congregational structure of the Dutch Reformed Church before the 1790s. Some strands of Calvinist theology were indifferent or even hostile to missions, and the Reformed churches had no tradition of clerical orders independent of local congregations, such as those from which mission societies had developed in Roman Catholicism. Nevertheless, the Dutch Reformed Church did conduct successful missions in this period; for example, in Formosa, Ceylon and Amboina. It did so, however, at the behest and at the expense of the VOC, which wanted to combat Islam and Roman Catholicism in these regions.⁵ These geopolitical motives did not obtain at the Cape.

Despite the absence of funds for proselytization a number of early Company officials and *predikanten* (ministers), influenced by precedents in Portuguese and Dutch spheres of the Indies, hoped that the Khoikhoi would adopt both Christianity and the Dutch language and culture. The first commander at the Cape, Jan van Riebeeck, promoted these ends by raising Khoikhoi children in his own home. One of his protégées, the famous Eva, learned fluent Dutch and Portuguese, wore western clothes, ate western food, and became a practising Christian. After Van Riebeeck's departure in 1662 she married the talented Danish surgeon Pieter van Meerhoff in a Christian wedding blessed and financed by the Company. On her husband's death a few years later Eva became a prostitute and drunkard. Wandering between two cultures in which she felt equally alien, she abandoned her children and was imprisoned at various times by the Council of Policy on Robben Island where, in 1674, she died.⁶

Along with the very public tragedy of Van Riebeeck's most promising assimilée, there were several other seventeenth-century Khoikhoi who declared their allegiance to Christianity and Dutch culture, but who were not baptised. One committed suicide, others renounced their new allegiance. Together these failures discouraged the Company from further ventures of proselytization and planned assimilation, though several clergy in the seventeenth century tried to learn the Khoikhoi language and engaged in minor, and usually unsuccessful, proselytization alongside their pastoral duties.[7] By the eighteenth century the inaction of the Reformed Church had hardened into a tradition. As Anders Sparrman observed in the 1770s:

> There is no doubt, but that the Hottentots might be easily converted to the Christian faith: but it is much to be doubted, whether any body will ever trouble themselves with the conversion of these plain honest people, unless it should appear to have more connexion than it seems to have at present with political advantages.[8]

VOC schools also exposed a tiny handful of Khoikhoi to European culture and religion. These schools, however, were far more influential in the Christianization of slaves. In the first decade of the colony Van Riebeeck's brother-in-law, Pieter van der Stael, founded a school for slaves, whose primary objects were the teaching of the Dutch language and Christian beliefs. Other spasmodic attempts followed until, in the wake of Commissioner H.A. van Reede's visit to the Cape in 1685, the VOC founded a slave school which lasted to the end of the Company period. In this institution the teachers were often slaves or free blacks. The school, however, affected only Company slaves in or near Cape Town. In the rural areas some *freeburghers,* who often hired *knechts* to educate their own children, possibly had their knechts teach their slaves as well; but only one contract has been found in which this duty was specified. Moreover, the number of knechts declined dramatically throughout the eighteenth century. Nevertheless, by 1779 a total of eight schools in the colony reported 696 pupils of whom, however, only 82 were slave children.[9] Clearly then, although Christianization was Company policy, the slave-holders were not overly zealous in educating or Christianizing their slaves.

In this light we may now examine the contention that a profession of Christianity at baptism was a passport to freedom and acceptance into European society. As for the Khoikhoi, so far as is now known Eva was the only full-blooded Khoikhoi baptised into the Reformed faith at the Cape in the Company period.[10] Thus for Khoikhoi the alleged benefits of baptism were purely academic. The more challenging aspect of MacCrone's view relates to the manumission of slaves, namely the proposition, earlier stated by G.M. Theal, that 'even in the case of pure blacks baptism and a profession of Christianity were always at this time [the seventeenth century] considered substantial grounds for claiming emancipation.'[11]

It is doubtless true that the Church's teachings had implications which, if taken seriously, would have undermined the practice of Christian colonists holding other Christians in bondage. The authoritative Council of Dort, which in 1618 had laid down basic doctrines and procedures for the Dutch Reformed Church, some decades before the VOC founded the Cape Colony, clearly supported the right of a Christian slave to his freedom:

[It was resolved] that those who had been baptised ought to enjoy equal right of liberty with the other Christians and ought not to be handed over again to the powers of the heathens by their Christian masters either by sale or by any other transfer of possession.[12]

The overlapping principles of Dort (namely that Christian slaves should be freed and not be sold) periodically pricked the consciences of clergymen concerned with Cape practice. In a letter received at the Cape in 1683 the Church Council at Batavia stated that slave children baptised at their masters' request were thereby freed and had to be brought up as children of their former owners.

In 1708 the Rev. E.F. Le Boucq roundly criticised the clergy of the colony for baptising as indiscriminately as Roman Catholic priests, and denounced the colonial authorities for allowing that 'baptised slaves, and their baptised children, even if they are church members, are frequently alienated here and used as slaves, which is contrary to Christian liberty'.[13] However, these clerical pronouncements lacked the force of law. Indeed, it seems that prior to 1770 no regulations or laws endeavoured to implement the Dort principles at the Cape. It is true that two influential commissioners — Goske in 1671 and Van Reede in 1685 — did declare that slave children of European fathers had the right of manumission, and Van Reede laid down regulations that they should be freed, males at age twenty-five and females at age twenty-two. However, these regulations (which in any event put primary emphasis on ancestry and the religion of the slave's father rather than on the slave's own religious profession) were ineffectual.[14]

The effect of the Dort principles — probably the source of Theal's and MacCrone's theories — can best be tested by compiling figures on slave baptisms at the Cape and then comparing them with figures for manumissions. According to one (incomplete) series of data 2,012 adult and young slaves were baptised between 1665 and 1795,[15] an average of fifteen every year. An analysis of these baptisms may be seen in Table 4.1.

As is apparent from Table 4.1, the overwhelming number of baptisms were of children, and need not necessarily have reflected profound inculcation of Christian teaching. The Company took its obligations far more seriously than did the burghers, baptising an average of twelve slaves a year. The rate of

Table 4.1 Baptism of slaves in the Cape district, 1665–1795¶
(*percentage of the population at risk in parentheses*)

Periods	Privately-owned slave children baptised	Government-owned slave children baptised	Privately-owned slave adults baptised	Government-owned slave adults baptised	Totals
1665—1678	23 (**)	30 (**)	2 (**)	0 (**)	55
1679—1695	49 (**)	172 (10.1)	11 (**)	44 (0.65)	276
1696—1712	32 (2.4)	102 (6.0)	1 (**)	2 (0.02)	137
1713—1729	82 (2.7)	244 (14.3)	1 (**)	0 (**)	327
1730—1746	90 (0.9)	352 (20.7)	30 (0.04)	6 (0.09)	478
1747—1763	34 (0.3)	231 (13.6)	38 (0.05)	0 (**)	303
1764—1780	1 (**)	194 (11.4)	33 (0.03)	0 (**)	228
1781—1795	8 (0.3)	192 (13.7)	8 (**)	0 (**)	208
Totals	319	1,517	124	52	2,012

Company baptisms remained very high during the eighteenth century. When we consider the size of the Company's slave force (about 600) and the number of slave children (about 100: see ch. 3, p. 86) it seems likely that a majority but certainly not all of the Company's slave children were baptised. The rates for privately owned slaves, by contrast, were extremely low and declined throughout the period, although the absolute number of slaves in the colony was increasing.

We must now consider the relation of baptism to manumission. For the seventeenth century we do not yet have complete statistics. However Dr A. J. Böeseken, after a thorough search of the Deeds Office, has found records of only about 100 manumissions in the seventeenth century, mostly after 1685. We know, too, that at least 331 slaves were baptised between 1665 and 1695.[16] Thus it is clear that the majority of baptised slaves were not freed in this period, as MacCrone's thesis would predict. As for the eighteenth century, during the years 1713—95 there were 1,075 manumissions and 1,535 slave baptisms. The close correspondence of these figures is illusory: almost all the baptised slaves belonged to the Company, and almost all the manumitted slaves to private parties. To further illustrate that the same slaves were not both baptised and manumitted, we have undertaken spot checks of specific decades. To take one example, between 1760 and 1769 the Company baptised forty-seven Madagascan slaves, yet manumitted none.

Moreover, not all manumitted slaves were baptised. For the period 1715—91 we have considerable information on every manumitted slave given in the *requesten* to the Council of Policy, which supervised manu-

¶ Double asterisks (**) indicate that figures are unavailable or impossible to compute.

missions. In this period 1,075 slaves were freed and in only 8.4 per cent of these cases was it argued in the slave's favour that he or she had been baptised: a small portion were in fact Muslim.[17] Thus for the eighteenth century we have a cogent, two-pronged argument against the notion that Christianity was an 'escape hatch' to freedom: most baptised slaves were not freed, most manumitted slaves apparently were not baptised. As for the seventeenth century, for which data are less precise, MacCrone's and Theal's views now seem questionable, though all relevant evidence has not yet been analysed.

In 1770 the implications of Christian doctrine for a slave society, up to this time ignored by most in theory and practice, were for the first time realised in legislation affecting the Cape. In that year the government in Batavia ruled, firstly, that Christians were bound to educate their slaves in Christianity and to allow baptism to those who wished it; secondly, that:

> ... such [slaves] as may have been confirmed in the Christian Religion shall never be sold, but their Master be under the obligation of emancipating them in the event of their departure from this country or at their death, or to give them away or bequeath them to others under the same obligation ... or, on the other hand to allow all such Slaves to purchase their freedom themselves at prime cost or by taxation if born in the family or presents from others . . .[18]

One should note that this statute did not oblige the colonists to free their slaves immediately after their baptism, nor without recompense. Nonetheless, it moved closer to Dort's identification of Christianity and freedom. Moreover, it unambiguously stated that owners should not sell their Christian slaves.

The tensions between Christianity and slavery now became stronger at the Cape. In practice this did not result in higher manumission rates, but it did result in lower baptism rates. Slave-owners were now aware that Christianity posed a threat to their property: even though they had never been overly energetic in attending 'to a circumstance of so little consequence in their eyes as the religion of their slaves',[19] they now had added incentive to neglect their slaves' formal Christian instruction. In October of 1772 Anders Sparrman observed in the hinterland:

> About ten o'clock I took shelter from the rain in a farmhouse, where I found the female slaves singing psalms, while they were at their needle work. Their master, being possessed with a zeal for religion quite unusual in this country, had prevailed with them to adopt this godly custom; but with the spirit of oeconomy [sic] which universally prevails among these colonists, he had not permitted them to be initiated into the community of Christians by baptism; since by that means, according to the laws of the land, they would have obtained their freedom and he would have lost them from his service.[20]

By the beginning of the nineteenth century it had become obvious to travellers that the spread of Christianity had been inhibited by the colonists' knowledge that they could not sell their Christian slaves, and by fears that they might lose them altogether.[21] By 1800 the benches in the *Groote Kerk*, which in recent decades had been set aside for Christian slaves, were empty.[22] Twelve years later the Rev. M.C. Vos, an early evangelist among the slaves, complained to the Cape authorities that:

> ... there is [a] great obstacle in this country to the progress of Christianity ... that a Slave who is baptized may not be sold. This circumstance is the occasion that the Proprietors of Slaves, who may perhaps possess truly Christian hearts and entertain a desire of them becoming incorporated in the Church of our Lord Jesus Christ, object to their being baptized.[23]

Consequently the British governor, Sir John Cradock, promptly repealed the 1770 statute which, he observed, 'had not been attended with the desired, but the opposite effect.'[24]

We may conclude, then, that in the Company period the spread of Christianity among slaves (other than Company slaves) was slow, and among the Khoikhoi negligible, and that its presence at the Cape did not narrow the social and cultural gulf between settlers and officials on the one hand and Khoikhoi and slaves on the other.

The generally Eurocentric historiography of the early Cape has over-emphasised the role of Christianity. Conversely, Islam has been unduly neglected. An Islamic community appeared at the Cape in the seventeenth century, grew slowly in the eighteenth century and spectacularly in the nineteenth. This growth was not solely due to the transplanting of Muslims from Indonesia, as has sometimes been supposed.[25] Rather it resulted chiefly from internal proselytization at the Cape, especially in Cape Town. Conversion to Islam was encouraged by the slaves' virtual exclusion from Christianity, but was also due to the ministry of the Muslim *imams* who, unlike the Christian clergy, identified with the black population and performed marriages and funerals which the slaves could not obtain in Christian churches. After a long commentary on the reluctance of the Cape clergy to baptise children of mixed ancestry, Sparrman quoted a case in point which occurred in another Dutch possession:

> 'There was a citizen in *Batavia*, who had often importuned the ministers of his church to baptize his illegitimate child, but had always found them inflexible. Well and good! says the man to them at last, it seems as if you alone wished to shut the door of heaven, the keys of which you imagine you have in your possession: but the Mahometan priests of the Malays are not so churlish and niggardly of salvation as you are; they have already promised me to incorporate my son this very day into their church, and make him a true Mussulman: for some kind of religion I am determined my child shall be of, as I hold that, in a well-regulated society no man ought to be without a religion'.[26]

The earliest mention of Islamic conversion among the slaves comes from the late seventeenth century, when the great leader of Bantamese resistance to the Dutch, Sheikh Yussuf, and his retinue of forty-nine Muslims were interned near modern Faure, twenty-five km from the port. According to K.M. Jeffreys this spot soon proved 'a rallying point for fugitive slaves and other orientals.' When Yussuf died on 23 May 1699, the local officials observed that, as a result of his stay at the Cape, 'these Mohammedans are multiplying rapidly and increasing in numbers.'[27]

In 1747 another important Muslim leader, Said Alochie of Mocha, was brought to Cape Town and sentenced to work on Robben Island for ten years. Mocha was formerly chief port of the Yemen, a flourishing export centre of coffee and Islam. According to the *bandiet* (convict) rolls, Said was a 'Mohammedan priest'. He served his sentence on Robben Island before being brought to Cape Town, where he was employed as a policeman; this might explain the pervasive legend among Cape Muslims that he entered the 'locked and guarded' slave quarters at night 'bearing a Koran under his arm'. This and other more anecdotal traditions attest to the considerable religious influence of Said, who was probably the first recognised imam in Cape Town.[28]

A further important figure in the establishment of Islam was Abdullah Kadi Abdu Salaam, 'a prince of Tidore'. Tidore was an intensively Islamised sultanate in the Moluccas. Exiled to the Cape in 1767, Abdullah became known as Tuan Guru (a Malay-Hindi combination of 'Lord' and 'Teacher'). One of his first accomplishments was writing a copy of the Koran from memory, a volume still in the possession of the Cape Muslim community.[29] In 1781 Tuan Guru completed a further work dealing with Islamic law, customs and mystical rites. This illuminated book, written in Malay with Arabic characters, should, once translated, provide a useful insight into the embryo Muslim community in the eighteenth century. Tuan Guru clearly assumed leadership of the Cape Muslims: in his will, dated 1801, he calls himself 'Kadi' (judge or leader).[30]

In 1772 Charles Thunberg attended a Muslim ceremony in Cape Town. His description of the 'Prince from Java' might well be of Tuan Guru:

> On the 28th June, the Javanese here celebrated their new year. For this purpose they had decorated an apartment in a house with carpets, that covered the cieling, [sic] walls, and floor. At some distance from the farthest wall an altar was raised . . . The women, who were all standing or sitting near the door were neatly dressed, and the men wore nightgowns of silk or cotton. Frankincense was burned. The men sat cross-legged on the floor, dispersed all over the room. Several yellow wax candles were lighted up. Many of the assembly had fans . . . Two priests were distinguished by a small conical cap from the rest, who wore handkerchiefs tied round their heads in the form of a turban. About eight in the evening the service commenced, when

they began to sing loud and soft alternately, sometimes the priests alone, at other times the whole congregation. After this a priest read out of the great book that lay on the cusion [sic] before the altar, the congregation at times reading aloud after him. I observed them reading after the oriental manner, from right to left, and imagined it to be the Alcoran that they were reading, the Javanese being mostly Mahometans. Between the singing and reciting, coffee was served up in cups, and the principal man of the congregation at intervals accompanied their singing on the violin. I understood afterwards, that this was a prince from Java, who had opposed the interests of the Dutch East India Company, and for that reason had been brought from his native country to the Cape, where he lives at the Company's expense.[31]

By 1799 the Muslim community felt large enough to require a mosque, and petitioned the authorities for permission to build one.[32] The same year Mirzu Abu Taleb Khan, a Persian visitor to Cape Town, provided a further tantalising glimpse of this growing group:

Among them [the free blacks] I met with many pious good Mussulmans, several of whom possessed considerable property. I had the pleasure of forming an acquaintance here with Sheikh Abdulla, the son of Abd al Aziz, a native of Mecca, who having come to the Cape on some commercial adventure, married the daughter of one of the Malays and settled here. He was very civil, introduced me to all his friends and anticipated all my wishes.[33]

By the turn of the nineteenth century, then, there was a flourishing Muslim community in Cape Town which included both slaves and free blacks (with wealthier members of the latter forming the leadership), and which enjoyed some contacts with the great centres of Islam. Unfortunately we cannot determine the size of this community before 1825, when it numbered 2,167.[34] But long before this the authorities were concerned about the spread of Islam. In the same regulations which forbade the sale of Christian slaves there was also an article which outlawed the Muslim imams' practice of circumcising slaves — suggestive evidence that conversion was already fairly widespread.[35]

Thus between 1652 and 1795 two great proselytizing religions appeared at the Cape. Among rural slaves the impact of Christianity was superficial, that of Islam negligible. Neither religion profoundly affected the Khoikhoi if we may ignore Schmidt's short-lived mission. Both religions had their greatest impact in Cape Town. There Christianity, the classical religion of slaves, made some progress, particularly among the Company's slaves, but the depth of the converts' understanding and commitment was possibly quite low: only a handful of slaves appear on the communion rolls of the Cape Church.[36] The spread of Islam was more spontaneous, arguably more profound, but also limited to the urban slaves and free blacks.

Yet, for all its limitations, the proselytization of the monotheistic religions contributed greatly to the regionalisation of the Cape Colony: it distanced the port town from its hinterland and enhanced its character as a residency city, closer in spirit to Asia than to the African continent on which it stood.

Miscegenation and intermarriage

A second possible avenue of advancement for slaves and Khoikhoi was miscegenation and intermarriage with the dominant European settlers and officials; theoretically such sexual unions might result in greater rights or opportunities for the black partners or their offspring. This theme of intermixture has caused several painful debates in the race-conscious historiography of South Africa, particularly where it has probed the 'purity' of the Afrikaners' ancestry. We must get beyond the simplistic question of whether there was miscegenation in the Cape Colony — there was — and determine as accurately as possible when, where and between which groups it occurred. The rates of miscegenation and intermarriage can help us identify the development of self-conscious groups and measure their sense of social distance from other groups. Much of the raw material is available in church registers, wills and *opgaaf* rolls; unfortunately no one has yet attempted a full-dress family reconstitution of the kind popular in French, English and American studies. Thus in this survey we have relied on aggregate analysis and, in part, on literary sources.

From the beginning, concubinage was illegal in the colony under the general Statutes of India. Moreover, in 1678 the Company issued a proclamation forbidding all kinds of concubinage on pain of penalties varying from a 50 rixdollar fine to thrashing and three years of hard labour on Robben Island. In 1681 the VOC issued prohibitions forbidding Europeans to attend parties with slave women or to enter the Company's slave lodge. The VOC reissued both these regulations in subsequent decades,[37] but there is little evidence that they were enforced.

On one occasion — an inland expedition — a special regulation was issued forbidding sexual relations between Europeans and female Khoikhoi. Such liaisons were, however, comparatively rare in the seventeenth century. Eva was the only full-blooded Khoikhoi to marry a European, and slaves vastly outnumbered the few Khoikhoi among prostitutes who hung around the docks. The Khoikhoi women, except for a few outcasts without family, were still subject to their fathers' and husbands' discipline and to the stringent traditional penalties (often death) for adultery. In the conditions of the seventeenth century, Khoikhoi were much less available and much less coercible than slaves. Moreover, the European male colonists preferred the

Asian and 'half-breed' women and considered the Khoikhoi, with their animal skins and grease, as objects of disgust.[38]

When historians discuss miscegenation at the Cape, they are usually referring to the Company slave lodge which, according to numerous travellers, was the leading brothel in Cape Town in the seventeenth and eighteenth centuries. Scholars frequently cite the anecdotes about the lodge and here we will only summarise the views of the most famous observer of this phenomenon. Otto Mentzel wrote that each evening European soldiers and sailors publicly entered the slave lodge; at 8 p.m. the VOC officials locked the gates and counted the slaves, and by 9 p.m. all European visitors had to leave. The men entertained the slave women in the taverns of the town in return for their favours and sometimes gave them hammocks and clothes superior to the Company issue. Even when semi-permanent unions existed between male and female slaves, the men often encouraged their women to take a European lover to augment the couples' income.[39]

Company officials often provided statistical evidence of miscegenation among Company slaves. In 1671 Commissioner Isbrand Goske reported that fully three-quarters of the children born to Company slave women were of mixed parentage. In 1685 Commissioner van Reede took an exact census which revealed only slightly less sensational results: of ninety-two Company slave children under twelve years, forty-four (or almost half) had European fathers. So appalled was Van Reede that he issued a number of instructions to stop further miscegenation (even through marriage) and at the same time to foster the rapid manumission and Christianization of the existing mixed-bloods and their absorption into the European community.[40] Historians have paid much attention to his guidelines, but the Cape authorities seem never to have seriously implemented them. Indeed, the Company officialdom was so lax in enforcing its regulations that visitors often believed it was conniving in the general licentiousness.[41] A complete muster of Company slaves was taken on 1 January 1693 and revealed that Van Reede's regulations had accomplished little. Though the pure-bloods outnumbered the mixed-bloods by 237 to 85, among school children 29 were mixed and 32 pure; among infants under 3 years old the mixed-bloods outnumbered the pure-bloods 23 to 15.[42]

A number of cautionary points must be raised lest we exaggerate the significance of this evidence. Firstly, we must remember that the slaves in the lodge comprised an ever diminishing proportion of Cape slaves, equalling only 3 per cent of the private slave force by 1795. Secondly, the slave lodge was also unrepresentative in that so many slaves were housed there in close proximity. Moreover, because of its central location in Cape Town, it naturally drew the attention of travellers and colonists. One cannot conclude that there was widespread prostitution in the lodge in all eras, nor may we extrapolate from the slave lodge in Cape Town to the slave population at large.

It is usually assumed that the high male to female ratios among the European settlers caused widespread miscegenation and intermarriage at the Cape. In assessing this view we must make a clear distinction between the Company and freeburgher sectors of the European community. Company servants rarely brought their wives to the Cape: in 1664 only 6 of 178 employees resident at the Cape had wives with them.[43] Furthermore, thousands of single Company soldiers and sailors disembarked each year at Cape Town for ten days to three weeks of recreation. For example, from 1701 to 1710 an average of 68 ships visited per year, in the 1780s an average of 133. On each of these ships were 70 to 300 or more sailors, most of them with money in their pockets and only a brief time to spend it.[44] It is a fair assumption that much of Cape miscegenation took place among the overwhelmingly male Company employees, both resident and transient, in Cape Town. The situation among the burghers was more complicated, as Table 4.2 will show.

Table 4.2 Sex ratios: Adult freeburgher population by districts[45]
(Figures indicate number of men per 100 women, rounded to the nearest ten)

Year	Cape district	Stellenbosch	~ Drakenstein	Swellendam	Entire colony
1660	290	—	—	—	—
1679	160	—	—	—	—
1690	220	280	350	—	260
1711	140	190	180	—	160
1730	130	170	160	—	150
1750	130	170	160	180	150
1770	120	180	140	160	140

The ratios in Table 4.2 show clear regional variation. In each newly settled district males predominated heavily, but these high sex ratios settled down in the course of time, although never reaching parity. Only in the Cape district did the ratios seem to approach parity by 1770, but we should remember that Cape Town had many male Company servants whose numbers were not recorded.

In general the male to female ratios were not very high for a colony of settlement, somewhat closer to those of New England (about 120 in the seventeenth century) than to colonial Virginia (between 300 and 400 in its first hundred years.)[46] Robert Ross has estimated that 11 per cent of the European males at the Cape could not possibly have found European wives and thus must have found sexual expression elsewhere. But 11 per cent of surplus males is not high, even for non-colonial regions: John Hajnal calculated a 10 per cent celibacy rate as the average norm for early modern Europe.[47] These figures, then, do not allow us to assume high rates of miscegenation in all parts of the colony at all times. They do, however, confirm what common sense suggests: that in any period the highest sex ratios among Europeans would be in the most remote and newly settled districts and (largely because of the anomalous Company sector) in Cape Town itself..

Our findings for Cape Town are confirmed by analyses of the literary sources on miscegenation compiled by Hoge and Franken.[48] Their seventeenth- and eighteenth-century evidence makes it abundantly clear that in Cape Town at least some burghers as well as Company servants consorted with black prostitutes and concubines. In the eighteenth century, according to Mentzel, it was common for teenage sons of wealthy, respectable Cape families to 'get entangled with a handsome slave girl belonging to the household' and get her pregnant. In such cases the girl ' is sternly rebuked for her wantonness', but as for the boy 'the offence is venial in the public estimation. It does not hurt [his] prospects; his escapade is a source of amusement, and he is dubbed a young fellow who has shown the stuff he is made of.'[49]

Closely related to miscegenation was intermarriage between European men and black women. Such marriages were very rare, and in some cases illegal, in colonies in the Americas.[50] The Cape authorities, however, did not discourage them and they took place steadily throughout the period. Three of the first interracial marriages (1656, 1658 and 1669) were with Bengali women. Bengalis continued to be the favourite pure-blood marriage partners in the seventeenth century, but Cape-born women, many of whom were likely of mixed ancestry, rapidly overtook their Asian counterparts. On the basis of Hoge's *Personalia,* Heese has found 191 Germans who, between 1660 and 1705, married or lived with women who were not pure-blood Europeans; of the 191 women, 114 were Cape-born, 29 were Bengali, 43 were from other Asian regions, and only 5 were Madagascans and Africans.

One of the first burghers to marry a black woman, Arnoldus Willemsz of Wessel, was among the prosperous farmers of the early colony, in 1686 reporting 40 head of cattle, 600 sheep and 16,000 grape vines. Once the authorities opened up the Stellenbosch and Drakenstein districts, a few of the new settlers took black wives with them so that in 1695, of twelve obviously mixed marriages listed on the rolls, ten were in the new districts. However, early in the eighteenth century a new pattern emerged which would last to the end of the Company period; namely, that almost all men whose wives were readily identifiable as black lived in the Cape district, were very poor, and had Cape-born wives, some of whom were probably of mixed descent. By 1770, for example, the opgaaf recorded eighteen such couples: sixteen of them lived in the Cape district, all but one were relatively poor (though many still owned slaves), and all but four had wives designated 'van de Kaap'. Of the four without Cape-born wives, two had wives from Bengal, two from Batavia.[51]

While it is important to note that the authorities tolerated mixed marriages at the Cape, one should not exaggerate the frequency of such unions. Hoge argued that they were 'very numerous' and 'increased markedly' in the eighteenth century, and a much-quoted 'anonymous researcher' estimated that 10 per cent of all Cape marriages between 1700 and 1795 were mixed.[52] A final calculation of the correct figure must await more thorough research than has yet been done. But even if later investigators should support a figure as high as 10 per cent, this would probably include not only marriages with pure-blood Asians and Africans, but also the (arguably more numerous) marriages of Europeans with women themselves of mixed blood. Marriages with pure-blood blacks are easiest to spot in the marriage records because such women tended to have toponyms (e.g., van Bengalen, van Batavia) in addition to, or instead of, 'European' names. A preliminary survey of selected years in the Cape church records suggests that the number of marriages with pure-blood Asians and Africans was far lower than 10 per cent (see Table 4.3).

Table 4.3 Marriages at the Cape Church[53]
(*percentage of total marriages in parentheses*)

Periods	Obviously mixed marriages	Marriages between free blacks	Marriages between persons with 'European' names	Totals
1665—1695	5 (2.3)	12 (5.5)	202 (92.2)	219
1696—1712	6 (2.9)	19 (9.0)	185 (88.1)	210
1713—1744	15 (2.4)	37 (5.9)	571 (91.7)	623
1780—1784	7 (1.8)	9 (0.2)	370 (95.9)	386
Totals	33 (2.3)	77 (5.4)	1,328 (92.4)	1,438

The European males involved in marriages with blacks originated partly in the Company sector. We do not have information on all of them, but nine or possibly ten were Company servants. Among these were one merchant, one widowed clerk, one messenger of the Council of Justice, one sailor, four soldiers, and two unspecified Company servants. Among the others were seven Cape district burghers (three widowed) and two burghers from the Stellenbosch district.

It may be significant that these Stellenbosch burghers chose to get married in Cape Town. A spot check of the Stellenbosch church records (1700—09, 1740—49, 1780—88) revealed no obviously interracial marriages at all.[54] If this is typical of rural areas, as seems likely, the low percentages cited in Table 4.3 should be even lower for the colony as a whole.

The low rates of intermarriage in agricultural areas parallel our impressions that miscegenation and concubinage in these areas was comparatively rare. Hoge cites a number of examples from Stellenbosch,[55] and there were doubtless many others. But travellers paid less attention to miscegenation and intermarriage in the southwestern Cape than in Cape Town and the more remote districts. It is possible that in the settled agricultural regions near Cape Town family structure was stable, and that moral attitudes against concubinage consequently stiffened, distancing burghers of these areas from the sexual habits of the port dwellers and the rougher morality of the trekboer. It is of course very difficult to build an argument on silence; but this hypothesis would fit in well with our regional breakdown of the sex ratios among Europeans and with comparative surveys of miscegenation in New World societies.[56]

There was apparently little sexual activity in any district between black males and European females. Heese has found references to only six such marriages,[57] and the authorities ruthlessly punished this sort of concubinage. In 1695 Jan of Batavia, a manumitted slave, had sexual relations with Adriana van Jaarsveld, a girl of fourteen living at the home of Jan's employer in Drakenstein. Though there was evidence of the girl's general promiscuity, the court sentenced Jan to be scourged and sent in chains to Mauritius for twenty years' hard labour. In 1713 Anthony of Mozambique was convicted of raping the fourteen-year-old daughter of his master. 'This being an execrable enormity and godless deed committed by the prisoner, a heathen, on a European girl . . . . the court sentenced Anthony to be bound to a cross and to have his flesh pinched from his body by hot irons; his body was then to be broken without *coup de grâce*, decapitated, and finally exposed to the birds; his head was to be affixed to a pole where he had first insulted the girl. In 1732 a similar sentence was inflicted on another slave, Hendrik of Nias.[58] The barbarity of these sentences was totally disproportionate to the mild, and rarely enforced, penalties against concubinage or rape between European males and black females.

What, then, was the sexual outlet for black males? The male-female ratio among blacks was even more unbalanced than among Europeans, and for the same reason: most new arrivals in the community were male. Figures in Table 4.4 (p. 132) illustrate the regional and chronological pattern among burghers' slaves.

Table 4.4 Sex ratios: Adult slaves owned by colonists[59]
(*Figures indicate number of men per 100 women, rounded to the nearest ten*)

	Cape district	Stellenbosch	Drakenstein	Swellendam	Entire colony
1660	110	—	—	—	—
1670	280	No women	—	—	—
1690	430	480	No women	—	460
1711	420	340	720	—	420
1730	400	620	700	—	480
1750	400	450	390	440	400
1770	380	430	330	310	360

As with the Europeans, the highest ratios are found in the country districts shortly after their founding: the overall trend is toward stabilisation, but even in 1770 the ratio for the whole colony was still 360, a high figure compared to those of other slave societies. Apparently Cape slaves were not reproducing themselves, and imports constantly had to replenish their numbers (see ch. 3, pp. 87—89). Among the always anomalous Company slaves, however, there seems to have been a surplus of women, at least in some periods. For example, in 1693 slave women outnumbered the males 125 to 98.[60]

Outside their own community almost the only possible sexual partners for black men were Khoikhoi. However, such opportunities were limited in the early years, except perhaps among the small group of urban Khoikhoi. In the seventeenth century there are hardly any references to black-Khoikhoi miscegenation. Of course European observers might have been unaware of such unions because the children would accompany their Khoikhoi mothers back to the *kraal*. The greatest opportunity and (in the light of the black sex ratios) the greatest need for black-Khoikhoi miscegenation occurred on the European-owned farms where, after the 1670s, the two groups began to work and live together. Even here there were inhibitions which would only slowly be overcome — the early pattern of Khoikhoi husbands and wives living together in huts separate from the master's house, and the frequently bitter hostility between Khoikhoi and slaves (see ch. 1, pp. 30—33).

An early indication of black-Khoikhoi miscegenation occurs in a letter of 1721 from several farmers to the Council of Policy. The colonists complained that the mixed children born to Khoikhoi women on their farms were, by virtue of their mothers' status, not slaves; yet these children had to be brought up at the farmers' expense, after which they deserted to other employers. The petitioners asked that such children be compelled to work for them for a stipulated number of years.[61] This suggestion, which would have created a form of indentured servitude for the Khoikhoi, was not acted on, though a similar proposal was implemented in 1775 in Stellenbosch (see ch. 1, p. 29).

De la Caille, Le Vaillant and Mentzel all confirm that black-Khoikhoi miscegenation was common on the farms throughout the eighteenth century. Some such unions were so permanent that some observers regarded the slave male as a 'husband'. Yet Le Vaillant claimed that black-Khoikhoi miscegenation was far less common than European-Khoikhoi miscegenation because Khoikhoi were proud to be associated with Europeans.[62] We have scarcely any way of assessing the claim of this often imaginative traveller. We do know that European-Khoikhoi *Bastaards* are mentioned more frequently in travel accounts than their black-Khoikhoi couterparts, but this might only reflect the interest or shock of travellers that Europeans participated in such unions.

Even more than black-Khoikhoi miscegenation, we should regard European-Khoikhoi mixing chiefly as a phenomenon of the eighteenth century, occurring on isolated farms, especially in the northwest. Sparrman argued that Khoikhoi women were not promiscuous by inclination, but once working on a European farm they could not resist the promises, presents or threats of their masters. It is impossible to estimate the number of trekboers who kept Khoikhoi women, but probably most of them were farmers in remote regions, and possibly some were wandering soldiers and sailors to whom respectable farmers refused to marry their daughters. In Houteniquasland in 1768 Jan Willem Cloppenberg found one European man with a Bastaard, another with a Khoikhoi partner. In Little Namaqualand, north of the Groen River, Robert Gordon reported that there were nineteen cattle farmers among which were 'five married farmers', the rest having 'mostly a Hottentot woman or two, whom they marry in their fashion . . .'[63] Le Vaillant even claimed that on rare occasions a Khoikhoi male might sleep with a European woman (we know of one such case which resulted in an elopement in 1811), and a case of homosexuality (on Robben Island) between a European sailor and a Khoikhoi appears in the judicial records.[64]

The offspring of European-Khoikhoi miscegenation were of course free and were known as Bastaards, sometimes distinguished from Bastaard-Hottentots, who were offspring of black-Khoikhoi unions. Both these mixed groups were so numerous that Le Vaillant estimated in 1781—82 that they numbered one sixth of the total Khoikhoi population of the colony[65] (see also ch. 8, p. 325).

Thus there emerged two groups of partially European ancestry: (1) some of the slaves and free blacks, mainly in and near Cape Town and (2) the Bastaards, mainly in remote trekboer regions. How many of these would become members of the 'white' settler community is a vexed and controversial question which cannot be fully answered by our present evidence. It is especially difficult to estimate how many Bastaards or children of European-Bastaard unions passed into the European group, for the social structure of the trekboer regions was fluid, locally differentiated, and largely beyond the ken or energy of the government's statistic-gathering agencies. For the southwestern Cape a fairly accurate estimate is in principle possible and, as indicated earlier, calculations from the colony's marriage and baptismal records have periodically been made by historians and genealogists trying to determine the ethnic antecedents of the modern Afrikaner. In 1902 H.T. Colenbrander published an influential study which put the percentage of 'non-white blood' in the Afrikaner at scarcely 1 per cent. Recently J.A. Heese, in a work which far surpasses Colenbrander's in sophistication, depth and precision, has revised the estimate up to approximately 7.2 per cent.[66]

Heese's calculation rests on the assumption that almost all children of extra-marital unions between Europeans and blacks became 'Coloureds' rather than Europeans. (Indeed, he argues that even some offspring of legal marriages became 'Coloureds'). Broadly speaking Heese is correct. Offspring of slave women were all legally illegitimate (slaves could not legally marry) and of course remained slaves; illegitimate offspring of free black women would normally (but not always) stay with their mothers and filter into the black community.

It is true that in many comparable societies of this period (including Dutch Batavia) it was very common for European fathers to legitimate their half-caste children and to manumit them if they were slaves. However, we know that this rarely happened at the Cape. Of 1,075 manumissions between 1715 and 1791 only 68 (6.3%) were of this type (see Fig. 4.4, p. 144).

If it was rare for Europeans to manumit their offspring, it was a great deal rarer for them to re-enact the ancient Roman *manumissio censu* (whereby the slave, once freed, became a citizen).[67] In only two of the 1,075 manumission cases was such a request for burghership made. On 1 August 1723 the Council of Policy was informed that Christiaan, the slave son of a wealthy deceased burgher, Jacobus Victor, and a slave girl, had reached his majority and wished to claim his freedom and burgher status. The long request ended by stating that 'Christiaan had made good progress as an apprentice blacksmith, and since January last had assisted in making iron work for the mills.' The Council agreed, on the grounds 'that such tradesmen are of the greatest service to the public and that therefore . . . he may be enrolled as a burgher.'[68]

The second such request occurred almost seventy years later, in 1790. The memorialist wished that his son, born of a slave woman, might be freed and enrolled on the burgher lists. He went on to quote three cases of European men whose sons, born of slave women, had achieved the status of burghers. He could cite more cases but did not want to waste the Council's precious time 'with the genealogical registers of those who are of humbler birth than his own children and yet [who] have been entrusted with burgher posts and duties'. This application circulated among officials for some years, apparently without their taking any action.[69]

Unlike in Iberian America, miscegenation and intermarriage at the Cape did not enable large numbers of blacks and Khoikhoi to obtain the privileges of the European citizens. For a black woman at the Cape, free-born or recently freed, there was a possibility of marrying a European and also a chance that her children would be regarded as 'white'. Few, however, were able to contract such marriages. The great bulk of intermixture was extra-marital and involved slaves. Neither mother nor child gained permanent social advantages from such liaisons: comparatively few of them obtained their freedom and a negligible number, as far as we can tell, achieved burgher status. In the Cape the mixing of races was limited — far below what one would expect if there were no preference among Europeans for racial endogamy. Miscegenation and intermarriage scarcely ever threatened European dominance at the Cape. There was no 'mulatto escape hatch' such as that which allegedly made Brazilian slave society comparatively fluid.

Patterns of miscegenation and intermarriage seem to have varied markedly from region to region. In Cape Town the rate of European-black concubinage was higher than in the settled agricultural regions, mainly because of the many Company bachelors and sailors on the outward- or homeward-bound fleets. In addition, there were more interracial marriages in the port than elsewhere in the colony. In the cultivating regions of the southwestern Cape the near equal sex ratios among Europeans reinforced stable family patterns and probably kept frequencies of miscegenation low. In the newly settled pastoral regions European sex ratios were very high, and considerable miscegenation, but not intermarriage, occurred.

Manumission

The rate at which slaves became free is another useful, but in itself incomplete, index of the openness of a slave society.[70] The crude rates must be combined with an analysis of the quality of the ex-slaves' freedom, a subject to which we shall return in our discussion of free blacks. For now, however, we shall examine the manumissions themselves — their frequency, distribution and social function — and draw comparisons with other slave societies.

Throughout the Company period the Cape government constantly tightened manumission regulations. Between 1652 and 1708 owners could manumit their slaves without Company approval. In 1708 Commissioner Joan Simons ruled that owners could manumit their slaves only upon guaranteeing that their freed slaves would not become charges of the church's poor fund for ten years. In 1722 the Council of Policy forbade owners to free their slaves without its permission, and extended the requirement of a guarantee to testamentary manumissions. In 1767 the high government in Batavia stipulated that the owner must place 20 rixdollars in the poor fund before each manumission. The authorities increased this sum to 50 rixdollars in 1777, and in 1783 they extended the bond period to twenty years.[71]

Our analysis of Cape manumissions is based on the applications submitted to the Council of Policy for the freeing of a slave or slaves. Fortunately almost all of these are preserved in the Company requesten: only four years are missing between 1715 and 1791. Spot checks in the resolutions of the Council of Policy suggest that all these requests were granted. Since manumissions for almost all of this period required Company approval, we may assume that the number of requests roughly equals the total number of manumissions. The requests vary greatly in length. Even the most terse indicate the owner's sex, origin and occupation as well as the sex and origin of the slave. In addition, the longer requests dwell on other topics such as the reasons for the manumission, the marital status of the owner, the family ancestry and age of the slave, and so on. This information has been coded and analysed by computer.[72]

From 1715 to 1791 the Council of Policy received a total of 1,075 manumission requests. Of these only 81 involved Company slaves while privately-owned slaves comprised the remainder. These seemingly large figures should not create the impression that manumission frequencies at the Cape were high and hence that Cape colonial society was relatively 'open'. If we turn these manumissions into percentages of the slave force per year, we find that the manumission rate in South Africa was low and remained so. Indeed, the average rate per year was 0.165 per cent of the slave force. In colonial Brazil and Peru approximately 1 per cent of the slaves could expect their freedom each year, a figure about six times higher than at the Cape.[73] The low rate at the Cape is one reason why the colony developed only a small free black population compared to those in Spanish and Portuguese America.

Some scholars of American slavery have claimed that many slave-owners manumitted old slaves who were past their productive years and that, in view of this fact, such manumission rates may be as much an index of cruelty as of benevolence. This practice was indeed a problem at the Cape, as an early *plakkaat* against manumitting *uitgeleefdes* (worn-out slaves) bears out.[74] However, it seems that this callous procedure gradually declined at the Cape, perhaps because of the government's vigilance. Be that as it may, between 1715 and 1791 owners rarely manumitted old slaves (see Fig. 4.1): only 12 (1.1%) of the 1,075 requests concern slaves 41 years or older. Moreover, none of these slaves were casually abandoned. Nine of the twelve

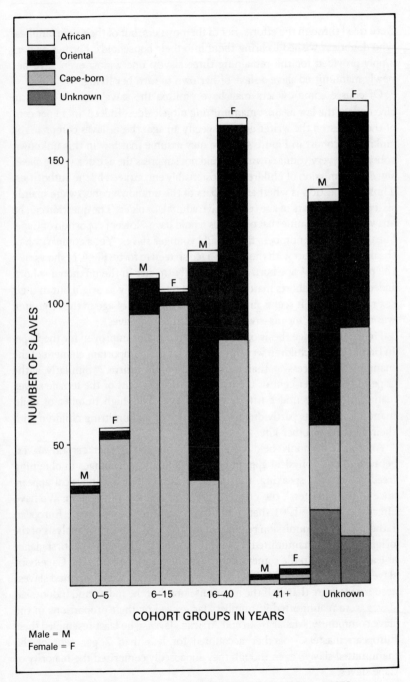

Figure 4.1 Origin, age and sex of manumitted slaves, 1715—1791 (n=1075)

were freed through the efforts, not of their owners, but of their own families, who doubtless wished to bring them into their households. Former owners amply provided for the remaining three slaves; one widow even gave her newly manumitted slave a slave of her own to earn her living.[75]

Of course some owners may have omitted the slave's age in order to circumvent the law against manumitting uitgeleefdes. Indeed, in 33 per cent of the requesten the writer did not specify an age: these slaves comprise the 'unknown' cohort in Figure 4.1. We may assume that few in this unknown cohort were very young: owners would not suppress the age of a young slave, since manumission of children was ostensibly encouraged by the authorities. Thus the question is whether members of the unknown cohort were mainly sixteen to forty years of age (productive adults), or older. The question can be answered if we assume that old slaves would have a lower proportion of Cape-born among their numbers than would younger slaves. Yet a comparison of the unknown cohort with the cohort aged sixteen to forty (Fig.4.1) shows that the proportion of Cape-born is only slightly smaller in the unknown cohort. Indeed, the two cohorts match almost exactly, not only in origin but in their sex ratios as well. It seems unlikely that the omission of age in the requesten was a camouflage for massive manumission of old slaves.

Hence the old age thesis of manumission remains unproven for the Cape. In Bahia (Brazil) children were 'probably a far more important element of the manumission process . . . than were the old and the infirm.'[76] Similarly, at the Cape fully 27.5 per cent of the male and 30.9 per cent of the female slaves manumitted were under fifteen years of age. This high number of child manumissions was partly due to the practice of manumitting children with their mothers or other kin.

Another commonly held view of manumission is that certain slaves, because of their physical appearance, had 'somatic' advantages in obtaining freedom: broadly speaking, the closer in skin colour and physical appearance to their masters', the greater were their chances of freedom. We have already noted (p. 120) that Van Reede favoured slaves with European fathers in his manumission regulations of 1685. Moreover, an analysis of the origins of slaves manumitted between 1715 and 1791 seems — at first glance at least – to sustain the somatic thesis (see Fig. 4.2). Not only did Cape-born slaves (who were more likely to be mixed-bloods than were imported slaves) account for more than half the manumissions, but the Indian and Indonesian slaves were manumitted in numbers far exceeding their proportions in the slave community. Madagascan and African slaves, who least resembled their European masters, together accounted for less than 2 per cent of the manumitted slaves, even though they supposedly comprised the majority of Cape slaves.

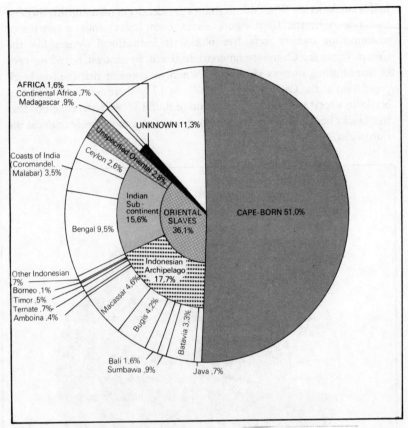

Figure 4.2 Origins of manumitted slaves, 1715—1791 (n=1075)

However, these dramatic figures do not necessarily confirm the somatic theory of manumission. One may argue, for example, that it was not so much the appearance as the culture of the Asians which drew them close to their European masters and created a bond which culminated in manumission. Even more likely is an economic explanation. The bulk of the rural slave force was probably Madagascan while almost all skilled artisan slaves in the city and on the large farms of the southwestern Cape were certainly Asian. Thus the low manumission rates for Madagascans might be rooted in the labour-intensive nature of Cape farming. Given the multi-correlated variables in our data, it is impossible, on the basis of statistical enquiry alone, to disentangle the relative importance of the somatic, cultural and economic forces which favoured Cape-born and Asian slaves in manumission.

We have noted that the manumission rate at the Cape was much lower than in Iberian America. When one examines the identity of manumitting owners, (see Fig. 4.3), the Cape figure seems even lower: fully a quarter of manumitting owners were free blacks (if institutional owners like the Company and the Church be ignored). In Brazil, by contrast, only 2 per cent of manumitting owners were black. When we consider that the free black population at the Cape was very small – in 1770 there were only 352 free blacks in a total freeburgher population of 8,088[77] – we must conclude that free blacks liberated their slaves many, many times more freely than did the Europeans.

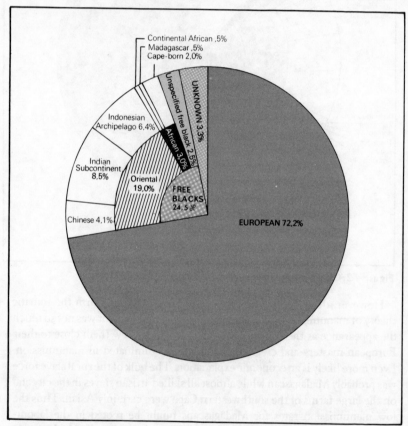

Figure 4.3 Origins of owners manumitting slaves, 1715–1791 (n=611)

Of the 609 private owners manumitting slaves between 1715 and 1791, 28 per cent were women, and at least half of these were widows. This high proportion of women and widows may be partly explained by a mistress's affection for her domestic slaves, whom she would free when she could, after her husband's death. Of particular interest is the relationship between the sex of owners and the sex of manumitted slaves. Woman owners manumitted roughly the same number of slaves of each sex (131 men and 135 women). Male owners, by contrast, manumitted 267 men and 368 women. This predilection of male owners for freeing females suggests amorous attachments between owner and slave. The text of the requesten rarely supports this hypothesis, except in the case of Chinese owners, who often specified that they were going to marry their manumitted slaves. But of course the requesten were not necessarily candid.

Students of comparative slavery have long debated whether slave-owners freed their slaves because they could no longer afford their upkeep. We have attempted an answer for the Cape by dividing manumitting owners into three categories: wealthy, middle-income and poor. The criteria for selection were admittedly subjective, since no readily quantifiable evidence of wealth is found in the requesten. However, we used no information that was not absolutely incontrovertible; consequently fully 70.3 per cent of the cases fell into the 'unknown' category. Nevertheless, enough information survived to make up Table 4.5.

Table 4.5 Wealth of owners of manumitted slaves, 1715—1791[78]

	Number	Percentage of total	Adjusted percentage of private owners for whom inference of wealth is possible
Wealthy	46	7.5	25.4
Middle-income	127	20.8	70.2
Poor	8	1.3	4.4
No inference possible	429	70.3	—
Totals	610	100	100

From the admittedly incomplete analysis in Table 4.5 one may suggest that slave-owners who manumitted slaves were not indigent to any great degree. Moreover, further regression analysis shows almost no correlation between the wealth of owners and the numbers of slaves manumitted.

This argument can be obliquely pursued by asking whether the owner imposed any service conditions on the freed slaves. One might reasonably expect that if owners were indigent they would insist on a service contract after manumission. This happened, but not as frequently as might be expected if the owners were extremely hard pressed. Fully 84 per cent of all slaves who obtained their freedom were under no restrictions, while only one slave was offered his freedom on condition that he spend the rest of his life working for his master. Forty-three slaves (4 per cent) were subject to a limited service contract of a few years, while twenty slaves (1.9 per cent) had to work for their owners until they (the owners) died. In a further sixty-three cases (5.9 per cent) there was some misunderstanding about service conditions which prompted the slave to appeal to the authorities. Finally, forty-six slaves (4.3 per cent) obtained their freedom by promising to accompany their masters as servants on their voyages to Holland or the Indies. In most cases, then, freed slaves did not become thinly disguised indentured servants, but were in reality free. This was so whether the owners were black or European, rich or poor.

Dr Anna Böeseken's newly published material for the seventeenth century manumissions parallels nearly all our findings for the eighteenth century, with two exceptions. Firstly, in the earlier period manumissions as often as not had service conditions. Secondly, privately owned slaves were more frequently manumitted by governors and high officials of the VOC than by burghers.[79]

In the eighteenth century it was not private owners but the Company that imposed the harshest conditions on its freed slaves. Many Company slaves who wanted their freedom had to provide a substitute slave. About half the requests concerning these slaves were in the following form:

> Cecilia, daughter of Angora, a slave in the lodge asks for the manumission of her daughter, Cecilia . . . 14 years old, offers in exchange a slave boy named Malda of Timor. [Attached to this request was the surgeon's report.] The chief surgeon V. Schoor declares that he has examined the boy, who is about 11 or 12 years old and finds him healthy and fairly strong.[80]

On the other hand, the Company manumitted twelve times as many slaves (in proportion to its total holdings) as did the private owners at the Cape. Indeed, the VOC manumitted proportionately twice as many slaves as Brazilian owners, even though its total from 1715 to 1791 was only eighty-one (see Table 4.6).

Table 4.6 Slaves freed by the Company, 1715—1791

1715—24	6	1755—64	15
1725—34	2	1765—74	13
1735—44	11	1775—84	12
1745—54	16	1785—91	6
		Total:	81

The regularity of Company manumissions in the mid-eighteenth century strikes a suspicious note. The VOC may well have used manumission as an incentive for its slave force, but we found no evidence for this.

Another form of manumission in which the owner's sacrifice was not very great was testamentary manumission. In these cases, which account for 17.5 per cent of the total manumissions by private parties, the owner had the best of both worlds: he continued to enjoy the services of his slaves until his own death, but still had the satisfaction of knowing he had freed them. Slave-owners sometimes used a fraudulent promise of manumission as an incentive. For example, in 1778 Johan Adolph Khuul told the Council of Policy that his aunt had bequeathed him certain slaves, including the elderly Manuel of Bengal. Manuel had always been under the impression that at his mistress's death he would be manumitted. Having learned that this was not to be the case, he became bitter and often treated Khuul and his wife 'in a most insolent manner', endeavouring thus to force his new owners to free him. Finally he threatened to commit suicide if he were not manumitted. Khuul, fearing for his own safety, had Manuel incarcerated. So much did he fear the slave's release that he begged the Council of Policy to take the slave over from him and banish him for life on Robben Island. The Council acceded to this request.[81]

In approximately half of the recorded manumissions the cause or occasion of the manumission is evident. These show not only that testamentary manumissions are the largest category, but also that manumissions for purely humanitarian reasons — and one would expect the documents to overemphasise the humanitarian aspect — were comparatively rare (see Fig. 4.4, p. 144).

In discussing religious change and miscegenation, we found dramatically different patterns between Cape Town and the arable southwestern Cape. A similar but even more startling regional pattern emerges from the manumission figures. There are flaws in our data; for instance, only 80 per cent of the requests mention the owner's place of residence, and some which specify the Cape district do not distinguish between town and country. Moreover, some distinctions are blurred by Company administrators and rich burghers who owned both a town house and a large farm. Yet, with all these problems, it is quite clear that Cape manumissions were predominantly urban.

The Company's manumissions were, by the nature of its economic enterprises, mainly in Cape Town. Moreover, of the 609 private slave-owners who manumitted slaves, only 29 lived outside the Cape district. And not all these rural owners were farmers: some were magistrates or Company officials in inland villages. A striking feature of these rural manumissions is that nearly as many men as women slaves were manumitted. By contrast, urban owners manumitted more women slaves than men. Perhaps many of these rural manumitted slaves were favoured domestic servants whose wives

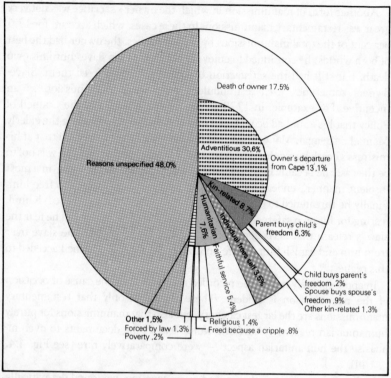

Figure 4.4 Reasons for manumissions, 1715—1791
(Subject to rounding error, ±1 per cent.)

and children were also freed: 54 per cent of these rural slaves were under fifteen years of age.

It is generally and probably correctly believed that rural owners preferred Madagascan and African slaves as fieldhands. These were far cheaper than skilled Asian slaves, whom urban owners imported from great distances at great cost. Yet 75 per cent of the slaves manumitted in the rural areas were Cape-born, 8 per cent were Bengali, 4.3 per cent were from other coastal areas of India, and the rest from the Indonesian Archipelago. Not one Madagascan fieldhand obtained his freedom. Evidently rural slave-owners did not use manumission as an incentive for their labourers. Although they owned the majority of slaves in the colony, they freed only a tiny proportion. In 1793, for example, only about .09 per cent of the rural slave force obtained their freedom.

Thus Indonesian and Indian slaves in Cape Town had much greater access than rural slaves, not only to Islam and Christianity, but also to freedom. The imperatives of the labour-intensive agricultural economy and its associated culture may have formed the main obstacles between the majority of Cape slaves and their freedom. As a result, by the late eighteenth century the Cape Colony had become one of the most closed and rigid slave societies so far analysed by historians.

The free blacks**

Neither separately nor together did conversion, miscegenation and manumission permit large numbers of blacks, Khoikhoi, or their mixed descendants to obtain the status and privileges of the European settlers and officials. However, as we have seen, each process contributed significantly to regional variation in the culture and society of the Cape Colony. In addition, each process helped form a small but visible status group—the free blacks.[82] Manumission brought the group into being; conversion and miscegenation further shaped its character.

In many American slave societies, free black populations sprang up with the explicit opposition of the authorities. This was not so at the Cape, where models were Asian rather than American. Consequently three of the greatest names of the early colony — Van Riebeeck, Van Reede and Simon van der Stel — advocated a society partly based on free black labour. Van Riebeeck continually urged his Batavian superiors to send *Mardijkers* (roughly the equivalent of free blacks) and Chinese to the Cape to introduce agricultural and fishing skills. Van der Stel, on the other hand, recommended freeing African (but not Asian) slaves who, 'by nature accustomed to hard labour', would expand the colony and cause no trouble. Still more ambitious was the vision of Commissioner van Reede, who wished eventually to entrust colonial agriculture to freed slaves of mixed blood, thinking that the Company 'could have no better subjects'.[83]

The positive attitude of these high officials derived from the European experience with Eastern colonies, where free blacks frequently played an important role. In the Indies the Dutch, drawing on Portuguese precedent, did not generally discriminate against free blacks in law (though they often paid free black employees less than their European counterparts). The Dutch also encouraged some residential segregation. The same patterns of mild discrimination and segregation were the practice in the first century of European colonisation at the Cape Colony. On the one hand the colonial authorities provided free blacks with land which they were free to buy and

** See footnote † (p. 116) for our definition of 'free black'.

sell; they gave them responsibilities by organising them in a citizen fire-fighting brigade (a dubious privilege); free blacks were entitled to the services of the Church in baptism, communion and marriage; they could borrow from the Church Council; they initiated cases in court; they owned livestock and slaves; they were free to return to Asia if they asked permission and paid costs; they apparently could carry weapons; and in 1722 they were given their own militia company (together with the Chinese) under free black officers.[84] By 1806 this company had developed into two important artillery companies which vigorously defended the colony against the British. Free blacks also paid taxes, a custom which was justified in a proclamation of 1752 on the grounds that they 'enjoy[ed] all privileges and rights of burghers.'[85]

On the other hand, however, the Company, and, more importantly, the burghers, did not always view free blacks as the complete equals of Europeans, at least in the eighteenth century. For instance, the authorities infrequently applied the term 'burgher' (or freeburgher) to the free blacks after the turn of the eighteenth century, and in the requesten from 1715 to 1795 there are no petitions from free blacks asking for burgher papers; Europeans, however, appear on every other page. We still need a thorough investigation of criminal and civil sentences to determine if free blacks received unfair treatment from the courts. One suspects discrimination in several cases; for example, in 1738 three free blacks and three slaves received equal punishment (a beating and costs) for being on the streets after curfew;[86] burghers were free to ignore curfew.

By the second half of the eighteenth century the laws had ceased to be colour-blind. In 1765 the government took notice of free black women who, by their dress, placed 'themselves not only on a par with other respectable burghers' wives, but often even push[ed] themselves above them.' The Council of Policy deemed such behaviour 'unseemly and vexing to the public'; henceforth no free black woman was to appear in public in coloured silk clothing, hoopskirts, fine laces, adorned bonnets, curled hair or ear-rings. In 1771 there was another instance of discrimination in a plakkaat against the purchase of clothing from Company slaves. The authorities laid down that Europeans were to pay fines on the first two offences and to be punished on the third: free blacks were to be treated as slaves, i.e., to be thrashed and set to work in chains for ten years.[87] By the 1790s there were other more disturbing practices. For example, free blacks now had to carry passes if they wished to leave town.[88] The evolution of the official attitudes to free blacks still awaits thorough investigation, but it would seem that the Dutch at the Cape followed the Roman precedent and developed a distinction between freeborn citizens and freedmen.

The vast majority of the free blacks were ex-slaves or their descendants.

However, a sizeable number had other origins. Firstly, there were a handful of Asian settlers such as Abdol Garisch, who came to the Cape in 1790 'a free man' (emphasis in the original document.) Abdol Garisch had left his native land, Amboina, in an English merchant vessel bound for various ports in the Indian Ocean. The ship was captured by a French privateer, only to be re-taken by an English man-of-war and brought to the Cape. Abdol Garish decided to stay on and eventually became a court interpreter and administrator of oaths to Muslim witnesses.[89] Another free immigrant was Abdol Wasie, who arrived at the Cape in the late eighteenth century 'as a free servant of his Batavian master', but elected to stay when his master returned to the East.[90] Though such settlers appear infrequently in the sources, their existence even in small numbers suggests that the Cape had some attractions for free persons of colour.

More influential than voluntary settlers, however, were Asian political figures banished by the Company from the Indies. Several of these exiles were eminent Indonesian princes who lived out their lives, often with a small retinue of family and servants, either on Robben Island or on farms largely isolated from the colony's life. Sometimes their children returned to the East on their parents' death; more often they stayed on. We have come across the names of approximately thirty such exiles, but possibly there were more.[91] With their retinues (De Rottij was reputed to have 100 slaves)[92] their total could not have amounted to much more than 250 in the period 1652—1795. At times the exiles exercised leadership among free blacks, but because of their isolation from the port and colonial life they seem not to have formed a permanent and recognised free black elite.[93]

A much larger number of Asians came to the Cape as convicts (bandieten). A particularly sizeable group arrived in 1743 to work on the breakwater, though most of them died shortly afterwards. On the basis of the bandiet rolls we have estimated that the VOC landed perhaps 200 or 300 convicts at the Cape in the eighteenth century. The authorities treated the convicts more or less as slaves.[94] However, they became free on the expiry of their sentences and trickled into the free black community. The numbers of ex-convicts among free blacks could not have been inconsequential, as the following irate resolution of the Council of Policy in 1749 bears out:

> Considering that this place is so full of Eastern convicts, sent hither from India [i.e., the East], who after the term of their imprisonment has expired, become free and remain free, competing with the poor whites of European descent in procuring their livelihood, and consequently very injurious to the latter . . . the council deem it necessary to take steps, in time, and write by first opportunity to Batavia for permission to send such convicts after the expiration of their terms of banishment back to the place whence they came.[95]

This correspondence to Batavia was apparently unsuccessful as we have found no indication that convicts left the Cape in increasing numbers after this date.[96]

It is clear that all or virtually all of the Chinese sector of the free black community were ex-convicts. By 1750 persons with obviously Chinese names numbered at least twenty-two, although in 1770 identifiable Chinese had fallen to seven.[97] This drop was perhaps due to their higher rate of return to Asia than other free blacks, perhaps also to their increasing intermarriage with other blacks. Such assimilation was not characteristic of the early eighteenth century, when Chinese apparently lived apart from other free blacks and even had their own cemetery. In the opgaaf rolls the Chinese nearly always appear as unmarried males, although Mentzel claimed that 'they practice[d] polygamy and obtain[ed] their wives by the purchase of female slaves'.[98]

The only systematic source for the size and make-up of the free black community is the annual opgaaf roll. James Armstrong has convincingly argued that we need not be unduly suspicious of these rolls as far as free blacks are concerned.[99] However, there are always a number of names which the researcher will find hard to identify as black or European. Tables 4.7A and B are based on a preliminary study of the rolls which, to the extent that it errs, does so in underestimating the number of free blacks.

The figures in Tables 4.7A and B show that free blacks were a small group, one whose numerical significance declined even further as both the European and slave populations outgrew it. In 1670 free blacks numbered 7.4 per cent of the total freeburgher community, but by 1770 only 4.4 per cent. Seen as a percentage of the total non-Company sector (including privately owned slaves and knechts but not Company servants and Company slaves), these figures

Table 4.7(A) Free blacks : Entire colony[100]

	Men	Women	Boys	Girls	Total	As percentage of free-burger population
1670	2	2	9*	—	13	7.4
1679	7	4	8	11	30	10.4
1690	15	13	20*	—	48	5.7
1701	16	16	8	11	51	4.0
1711	25	20	10	8	63	3.6
1719	47	46	26	17	136	6.6
1730	56	62	52	51	221	8.0
1740	60	92	85	80	317	8.4
1750	94	98	69	88	349	7.2
1760	93	118	51	51	313	5.1
1770	98	141	53	60	352	4.4

* Not known whether boys or girls

Table 4.7(B) Free blacks : Cape district only

	Men	Women	Boys	Girls	Total	As percentage of free-burgher population
1685	4	2	6	2	14	7.6
1711	18	18	1	5	42	6.0
1730	55	61	52	51	219	16.3
1750	94	98	69	88	349	15.8
1770	97	139	51	58	345	12.8

are of course even lower: 5.7 per cent and 2.1 per cent respectively. These proportions are very low when compared to those of free black communities in contemporary Spanish and Portuguese colonies, but in the same range or only slightly lower than those of French and British colonies in the Caribbean and North America. However, in the Cape district free blacks formed a significant and visible part of the population, representing, for example in 1730, 16.3 per cent of the freeburgher population. In Cape Town itself, where most free blacks lived, the percentage was doubtless much higher. Unfortunately we have no figures for the town alone in the Company period, but we do know that by 1827 free blacks comprised at least about 25 per cent of the free urban population, excluding troops.[101]

The free black group was unique at the Cape in having a sex ratio below 100. Despite this preponderance of women over men — a result of manumission practices (discussed on p. 141) — the free blacks had a very low fertility rate. In 1760 the ratio of European children to European women in the colony was 2.7:1; among free blacks this ratio was .86:1 — that is, considerably below replacement rates. Although the numbers of free blacks were increasing through manumission and, much less importantly, through the freeing of convicts and exiles, their natural increase was too small for them to survive as a community. This may have been due to high infant mortality, itself a result of poverty. Or the free blacks, who were a far more urbanised group than the Europeans, may have undergone the decline in birth rates which normally accompanies urbanisation. However, the subtle psychological mechanisms whereby a group controls its population rarely rise to historical visibility. The other indications we have of low fertility are celibacy and nuptial rates, which at best are only suggestive. Despite the nearly equal numbers of free black men and women, the number of stable unions in the community — if we can trust the opgaaf rolls — was small and declining in the eighteenth century. In 1705 the opgaaf listed 41 free black adults, 20 (48.8%) of them in couples; by 1735 only 24 of 130 adults (18.5%) were listed in this way; and in 1770 the returns recorded only 44 of 239 (18.4%) as being together. Moreover, the admittedly incomplete figures in

Table 4.3 (p. 130) suggest that the number of marriages among free blacks, although reasonably high at the beginning, may also have declined in the eighteenth century.

In the early decades, when there were few free blacks and comparatively numerous stable unions among them, most unions were formed between persons of similar ethnic background. In time these cultural cleavages among the free blacks tended to dissolve and the opgaaf shows that few stable unions were contracted within ethnic groups. For example, of the twenty-two stable unions recorded in the opgaaf of 1770, only two were between partners with the same toponym, and only three more were between partners from the same region (e.g. modern India or Indonesia). Fully sixteen were between persons born in different regions.

The opgaaf rolls give a picture of the ethnic origins of free blacks which is almost fully in accord with what we would expect from the manumission figures; i.e., an overwhelming number of Asians divided about equally between persons from modern India (chiefly Bengalis) and persons from modern Indonesia (largely Macassarese/Buginese), with only a smattering of Africans, Madagascans and Chinese ex-convicts.

Figure 4.5 illustrates the increasing incidence from 1705 to 1770 of European names among free blacks, who apparently took these names from masters, protectors, employers and putative fathers, or simply from the European master culture. Most of these blacks would be Cape-born, and could probably be bracketed with the 'van de Kaaps'. Together these groups numbered 22 per cent of the free black population in 1705, 34 per cent in 1735 and 40 per cent in 1770. Thus, as would be expected, the Cape-born component grew over time.

In the seventeenth century the free blacks did not all live in the Cape district, nor were they all poor. Indeed, after the founding of Stellenbosch (1679) the larger part of the tiny group set up farming in the new region. By 1688 there were six free black households in Stellenbosch listed as owning livestock, planting crops, or both. Only two or three free black farmers continued to prosper (for example, Anthony of Angola and Jan of Ceylon), and by 1690 almost all were back in the Cape district. By 1714 the pattern for the coming century had been set: there were then only six free blacks in Stellenbosch-Drakenstein, of whom only one had livestock property, and of whom none planted. Even in the Cape district, where thirty-two free blacks lived, most had no property entered on the rolls, except for six who owned slaves and three who had a horse or two.

But one cannot conclude from these figures[102] alone that free blacks had become an under-class separated from Europeans by their poverty. Firstly, free blacks comprised only a minority — though a significant one — of

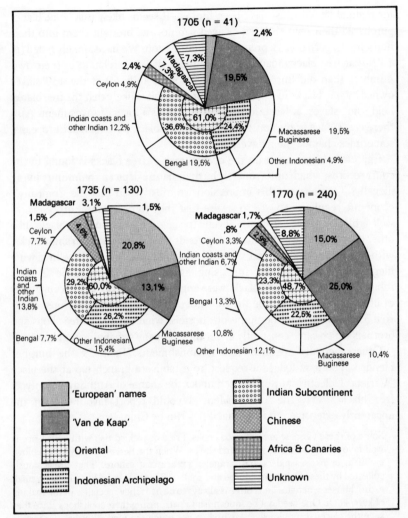

Figure 4.5 Ethnic composition of adult free black community
(As reflected in their names and toponyms recorded in opgaaf rolls in selected years)

persons listed without property on the rolls. Secondly, since most lived in Cape Town, they may have possessed other types of property (including cash) which the opgaaf did not enumerate. The one form of registered property which free blacks did possess in increasing numbers was slaves; for example, in 1735 the 132 free black adults owned 139 slaves (adults and children). Since most had neither land nor a large home, their purely economic need for manual labour must have been limited. It seems likely that some blacks purchased their own children or aged parents and brought them into their households, perhaps as a prelude to manumission. We have already noted (p. 140) that free blacks manumitted far more slaves in relation to their own numbers than did Europeans. However, since fully 69 of the 139 slaves owned by free blacks in 1735 were adult males, it is likely that the free blacks held some slaves, at least, for their labour or as a form of investment. Also there is evidence in the court records that free black owners, like Europeans, sometimes chained their slaves.[103]

Important information on the occupations of free blacks is found in the court records, which unfortunately by their nature depict a community living illegally. To moderate this impression we must recall that the Company's economic regulations were so severe that they forced many Europeans, as well as blacks, to live constantly beyond the law. Thus we find free blacks, like other burghers, charged with stealing goods washed ashore from shipwrecks, with shooting game beyond the permitted borders, and with selling wine illegally.[104] This was not surprising as the majority of Cape Town's inhabitants, European and black, were engaged in the associated occupations of housing and entertaining the transitory population from the ships. Many free blacks worked in the numerous hostels, wine outlets, coffee shops and brothels which came constantly under the Company's changing regulations.

Others actually operated such establishments. In 1729 the burgher Hendrik Thomasz lodged a request 'to establish a branch tap at the place "Varietas Delectus" at Rondebosch under the charge of Anthony Valentyn a free black'.[105] By the 1740s Mentzel could report favourably on the apparently extensive restaurant facilities run by Chinese:

> Some of these Chinese are . . . good cooks. Fried or pickled fish with boiled rice is well-favoured by soldiers, sailors and slaves. When the fierce North-Westers blow, crayfish, crabs, seaspiders and 'granelen'†† are cast ashore. They are jealously collected by these Orientals, cooked and sold . . . These Asiatics likewise keep small eating houses where tea and coffee is always to be had; they specialise in the making of kerri-kerri. One need not be squeamish in patronising their cookshops since they keep the places scrupulously clean and do not touch the food with their fingers.[106]

Later travellers' accounts seldom mention these eating houses, an almost certain indication that they did not flourish. Only a few scattered entries in the nineteenth-century street directories suggest that they survived at all.[107]

Other sources indicate that the free blacks had a substantial hold on the artisanry. Many were tailors and shoemakers in Cape Town, probably because of the great number of military and naval personnel who needed uniforms. Business prospered so well that in the winter months, when the only secure

†† A diminutive species of crab with a soft, edible shell (footnote in original).

anchorage was in Simonstown, many free black tailors and haberdashers shuttled across the peninsula to set up shop and swell the village population. There were so many free black Muslims in Simonstown by the middle of the nineteenth century that the butcher there would not sell pork 'for fear of giving offence to his mohammedan customers'.[108]

Cape Dutch architecture was fundamentally influenced by the 'Malay' masons (presumably free blacks as well as slaves), who were responsible for the many stylish gables which are seen on old Cape homes and farms. Indonesian craftsmen also influenced Cape carpentry and cabinet-making. As L.E. van Onselen comments:

[The Malays] were probably the first real furniture-makers to arrive at the Cape. The furniture they made would, undoubtedly, have incorporated designs of Eastern origin. Their influence can be seen in the cane and ratan used in some Cape antique furniture and they were probably responsible for the ball and claw foot which was originally a dragon's foot clutching a pearl. The cabriole leg which graces some Cape furniture is Eastern in origin and was, probably, first introduced by them. They would [also] have introduced the marquetry and lacquer work which is Eastern in conception and which was to be universally adopted in Europe during the eighteenth century.[109]

Free black coopers, saddlers, basketmakers and hatmakers are also mentioned in the travellers' accounts and secondary sources.[110]

Fishing was one of the many occupations in which free blacks early established themselves and in which they remain today, as the 'Coloured' fishing communities around the Cape bear witness. Free black fishing began at least as early as 1722, when we have a memorial requesting fishing rights signed by both European and black fishermen. Among them was one Chinese, Sobinko, and two Indonesians, Jacob of Bugis and Jonker of Macassar.[111] Fishing was organised collectively because of the large capital outlay; as Mentzel indicates:

No single person or boat-owner is in a position to engage in fishing on a large scale because the co-operative labour of several persons, boats and a net is essential for success. The usual practice at the Cape is as follows. Two men provide a boat each, another supplies the net, and various other people the slaves to man the boats. Each boat requires five persons.[112]

Free blacks were engaged in the retail trades as well. Very early on there were complaints about their competition. For instance, in 1727 several European bakers submitted to the authorities that 'certain burghers and Chinese were in the habit of sending their boys about the streets to sell different sorts of cakes, and pray that this should be forbidden as it causes the memorialists great injury'. Mentzel also noted that the Chinese made money 'by the sale of vegetables cultivated on their private plots of land'. Nor did these traders disappear. Thunberg noted their zeal in 1772 when he arrived in the port: 'We were hardly come to an [sic] anchor, before a crowd of black slaves and Chinese came in their small boats to sell and barter, for clothes and other goods, fresh meat, vegetables, and fruit, all of which our crews were eager to procure.'[113] Cape paintings of the period depict numbers of Chinese and Malay traders (easily differentiated by their conical straw hats or *toerangs*) busily serving the ships' needs in the roadstead.

By 1745 the colonists had convinced themselves that these incipient free black traders were not only 'injuring them' but also corrupting 'the slaves by purchasing from them stolen property, and thus [inciting] them to rob and pilfer'. They even convinced the French traveller Abbé de la Caille, who duly noted their views. Mentzel tried to refute this charge. He admitted that some 'East Indian hucksters are as sharp as needles and will cheat the Devil himself', but argued that they received stolen goods, not from slaves, but from European sailors who smuggled them from the ships. Moreover, he said about the Cape Chinese traders:

> ... it is dangerous to generalize, and condemn them all as rogues. Some of them will show more consideration to those who owe them money than Europeans do. I have met people to whom Asiatic dealers had given various commodities such as tea, chinaware and Eastern fabrics on long credit, even until their return from Holland. On the whole, these Chinese live a humble, quiet and orderly life at the Cape.[114]

A profitable trade which the Chinese free blacks monopolised was chandlering. They obtained waste fat from the Cape butchers at a nominal price and then made it into shapely candles which were much in demand at the Cape. Mentzel remarked: 'The Chinese are the only candlemakers at the Cape, for though the homemade farm candle is serviceable, it cannot be compared in appearance with the handiwork of the Chinamen [sic]. Though made of mutton fat [these candles] are as white and well-shaped as wax candles'.[115]

Thus some free blacks, particularly the Chinese, flourished in the small-scale trades and crafts of the port city. However, the free blacks did not succeed in agriculture, despite their promising start in Stellenbosch. Perhaps part of the problem was lack of capital or credit. Unlike Chinese, Lebanese and Indian traders in nineteenth- and twentieth-century colonies, they did not arrive with an extended family structure in which capital could be accumulated, nor did they have close financial links with their homelands. The colonists and officials could very easily stop the free blacks from rising beyond a certain point by not extending credit, by not granting licensing privileges for butchers and bakers, and so on. However, no evidence for such discrimination has yet been found, except that in the requesten (1715–91) no free black ever applied for a licence to ply any of the more lucrative trades, whereas European burghers' applications appear throughout the series.

Whatever the reasons, the retreat of the free blacks to Cape Town, and their failure to participate in the town's leading wholesale trades, was of crucial importance in the shaping of the entire colony. For the free blacks were left behind in a society which came to be dominated by agriculture and intercontinental commerce, where Europeans normally ruled over a black labouring force, and where European settlers soon owned virtually all the land and possessed most of the great fortunes. The free blacks' only means of livelihood were handicrafts and petty retailing, and their fortunes must have oscillated wildly with the presence or absence of ships in the bay. Their slow demographic growth ensured that they never posed a real threat to the ever-burgeoning European settler population. They always appear as a marginal group whose legal status — like the freedman in Roman law — was ambiguous and, as the power of the colonists waxed and that of the VOC waned, increasingly subject to local (European) interpretation.

Changes in culture

Earlier in this chapter we discussed religious proselytization. We must now turn to more spontaneous aspects of cultural change, by-products of the incorporation of Khoikhoi and slaves into a colony whose dominant members were European in culture. Cape historians have written a great deal on the culture of Europeans, very little on that of slaves, free blacks and colonial Khoikhoi. Hence our analysis will be very sketchy.

The most obvious features of Cape cultural history were the borrowing of cultural traits among groups and the emergence of syncretic cultural complexes. But borrowing was not simply a matter of European culture being transferred to Asians and Africans. It is in any event imprecise to speak simply of 'European' culture: many Company servants arrived at the Cape after a long sojourn — or even a lifetime — in the East Indies, where they had been affected by the mores of the *Indische* (Eurasian) culture in the Company's holdings.[116] Many of these were high Company officials who would have been influential cultural models, particularly in Cape Town. We can discern evidence of the importance of Indische culture in the wide use of Low Portuguese (the 'lingua franca') among Europeans at the Cape,[117] in Cape Dutch architecture, and in Cape cuisine. On the other hand, the Cape was much closer to Europe than was Batavia, and it received a considerable influx of new settlers directly from the Netherlands, Germany, France, etc. These immigrants probably to some extent diluted Indische influences in the Cape Colony, particularly in agricultural regions beyond Cape Town.

Moreover, just as the mixed Indische culture testified to the cultural impact of subjects on their masters in the Orient, so at the Cape cultural transfer was also mutual. In Cape Town the impress of various Indian and Indonesian cultures continued to be felt on Europeans, particularly through the agency of the skilled Eastern artisan and domestic slaves and the free blacks.

In the arable regions of the southwestern Cape, slaves probably accepted European culture rather more rapidly. We cannot yet support this assertion with detailed evidence, but we base our opinion on an analysis of the social and demographic framework of slavery in this region. With the possible exception of the Madagascans, there was never a large group of slaves at the Cape with a single cultural heritage, and no ethnic group was intentionally concentrated in one locale (ch. 3, pp. 82—83). The only common and visible culture for slaves to acquire was that of their masters.

Moreover, Cape slaves, unlike plantation slaves, were evenly distributed among the burgher population, more than half of them (in 1750) being in groups of five or fewer (ch. 3, p. 97). Many of these slaves were domestic servants in close contact with Europeans; in poorer locales many lived in the same quarters with their masters; some, as we have seen, had permanent or semi-permanent sexual liaisons with Europeans. All these conditions must have accelerated the acquisition of the hegemonic European culture among the rural slaves. At the same time they encouraged the development of Dutch, and the preservation of Low Portuguese, as a means of communication among slaves and between slaves and masters.

The Khoikhoi in arable areas adopted their rulers' culture more slowly and more selectively than did the slaves.[118] This was partly because they, unlike the slaves, were only gradually incorporated into the colonial economy and society. In the seventeenth century few Khoikhoi spent all of their time on European farms, and even in the eighteenth century, after the collapse of the strong Khoikhoi chiefdoms, opportunities for periodic withdrawal from the colony abounded. Moreover, the Khoikhoi, much more than the slaves, possessed a homogeneous culture and a family structure, undamaged by slavery, to transfer to their young: independent domicile and family solidarity often continued undisturbed even among Khoikhoi on the European-owned farms.

Khoikhoi came into contact with Western culture only as servants. Not surprisingly, their main acquisitions tended to be useful skills or items of material culture. This pattern first appeared among the Strandlopers, the core of the growing population of Khoikhoi in Cape Town from the 1650s onward. But it soon reappeared among the more numerous Khoikhoi who, after the 1670s, came into contact with European culture by spending at least part of their year on the farms of the southwestern Cape. These Khoikhoi, like their urban counterparts, were attracted by European products, which rapidly became part of their own culture — green vegetables, bread, rice, tobacco, brandy and arak (an East Indian liquor). They learned various forms of pidgin Dutch (one of which was also spoken by slaves and which in some respects resembled modern Afrikaans); on Huguenot farms they learned French.[119] Unlike many of the urban Khoikhoi, their family life persisted in the traditional mat huts which they brought on to the farms: they continued to dress in traditional skins, greased their bodies, and carried *assegais* in the colony. Presumably other undocumented aspects of their culture also changed only slowly, particularly their mythology, music and religion.

The smallpox epidemic of 1713 drastically altered the patterns of cultural exchange. It eliminated the majority of Khoikhoi in both Cape Town and the southwestern Cape and destroyed the remnants of their traditional social structure in these areas. It thus impelled the few survivors to more rapid adaptation of European culture and determined that, as a few Khoikhoi filtered back into the region in the eighteenth century, they would find themselves vastly outnumbered by Europeans and slaves, whose culture was now clearly dominant.

Very different was the case of the vast region occupied by trekboers and their slaves after the 1690s. For here the arid climate, rough terrain, and distance from markets encouraged the abandonment of intensive cultivation and favoured the traditional pastoral economy of the Khoikhoi and its associated cultural patterns. Furthermore, in regions remote from Cape Town, the population density of both Europeans and slaves declined, as did the material wealth of the farmers and their opportunity for regular contact with Cape Town and Europe. Such circumstances stimulated the rise of a composite culture in which Khoikhoi influence was apparent, and also completed the submergence of the Asian slave cultures which — apart from the lingua franca — could not survive when few countrymen lived in regular contact with one another.

During the eighteenth century the rise of this composite culture provoked fears that European trekboers would sink to the level of the despised Khoikhoi, losing their culture and, even worse, their religion. Inhabitants of Cape Town conventionally informed overseas visitors that the European colonists in the interior 'both in their manners and appearance more resembled Hottentots than Christians.' Knowledgeable and influential officials who had travelled widely in the interior endorsed these views. For example, in 1768 the secunde Jan W. Cloppenburg, noting that Europeans were becoming 'unmannerly and unchristian', advanced a scheme to separate Europeans from contamination by depriving them of Khoikhoi and slave labour. Similar views were expressed for the rest of the century.[120]

At the root of this phenomenon was the adoption by colonists (and their slaves) of a pastoral and hunting economy formerly monopolised by Khoikhoi. The Europeans modified certain aspects of this economy by introducing the controlled breeding of sheep, extensive slaughter of animals for regular human consumption, and a more intensive grazing which ultimately led to soil erosion.[121] They were also more inclined than Khoikhoi to sell their livestock for slaughter in Cape Town (ch. 2, p. 60). However, all these innovations did not fundamentally alter the isolation, semi-nomadism and comparative self-reliance of the inland pastoralist.

Thus the values and aesthetic standards of the trekboers tended to centre, as Sparrman noted even of the wealthiest trekboers, on 'the number and beauty of their herds and flocks.' Trekboers exchanged livestock at births and marriages and created bonds of clientage by pasturing out sheep and cattle with their neighbours.[122] In these respects trekboer culture resembled Khoikhoi culture, but the extent to which it derived from Khoikhoi culture cannot be accurately determined.

It is only on comparatively superficial matters of material culture that our sources are abundant and easily interpreted. These show a remarkable convergence of the material culture of Europeans, slaves and Khoikhoi, and suggest a considerable influence of the Khoikhoi on the others. In some more settled pastoral locales, Europeans had built stone houses; but the typical dwelling seems to have had one or two rooms with clay walls, a straw roof, mere holes for windows, and a door made of reed mats. The water-resistant reed mats were derived from Khoikhoi culture and were also used under tarpaulins as covering for the farmers' wagons.[123] On farms like these, Khoikhoi servants either lived in their own huts with their families, or pell-mell with slaves and Europeans in the main house. Many Europeans, however, lived more simply than this in mat huts, which travellers found indistinguishable from those of Khoikhoi. Perhaps many of these were temporary buildings of new settlers, or a result of the shortage of timber, but there were several remote regions where Europeans used mat houses, tents or wagons as dwellings — or simply slept under a tree — because their lives were as nomadic as those of the Khoikhoi.[124]

Europeans and slaves adopted other aspects of the Khoikhoi cattle culture. Early in the eighteenth century they began to burn the veld, just as the Khoikhoi did, to improve pasture. Thunberg noted poor colonists who stored milk in skin sacks made like those of Khoikhoi, and Sparrman saw Europeans dry strips of game (later called *biltong*) on trees and bushes like Khoikhoi hunters. Generally the trekboers did not adopt Khoikhoi dress; however, sometimes their children ran about in sheepskins, and an occasional farmer like Willem van Wijk, who married the daughter of a Nama chief in a Khoikhoi ceremony, dressed and bore himself as a Khoikhoi. Travellers frequently remarked on the widespread adoption of *veldschoenen* (Khoikhoi sandals made of cattle hide or animal skin) which were to be found even in Cape Town.[125]

As the colony expanded, this composite culture spread and consolidated itself in new regions. Khoikhoi who were newly incorporated into the colony had to adapt to it to a far lesser extent than did the Europeans who came to the trekboer regions from Cape Town. Indeed, because the bearers of European culture were few, the alteration of Khoikhoi culture was probably even slower than it had been in the southwestern Cape in the seventeenth century. Again our evidence suggests changes mainly in consumption patterns — the adoption of European food, drink and tobacco. Khoikhoi on farms smoked tobacco in pipes which they made themselves from wood or the horns of gazelle or antelope, though they preferred European pipes when they could obtain them. They continued to adorn themselves in the traditional skins and grease, even near Company posts or on farms as close to Cape Town as Paarl.[126] When hunting, herding, or travelling long distances, they wore veldschoenen, but otherwise went barefoot. In this they differed from the Bastaard offspring of European-Khoikhoi unions, who favoured European clothes, and also from the few Khoikhoi in wealthy homes in and near Cape Town who were sometimes clad in the costume of domestic slaves.[127]

On the more complex aspects of culture our sources are less helpful. However, travellers often noted that Khoikhoi observed their traditional festivals and dances on the farms (though these were sometimes modified by contacts with Europeans), and that they continued to practice customs which were either abhorrent or strange to the travellers, like burying a child alive whose mother had died in childbirth, or feeling compelled to move from a farm where someone had recently died.[128]

A major exception to Khoikhoi conservatism was language. The languages of the immigrants (Dutch among Europeans and Portuguese among slaves) rather than that of the indigenous Khoikhoi became the means of communication in trekboer society. This was due largely to the extraordinary difficulty of the Khoikhoi language; in the seventeenth century the Dutch, famed for their linguistic ability in the Orient, failed to produce one fluent speaker of Khoikhoi although, according to Anna Böeseken, at least two officials, G.F. Wrede and J.W. de Grevenbroek, had a working knowledge of the Khoikhoi language.[129] In the trekboer regions of the eighteenth century, children often learned Khoikhoi (along with Malay and Portuguese) from their playmates, but there is little evidence that they used it later as adults in talking to Khoikhoi labourers on their farms, who normally spoke Dutch and often Portuguese. Travellers give different accounts of the quality of their Dutch, some finding it as good as that of the colonists — though they did not intend this as a compliment — others finding it just passable. Khoikhoi, of course, for a long time continued to speak their own language among themselves, although they took into it many words of Dutch derivation (like the words for wagon, bread and wheat) and coined words, sometimes by onomatopoeia, to describe new cultural items (such as firelock and gunpowder). In 1772 Thunberg heard Khoikhoi spoken at Paarl. However, the language slowly died out, and by the turn of the nineteenth century the well-travelled Lichtenstein heard it only on the colony's borders, and even then with a heavy European admixture.[130]

The prevailing trend in the cultural history of the period we are discussing was towards homogeneity within regions. Various European cultures (Dutch, French, etc.) and various slave cultures (Bengali, Indonesian, Madagascan, etc.) were merging with one another and with the culture of the Khoikhoi. By the late eighteenth century the main cultural cleavages were no longer between ethnic or status groups (European versus non-European, or slave versus Khoikhoi) but between regions. In Cape Town a mixed European and Asian culture was shared by Company officials, some burghers, and slaves, though some of the latter managed to retain more traditionally Asian traits, especially through conversion to Islam. In the agrarian southwestern Cape, slaves and Europeans seem to have shared in a culture which was predominantly of European origin. In the trekboer regions the prevailing languages were Dutch and Portuguese, but otherwise the culture of slaves and colonists was a composite of European and Khoikhoi influences, appropriate to a livestock economy. Here the remaining cultural cleavages were between Europeans, slaves, Bastaards and a few acculturated Khoikhoi on the one hand, and the more traditional Khoikhoi on the other.

Conclusion

We have seen distinct regional variations in our study of conversion, miscegenation, manumission, the history of the free blacks, and cultural change. These regional differentials are hard to quantify, largely because the 'districts' in the Company's statistics did not neatly correspond with our regions: the Cape district was both rural and urban; the Stellenbosch district included both arable and pastoral sections; and the trekboer region was divided among two (later three) districts and one subdistrict. Nevertheless, evidence of regional variations intrude on all sides, and the cumulative case for a regional analysis is compelling.

Cape Town was a seaward-looking community, a caravanserai on the periphery of the global spice trade. European and Asian cultures flourished in the port; so, too, did Christianity and Islam, though the former had only superficial success among people of colour, being largely confined to the Company's slave lodge. Manumissions, too, were more frequent in Cape Town, partly because some of the slave-owning population was in transit, but mainly because the seasonal fluctuations in economic activity made wage labour a flexible alternative to slavery. Moreover, there were fairly high rates of miscegenation in Cape Town, necessitated by the numerous Company sailors and soldiers who lived or visited there. And, finally, Cape Town was the home of a significant population of free blacks, many of whom were Muslim and a handful Christian. A few of the former were modestly prosperous.

In contrast to Cape Town, the arable lands of the southwestern Cape were more insulated from the influx of new people and ideas, and more dominated by a labour-intensive economy. Here the European settlers soon achieved comparatively balanced sex ratios and the formation of stable European families was possible. Consequently there was little pressure toward miscegenation, and hostility to concubinage intensified. There was also little manumission, even though most of the colony's slaves lived in these areas. Without the ginger group of free blacks who gave Cape Town its rather cosmopolitan air, this region was soon characterised by the assimilation of blacks to European culture, but not by their incorporation into the church or freeburgher society. A clear social distinction between Europeans and blacks was established soon after settlement. Prestige and local power became associated with land-holding, and almost all land-holders were European.

The trekboer pastoralists required a less extensive labour force and, because of their comparative poverty, they relied less on slaves than on Khoikhoi who were subject to informal controls. Their farms were even further from Cape Town, and among them Asian (and to some extent European) culture soon became diluted. Because of a shortage of manufactured goods, a new material culture arose based on the products of pastoralism and the immediate environment. European women were few, and the consequent miscegenation produced a new group, the Bastaards. However, the Bastaards, even if baptised, found it hard to become full-fledged burghers; and ultimately, as the frontier closed (see ch. 8, pp. 316 ff.), they were squeezed out of the colony.

Our emphasis on regionalism should not obscure important features common to the whole colony. Cape colonial society was rigid, even by some contemporary standards. The position of the lower status groups did not improve. Slaves had comparatively little opportunity to become free, even in Cape Town. Khoikhoi never enjoyed the rights of burghers, and free blacks and baptised Bastaards gradually lost the privileges they had once had. All these groups lived in a twilight world, neither slave nor wholly free. Mobility of individuals into the dominant European settler group was quite uncommon. For free blacks, Khoikhoi and their descendants the era 1652 to 1795—at the end no less than at the beginning — was no golden age.

Chapter Four   Notes

1. In a stimulating essay, 'The Rule of Law at the Cape in the Eighteenth Century' (mimeo, 1977), Robert Ross has taken issue with Rodney Davenport's statement in the *Oxford History of South Africa* that 'the rule of law did not exist in the Company period' and concluded that the VOC was all too successful in its application of law (p. 17).

2. I.D. MacCrone, *Race Attitudes in South Africa: Historical, Experimental and Psychological Studies* (Johannesburg, 1937), p. 41; see also pp. 7, 40—46, 76—78, 129 fn. 1, 134—35.

3. George McCall Theal, *History of South Africa* (Cape Town, 1964), III, 272; cf. V, 268.

4. See Bernhard Krüger, *The Pear Tree Blossoms. A History of the Moravian Mission Stations in South Africa, 1737—1869* (Genadendal, 1966), pp. 18—44.

5. C.R. Boxer, *The Dutch Seaborne Empire, 1600—1800* (New York, 1965), pp. 138—49.

6. Richard Elphick, *Kraal and Castle: Khoikhoi and the Founding of White South Africa* (New Haven and London, 1977), pp. 106—08, 201—03.

7. *Ibid*, pp. 203—07. For an early scheme for evangelising Khoikhoi which in some ways foreshadowed nineteenth-century missions see VC 168, Simond — XVII, 1298 ff. We are indebted to Dr Pieter Coertzen for a copy of this document.

8. Anders Sparrman, *A Voyage to the Cape of Good Hope towards the Antarctic Polar Circle Round the World and to the Country of the Hottentots and the Caffres from the year 1772—1776* (Cape Town, 1975), I, 208, cf. I, 263—64.

9. H.P. Cruse, *Die Opheffing van die Kleurlingbevolking: Aanvangsjare, 1652—1795* (Stellenbosch, 1947), I, 83, 101, 106; Res 2 Sept. 1779. We are indebted to James Armstrong for this last reference.

10. One Khoikhoi was baptised in the Netherlands by the Rev. Petrus Kalden.

11. Theal, *History*, III, 150. See also III, 59—60: 'A hundred years later very different views were held, but in the middle of the seventeenth century no distinction whatever appears to have been made between people on account of colour. A profession of Christianity placed black and white upon the same level. The possessions of the heathens were the inheritance of God's people, and could be taken from them without sin. The heathen themselves could be enslaved, but Christians could not be kept in bondage. The archives of the Cape Colony contain numerous illustrations of this doctrine.'

12. Cruse, *Opheffing*, I, 224 (Robin Whiteford translated the Latin citation).

13. Adriaan Moorees, *Die Nederduitse Gereformeerde Kerk in Suid-Afrika, 1652—1873* (Cape Town, 1937), pp. 36—38; MacCrone, *Race Attitudes*, pp. 77—78; Cruse, *Opheffing*, p. 226. The quotation is in Moorees, *Kerk*, p. 38.
14. Donald Moodie, *The Record* (Amsterdam and Cape Town, 1960), p. 309; MacCrone, *Race Attitudes*, p. 76.
15. Dutch Reformed Church Archives (Cape Town), G1 4/34, Lyst aanweizende hoe veel slavenkinderen . . . gedoopt zyn geworden . . . A copy of this document was kindly provided to us by James Armstrong. We have not had an opportunity to check all of these figures against the original baptismal records: spot checks suggest that in some periods these figures are exact, in some periods too low. Because of strange recording procedures in the original, we have had to use seventeen-year intervals except for the first and last intervals: the mean percentages have been adjusted accordingly. The 'population at risk' refers to the total number of slaves who were eligible for baptism or freedom. Thus slaves who were already baptised or freed have to be excluded from these denominators.
16. On manumissions see Anna J. Böeseken, *Slaves and Free Blacks at the Cape 1658—1700* (Cape Town, 1977), appendices *passim*. The figure for baptisms are based on Table 4.1. However, we know that this series' figures for this era may be far too low: a spot check of the church records shows 143 privately owned slave children baptised between 1695 and 1712, while the series on which Table 4.1 is based gives only 32.
17. For information on manumissions see pp. 135—45.
18. *RCC*, IX, 131—32.
19. George Forster, *A Voyage Round the World . . . in his Britannic Majesty's Sloop, Resolution*, 2 vols. (London, 1777), I, 60.
20. Sparrman, *Voyage*, I, 90; cf. O.F. Mentzel, *A Complete and Authentic Geographical and Topographical Description of the . . . Cape of Good Hope* (Cape Town, 1921, 1925, 1944), II, 130—31.
21. Robert Percival, *An Account of the Cape of Good Hope* (London, 1804), pp. 274—75.
22. Johannes Stephanus Marais, *The Cape Coloured People: 1652—1937* (Johannesburg, 1957), p. 168.
23. *RCC*, IX, 133.
24. *Select Constitutional Documents Illustrating South African History*, G.W. Eybers ed. (London, 1918), p. 18.
25. I.D. du Plessis, *The Cape Malays: History, Religion, Traditions, Folk Tales, The Malay Quarter* (Cape Town, 1972), pp. 1—2. Du Plessis does admit there was conversion, but seems to emphasise the theory of transplanting of Muslims from the Indonesian Archipelago.
26. Sparrman, *Voyage*, I, 264—65.
27. Robert C.-H. Shell, 'The Establishment and Spread of Islam at the Cape from the Beginning of Company Rule to 1838' (Honours thesis, University of Cape Town, 1974), p. 20.
28. *Ibid.*, p. 32.
29. *Ibid.*, p. 33.
30. MOOC 7/1/53, no. 66 and no. 66½.
31. Charles Thunberg, *Travels in Europe, Africa and Asia performed between the years 1770 and 1779* (London, 1795), I, 132—34.
32. Burgherraad, Incoming letters, 17, Barnard/1st Feb. 1800; British Occupation

154, Item 236; Samuel Abraham Rochlin, 'The first mosque at the Cape', *South African Journal of Science*, XXXIII (1937), pp. 1100—03.

33. Mirza Abu Taleb Khan, *The Travels of Mirza Abu Taleb Khan in Asia, Africa and Europe in the years 1799, 1800, 1801, 1802 and 1803, written by himself in the Persian language and translated by Charles Stewart* (London, 1810), pp. 72—73; we probably would have learnt more about this group of Muslims had the translator not decided to curtail 'the long list of his friends at the principal places he visited', see preface, p. viii.

34. Shell, 'Establishment', p. 41; *RCC,* XXXV, 367.

35. *RCC*, IX, 131—32, article 11, p. 147.

36. Dutch Reformed Church Archives, Cape Town, G1: 1/1, 8/1, 13/1, 12a/4.

37. Anna J. Böeseken, 'Die verhouding tussen blank en nie-blank in Suid-Afrika aan die hand van die vroegste dokumente', *South African Historical Journal,* II (1970), p. 14; *KP*, I, 152 (1678), 179 (1681), 266 (1692), 331 (1704); *KP*, II, 73 (1718).

38. Elphick, *Kraal and Castle*, pp. 204—05.

39. Mentzel, *Description*, I, 116; II, 81, 124, 130.

40. Theal, *History,* III, 273; A. Hulshof, 'H.A. van Reede tot Drakenstein, Journaal van zijn Verblijf aan die Kaap', *Bijdragen en Mededeelingen van het Historisch Genootschap*, LXII (1941), p. 213; Cruse, *Opheffing*, pp. 91—101; MacCrone, *Race Attitudes*, pp. 76—78.

41. E.g., Charles Lockyer, *An Account of the Trade in India* (London, 1711), p. 297; Capt. Daniel Beeckman, 'A Voyage to Borneo in 1714', *Colleçtanea* (Cape Town, 1924), p. 114; A.J. Böeseken, *Slaves and Free Blacks*, p. 45 and n. 38.

42. KA 4007, Generale Opneming en monster rolle van 's Comp soo slaven als bandieten, 1 Jan. 1693, pp. 359—68.

43. KA 3976, Muster of 1664, n.p.

44. Numbers of ships determined from annual port records in KA. Numbers of men per ship derived from KA 3996, Oncostboeck van verstreckte ververssingen en scheeps nootwendigheden . . ., 1683, pp. 689—708.

45. Table based on opgaaf rolls of designated years.

46. Herbert Moller, 'Sex Composition and Correlated Culture Patterns of Colonial America', *William and Mary Quarterly*, II (1945), pp. 113—53.

47. Robert Ross, 'The "white" population of South Africa in the eighteenth century', *Population Studies*, XXIX (1975), p. 230; John Hajnal, 'European marriage patterns in perspective' in *Population in History: Essays in Historical Demography,* ed. D.V. Glass and D.E.C. Eversley (London, 1965), Table 2, p. 102 and *passim.*

48. J. Hoge, 'Miscegenation in South Africa in the seventeenth and eighteenth centuries'; Marius V. Valkhoff ed., *New Light on Afrikaans and 'Malayo-Portuguese'* (Louvain, 1972), pp. 99—118; J.L.M. Franken, *Taalhistoriese Bydraes* (Amsterdam and Cape Town, 1953), pp. 16—26.

49. Mentzel, *Description*, II, 109—10.

50. David W. Cohen and Jack P. Greene, *Neither Slave nor Free: The Freedman of African Descent in the Slave Societies of the New World* (Baltimore and London, 1972), pp. 55, 78, 142—43, 154—55, 210, 262, 322.

51. Böeseken, 'Verhouding', pp. 12, 17; opgaafs of 1686 (KA 3999), 1695 (KA 4013), 1730 (KA 4091), 1770 (KA 4240); personal communication from J.A. Heese.

52. Hoge, 'Miscegenation', pp. 110—11; [Anon.], 'The origin and incidence of miscegenation at the Cape during the Dutch East India Company's regime, 1652—1795', *Race Relations Journal*, XX (1953), p. 27.

53. Based on Dutch Reformed Church Archives (Cape Town), G1 1/1, 8/1 13/1, 13/2. We have considered as free blacks (1) those so identifiable by toponym, (2) those identified as free blacks in the documents, (3) those known to be free blacks by prior knowledge. As we have indicated in the text, these crude methods doubtless miss many Cape-born free blacks.

54. Dutch Reformed Church Archives, G2 7/1.

55. Hoge, 'Miscegenation', p. 109.

56. Moller, 'Sex composition', pp. 113—53.

57. Personal communication.

58. KA 4013, DR, 1 June 1695, pp. 745—48; KA 4048, DR, 4 July 1713, pp. 192—205; KA 4098, Landdrost vs. Hendrik van Nias, 2 Oct. 1732, p. 958.

59. As in n. 45.

60. KA 4007, Generale opneming en monster rolle van 's Comp. soo slaven als bandieten, 1 Jan. 1693, pp. 359—68.

61. C 228, pp. 291—92, Requesten, no. 73, 9 Sept. 1721; *Res*, VI, 128 (2 Sept. 1721).

62. Abbé de la Caille, *Journal Historique du Voyage fait au Cap de Bonne-Espérance* (Paris, 1763), p. 324; François le Vaillant, *Voyage de Monsieur le Vaillant dans l'Intérieur de l'Afrique* (Paris, 1790), II, 133–41; Mentzel, *Description*, II, 126. See also KA 4146, Prosecution of Jephta van Sambouwa *et al.*, 5 May 1746, p. 963 v.

63. Anders Sparrman, *Voyage*, I, 262–63; AR, Aanwinsten 1881, A viii, Kol. Aanw. 242, [Jan Willem Cloppenburg] Journaal, p. 8; Staf D 593/U/4/3/3, Journaal van de vierde reyse van Captein R.J. Gordon . . ., 23 Sept. 1779, n.p.

64. Le Vaillant, *Voyage*, II, 141; KA 4106, Prosecution of Rijkaart Jacobse and Hottentot Claas Blank, 18 Aug. 1735, pp. 770—76. A Khoikhoi named Cobus eloped with the daughter of Pieter Terblans and went to an abandoned loan farm on the upper Elands River. The couple were met by a raiding Xhosa group who killed the man and left the woman for dead. Uitenhage 15/1, Cuyler-Truter, 6 Feb. 1811. We are indebted to John Hopper for information on this incident.

65. Le Vaillant, *Voyage*, II, 140.

66. H.T. Colenbrander, *De Afkomst der Boeren*, 2nd edn (Cape Town, 1946), p. 121; J.A. Heese, *Die Herkoms van die Afrikaner 1657 –1867* (Cape Town, 1971), p. 21.

67. Paul van Warmelo, *An Introduction to the Principles of Roman Law* (Cape Town, 1976), p. 39, para. 95.

68. C 231, pp. 132—33, Requesten no. 69, 1 Aug. 1724. (H.C.V. Leibbrandt erroneously numbered this as 64 and dated it 1723 in his *Requesten* (Cape Town, 1905—06), I, 57.

69. C 287, pp. 1139—45, Requesten no. 22, 19 Nov. 1790.

70. This debate began when Frank Tannenbaum claimed that 'the attitude toward manumission is the crucial element in slavery: it implies the judgment of the moral status of the slave, and foreshadows his role in case of freedom'; see *Slave and Citizen, The Negro in the Americas* (New York, 1947), p. 69 ff. For attacks on Tannenbaum see Marvin Harris, *Patterns of Race in the Americas* (New York, 1974), p. 86 ff. and Harmannus Hoetink, *Caribbean Race Relations: A*

Study in Two Variants (New York, 1971), *passim,* and his *Slavery and Race Relations in the Americas* (New York, 1973), pp. 192—210; for an incisive commentary on the ensuing historiography, see Eugene Genovese, 'The treatment of slaves in different countries: Problems in the application of the comparative method', *Slavery in the New World: A Reader in Comparative History,* ed. Laura Foner and Eugene Genovese (Englewood Cliffs, New Jersey, 1969) pp. 202—11.

71. Isobel Edwards, *Towards Emancipation: A Study in South African Slavery* (Cardiff, 1942), p. 29; James C. Armstrong, 'The Free Black Community at the Cape of Good Hope in the Seventeenth and Eighteenth Centuries' (unpublished paper, 1973), pp. 8—9.

72. The material on manumission was found in H.C.V. Leibbrandt's summarised and published *Requesten* I and II, and the summarised but unpublished typescript manuscripts, *LM* 15, *LM* 16 and *LM* 17 (*LM* =Leibbrandt's manuscript). Where we quoted a manumission request, we referred to the original archival volume and cited it, but we also retained the Leibbrandt reference in the footnote. The archival series is complete except for a few years (1717, 1722, 1777 and 1788) which are not serious flaws. The breaks in 1717 and 1722 are at the beginning of the series, when manumission frequencies were very low. The later missing years could mean that our total of 1,075 manumitted slaves represents a slight (1—2 %) underestimation. If a request appeared in one year but referred to another year in which the slave would obtain his freedom, we dated the manumission to the latter date. We counted 1,075 manumitted slaves in the period 1715—1791; each slave had 52 variables, all coded in SPSS format.

73. Stuart B. Schwartz, 'The manumission of slaves in colonial Brazil, 1684—1745', *Hispanic American Historical Review,* LIV (1974) p. 604, n. 4. Robert Wayne Selenes in his Ph.D. dissertation 'The Demography and Economics of Brazilian Slavery 1850—1888' (Stanford, 1975), has calculated even higher rates of manumission for this later period. See pp. 484—573.

74. *Res,* III, 40 (8 April 1682); *PB* I, 184 (8 April 1682).

75. C 265, pp. 184—85, Requesten no. 44, 1766, LM 16, p. 1087.

76. Schwartz, 'Manumission', p. 619.

77. KA 4240, Opgaaf of 1770.

78. 'Wealthy' owners were those who were known to be 'rich', either as Company administrators or as farmers, e.g., Martin Melck, the plantation owner: see John Splinter Stavorinus, *Voyage to the East Indies . . .,* 2 vols. (London, 1798), II, 61—2. For Company servants we approximated eighteenth-century wage scales by using C. Boxer's *The Dutch Seaborne Empire,* pp. 300—303, appendix II, 'Some Salary Scales of Sea-faring and Overseas Personnel.' Thus Michiel Brik, a quartermaster, who wished to emancipate two slaves (Leibbrandt, *Requesten,* II, 173 [no. 44 of 1787]) would have been an 'average' owner, as Boxer claims a quartermaster would have received 14 guilders a month (*Dutch Seaborne Empire,* p. 300). Sailors, who received half this salary and who were the second lowest paid personnel, were regarded as 'poor'. Sometimes the requesten themselves provided evidence of indigence; for example, an owner might ask to be excused from paying the guarantee, on grounds of poverty. Admittedly these are coarse, subjective approximations only. A more severe test would be to compare the wealth of manumitting owners with that of non-manumitting owners, but this was beyond the scope of this chapter.

79. Böeseken, *Slaves and Free Blacks*, appendices.
80. C 241, pp. 121—23 and surgeon's report p. 125, Requesten no. 33, 1742. (Leibbrandt has made a small mistake here; although listed under 1741 in his *Requesten* (I, p. 245), the numerical sequence of the other Requesten clearly indicates that this item belongs to 1742.
81. C 276, pp. 309—11, Requesten no. 91, 1779; *Requesten* II, 643.
82. On free blacks see Victor de Kock, *Those in Bondage* (Cape Town, 1950), pp. 198—223; MacCrone, *Race Attitudes*, pp. 70—80; Sheila Patterson 'Some Speculations on the Status and Role of the Free People of Colour in the Western Cape', *Studies in African Social Anthropology*, ed. Meyer Fortes and Sheila Patterson (London, 1975), pp. 159—205; Armstrong, 'Free Black Community'; Shell, 'Establishment'; and Böeseken, *Slaves and Free Blacks*.
83. KA 3969, Van Riebeeck — Batavia, 14 Aug. 1656, p. 41v; KA 3993, S. van der Stel — XVII, 20 March 1681, pp. 11v—12; Hulshof, 'H.A. van Reede . . . Journaal', p. 204.
84. Böeseken, 'Verhouding', pp. 15—16; *KP*, II, 93 (29 Sept./13 Oct. 1722), 116 (1 Feb. 1727), 182 (11 Oct. 1740); *RCC*, XXXV, 191; KA 4039, Church Council vs. Louis of Bengal, 18 Oct. 1708, p. 623; *Res*, V, 282 (10 May 1718), 348 (20 June 1719); *Res*, VI, 211 (13 Oct. 1722).
85. Theal, *History of South Africa*, V, 189—90; Brian Aldridge, 'Cape Malays in action', *Quarterly Bulletin of the South African Library* XXVII (1972), p. 26; the quotation is in *KP*, II, 239 (1 Feb. 1752).
86. KA 4116, Interim Fiscal vs. Three Slaves and Three Free Blacks, 2 Jan. 1738, p. 799—99v. The prosecutor justified the punishment by noting that 'from that sort of people at such an hour [after 11 p.m.] nothing is to be expected but roguery'. But this observation is not necessarily 'racist'. Company servants were also subject to curfew (see KA 4116, Dictum ter Rolle, 2 Jan. 1738, p. 859.
87. *KP*, III, 62 (12 Nov. 1765); 80 (19/20 June 1771).
88. *RCC*, XXXV, 146—47.
89. CO 3956, item 111. We are indebted to Shirley Judges for this and the following reference.
90. CO 3949, item 344.
91. Shell, 'Establishment', pp. 15—28.
92. De Kock, *Those in Bondage*, p. 194.
93. Shell, 'Establishment', p. 28.
94. They were housed together with slaves in the slave lodge and were often indistinguishable from slaves: see Cruse's enumeration in *Opheffing*, I, 221 ff.
95. LM 7, pp. 75—76, Res, 16 Sept. 1749, s.v. 'convicts'.
96. CJ 3321, cf. CJ 3318.
97. KA 4158, opgaaf 1750; KA 4240, opgaaf 1770.
98. Mentzel, *Description*, II, 149.
99. Armstrong, 'Free Black Community', pp. 4—6.
100. The figures in this Table are probably more complete than those in Table 4.3, because the opgaaf, unlike the marriage records, sometimes listed free blacks (other than those married to Europeans) separately. In 1725 their names were explicitly set apart under the heading 'free blacks'. As a result of this feature one can spot free blacks whose names give no hint that they are not Europeans.
101. Cohen and Greene, *Neither Slave nor Free*, p. 4; Shirley Judges, personal communication.

102. This and the previous four paragraphs are based on the opgaaf rolls for the years cited.

103. KA 4095, Independent Fiscal vs. Robbert Schot of Bengal, 27 Dec. 1731, pp. 686v–87.

104. E.g., KA 4069, 19 June 1722, pp. 1312 ff; KA 4010, Landdrost vs. Hans Henske *et al.*, 4 Dec. 1692, p 239v; KA 4039, Provisional Landdrost vs. Willem Carelsz van de Caab, 18 Oct. 1708, p. 623; KA 4075, Provisional Fiscal vs. Susanna van Gildenhuysen (vryswartin), 12 Oct. 1724, p. 1049.

105. C 235, pp. 215–16, Requesten, no. 50, 1729–32.

106. Mentzel, *Description*, II, 92.

107. *Cape of Good Hope Almanacs 1812–1838, passim.*

108. Karl Scherzer, *Narrative of the Circumnavigation of the Globe by the Austrian frigate Novara in the years 1857, 1858 and 1859*, 3 vols. (London, 1861), I, 198–99.

109. L.E. van Onselen, *Cape Antique Furniture* (Cape Town, 1959), p. 7.

110. W. Burchell, *Travels in the Interior of Southern Africa* (London, 1822–24), I, 27–28; David Lewis, 'Malay Arts and Crafts', *Handbook on Race Relations in South Africa*, ed. Ellen Hellmann (Cape Town, 1949), pp. 646–50.

111. C 229, p. 149, *Requesten*, II, 444 (no. 86, 1722).

112. Mentzel, *Description*, II, 88–89.

113. C 234, p. 17, *Requesten*, I, 60 (no. 4, 1727); Mentzel, *Description*, II, 92; Charles Peter Thunberg, *Travels in Europe, Africa and Asia performed between the years 1770 and 1779* (London, 1795), I, 99.

114. Mentzel, *Description*, II, 149–50; see also 91, 92; Mentzel mentions *Journal Historique du Voyage au Cap de Bonne Espérance* (1763), but does not cite the page on which Abbé de la Caille repeats this story.

115. Mentzel, *Description*, II, 92.

116. On this culture see Pauline Dublin Milone, 'Indische culture, and its relationship to urban life', *Comparative Studies in Society and History*, IX (1966–67), pp. 407–26.

117. Marius F. Valkhoff, *Studies in Portuguese and Creole, with Special Reference to South Africa* (Johannesburg, 1966), pp. 146–91.

118. The following two paragraphs are based on Elphick, *Kraal and Castle*, pp. 207–14.

119. KA 4037, Vraagpoincten . . . Pieter Cronje, 3 March 1707, p. 781v.

120. Quotations are from John Splinter Stavorinus, *Voyages to the East Indies by the late John Splinter Stavorinus* (London, 1798), II, 57; and AR, Aanwinsten 188, A viii, Kol. Aanw. 242, Cloppenburg Journal, p. 12. But see also Mentzel, *Description*, III, 115 and Henry Lichtenstein, *Travels in Southern Africa in the Years 1803, 1804, 1805, and 1806* (Cape Town, 1928, 1930), I, 448.

121. Mentzel, *Description*, I, 56; André Sparrman, *Voyage au Cap de Bonne-Espérance et autour du Monde* (Paris, 1787), I, 269–73.

122. Mentzel, *Description*, III, 112; KA 4119, Res 21 July 1739, pp. 313–14v; The quotation is from Sparrman, *Voyage au Cap*, II, 182: 'Ce n'est pas, à la verité, sur la parure que tombe l'émulation des colons; c'est par le nombre et la beauté de leurs troupeaux, et surtout par la force de leurs boeufs de trait, qu'ils [the trekboers] ambitionnent de se surpasser.'

123. Sparrman, *Voyage*, I, 137–193; Vernon S. Forbes, *Pioneer Travellers in South*

Africa (Cape Town and Amsterdam, 1965), p. 68; *RZA*, II, 'Dagverhaal . . . Plettenberg', p. 74.

124. KZ, Dag register . . . Jan de la Fontaine, 20 July 1734, n.p.; Staf D 593 /4/1/3, Vierde Reyse . . . Gordon, 25 July 1779, n.p.; William Paterson, *A Narrative of Four Journeys into the Country of the Hottentots* . . . (London, 1790), pp. 47, 58; Lichtenstein, *Travels*, II, 83.

125. C.P. Thunberg, *Voyages de C.P. Thunberg au Japon par le Cap de Bonne-Espérance* (Paris, 1796), I, 143; Sparrman, *Voyage,* I, 98 and note, 251, 288; II, 21; Jacob Haafner, *Lotgevallen en Vroegere Zeereizen van Jacob Haafner* (Amsterdam, 1820), pp. 68—69; KA 4119, Res 13 March 1739, p. 241v.

126. Mentzel, *Description*, III, 307; Thunberg, *Voyage*, I, 98, 128; AR, Aanwinsten 1881, A viii, Kol. Aanw. 242, Cloppenburg Journal, p. 11.

127. Mentzel, *Description*, III, 318; De la Caille, *Journal Historique*, p. 326; L. Degrandpré, *Voyage à la côte occidentale d'Afrique* . . . (Paris, 1801), II, 189; Sparrman, *Voyage*, II, 68; Lichtenstein, *Travels*, I, 193.

128. Sparrman, *Voyage*, I, 277, 283; Lichtenstein, II, 291—92. Lichtenstein commented on Khoikhoi festivities that 'these pastimes, however, had not much of national character, since the present generation of Hottentots in the interior of the colony have, in this respect, very much adopted the European customs'. However, several features of the activities described by Lichtenstein are traditional: e.g. mock combats, and dancing by the full moon.

129. Personal communication.

130. Sparrman, *Voyage*, I, 202; II, 328; Thunberg, *Voyage*, I, 98, 131, 234; Le Vaillant, *Voyage*, II, 144-54; AR, Aanwinsten 1881, A viii, Kol. Aanw. 242, Cloppenburg Journal, p. 11; Mentzel, *Description*, I, 49, 56; III, 302; Lichtenstein, *Travels*, II, 463.

PART II

Rulers and ruled in the Cape Colony

Company and colonists at the Cape*

Gerrit Schutte

Any attempt to describe relations between freeburghers and the Dutch East India Company yields, at first, more questions than answers. True, the broad outlines are known. Much has been written on the Cape burghers' conflict with Governor Willem Adriaan van der Stel, the Cape Patriot movement, and the evolution of the *trekboer*. By contrast, only slight attention has been paid to stratification and socio-economic conditions among the freeburghers in and around Cape Town, who have on occasion been dismissed as unimportant,[1] or at least as lacking a character of their own. We also know little about the history of ideas at the Cape: political, religious, racial and social.

Equally serious is the scant attention paid to the colonial character of the Cape community. What place did the Cape have in the global strategy of the *VOC*? How did its colonial character make it different from contemporary European states? Is anything to be gained by comparing it with North and South American colonies or with similar Dutch settlements like Ceylon, Batavia, Surinam, Curaçao, etc.? Or was C.R. Boxer correct in calling the Cape a colony *sui generis*?[2]

Curiously, we lack information even on the VOC establishment at the Cape. Apart from some scattered generalisations and a number of studies on specific persons, there seems to be nothing on the composition of the official group — its recruitment, training, social character and behaviour — and little on the personal and official relations that VOC servants had with one another, with the residents of the Cape,[3] or with the *Heren XVII* in the fatherland. Similarly, there is no detailed economic history of the Cape, despite historians' repeated criticisms of the Company's economic policies there.[4]

In this chapter I shall explore some of these more neglected themes and reconsider some of the less neglected. This is a big undertaking, particularly

* Translated from Dutch by Henry Snyders and Richard Elphick.

when so many essential preparatory studies are lacking. Hence this must be regarded only as a first attempt. I shall describe the social structures of Cape society and the place of the colony in the VOC system. This will provide a background for a more detailed consideration of three specific episodes: the campaign against Willem Adriaan van der Stel (1705—07), Barbier's rebellion (1739), and the Patriot movement (1778—87). I shall try to demonstrate the similarity of these conflicts between ruler and ruled at the Cape, a similarity which was rooted in the striking continuities in the internal structure and external relations of Cape society.[5]

The Heren XVII and their subordinates

Historians often forget that the Cape settlement was only a part of the extensive interests of the East India Company, and thus divorce it from the overall structure to which it belonged: the world of the VOC and the policies of its directors.[6]

It should be grasped at the outset that the VOC was a private commercial undertaking, owned by a number of shareholders (*actionarissen, participanten*) and managed by an executive council (Heren XVII or Lords XVII). Day-to-day affairs were managed by the First Advocate (*Eerste Advocaat*) and his staff of officials.

The VOC (*Verenigde Oostindische Compagnie*) had been formed in 1602 by uniting a number of commercial undertakings, each of which retained a measure of autonomy. These so-called *kamers* (chambers) were each managed by a number of shareholding directors (*bewindhebbers*) — Amsterdam had twenty; Zeeland twelve; Delft, Rotterdam, Enkhuizen and Hoorn seven each — who were nominated by the incumbent directors and then appointed by provincial states or municipal governments. A number of them (eight from Amsterdam, four from Zeeland, two from Rotterdam/Delft, two from Hoorn/Enkhuizen, and the seventeenth by rotation from the Chambers outside Amsterdam) formed the Heren XVII, the central policy-making body. The directors almost invariably came from the ranks of the local governing patriciate of the chamber cities.

Abroad the Company's affairs were managed by the Governor-General and Council of India (sitting in Batavia, on Java) and the corps of officials under their command. In theory the Indian authorities were entirely bound by the many and often detailed instructions sent from the fatherland; in practice slow communications and the need for expeditious and energetic management gave them considerable autonomy. Until 1732 the Cape was governed by instructions both from the Heren XVII and from Batavia, but after that date instructions came from the fatherland alone. A measure of inspection and control over the Cape was exercised by passing admirals of the return fleets, acting as commissioners. However, their activities were restricted by the brief duration of their visits and by their need to cooperate with Cape officials. In addition, special Commissioners-General (e.g., Van Reede, Nederburgh, and Frykenius) were occasionally sent to introduce really significant measures, mostly on specific instructions from the Heren XVII.

As with any commercial firm, the object of the VOC was to make a profit. Since the shareholders' capital was kept low, a large part of the profits went towards financing investments internally. The ownership of overseas territories was by no means the object of VOC policy; it simply appeared to be, in places, the inevitable solution to problems of security posed by competitors. Even when, in the eighteenth century, the Company became more and more the *de facto* sovereign of diverse territories, it hesitated to acknowledge its sovereignty openly.[7]

The VOC at first brought only comparatively small, though profitable, quantities of luxury products into the European market. It had a monopoly on the sale of products originating in its own possessions; but this monopoly was naturally valid only for sales in the Republic, where it could anyway be fairly easily evaded. A larger share of the European market for colonial goods could be obtained only by supplying goods cheaply. To this end overheads had to be kept as low as possible, and consequently the directorate of the Company showed scant enthusiasm for expensive settlements.

It was of course an important aim of the Company to thwart competitors at the sources of overseas production: hence it strove to obtain monopolistic contracts with Asiatic potentates. At times it even tried to control production, but succeeded in this aim with only a few products of decreasing importance. To achieve and maintain its trading advantages, the Company had to establish itself as an Asian power, for which possession of the Cape was essential; such political authority was also crucial to support its inter-Asiatic trade. The profits were used by the Company to finance much of its operation and to purchase return freight. There was very little direct exchange of products between Europe and Asia, since Europe could offer Asia little except precious metals.[8]

In 1602 the States-General had conferred upon the VOC a charter 'in order to promote the welfare of the United Netherlands, to secure and develop trade, and to operate for the profit of the Company and the inhabitants of the Country.'[9] It was, above all, the Company's contribution to the Dutch staple market economy and its share in the struggle against the Republic's competitors (Spain, Portugal, England and France) that made the VOC important to the Republican government. It is true that contemporaries overestimated the contribution of the VOC to the Dutch economy. Still, it amounted to about 15 per cent, and became relatively larger toward the end of the eighteenth century. Moreover, the Company contributed directly to the state by paying for its charter and its licences, by paying import and export duties (*convooi- en licentgelden*), and by providing ships and sailors in time of war.[10]

The statesmen — themselves merchants and steeped in the merchant tradition[11] — were perfectly aware of how much the VOC could contribute to the power of the Republic. In their merchant world, power was mainly identified with economic and maritime prosperity. It is no wonder, then, that the Dutch rulers adopted measures founded on mercantilist principles (such as protection, monopoly, and the exploitation of overseas territories) to entrench the VOC.

An understanding of the VOC must begin with the decentralised structure of the Republic of the United Netherlands. The Republic was by no means a unitary state but rather an alliance of provinces composed, in their turn, of cities and rural districts strongly concerned with their own interests and liberties. It was to placate regional sentiments that the VOC remained divided into six chambers, an arrangement that fitted in well with the form of commercial concerns of the time. The decentralisation of Dutch government also explains the nature of the Company's ties with the state. The virtual absence of central executive bodies in the Republic (and the prevailing distaste for them) prevented direct intervention by the state in the colonies, as happened in the case of France and the Iberian countries. However, the States-General — the deliberating body of the seven regions, entrusted with powers over a number of matters affecting the Union, like defense and foreign policy — granted and extended the Company's charter for a fee, while reserving the right to receive regular reports and to supervise policy-making; furthermore, the Prince of Orange, whom one might call the head of what there was of a central executive power, became the Company's Chief Director (*Opperbewindhebber*) from 1747 onwards.

In practice, however, the supervision of the States-General did not amount to much and was exercised in a somewhat unusual manner by combining the functions of Company directors and local regents in the same hands. By virtue of their wealth and prestige, the regents formed an elite in the Republic, holding local power and maintaining it by co-option. From this local power base some of them were sent to the provincial States and the States-General, and were appointed to various executive posts. Although the Republic had a less centralistic, absolutistic character than neighbouring countries, one should not form a too democratic conception of freedom in the Netherlands. The regents jealously guarded their position and tolerated no popular infringements of it. Politically, socially and economically their status and power were virtually absolute; even the church was under their control, and the judiciary was an extension of their authority.

Just as the regents governed their cities or provinces in virtual autonomy, so the regent-directors governed their company; personal alliances were considered adequate guarantees of the interests of the state.[12] But the VOC, no matter how strong it was in relation to the state or how like an *imperium in imperio* it appeared, was always a Dutch company. Attempts to create friction between the state and the Company were not lacking. Jealous merchants tried to break the monopoly of the VOC, and disgruntled regents tried to curb the power of the directors, especially towards the end of the eighteenth century, when the mostly Orangist regent-directors were embroiled in a struggle for power with Patriot adversaries.

In comparison with the Dutch Republic, the VOC itself was centralised, bureaucratic and hierarchic. The Heren XVII and their confidants had immense power. By the terms of its charter the VOC had sovereign rights in its territories; for instance, it could enter into international agreements, issue edicts, execute high and low justice, and exercise any governmental authority it deemed necessary. The contract setting out the legal position of VOC officials (*artikelbrief*) bound them to absolute loyalty to the Heren XVII and restricted their liberty in many spheres.

It is clear that the community of freeburghers at the Cape was created for the Company's benefit. They could produce, more efficiently and more cheaply than the personnel of the Company, the commodities needed by the Cape settlement and by passing ships. It is true that there was a second motive as well, namely to provide a livelihood for the poor, but this was a very minor consideration. Commissioner van Reede stated quite clearly in 1685: 'The Company's interest . . . above all, must be the first and foremost object of this settlement.'[13] And a century later fiscal W.C. Boers explained that

> One would be greatly mistaken if one were to draw a comparison between the inhabitants of a colony such as this and the privileged citizens of our large cities in the Republic.[14]

Like the settlement itself the colony's inhabitants were, in accordance with mercantilistic thinking, subservient to the interests of the mother country (in this case the Company). Theirs was a second-class citizenship. It was official VOC policy that the freeburghers, like the officials of the Company, had to take an oath of loyalty not only to the States-General, but also to the VOC directors and their servants abroad.

. So, too, people born in the colonies, on moving to the Republic, had to secure their civil rights by obtaining letters of naturalisation.[15] The proposal in 1786 that the confusing term 'civil rights' (*burgerregten*) be deleted from the letters conferring freeburgher status was fully in accord with Company views.[16] The clause, in the same letters, that freeburghers who misbehaved could be brought back under direct VOC discipline, underlines the limited nature of their freedom. The Company in fact exercised this right. The best-known example was the banishment of the freeburgher Hendrik Buytendagh to Batavia in 1779; but one of Willem Adriaan van der Stel's adversaries, the ex-burgher councillor Johannes Rotterdam, had suffered the same fate.[17] For the rest, however, the VOC seems to have allowed the freeburghers as much practical liberty and autonomy as was reconcilable with its own interests.

Understandably the freeburghers themselves saw their position differently. What was the sense in the VOC charter calling the States-General their sovereign, or their letters of freeburgher status speaking of civil rights, if the Company could act arbitrarily and treat them as slaves?[18] They naturally considered themselves 'free-born men and subjects of Their High Mightinesses' (i.e., the States-General).[19] By the end of the eighteenth century, moreover, Enlightenment concepts of the rights of subjects were coming into conflict with a political order which many were ready to label 'feudal'.[20]

The modern observer is likely to sympathise with the views of the freeburghers. But one should bear in mind that the VOC was in a strong position in terms of contemporary law. Furthermore, it is hard to imagine what concrete meaning free citizenship under the States-General could have had at the time. In practice the burghers in the Netherlands itself were not the subjects of the States-General but of the local and regional authorities. The law differed from place to place, as did the degree of political influence exerted by the inhabitants. But in all fields of life there were so many repressive regulations and discriminatory privileges that in the Republic itself 'free citizenship' was an aspiration rather than a reality.

The Cape in the VOC system

The Cape occupied a somewhat peculiar position among the settlements of the VOC: its founding derived not from any direct commercial interest, but from the need for a refreshment station and harbour. During the eighteenth century the settlement's value as the 'gateway to the East' increased enormously as the maritime power of the Republic and the Company steadily declined[21] and that of their competitors grew. Consequently in the eighteenth century, the loss of the Cape would have been regarded as a disaster; only the spice-producing and directly governed territories (Ceylon, Java, the Moluccas) were considered more important for the prosperity of the Company.[22]

No matter how important the Cape Colony may have been as a refreshment station and seaport, the Company never lost its commercial attitude towards it. The Cape was an expensive undertaking; therefore the cheaper the produce it supplied to the ships, and the lower the costs of its administration and defense, the better. Numerous attempts were made to increase the revenues at the Cape: there were experiments with all kinds of crops, and repeated attempts to find ores and timber and to develop fishing, seal hunting, etc. On the whole the results were disappointing.

It transpired that the Cape had little to offer apart from some agricultural produce; even this was not very promising considering its quality, its prices, and the distance to possible markets. The authorities could see no way to contain the ever-rising costs, except to buy produce at low prices, to transport and sell imports at the highest possible profits, and to keep administrative costs at a minimum. This explains why, shortly after 1652, production of refreshment foodstuffs was shifted on to the freeburghers who, in addition, were given military obligations; their free labour seemed to be cheaper than that of Company personnel or slaves, and in this fashion the size of the garrison could be restricted. The freeburghers would have to pay import, export and excise duties and various other taxes such as *pachtgeld,* stamp duty, and a tithe on wheat. Thus they would make good the costs which the Company incurred in settling and governing them.[23]

The military expectations that the Company had of the freeburghers were not fulfilled. They were of little use in defence against attacks from the sea, because they lived too far inland and were reluctant to leave their homes and occupations to perform poorly paid military service for a Company they did not love. Though they were required to participate in regular drills, the burghers were regarded by military men as more of a nuisance than a reinforcement of the Cape defenses: they were considered as undisciplined, inadequately trained in formal military skills, and rebellious. As the eighteenth century progressed the officials became more and more gloomy about the freeburghers, and during the troublesome final decades they scarcely trusted them at all. Thus it became necessary to spend more on defense, especially fortifications, and correspondingly less on economic experiments.[24]

The Cape was neither the first nor the only VOC territory that had freeburghers; the most important concentrations elsewhere in its dominions were at Batavia, Ceylon and the Moluccas. The directors had hoped that the freeburghers would form a core of reliable subjects among the native populations and thus permit a retrenchment of the Company's garrisons. They also thought that the burghers, like the nutmeg planters on Banda, would regularly supply certain products needed by the Company. In the seventeenth century, then, both inside and outside Company circles there were those who advocated the colonisation of non-European territories by European settlers. The principal motives were relief of poverty at home and the expansion of Dutch economic, political and religious spheres of influence.

But experiences in the VOC territories were not very encouraging. Many of the freeburghers in the East were not colonists in the true sense of the word but people who hoped that, outside the service of the Company, they would more quickly accumulate enough riches to be able to return to the fatherland. Furthermore, many freeburghers survived on the peripheries of the Company's activity, as purveyors of liquor, food and lodging, and as shopkeepers and merchants in produce that did not particularly interest the Company. The instability and lawlessness of the freeburgher groups, as well as their meagre economic achievements, scarcely confirmed the high hopes the Company had had for them. Although the Company was prepared to assist freeburghers in cases of extreme need, it did little to improve their position. It tolerated them only as long as they did not prejudice the Company, excluding them from certain territories and certain enterprises.

At the Cape the burghers also felt powerless in political matters. The only policy-making body of any importance, the Council of Policy, consisted entirely of officials, as did three-quarters of the highest judicial body, the Council of Justice. It is true that the three burgher councillors on the Council of Justice could also be consulted on matters of government, but this was not obligatory. It was only in 1783 that the numbers of freeburghers and officials were made equal on the Council of Justice (six members each), provided that the thirteenth member — the chairman — was an official. There was a similar division in the Court of Petty Cases (*Hof voor Kleine Zaken*), the Court of Marital Cases (*Hof voor Huwelijkse Zaken*), the Orphan Chamber (*Weeskamer*), and the board of directors of the Bank, founded in 1793. The freeburgher members were chosen from a double list by the Council of Policy, which also had to approve the elected members of the Civil Defense Council (*Burgerkrijgsraad*).

Even members of the Church Council were nominated by the governor and Council of Policy. In Cape Town, as also for example in Batavia, many seats on the Church Council were filled by men from the VOC hierarchy. In the territories of the VOC, even more so than in the Republic, the Reformed Church was controlled by the authorities. The ministers were in fact officials in the service of the Company which, until the second half of the eighteenth century, allowed no other denomination in its territories.

In rural areas at the Cape, government was in the hands of the *landdrost*, the *heemraden*, and the field-cornets. These acted as the local government, as a court of law in minor civil matters, and as executive officers for decisions taken in Cape Town. The landdrost was a full-time official; the others were nominated by the heemraden and chosen by the Council of Policy.

Until a closer study has been made it is difficult to assess what influence the freeburghers actually had on the government of the Cape.[25] It is clear that the Company's authority was not very effective in the interior; there colonists decided on their own day-to-day affairs, and the field-cornet — a farmer among farmers — was a man of authority.[26] But in important matters (border conflicts, legal matters, wars, etc.) the landdrost played an active role: a high Company official, he was a stranger assisted by a secretary, a messenger, and a number of soldiers, who were all equally foreign to the district. It seems significant that quite a few landdrosts clashed with the citizenry of their districts — not only Maynier and Bresler but, even earlier, Starrenburg and Marthinus Bergh (before he became a Patriot). Moreover, in judging the influence of all the burgher functionaries we should remember that the Company reserved the rights of supervision and veto; and that in all matters of policy it could make its will effective, in Cape Town at least, through the large majorities it commanded on all the councils.

To what extent did the office-holding burghers consider themselves as representatives of their fellow citizens? Caution should be observed in answering this question, but it does seem that the heemraden and burgher councillors saw themselves in this light: they were, at least occasionally, at the head of protest movements, especially so in the second half of the eighteenth century.

Prominent freeburghers also served on lower government bodies in some of the Company's Eastern territories, e.g., the court of aldermen (*Schepenbank*), the board of heemraden, the Court of Marital Cases, the Orphan Chamber and the Church Council. At Batavia, moreover, the freeburghers were a majority on such councils. Nevertheless, as at the Cape, the freeburghers felt themselves to be dominated and slighted by the Company's policy and its officials. As at the Cape, they sometimes protested and made demands, usually to little effect. Occasionally they were forcibly re-enlisted by the Company or were banned from the Company's territory. It seems, therefore, that the position of the freeburghers at the Cape was in accordance with the general pattern of the VOC, except that at the Cape the burghers were relatively more numerous and hence perhaps more self-conscious and self-assertive than freeburghers elsewhere. In other territories where the numerical proportion was more favourable to the officials and where the burghers were mostly concerned with trading in commodities, they may have been more directly dependent upon the VOC than were most freeburghers at the Cape; their closest counterparts at the Cape were the burghers in Cape Town itself.

Inevitably the mercantilist views of the directors and the commercial principles of the time led to economic conflicts with the Cape freeburghers. The burghers were dependent upon the Company not only for an outlet for their produce, but also for the delivery of numerous commodities and services. Moreover, the Cape economy was regulated strictly for the benefit of the Company and left little scope for private initiative. Within the framework of the eighteenth century much of this must be accepted as normal. To condemn the VOC economy as the epitome of heartlessness and selfishness, as writers such as Scholtz[27] have done from their twentieth-century viewpoint, is to ignore the values and presuppositions of the time.

The attitude of the VOC to indigenous peoples was also strongly determined by its character as a commercial firm. In general it tried to maintain good relations with the peoples with whom it traded, preferring to draw up treaties with them in terms of western international law. Even where the Company exercised authority over indigenous peoples, it preferred indirect rule: the Khoikhoi in southern Africa were, like the natives of Java, governed as much as possible through their own chiefs.

This policy was founded on practical considerations (the need for economy, and lack of power), but was also a logical consequence of the VOC's commercial character: empire-building was contrary to the mentality of the Dutch merchant-regents. They were set on restricting rather than expanding territory, as may be seen from their policy in Europe, in North and South America (Brazil), and in Asia and Africa.

Thus the attitude of the Company towards the Khoikhoi (and later the 'Bushmen') was, virtually from the time of Van Riebeeck's landing, a mixture of goodwill and a hardness born of the need to achieve and maintain its own objectives. This was clearly stated in 1685 by Commissioner Van Reede, who emphasised the Company's objectives but also praised Simon van der Stel's treatment of the Khoikhoi because it 'served very well to gain us their goodwill and friendship, mainly because they were not handled contemptuously or unjustly but were heard and treated courteously and patiently.'[28] In Van Reede's words one still perceives a tone of respect for others and a Christian sense of responsibility, to which the Enlightenment would later add a nuance of its own. It is not surprising that in relations with the indigenes, in particular, the VOC officials and the freeburghers would clash sharply, the frontier farmer having been brought to a harsher view by his circumstances. It should be borne in mind that the VOC, whose interests lay in and about Cape Town, paid little attention to the interior; if it did so it usually acted unobtrusively and correctively. The white population could hardly have prized either the neglect or the correction, even if this scant supervision meant that they were free to go their own way.

This freedom applied not least of all to the occupation of new land. As we have shown, the VOC did not like expansion, elsewhere or at the Cape. Van Riebeeck's hedge and Van Goens' proposed canal were graphic symbols of the Company's insularism.[29] At the outset a measure of expansion proved inevitable for military purposes, to make the Cape self-supporting and to enable it to serve as a refreshment station. When both objectives were achieved in the time of W.A. van der Stel, the Heren XVII considered further immigration unnecessary.[30]

Nevertheless, the Cape population grew and expanded into new regions. P.J. van der Merwe has noted that the limitations of the Cape market stimulated the expansion of stock farming, which was fairly independent of the market (see ch. 2, pp. 67—71).[31] But the VOC accepted the expansion reluctantly. It is characteristic of VOC policy that the granting of freehold was replaced by the granting of grazing rights, which were of course intended to be temporary.[32] The stock farmers had to pay taxes on their land, yet they had no legal security of tenure. Obviously such inconsistency would irritate them. Once the Cape settlement had grown into a colony in spite of the VOC, the Company was faced with problems it could not solve without prejudice to its own commercial character. This irreconcilable conflict of interests — the essential dualism of a commercial company with extensive territorial possessions — gave birth to tragedy in the colonial relations not only of the Netherlands, but of other European powers of the time.

The Company's personnel

It will now be clear that the structure of the Company had certain consequences for social relations in its territories. Before dealing with these consequences, we need to consider two major social groupings: in this section the officials, in the next the citizenry.

A study of the officials of the Company produces conflicting impressions.[33] On the one hand there were many complaints about their poor qualities and bad behaviour; on the other hand it is clear that a rather small number of them conducted the very extensive and varied activities of the Company with considerable success.[34] Let us remember that the limited population of the Netherlands could find employment elsewhere than in the East, which was popularly regarded as a man-eating Moloch. The Dutch were not very willing to enter the service of the VOC — even ex-Company employees such as Mentzel advised against it.[35] Those who did join often did so out of need. The large percentage of foreigners in the Company's personnel, which grew steadily during the eighteenth century (57 per cent in 1700, 80 per cent in

1779),[36] is explicable in terms of the poverty and over-population of their countries of origin (Germany, Scandinavia, Switzerland, etc.). In the stable, stratified society of the eighteenth century the VOC provided not only an escape from unpleasant circumstances and the pleasure of adventure, but real opportunities for financial gain and social advancement. Those who were capable (and who survived) could make a decent career.[37]

Apart from certain specialised fields (military, technical and legal), a career with the VOC usually started at the bottom of the ladder. A man who had enlisted as a soldier could 'take up the pen' and rise, via all sorts of activities, to assistant, under-merchant (*onderkoopman*), merchant, chief merchant (*opperkoopman*), Councillor of India. The rapidity of promotion naturally depended on training and ability, but personal and family ties undoubtedly played a large part too, as they did everywhere in eighteenth-century society. It is known, for example, that Governor-General van Diemen's fellow-Culemborgians (amongst them Jan van Riebeeck) did well in the service of the Company, as did officials from Groningen later under Governor-General Alting. Similarly, a marriage with the daughter of one's superior was usually a promising start to a successful career.

But having the right ancestors and relatives was not everything. The VOC never lost sight of its profit motive, and profit-making demands capable and efficient workers. The Heren XVII made stringent demands on their servants, in practice as well as in theory. Every promotion had to be approved in the fatherland, and promotion was by no means automatic, particularly to the higher ranks.

Given the comparative independence which the Indian government had attained from the fatherland, both because of distance and administrative precedent, it was the local hierarchy of officials that was of most direct importance to the career-conscious. This led to untiring efforts to gain the favour of superiors and to score over competitors. If one remembers that the VOC officials usually lived in small white enclaves in the midst of foreign peoples, it is not surprising that there was so much petty politics and quarrelling among them, so many betrayals and cover-ups.

The salaries of VOC officials have often aroused astonishment. A soldier, for example, earned 9 guilders a month, an assistant about twice that, an under-merchant some 60 guilders, and a chief merchant about 100 guilders. Only one half of these salaries was paid abroad. But nobody, not even the directors, reckoned with the nominal salary alone. Apart from their monthly salaries, Company officials received board and numerous other emoluments. Thus the fiscal (prosecutor) kept certain fines he imposed, the victualling officer and the auctioneer certain surtaxes, etc. In 1710 the Cape governor received a nominal salary of 2,400 guilders per annum. But Valentyn calculated that subsistence allowances and payments in kind quadrupled this amount.[38] By the end of the eighteenth century the tithe on the wheat planted at the Cape ensured the governor of a tidy supplementary income, and by that time the nominal salary, too, was much higher.

Similar augmentations of salary occurred in the lower ranks. For example, no clerk at the Cape copied a document without claiming sixpence in payment.[39] Both Mentzel and the petitioning Patriots could report many anecdotes of extortions committed by officials. Those who travelled to the fatherland were burdened with letters, bills of exchange and parcels — the sea chest which was transported free of charge seems to have been rather elastic.

No doubt the VOC winked at such practices as were deemed marginal to its business, and applied its prohibitions flexibly. But in a situation where every one, from high to low, tried to enrich himself by more or less permissible means, excesses easily occurred. These were vigorously attacked from time to time, but not the system as such; towards the end of its existence (1791) the Company in fact gave legal sanction to this system by introducing a levy on real rather than nominal incomes.[40]

Under the *ancien régime*, when norms for official behaviour differed totally from modern ones, such a system of payment was by no means rare. The manner in which officials systematically abused their offices was in accordance with custom and had long enjoyed social tolerance. It should be emphasised that such practices had to observe reasonable limits; in time of crisis, especially, those hurt by the system would resist it. And conflict became almost inevitable when, towards the end of the eighteenth century, radically new notions about the character and the performance of official duties gained influence.

At the Cape the number of officials was fairly large: for example, in the second half of the eighteenth century only Batavia, Ceylon and the district of the northeast coast of Java had more. The Cape official establishment rose from approximately 120 in 1660 to 545 in 1700 and some 2,000 by 1795.[41] Until far into the eighteenth century there were more VOC officials than adult male freeburghers at the Cape: 545 as against 487 in 1700, 1,016 as against 717 in 1732.[42] It was only around 1755 that the number of male adult freeburghers exceeded the number of officials; in 1795 the proportion was still about two to one. A comparison with the total freeburgher population (men, women and children) shows that the numbers were roughly even in 1660, but in 1700 there were already 1,334 freeburghers as against 545 officials; in 1795 the proportion was 15 to 2, and if the slaves were added, 15 to 1.

VOC officials could be roughly divided into four groups according to function. Those employed in administration and internal services fell from

10 per cent of the total in 1670[43] to 8 per cent in 1700 and 6 per cent in 1779. In 1670 the artisans accounted for 14 per cent, in 1779 for 15 per cent. In the agrarian sector (gardeners, herdsmen) there was a reduction from 19 per cent in 1670 to 5 per cent in the eighteenth century. In reality this decrease was not as large as it seems, because many soldiers later did the work of herdsmen at outlying posts (whether or not assisted by Company slaves). In the light of the Cape's strategic value there was naturally a sizeable garrison at all times; it accounted for 50 per cent of the Company's establishment in 1670, 70 per cent in 1700 and almost as much in 1779. In accordance with its priorities the Company often sent governors to the Cape who had a military background: four of the ten eighteenth-century governors were professional military men.† Frequent contacts with the passing subjects of foreign powers demanded an official corps at the Cape that could cope socially, diplomatically and militarily. Thus among the high officials there were quite a few who had a patrician background or whose fathers had reached a responsible position in the Company's service.

Probably the increase in the rank and status of the governors at the Cape was related not only to the expansion of the settlement, but to this need for a show of power. Van Riebeeck was only a chief merchant, as were most of his successors.‡ It was only in 1690 that Simon van der Stel was given the title of governor, and in the next year the rank of councillor-extraordinary of India. The eighteenth-century governors were almost all councillors of India — a rank shared only by the governors of Ceylon, Coromandel, the Moluccas, Macassar and Java.

There were great differences in rank and social standing among the officials at the Cape. The gap between a councillor of India and a bookkeeper was enormous, and perhaps even greater was that between a colonel and a surgeon, even though they all had the prestige of having their names on the exclusive Roll of the Qualified (*Rolle der Gequalificeerden*) which included only 2.5 to 5 per cent of the total number of VOC servants.[44] In times of class consciousness and preoccupation with protocol, such differences gave ample opportunity for friction.[45] Quarrels among government factions were normal phenomena during the *ancien régime*, and they were not lacking at the Cape.[46]

Family relationships played a part in faction conflicts, as elsewhere. It was because of the support of friends and relations that Willem Adriaan van der Stel could take over the governorship from his father in 1699. Governor Hendrik Swellengrebel (1740—51) had a very extensive network of blood

† Assenburg, De Chavonnes, Noodt, Van de Graaff. Commissioner-General Frykenius was a naval officer.
‡ Goske (1672—76) and Bax (1676—78) were exceptions.

relationships at the Cape, and this his brother-in-law and successor, Rijk Tulbagh (1751–71), inherited from him. Like the regents of the fatherland, the elite at the Cape built up a clientele behind each faction; thus the phenomenon penetrated to the lower ranks as well, as may be observed in the way numerous appointments were made.

Officials generally considered their stay at the Cape as merely a temporary phase in their careers or a means of gaining enough wealth to be able to return to the fatherland (or even, as in the case of H. Swellengrebel, who was born and raised at the Cape, to settle there for the first time.) The faction system worked in such a way as to exclude from office permanent residents of the Cape: sons of freeburghers did not readily gain entrance to the official stronghold. Of the ninety-four officials employed in the central administration in Cape Town in 1779, forty-eight were of Cape birth; however, they were all sons of VOC officials. Even when certain official families had settled at the Cape, sometimes for generations, they retained the stamp of belonging to the Company rather than to the citizenry. This was particularly true of officials in higher ranks; among the lower ranks there seems to have been a stronger inclination to settle.

In all these respects Cape officialdom was by no means exceptional, not even in the world of the VOC: the nepotistic government in Batavia, where the principal functions were in the hands of a small coterie, tightly linked by blood and friendship, became virtually proverbial. But the high Cape officials were more vulnerable to criticism than similar groups elsewhere, perhaps because of the small size of the Cape settlement. Cape Town was like a gossipy village where the European population kept a close watch on the officials. Here pomp and luxury could not be defended, as they were in Batavia, by the claim that a large indigenous population needed to be impressed. The richer and more advanced freeburghers were the ones that most readily and frequently took umbrage at the actions of officials who, owing to the structure of government and the legal position of the freeburghers, exercised authority in the somewhat arrogant manner of the regents in the Netherlands.

The freeburghers at the Cape

The first deeds of freeburgher status were issued to nine men in 1657. By 1660 the burghers, with women, children and servants, numbered 105. Their population had grown to 1,334 by 1700, and by the end of the VOC period (1795) to some 15,000.

The increase was at first sluggish in the seventeenth century, but the arrival of some 180 Huguenots in the 1680s provided a considerable boost. In the first half of the eighteenth century the rate of increase rose from an average of 400 in the first decade to about twice as much in the fifth. After only a slight rise during the 1750s (smallpox struck during this period) there was a strong surge in the second half of the century.[47] New settlers had accounted for the bulk of the increase in the seventeenth century, but increase by birth was most important in the eighteenth. The colonists tended to marry very young (the median age for first marriages among women was 19.6 years in the eighteenth century) and had large families (the median number of children per married woman was at least six in the same period).[48]

Little concrete information is as yet available on the social origins of the settlers, except that the bulk of them apparently originated among the lower strata of European society: the urban proletariat, minor tradesmen and farmers. The growth of the Cape population brought increasing differentiation among the settlers, not only geographically but socially. This was so despite the rather similar origins of the burghers in Europe, and despite the fact that less attention was paid to social background at the Cape than was the case in the older and more stable societies of Europe.

The natural character of the country, and the need for good land for planting and grazing, soon drove the settlers further and further away from Cape Town. In 1679 (when there were only about 100 male freeburghers) Stellenbosch was founded, in 1687 Drakenstein. The Cape district had 393 freeburgher inhabitants in 1691,[49] 615 in 1700, and ten times as many in 1795. The 'Cape hamlet', as the mother city was called until late in the eighteenth century, grew slowly and steadily, although for a long time it remained no more than a thriving village. In 1710 there were about 155 houses which, together with the Company buildings, served to house some 500 VOC servants and about the same number of freeburghers and their slaves.[50] According to Stavorinus[51] there were approximately 500 houses by about 1770, most of these still single-storeyed.

The district of Stellenbosch had a freeburgher population of 464 in 1706 and 957 in 1783, and Drakenstein had 525 and 4,081 in the same years respectively. In 1795 their combined population was 4,654, the decline in the number of inhabitants being due to the administrative separation of Graaff-Reinet. In 1795, nine years after the first magistrate had been appointed to the district of Graaff-Reinet, it already had 3,079 inhabitants. There had been a similar decline in the population of Drakenstein after the founding of Swellendam (1743), which had 551 freeburghers in 1748 and 2,247 in 1795.

In the Cape Colony, agriculture and stock breeding were the most important economic activities, and many (particularly tradesmen) were directly or indirectly dependent upon these activities. But this phenomenon must be more closely examined. Although in theory they were permitted hardly any trading, many Capetonians lived by some form of craft, enterprise or service: according to passing seamen every house in Cape Town was a public house or inn. Even in 1660 only twenty of the thirty-five independent freeburghers were directly involved in the agrarian sector (agriculture, horticulture and stock breeding); of the rest three were boatmen, two fishermen, three carpenters, and two masons; the remaining five consisted of a barber, tailor, miller, thatcher and messenger. Three-quarters of a century later roughly the same percentage (i.e., 57 per cent) were engaged in agriculture.

Thanks to Governor de la Fontaine[52] we know the professions of most of the freeburghers in 1732 (see Table 5.1). In De la Fontaine's survey the agrarian character of the Cape community shows up clearly: the figures for Stellenbosch and Drakenstein leave no doubt as to the predominance of stock

Table 5.1 Freeburghers' occupations by district, 1732

Profession	Cape District	Stellenbosch	Drakenstein
unknown	7	7	3
retired	21	—	1
poor, indigent, decrepit	55	33	26
bachelor, employed by parents	29	32	58
agriculture, stockbreeding	66	48	193
gardener	24	5	—
fisherman	4	—	—
monopoly operator *(pachter)*	13	1	—
brewer	1	—	—
vintner	1	—	—
inn-keeper, vintner	26	—	—
shopkeeper	7	—	—
miller	1	2	1
butcher	6	1	—
baker	11	—	—
surgeon	1	—	—
wagoner	5	1	—
barber	4	—	—
midwife	1	—	—
nurse	1	—	—
bellringer	1	—	—
nightwatchman	1	—	—
messenger	1	—	—
beadle	—	1	1
teacher	3	—	—
artisan	72	8	5
free black, ex-convict	54	—	—
Company employee	—	2	—
Total	416	141	288

breeding and, particularly in Stellenbosch, of cultivation. In Drakenstein the artisans were restricted to a cobbler, a tailor, a carpenter, a saddler and a mason. In Stellenbosch there were, in addition, a smith, two thatchers and two wagon-makers (but no carpenter or saddler). In the Cape district, however, three-quarters of the freeburghers were in non-agrarian employment. One is also struck by the high number of people involved in inn-keeping (often linked with wine-selling) as a primary source of income. One should not overlook the 20 per cent who were tradesmen (divided among sixteen trades) and the 12 per cent in services and 'middle-class' professions.

It is clear that the various economic activities would not only yield varying profits but would also give rise to social distinctions. Roughly speaking, the Cape Town population may be divided into a labouring class, a modest middle class, and a well-established bourgeoisie. The free blacks and indigents on De la Fontaine's list — jointly a notable section of the Cape population — probably belonged mainly to the first group, as indicated by De la Fontaine's notes on them being 'poorer than poor', etc. All in all, the picture he draws of Cape prosperity in 1732 is rather sombre, though it is difficult to know how much weight to attach to his remarks. At the very least, however, they indicate a stratification that is also apparent from other sources and that deserves closer investigation.

As Cape Town grew, so did its distance from its rural environs. However, the rural areas, too, cannot simply be classed under one heading: more and more distinctions arose — geographically, socially and culturally — between the wheat and wine farmers of the Western Cape and the stock farmers further to the north and east. Like the arable farmers, stock farmers were by no means all equally rich (even if one ignores the servants and retainers), but there was a great deal of homogeneity in their customs and culture. They were migrant farmers, more or less nomadic, far from Cape Town and very isolated. Under the circumstances they had to shed their European background and adapt themselves to African conditions; their frontier existence gave them few opportunities for refined cultural expression. The Bible and a few other devotional works were their only literature, hunting their main recreation. They lived a patriarchal life, austere and adapted to the demands of nature, which led some observers to fear that they might sink to the level of their Khoikhoi neighbours.

In the vicinity of Cape Town and the older villages the farmers were different from those in Swellendam, Graaff-Reinet, or further districts. Here the initial problems of adjustment and settlement had already been overcome. The lands of the farmers in the Western Cape, worked with the assistance of European and non-European labourers, and especially slaves (whose numbers soon exceeded those of the whites), were quite extensive by European standards and invite comparison with the holdings of the gentleman farmers and lesser landed gentry in Europe. These settlers lived in the vicinity of the city, with which numerous economic and social contacts were retained. They met with one another as well as with outsiders, including a fair number of passengers from ships. Not isolated like the migrant farmers, they enjoyed social contacts, education, literature. The naval officer C. de Jong illustrated these characteristics by commenting on external factors: 'In the vicinity of the Cape the country people are dressed like first citizens, their wives like ladies; many even have coiffures.'[53] Further evidence is found in the diary of Adam Tas and the comments by many visitors on the open court that Hendrik Cloete kept at Constantia.[54]

The various groups of whites at the Cape did not live in impenetrable compartments; on the contrary, in such a small community there were all kinds of contacts — both commercial and personal — between various classes of burghers and between burghers and officials. Marriage, in particular, was an institution that bridged all divisions although, especially in the rural areas, marriages within an extended family were common.[55] Younger sons of freeburghers sometimes entered the service of the Company, while many of the Company's officials became burghers. Sometimes they did so after scouting out the field as a *pasganger* or *knecht* (Company servant temporarily hired by a burgher), sometimes by settling with their accumulated savings, and sometimes when, having married, they were driven to it by the expenses of keeping a family. In general, however, it was the sons of established farmers, and not ex-officials, who, forced by lack of land, moved to the northeast and became trekboers.

Naturally there was also some upward mobility: VOC officials were promoted and thus moved into higher social classes, or freeburghers succeeded in their undertakings. Thus Henning Husing, Johannes Swellengrebel, Martin Melck, Joachim von Dessin and Rijk Tulbagh all arrived at the Cape as soldiers and ended in high positions or became very rich. Visitors from overseas tended to complain about the parvenu character and behaviour of the Cape citizenry. 'Here no one loves anything but money', wrote Valentyn in 1726. Half a century later Stavorinus stated that avarice was the dominant characteristic of people at the Cape and condemned their laziness. According to Cornelius de Jong, the Capetonians' 'high opinions of themselves' made them despise manual labour as being work for slaves.[56] This was, however, a typical complaint about colonists, by no means peculiar to the Cape.

The various groupings among the Cape population had conceptions of one another that clearly underlined the differences between them. Both the Western Cape gentry and the high officials considered the migrant stock farmers as the worst sector of the population: degenerate, uncultured and lazy, almost less civilised than the 'Hottentots'.[57] Conversely, these so-called 'canaille' held no very high opinion of the urban merchant,[58] not to mention the vain and avaricious official.

Among the population groups of the Western Cape, prejudices were no less severe. In general, the higher officials had the same attitudes to the Cape citizens as those of overseas visitors, namely that they were greedy for wealth and comfort but unwilling to work or make an intellectual effort. This reproach was directed not so much at the common man as at the higher classes: it was brought against both Van der Stel's adversaries and the Cape Patriots. On their side, the burghers of means and status—including many of the Patriots — did not deem themselves less than the highest officials, and they indulged in considerable prejudices against the common man. A well-established and prosperous farmer such as Adam Tas did not consider attending the funeral of his poor white servant; he and his friends looked down upon the 'common' people in the Cape who signed the petition in favour of Van der Stel and who included so many 'blacks'.[59] An aristocrat such as Hendrik Swellengrebel, the younger son of a governor, did not deem it necessary to mention the name of the common soldier who illustrated his travel diaries.[60]

It will be obvious that these entrenched prejudices between Cape citizens and officials, and to a lesser degree among the burghers themselves, would intensify the repeated conflicts which broke out in Cape society. We must now pay closer attention to these conflicts themselves, firstly by examining three specific episodes in detail, and then by considering the features which lay at the root of them all.

The struggle against Willem Adriaan van der Stel

This is not the place for a detailed account of the well-known conflict between Governor van der Stel (1699—1707) and a group of self-conscious freeburghers during the years 1705-07. Here we shall merely draw attention to some important events and the issues surrounding them. Some years before Van der Stel took over the government from his father in 1699, there had been complaints that food production was inadequate for the needs of the ships and of the Cape itself. Willem Adriaan therefore knew what the Heren XVII expected of him. Like his father before him, he took up his task energetically. In order to obtain a good supply of slaughtering stock, he issued licences allowing farmers to graze in the Land of Waveren, and even suspended the prohibition on stock bartering with the Khoikhoi. He also stimulated grain and wine farming.

In all this Willem Adriaan did not forget his own interests. Since Van Riebeeck's time the Cape governors had done their own farming, mostly on a considerable scale. Van der Stel, too, farmed in the grand manner, and also favoured his friends with grants of land. Secundus Elsevier owned 110 morgen; the Rev. Petrus Kalden 100 morgen; the surgeon Ten Damme, the quartermaster Jacobus de Wet and Landdrost Starrenburg, 60 morgen each. But all these properties were insignificant compared with the Van der Stels' own: Willem Adriaan owned 613 morgen and his father, Simon, 891 morgen; their estates at Vergelegen and Constantia respectively were planned like country estates in the tradition of the Dutch regents. In addition, Willem Adriaan's brother Frans had 240 morgen, and each of the three had extensive grazing grounds at his disposal.

The policy of stimulating agricultural production bore results. In these years the Cape reached a stage of overproduction, but in the mean time the Company had failed to provide a single new outlet. The various groups of producers — freeburgher farmers and farming officials — consequently waged a desperate battle for the available market. Van der Stel himself, true to the VOC tradition, exploited his official power in this conflict of business rivals; because the Van der Stel faction was fairly small they formed a compact marketing cartel. In 1702 the governor, after receiving complaints about abuses, withdrew the rights of burghers to trade with Khoikhoi. In August 1705 he inaugurated a new variant of the wine concession, which he defended as more advantageous to both the small consumer and the Company, but which in any event secured him a market for his own produce.

The issue of the wine concession goaded into action a group of freeburgher entrepreneurs who had long observed the activities of the governor and his friends with dissatisfaction. They drafted a petition and started collecting evidence against their adversaries. Their leader was Henning Husing, a former soldier who had worked himself up to being the richest man in Cape Town. His wealth had been obtained, for the most part, from a typical institution of the VOC system, the meat monopoly. Husing's principal allies were the Stellenbosch burghers Jacob van der Heijden (a very rich farmer, money-lender and livestock dealer), Jan van Meerland, Pieter van der Bijl, Ferdinand Appel and Adam Tas — also by no means poor men.[61] Tas, for instance, owned 184 morgen. These men gained a following among their neighbours and friends and also obtained support from the Huguenots in Franschhoek.

Thus two groups were contending for control of the monopoly. But there was a social conflict as well. Van der Stel had lost sight of the limits on official behaviour which custom would tolerate. Given his social background, this is perhaps not incomprehensible: why should an Amsterdam regent and former city magistrate such as Willem Adriaan pay any attention to a huddle of Cape freeburghers? Was he not the supreme authority in the land? As the conflict developed, Willem Adriaan abused his position in typical Dutch regent style. Alluding to the fate of the Amsterdamers who had rebelled against the regents some years before, he threatened to string up his adversaries, and in fact had the former burgher councillor Johannes Rotterdam, who had clearly shown his contempt for the governor, banished to Batavia by the Council of Justice.

Once it became clear to Van der Stel that his adversaries' complaints had reached the Council of India and the Heren XVII, he obtained signatures for a counter-petition or 'testimonial'. Among the 240 Cape inhabitants who signed this petition there appeared — by no means fortuitously — the governor's favourites and protégés, such as the gardener Jan Hartog, and Jan Mahieu, the secretary of the heemraden in Stellenbosch. It was normal for Dutch regents to build up a following by bestowing favours, positions and presents, and to call upon it in times of need. In explaining Van der Stel's behaviour, including his browbeating of arrested opponents, it is of course nonsense to indulge in fantasies about his 'Oriental character' or 'slavish following'. What showed itself here was his recent past as a regent in Amsterdam and not his remote Eastern origins (his great-grandmother had been an Indian).[62]

On the other hand, the actions of his adversaries were by no means free from self-interest. Henning Husing was, after all, as eager to obtain monopolies as was Van der Stel. Before the two quarrelled, Husing had had no objection to close and profitable cooperation with the governor, and had paid him liberally for services rendered.[63] Nor did the obstinate Van der Heyden[64] endure his many months of imprisonment purely for universal liberty or the public weal. He had been willing to pay high prices to obtain a great deal of land from the governor. Probably his anger at being robbed of the profitable barter with Khoikhoi was one of his strongest incentives to revolt.[65] None of these people objected to cheating the Company when they reported their taxable assets — in his diary Tas merely records, sourly, that compared with others he was still reporting too high a percentage of his wealth. Tas, by birth a member of the occasionally anti-regent middle class, cleverly publicised the idea that he had joined battle against Van der Stel for the sake of freedom — the new name of his farm, Liber-tas, could be translated either as 'freedom' or as 'Tas is free'.

Thus this was not a conflict in which the freedom-loving Afrikaners obtained justice against tyrannical, oppressive officials. Nor was it a frontier rebellion, as Eric Walker supposed, for it was mainly men from the Western Cape who were involved.[66] The burghers' petition was cleverly drafted to gain the favour of the directors; it represented Van der Stel and his group as incompetent officials who robbed the Company. The impression was created that only the interests of the Company led the plaintiffs to draw up their petition; only in passing did they point out the harmful economic consequences which the behaviour of the officials had for the freeburghers, and in this regard they appealed to the fatherly sentiments of the Heren XVII. Their lamentations, in which they represented themselves as sorely tried victims of official caprice and contempt, concluded with a warning, wrapped in velvet, but clear nonetheless: they threatened disruption.

In his *Korte Deductie* (Brief Statement) Van der Stel naturally concentrated on the weak points in the accusations. He attempted to cast doubts on the characters of his adversaries, pointing out that they had misrepresented themselves as being concerned solely for the interests of the Company. He also tried to minimise the force of the complaints and to defend his own actions by comparing them to practices permitted in the past. Significantly he elaborated on the aversion of the Cape burghers to law and order. The freeburghers had accused Van der Stel of dictatorial action; he hit back by complaining of their anarchic behaviour and virtually democratic aspirations. This was not simply the obvious retort to make; it seems that he wanted the Heren XVII to draw comparisons between the Cape unrest and similar movements (the *Aansprekers* riot and the *Plooierijen*) that had some years previously disturbed the peace of the regents in the fatherland. It is noteworthy that again in the Patriot unrest after 1778 both Cape factions would try similar gambits to curry favour with the parties in the fatherland, branding each other as contemptible aristocrats, or revolutionaries 'driven by an American spirit'.

It seems unlikely that the Heren XVII recalled Van der Stel because they were fully convinced of his despotic behaviour or of the harm he had allegedly done to the Company. They discharged him and summoned him home, but they allowed him to retain his salary during the homeward passage and otherwise hardly bothered him. Rev. Kalden, who had been as violently attacked as the governor, later obtained a good post with the Company as rector of the seminary on Ceylon. Bergh, Blesius, Ten Damme, De Wet and Starrenburg simply retained their posts.

It may be that the directors merely wanted quiet at the Cape during those times of war (the War of the Spanish Succession, 1701–14), or that they genuinely felt the governor had overstepped the bounds of propriety. Or, alternatively, Van der Stel may have been the victim of a typical eighteenth-century feud. Of the seventeen Amsterdam directors who were responsible for his discharge, half had assumed their posts after Willem Adriaan's appointment in 1697; the same applied to the Company's Advocate, Everard

Scott. Most of the new incumbents belonged to the following of Joan Corver (a director since 1688), who was the most powerful man in the Amsterdam regents' circles after 1702. Because of Corver, Van der Stel's patron, Nicolas Witsen, had lost much of his influence. A number of other men who had been prominent in 1697 had died by 1706. It was not unusual for such a shift of power in the Amsterdam government to have far-reaching effects on the followers of the factions concerned.[67]

Van der Stel's discharge was naturally an important victory for the freeburghers, though hardly an occasion for unrestrained rejoicing. The final settlement of the dispute — including the sale of the property of the accused — took years and did not always work out to the advantage of the petitioners. After 1707 monopoly contracts remained; officials continued to farm extensive lands and engage in trading; and cattle bartering was still forbidden to the colonists.

Some officials had disappeared, but not the VOC system itself. The real problem, the discrepancy between production and marketing outlets, had not been solved. The Heren XVII did try to do something about it by stopping further immigration (1705) and by creating some further possibilities for marketing. But the mercantilist VOC system was not abandoned.

The absence of major conflicts in the following decades was due to several more or less fortuitous circumstances that dissipated tensions. Thus, for instance, grain harvests in this period were just as irregular as the marketing possibilities.[68] More importantly, the position of the freeburghers changed: the expansion by the trekboers gathered momentum, and the stock farmer was temporarily less concerned with the problems of marketing than his counterpart in the southwestern Cape. Furthermore, this expansion was not seriously hampered either by the Company or by the indigenous population. The migration of the white freeburghers to the interior prevented the simmering economic and political conflict at the Cape from reaching boiling point.

The Barbier Rebellion

The Van der Stel episode was an internal dispute in the white community; apart from the question of barter with the Khoikhoi, policy toward native peoples played no part.[69] But in the rebellion of 1795 on the Eastern Frontier (see ch. 9), and repeatedly later in South African history, this issue would be at the heart of settlers' disputes with the government.

That the problem had existed even earlier is apparent from the episode of 1738–39 in which Estienne Barbier played the principal part: here the policy of the Company, which was founded on good relations with the independent Khoikhoi, quite clearly clashed with the interests of white stock farmers. In the 1730s younger, and as yet unsettled, freeburghers were doing what had long been customary: crossing the borders of the colony to hunt, to 'barter' cattle, and to find pasture.[70] In general the Company was opposed to these movements and took sporadic action to control them, as in 1738, when it again prohibited stock bartering after receiving complaints about the misdeeds of barterers.

In 1739 a group of frontier farmers rebelled against this prohibition, incited by Estienne Barbier, a French-born sergeant in the service of the Company.[71] Barbier had served at the Cape since 1735 and does not seem to have been a very cooperative character: he was unwise enough to publicly attack one of his highest superiors, Ensign R.S. Allemann, with complaints about malpractice. When Barbier brought these charges a second time, he was imprisoned in the Castle.

On 24 March 1738 he managed to escape from the Castle and made his way to the interior, where he found refuge in the Drakenstein Valley. His tales of the iniquities of high Company officials were eagerly accepted, especially since a number of frontier farmers had recently suffered legal action following the complaints of Nama victims of a stock-bartering expedition. At the head of about ten young frontier farmers Barbier began his rebellion. At the Paarl church he and his followers ripped down the Company notice against stock-bartering (1 March 1739); they then incited others to disobedience, and threatened violence. Barbier, whose leadership abilities seem to have been meagre, managed to gather only a small number of desperados behind him. He was arrested on 17 March 1739 through the deft and tactful action of the local authorities (the heemraden).

But the Council of Policy itself acknowledged the broad sympathy in the colony for Barbier's action, and hence acted cautiously.[72] They even granted amnesty to Barbier's followers, although not to him: he was executed on 14 November 1739, after conviction on charges of *lèse-majesté* and rebellion. At the same time the government sent — perhaps as a distraction and a token of goodwill — a punitive commando against the Khoisan, and ordered the pardoned men and some who had been accused of raiding the Khoikhoi to take part!

The importance of Barbier's 'rebellion' lies not in his rather inconsequential actions, but in the wide sympathy he elicited among the local population — a sympathy that had allowed him to elude justice for about a year. The two-fold complaint that Barbier voiced was widely shared: firstly, that the Company paid too much attention to 'the word of unbaptised Hottentots, who know neither salvation nor damnation',[73] and secondly, that by illegal and semi-legal means the officials made economic enterprise nearly impossible for the burghers of the Cape. With regard to the second point, they charged that officials traded and farmed illicitly and demanded presents from those who wanted to have loan farms registered in their names (the same charge had been brought against Van der Stel). All these practices made life expensive, as did excessive taxes for people with low incomes. These complaints contain clear echoes of those of 1705 and 1779, and it is not surprising that half a century later the Patriots would pass favourable judgement on Barbier.[74] The complaint that heathenish Hottentots were protected and advanced above Christians would also be frequently voiced in the future.[75]

The Cape Patriot movement[76]

In May 1778 a number of secret meetings were convened in and around Cape Town. At about the same time a pamphlet was circulated, mainly by night. In this pamphlet 'the powers and freedoms of a society of citizens' were 'defended by the opinions of the foremost lawyers, and dedicated to the judgement of the Cape citizenry'.[77] The 'power' of the burghers was the freedom — in fact, the duty — to change the form of government by violence if necessary, should the authorities no longer perform their natural task of 'standing for the people, and defending their lives, property, and liberty.'

This pamphlet was clearly a theoretical justification of the right of revolt: it was intended as a preamble to a request that the governor redress grievances — or so one can deduce from its wording — but no such request was ever made. What did happen, almost a year later, was that the burgher Hendrik Buytendagh was arrested, forcibly re-enlisted in the Company's service, and sent to Batavia.

The freeburghers now felt that their rights and liberties were truly at stake, and 400 of them signed a petition to the governor asking permission to send a delegation to lay complaints before the Heren XVII. This request was naturally refused by the governor: if there were complaints he, the governor, was the one to whom they should be addressed. The burghers calmly proceeded to designate Barend Jacob Artoys, Nicolaas Godfried Heyns, Tielman Roos and Jacobus van Reenen 'as joint representatives of the entire citizenry' (7 May 1779). The four men left for Europe, and on 9 October 1779 submitted an elaborate petition to the Heren XVII. This petition, the so-called Memorandum of 1779, consisted of three sections. The first set out the bad economic circumstances of the Cape freeburghers. The second showed how these were aggravated by the actions of officials, whose selfish and tyrannical character was illustrated with numerous examples. The third section contained a number of economic proposals: that burghers be permitted to trade freely with foreign ships in the harbour, and that they obtain better prices for goods they sold to and bought from the Company. There were also some political requests: the petitioners wanted half the members of the Council of Policy to be freeburghers, who would also have the right to report to the Heren XVII. In addition, they called for the codification of laws and delineation of the powers of officials and, of course, for a strict prohibition on their private economic activity.

In keeping with Company practice, the accused officials were called upon to explain their actions. The wording of their defence was strikingly reminiscent of that adopted by Willem Adriaan van der Stel. In his 'Considerations' (submitted on 20 March 1782) Governor Plettenberg declared that the signatories of the Memorandum were by no means representative of all freeburghers, but merely a small and insignificant group. The economic privation of which they complained could not be squared with the facts: great prosperity and luxury prevailed at the Cape. It was because the Cape burghers were lazy and refused to exert themselves that they did not prosper. The complainants were merely jealous of the hard-won success of officials, whose private trading activities remained well within the bounds of established custom. Fiscal Willem Cornelis Boers, who had been sharply attacked in the Memorandum for his extortionate actions, defended himself with a frontal assault on the political pretensions of the signatories. Government at the Cape, he held, was the sole prerogative of the officials; it was, after all, solely for the Company's benefit that the Cape settlement had been founded and maintained.

The mills of the VOC could grind very slowly. The Heren XVII gave their judgement only in December 1783, and then for the most part they exonerated the officials. This could not be a definitive judgement, however, for in 1782 the Cape representatives had submitted a Further Memorandum, repeating and augmenting earlier complaints. But it was not only the Heren XVII who had to deal with the complaints of the Cape citizenry. Having become wiser about affairs in the fatherland, where the Patriots were embroiled in an intense struggle with the Orangist establishment, the burghers also appealed to the States-General and to the States of Holland (in addresses dated December 1784, but submitted in 1785).

Events in the fatherland (where the Prince of Orange and his faction were losing ground), as well as those in North America, were closely followed at the Cape; and their echoes were noticeable. In 1784 the dissidents at the Cape showed signs of organising themselves. A representative body ('Commissioned Representatives of the People') was chosen to coordinate activities, which consisted mainly of drafting the above-mentioned appeals to the States-

General and of electing and briefing four new delegates to the Netherlands (Martinus Adrianus Bergh, Johannes Roos, Johannes Henricus Redelinghuys, and Johannes Augustus Bresler). After this, few new developments appear to have taken place at the Cape. The Patriots apparently fell out among themselves.

Meanwhile the second delegation to the Netherlands, having gained legal advice, submitted their petition to the States-General, and in April 1786 yet another. Moreover, they tried, through a number of publications, to influence public opinion, and especially to persuade the Dutch Patriots that the two movements were similar. In temperament, revolutionary intentions, and methods the four delegates differed widely. Bergh even distanced himself publicly from his co-delegates. They did not achieve much, although the postponement of the appointment of a new fiscal in 1785 was perhaps due to their efforts. Compelled by the States-General, which demanded information, the directors of the VOC closely examined Cape affairs in 1785. In the end, however, they upheld their judgements of December 1783. The most important concessions they were prepared to allow were free trade with foreign ships and the purchase of surplus produce at fixed prices — all this, of course, after the normal demands of the Company had been met. One could hardly call these radical solutions to the marketing problems of the Cape producers – many uninvolved observers recognised this – but within the framework of the VOC they were probably realistic.

In general the directors were determined to protect their servants, even when the States-General became involved. The strategy of the Cape Patriots in publicising their grievances and seeking contacts with the Dutch Patriots probably turned the directors against them. In these years the Company was facing growing financial problems as well as increasing attacks on its privileged position, its structure, and its mode of operation. One must not, of course, assume that these attacks came entirely from theorists questioning the value of all monopoly companies like the VOC; many who called for greater supervision of the VOC by the state were self-interested.

Since the directors were Orangists and supporters of the status quo, one could hardly expect them to be sympathetic to the Cape petitioners, who were so patently supported by their political opponents. In September 1787 the Prince of Orange, backed by British diplomacy and a Prussian army, resumed full powers; his Patriot opponents were chased out of their offices and the country. This meant that the Cape Patriots could gain no further hearing. Indeed, their representatives in the Netherlands were even obstructed when they tried to return to the Cape. As is shown by the VOC's decisions, including the reforms made by Commissioners-General Nederburgh and Frykenius during their stay at the Cape in 1791—92, the achievements of the Cape Patriot movement were meagre indeed.

As in the movement against Van der Stel at the beginning of the eighteenth century, the local economic and social situation formed the background to the Patriot movement. But in the three-quarters of a century between the two conflicts the population of the Cape had expanded considerably, society had become more stratified, and problems of the economy had become more severe and complex. The Cape burghers had become more deeply rooted in the colony, and hence more alienated from the governing class. There was also, on both sides, a stronger urge to express complaints and demands in theoretical terms.

At the end of the eighteenth century certain centuries-old institutions were under strong attack from ideas associated with the Enlightenment. Many thinkers, proceeding from the idea of equality among men, were rejecting all forms of aristocracy and group privilege, and advocating government for and by the people instead of by remote ruling bodies like the VOC. They were also demanding the abolition of monopolies, nepotistic politics, and secretive procedures in government — all of which made it difficult for popular policies to prevail.

It is still too early to assess the degree to which Cape leaders were influenced by the Enlightenment. For instance, we hardly know what literature reached the Cape — a good deal it seems — nor, more importantly, who read it. It would seem, however, that the closer one lived to Cape Town, the greater one's chances were of being influenced by Enlightenment thinking. It has been proved, for example, that the events of the American Revolution and the conflict between Patriots and Orangists in the Netherlands were followed closely in the southwestern Cape. Even more, of course, those Cape citizens who went to Europe would imbibe new ideas. The most radical and explicitly Enlightenment pronouncements of the Patriot movement came from those who had visited the Netherlands: their statements should not be uncritically regarded as products of the intellectual climate at the Cape.[78]

One should also note that the Patriots need not have derived their ideas solely from Enlightenment thinkers, but that they may have been drawing on a long Dutch tradition of revolt. Among the 'gentry' and bourgeoisie of the southwestern Cape there were men with administrative experience — not only officials who had formerly been burghers, but also field-cornets, heemraden, militia officers, and burgher councillors. Such people were likely to find some inspiration in the 'democratic' tendencies which had cropped up from time to time in Dutch history: e.g., during the war of 1672, in the decade after the death of William III in 1702 (the 'Plooierijen'), and in 1747—48 when broad layers of the population revolted against the economic and political dominance of the regent classes (the tax farmer riots and *Doelisten* movement).[79]

However, the main inspiration for the Patriots' ideas was neither the Enlightenment nor Dutch history, but the situation at the Cape. In fact their grievances, as reflected in their Memorandum of 1779, hardly differed from those of Van der Stel's opponents: a precarious economic situation aggravated by the actions of officials who abused their position for private purposes, and high-handed action by officials against freeburghers who had no rights. Their recommendations to improve the situation were mainly economic and did little more than demand affirmation in practice of what already existed in theory. All that struck a new note was the request for a clearer definition of the rights of the burghers, and for more burgher councillors with greater powers. This, too, was by no means revolutionary.

Once again, it seems as if the background of the Cape Patriot movement was mainly economic and social. The discrepancy between production and marketing was again very strong. The avaricious actions of the officials above all affected those who were economically weak; but strong and active entrepreneurs were also annoyed with the restrictions imposed by the officials on their undertakings.

The leaders among the Cape Patriots were clearly inhabitants of the city and of the Western Cape. Among the former one notices a number of more or less intellectually trained men (Artoys, Heyns, Redelinghuys) and a fairly large number of ambitious bourgeoisie: entrepreneurs, merchants (the Van Reenens, Roos, Verweij, J. Smith Jurriaansz), and people who had savoured participation in government and who wanted more, such as burgher councillors Meyer, Van der Poel, Maasdorp and Bergh. This was a kind of colonial elite that came into conflict with officials from abroad and that could gain influence by exploiting feelings of dissatisfaction in wider circles.

The relationship between the urban and the rural members of the Patriot movement did not remain good for very long: Redelinghuys later complained[80] that the rural leaders had left him in the lurch. In fact, the Western Cape gentry were not undivided in their support of the Memorandum. It is significant that a number of the most prominent Western Cape farmers submitted a separate request (1784) in which better economic arrangements were called for, but which contained none of the political and social acrimony of the Memorandum.[81]

During the last five years of Company rule, relations between burghers and government became even worse. In 1789 the Heren XVII recalled the free-spending Governor C.J. van de Graaff and withdrew a large part of the garrison from the Cape.[82] In 1791 Commissioners Nederburgh and Frykenius visited the Cape and attempted to grapple with the distressing state of the

Company's finances by curtailing government spending, tightening the collection of existing taxes, and levying new ones.

At the same time the export economy was suffering from a decline in the number of foreign ships which visited the Cape as a result of the war which had broken out in Europe in 1792. Nederburgh and Frykenius made some concessions to the burghers, such as allowing them to export colonial products with their own ships, and to engage in the slave trade on the East African coast and at Madagascar. But these measures, being adaptations rather than reforms, were too little and too late to revive the economy. Great discontent arose among the burghers about economic matters, particularly the declining value of the rixdollar. With a weakened garrison, Company authority seemed insubstantial. Burghers expressed contempt for the government and openly defied its authority. Nederburgh spoke of 'a spirit of confusion and insubordination toward all authority without exception.'[83] J.F. Kirsten said 'Government had lost its respect . . . Everybody would command here and nobody would obey.'[84] Among the burghers, revolutionary voices were increasingly heard. Some wanted the Cape to be governed directly by the States-General, others wanted total independence.[85]

In the eastern districts the settlers became more and more aware that the Company could neither protect them against their indigenous enemies nor punish them for insubordination. In 1795 the burghers of Graaff-Reinet and Swellendam rose in rebellion.

The world of the VOC was breaking up.

Conclusion: The framework of conflict

The conflicts between freeburghers and VOC officials at the Cape were largely rooted in the social, economic and administrative structures of the Cape settlement. Since these structures remained essentially unchanged, there was a constant element in the various conflicts: from the freeburghers who in 1658 complained to Van Riebeeck about their economic subservience to Company interest, to the Memorandum of the Cape Patriots in 1779, or — to give another example — Hendrik Cloete's attempts in the 1780s to find better marketing outlets for his famous Constantia wines.

In the interior, most conflicts between stock farmers and officials concerned land policies, taxes, and relations with the indigenous peoples. Stock trading with the Khoikhoi was a point of contention virtually from the beginning of the settlement, as were hunting and grazing beyond the borders. Why could grazing concessions or loan farms not be obtained more readily and cheaply? Why was stock bartering prohibited when the Company itself engaged in it? Why were boundaries which were recognised by the government always years behind the actual ones? Why must farmers pay high prices and high taxes on goods from the Company's stores when their own produce could be sold only at fixed, low prices? Why were taxes not used for better defence of the borders or to establish churches and administrative centres deeper in the interior?

A second set of grievances held by stock farmers centred on the different attitudes which officials often had to the threat from Khoisan and later Xhosa. In brief, the farmers wanted to know why Cape Town and its agents paid serious attention to complaints from native spokesmen, yet left the frontiersmen to fight their battles alone. Grievances regarding native policy rankled throughout the century, coming into brief prominence in Barbier's rebellion, but not giving rise to a major revolt until the frontier uprisings of 1795 (see ch. 9).

Clearly the conflict between officials and stock farmers owed a great deal to the social and cultural differences between them. While the gap was smaller in Cape Town and surrounding districts, it still existed, however, and was aggravated by the constant contact between the two groups which took place there. It was the city-dweller who knew the officials best, and it was he who was most dependent upon them for jobs, favours, commodities and services. And, as we have seen, the city-dweller played a significant part in the conflict with officials and, by extension, in the formation of the Afrikaner people.[86] While social and administrative contacts between officials and freeburghers produced ample occasion for conflicts, it was the economic structure of the Cape that made such conflicts virtually inevitable. By about the beginning of the eighteenth century the Cape could produce enough for its own needs, for the passing VOC ships, and even for export. The VOC realised this and allowed exports, but only on its own conditions. Its claims always had to be satisfied first, at fixed and low prices, and even then the producers were tied hand and foot to the Company. The production of the Cape was too large for the local market. Chance circumstances such as failed harvests, unusually large numbers of passing ships, expanded garrisons, or temporary measures by the Company could conceal this structural problem from time to time, but it always remained. The importation of many products also fluctuated, owing to all kinds of circumstances, but here, too, the freeburghers remained dependent upon bodies and persons who were primarily serving other interests. Although the Company tried from time to time to reconcile these opposed interests by a variety of measures (supplying import goods by order, free auctions, buying up surpluses, fixing prices), such measures remained no more than patchwork as long as their execution was organised in such a way that officials had every opportunity for profiteering, nepotism and bribery.

If, as we have argued, the constitution of the Cape was structurally unsound, we will no longer need to explain the endemic conflict with stereotypes of either the lazy, self-opinionated and uncultured Afrikaner or the vain, avaricious and tyrannical VOC official. While some members of both groups clearly deserved these labels, the stereotypes were created in the struggle itself and have no value as historical explanations. Nor need we be misled into exaggerating the role of ideology among the burghers. 'Freedom', 'national sentiment', 'democratic liberalism' and such characterisations seem to have had little bearing on the realities of these conflicts. Those, for example, who treat the Cape Patriots too ideologically and who see in the Great Trek, in Paul Kruger, and in the declaration of the Republic (1961) 'the continuation of their [the Patriots] ideas'[87] are guilty of facile simplification by hindsight.

But to say that the conflict was rooted in the specific conditions of the Cape's society and economy is not necessarily to say that such conditions were unique. The settlement at the Cape was, after all, only one of the territories of the VOC, and the VOC formed part of the Republic of the United Netherlands. This means that Cape structures and events should be seen in the context of the Netherlands and of common Dutch colonial patterns, which in turn reveal certain similarities with the general and colonial history of the time.

Chapter Five Notes

1. This is implied by Leo Fouché, *Dagboek van Adam Tas 1705—1706* (Cape Town, 1970), p. 390 and Gert D. Scholtz, *Die Ontwikkeling van die politieke denke van die Afrikaner* (Johannesburg, 1967), I, 176.
2. Cited in M.F. Katzen, 'White Settlers and the Origin of a New Society', *The Oxford History of South Africa*, ed. Monica Wilson and Leonard Thompson (Oxford, 1969), I, 231. For information on the social system of other Dutch colonies see H. Hoetink, *Het patroon van de oude Curaçaose samenleving* (Assen, 1958); R.A.J. van Lier, *Frontier Society: A Social Analysis of the History of Surinam* (The Hague, 1971).
3. Anna J. Böeseken, 'Die Nederlandse Kommissarisse en die 18e eeuse samelewing aan die Kaap', *AYB*, VII (1944) p. 25 states that only a few traces can be found of cooperation between officials and freeburghers, but does not explain this phenomenon.
4. Scholtz, *Ontwikkeling*, I, ch. 5 and Katzen, 'New Society', pp. 189—190, 202, 217.
5. For complaints that South African historiography lacks structural analysis see W. Ph. Coolhaas, 'Twee nieuwe werken over de geschiedenis van Zuid-Afrika', *Zuid-Afrika*, XLVI (1969), pp. 166—69; F.J. du T. Spies, 'Leemtes in die Suid-Afrikaanse Geskiedskrywing', *South African Historical Journal*, III (1971), pp. 82—92; Phyllis Lewsen, 'The Oxford History of South Africa: An Attempt at

Re-evaluation', *South African Historical Journal*, V (1973), pp. 103–08.

6. Still indispensable for a study of the Company is a work completed around 1700 by the Company's advocate, Pieter van Dam, *Beschrijvinge van de Oost-Indische Compagnie,* ed. F.W. Stapel and C.W. Th. van Boetzelaer (7 vols., The Hague, 1927–54). For a brief overview see the article by J.E. Heeres in *Encyclopaedie van Nederlandsch-Indië* (The Hague, 1917), I, 498–517. See also W.M.F. Mansvelt, *Rechtsvorm en geldelijk beheer bij de Oost-Indische Compagnie* (Amsterdam, 1922); C. de Heer, *Bijdrage tot de financieele geschiedenis der Oost-Indische Compagnie* (The Hague, 1929).

7. Leslie H. Palmier, 'The Javanese Nobility under the Dutch', *Comparative Studies in Society and History*, II (1959–60), p. 208.

8. Kristof Glamann, *Dutch-Asiatic Trade, 1620–1740* (Copenhagen, 1958), ch. 3; F.S. Gaastra, 'De VOC in de zeventiende en achttiende eeuw: de groei van een bedrijf; geld tegen goederen', *Bijdragen en Mededelingen betreffende de Geschiedenis der Nederlanden*, XCI (1976), pp. 249–72.

9. Van Dam, *Beschrijvinge*, I. 78.

10. I.J. Brugmans, 'De Oost-Indische Compagnie en de welvaart in de Republiek', *Welvaart en Historie*, ed. I.J. Brugmans (The Hague, 1950), pp. 28–37; Johan de Vries, *De economische achteruitgang der Republiek in de achttiende eeuw* (Leiden, 1968).

11. Johannes C. Boogman, 'Die holländische Tradition in der niederländischen Geschichte', *Westfälische Forschungen*, XV (1962), pp. 96–105.

12. Van Dam, *Beschrijvinge*, I, 80. Toward the end of the eighteenth century attempts were made to put the VOC under the supervision of the state; see Gerrit J. Schutte, *De Nederlandse Patriotten en de koloniën. Een onderzoek naar hun denkbeelden en optreden, 1770–1800* (Groningen, 1974), chs. 3, 5.

13. H.A. van Reede tot Drakenstein, 'Journaal van zijn verblijf aan de Kaap', ed. A. Hulshof, *Bijdragen en Mededelingen van het Historisch Genootschap te Utrecht*, LXII (1941), p. 123.

14. AR, Nederburgh Collection, no. 143, Kaapsche Stukken 1785, III, 136.

15. Eduard van Zurck, *Codex Batavus* (Delft, 1711), pp. 413, 565.

16. AR, Nederburgh Collection, no. 149, Van de Graaff — Heren XVII, 19 April 1786, p. 70.

17. Banishment also occurred at Batavia: Abraham Bogaert, *Historische Reizen door d'oostersche Deelen van Asia . . .* (Amsterdam, 1711), pp. 129–30.

18. This phrase was already used in 1658. See Foort C. Dominicus, *Het ontslag van Wilhem Adriaen van der Stel* (Rotterdam, 1928), p. 12.

19. Bogaert, *Reizen,* p. 495.

20. C.W. de Kiewiet's use of this term is an unjustifiable concession to eighteenth-century sentiment: see his *A History of South Africa — Social and Economic* (Oxford, 1946), p. 5. The same objection can be made to Katzen, 'New Society', pp. 213ff.

21. Taco H. Milo, *De invloed van de zeemacht op de geschiedenis der VOC* (The Hague, 1946).

22. This was still the opinion in 1802: Schutte, *Nederlandse Patriotten*, p. 211.

23. After 1740 the annual losses of the Cape settlement averaged 300,000 guilders (*Nieuwe Nederlandsche Jaarboeken*, 1790, p. 1014; AR, Nederburgh Collection, no. 106). There is a need for closer study of the taxes imposed at the Cape to compensate for expenses, and for a comparison of these with taxes in other

colonies and in the Netherlands itself. On the politics behind the settlement of burghers, see Van Dam, *Beschrijvinge,* Book II, part 3, 500ff; *The Reports of Chavonnes and his Council, and of Van Imhoff, on the Cape* (Cape Town, 1918), pp. 25—32.

24. Van Reede, 'Journaal', p. 125; O.F. Mentzel, *Life at the Cape in Mid-Eighteenth Century, being the Biography of Rudolf Siegfried Alleman* (Cape Town, 1920), p. 151. In the 1780s and 1790s the VOC increasingly based the security of the Cape on Anglo-French rivalry: *Nieuwe Nederlandsche Jaarboeken,* 1790, pp. 1011—64.

25. We still lack a thorough study of the governmental and judicial structure of the colony. Scattered data on the burghers' role in government are found in Böeseken, 'Kommissarisse', ch. 4; P.J. Venter, 'Landdros en Heemrade', *AYB,* III (1940); *Bepalingen en Instructiën voor het bestuur van de buitendistricten van de Kaap de Goede Hoop,* ed. G.W. Eybers (Amsterdam, 1922); J.C. Visagie, 'Die ontstaan van die Burgerraad' *Kleio: Bulletin of the Department of History of the University of South Africa,* V (1973), pp. 33—36; Scholtz, *Ontwikkeling,* I, 143. Scholtz's comments are rather confused. On the one hand he gives the impression that Cape colonists, like the Netherlanders, had little political influence at the time (I, 145), that they did not desire it (I, 220) and that their behaviour always had an economic motivation (I, 221). On the other hand he emphasises the political significance of 1706 and 1779 (I, 234—35, 243—44, 256ff) and speaks of the colonists' burgeoning political activity (I, 220ff).

26. Still the farmers sometimes mistrusted the field-cornets. See J.S. Marais, *Maynier and the First Boer Republic* (Cape Town, 1944), pp. 10ff, and L.C. van Oordt, 'Die Kaapse Taalargief 10: Een-en-dertig Afrikaans-Hollandse briewe uit die jare 1712—1795, hoofsaaklik afkomstig van veldwagmeesters', *Tydskrif vir Weten-skap en Kuns,* XVI (1956), no. 303.

27. Scholtz, *Ontwikkeling,* I, 85.

28. Van Reede, 'Journaal', pp. 202—03. Compare his 'Instructie voor Simon van der Stel', *Belangrijke Historische Dokumenten,* ed. George McCall Theal (Cape Town, 1896), I.

29. The renowned political publicist Pieter de la Court had recommended such insularism for Holland in a book of 1669: see Boogman, 'Holländische Tradition'.

30. Plans for colonisation in the East Indies by Governor-General J.P. Coen had earlier been rejected and the West India Company had given up Brazil. See also Van Dam, *Beschrijvinge,* II (3), pp. 500ff; for the decision to stop immigration to the Cape, see Theal, *Belangrijke Dokumenten,* III, 2, 4, 6. Scholtz's jeremiads about this decision totally ignore contemporary values (*Ontwikkeling,* I, 62).

31. P.J. van der Merwe, *Die Trekboer in die Geskiedenis van die Kaapkolonie* (Cape Town, 1938), ch. 2.

32. *Ibid.* See also P.J. van der Merwe, 'Van Verversingspos tot Landbou-Kolonie', *Geskiedenis van Suid-Afrika,* ed. A.J.H. van der Walt, J.A. Wiid and A.L. Geyer (Cape Town, 1965), pp. 88—89.

33. The material is scattered in pamphlets and travel journals and has never been systematically studied. For the late eighteenth century see Schutte, *Nederlandse Patriotten.* The qualities of officials can be deduced from their letters to their successors. Those for the Cape before 1700 are found in *Memoriën en Instructiën,* ed. Anna J. Böeseken (Cape Town, 1966).

34. The Generale Monsterrollen (lists of employees) of 1700 (KA 8518) give a total

of 13,204, though this omits a few minor factories. The rolls of 1779 (KA 9314) give a total of 17,267; those of 1789 (KA 9314), 19,006.

35. Mentzel, *The Cape*, p. 162.

36. Generale Monsterrollen, see fn. 34.

37. Schutte, *Nederlandse Patriotten*, pp. 32—38.

38. François Valentyn, *Beschryvinge van de Kaap der Goede Hoope* (Cape Town, 1973), II, 250.

39. Böeseken, 'Kommissarisse', p. 33. Many other forms of income are discussed by Mentzel.

40. Schutte, *Nederlandse Patriotten*, p. 50. The proclamation of 25 Oct. 1791 is in J.A. van der Chijs, *Nederlandsch-Indisch Plakkaatboek* (Batavia, 1893), XI, 358.

41. KA 3973 and KA 4022.

42. Katzen, 'New Society', p. 217. Figures on the burgher population after 1700 are in Coenraad Beyers, *Die Kaapse Patriotte gedurende die laaste kwart van die agtiende eeu en die voortlewing van hul denkbeelde* (Pretoria, 1967), appendix H.

43. KA 3983.

44. Based on a sample of the years 1700 to 1769.

45. Already noted by J.S. Stavorinus in his *Reize van Zeeland over de Kaap de Goede Hoop, . . . in de jaaren 1768 tot 1771 . . .* (Leiden, 1793), I, 243. For excellent introductions to the factional character of the Ancien Régime, see Lewis B. Namier, *The Structure of Politics at the Accession of George III* (London, 1961); Daniel J. Roorda, *Partij en Factie* (Groningen, 1961).

46. The faction of Van der Stel, Elsevier, Starrenburg and Kalden was opposed by one led by Johannes Swellengrebel (nicknamed Zwelling Rebel) and Oortmans. Factional disputes were rife under Governors d'Ableing (1707—08), Van Assenburgh (1708—11) and Pasques de Chavonnes (1714—24); See *Res, IV*, 79, 400; D.B. Bosman, *Briewe van Johanna Maria van Riebeeck en ander Riebeeckiana* (Amsterdam, 1952), pp. 78, 110—11, 115. A vehement conflict arose in the late 1730s about the successor to Governor van Kervel between the fiscal Van den Henghel and the secunde Hendrik Swellengrebel (R.P.J. Tutein Nolthenius, *Het geslacht Nolthenius* (*Tutein Nolthenius*) [Haarlem, 1914], pp. 459, 1039 ff, 1055 ff); Governor van de Graaff was opposed by a faction too: see AR, Admiraliteiten, Aanhangsel 39, Van der Hoop no. 80; H.C.V. Leibbrandt and J.E. Heeres, 'Memoriën van den Gouverneur van de Graaff over de gebeurtenissen aan de Kaap de Goede Hoop in 1780—1806', *Bijdragen en Mededelingen van het Historisch Genootschap te Utrecht*, XV (1894), pp. 180—256.

47. H.T. Colenbrander, *De afkomst der Boeren* (Cape Town, 1964); Beyers, *Patriotte*, appendix H; J.A. Heese, *Die herkoms van die Afrikaner* (Cape Town, 1971); Robert Ross, 'The "White" Population of South Africa in the Eighteenth Century', *Population Studies*, XXIX (1975), pp. 217—30. Figures for burghers include free blacks.

48. Ross, ' "White" Population', pp. 224—28.

49. KA 4005.

50. Valentyn, *Beschryvinge*, II, 238.

51. Stavorinus, *Reize 1768*, II, 127.

52. AR, Radermacher collection, no. 507, Letter of Jan de la Fontaine, 30 Jan. 1732, and appendices.

53. Cornelius de Jong, *Reizen naar de Kaap de Goede Hoop, Ierland en Noorwegen,*

in de jaren 1791 tot 1797 (Haarlem, 1802), I, 99.

54. *Ibid.*, I, 79—84. See also Cloete's correspondence with H. Swellengrebel Jr (publication in preparation).

55. This is the impression one gets from travel journals and from C.C. de Villiers and C. Pama, *Geslagsregisters van die ou Kaapse families* (Cape Town, 1966).

56. Valentyn, *Beschryvinge*, I, 134; Stavorinus, *Reize 1774—1778*, II, 309—11; De Jong, *Reizen*, I, 134.

57. Van Reede, 'Journaal', p. 149; Bogaert, *Reizen*, p. 565; Fouché, *Dagboek Adam Tas*, I, 2, 4; Fiscal Cloppenburg cited in Van der Merwe, *Trekboer*, p. 139; Journal of Hendrik Swellengrebel Jr (in preparation).

58. Fouché, *Dagboek Adam Tas*, p. 138; Bogaert, *Reizen*, p. 468.

59. Fouché, *Dagboek Adam Tas*, p. 122; Bogaert, *Reizen*, p. 501—02; Anna J. Böeseken, *Simon van der Stel en sy kinders* (Cape Town, 1964), p. 183.

60. Journal of Hendrik Swellengrebel Jr (in preparation).

61. KA 4022, Generale Opneeminge der Vryluiden Gedoente en Effecten, 1700.

62. Fouché, *Dagboek Adam Tas,* pp. 10, 12; George McCall Theal, *History of South Africa before 1795* (Cape Town, 1964), III, 384, 386, 414.

63. Husing paid 10,300 guilders for the meat monopoly: Bogaert, *Reizen*, p. 478; Fouché, *Dagboek Adam Tas*, p. 154.

64. On Van der Heyden see Dominicus, *Het Ontslag*, p. 68.

65. It is going quite too far to say, as Fouché does (*Dagboek Adam Tas,* p. 8), that the resistance to Van der Stel was rooted in 'the most extreme hardship' suffered by his opponents. The behaviour of, for example, Van der Heyden in later years suggests other motives: *Res*, VII, 127.

66. Eric Walker, *The Frontier Tradition in South Africa* (London, 1930), p. 8; S.F.N. Gie, *Geskiedenis van Suid-Afrika of ons Verlede* (Stellenbosch, 1924), p. 137. Formulated better, the rebels wanted no constitutional changes; their main demands were economic. Theal (in *History of South Africa*, III, 451) supports Gie's view, but elsewhere contradicts him (*ibid.*, 444—45) by stating that this was a struggle for freedom.

67. It is not certain whether Corver's main opponent, Jeronimus de Haze, was related to Willem Adriaan's wife, Maria de Haze. See Johan E. Elias, *De vroedschap van Amsterdam* (Amsterdam, 1923); A. Porta, *Johan en Gerrit Corver* (Assen, 1975).

68. The middle decades of the eighteenth century — roughly the Swellengrebel and Tulbagh period — have been inadequately investigated. It is possible that the many wars of the time benefitted the Cape economy: 'Father Tulbagh' might owe his nickname to these benefits.

69. Fouché (*Dagboek Adam Tas*, pp. 364ff) correctly argues that Van der Stel was not a victim of his protective policies toward the Khoikhoi. It was not protection of Khoikhoi that was in contention, but the question of who would conduct the profitable trade with them.

70. There is no reason to separate such trekkers and hunters from the general population by labelling them 'riff-raff': Fouché, *Dagboek Adam Tas*, p. 244; Theal, *History of South Africa*, III, 416—17.

71. KA 4118, 4119, 4120; Theal, *Dokumenten, I*. For Barbier see also bibliography in *Suid-Afrikaanse Biografiese Woordeboek*, I, 54—55 and R.H. Pheiffer, 'Hernuwde aandag vir 'n verloopte Fransman: Tekste in gebroke Nederlands van Estienne Barbier', *Tydskrif vir Geesteswetenskappe*, XV (1975), pp. 34—93.

72. KA 4119, Governor and Council, 21 March 1739, p. 252v.
73. Theal, *Dokumenten,* I, 2.
74. Schutte, *Nederlandse Patriotten,* pp. 77, 84.
75. Investigation is needed into such complaints for the period up to and including the Great Trek.
76. Schutte, *Nederlandse Patriotten,* ch. 4, where primary and secondary sources are cited and information is given on the interest shown towards the Cape Patriots in the Netherlands. See also Beyers, *Patriotte* and *Kaapsche Stukken* (4 vols., VOC publication, 1785).
77. Schutte, *Nederlandse Patriotten,* pp. 61—62. I.L. Leeb, *The Ideological Origins of the Batavian Revolution* (The Hague, 1973).
78. See e.g. anon., *L'Afrique Hollandaise* (n.p., 1783); Schutte, *Nederlandse Patriotten,* pp. 78—82; Gerrit J. Schutte, 'Johannes Henricus Redelinghuys: een Revolutionair Kapenaar', *South African Historical Journal,* III (1971), pp. 49—62.
79. Pieter Geyl, 'Democratische tendenties in 1672', *Pennestrijd over staat en historie,* ed. Pieter Geyl (Groningen, 1971); Leeb, *Ideological Origins;* H.A. Wertheim and Gijse Weenink, *Democratische bewegingen in Gelderland* (Amsterdam, 1973); Pieter Geyl, *Revolutiedagen te Amsterdam, Aug.—Sept. 1748* (The Hague, 1936).
80. Schutte, 'Redelinghuys'.
81. Beyers, *Patriotte,* appendix E. Details on the origins of this petition are in the Swellengrebel archive (publication in preparation).
82. On the costs of the Cape during Van de Graaff's governorship see *Nieuwe Nederlandsche Jaarboeken,* 'Memorial of Falck, Craeyvanger and Scholten (1790)', pp. 1011—64.
83. AR, Nederburgh Collection, no. 531.
84. C.F.J. Muller, *Johannes Frederick Kirsten oor die toestand van die Kaapkolonie in 1795* (Pretoria, 1960), pp. 54—55.
85. Hermann B. Giliomee, *Die Kaap tydens die eerste Britse Bewind* (Cape Town, 1975), p. 31.
86. Leo Fouché, *Die Evolusie van die Trekboer* (Pretoria, 1909), p. 1; Scholtz, *Ontwikkeling,* p. 176.
87. Beyers, *Patriotte,* pp. 281—95.

The Cape under the transitional governments, 1795—1814[*]

William M. Freund

The transitional years, 1795—1814: An introduction

In September 1795 a British force took command at the Castle and put an end to almost 150 years of *VOC* rule. The Cape Colony was not in a position to defend itself against European invaders from overseas and perhaps not even from the Xhosa chiefdoms that lay to the east; yet despite its weakness and small population it had developed into a society with its own characteristic social forces. The development of the colony was only in part a direct result of the policies and wishes of the *Heren XVII*; the successor regimes would find, often to their disgust or to their cost, that the Cape social structure was sufficiently resilient and deeply rooted to defy administrative attempts at change.

The VOC regime, because of its venality and inability to provide the colonists with security or scope for enterprise, had no deep hold on their loyalties. Its weakness in the last years opened the possibility for revolt; yet, if the *freeburghers* had much to dispute with the VOC, it was also true that the VOC had endorsed their internal position as masters of thousands of slaves and landless servants. This fact would continue to lie at the heart of the relationship of the Cape freeburghers with the colonial regimes.

Between 1795 and 1814 the Cape Colony changed hands three times, finally coming permanently under the control of the British. These years may conveniently considered as a transitional period divided into three phases:

* While writing my dissertation, on which part of this chapter is based, I worked in the Algemeen Rijksarchief (The Hague), the Cape Archives (Cape Town), the Kerkargief (Cape Town), the London Missionary Society Archives (London) and the South African Public Library (Cape Town). I wish especially to thank the editors of this work for their painstaking and valuable criticisms of this chapter.

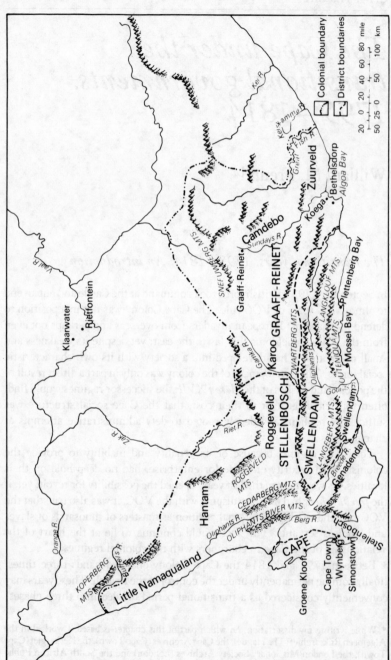

Figure 6.1 The colony in 1803

the first British occupation lasting from 1795 to 1803; the Batavian interlude when the Cape fell under the rule of the Batavian Republic that had been established in the Netherlands; and the second British occupation resulting from the reconquest of 1806.† The transitional period ended when the Dutch permanently ceded the Cape at the London Convention of 13 August 1814.

The first British occupation was a time of convulsive disorder at the Cape.[1] The frontier Khoikhoi rose twice in conjunction with the Xhosa (1799 and 1802) while the frontier settlers, already in revolt when the British took over, challenged the authority of the government again in 1799 and 1801 (see ch. 8 and ch. 9). Considerable hostility towards the British, marked by passive resistance, existed in the west as well. Consequently the British regime was authoritarian, in fact much more effectively so than the VOC had been in its final days. At the same time the British were not interested in transforming the Cape. British official opinion was divided on the question of retaining the colony, and ultimately the anti-retention party negotiated the return of the Cape to the Dutch by the treaty of Amiens.[2]

The Batavian interlude between 1803 and 1806 appears superficially to present a striking contrast to the first British occupation. Batavian policy aimed at making a real and permanent impact at the Cape. After the treaty of Amiens a specially appointed commissioner-general, J.A. de Mist, was sent out to the Cape to implement a memorandum, which he himself had written, proposing reforms that would make the colony both prosperous and orderly.[3] In fact, however, De Mist was prevented from accomplishing much, both by a lack of resources and by his need to preserve the shaky social order.

Many historians have extolled the Batavians.[4] De Mist has been seen as everything from an enlightened innovator to an inventor of apartheid. These writers have ignored both the extent to which the Batavian reform ideas were a continuation of the ideas expressed during the first British occupation and VOC times, and how little change the Batavians actually succeeded in bringing about at the Cape. George McCall Theal wrote that the Batavian school and church ordinances awoke a storm of protest at the Cape which was not yet ready for radical notions, but all evidence indicates that, to the extent that these ordinances were new, they were rather popular.[5] Both De Mist and Janssens were quickly disillusioned with the Cape and especially with its economic prospects. Neither advocated that the Dutch recover it after it fell to the British in 1806.

The years after 1806 were marked by a consolidation of British authority at

† For the reader's convenience I have appended to this chapter a chronology of major events in this period (p. 237).

the Cape. Although little structural change, even of the administration, could be envisaged until a formal treaty recognised British rule, home opposition to the retention of the Cape had dwindled. On the whole the post-1806 period was more stable and less conflict-ridden. Despite its importance for economic and social change, historians have generally paid much less attention to this phase than to its predecessors.[6]

If all three periods have their special characteristics, the transitional era as a whole exhibits considerable unity. In the problems they faced as well as in the solutions they considered, the early British governors and Batavians had much in common, and there is remarkable continuity in economic, social and administrative concerns throughout the period.

This continuity resulted from the essentially similar aims of the Cape's rulers: prosperity and order. The Cape, undercapitalised, sparsely populated and lacking decent transport, produced little for international trade. The colonial accounts were unbalanced and the currency unstable, yet in Europe the hope remained that successful policies could transform the Cape economy. The proposed remedies of the era, taken up and passed on from one administration to the next, were diverse. Yet the limited resources or commitments of the regimes did not allow for much innovation, and the economic problems of the Cape remained similar in 1814 to what they had been twenty years earlier.

In maintaining order the governments of the transitional era were more successful than the VOC had been in its last years. This was a period of consolidation of white control in the countryside. In the master-servant relationship the British and the Batavians intervened with increasing decisiveness on the side of the masters. Social control was also served by increased bureaucratization of an administration, the basic structure of which, however, was only gradually altered.

If one can regard this period as a whole from the vantage point of the rulers of the Cape, there is an even stronger justification for doing so from the perspective of the people of the Cape. Because of uncertainty about retaining the Cape (on the part of the British) and because of their limited financial resources, the colonial authorities did not succeed in dramatically altering the lives of South Africans. The larger social developments of the turn of the nineteenth century, notably the mission movement, developed at their own pace and not at one imposed from the Castle.

Our analysis will focus on broad themes covering the entire transitional period: firstly economic policy and economic change at the Cape; secondly, relations among masters, slaves and servants; thirdly, the impact of the missionaries on Cape society; and finally, the relationship between rulers and ruled.

Economic policy and economic change at the Cape

The economic structure of Cape life changed in some important respects during the era of transition, partly as the result of internal developments and partly of new administrative policies. Consequently by 1814 the Cape was ready to receive new impulses — notably the development of the wool trade — which would greatly increase its importance in world commerce.

As for the international linkages of the Cape economy, the most obvious change after 1795 was the development of a British trade connection. During the first British occupation, British shipping bearing British and Eastern manufactures quickly came to dominate Cape commerce.[7] After the Batavian interlude British merchants and shipping became even more important than before. Traders such as Alexander Tennant, Michael Hogan and John Murray had settled at the Cape after 1795 and gained ascendancy over foreign trade, largely because they had the commercial and financial connections in England and with British officials at the Cape that the older Cape merchants lacked. Those older entrepreneurs whose careers have been most carefully documented, D.G. van Reenen, J.F. Kirsten and W.S. van Ryneveld, all fared poorly under British rule.[8] There was thus a greater distance between officials and merchants in this period; the educated and wealthy Cape officials continued to serve in important positions because of their knowledge of local law, customs and language while a new, relatively small, group of British immigrants achieved commercial mastery. By the early 1820s W.W. Bird described the Cape traders as mainly agents for British firms.[9]

This was only one aspect of the incorporation of the Cape into the British imperial system, vastly larger and more dynamic than that of the VOC. The scale of trade increased greatly, although before 1814 the continued role of monopolist companies and restrictions on external and internal trade prevented any important development of local private enterprise. Under the first British occupation imports rose and a sharp inflation set in. In 1798 over one million rixdollars worth of British goods were brought to the Cape.[10] Thereafter, with the Cape market sated, trade took a downturn. These slow years were followed by the depressed Batavian period when the Cape was partially closed off to world commerce by the resumption of the Napoleonic wars.

Through its monopoly over Eastern trade and over the arms traffic, the English East India Company in many ways fulfilled the part which the VOC played in the commercial field until 1795. During the first British occupation one governor, Lord Macartney, sought to give it political power over the Cape as well. In actual fact the East India Company had little interest in the Cape apart from its fear of smugglers cutting into its monopolistic profits. It proved so ineffective at supplying the Cape with foodstuffs during bad harvests that the Cape government was henceforth obliged to contact authorities directly in India to ship badly needed rice to the Cape.[11] During the Batavian period most of the Eastern trade was officially in the hands of a monopoly run by the *Aziatische Raad*, a government agency that had both political and economic authority. However in practice, as a result of wartime conditions, neutral ships, particularly from Denmark and the United States, did most of the carrying trade.

After 1806 there was again a large increase in trade, notably in re-exported goods. According to Kantor's calculations, exports (together with re-exports) rose in value from 180,000 rixdollars in 1807 to 630,000 in 1811 and 1,320,000 in 1815, and imports increased correspondingly.[12] The increase in imports reflected the swollen size of the garrison, at its peak numbering 6,407 men — more than were stationed at Gibraltar or Malta[13] — and the presence of a growing number of highly paid British officials demanding British goods. British cotton manufactures were by far the most important imported item by 1813 while British iron and steel goods were increasing in value.[14]

The British had begun to free internal trade in 1795, but all the transitional governments continued to set the prices of staples and to tax produce entering Cape Town. Moreover, the *pachten*, or monopolistic farms — whose owners purchased from the government the sole rights to distribute valuable commodities, notably spirits — although under attack from the Batavian period onwards, were only very slowly replaced by licensing arrangements.[15] During the second occupation legislation gradually brought the Cape into the system of British imperial preferences, even though the English East India Company held on to most of its old prerogatives, only losing its Eastern trade monopoly (excluding tea) in 1815. By far the most important of these measures was the reduction of duty on Cape wines entering Britain in 1813. As a result the Cape could for the first time compete effectively with continental wine-growers in a foreign market. There followed an enormous increase in the production and export of wine. By 1822 Cape wine represented 10.4 per cent of the wine consumed in Britain.[16] Government revenues, devoted largely to official salaries and administrative expenses, grew rapidly in consequence.

The significance of these changing trade patterns emerges only in an analysis of the productive forces in Cape society. The Cape population grew rather substantially over this period, but overall increases mask two important shifts: the declining proportion of slaves and the declining proportion of people in the capital. That category of people labelled 'inhabitants' or 'Christians' in the census, which included free blacks as well as whites, grew from 22,000 in the relatively accurate count of 1798 to 37,000 in 1815. These figures are not exact but they indicate the general scale of growth. The number of 'Hottentots', by the same set of figures, grew from 14,000 to 17,000, but these are certainly underestimates and too inaccurate for the historian to formulate any conclusions from them. The slave population is recorded as growing from 25,000 to 30,000 between 1798 and 1815, although the last figure is definitely too low. Almost all the increase among slaves took place before the abolition of the slave trade in 1807.

Population trends were not uniform throughout the colony. In particular Cape Town grew far more slowly than outlying rural districts. Its population was estimated at 15,500 in 1798 and 15,600 in 1815. This was in part because so many slaves were sold to the country districts after 1807, but even the free population experienced only a moderate increase. By far the biggest population growth occurred in the east, especially in the Graaff-Reinet district. In 1798 the 'Christian' population there was counted as 4,262; in 1815, together with the now detached Uitenhage district, that total was 11,650. In the other rural districts it increased at rates of 25 to 50 per cent per decade.

In general, agricultural production seems to have increased, but not as rapidly as the population. Between 1795 and 1804 wine production doubled from 6,000 to 12,000 leaguers, doubtless affected by the demands of fleet and garrison; but thereafter decline set in. In 1813, an especially poor year, wine production was again below 7,000 leaguers. However, from this date there was a rapid increase.[17]

There was an overall, if uneven, increase in quantities of cereals grown at the Cape. In 1798, a good year for grain production, 138,000 *muiden* of wheat were grown and 44,000 brought to market; 186,000 muiden were grown in an excellent harvest in 1815 and 63,000 muiden brought to market. The remainder of the increase was absorbed by the expanding rural population. To compare good years, however, is to ignore the bad years when so little grain was brought to Cape Town that imports were required; this continued to happen throughout the transitional era and after. Grain was no more reliable as an export crop than it had been in earlier times. Shortages dashed the hopes — both of the British in 1795 and the Batavians in 1803 — that the Cape could be a granary for the East. Part of the increase in production which did occur took place in the eastern districts of Graaff-Reinet and Uitenhage, which grew only about 5 per cent of the colonial wheat in 1795 but about 15 per cent twenty years later.[18]

The census rolls show still greater variations in the livestock population, concentrated in the north and the east. Between 1798 and 1806, largely because of frontier wars, the number of cattle decreased considerably at the Cape, by perhaps 25 per cent overall. Thereafter the totals rose, surpassing the 1798 figures by 1815. Nevertheless this meant an overall decline in the number of cattle per household. By contrast the 1807 census roll indicated a considerable increase in the number of sheep over the preceding decade,[19] with the increase occurring in the eastern rather than the northern pastoral zones. The number of colonial sheep peaked in 1811, on the eve of the expulsion of the Xhosa from the Zuurveld, and thereafter declined as a result of losses in the Graaff-Reinet district. By 1815 there were somewhat fewer sheep per farmer than there had been twenty years before. Whether the quality of stock altered is difficult to ascertain.

Population growth was not coupled with significant expansion of colonial territory. The result was increasing pressure on land, a phenomenon that P.J. van der Merwe has dated to the end of the eastward movement of the *trekboers* around 1780.[20] Over the entire period the census roles show an increasing ratio of farmers to registered farms. It is not clear whether this had a severe effect on living standards. Farms could often provide a living for more than one family and were frequently subdivided informally, since loan farms could not legally be partitioned. There were definitely some areas where land-hunger was especially severe and an impoverishment of the population resulted. Such an area was the Baviaans River section where the Slachtersnek rebellion took place in 1815. This area was more populous at that date than it is today.[21] By 1813 some 2,000 applications for new loan farms had collected in the Castle, as many loan farms as were then in existence.

The loan farm system, the characteristic form of land tenure in outlying areas, was itself under attack during the transitional era. Critics of the system believed that it had encouraged the population to spread out so widely that the remoter countryside was ungovernable and prone to rebellion. They also feared that the cheapness of loan farm land discouraged capital investment and the development of a more productive agriculture. Finally there was the nagging issue of the annual rents which were invariably badly in arrears. Government attempts to improve collection played an important role in provoking the rebellions of 1795 and 1799 (see ch. 9, pp. 338–43).

But the loan farm system survived. Until 1806 both Governors Dundas and Janssens recognised that despite its flaws it functioned reasonably efficiently, especially on the cattle and sheep farms and in arid country. More commercially productive land tended to be converted to freehold voluntarily.

The second British occupation saw a renewed attack on the loan farm. On 6 August 1813 Governor Cradock issued a proclamation prohibiting the further granting of land in loan and created a mechanism to speed conversion into quitrent tenure which would prove more profitable to the government. Though the loan farms survived for a long period thereafter, the decree gradually had its effect; it became far more expensive for cattle boers to acquire new land and discriminated against the large number of squatters who were unable to apply for the purchase of land on which they were squatting. The 1813 proclamation contributed to the origins of the Slachtersnek rebellion and to an overall land squeeze that played a major role in bringing about the Great Trek. In the agrarian southwestern Cape the new policy had no effect as land had generally already been converted to other forms of tenure, suitable to more intensive land use.[22]

Though the end of the loan farm system caused some hardship, this was perhaps mitigated by the increasing prosperity of the eastern part of the colony. Despite the insecurity caused by war and rebellion, the east experienced a striking growth of population, grain production and ownership of slaves. Qualitative change was noticed by officials and visitors after 1806. In the northeast, especially in the Sneeuwberg, Tarka and Nieuwveld, farmers benefitted from the establishment of better relations with the 'Bushmen', increasing numbers of whom came to work on their farms.[23] Further south, travellers reported the growing wealth of the Camdebo and the resulting transformation of Graaff-Reinet after 1806 into a prosperous-looking village.[24] In the southeast, colonial policy culminating in the 1811—12 war did not succeed in reducing Xhosa raids or repopulating the Zuurveld with whites, but the war itself, by bringing a large garrison to the east, considerably stimulated agriculture and trade.[25] In 1812 the firm of Pohl and Company began direct exports from Algoa Bay: this was the beginning of improvements in transport and the general economic growth of the east that laid the foundations for the wool economy to come.

The export of wool was one of several administrators' dreams that did not achieve much substance before 1814. Merino sheep had first been introduced in VOC times. The Batavian Agricultural Commission tried to force farmers to pure-breed their sheep, but to little avail. Caledon's attempts to encourage the breeding of wool-bearing sheep also failed. The meat and fat products of the Cape sheep continued to be surer market commodities to the farmer than wool. Efforts to encourage the development of other potential exports at best met with indifferent success. The whale fisheries had many unproductive years and provided little scope for entrepreneurs, despite government attention and assistance. Somewhat more important was the increasing export of aloes for medicinal purposes, of hides and skins, and of ivory. However, none of these commodities remotely rivalled wine as an export. Nor did new, planned European settlements develop at the Cape despite a number of schemes suggested to this end.[26] During the transitional era, immigration from Europe continued as a steady trickle with a preponderance of ex-soldiers from the garrison.

The undercapitalised Cape economy rested upon the insecure foundation of the inconvertible rixdollar. The financial and monetary weakness of the Cape continued throughout the whole transitional era. Despite ensuing inflation, all the transitional administrations found it easiest to increase the supply of paper rixdollars and thus to encourage commerce and finance extraordinary government expenditure. When the regime was stable and the economy expanding, the reign of the rixdollar was in some ways advantageous. There is some evidence that prices for produce kept abreast of inflation in better times.[27] However, when the economy stagnated, lack of confidence in the currency, which lost half its exchange value over twenty years, continued to provoke serious crises.

The transitional economy, then, was characterised by certain changes of considerable significance: the development of the British connection, the gradual dismantling of monopolies, the increasing prosperity of the eastern districts, the growth of population, the smaller growth of agricultural production and (at the close of the period) the reduction of duties on wine imported to Britain, and the land tenure legislation of 1813. These changes were not sweeping or sudden; they came singly without building up to a quantum leap or visibly changing the overall economic pattern. The Cape was not yet transformed from an entrepot, essentially dependent on its marginal role in the Europe-Asia trade, to a colonial export economy. However, it was moving in this direction. It was perhaps indicative of the intensification of commercial activity that after 1806 the all-purpose Cape Town inn-emporia were gradually replaced by specialised hotels and shops.[28] By 1814 the Cape was far more ready than twenty years before to be engaged to new productive forces.

Masters, servants and slaves

The crucial social relationship in early Cape society was that between the free population and a subordinate majority of slaves and servants. The indigenous population of the Cape, although not enslaved, had, in losing their lands and herds, effectively lost their freedom. It was they rather than the slave population who posed a crisis of order for the transitional regimes, a crisis which focused in the border regions of the colony and which is discussed later in this volume (ch. 8, p. 310). The British, in order to forge some sort of peace that would restore the cattle and sheep economy, were obliged to come to grips with the master-servant relationship in the colony. For the next decade the evolution of a policy governing this relationship was a major administrative priority.

By contrast the slaves remained a docile force in Cape society. The one slave rising of the era, which took place in 1808, was not sufficiently serious to challenge colonial authority. The most important change came in the increasing European criticism of the slave trade, leading to its abolition in 1807. The institution of slavery, however, survived intact throughout the period.

European administrators and those Cape officials who worked for them during this period (Van Ryneveld, Van Reenen, Stockenstrom, Maynier) had mixed and often contradictory feelings about the condition of slaves and servants. On the one hand the complaints of the servants were clearly not without justification, and slavery increasingly seemed a socially noxious and economically deleterious institution. On the other hand the colonial order rested on an economic basis of rigid labour subordination and on the political cooperation of the white masters who effectively controlled the means of production. The solution was to find a balanced policy between master and servant; but as the threat of rebellion gradually diminished on all sides, the ideal balance in the official mind increasingly lay in strong support for the white farmer with some protection for the servant and some mitigation of abuses for the slave.

The most powerful argument for better treatment which the servant offered the government was the rebellion of 1799 (ch. 8, pp. 310 ff.). General Dundas negotiated a truce with the rebels which did not oblige them to return to work for the farmers and which granted land to several of their leaders, including the famous Stuurman brothers. At the same time, in order to encourage the re-establishment of the eastern farms, returning servants were offered a contractual system of employment. The contract had to be signed by both employer and employee in the presence of the *landdrost* and it could not be fixed for a period of over a year.[29]

The Batavian government was more hostile than Dundas to the maintenance of any autonomy by the Khoikhoi. It stressed the need to get the Khoikhoi back to the farms. The Batavian contract system, established in 1803, was more weighted towards masters as opposed to servants than its British predecessor. Surviving contracts show that there were violations of the one year maximum; moreover field-cornets, themselves local employers, were now authorised to approve contracts.

During the second British occupation, government policy was further refined and developed. Memories of rebellion began to recede and, once the French had been driven from Mauritius in 1810 and a large garrison sat idle in Cape Town, the government acted with more energy and force on the frontier than before. The new British authorities stood for a policy of rigidly subordinating the servants while also protecting them against contractual abuses; this policy was epitomised in the Hottentot Proclamation of 1809, the institution of circuit courts in 1811, and the apprenticeship legislation of 1812. Caledon and Cradock also moved against the last remaining independent kraals at the Cape, turning several of them into mission stations.

The new legislation enabled fair-minded magistrates like the Stockenstroms to eliminate the most brutal abuses of the labour system, but it entrenched the position of the servants as landless labourers with no opportunity for independence or advancement.[30] Travellers in the second and third decades of the nineteenth century, such as Campbell, Latrobe and Burchell, all recorded the continued frequency of contract abuse. The judicial and administrative organisation of the colony could hardly alter this, for it consisted of white officials, judges and advocates who condoned the use of corporal punishment by employers and strongly disliked imposing harsh sentences on whites in disputes involving slaves or Khoikhoi. Furthermore its effectiveness was limited by its reliance on the pivotal role of the field-cornets.[31]

A special feature of the government's policy towards masters and servants was the maintenance throughout the transitional period of the Hottentot Corps. The corps, founded in the last days of the VOC, was expanded and strengthened after 1795 with the specific intention of posing a counterweight to the suspect freeburgher population.[32] The Batavians wished at first to dismantle it, but after the outbreak of war in Europe in 1803 they recruited so actively that the corps resembled a forced labour venture. There was renewed expansion and contraction after the British reconquest. Although loyal both to the Batavians in 1806 and to the British in 1811–12, the Khoikhoi soldiers disliked army service when it entailed separation from their families, and there is some evidence that they resented recruitment.[33] The white farmers opposed the corps because it cut into their labour supply and because it was potentially a stick which the British and Batavians could use to beat them. Yet from 1803 the corps was increasingly intended for use not against rebellious whites but against Khoikhoi and Xhosa as well as potential foreign foes. The corps was thus no real escape from the master-servant nexus at the Cape and served rather to reinforce it.

Slavery was an essential feature of Cape society in 1795, slaves forming the largest sector of the population. The transitional era witnessed an increasing outcry in Europe against the slave trade and the social effects of slavery which posed a challenge to its continued existence. Yet colonial administrators on the whole agreed with Governor Janssens that 'the abolition of slavery in South Africa would overturn all property and leave the colony [in misery], possibly irredeemably.'[34] Pressure to end the slave trade came from outside. Both during the first British occupation and the Batavian period the home authorities weighed the future of the trade and put temporary or partial checks on it.

During the first decade after 1795 perhaps only 3,000 slaves were imported to the Cape (2,000 during the first British occupation, more than 1,000 during the Batavian period) mainly from Mozambique; and the price of slaves consequently climbed steeply.[35] In 1808 the abolition of the slave trade in the British Empire took effect at the Cape. The slave population, heavily unbalanced in favour of adult males, had according to the census rolls climbed from 25,000 in 1798 to nearly 30,000 in 1806. After abolition of the trade it grew very slightly, if at all, in the next decade. (The 1817 count of 32,046 seems not far from accurate.) Slaves ceased to be the largest element in the population from 1810 and ceased to form a majority in Cape Town from 1815.

Slave labour declined in the non-agricultural sector of the economy. In the capital, where slaves were often owned for speculative purposes, hired out as artisans, or used for exclusively domestic tasks, their population shrank by some 2,000 (or more than 20 per cent) between 1806 and 1815. Slaves were increasingly sold up-country to farmers, where their numbers increased especially in the more outlying areas, although the bulk continued to live in the southwestern Cape.[36] By this means the population in the agricultural economy continued to grow reasonably rapidly and the Cape economy managed to weather the new situation.

After 1808 labour needs in town were partly filled by the prize Negroes brought to the Cape from slave vessels captured by the Royal Navy.[37] Prize Negroes could be apprenticed to employers for fourteen years, although the government was supposed to ensure their decent treatment. With the growth of the apprentice and free black population, especially in Cape Town, the overall trend in the west, even before 1815, was away from slavery to free labour: in 1806 the slaves had constituted about 85 per cent of the population considered non-European in Cape Town; in 1817 perhaps only 70 per cent. Most manumissions also took place in Cape Town (92 per cent of the 1,245 manumissions between 1815 and 1830.)[38]

In 1812, on the advice of the Rev. M.C. Vos, Governor Cradock abolished the VOC statute forbidding the sale of Christian slaves. This was done largely to facilitate the conversion of more slaves to Christianity, which the statute had hindered. The following year the government limited to thirty-nine the number of lashes a slave could receive in punishment; this was the beginning of ameliorative legislation for slaves that would continue until the final abolition of slavery twenty years later. In 1797 the British eliminated the more brutal forms of torture used on suspected and convicted criminals; this reform, which was introduced despite opposition from local officials, was probably for slaves the most beneficial consequence of British rule before 1815.[39]

The one slave rising of consequence during the transitional period came in response to the hopes that were aroused among slaves by the abolition of the slave trade. The 1808 rising began in the Zwartland where its leader, Louis, had contacts. Louis was a Cape Town slave born in Mauritius, light enough to pass for white. He led a band of slaves south towards Cape Town where they hoped the governor would announce their freedom. After they had caused some damage to property but little physical harm, they were met by a government force and disarmed. Severe punishments and the execution of five leaders followed. The remainder of the slaves were returned to their masters. Unlike the handful of original plotters, who genuinely hoped to overthrow the social order, most of the slaves had expected a benign government to confirm the rumours of coming freedom. The initial conspiracy had involved two Irishmen, both of whom abandoned the slaves before the rising had begun and one of whom became a witness for the prosecution; several 'Hottentot' servants also participated.

During the 1795–1814 era the inequities of the Cape social system were sharply attacked not only by missionaries and private travellers but by high officials. Yet the colonial order had become reliant over a century on the strict subordination of labour. The British achievement of gaining the support of the white population by 1815 was an enormous one, and suppressing qualms about the inequities of the system seemed a moderate price to pay for it. As long as the servants and the slaves could not themselves challenge their treatment, retention of the status quo was certainly the cheapest and easiest way for the colonial regime to function. As a result the transitional era, which began with a severe crisis of master-servant relations, ended in powerfully confirming the existing order.

The coming of the missionary

The transitional era marked the beginning of the age of the missionary at the Cape. In 1795 mission activity consisted of the newly refounded Moravian settlement at Baviaanskloof and some local preaching. Over the next two decades the mission field vastly expanded. The London Missionary Society (LMS) began work in 1799 and in 1803 established its first permanent settlement at Bethelsdorp on the Eastern Frontier. Under the guidance of Johannes Theodorus van der Kemp, a Dutchman, Bethelsdorp served as a focal point for mission protest against government policies towards the Khoikhoi and the Xhosa. Other LMS missionaries — British, German and Dutch — worked beyond the Northern Frontier and established settlements in the colony at Zuurbraak (1812), Hoogekraal (1813) and Theopolis (1814).[40] Cape colonists themselves organised the South African Missionary Society in 1799 with the assistance of Van der Kemp and J.J. Kicherer. As a result of secessions, separate mission societies were later formed in Stellenbosch and Paarl. The South African society had gained a membership of several hundred within a few years and supported a wide range of mission activities, mainly within the colonial borders, founding no special settlements. Finally, the Moravian Brethren continued to direct the establishment at Baviaanskloof (renamed Genadendal in 1805), the largest colonial institution, and founded a second station at Groene Kloof in 1808. By 1815 more than 2,500 Khoikhoi and others were affiliated to missionary settlements while thousands of servants and slaves had come into contact with them.

To the extent that they created new communities, the missionaries represented a threat to Cape employers that their labourers would desert them and find champions for their grievances. As a result, despite widespread belief that Christians must work for the conversion of the heathen, the mission stations evoked much opposition among employers. Moreover the government, increasingly anxious to support the farmers, came into conflict with the missionaries. At the same time both government and employers could appreciate the advantage for the colony if the mission stations could add to the stability of the social order. As a result of these ambiguous attitudes, phases of cooperation between government and missionaries were juxtaposed with phases of conflict.

The missionaries themselves differed in their attitudes towards politics. The Moravians were not insensitive to the difficulties faced by the Khoikhoi and indeed met with enormous hostility from local farmers in the first decade after they returned to the Cape in 1792. Yet they had a tradition of quietism toward secular power and an authoritarian, paternalistic attitude to their flock that enabled them to settle down within the confines of Cape society and government policy. H.R. van Lier, the Cape pastor who really inspired the local mission movement, and his influential associate, M.C. Vos, believed that the concern of missionaries was exclusively with the spiritual life and not the social condition of the slaves to whom they preached. Even among the LMS missionaries most, like J.J. Kicherer or the Englishman, William Anderson, were hardly social critics. By contrast, Van der Kemp and Read fought against administrative demands for unpaid corvée and military labour, for the right to preach to whom they willed, and against the enforcement of contractual obligations made under duress or false pretences. Van der Kemp championed the cause of the Khoikhoi on the Eastern Frontier and strongly opposed slavery. He married the daughter of a Malagasy slave woman in the belief that a missionary should throw in his lot with the people he was trying to convert.[41] Van der Kemp's opposition to the master-servant system was further developed by John Philip and continued as a critical tradition into the twentieth century.

Officials of the first British occupation originally favoured the missionaries in the hope that they could prove effective intermediaries with the Xhosa and the rebel Khoikhoi.‡ Van der Kemp played a major role in this capacity. Support for him diminished towards the end of the period as he became more hostile to the labour system in the east, although no real confrontation took place before 1803. At the same time the neat Moravian settlement of Genadendal, with a more cooperative attitude toward the authorities, won official approbation.

The Batavians held similar hopes that missionaries would support their politics of stability and made the grant of Bethelsdorp to Van der Kemp. However, they soon turned sharply against the missions, partly because of their mistrust of the LMS link to Britain, partly because of the hostility of the established Reformed ministers to 'enthusiastic' preaching and, above all, because they resented resistance to their labour policies. Van der Kemp was forced to leave Bethelsdorp in 1805 and Janssens hoped to ban mission activity, including that of colonists, entirely. Again, however, the Moravians were exempted from government disapproval.

After 1806 clashes between the British administration and the missions continued. Acrimonious relations between Colonel Jacob Glen Cuyler, the *landdrost* of Uitenhage, and Van der Kemp led the Bethelsdorp missionaries to appeal over the heads of the Cape administration to Britain for help in ensuring juster treatment for their charges. As a result the Cape government instituted the so-called Black Circuit of 1812, which vindicated many of the accused colonists but showed the potential influence which missionaries could wield in a colonial cause. Other signs of hostility during the second occupation were the continually voiced suspicion that the Orange River missionaries harboured runaway slaves and servants, and the opposition by Cradock and Lord Somerset to the Groene Kloof mission, which they would have preferred as a country residence for themselves.

At the same time British government officials to an increasing extent saw the value of the mission institutions as fixed locations from which the Khoikhoi could emerge to work for farmers. They also valued them as a means of blunting the disaffection of servants, at least as long as the

‡ With the notable exception of Governor Yonge, who was extremely hostile to missionaries.

missionaries did not overtly challenge the administration. Government priorities became central to the planning of new mission stations. Groene Kloof was founded in 1808 by the Moravians on the invitation of Lord Caledon despite the opposition of Hans Klapmuts, the still independent captain and Hottentot Corps veteran on whose kraal the institution was established.[42] Zuurbraak and Hoogekraal were also founded on the sites of some of the last surviving independent kraals in the colony; Hoogekraal especially was intended by the government as a labour reserve to serve farmers in a poor stretch of countryside.[43] Theopolis was placed near the eastern border in order to establish colonial security at a strategic point where white farmers feared to settle. By 1815 the mission stations were surviving and, despite some underlying tensions, had come to terms with the colonial government.

The mission stations and the mission movement had a profound influence on Khoikhoi society. Between 1795 and 1815 thousands became Christians. During this period conversions at Bethelsdorp, at first on a small scale, became numerous, while most residents of Genadendal, the oldest institution, were baptised by 1815. The intensity of the converts' zeal was often striking. Bethelsdorp in particular spawned numerous preachers from an early date.

Christianization went hand in hand with the destruction of the older Khoikhoi culture. William Burchell's travels, published in the 1820s, described baptised Khoikhoi who refused to eat zebra meat — a prejudice he believed derived from Europeans — and others who looked down on the 'Hottentotten'. Burchell also noted adult Khoikhoi (not 'Bastaards') in the Graaff-Reinet district who could speak no language but Dutch.[44] This new class that despised its 'Hottentot' roots was on its way to becoming what would later be called the Cape Coloured people. As the last Khoikhoi kraals were replaced by mission stations or broken up, the remains of Khoikhoi political and cultural independence dissolved.

The South African Society (SAS) worked primarily with slaves and free blacks. Their work flourished, but on a smaller scale than that in the mission settlements. The administration supported the SAS partly because it feared the spread of Islam. Increasing numbers of slaves and free blacks were baptised in the Reformed and Lutheran churches, and their conversion facilitated their adoption of the dominant European culture of the colony.

The conversion of slaves and servants to both the European's religion and to his ways did not provide them with a higher status at the Cape. Despite the efforts of Van der Kemp and Read, the missionaries were rather ineffective at challenging the treatment of labourers in Cape society. None of the mission stations in the colony was big enough or productive enough to provide its inhabitants with much of a livelihood. Genadendal was fairly fertile but small; the Moravians favoured communal labour under the supervision of the missionaries, thus discouraging any initiative from the people. Moreover, their land was unsuitable for livestock. Bethelsdorp was far poorer; cattle and sheep only flourished in the better years, while cultivation was impossible.

In general, adult male inhabitants of the mission stations had to support themselves and their families by going to work for the colonial farmers: for example, the census of 1 April 1813 recorded only 94 adult males among Bethelsdorp's 608 residents.[45] The principal alternative lay in the practice of crafts or some other kind of enterprise. At Genadendal the Khoikhoi made high-quality knives which were widely used in the colony, but this enterprise was entirely under mission direction. Bethelsdorp, despite its less pre-possessing appearance, was a far more active centre for artisans and transporters, especially after the establishment of a large garrison at nearby Fort Frederick.[46]

The really new features in the mission movement for Cape society were the incentive provided to Khoisan cultural assimilation and the thread of articulate protest first picked up by Van der Kemp. Yet the mission establishments also served to mute protest. Unable to alter the course of labour relations at the Cape, the mission stations became palliatives that sweetened the bitter pill of social subordination for the Khoikhoi. On the station a family could live in domestic peace, somewhat sheltered from the harsh conditions of life outside, while it acquired cultural attributes of the dominant colonial society. On a small and crude scale, the mission Khoikhoi were anticipating the lives of millions of Africans in the reserve system of a future industrialised South Africa.

Ruler and ruled at the Cape

After a fairly detailed examination of the attitude of the transitional administrations to economic development and labour relations at the Cape, we should now consider their general philosophy of colonial rule. British as well as Batavian governors were influenced by Enlightenment thinking which, above all, favoured the formation of a new sense of community and the destruction of ancient barriers of caste and estate. Linked to this was the new secularism, the cult of the energetic and enlightened ruler, a growing concern with technical efficiency in economic and administrative activities, and the ideal of an informed and loyal citizenry. Two factors modified the application of Enlightenment ideas at the Cape: the inherently extractive nature of the colonial relationship in which the colony existed for the benefit of the European government,¶ and the inhibiting influence of the counter-revolution of the 1790s, concerned with combating the pull of events in France, the United States and Haiti.

At the Cape the means at hand for altering the nature of society were limited. The government had little money to spend on economic improvements or education. Above all, and especially while the war continued in Europe, the social order was too delicately poised for administrators to dare to initiate sweeping, perhaps unpopular, changes. Their very first priority was to preserve tranquility and so avoid any large expenditure of money and effort on South African affairs. The Batavians were especially hampered by limited funds as well as a fear, ultimately justified, of renewed attack from the sea. De Mist was the most explicitly reforming administrator at the Cape during the transitional era and for this reason his quick retreat into an acceptance of local conditions was especially striking. Particularly before 1803 the British did not act decisively because their legal control over the colony remained uncertain and their commitment to retaining it was not yet total. Even after the reconquest the home government urged avoidance of fundamental changes for this reason. Anglicisation of the law and the official use of the English language had hardly begun before 1814, although General Grey and Governor Cradock had started to talk about changes along these lines.

Moreover, during the second occupation civil peace, the quickening economic tempo, and increasing closeness of view between the British and the white farmers on master-servant relations and frontier security, greatly blunted the critical acuity that had earlier characterised administrators' attitudes to the colony and the VOC system. By 1814 administrative dispatches had become self-satisfied and conventional compared to the crisis-ridden hand-wringings of the first occupation and Batavian times.

On the whole administrative forms did not alter greatly between 1795 and 1814. Two tendencies, however, stand out: a growth of professionalism in government, and continuing adamant opposition to a greater representative role for colonists. The first tendency resulted in a significant but measured advance before 1814; the second accorded perfectly with the administrators' authoritarian inclinations and their fear of radical ideas originating in the French Revolution.

In 1797 the British raised official salaries and created some where none had existed before; they also suppressed certain perquisites which had formerly been the principal income of officials. These important innovations were

¶ As Janssens put it, 'Members of the government must realize, and have before their eyes always [the fact] that the Colony exists for the sake of the Republic, not the Republic for the sake of the Colony', Batavian Republic Inventory, 11, Janssens—Raad van Politie, 23 April 1805, p. 1347, my translation.

designed to stamp out the corruption associated with the VOC administration. Officials brought out from England were paid handsomely in pounds rather than in rixdollars; henceforth official salaries became by far the largest item in government expenditures. During the first British occupation there was a major scandal involving favouritism which in 1801 led to the recall of Governor Yonge. In the long run, however, the calibre of officials improved; most of the major transitional administrators such as De Mist, Janssens, Cradock and Caledon were honest and set an example for improving standards.

In his memorandum De Mist promised a further advance in professionalism and greater inclusion of colonists in the administration. His most lasting reform in the first direction was the introduction of several Dutch graduate lawyers into the Council of Justice. He also created a central accounting office, the *Rekenkamer,* which was however eliminated by Janssens in 1805. De Mist's second promise was not kept. The number of Cape-born officials tended to decrease rather than increase during the Batavian period, and De Mist's original intention of making the Burgher Council or *Burgerraad*** elective was quietly dropped.

After 1806 the number of British civil servants at the Cape increased steadily, perhaps somewhat at the expense of the old official class. Yet the official class, because of its command of Dutch and knowledge of local conditions, continued to play a crucial role before 1815. Its most prominent member until his death in 1812 was Willem Stephanus van Ryneveld, who served the British as fiscal. Van Ryneveld's reports on social and economic conditions still read impressively today. Local officials continued to monopolise other offices, but as we have seen above their economic position was in good part usurped by a new group of British merchants.

The Burgher Senate remained an appointive body, and the governments, both British and Batavian, sought to reduce its functions more or less to those of a municipal council. Members continued to petition the government in the name of the colonial population and thus claimed for the Senate a representative role. Their petitions, however, tended to be turned down with the advice that senators should confine themselves to narrower tasks which lay within their legitimate sphere.[47]

In the transitional era the power of the governors over the colonists expanded beyond what it had been in VOC times. Under the British and the Batavians there was no longer a *secunde* (lieutenant governor) nor a fiscal (prosecutor) independent of the governor and his council. (The fiscal's independence had in any event been largely curtailed after the Nederburgh-

** Renamed the Burgher Senate by the British and *Raad der Gemeente* by the Batavians.

Frykenius mission to the Cape in 1792—93). Furthermore, the VOC officials in Batavia no longer remained as countervalent influences to the governor and the company regime in Holland. The Council of Policy was abolished by the first British occupation; the Batavians restored it, but for most of their administration its membership consisted entirely of Hollanders. There were numerous limitations on the power of British governors, notably the division of civil and military jurisdictions before 1811 and the possibility that colonists could exert influence on the Colonial Office in Britain, as the missionaries attempted to do. Yet for most Cape colonists, who had no friends or associates in Britain, these avenues were not of much use. Nor was the Batavian period a democratic interval. Between 1804 and 1806 Governor Janssens moved in a more and more authoritarian and centralising direction, regarding his role as that of a viceroy with responsibility exclusively to his home office and with no check on his will in the colony. The British governors were content that local influences, if present at all, should be mediated through a few trusted officials such as Van Ryneveld.

In the countryside the administrative system changed even less. There was a striking continuity of office-holders, particularly at the level of the field-cornets. The landdrosts continued to be selected from the Cape Town elite while the local farmers played their crucial role as *heemraden* and as field-cornets. Before 1814 no British officials served in these offices, apart from the landdrost of Uitenhage, Colonel Cuyler, a Dutch-speaking military officer born in New York. However, the formal duties of local officials were codified with increasing precision, notably in the 1797 ordinance for *veldwacht-meesters* and in the 1805 ordinance for the administration of outlying areas.

There was some intensification of central authority through the creation of new districts and sub-districts. In 1804 the Batavian regime formed two districts to encompass the northwestern and southeastern frontier zones, with headquarters at Tulbagh and Uitenhage respectively. In 1808 a new district was created in eastern Swellendam, centred on George. During the second British occupation five subdistricts were established by 1814. In the countryside there were as a result more administrators directly responsible to the Castle, which thus gained a closer control over local circumstances. The churches and schools which were built in the new *drostdies* also spread commercial and 'civilising' influences which the government viewed with favour. Another reform that had the same tendency was the institution of the circuit court in 1811. This deepening of central government influence played a role in the apparent extinction of the rebellious embers that had flared up between 1795 and 1801.

The British were slow to introduce legal changes at the Cape. They made only a beginning in modifying Cape law to conform to imperial models.[48] The growing British community, however, was subject to British law, an inconsistency which occasioned nagging disputes. This legal continuity further retarded social change during the transitional period.

The governments of the transitional period were concerned with transforming the population into a more orderly, more loyal, more enlightened citizenry: this was to be done by means of formal education. In 1795 the Cape educational system was weak. Though there were numerous small schools in Cape Town, they were quite uncoordinated with each other, and there was no secondary education outside the feeble Latin School. In the countryside, education was largely in the hands of wandering tutors, often demissioned soldiers. There were virtually no schools, and illiteracy was fairly common among whites and the norm among slaves and servants. From the first British occupation onwards the administration became increasingly concerned about improving the quality of education. This was especially true of the Batavians, who frequently wrote about the problem and promulgated the *Schoolorde* of 1805. The Schoolorde attempted to systematize the colonial education structure and created a school commission consisting of officials and ministers to preside over education matters. The second British occupation saw further advances, notably the establishment in 1812 of local Bible and school committees that began to further education in the countryside.

According to Theal the Schoolorde was deeply resented at the Cape, because it was seen as an attempt to dragoon the pious citizenry into secular schools which emitted unwelcome Enlightenment propaganda. Actually there is no record of such resentment. Advances in formal education were welcomed by the local population, even in remote areas, and the Schoolorde largely continued the tradition of church-state collaboration which was typical of education under the VOC and in contemporary Dutch society generally. The principal brake on educational improvements was financial: the colonial governments were unable or unwilling to set aside much money for schools. The second part of the Schoolorde, dealing with financial regulations, was never issued: the Batavian government had learned through various protests that new taxes for education would be most unwelcome.

Yet education moved forward in fits and starts with general government approbation. During this era the 'Tot Nut van het Algemeen' school, the first good private school in Cape Town, was established and supported by well-to-do Cape officials and merchants. The real inspiration behind the 'Tot Nut' society was H.A. Vermaak who, as a Patriot, spent the years of the first British occupation in Holland and was much impressed with the work of the Dutch parent society, an important Enlightenment institution. In 1813 the Cape Town Free School for the needy was founded, and before the end of 1814 it was educating over 200 students of both sexes and all races.[49] Outside the capital little schools sprang up in the country villages while missionaries had an educational impact on slaves and other brown and black peoples. In 1803 the Batavians, afraid of this impact, had forbidden mission stations to teach reading and writing; however, this decree, which remained in force after the British re-conquest, was in practice ignored.

Even as late as 1814 formal education at the Cape was unimpressive. Facilities for rural children were still rare and the population mostly lived far from any urban centre. More crucially, given the hopes of the colonial regimes, no elite institutions had been created that functioned effectively as socialising agents. De Mist's model of such an institution, a secondary school for the training of teachers and officials, firmly reflecting Batavian ideals and prerogatives, was reluctantly dismissed by the school commission as an impossibly expensive and visionary proposal, at least at the time. Certain British officials of the second occupation, notably General Grey and Governor Cradock, wanted to further the use of English by means of the schools. Yet they had not progressed very far before 1814. By that time British children attended separate English-medium schools; to an increasing extent the other schools taught English as a subject, but they were not yet seriously used as instruments for Anglicisation.[50]

The Cape press was created during the transitional era to serve an educative purpose. The *Cape Gazette*, a government organ, was founded in 1800 and continued to operate throughout the period as the only Cape newspaper. It was a dull sheet which, apart from commercial advertisements, consisted mainly of government exhortations and announcements. Both the British and the Batavians were hostile to the notion of a free press and thus banned private printing. Their attitude to the press sharply reflected the view that education should set youth on a road that led in but one direction — towards loyalty and better performance of duty within the colonial order.

How successful were the transitional administrations in transforming the Cape population into the desired loyal citizenry? Administrative priorities and limited finances would obviously prevent ambitious schemes for social reformation from getting very far. At the same time, however, there was a strong evolution between 1795 and 1814 of a more positive feeling on the part of the authorities towards the dominant freeburgher class. During the first British occupation the regime feared rebellion, and officials such as Barrow had a low opinion of all but the most distinguished and Anglophile civil servants at the Cape. This antagonism dwindled considerably during the Batavian period and virtually disappeared during the second British occupation. Contrasting with Barrow's hostile view is the far more sympathetic commentary of Hinrich Lichtenstein, the most distinguished official traveller and commentator of Batavian times, and the even more pro-colonist views of

Colonel Collins, perhaps the most influential British official of the first decade of the second occupation.

The colonists, although disaffected with the VOC, did not greet the British with much warmth in 1795. During the first British occupation there remained a large number of Dutch sympathisers at the colony, including pockets of Patriot supporters who were labelled Jacobins by the British and their colonial opponents. There were incidents of sabotage, refusal or reluctance to take the British oath of loyalty and other acts of passive resistance. That acute observer, Lady Anne Barnard, saw little loyalty to the British developing before 1803. During the same period rebellion broke out on the Eastern Frontier on three occasions. However, the British proved more able and determined than the VOC in stifling protest and enforcing compliance.

Relations between the Batavians and the colonists were better. In the southwest, resistance to Batavian rule was insignificant and no further rebellions took place in the east. At the same time the regime kept a tight grip on the population and was suspicious of popular loyalties.

The first decade of renewed British rule was even more placid. Little resistance took place; the Patriot flames had apparently died down and the last of the eastern rebellions, that of Slachtersnek in 1815, was by far the least serious and the most easily contained (see. ch. 9, p. 348).[51] Part of this conciliation came about because the British ever more clearly espoused the cause of employers and slave-owners and because they were won over to the views of frontier farmers on Xhosa policy. Partly, too, it was the result of British strength. Throughout the transitional era thousands of European troops were stationed at the Cape, a very formidable force to the small colonial population of the day. Serious military action against the British was not feasible, especially once the possibility of a French attack on the Cape was removed by the British conquest of the Mascarene islands (Mauritius and Réunion) in 1810. The greater prosperity of the period after 1806 also soothed rebellious spirits. So, too, did the fact that while the British brought to the Cape new ways, a new language and a new church, their policy before 1815 was quite conciliatory on cultural matters and they showed little inclination to impose change beyond the purview of the Castle.

Helping to adjust the population to the changes in rule were the high officials and prominent merchants of Cape Town. A few, such as H.A. Vermaak or the Van Reenen family, were genuinely Patriot and anti-British but, in general, partisan divisions merely reflected family feuds and rivalries. These citizens gave their loyalty either to the British or Dutch in their role as keepers of order, holders of economic privilege and employers of bureaucrats. As J.J. Oberholster has written about the reaction of the Burgher Senate to the British re-conquest of 1806:

> So complete was the continuity of the Burgher Senate, that no interruption took place in its sessions. From the arrival of the British fleet on January 4 to January 10, the day Cape Town was occupied, the Burgher Senate sat day after day to support Janssens in his war operations; from January 10 to January 18, the day Janssens capitulated, they held daily sessions to help provide the necessary wagons and horses for the English.[52]

During the transitional period a growing alienation between church and state took place. The British interfered very little with the Reformed church during their first occupation. By contrast the Batavians were much concerned with church organisation and reorganisation. They extended toleration for Christians outside the Reformed church and in the *Kerkorde* of 1804 provided for a new and more self-supporting church administration. Despite assertions by Theal and others, contemporary evidence shows a great deal of support by church boards and ministers for the Kerkorde. In fact the new role of the state in education and the solemnisation of marriages did not signally differ from VOC tradition, and ministers welcomed Batavian financial assistance. After 1806, however, the continued role of the government in church affairs was resented because the government was no longer in the hands of Reformed church members. Extensive controversy developed over British insistence on helping to select deacons (despite the fact that this was no longer required by the Batavian Kerkorde), and over the interference of the *Commissaris-politiek*, the government representative in church affairs.[53]

To the majority of the colonial population, the slaves and servants, the various transfers of power meant relatively little. The Khoikhoi responded positively to the rather open policies of General Dundas towards the rebels of 1799 and to British attempts to use the Khoikhoi as a lever against whites. There are a few indications that Khoikhoi regretted the Batavian take-over in 1803 and that they had high hopes when the British returned in 1806; however, these hopes were dashed when the British sided increasingly with white farmers. What is known of the slave rebellion of 1808 hints at the expectations the British must have aroused among slaves by abolishing the slave trade. On the whole, however, the increasing tendency of the transitional administrations to maintain the status quo prevented any change in role for the slaves or servants.

By 1815 the relationship of ruler to ruled had once more settled into a stable pattern. Part of the special interest of the earlier years of the transitional period lies in the instability of this relationship: the British and the Batavians were initially suspicious of the existing order. Critical reports questioned, or at least discussed from an outsider's point of view, fundamental social institutions, while the regimes seemed to require substantial reforms in order to meet their goals. Yet without important reforms the new colonial administrations were able to cement a firm working arrangement with the dominant class at the Cape and to reaffirm the essentials of the Cape social structure as it had developed before 1795.

Conclusion

The era of transition began in a time of crisis and conflict in Cape society; gradually the crisis dissipated and calm was restored. On the whole the recreated order was not the result of bold reforms by the government nor of dramatic social transformation. The reformist impulse which figured in the schemes of Governor Yonge and Sir John Barrow, or of De Mist and officials such as Alberti or Van Ryneveld, declined markedly after 1806. Changes in Cape institutions, whether educational, administrative or legal, came slowly.

The slack pace of change in the transitional period, and the continuation of social process from VOC times, makes it fitting to include the period in this volume. On the whole the next twenty years of Cape history, which would encompass the beginnings of the Great Trek, the coming of the 1820 settlers, the rise of the wool industry, Ordinance 50, the abolition of slavery, the full onslaught of Anglicisation and the buildup of conflict with Xhosa on the far side of the Fish River, is both a more dramatic era and one that made a far more emphatic break with the past. Nevertheless, the transitional period was not without change, and important trends that can be observed before 1814 point to later events. Foremost among these were economic changes: the gradual dismantling of monopoly, increasing economic growth dramatised by the expansion of wine exports towards the end of the period, and the rapid rise of British traders and British trade. One may also regard the abolition of the slave trade and the increasing importance of tightly controlled but free labour as early steps away from the slave system. The expulsion of the Xhosa across the Fish River in 1811—12 was decisive in putting an end to the longstanding power-vacuum on the Eastern Frontier and in throwing the weight of the British army on the side of the colonists. Finally, the expanding mission movement, which would dramatically affect the culture and society of brown and black peoples at the Cape, was perhaps the most striking new social phenomenon of the period, and the one with the greatest long-range significance.

Chapter Six   Chronology

1795	16 Sept.	British take possession of Cape Town. General James Craig, acting governor.
1797	January	Conclusion of the Graaff-Reinet rebellion.
	5 May	Arrival of Lord Macartney, governor.
1798	20 Nov.	Departure of Lord Macartney; Major-General Francis Dundas, acting governor.
1799	Jan.—April	'Van Jaarsveld' rebellion.
	April—Oct.	Khoikhoi rising.
	31 March	Arrival of the first LMS missionaries.
	10 Dec.	Sir George Yonge, governor.
1801	20 April	Resignation of Yonge; Dundas, acting governor.
	April	General introduction of the contract system for farm labourers.
	October	Graaff-Reinet rebellion.
	December	Resumption of hostilities on the frontier.
1802	1 April	J.A. de Mist appointed Commissioner-General.
	23 Dec.	Arrival of De Mist and Governor Jan Willem Janssens at the Cape.
1803	1 March	Batavian rule proclaimed.
	2 June	Van der Kemp takes possession of Bethelsdorp.
	25 July	*Kerkorde*.
1804	11 Sept.	*Schoolorde*.
	25 Sept.	Resignation of De Mist.
1805	23 April	Expulsion of Van der Kemp from Bethelsdorp.
1806	18 Jan.	Capitulation of Janssens to the British. Major General David Baird, acting governor.
1807	17 Jan.	Lieutenant-General Sir Henry George Grey, acting governor.
	22 May	Du Pré Alexander, Earl of Caledon, governor.
1808	29 April	End of the slave trade proclaimed at the Cape.
	October	Slave rising in the Zwartland. Introduction of first apprentices to the Cape from among Prize Negroes.
1809	1 Nov.	Hottentot Proclamation.
1811	4 July	Departure of Caledon.
	6 Sept.	Sir John Cradock, governor.
	October—March 1812	Attack on the Zuurveld Xhosa; their expulsion across the Fish.
	December	Death of Van der Kemp.
1812	23 April	Apprenticeship of Servants law.
	23 Sept.	Black Circuit initiated.
1813		Reduction of duties on Cape wine.
	6 August	Land tenure proclamation.
1814	6 April	Lord Charles Somerset, governor.
	13 August	London convention, whereby the Netherlands acknowledges British right to the Cape.
1815	November	**Slachtersnek Rebellion.**

Chapter Six   Notes

1. A recent major work on the first British occupation is Hermann Giliomee, *Die Kaap Tydens die Eerste Britse Bewind 1795—1803* (Cape Town, 1975).
2. A good discussion of the debate in British government circles can be found in Vincent Harlow, 'The British Occupations 1795—1806', *Cambridge History of the British Empire*, VIII (Cambridge, 1936). See also L.C.F. Turner, 'The Cape of Good Hope and the Anglo-French Conflict 1797—1806', *Historical Studies of Australia and New Zealand*, IX (1961).
3. J.A. de Mist, *The Memorandum of Commissary J.A. de Mist*, trans. K.M. Jeffreys (Cape Town, 1920).
4. A.H. Murray, *The Political Philosophy of J.A. de Mist* (Cape Town, n.d.) and Harlow, 'British Occupations'. A detailed work on the period, basically in the conservative camp, is J.P. van der Merwe, *Die Kaap onder die Bataafse Republiek 1803—06* (Amsterdam, 1926). The historiography of the period is discussed in William M. Freund, 'Society and Government in Dutch South Africa, The Cape and the Batavians 1803–06' (Unpublished Ph.D. thesis, Yale University, 1971).
5. George McCall Theal, *A History of South Africa since 1795* (London, 1906), I, 121.
6. The principal exception is Hermann Giliomee, 'Die Administrasietydperk van Lord Caledon 1807—11', *AYB*, XXIX (2), 1966.
7. Giliomee, *Eerste Britse Bewind*, p. 202, gives pertinent figures. Apart from coasters, of 742 vessels calling at the Cape between 1795 and 1800, 458 were British: Theal, *History*, I, 41.
8. C.F.J. Muller, *Johannes Frederik Kirsten oor die Toestand van die Kaapkolonie in 1795* (Pretoria, 1960); H.B. Thom, introduction and notes to W.S. van Ryneveld, *Aanmerking over de Verbetering van het Vee aan het Kaap de Goede Hoop* (Cape Town, 1942); W. Blommaert, Biographical sketch in Dirk Gysbert van Reenen, *Die Joernaal van Dirk Gysbert van Reenen* (Cape Town, 1937).
9. [W.W. Bird], *State of the Cape in 1822 by a Civil Servant* (Cape Town, 1966), p. 147.
10. Giliomee, *Eerste Britse Bewind*, p. 147.
11. *RCC*, II, General Fraser—Clive, 12 Feb. 1799, pp. 504—05.
12. Brian Kantor, 'The Rixdollar and the Foreign Exchange', *South African Journal of Economics*, XXXVIII (1970). The value of exports rose to over 3,000,000 rixdollars in 1817, declining thereafter. Imports rose above 2,000,000 in 1813 and reached almost 5,000,000 in 1817 and 1818.
13. *RCC*, VII, Gordon—Harrison, 4 April 1810, p. 274.
14. *RCC*, XI, Account of Imports from and Exports to Cape of Good Hope, 1813—1817, pp. 293—94.
15. Bird, *State of the Cape*, pp. 41—43, for a discussion of the pachten as they were in the early 1820s.
16. René F.M. Immelman, *Men of Good Hope: The Romantic Story of the Cape Town Chamber of Commerce 1804—1954* (Cape Town, 1955), p. 72. See also the exhausive new study on Cape wine: D.J. van Zyl, *Kaapse Wyn en Brandewyn, 1795—1860* (Cape Town, 1975).
17. Between 1811 and 1819 some 9,000,000 vines were planted and in 1815, a record year, production already exceeded 14,000 leaguers. Figures are from

annual returns in the volumes of *RCC* and Immelman, *Men of Good Hope*, which discusses the rise of wine export and production.

18. Figures are from *RCC* and Dirk Jacobus van Zyl, 'Die Geskiedenis van Graanbou aan die Kaap 1795—1826'. *AYB* XXXI (1), 1968, p. 275.

19. The 1806 figures are so low as to fit no rational sequence.

20. The most important source on the land question at this time remains P.J. van der Merwe, *Die Trekboer in die Geskiedenis van die Kaapkolonie* (Cape Town, 1938). See also Freund, 'Society and Government', pp. 70—71.

21. J.A Heese, *Slagtersnek en sy Mense* (Cape Town, 1973), pp. 67—71.

22. *RCC*, IX, Proclamation by Cradock, 6 Aug. 1813, pp. 204—08. The best discussion of Cape government land policy is Leslie C. Duly, *British Land Policy at the Cape 1795—1844: A Study of Administrative Procedures in the Empire* (Durham, 1968).

23. For the 1808 turn in colonist-'Bushman' relations in the northeast, see Giliomee, 'Caledon', pp. 267—69. There is an important discussion in chapter five of P.J. van der Merwe, *Die Noordwaartse Beweging van die Boere voor die Groot Trek (1770—1842)* (The Hague, 1937). A crucial contemporary account is the report of Richard Collins in *RCC*, VII, 201.

24. See *RCC*, VIII, Report of the Circuit Court Commission, 28 Jan. 1812, p. 299; William J. Burchell, *Travels in the Interior of Southern Africa* (Cape Town, 1967), II, 143—46 and the enclosed reprint of Burchell, 'Hints on Emigration', I, 38.

25. For the career of one later famous trekker who went east to seek his fortune as an entrepreneur at this time, see J.L.M. Franken, *Piet Retief se Lewe in die Kolonie* (Pretoria, 1949).

26. The considerable and controversial literature about the failure of the Van Hogendorp scheme during the Batavian period is reviewed in Freund, 'Society and Government', pp. 415—30.

27. Van Zyl, 'Graanbou', pp. 271—72.

28. Immelman, *Men of Good Hope*, p. 25.

29. See the crucial report prepared for Dundas by Van Ryneveld, *RCC*, IV, 88—96.

30. For discussion of labour policies with special relevance to the Eastern Frontier, see chapters 8 and 9 in this volume.

31. For the strong comments by the generally conservative Governor Cradock on the light sentences passed on whites in such crimes, see *RCC*, X, Cradock—Bathurst, 15 April 1814, pp. 1—5.

32. *RCC*, I, Craig—Henry Dundas, 12 April 1796, pp. 353—56.

33. Collins—Caledon, 6 Aug. 1809, in *The Record; or a series of official papers relative to the conditions and treatment of the native tribes of South Africa*, ed. Donald Moodie (Amsterdam and Cape Town, 1960), p. 22; George Thompson, *Travels and Adventures in South Africa* (Cape Town, 1967), II, 74.

34. AR, Inventory Aziatische Raad, 311, Janssens—Staats-Bewind, 21 Dec. 1804, p. 171.

35. Before 1795, 600 slave arrivals a year was a normal figure: Giliomee, *Eerste Britse Bewind*, p. 182.

36. In 1798 there were 964 slaves in Graaff-Reinet district. The figure rose to 1,905 in 1806 and 2,874 for the combined districts of Graaff-Reinet and Uitenhage. These figures are taken from the census rolls in *RCC*.

37. Some 2,000 arrived at the Cape between 1808 and 1816: J.S. Marais, *The Cape*

Coloured People 1652—1937 (Johannesburg, 1957), p. 161.

38. *Ibid.*, p. 167.

39. *RCC,* I, Court of Justice—Craig, 14 Jan. 1796, pp. 302—09.

40. The first two were later renamed Caledon Institute and Pacaltsdorp.

41. For Van der Kemp, see W.M. Freund, 'The Career of Johannes Theodorus van der Kemp and his role in the history of South Africa', *Tijdschrift voor Geschiedenis.* LXXXVI (1973), pp. 376—90 and the sources quoted there.

42. Christian I. Latrobe, *Journal of a Visit to South Africa in 1815 and 1816 with some Account of the Missionary Settlements of the United Brethren Near the Cape of Good Hope* (New York, 1969), p. 47; Bernhard Krüger, *The Pear Tree Blossoms, a History of the Moravian Mission Stations in South Africa 1737—1869* (Genadendal, 1966), pp. 102—03.

43. *RCC,* IX, Report of the circuit commissioners for Graaff-Reinet, Uitenhage and George, 1812, pp. 76—77.

44. Burchell, *Travels,* II, 179, 238, 286.

45. For evidence on the economy of Genadendal see, among others, Van Reenen, *VRS* 18, p. 23 and *Periodical Accounts Relating to the Mission of the Church of the United Brethren 1795—1834* (translated typescript, South African Public Library), 2.39. For Bethelsdorp see John Campbell, *Travels in South Africa undertaken at the request of the London Missionary Society* (London, 1812), pp. 84, 90—93. Campbell wrote (p. 90) that '. . . those who have obtained most property, are such as have remained most constantly at the settlement, while those who have been much in the service of the boors, have gained little.'

46. Important and sympathetic accounts of the missions at the close of the transitional era are Latrobe on the Moravians and Campbell on the LMS. An interesting comparison of the two mission traditions by H.T. Colebrooke is to be found in Bird, *State of the Cape,* p. 350.

47. The best source on this institution is J.J. Oberholster, 'Die Burger-Senaat 1795—1828' (unpublished M.A. thesis, University of Stellenbosch, 1936).

48. C. Graham Botha, 'The Early Inferior Courts of Justice at the Cape', *South African Law Journal,* XXXVIII (1921), pp. 406—23.

49. W.S. van der Westhuyzen, 'Onderwys onder die Algemeene Skoolkommissie: Die Periode 1804—30', *AYB,* XVI (2), 1953, p. 40.

50. For education during the transitional era, see Giliomee, *Eerste Britse Bewind,* pp. 231—33 and Freund, 'Society and Government', pp. 227—39. This subject has been covered in depth in Van der Westhuyzen, 'Onderwys', and in several works by P.S. du Toit, especially *Onderwys aan die Kaap onder die Bataafse Republiek 1803—06* (Pretoria, 1944).

51. The most recent account of Slachtersnek is Heese, *Slagtersnek.*

52. Oberholster, 'Burger-Senaat' p. 36.

53. The conflict is documented in *Boustowwe vir die Geskiedenis van die Nederduits-Gereformeerde Kerke in Suid-Afrika,* ed. A. Dreyer (Cape Town, 1936), III, 88—135.

PART III

The colonial frontiers, c. 1770—1820

The Northern Frontier to 1820: The emergence of the Griqua people [*]

Martin Legassick

Introduction

This chapter is, broadly speaking, concerned with the history of the peoples who inhabited Namaqualand,[†] Bushmanland,[‡] and central Transorangia[¶] during the eighteenth and early nineteenth centuries. At that time this region had long been occupied by a variety of communities, each with its own specific history. The major theme of this chapter is the increasing domination of these communities, and of this region, by the social relationships emanating from the *VOC* (and, later, Batavian and British) colony at the Cape. Its minor theme is the emergence, in this period and in this area, of a distinctive new community with its own way of life, distinct from the way of life of the settled Cape Colony and distinct from the ways of life of the preceding peoples. This community was the Griqua people.

The social relationships characteristic of the Cape Colony, and the history of their expansion and consequent domination over the pre-existing communities of southern Africa, have been viewed in a number of different ways. In this chapter we begin with the comparatively uncontroversial assumption that the Cape Colony itself must be seen as a product of the world

---

[*] This is a revision of parts of my Ph.D. thesis (University of California, Los Angeles, 1969) entitled 'The Griqua, the Sotho-Tswana, and the Missionaries, 1780–1840: The Politics of a Frontier Zone.' I am much indebted to Professor L.M. Thompson both for supervising my thesis and for comments on an earlier draft of this chapter. The chapter has also benefitted from extensive comments on the thesis by Professor Jeffrey Butler, and on various drafts by the editors of this volume. I am grateful also to Bill Freund and Christopher Saunders who at different times provided material.
[†] The mountainous and rugged granite terrain along the escarpment south of the lower Orange was regarded as Little Namaqualand; the area extending from the Orange River to Rehoboth in the north and from the great escarpment to the Kalahari sands was called Great Namaqualand.
[‡] Bushmanland was the dry plain east of Little Namaqualand and south of the lower Orange.
[¶] This was the region to the north of the middle Orange River mainly comprising Griqualand West and what was once called British Bechuanaland.

expansion of Europe, starting from the fifteenth century, which began to integrate ever larger areas of the world into a single economic system.[1] The central characteristic of this economic system was that it involved the exchange of *commodities* — those peculiar things which, as was discovered by Karl Marx, embodied labour in two different ways.[2] The implications of exchange of commodities for the analysis of social relationships in the Cape Colony, or for the analysis of the extension of those social relationships into what we have called the 'Northern Frontier', cannot be fully explored in a piece of such limited length. At the same time it would be dishonest of the author not to express his conviction that it is through a full understanding of the implications of the commodity that the material presented in this chapter will be better understood.[3]

A major theme in the twentieth-century historiography of South Africa has been an explanation, whether as affirmation or critique, of the forms of exploitation, domination and dependence which have existed, and the conflicts which have resulted from them. Most frequently these structures of domination and conflict have been analysed in 'racial' terms, and assumed to have developed historically along unambiguously 'racial' lines. Thus, in discussing the expansion of the social relationships of the Cape Colony, there was a tendency, from Theal and Cory to Macmillan, to focus on the 'remorseless advance of white agricultural colonisation'[4] occurring either in a vacuum or in the form of establishing domination over the indigenous population of South Africa. The major alternative explanation of these phenomena has been that offered by the liberal school of South African historiography of which Macmillan was, ambivalently, a founder, and whose increasing domination in the field is reflected in the recent *Oxford History of South Africa*. A central theme in this school has been the expansion of the social relationships of trade (or, in other words, of commodity exchange) as the mode through which 'cooperative' relationships were established between the Cape Colony and indigenous societies, and through which a 'new' South African society came into being. The task of this school, therefore, has been to explain how the harmony generated by trade has become 'distorted' into historic and contemporary forms of racial conflict.[5] This they have achieved with various measures of empirical success, but on the basis of theoretical deficiencies.[6]

It is true that, at one level, the exchange of commodities generates relationships between men as equals. If this is the only level at which exchange is seen, then all conflict must be viewed as a product of relationships created and developed outside the market. But, for Marx, commodity exchange was not a universal mode of social relationship, but a historical mode. Its appearance progressively disguised and fetishised the social relationships of class which it expressed. Its appearance, indeed, could be said to have created the potential for relations of class exploitation and domination to take on 'racial' forms.

It is a matter of regret to the author that when he originally undertook the research for this chapter (which was presented in his thesis) and when he undertook to revise this research for the current book, he was not yet equipped to re-present the material to illustrate this theme adequately. His critique of the liberal school at that point was couched within the terms established by John Rex and Andre Gunder Frank.[7] Both of these writers were implicitly concerned, if in different ways, with the existence of *unequal* forms of exchange consequent on the establishment of colonial societies. Frank saw the colonial relationship as constituting a relationship of class directly expressed in the unequal exchange between colony and metropolis. Rex saw the unequal exchange as predicated on the act of conquest through which the colony came into being and the forms of political domination through which the colonial relationship was maintained. These were valuable insights, but they were not able to establish a systematic theoretical link between 'economic' and 'political' relationships, and to establish their unity in the class relationships of pre-capitalism and capitalism, or the distinct forms in which they could appear as a result of the development of exchange. It must therefore be borne in mind by the reader that in the view of the author much of the material in this chapter requires reinterpretation, although as it stands (as will be seen) it challenges the liberal school at many central points.

The concept of white agricultural colonisation, used to analyse the extension of colonial social relationships, conflates a number of processes which must be disentangled and examined separately. What, in the Cape, was the relationship between the expansion of the territorial authority of the ruling power and the expansion of white settlement? What was the relationship between the extension of trade, the extension of commodity relationships, and the expansion of white settlement? Were all European immigrants who moved away from the Cape Peninsula agriculturalists? Were all European immigrant agriculturalists bearers of 'colonial' political and economic relationships? Did not some of the indigenous population come to perform 'colonial' political and economic roles? And, if exchange was the 'cooperative' act assumed by the liberal historians, what then were the factors which led to domination and conflict, whether in class or racial forms? Who were the bearers of this trade? And, if they were both white and non-white, to the extent that the trade was exploitative or created relationships of exploitation and domination, were these not class relationships?

The first of the settlers with whom we are concerned were the *freeburghers*, a social category created in the seventeenth century under the auspices of the Dutch East India Company (VOC) regime. As these expanded inland from the Western Cape heartland, they were not initially agriculturalists, but traders and hunters. Up to that historical point the trade in cattle and other goods to Cape Town had been by Company officials through direct purchase from Khoikhoi or their middlemen: the mercantile VOC was the initial agency of expansion of the commodity system. Insofar as freeburghers began to usurp the middleman role from the Khoikhoi or from Company officials, they became the bearers of the expansion of commodity exchange. This occurred both through the trade in cattle and through trading in other products of pastoralism or of hunting. This had no necessary political consequences, no necessary establishment of relationships of political domination. Trading or hunting could be carried out with the permission of the political leadership (such as it was) of the Khoikhoi. But in practice the bearers of trade came to be the bearers of *de jure* or *de facto* political authority. Created by exchange as equals, colonists and Khoikhoi were simultaneously the expression of vastly different forms of social relationship within their communities. In the same way (but under different conditions, as we shall see) missionaries, bearers of ideology, came to be bearers of trade and political domination (see pp. 263 ff.).

Thus for the settlers the appropriation of products of the hunt might be pursued without reference to the political authority of the community on whose territory the hunt was being conducted. Equally, simple trading could develop into coerced exchange, into raiding, and into pure robbery. 'A few colonists, well armed, assemble together: then, falling suddenly on some solitary horde, they compel those who compose it to bring them all their cattle, from which they select such as may suit them, and give in return what they think proper'.[8] In 1738, on what may have been the first trading expedition from the Cape Colony to reach the Orange River, a simple exchange of cattle was supplemented by theft. After departing, the colonists on the following day sent their Khoisan dependants to seize further cattle. In no single instance was the transformation of a trading relationship into one of coercion inevitable or necessary; that it came to occur reflected the ultimate relationship between European metropolis and indigenous community, mediated only by the settlers. This raiding of cattle and other commodities could also lead to the seizure of people as captives, to be subordinated as dependants, or distributed or sold. Again, the possibilities for this in any individual instance reflected the establishment by the VOC of the Cape heartland as a colony based on slave production.

In trading, the weakness of the freeburghers vis-à-vis the monopolistic VOC made direct coercion more necessary to the establishment of their role. And the force that emerged from such activities then became a means for the appropriation of land. In the Cape heartland, land was allocated through the law: the VOC law. In the eighteenth century, land allocation grew progressively beyond the power of the VOC in the regions of freeburgher expansion.[9] Although it claimed to rule the limits of the domain into which freeburghers and other immigrants (*knechts*, deserters, escaped sailors, etc.) were moving, it could not exert a uniformly effective authority. In other parts of the colonial world of the period the colonial regime abandoned all pretence: the settlers were left to 'go native' and to integrate themselves into roles in the indigenous society. But in the Cape Colony this did not occur. The reasons for this resolute, if ineffective, legalism of the VOC and the reasons for this clinging to the umbilical cord by the freeburghers — these are among the fundamental problems of South African history.[10] They can be described, though not explained, through the concept of the 'frontier zone'.[11] The freeburghers (and those who became attached to them) were neither autonomous from the VOC nor from the indigenous societies. They lived in a 'frontier zone', a fluid region of social transition, relatively autonomous from both colonial base and the indigenous social systems, but dependent on both. Within its own dimensions there was no necessary history to the frontier zone. The frontier zone of the eighteenth-century Cape for three generations remained in limbo. Only as industrial capitalism came to displace mercantile capitalism in Europe, only as Britain displaced the VOC and Batavians in South Africa, were the processes set in motion for the reincorporation of the frontier zone into the Cape colonial system. In Giliomee's terms, what had been an 'open frontier' became a 'closed frontier' (see ch. 8, pp. 316—17). As we shall see in the second part of this chapter, this was associated with a new relationship between political and economic forms, and with new bearers of these forms.

The major institution of the open frontier zone was the commando. Its tasks were simultaneously political and economic. It drew from both the indigenous and colonial systems but, as a band of armed retainers, had feudal characteristics which distinguished it from each. Dependent for its existence on firearms and, more crucial in the short term, on a constant supply of powder, the commando, like the frontier zone, was ultimately subordinate to its colonial base. For the freeburgher frontiersmen the commando was the military form of the hunting and trading party. The VOC's attempt to preserve a trade monopoly by declaring *all* intercourse between colonists and the indigenous population illegal, encouraged the frontiersmen to maximise their illegal gains by the most coercive means. Raiding, which was the result, exacerbated social conflict and confirmed the VOC in its attempt to prevent contacts. But at the same time, from about 1715, the commando replaced the VOC soldiery as the main agency for the defence of the colonial interior against attack. Coerced trade, unregulated hunting, and raiding bred resistance by the Khoisan peoples in the eighteenth century; and the VOC was compelled to depend on the commando to defeat them.[12] Thus the VOC was forced to permit the supply of firearms and powder for political purposes to an institution to which it was economically opposed. Only in 1795, when eastern frontiersmen rebelled against the colony, was the powder-supply actually suspended as a sanction.

These separate political and economic tasks became reunited in the role of the commando in the appropriation of land. It is true that there was no one-to-one relationship between military conquest and land allocation. On the other hand, in the absence of an effective legal power, it was the commando system which created the possibilities for the replacement of an indigenous system of usufruct of common land by a system of private land-holding. This transformation was, for the most part, initially effected on the spot by *de facto* occupation; only thereafter would the land-owner seek to guarantee his occupation in perpetuity through registration of a land title with the colony. Strictly speaking it is only such land-owners who turned to agricultural production on colonially registered land who can be regarded as white agricultural colonisers. Nor, as will be seen, were they uniformly white. Moreover, to the extent that such production became the most important aspect of their subsistence, they tended to delegate the tasks of trading and hunting and the *de facto* extension of land appropriation to others: their family and their dependants. Colonisation in this sense was a form of closing the frontier zone, not of extending its openness.

There were, broadly speaking, two main northward thrusts in the eighteenth-century expansion of the open frontier of the commando. The first of these was along the coastal plains, over the Oliphants River, to the Khamiesberg, to Little Namaqualand and into present-day Namibia (South West Africa). The particular significance of this thrust was — as Marais pointed out in his classic though dated study — that it was pioneered largely by non-whites.[13] Marais, concentrating on a particular period, exaggerated: until the 1730s whites predominated in this thrust. Only as they moved across the mountains south of Bushmanland was a space created for a frontier of mixed racial descent.

A second northward thrust came much further to the east. From about 1810 the frontier north of Graaff-Reinet and the Sneeuwberg began to open as the resistance of 'Bushman' hunters crumbled; the descendants of those who had turned across the mountains in the 1730s began to push to the north. In the mean time the northward penetration along the coast had turned eastwards along the valley of the Orange River. By 1820 the two streams were meeting in central Transorangia. Here again there was a

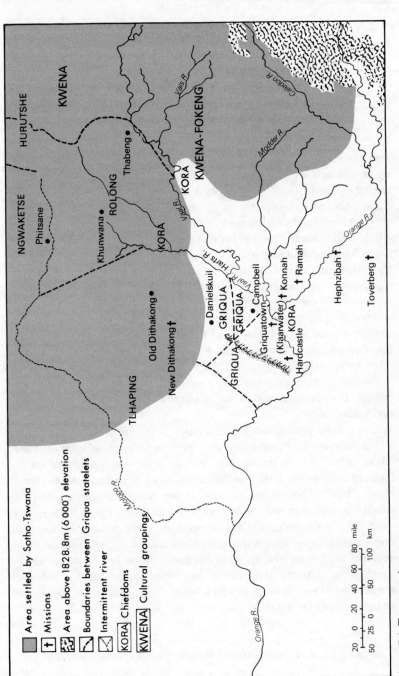

Figure 7.1 Transorangia

It is probable that Sotho-Tswana settlement between the Vaal and the Modder was overlaid by a northeast thrust of the Kora between 1800 and 1820.

Legend:

- Area settled by Sotho-Tswana
- † Missions
- Area above 1828.8m (6 000') elevation
- Boundaries between Griqua statelets
- Intermittent river
- KORA Chiefdoms
- KWENA Cultural groupings

Scale:
20 25 0 20 40 60 80 mile
50 0 50 100 km

Map labels:

NGWAKETSE · Phitsane

HURUTSHE

KWENA

ROLONG · Khunwana

· Thabeng

KORA

KORA

KWENA-FOKENG

Vals R.

Modder R.

Caledon R.

Vaal R.

Harts R.

TLHAPING

Old Dithakong †

· Danielskuil

New Dithakong

GRIQUA

GRIQUA

GRIQUA

Griquatown ·

· Campbell

(Klaarwater) † Konnah

KORA

† Hardcastle

† Ramah

Hephzibah †

Toverberg †

Orange R.

Orange R.

Molopo R.

predominant, though not exclusive role played by non-whites (see Fig. 7.1).

The minor theme of this chapter, we have said, is the emergence of a distinctive new community. As has been suggested, this new community was formed in the crucible of the frontier zone and shaped by the institutions of the commando. But if a general history of the eighteenth-century frontier would see this new community as that of the freeburghers, for a historian of the Northern Frontier it is essentially the community of the Griqua. The term 'non-white' is at least partially anachronistic in its application to the eighteenth century: the economic and political conditions in which racial categories could become established did not as yet firmly exist. The eighteenth-century colour line was, to say the least, a blurred one in which the criteria of legal and social status by no means always coincided with those of ethnic origin. Many who later became assimilated into the white side of the South African colour line descended from a biological and cultural mixture in the eighteenth century. At the same time there emerged in the eighteenth century a social category denominated 'Bastaards'. If these originated as dependants or commando-members in the open frontier system, they could also become property owners under colonial law. Like the freeburghers, they initially aspired to Christianity and to citizenship of the colony. From this Bastaard nucleus, through various forms of accretion in a variety of social relationships, there emerged in the early nineteenth century a series of communities (along and north of the valley of the Orange, from Namibia to central Transorangia) with a social identity which is most conveniently denoted as 'Griqua'.[14]

This chapter proceeds with a description of the indigenous communities which occupied the Northern Frontier prior to its 'opening' from the Cape. There follow sections on the open frontier of the commando, and on the forms of stabilisation of the frontier zone through land claims and territorial rights. The main body of the chapter discusses the attempts by the post-1800 colonial government and the bearers of its authority, the missionaries, to close the frontier zone, and the consequent emergence of new forms of domination and exploitation (not along racial lines) along with a failure in the attempts at closure. The epilogue discusses, all too briefly, the processes which, after 1820, sealed the fate of the Griqua and secured the 'closing' of the Northern Frontier in terms which began to entrench the ideology of race and the power of white colonists.

The indigenous communities: Bantu-speakers and Khoisan

The inhabitants of the region on whom the eighteenth-century commando frontier impinged were Bantu-speakers and Khoisan. ('Khoisan' includes both the pastoral Khoikhoi and groups of hunter-gatherers whom Khoikhoi called 'San' and whom the colonists called 'Bushmen'). In central Namibia, south of the Ovambo peoples, were the Bantu-speaking Herero, cattle-keepers par excellence.[15] East of the Kalahari (which may not have been as extensive then as it is now) the highveld and central and eastern Transorangia were dominated by the Bantu-speaking Sotho-Tswana peoples, who were cultivators as well as pastoralists. The southernmost of these in the eighteenth century were the Rolong (south of the Molopo) and, moving eastward, the Fokeng, Ghoya and Taung spread as far south as the Caledon River (see Fig. 7.1, p. 249).[16]

South of the Bantu-speakers, and interspersed among them, were the Khoisan.[17] Prior to the eighteenth century there is evidence that cattle-keeping Khoikhoi were living adjacent to Bantu-speaking communities, at least in Namibia and along the middle Orange.[18] By the early nineteenth century these Khoikhoi north and south of the lower Orange were known generically as 'Nama', and those north and south of the middle Orange as 'Kora'. In contrast, the region of eastern Transorangia (roughly the present-day Orange Free State) was, in the eighteenth century, occupied only by Khoisan hunter-gatherers alongside Bantu-speakers.[19] In all these cases, and specifically regarding Nama and Kora, it is almost impossible to disentangle which elements were long-established inhabitants of the area, and which had retreated from the Cape during the seventeenth or eighteenth centuries, though there is fragmented evidence of both situations.[20] The resulting tangle of social relationships, exacerbated in the frontier zone period, makes it well-nigh impossible to link Khoisan political groupings in the nineteenth century to any earlier Khoisan political history.[21]

The obsession in the historiography of South Africa with the analysis of society in the 'racial' terms in which it presents itself produces endless attempts to differentiate Bantu-speakers from Khoisan, Sotho from Nguni, and, within each, tribes and sub-tribes, Khoikhoi and 'San', and so on. Though liberal historiography has at times resisted this tendency, insisting on the separation of language from mode of livelihood, from other cultural practices, or from genealogies of descent, the trend to re-conflate these different phenomena in a mechanistic way remains. Thus, as Johnstone has argued recently, 'plural society' theory reduces, in its essence, to a new liberal variant of the philosophy of *apartheid*. It is only through an analysis which begins from the social relations of production that this tendency can be overcome.[22] Indeed, for the purposes of this chapter, the fundamental proposition concerning the societies being discussed here is their similarity.

As liberalism recognised in its hey-day, all were small-scale societies in which persons were dependent on forces of nature over which they had but little control.[23] Some communities gathered for subsistence, others hunted, kept cattle or grew crops. Some indulged in more than one, or all of these practices. This is of interest to the economic historian in terms of the origin and spread of technological practices; it is not central to the present chapter. We are concerned here with those features of indigenous society which were relevant at the time of impact of the commando frontier. The commando frontier was interested in the appropriation of resources, and resources in various forms were available. These resources were produced under a variety of social relationships, and their production was characterised by a limited and variable surplus. Hence appropriation, even of a minimal amount, had vastly disproportionate effects on each community. At the same time it was through this appropriation expressed as exchange that these communities, each with their separate histories, became forcibly integrated into the history of the frontier, of the Cape Colony, of Holland, and of world capitalism.

The question of the social relations of production in such communities has been inadequately explored. Certainly there was a sexual division of labour, although this was more pronounced among agriculturalists and mixed-production communities than among pure pastoralists or hunter-gatherers. There were craft specialists: blacksmiths, herbalists, rainmakers. Mostly these were in Bantu-speaking communities, but who is to say their origins were the same as those of their communities? Mining was carried on, of metals for example, or of a decorative yellow ochre called *sibello*: we do not know who did the mining, and under what compulsions or incentives.[24] More important is the extent to which the existence of relationships of class can be established.

The community was in all cases constituted on the basis of relationships expressed neither economically nor politically, but in terms of kinship. Kinship was the language of social interaction, disguising the relations of production. The only potential for class relationships existed in societies where there was chieftainship. This office was inherited through lineage descent, and could therefore emerge or disappear in kin-based communities without any basic alteration in language or structure. Where it became institutionalised, it was surrounded by a structure of government based on leading lineages: lineage-members, the counsellors, were the assistants to the chief. The officers of government had the obligation to redistribute resources for the benefit of the community, but these obligations necessitated the simultaneous appropriation of resources which could be redistributed.[25]

It is these forms of appropriation which have been inadequately investigated. Clearly they involve the appropriation either of labour-time, or of products, or of both. The prerogative of chiefs to receive tribute labour was well established in many Bantu-speaking societies by the nineteenth century (though this practice may have post-dated the Mfecane). Equally, the presence of mining products, handicrafts and cattle provided a potential basis for appropriation and for either redistribution or private accumulation.

If redistribution, to provide social insurance and attract new members, was the main form of *internal* recycling of goods, a limited amount of trading was the main form of *external* recycling of goods. To refer to this trade as 'exchange' in the period prior to the impact of the frontier is problematic; we do not know to what extent it was bound up with relationships of tribute or worship between communities. This is not a matter of the existence or non-existence of money, currency or markets; it is a matter of distinguishing between the circulation of use-values and the circulation of commodities.

In the period that we are considering, trade was already conditioned by merchant capital: Khoisan traded cattle southward to the Cape; Bantu-speakers exported metals, *karosses* (hides), finished furs and, increasingly, ivory to the Portuguese settlements of the East Coast.[26] This trade was not carried out by long-distance traders but through a series of relays. It seems likely, therefore, that it grew out of local circulation rather than the reverse. Exchanges of goods between specific trading mates customarily took place either at the neutral frontier between communities or at the *kgotla* (forum) in the town centre of the community. Where a chiefly structure existed, the chief attempted internally and externally to monopolise this trade. Trading disputes may well have been the main cause of the occasional inter-community warfare which took place, warfare which was clearly (as will be seen) exacerbated by the impact of the frontier. Disputes over succession, or over the definition of access to limited resources such as water, would also have led to conflict.

Chiefs, and the heads of lineages, would gather around them 'as many Men as their wealth would admit, to each of which they assign the milk of one or two cows which, together with the efforts of the Men's wife in gathering roots, wild fruit, locusts, and the cultivation of a Garden, is generally sufficient to enable him to maintain his family'.[27] At one level this social relationship of clientage was simply one of the major ways through which communities could grow on a non- or quasi-kin basis. At another level it was a protofeudal relationship of personal dependence which acquired the name of the *fhisa* or *mafisa* system in the nineteenth century. It clearly provided the basis for the emergence of a class differentiation between property-owners and serfs. Powerful communities might, through their chief, also hold as tributaries not single individuals or families, but internally coherent (kin-based) groups of herders or cultivators. Hunter-gatherers might also become dependants, acquiring dogs, old iron weapons or tobacco from their patrons in return for supplying karosses.[28]

Many of these forms of dependence became possible only to the extent that an export trade existed; equally, the development of an export trade, dominated by the chief and his associated lineage-heads, made such forms of class relationship the more necessary. It is, however, important to emphasise that in any instance of a particular community the existence and nature of class relationships remained fluid. Dependent groups or individuals could leave a particular dependency relationship, either for autonomy or for a different relationship with another community. Previously autonomous groups or individuals could become dependent. Over all, mobility was possible. But to the extent that all communities tended towards the development of chieftainship or absorption into a chieftainship, and to the extent that trade was expanding, the situation was ripe for the overall emergence of a class society.

This process was interrupted in southern Namibia and central Transorangia in the eighteenth century by the arrival of Khoisan pastoralists and hunter-gatherers. Their pressure was one of the factors in the demise, south of the Molopo, of the hegemony of the Rolong ruled by Tau, whose sway, one source relates, 'extended from the Bahurutsian mountains to the Hamhanna hills, a distance of two hundred miles' (and a considerable sway it was, considering the conditions of communication of the time).[29] Another factor in the Rolong demise was probably the emergence, north of the Molopo, of the Ngwaketse, who competed with the Rolong for the ivory and pelts of the Kalahari borderlands.[30] The Rolong disintegrated into five smaller chiefdoms, some of them moving north and eastwards. Some Rolong tributaries (whether as a group or as fragments is unclear) asserted their autonomy and became known as the Tlhaping. Central Transorangia, as a result, came under the sway of Khoikhoi under their name of Kora, of the Tlhaping, and of lesser Sotho-Tswana groups.[31]

Of these the most important were the Tlhaping. In 1801 their chief settlement had a population of some 16,000 and was described as being 'in circumference as large as Cape Town'.[32] For the first time in the history of the Cape a social relationship existed between the colonial capital and a town of equal size. The hegemony of the Tlhaping extended from the Langeberg in the west to the Harts River in the east, a substantial area (see Fig. 7.1, p. 249).[33] This state was 'multi-ethnic' even in the origins of its rulers. Molehabangwe, then Tlhaping chief, was probably the son of a Kora woman and had at least one Kora wife. His half-Kora son Mothibi, who succeeded him, married a Kora woman (like others of the ruling lineage), and later confided to a missionary that having 'grown up among the Corannas', he was sceptical of many Tlhaping customs.[34] This state, embracing Sotho-Tswana and Kora, testifies to the irrelevance of the ethnic characterisations of South African historical pseudo-anthropology. It had, it was later claimed, never been 'so rich or so numerous as in the late eighteenth century'.[35]

Trading, hunting and raiding in the Northern Frontier zone

From the 1730s the northward thrust of colonial expansion, defined in terms of the registration of farms, turned eastwards from the Oliphants River across the mountains. Apart from an occasional official expedition, the area north of the Oliphants River was left predominantly for the trading, hunting and raiding dimensions of frontier expansion. Until the last two decades of the eighteenth century it is difficult, however, to trace either the chronology of geographic extension of the frontier or much about the activities of frontiersmen.[36] The emergence of the commando-like band, which was the vehicle for the hunting, trading and raiding of the frontier zone, depended on access to firearms, horses and gunpowder. Underlying much of the politics of the frontier zone was a struggle to gain access to arms. The 'opening up' of the Northern Frontier zone and the long persistence of its 'openness' was partly rooted in the multiplicity of channels for the diffusion of arms. Much of the colonial governments' struggle to 'close' the frontier zone was the attempt to exert control over the firearms trade.[37]

The commando-like bands of the Northern Frontier zone consisted of both whites and non-whites, with white and non-white leaders. But at first it was colonial citizens who could distribute the crucial resources of arms and powder. As they moved out to tap new trade routes or new hunting-grounds, they would have found Khoikhoi eager to accept arms and powder in return for serving as guides. Such a relationship of exchange could become transformed into the pattern of the commando band in two overlapping ways. In the first place, Khoikhoi who had lost their cattle and pasture land would attach themselves to frontiersmen, probably be given the use of a cow or two, and hope to acquire more cattle, a horse and a gun. By the end of the eighteenth century this class of Khoikhoi dependants, some of them having regained autonomy, had become sufficiently numerous to become known as *Oorlams*, 'that is, Hottentots who come from the upper country [i.e. beyond the "frontier"] and are born and bred with the farmers; most of whom understand and speak the low Dutch language.'[38]

In the second place, frontiersmen might be invited to intervene in a dispute between indigenous groups. Although also coercive, such intervention differed from raiding. Both forms of coercion, however, involved the risks of detection and consequent deprivation of access to arms. Thus *veldwachtmeester* Adriaan van Zyl, who led a commando to participate in a Kora dispute on the middle Orange, probably in 1786, was banished from the colony in consequence.[39] In the 1790s Guilliam Visagie had his grant of a farm at present-day Keetmanshoop in Namibia revoked for leading a band of 'half-breed and Hottentot' raiders, and was returned to the colony by an Oorlam-led colonial commando.[40] It was somewhat less risky for those with official positions or titles to land to trade in arms and powder, though even here their actions could bring punishment.[41] To avoid difficulties with the colonial government, some 'respectable' frontiersmen retained the services of trustworthy commando leaders whom they recruited either from deserters or from among the Oorlams.[42]

A case in point was veldwachtmeester Petrus Pienaar, a man well respected among his fellows.[43] The owner of several farms in the northwest, he turned his attention in the 1780s to the valley of the middle Orange. There he met Jan Bloem, a German from Thuringia who had deserted from a ship in Cape Town in 1780, murdered his wife, and fled to the Orange.[44] Pienaar established Bloem on his farm on the Orange, provided him with powder, and sold the cattle which Bloem was able to capture. Bloem acquired a following of Kora and began to raid not only other Kora communities but Sotho-Tswana as well, moving his base of operations further into central Transorangia. Indeed, this was the 'firearm frontier' which intervened in the Kora thrust to roll back the area of Sotha-Tswana hegemony on the middle Orange. As Bloem moved towards central Transorangia, Pienaar acquired another commando leader, an Oorlam named Klaas Afrikaner, who had earned a reputation for his role in large colonially-authorised commandos against the Khoisan in 1792. After refusing to be conscripted into military service in Cape Town, he settled at Pienaar's farm on the Orange and began to raid. Afrikaner soon began to complement Bloem's activities in central Transorangia, making southern Namibia his sphere of operations.[45]

Besides white frontiersmen and Khoikhoi-Oorlam dependants, the so-called Bastaards began to play an increasingly important role in the Northern Frontier zone. The meaning of the word 'bastaard' of course indicates illegitimate birth. Within the social system of the Cape Colony, however, it acquired two further meanings. In the first place it came to specifically denote the children of mixed parentage, particularly between white and Khoikhoi, but also between slave and Khoikhoi.[46] Initially such persons acquired a stigma because of their illegitimacy as much as their colour; indeed, children born out of inter-ethnic *marriage* could be more readily absorbed into the white community. Moreover, the term Bastaard apparently denoted an economic category as much as a social status of illegitimacy or colour. Thus Maynier described the Bastaards as 'such Hottentots, *particularly* [i.e. not only] of the mixed race, who possessed some property, were more civilised.'[47]

Partly, no doubt, because of their descent from higher status groups, the 'Bastaards' tended to be in less menial jobs than hired farm labour or domestic service. They were transport riders, day labourers, craftsmen or small farmers. Or they were 'a superior and confidential type of servant', trusted to take charge of a farm during the owner's absence, or to act as overseers on loan farms. When his master died, wrote Lichtenstein, such a servant would often assume his name, 'and not infrequently sought himself some little spot, to which he retired with all belonging to him, and gained a subsistence for himself and his family by the breeding of cattle.'[48]

The colonial affiliations of the Bastaards through descent encouraged the acquisition of other accoutrements of colonial status. Such people, wrote Lichtenstein, 'were educated in Christianity: they learnt to sing psalms, and to read: and were, even to receiving the sacrament of baptism, as good Christians as the offspring of Europeans.'[49] At the turn of the century the Bastaards of the Orange River valley saw themselves as 'swarthy Hollanders' and 'in their behaviour there was a certain good-natured ostentation, a sort of vanity, which seemed to show that they considered themselves as much superior to the rude Hottentots.'[50] Others who were not necessarily illegitimate or of mixed descent (especially not of part white descent) might aspire to Bastaard status. Among them were slaves and Khoikhoi as well as people of mixed descent who were trusted as overseers or who acquired the independence of small property-owners. Colonial officials claimed that runaway slaves, particularly those of part-Khoikhoi descent, found it easy to pass themselves off as Bastaards in the interior.[51] It is significant that both the two most wealthy and powerful Bastaard families of the Orange appear to have had slave origins. One of these was the Koks: Adam Kok and his sons Cornelius and Salomon. Adam Kok was a manumitted slave who acquired a farm at Piketberg in the mid-eighteenth century.[52] The other was the Berends family, including the brothers Klaas and Piet, though whether they were by origin slaves or true 'mixed' Bastaards is not so clear.[53] Oorlams and other Khoikhoi may also have aspired to the status of Bastaards.[54]

Bastaards certainly participated, along with white frontiersmen, Oorlams and Khoikhoi, in the raiding expeditions of the Northern Frontier zone.[55] But apparently some leading Bastaard families were attempting towards the end of the eighteenth century to create, or recreate, more stable patterns of trading. This attempt may well have been associated with the emergence of an ivory trade on the frontier which complemented the cattle trading that dominated throughout the eighteenth century. In 1780 Klaas Berends and his followers probably formed the vanguard of the trading frontier among Khoikhoi in southern Namibia and even higher up on the Orange.[56] Within two decades both the Kok and the Berends families had begun to establish relationships with the Tlhaping, and Cornelius Kok and a follower had even ventured further on at least one trading expedition to the Rolong.[57]

Two factors may have contributed toward the stabilisation of trade with the Sotho-Tswana. The Sotho-Tswana were less easily raided than the Khoisan communities. Secondly, the dwindling number of elephants in the Orange River valley[58] forced traders to tap the north-easterly trade routes controlled by the Sotho-Tswana. A desire to sell ivory directly to Cape Town,[59] instead of through white farmers acting as agents, probably also encouraged the Bastaards to build a stable order and trading relationships in the frontier zone. For, by assisting the colonial authorities in the establishment of stability, they could hope to have their rights and privileges of access protected by the colonial government.[60]

Between 1800 and 1820 Bastaard-Tlhaping trade relationships became firmly institutionalised.[61] However, the Bastaards were not able to significantly extend their trading hinterland beyond the Tlhaping. This was partly a result of Tlhaping success in defending their monopoly by blocking the movements of white and Bastaard traders. The Tlhaping, moreover, were very selective about what they would accept in exchange for cattle or ivory. They sold ivory for sheep, which they did not possess, or for tobacco or *dagga*, which they did not grow but which the Bastaards did. Cattle were sold for carefully selected beads, for raw iron, or for cloth.[62] In 1801 the Tlhaping were unimpressed by the looking-glasses, linen handkerchiefs, tinderboxes and knives brought by an official colonial expedition, regarding their own knives as superior; indeed, they were at the time selling knives, hatchets and other metalware to the Bastaards.[63] Nevertheless, trading with the Tlhaping and hunting in their territory proved fairly profitable for the Bastaards and others. A profit of some 8 rixdollars (nearly 100 per cent) could be made on a cow sold in the colony, and anything from 18 rixdollars (900 per cent) upwards to 100 rixdollars (500 per cent) on a tusk of ivory.[64] Certainly the first missionaries on the Orange, who engaged in ivory trading, did well.[65]

Stable ivory hunting and trading, in the control of the leading Bastaard families, overlaid but by no means supplanted illegal trading and raiding of cattle in the Northern Frontier zone and their sale, in exchange for arms, to the frontier farmers. On the lower Orange this illegal trading dominated. On the middle Orange after 1800 the Bastaard-Tlhaping relationships seemed to presage a new pattern, the continuation of which, however, depended on the ability of the Bastaards to control the channels for the diffusion of arms, a well-nigh impossible task as the edge of land registration moved more widely towards the Orange.

In particular, a new threat emerged from the extension to the Kora of the illegal arms trading conducted by frontiersmen like Coenraad Bezuidenhout,

Cobus Vry, Gerrit Coetzee and Coenraad de Buys.[66] From about 1810 into the 1820s and 1830s the illegal trade in arms into central and eastern Transorangia flourished with such people as intermediaries, and led to cattle raiding and the seizure of hunter-gatherer 'apprentices'.[67] Such Bastaards, wrote Governor Somerset in 1817, were 'expert in the use of firearms' and subsisted 'in great measure from the game they kill'. However, he continued, 'to procure firearms they must revisit the Colony and bring with them something which will induce the itinerant traders to supply them with these prohibited articles. The consequence is that they plunder the distant tribes and traffic with the booty'.[68] This eruption of the firearms frontier in the hands of new people both weaned followers away from the leading Bastaard families and placed firearms in the hands of Kora and Sotho-Tswana groups in Transorangia, something that the Bastaard ivory traders had sought to prevent.[69]

Land claims and territorial rights in the Northern Frontier zone

On the Eastern Frontier the stabilisation of social relationships was achieved by the colonial government from 1811—12 through the 'closing' of the frontier zone. It established effective colonial control and entrenched the occupation of a community of almost exclusively white farms. The initial attempt to normalise relationships in the Northern Frontier zone was, by contrast, undertaken by non-white frontiersmen — the leading Bastaard families — both with and without colonial cooperation. They tried not only to regularise trade, as we have seen, but also to assert effective claims to territory and political authority.

For both whites and non-whites in the frontier zone the retention of land once claimed *de facto* through the power of the commando became increasingly a matter of colonial 'legitimisation' of that title. It was possible for a Khoikhoi to retain legitimate title by obtaining colonial recognition of his status as chief, with a staff of office and rights to territory.[70] But, to the extent that there were competing claims to territory, registration of an individual title was a more secure long-term guarantee. For some non-whites, particularly baptised Bastaards, it was possible to register colonial land titles in the same way as whites.[71] Moreover, Bastaards held on to land, whether registered or unregistered, in isolated areas in the Zwartberg, the Cedarberg, De Koup and Nieuwveld, the Zak River and elsewhere.[72]

A good example of Bastaard land ownership was Little Namaqualand. In general, the northward extension of *de jure* settlement was slow north of the Oliphants River,[73] for in terms of agricultural or pastoral production the region was unattractive.[74] Here Bastaards could still obtain farms easily, as is apparent from the farms which Kok, Diedericks, Brand, Meyer and other baptised Bastaards received.[75] Of these the most prominent family were undoubtedly the Koks. Adam Kok, the manumitted slave, was granted the farm Stinkfontein between 1751 and 1760 and received 'burgher rights' at apparently the same time.[76] Adam died in 1795, but his son Cornelius had already registered at least four other Namaqualand farms to his name. In 1799 the local veldwachtmeester wrote that Cornelius had become his 'one great help', and contemporary accounts indicate his considerable wealth and status. He even had white *bijwoners* (tenant farmers), and was baptised some time between 1795 and 1803.[77]

Such a concentration of Bastaards in Little Namaqualand may already have been a consequence of their extrusion from less remote areas by white frontiersmen.[78] The later movement, at the turn of the century, of Bastaards, Oorlams and other non-whites from Little Namaqualand to the middle Orange may have been partly a result of the same pressures as well as the attraction of hunting and trading in Tlhaping territory. It was also caused by new pressures on non-whites within the colony. One of these was changes in the terms of military service. Throughout the eighteenth century, Bas-taards and Khoikhoi were active participants in officially authorised com-mandos. Indeed, in many instances whites sent their non-white dependants on commando as their substitutes.[79] This in itself may have been conceived as an onerous activity: 'All the Hottentots and Bastaards fit for commandos', complained a veldwachtmeester in 1778, 'are going away to Namaqua country to evade serving on commandos . . . [they are] trafficking and bartering with the Namaquas.'[80] The position became worse with the formation of the *Corps Pandoeren* in Cape Town in 1781—82. Not only did this require military service away from the frontier, but for Bastaards it meant enrolling under the lower status of 'Hottentot'. It was the summons to the Corps Pandoeren which induced Klaas Afrikaner to set himself up as a raider in the 1790s and which in 1814 provoked a revolt among Bastaards and Oorlams of the middle Orange.[81]

Secondly, the regulations governing dependants apparently began to be tightened towards the end of the eighteenth century and to impinge more directly on Bastaards. By 1783 there were people in the colony who argued that the emergence of the Bastaards must be 'mischievous' since they might produce 'a leader of talent to unite the injured Hottentots, and perhaps the slaves, against the white inhabitants.'[82] In the 1770s there were moves to compel Bastaards to carry passes and to 'apprentice' slave-Khoikhoi offspring, though to what extent these were a result or a cause of the Bastaard movement to the frontier zone is not clear.[83] This movement or 'desertion' may well have been encouraged by the abolition of the slave trade in 1807 and by the more stringent regulation of 'Hottentot' labour in the Caledon and Cradock codes of 1809 and 1812 respectively.[84] From this time, it would seem, the colonial mind steadily assimilated the Bastaards into the category of a homogeneous 'Hottentot' (Coloured) labouring class. Commissioner Bigge referred to 'the Hottentots . . . in which class is generally included the mixed race of Hottentots and the white and free coloured inhabitants denominated "Bastaards".'[85]

These were the conditions under which leading Bastaard families attempted, after 1800, to establish new claims to land on the middle Orange. In doing so they were not alone. Thus Jan Bloem in the 1780s and 1790s seems to have welded together disparate Kora and Khoisan hunter-gatherers into a multi-ethnic unit, taking a wife from each new group. His final venture to construct a wider military alliance against the Ngwaketse failed, and on his return Bloem died of poisoning.[86]

Petrus Pienaar's other protégé, Klaas Afrikaner, was in the long run more successful in building a new social order in the frontier zone. In the mid-1790s Afrikaner and his sons fell out with Pienaar, killed him at his farm, and from an island base on the Orange began to accumulate an increasing following of Khoisan of the lower Orange valley, and even a scattering of Xhosa displaced from the Eastern Frontier. For a short period this political grouping fought against the colony in a war contemporary and perhaps even coordinated with the 1799 Khoikhoi rebellion on the Eastern Frontier. Afrikaner was joined by rebellious dependants and opposed by the colonial commandos, including both white and leading Bastaard families.[87] A state of mistrustful peace was restored between the colony and Afrikaner at the same time that the Eastern Frontier rebellion died away. For a time some missionaries had hopes of the emergence of an Oorlam-led state on the lower Orange parallel to that of the Bastaards in central Transorangia. But the dependence of Afrikaner's community on raiding militated against this and prompted a move further northwards into Namibia in the 1820s, where both the Afrikaner family and other Oorlam groups came to exert substantial hegemony through much of the nineteenth century.[88]

From shortly after the turn of the century, attempts to consolidate Transorangia politically came from the southeast rather than the southwest. Between 1805 and about 1814 the communities of the middle Orange valley and central Transorangia — Kora, Sotho-Tswana, and Bastaards alike — were harassed by a Xhosa-led raiding community, numbering perhaps three to five hundred, which appears to have been obtaining supplies of firearms from frontier farmers.[89] One of its original leaders was one Danster, a Xhosa who was for a while a follower of Afrikaner. In 1814 he was acting as a guide to the former Eastern Frontier 'rebel', Coenraad de Buys, in Transorangia. From this time it was De Buys who built up and led the most prominent Transorangian raiding community. He was able to win supporters from the Xhosa and dissident Bastaards and Oorlams by providing them with arms.[90] Like Bloem, his last venture in the Transorangia frontier zone was to construct a military alliance from Tlhaping, Rolong and others against the Kwena or Fokeng chiefdom, the Motlala. His venture was as unsuccessful as Bloem's. Thereafter he decisively separated himself from the trade links to the south and attached himself successively to a number of Sotho-Tswana communities, moving along the lines of trade with the Portuguese settlements on the east coast.[91]

The firearms frontier, and the commando-like organisation which was its corollary, tended therefore to create a need for social and political stability along the whole length of the Orange River valley. Over a period of a century the expansion of the northern colonial frontier zone had drastically compressed the belt where Khoisan lived, squeezing them against the southernmost limit of the Sotho-Tswana and intensifying conflict amongst themselves and between them and the Sotho-Tswana. Those who were dispossessed saw little alternative than plundering to reappropriate cattle; those who retained their cattle sought the means to defend them. In both cases the means were greater access, and privileged access, to arms and powder. But obtaining these goods generally meant selling cattle, or selling 'apprentices', along the southward trade routes, and this perpetuated and extended the cycle of raiding and dispossession.

Firearms not only caused the breakdown of existing social structures but also transformed them. The forms of political organisation which were re-created on the basis of firearms alone were, as Moorsom has argued, essentially parasitic.[92] The commando-based bands of the frontier zone became dependent on appropriating the production of others through raiding. As such productive resources became exhausted, the tendency was to seek them further afield rather than to create the conditions for renewed production. The hunting and trading in ivory was different from the trading and raiding of cattle, for at least ivory was *solely* a trade item, whereas cattle were both a means of subsistence and a potentially exchangeable commodity. Hence the depletion of ivory resources did not drain the vital resources of the existing communities of the area as did the depletion of cattle to levels where they could not reproduce fast enough to maintain the size of the herds.

The missionaries, who in 1801 came to live among the Bastaards of the middle Orange, dogmatically believed that greater economic and political stability could be achieved by the introduction of agriculture by the Bastaards themselves. But in fact, as a non-white frontiersman later argued to Andrew

Smith, either pastoralism or agriculture or both would have provided an economic basis.[93] This was partly an ecological question. It was also a political one: under what conditions could the necessary military power and political authority be generated to protect such an economic base?

The colonial government, the missionaries, and the evolution of the Griqua state, 1800—1814

The decisive step in the move of the leading Bastaard families from Little Namaqualand towards the middle Orange took place in 1800. At that time Jan Bloem died in central Transorangia, and on the lower Orange Afrikaner's powerful anti-colonial force had emerged which was disrupting trade into Namibia.[94] For several years drought and the activities of Afrikaner made the Bastaards uncertain where to establish themselves, but in 1804—05 crops were planted at a number of fountains around Klaarwater (later Griquatown) with good results. In April 1805 a beginning was made on the construction of houses in stone, and the Bastaards and their followers, numbering perhaps 400 to 500, took possession of a line of springs running some fifty miles southwest and northeast of Klaarwater. Other more distant fountains – they were to become Campbell and Danielskuil — were also identified at this time, though only settled later.[95]

It was from this time that the development of a new Bastaard-dominated political community in Transorangia became inextricably entangled with the activities of missionaries of the London Missionary Society, who in 1799 had started to arrive at the Cape. The British and Batavian regimes took some time to come to terms with the phenomenon of missionary activity: were its social affects to be regarded as dangerous or desirable? At the turn of the nineteenth century, missionaries were beginning to establish mission stations for the incipient 'Coloured' community whose economic function, at least so far as the Coloured occupants were concerned, was to provide a measure of subsistence for themselves, a guarantee of a separated sphere of property relationships which would reduce their dependence on service with colonial farmers. As far as the colonial government was concerned, however, the role of these institutions was to maintain social order and to preach the dignity of wage-labour. Missionaries were thus faced with pressures exerted by their conflicting socio-political roles, and adopted a variety of responses.[96]

It was the Bastaards themselves, and probably the Berends family, who first invited the London Missionary Society (LMS) to move to the middle Orange from the station they had established among Bastaards and Khoisan hunter-gatherers at the Zak River.[97] Here on the middle Orange there existed a fairly continuous missionary presence, until 1820 under the leadership of William Anderson, who arrived in April 1801 at the age of thirty-three.[98]

The Bastaards who invited the missionaries to the middle Orange apparently wanted to retain, and even strengthen, certain kinds of links with the colony at the same time that they were separating themselves from it geographically. They wanted access to the Cape Town market and a legal means of procuring arms and powder. They wanted to sustain their status as Christians, since, in colonial eyes, membership of this faith had a close correlation with citizenship.[99] In this sense they saw the missionaries as something like representatives of the colonial government, expecting them to ensure their equality of status with colonists. At the same time they were concerned to develop a polity with some form of autonomous economic base to supplement their trading activities. For this, too, they wanted the missionaries' support, desiring them to represent to the colony their collective rather than their individual interests. These contrary expectations of, on the one hand, colonial citizenship and, on the other, political independence, created tensions which were compounded by the suspicions held by the colonial authorities. The Batavian distrust of missions beyond the colony led to the recall of Van der Kemp from among the Xhosa. Two official colonial expeditions to Klaarwater, in 1801 and 1805, however reported favourably both on the mission at Klaarwater and on the Bastaards.[100]

The 1801 expedition appears to have regarded the Bastaard community as autonomous and under the authority of the Kok and Berends families, but favourably disposed towards the colony, and was prepared to allocate to Anderson and the Bastaards a supply of powder for the defence of the mission station.[101] The expedition of 1805, led by the landdrost of the newly-established district of Tulbagh, laid down much firmer regulations for the conduct of the mission, based on Governor Janssens's edict of February 1805. This edict recognised the right of accredited missionaries to teach and promote 'religion and cultivation among the heathen nations' beyond the colonial borders. But such stations should be established sufficiently far beyond the established boundaries that they had 'no communication with the inhabitants upon these boundaries, much less with those that live within them, either Christians or Heathens'. Moreover, the missionaries had the obligation to teach 'the first ideas of social order such as exists in the mother-country . . . as far as the capacity of the Natives is fit for comprehending [it]'. The teaching of writing was forbidden (though this part of the edict may not have been confirmed).[102] The landdrost elaborated on the edict by lecturing to the inhabitants of the Klaarwater settlement on 'obedience' to Anderson as 'one of their first duties; assuring them that the neglect of it would be considered as an offence against government, and would be punished accordingly.'[103]

The terms of this edict attempted a dramatic transformation in the relationship of the Bastaards and their followers with the colony. It expressly precluded them from trading with frontier farmers or with Cape Town, except through the missionaries themselves.[104] By implication it therefore encouraged them to become subsistence agriculturalists and pastoralists. But could such a transformation be effectively implemented? Sanctions could be exerted against Bastaards who came within the area of effective colonial authority, but not within the frontier zone itself.[105]

It was the missionaries who were ultimately most dependent on their attachments to the colony, logistically, culturally and personally. Sanctions could effectively be imposed on them by the colonial authorities and through them on the Bastaards. Indeed, the missionaries were quick to make use of the authority thus bestowed upon them by the colonial authorities. People who refused to help build a mission-house were threatened with government retribution; potential dissidents were warned that leaving the station would mean loss of their guns and of access to the colony. They distributed powder to ensure the loyalty of those at the settlement and to encourage the adherence of new members. They negotiated with groups hostile to the settlement, allocated and redistributed land and water resources, adjudicated disputes, and punished crimes.[106]

The community over which the missionaries attempted to exert such an authority was a growing one with considerable social stratification and with its forms of economic activity in a state of transformation. The Berends following, which invited Anderson to the Orange in 1801, may have numbered about 200 people. In 1813 the numbers appear to have increased to 1,266 Bastaards (including 291 adult males) and 1,341 Kora.[107] This increase partly represented an increasing drift from the area of the lower Orange and the Eastern Frontier region, and partly the incorporation of Khoisan communities on the spot. Among this population there were considerable gradations of wealth and status. At the head were the prominent Bastaard families. Cornelius Kok, who in 1816 moved to the middle Orange with 500 followers, owned perhaps some 45,000 sheep at his various farms.[108] Of the 3,000 cattle estimated at Klaarwater in 1812, Adam J. Kok (son of Cornelius) may have owned as many as 400, besides his 1,000 sheep, 800 goats and 3 teams of oxen . Other 'big men' among the Bastaards might have herds of 50 to 200 cows, while poorer Bastaards and others might have 2 or 3 cattle each.[109] The wealthier families had dependants whose treatment varied widely. While the Koks were noted for their benevolence, others among the Bastaards acted 'with great severity flogging and abusing them like slaves'.[110] Kora dependants were considered indolent and 'Bushman' dependants were preferred, especially for herding cattle at a distance from where the owner lived. By the 1820s it was very common for Bastaard cattle-owners to contract 'Bushmen' for hire, the men herding the cattle and the women guarding the cornfields.[111]

The main form of production was clearly pastoral, and cow's or goat's milk, supplemented by meat, was the basic diet. After 1804 crop cultivation, predominantly of maize and wheat, though with some vegetables, increased. The basic problem was the drying up of the fountains around Klaarwater. In 1812 Anderson stated that the maize crop was insufficient for subsistence needs. In the following decade cultivation by irrigation started at Campbell and Danielskuil.[112]

The political structure of the Klaarwater community resembled forms which had already existed in Little Namaqualand. Of these, three can be identified which shaded off into one another. The first was the authority of a Khoikhoi chief, which could become recognised by the colony. The second, characteristic of the frontier zone, was the authority of commando band leaders, created through their access to arms and powder and sustained through the distribution of spoils. The third was the power, implicitly reinforced in colonial law, of the head of a colonial family over its members and dependants. Colonial farms, argued Lichtenstein, were almost 'states in miniature'.[113] In all these respects the dominant figure of authority for the Bastaards in 1800 was Cornelius Kok, a wealthy farm-owner, a leading hunter and trader, and possibly already the possessor of a 'staff of office' from the colonial government.[114] In 1801 Cornelius 'appeared not only to command love and respect but also . . . to maintain his directions by the good feeling and co-operation of those about him. His followers . . . bore him willing allegiance from affection: his interests seemed closely connected with theirs, and his superiority as chief or captain was tacitly acknowledged'.[115]

In 1804 or 1805, relates Lichtenstein, 'the persons of most distinction among the Bastaard Hottentots were appointed as magistrates to inspect and take care of the rest'.[116] This new office of magistrate represented, at least potentially, a change in the form of political authority away from the patriarchy of the leading families, the Koks and the Berends. It seems plausible that, as a number of historians have implied, this innovation was stimulated by the missionaries. In the initial instance, however, the actual appointments made (and it is not clear how they were made) seem to have confirmed the authority of the leading families. Two of the magistrates, Salomon Kok and 'Kort Adam' Kok, were members of the Kok family and a third, Hans Lucas, was a close Kok associate. Two others, Piet and Klaas Berends, were from the second leading family, and another, Jan Hendrick, was a close Berends associate.[117] At this time the magistrates, asserted a later *kaptyn* at Griquatown, 'governed . . . in the name of old Cornelius Kok, as his deputies'.[118]

But whatever the basis and the practice of these initial appointments, the establishment of this new office created the potential for the development of 'popular' or at least anti-patriarchal power embodied in the magistrates. This tension was not dissimilar to that between the patriarchal military leader and the 'Volksraad' party which can be traced to as early as the Eastern Frontier 'republics' of the period, and which characterised much post-Trek frontier politics on the Highveld.[119]

In the case of the Klaarwater settlement, the potential tensions involved an additional factor: the role of the missionaries. Although, as Lichtenstein wrote, 'Anderson, with Kramer performed the office of pastor', the Janssens edict of 1805 gave the missionaries a political mandate. It brought them into potential conflict with the patriarchal structure of power, or with the magistrates, as they implemented the terms of the edict in the ways already outlined (see above, p. 264). At the same time the missionaries were increasingly not 'above and outside' the Klaarwater community, but actively involved in its social nexus, and this in two ways. Firstly, through marriages: the missionaries married into both the Pienaar and Engelbrecht families.[120] Secondly, through the emergence of a church membership at Klaarwater. Baptism commenced in 1807, and within two years the church had twenty-six adult and forty-six child members; by 1813 there were forty-two adults.[121]

Whatever the religious motivations involved, the development of a church had a two-fold political effect. Firstly, church members formed a cohesive political grouping, subject to the discipline of the missionaries, which could exert a powerful influence on the community either in its own interests or those of the missionaries. Secondly, it offered to less powerful and less wealthy members of the community, those not close to the leading families, a new status which could be used politically to challenge old elites. Early converts included members of the Pienaar, Hendrick and Goeyman families, as well as 'diligent' agriculturalists such as Moses Adam Renoseros or Willem Fortuin.[122] Another early convert was Andries Waterboer, who was to become kaptyn in 1820. Born in 1789, he was of 'Bushman' extraction with apparently no white ancestry and, according to some accounts, came to Klaarwater as a dependant of Adam J. Kok. The missionaries saw him as a 'truly serious young man' who had 'distinguished himself above all our people in receiving instruction' and he soon became their principal interpreter.[123] Moreover, some of the appointed magistrates soon gravitated to the 'church party' and became church members.

Although the records are obscure on these points, it may have been the growing influence of the missionaries through the church party, even to the extent of weaning the magistrates away from their client-like dependence on the leading families, which provoked counter-reaction. Certainly between 1807 and 1809 the magistrates were dismissed and replaced by Adam J. Kok and Berend Berends. In 1809 Anderson, travelling to Cape Town, obtained the sanction of Governor Caledon for these appointments, but he regarded them as 'chiefs' rather than as 'magistrates' and granted each of them a staff of office as 'chiefs'. It is significant that in the same memorial Anderson made an appeal to the colony for baptised members of the mission to be granted 'common privileges' with other colonial citizens, particularly free access to the colony.[124] The counter-reaction of the leading families against the influence of the church party may have won support by pointing out that increased missionary influence had been associated with greater exclusion from the colony rather than with any secular benefits.

Four years later, in 1813, there was a fresh attempt to establish a political structure for the community which could integrate the claims of the leading families with the increasing influence of the church and popular elements, and give a due place to the missionaries. These innovations were introduced by John Campbell, a director of the LMS, on a tour of South African stations.

One of Campbell's proposals was that the Bastaards change their name to 'Griqua' and that Klaarwater be renamed Griquatown, because 'on consulting among themselves they found a majority were descended from a person of the name of Griqua', that is, from the eponymous ancestor of the Khoikhoi clan, the /Karihur ('Chariguriqua').[125] The truth of this contention is less important than its bearing on the self-perception of the Bastaards. The change of name implied a change in reference-point from the colonial origins of the Bastaards to their claims of indigenous ancestry. It aimed, therefore, to break down the distinction between those who saw themselves as 'swarthy Hollanders' and those who were Oorlams, Kora or 'Bushmen', and to provide a basis through which indigenous Khoisan could become integrated into the polity. However, the distinction and concomitant tension persisted for some time, being constantly reinforced by those Bastaards who moved to Transorangia from the colony, and by the persistence of aboriginal Khoisan identities. But as early as the 1820s the distinctions between 'descendants of the colonists and of the aboriginal tribes' were reported to be breaking down.[126] And it was the name 'Griqua' which survived into the late nineteenth and early twentieth centuries in nostalgic remembrance of a better past.

Campbell also drew up a constitution. Adam J. Kok and Berend Berends were to remain as chiefs or kaptyns to act as 'commanders in things requiring the public safety' and, jointly with the missionaries, as a court of appeal. Thus was the status of the leading families protected. But by this time their influence was again on the wane: it extended, it was reported in 1811, 'very little beyond a voluntary submission on the part of the people. It is confined principally to that of ordering out the force of the tribe to attack an enemy, or to take up arms in defence of the settlement . . . But in ordinary cases, their power does not seem to be so strong, as the good of their society requires'.[127] Under the Campbell constitution, therefore, the popular elements secured their representation by electing nine magistrates who would be responsible for enforcing a constitution of thirteen clauses. For the most part this constitution affirmed existing prohibitions, those which had derived from the missionary interpretation of the 1805 edict. It also imposed severe punishments. Murder would be punished by execution; house-breaking, theft or bribery by flogging or hard labour. In 1816 important amendments provided for fines for failing to clear irrigation channels or failing to cultivate land.[128]

The final innovation concerned the church, and was probably the work of the Eastern Frontier missionary, James Read, who accompanied Campbell. At Bethelsdorp Van der Kemp had sought to involve Khoikhoi converts rapidly as officers of the church and itinerant evangelists. Campbell supported such a 'native agency' because a self-propagating church would release missionaries to begin work in more distant areas of southern Africa.[129] Therefore Campbell's visit was rapidly followed by the election of deacons in the Griquatown church and, in August 1814 at Graaff-Reinet, by the appointment of six 'native agents' for Transorangia, two from Bethelsdorp and four from Griquatown.[130]

All these innovations together provided the political basis for the strengthening of the Griquatown community, and indeed constructed a 'democratic oligarchy' which, as Ross has argued, formed the basis for most subsequent Griqua captaincies.[131] The native agency also provided a potential basis for the geographical extension of political authority over new territory and peoples. Thus, in the years after 1814, the native agents appointed at Graaff-Reinet, and others, settled themselves above and below Griquatown on the lower Orange and began to move north and east into Transorangia.[132] Their immediate purpose was evangelisation. But, as 'leaders' of the communities in which they were situated, they had a latent political role either for or against the Griquatown polity. In some cases individuals combined political and religious functions explicitly. Thus Berend Berends (kaptyn, deacon and native agent) and Peter David (magistrate, deacon and native agent) were initially at Kloof (formerly Hardcastle) after 1814, but before 1820 had moved to Danielskuil on the northeastern border of Griqua territory.[133] Equally, members of the Kok family, although not so woven into the Griquatown political or church structure, moved from the core of the polity to the settlement of Campbell.[134] Significantly both Danielskuil and Campbell had much greater potential for crop cultivation than did Griquatown itself.

In 1816 James Read, moving to the Tlhaping to re-establish an LMS station there in the wake of abortive attempts earlier in the century, took with him a number of native agents. Read concentrated on attempts to introduce improvements in agriculture and left religious instruction to Jan Hendrick, Griquatown magistrate, deacon and native agent.[135] At the same time native agents from Bethelsdorp were established both among the Kora in the Harts-Vaal area and at several stations for hunter-gatherers along the upper reaches of the Orange.[136]

Thus the native agency after 1814 created a core of Bastaards and Khoisan, exerting religious authority over a wide geographic spread of peoples from the lower Orange to the Tlhaping and across to the Harts-Vaal area. Nominally these people were subject to the religious authority of the LMS. But where did their political allegiances lie? Depending on the character of this political allegiance, they could act as foci for the extension of the hegemony of the Griquatown state, as nuclei for revolt against it, or as centres of autonomous political authority. In fact, in the ensuing years some of them played each of these roles.

The colonial government, the missionaries, and the peoples of the central Transorangia frontier zone, 1814–1820

In January 1814 the colonial government commanded William Anderson to supply twenty youths between the ages of seventeen and twenty from the Griquatown mission for the Cape (Hottentot) Regiment.[137] This command represented the first serious attempt by the colonial government to 'close' the Northern Frontier zone, at precisely the time when it had successfully completed this task on the Eastern Frontier. Because of the different conditions of the Northern Frontier zone, however, this attempt not only precipitated a rebellion which dislocated such political stability as had been achieved by the Griqua, but also prolonged the 'open' character of the frontier zone in Transorangia for another three decades.

The colonial government, in a letter to Anderson, defined the relationship between Griquatown and the colony. It stated: 'you may urge that your Institution is without the Colonial Border and therefore not properly subject to the Government of this Territory, but it is also to be remarked that you have on every occasion received protection from the Colony . . . If you then wish that this protection should be continued the Condition imposed must be that, by which every Society is bound, viz that of contributing to the General Protection.'[138] While the Janssens edict had demanded that no colonial subjects be accepted at Griquatown, the colony was now urging the Griqua to seek out and return to the colony any 'deserters' — slaves, Khoikhoi, Bastaards and criminals — along the Orange River valley.[139] This represented a new level of intervention by the colonial government which wished both to tighten its authority and to make fuller use of the labour resources of the colony.[140]

From Anderson's point of view the 'protection' accorded hitherto by the colony had been far from satisfactory. He had had to struggle to secure that access to arms, powder and the colonial market which would foster Bastaard hegemony in central Transorangia. For the Griqua the demand for military service in the colony, made more unpalatable by the low and segregated status of a 'Hottentot' regiment, was the breaking point. It seemed to represent a denial of the degree of autonomy, even if a *de facto* dependent autonomy, which had been guaranteed by the colonial recognition of the kaptyns in 1809, and the institution of Campbell's constitution in 1813. They would serve the colony in their 'native place', they insisted, but they would not furnish recruits. Anderson hastened to the colony to plead with the authorities. Annoyed that Campbell had seen fit to institute a constitution without its authorisation, the colonial government withdrew its support from the kaptyns, insisted that the Griqua would be regarded as subject to colonial law,[141] and told Anderson that the Griqua could expect no assistance or protection.

Anderson returned to Griquatown in February 1815 to find, not surprisingly, severe demoralisation and dissension. This soon escalated into actual revolt against the Griquatown polity as many of its subjects moved to the Harts River (some eighty km away) and styled themselves the 'Hartenaars'. At one level this was nothing more than a reversion to the trading-raiding patterns that had predominated in the Northern Frontier zone up to 1800 and which were continuing even as the Griquatown polity evolved. The dissidents linked up with the networks of illegal trade in arms and powder that existed and began to raid Khoisan communities for cattle and 'apprentices'.[142]

The dissidence had other, more important, dimensions. The rebellion was a rejection by a frontier zone community of attempts to 'close' the frontier by extending the sphere of effective colonial control, and as such was related to the revolts by white Eastern frontiersmen between 1795 and 1815. It was, indeed, contemporaneous with Slachtersnek and the Griqua rebels likewise became known as the 'Patriots'.[143] Significantly Coenraad de Buys, the former Eastern Frontier rebel who had crossed the Orange in 1814, was present among the Hartenaars. He did not instigate the revolt, but he could extend and confirm the participants' perceptions of their grievances.[144]

The revolt was therefore directed ultimately against the colony and the attempt to extend its authority. But since this authority was mediated through both the missionaries and the political structures established by the Campbell constitution of 1813, these, too, became objects of attack. Significantly, however, it was the kaptyns (the bearers of patriarchal authority, now sanctioned by the colonial government in weaker form) rather than the magistrates who were the major focus of hostility.

The dissidents commenced their revolt by refusing to cultivate, and by referring to Campbell's laws as the 'punishments'. Anderson and the kaptyns were blamed for the demand for conscripts, for the lack of gunpowder and for the prohibition on legal entry to the colony. 'You may compel me to stay, but you can't compel me to work' said one leader to Anderson. This hostility to the political role of the missionaries extended to their educational and evangelical activities.[145] 'As to losing their teachers they did very well before they came and could do again as well without them', said another. At the Harts, it was reported, the rebels 'had given up all religious worship' and some went so far as to 'testify their aversion to it'. Anticipating that many still at the station would support them, they planned to attack Griquatown, seize the gunpowder, and shoot Anderson and Kaptyn Kok (but not Berends). The Hartenaars, it was said 'had bound themselves not to speak Dutch, nor to ask after each other's welfare' (the latter point no doubt being a reference to habits of bourgeois politeness which had been inculcated by the missionaries).[146] Since former pillars of the community and the church (such as Jacob Cloete, church member and elected magistrate) were among the leaders of the revolt, those who remained in support of the church were also particular foci for hostility.[147]

Anderson's first response to the widespread rebellion was a renewed attempt to win the right for those authorised by the mission to have free access to the colony. In return, he said, the Griqua would try to capture and return deserters.[148] The colonial authorities were not interested in this compromise. Anderson then fell back on an attempt to boost the authority of the leading families, including summoning the patriarch, Cornelius Kok, to move to the area from the lower Orange. This, too, was of no avail: the Campbell constitution had already connived in the creation of a new source of authority (the elected magistrates), and the popular aspirations this aroused could not now be denied.[149] Anderson therefore shifted his position and began to make overtures to the rebels, saying that he would withdraw support from the kaptyns and bolster the authority of the council of magistrates.

It was on this basis that the Hartenaars began to return to Griquatown, and by the middle of 1817 most of them had been pardoned and re-admitted to the church. Berends and Kok, related Waterboer later, were summoned several times before the council of magistrates (an unprecedented occurrence), and reprimanded for their neglect of duty until 'they became dissatisfied, went from the presence of the Council, and Captain A. Kok threw away his Captain's Staff and immediately removed from the place, with his whole family, to the Great Orange River. Berend Berends also left the place, with a small following.'[150] In withdrawing, Berends and Kok accused Anderson of unwarranted leniency towards the rebels: 'his system is contrary to the Bible and he wishes to be a terror to them that do well and protect them that do evil'.[151]

Neither the return of the Hartenaars, nor the departure of Kok and Berends to Campbell and Danielskuil respectively, restored complete tranquillity. Although there was more cultivation of crops and good harvests in 1817 and 1818, conflict resumed. Waterboer later wrote of the destruction of gardens, the hamstringing of cattle, and renewed threats on the life of Anderson. Anderson himself began to complain increasingly of spiritual and temporal 'backsliding' and 'degeneracy'. Finally, in February 1820, the situation grew too much for him and he left Griquatown for the colony.[152]

In despair Anderson now abandoned all his attempts to construct an independent Griqua polity, whether under the leadership of the patriarchs, the magistrates, or a combination of both. 'Were some measures not adopted to crush the existence of the Bastaard Independency', he wrote to the colonial authorities, 'it would prove ruinous to them, and most detrimental to the prosperity of the Colony'.[153]

This was exactly the direction in which the thinking of the colonial authorities had been developing since the Griqua defiance in 1814. In addition to the refusal to send conscripts, the colonial government believed that desertions to the Northern Frontier zone were increasing, and that trading of arms and powder, and raiding of cattle and 'apprentices' were also on the increase.[154] This was true; white and Bastaard frontiersmen were, from the time of De Buys, pioneering new routes from the Graaff-Reinet area into Transorangia. The response of the government was, however, to act against missionaries rather than such persons. In 1817 the government ordered the closure of the upper Orange River out-stations for the Khoisan hunter-gatherers, staffed by the Bethelsdorp native agents and others (including a West Indian). It also refused to allow four newly-arrived LMS missionaries, including Robert Moffat, to take up their positions at stations outside the colony.[155] It recommended that the Griquatown mission should become directly subject to colonial law under the authority of the nearest magistracy (the newly created one of Beaufort West).[156] In June 1819 Governor Somerset went further, arguing to the recently arrived LMS superintendent, John Philip, that the Griquatown mission should be broken up and re-established 'either within the Colonial border or at least so close to it as to be considered under the control of the Colonial government'.[157]

It was this last recommendation that, in February 1820, Anderson was endorsing. Acting governor Donkin responded rapidly, ordering Andries Stockenstrom, landdrost of Graaff-Reinet, to take Griquatown by surprise with two companies of Cape Infantry and a burgher commando, to seize the Griqua firearms and cattle, and to return all the Griqua to the colony. Stockenstrom, who had visited Griquatown in 1818 and who had obtained a rather different picture of events from the kaptyns than that presented by Anderson, demurred. An attack on Griquatown, he argued, would force the Griqua to flee further into the interior.[158] Stockenstrom recommended as the most desirable course that the colonial boundary should be extended to include Griquatown, and a landdrost appointed to the settlement. If this was regarded as too expensive, he suggested as an alternative that the Griqua should be given renewed recognition as an independent community.[159]

The basis on which Stockenstrom supported this second proposal was a novel one. Bringing them back into the colony, he maintained, would 'generate the entire dissolution of the shadow of restraint which, little as it is, keeps the Corannas [i.e., Kora] from those depradations of which the colony formerly had to complain'. He did not, in other words, present the Griqua as a force essentially hostile and menacing to the colony. Nor did he present the missionaries as the only force for stability and 'civilisation' in the Northern Frontier zone. He was, in fact, suggesting that the Griqua should be seen in their own right as potential allies of the colony, as active agents and collaborators in 'closing' the Northern Frontier zone by extending stability in the area.[160] It was this view of the Griqua which began to inform colonial Northern Frontier policy after 1820, although it did not come to full (if belated) fruition until the 1830s in the treaty state policy.

However, even as the colonial government began to accord recognition to the Griqua as a stabilising force with the appointment of a government agent in 1822 to establish a liaison with the Griquatown kaptyn, the inner fissures which had generated the problems of the previous decade began to re-emerge. On 20 December 1820 Berends was forced to follow Adam Kok into resigning his office at Griquatown. In his place Andries Waterboer was elected as kaptyn. This replacement of the authority of the two leading Bastaard families by an elected kaptyn of 'Bushman' extraction was a step which reinforced the 'popular' party in the polity. But Waterboer did not continue to command universal support. Adam Kok and Berend Berends, established at Campbell and Danielskuil, formed competing poles of political allegiance. These latent conflicts were compounded by the existence of other settlement centres which were led by the native agents who had been established there in the previous decade.

As the firearms frontier penetrated more deeply and widely through Transorangia, these separate centres acted to weaken the hegemony of the Griquatown polity rather than acting as a religious-political spine which could strengthen and extend that hegemony. A number of the native agents were themselves involved in illegal arms trading and, possibly, raiding, and situated themselves at the major ford over the upper Orange at Philippolis. Twenty years later Philippolis, as the centre of a new Griqua polity headed by the Kok family, was to become the fulcrum of a struggle for leadership in the establishment of a stable hegemony in Transorangia, a struggle between the Griqua and the Voortrekkers.

Epilogue

By 1820, then, the northern economic frontier of the Cape Colony had been extended by Bastaard-Oorlam-Griqua frontiersmen into southern Namibia, lapped at the southernmost Sotho-Tswana communities in central Transorangia, and was spreading among the Kora and Khoisan hunter-gatherers of eastern Transorangia. This northern expansion of the colonial frontier had been accompanied both by conflict and by forms of cooperation, inextricably linked. The commando involved persons cooperating in order to engage in conflict. The establishment of the Griquatown state necessitated cooperation but inflamed old, and generated new, lines of conflict.

What was also evident, however, was the emergence of new patterns of domination and exploitation. Increasingly dominance was falling to those with firearms and those who could, directly or indirectly, muster the support of the colonial government. Moreover, whatever the forms of differential distribution of property in Bantu-speaking and Khoisan societies, the impact of the frontier was beginning to sharpen and transform those differences. On the one hand there were the owners of land, of cattle, of instruments of production; on the other there were dependants, servants, even wage-labourers. The specific features of the Northern Frontier zone in 1820 were, in comparison with the Eastern Frontier, twofold. In the first place those who held political authority, who dominated, who were property-owners, who exploited, were not all white; indeed, they were predominantly non-white. Secondly, by 1820 the Northern Frontier zone had not come within the effective control of the Cape government: the possibility existed for the consolidation of political and social relationships on the basis of Bastaard-Oorlam-Griqua hegemony.

But what were the prospects for Griqua hegemony? This is an important question which has not received enough attention in a historiography preoccupied by the Great Trek and the establishment of the Republic of the Orange Free State based on a democratic oligarchy of whites alone. Although the Northern Frontier for most of the period under discussion had been characterised by hunting, trading and raiding, there were centres of more stable settlement and attempts to establish new forms of political organisation, authority and legitimacy. This was true not only of the Griqua on the middle Orange but also of the community dominated by the Afrikaner family in southern Namibia, and even of the small clusters of Bastaard and Griqua families strung out along the upper Orange. By the early 1830s there were at least three centres of Griqua power in Transorangia, centred on Andries Waterboer at Griquatown, Adam Kok at Philippolis and Berend Berends on the Harts River at Boetsap.[161] Bastaards, or armed and mounted Kora groups aspiring to the condition of Griqua polities, were also dotted across southeastern Transorangia. Most of these communities had a missionary presence, a potential form of mediation with the colonial authorities; and some aspired to a closer relationship with the Cape government through treaties. In the 1830s the parasitism of raiding was complemented by hunting and trading, by pastoralism, and by some engagement with agriculture. Throughout eastern Transorangia clients and dependants were predominantly Khoisan, but in the region of Philippolis there were also groups of Sotho-Tswana.

In many respects the forms of social relationships in this region, the political and economic structures of society, were not dissimilar to those of the early Trekker societies. As has recently been argued, the Boer Republics were not based on 'yeomen farmers but on the domination of a class of land-owning notables over lesser whites and, more fundamentally, over Khoisan and African captives and tributary groups.'[162] Peter Wright, the missionary at Griquatown, began to develop a rationale for Griqua domination over the Sotho-Tswana which bears comparison with that of the early Trekker claims. The Griqua, he argued, were right in leaving the production of their food-crops to the Tswana, whose methods of cultivating the arid Griquatown area were more efficient.[163] With the time saved by this rational division of labour the Griqua could devote themselves to the defence of the district, thus sparing the 'timid' and 'defenceless' Tswana the expense, labour and risk of 'public duty in the general defence'. Here, in truth, was the emerging ideology of a 'democratic oligarchy' of armed warriors (and hunters and traders) justifying their domination over tributary producers.

The question arises: why were the Griqua unable to sustain a comparable hegemony based on similar forms of domination and exploitation? Focussing on Griquatown, J.S. Marais gave as reasons for their failure nomadism, lack of individual land tenure, and improvidence.[164] However, these characteristics were also found at the vanguard of the Trekker frontier and were associated, firstly, with the predominance of hunting, trading and raiding.

Part of the blame has also been laid on the political squabbles among the Griqua and their inability to create effective forms of political authority. It is true that the Griqua were divided; yet the Trekker Republics in Transvaal were also riddled with conflicts, and an *effective* unified political authority was not created earlier than the 1870s. The indecision of the Cape government, together with their ineffective protection of Griqua interests, have also been taken into account.[165]

Yet even more important were the detrimental policies of the missionaries. Their commitment to the economically unviable and politically peripheral Griquatown state of Andries Waterboer was unsound and tended to exacerbate conflict with other Griqua communities. Their efforts should rather have been directed to a Griqua concentration further east, perhaps securing at an early stage a treaty between the Cape government and the Philippolis Griqua who were in line with the major advance of white frontiersmen.[166]

However, it would be implausible to place the weight of the explanation for the failure of Griqua hegemony on the actions of either the Cape government or the missionaries. At least two other factors need to be considered. The first is the effects of the *Mfecane* on the attempts at Griqua consolidation in the 1820s and 1830s. The Bantu-speaking raiding groups, which after 1822 erupted onto the Highveld and into Transorangia, delayed by at least a decade the consolidation of Griqua hegemony and retarded the geographical expansion of hunting and trading, which might have provided a firmer base for settled Griqua polities. Based on the commando, the Griqua were unable to establish a military superiority over the Bantu-speaking armies and lost the opportunity to present themselves as the hegemonic force in Transorangia. It was seized by the Voortrekkers, whose immediate advantage lay in the defensive possiblities of the *laager* (circle of ox-wagons), added to the aggressive advantages of the commando.

The second factor to be assessed is whether, after the Great Trek, the Griqua might not have secured a different place in the social structure of Transorangia. It would be a mistake to imagine that the Griqua were to be excluded automatically from citizenship in the Voortrekker Republics, that there was some inherent 'race-feeling' among white frontiersmen which precluded the possibility of an interracial hegemony over Khoisan and Sotho-Tswana dependants. It is true that the first Trekker political document mentioning non-white political rights (the Thirty-Three Articles) stipulated that 'No half-caste down to the tenth degree shall be entitled to sit in our meetings as a member or judge'. Yet the same Hendrik Potgieter who played a leading role in drawing up this document wrote some months later to Adam Kok at Philippolis: 'We are emigrants together with you and are regarded as such and regard ourselves as emigrants who together with you dwell in the same strange land, and we desire to be regarded as neither more nor less than your fellow-emigrants, inhabitants of the country, enjoying the same privileges with you'.[167]

It can be cogently argued that it was from the British annexation of the Orange River Sovereignty in 1848, and not from the time of the Great Trek, that the Griqua claims to participation in hegemony in Transorangia were undermined. This undermining was not a consequence of a dramatic increase in the power of the white frontiersmen. The economic and political changes in the era of British hegemony in the sovereignty appear to have been more crucial. From the 1840s the large amounts of capital which were being invested in the Cape in wool production and speculation began to spread into Transorangia. The large traders and land speculators tended to base themselves in Bloemfontein rather than Philippolis, where the Griqua had also taken up sheep farming with considerable success.[168] It has been argued that this 'English party' was largely responsible for the constitution of the independent Free State, which restricted the franchise and the obligations of military service to whites alone,[169] thereby excluding the Griqua. If, as Houghton has written, the 'economic impact of international markets were carried into the interior, not in the wagons of the Voortrekkers, but upon the backs of merino sheep',[170] it was the effects of that international market, of those merino sheep, which created the Orange Free State and sealed the fate of the Griqua.

Chapter Seven   Notes

1. See, for example, I. Wallerstein, *The Modern World-System: Capitalist Agriculture and the Origins of the European World-Economy in the Sixteenth Century* (New York, 1974).
2. See particularly K. Marx, *Capital*, I, chs. 1–3; E.B. Pashukanis, *The General Theory of Law and Marxism* (forthcoming).
3. I have learned that it is unwise to advertise one's writings prior to publication; it is the way to inhibit their production, and can lead to their misrepresentation. However, I hope to deal with this theme in *Capitalism and Segregation* (forthcoming).
4. See W.M. Macmillan, *The Cape Colour Question* (Cape Town, 1969), p. 11.
5. Among the first to discuss the concept of 'cooperation' was H.M. Robertson, '150 Years of Economic Contact between White and Black', *South African Journal of Economics,* II (1934) and III (1935).
6. For discussion and criticism of the assumptions of this school, see M. Legassick, 'The Frontier Tradition in South African Historiography', *Collected Seminar*

Papers on the Societies of Southern Africa in the Nineteenth and Twentieth Centuries, II (London, 1971); 'The Dynamics of Modernization in South Africa', *Journal of African History,* XIII, I (1972), pp. 145–50; *The Analysis of 'Racism' in South Africa,* Dar es Salaam: United Nations/African Institute for Economic Development and Planning, 1975.

7. J. Rex, *Race Relations in Sociological Theory* (London, 1970); A.G. Frank, *Capitalism and Underdevelopment in Latin America* (London, 1967). For a critique of Frank and others see M. Legassick, 'Perspectives on African "Underdevelopment"', *JAH,* XVII (1976).

8. KA 4119, Res 13 March 1739. (I am grateful to Richard Elphick for this reference.) Those involved were in this instance summoned to a colonial court and instigated a petty and unsuccessful frontier revolt: the government then issued a severe general plakkaat against any trading with the indigenous population. See E.A. Walker, *A History of South Africa* (London, 1928), pp. 97–98. The quotation is from F. le Vaillant, *Travels into the Interior Parts of Africa by way of the Cape of Good Hope in the years 1780–1785* (London, 1790), II, 72–73.

9. L. Duly, *British Land Policy at the Cape 1795–1844: A Study of Administrative Procedures in the Empire* (Durban, 1968) discusses the chaos in the land tenure system by the early nineteenth century.

10. The tradition of explanations based on 'trekgeest', which can involve certain philosophical assumptions about man's essentially migratory nature, and which stressed the *detachment* of frontier society from Western Cape society, was empirically challenged by S.D. Neumark, *Economic Influences on the South African Frontier, 1652–1836* (Stanford, 1957). Neumark emphasises the frontiersmen as bearers of commodity relationships; and his argument is not wholly refuted by W.K. Hancock, 'Trek', *Economic History Review,* 2nd series, X (1958), pp. 331–59. There is perceptive discussion of these issues in M. Moerane, 'Towards a Theory of Class Struggle in South Africa: Historical Perspectives', *Maji-Maji* (Dar es Salaam), 21 July 1975; and important theoretical and empirical investigation of this issue among others is being undertaken by Stanley Trapido, Institute of Commonwealth Studies, Oxford.

11. For the concept of a frontier zone see M. Legassick, 'The Griqua, the Sotho-Tswana, and the missionaries, 1780–1840: the Politics of a Frontier Zone' (Ph.D., University of California, 1969), pp. 1–22. I must acknowledge my debt to W.K. Hancock in thinking through this concept.

12. The commando system has not been adequately treated; but see G. Tylden, 'The development of the Commando System in South Africa, 1715–1792', *Africana Notes and News,* XII, December 1959, pp. 303–13; P.E. Roux, 'Die geskiedenis van burger-kommando's in die Kaapkolonie, 1652–1878' (Ph.D., University of Stellenbosch, 1946). The best treatment of Khoisan resistance in this period is S. Marks, 'Khoisan Resistance to the Dutch in the Seventeenth and Eighteenth Centuries', *JAH,* XIII (1972).

13. J.S. Marais, *The Cape Coloured People, 1652–1937* (Johannesburg, 1937), pp. 11–12, 26, 32, 74. See also P.J. van der Merwe, *Trek* (Cape Town, 1945), p. 207; W.P. Carstens, *The Social Structure of a Cape Coloured Reserve* (Cape Town, 1966), p. 19.

14. The specific weighting of the discussion cannot but be influenced by the volume and character of the sources available. For much of the time the indigenous

peoples left few literary sources, and usable oral traditions did not generally survive. Moreover, the preoccupations of racist and liberal South African historiography and anthropology have mystified almost all the available subsequent records. For the earlier period travellers' accounts, the Cape Archives and oral tradition recorded in the early nineteenth century are valuable; subsequent footnotes criticise the interpretation of such sources. From 1800 the almost continuous presence of missionaries provides a systematic, though partisan, eye-witness record of events, supplemented by travellers, the Cape Archives and oral traditions.

15. The standard, though seriously outmoded, account of the indigenous inhabitants of Namibia is H. Vedder, *South West Africa in Early Times* (London, 1938). It is preoccupied with 'origins and movements' on the one hand, and a static ethnic description of social structure in the timeless anthropological present on the other. Namibian history is good only on the period of German colonisation, except for the valuable recent reinterpretation of the nineteenth century by R. Moorsom, 'The Political Economy of Namibia until 1945' (M.A., University of Sussex, 1973). In a truly independent South West Africa/Namibia we may expect a revival of serious scientific historical work.

16. The literature on the Sotho-Tswana is surveyed, and some reinterpretation offered, in M. Legassick, 'The Sotho-Tswana peoples before 1800', *African Societies,* ed. L.M. Thompson (London, 1969), pp. 86–125. The furthest expansion of Sotho to the southeast is discussed in PEMS, G.M. Theal – H.M. Dyke, 4 Oct. 1883; H.M. Dyke – G.M. Theal, 23 April 1883; and D.F. Ellenberger, 'Preamble to Third Period of History of the Basutos 1833–1854' (Ellenberger Archives). I am grateful to William Lye for providing these sources.

17. Prior to Elphick, the most comprehensive account is I. Schapera, *The Khoisan Peoples of South Africa* (London, 1930), which suffers from defects similar to those in Vedder's account (see note 15).

18. The first documentary evidence supporting the existence of Khoikhoi (herding) communities north of and along the Orange comes, for the coastal areas, from the seventeenth century and, for the middle Orange, from the journeys of Wikar and Gordon. See Richard Elphick, *Kraal and Castle: Khoikhoi and the Founding of White South Africa* (New Haven, 1977), p. 20; *The Journal of Hendrik Jakob Wikar (1779) and the Journals of Jacobus Coetsé Jansz (1760) and Willem van Reenen (1791),* ed. E.E. Mossop (Cape Town, 1935); Staffordshire County Record Office D 593/U/4/1 to 5, Four Journals of Captain R.J. Gordon.

19. The first Kora penetration north of the Vaal seems to have occurred after 1800; see *inter alia* John Campbell, *Travels in South Africa . . . Second Journey* (London, 1822), II, 293; MMS, S. Broadbent, 1 June 1823; T. Wangemann, *Geschichte der Berliner Missiongesellschaft und ihrer Arbeiten in Süd Afrika* (Berlin, 1872), II, 6 ff. However, T.M.O'C Maggs, 'Pastoral Settlements on the Riet River', *South African Archaeological Bulletin* (1971), p. 37-61 posits pre-nineteenth-century pastoralism in this area.

20. See Legassick, 'The Griqua', p. 62.

21. The problems in such a venture are illustrated by any attempt to use for the purpose Vedder, *South West Africa,* J. Engelbrecht, *The Korana* (Cape Town, 1936), and L.F. Maingard, 'The Lost Tribes of the Cape', *South African Journal of Science,* XXVII (1931), pp. 487–504; 'Studies in Korana History, Customs, and Language', *Bantu Studies,* VI (1932), pp. 103–62. On the other hand,

these scholars evinced an interest in the 'peoples discarded by history', such as the Khoikhoi – an interest which has atrophied until the 1960s.

22. See, as a recent attempt along these lines, R. Moorsom, 'Political Economy'. *The Oxford History of South Africa* claimed in its introduction to be replacing 'ethnic' by 'economic' categories, but achieved variable success in this respect.

23. G. and M. Wilson, *The Analysis of Social Change* (Manchester, 1945).

24. For the Tlhaping *sibello* quarry see Campbell, *Second Journey,* II, 194—96.

25. The classic, but dated, accounts of Tswana political structure are by I. Schapera, *Handbook of Tswana Law and Custom* (London, 1938); *Government and Politics in Tribal Societies* (London, 1956) (which deals also with Khoisan). But the brief comments here are confirmed by every early traveller: see Legassick, 'Griqua', pp. 30—39.

26. C. Saunders, 'Early Knowledge of the Sotho: Seventeenth and Eighteenth Century Accounts of the Tswana', *Quarterly Bulletin of the South African Library* (1966), pp. 60—70; Legassick, 'Sotho-Tswana', pp. 107—10; Alan Smith, 'Delagoa Bay and the Trade of South-Eastern Africa', *Precolonial African Trade,* ed. R. Gray and D. Birmingham (London, 1970), pp. 265—89.

27. MMS, Hodgson and Archbell, 31 March 1827. Also Campbell, *Second Journey,* II, 214; W.J. Burchell, *Travels in the Interior of South Africa* (London, 1953), II, 216, 247—48.

28. See Legassick, 'The Griqua' pp. 51—55.

29. R. Moffat, *Missionary Labours and Scenes in South Africa* (London, 1842), ch. XXIII.

30. I. Schapera, 'A Short History of the Bangwaketse', *African Studies,* I (1942), pp. 1—26.

31. On these events see Legassick, 'Griqua', pp. 60—68.

32. *RCC,* IV, 380.

33. Legassick, 'Griqua', pp. 69–70, 251–54, 271–72.

34. LMS, Read, 15 March 1817. On the existence of ruling lineage intermarriage and its origins see Legassick, 'Griqua', pp. 61, 68—70.

35. LMS, Mothibi, quoted in R. Moffat, 23 Nov. 1836.

36. The trading-raiding expedition of 1738 mentioned in note 8 may have been the first party of frontiersmen to reach the Orange; official expeditions travelled to and across the lower Orange in 1760 and 1761—62. Both these expeditions were accompanied by the Bastaard Klaas Berends who, by the time of the next recorded journeys, had a cattle-kraal near the junction of the Hartebeest and Orange, and appears to have been trading both into Great Namaqualand and up the Orange valley.

37. In 1797 Lord Macartney, for the British administration, reconfirmed the regulations stipulating that gunpowder was to be purchased from the government alone, and forbidding resale. Official statistics on powder and arms sales thereafter may be found in Great Britain Government Publication 252 of 1835, Wade – Stanley, 14 Jan. 1834, pp. 75—84.

38. This, the earliest definition I have traced of a term which became widely used in the nineteenth century (especially in Namibia) is from Albrecht and Siedenfaden, entry 12 Oct. 1805 (LMS Journals).

39. Smith, *Diary,* I, 203—4. The date is derived by J.A. Engelbrecht, *The Korana: An Account of their Customs and their History* (Cape Town, 1936), p. 20, from documents in the Cape Archives; the dispute was between Kora chiefs named

Taaibosch and Philip. For Van Zyl's complaints a few years earlier about Bastaards trading with the Nama, see note 80 below.

40. *The Journals of Brink and Rhenius,* ed. E.E. Mossop (Cape Town, 1947), pp. 114—15. See Moffat's comments in Smith, *Diary,* I, 255—56; Moffat, *Missionary Labours,* ch. 5.

41. See, for example, LMS Journals, Albrecht etc., entry Aug. 1805; Carstens, *Social Structure,* pp. 107—8; A. Smith, *The Diary of Dr. Andrew Smith* (Cape Town, 1939), I, 203.

42. For more information on deserters such as the Kruger brothers and Stephanus see Legassick, 'The Griqua', pp. 137—38, 140, 147—48.

43. On Pienaar see Legassick, 'The Griqua', pp. 133—34, 143.

44. On Bloem see Legassick, 'The Griqua', pp. 133—37, 251.

45. For Klaas Afrikaner and his sons see Legassick, 'The Griqua', pp. 141—42. Possibly the first mention of Afrikaner is in the Gordon Collection: Staffordshire County Record Office, D 593/U/4/1/6, entry of 8 Dec., n.p. (I am indebted to Richard Elphick for this reference.)

46. See also ch. 3 in this volume.

47. *RCC,* XXI, Evidence by Maynier, 25 April 1825, p. 394.

48. Lichteinstein, *Travels,* II, 303. Also I.D. MacCrone, *Race Attitudes in South Africa* (Oxford, 1937), p. 98. Contemporary sources, and later research, provide much evidence of both 'white' and 'Bastaard' descendants of late eighteenth-century white frontiersmen: Engelbrechts, Van der Westhuizens, Bloems, Krugers, Pienaars. See Legassick, 'Griqua', pp. 115—17, 138—39, 172, 186, 190, 199, 218, 220, 317ff., 356—58, 512, 547, 549ff. Also E. Fischer, *Die Rehobother Bastards und das Bastardierungsproblem beim Menschen* (Jena, 1913); J.A. Heese, 'Onderwys in Namakwaland: 1750—1940' (D. Ed. thesis, University of Stellenbosch), pp. 79—82.

49. H. Lichtenstein, *Travels in Southern Africa in the Years 1803, 1804, 1805* (Cape Town, 1928), II, 241; Heese, 'Onderwys', p. 80.

50. LMS, Anderson, 12 Aug. 1806; Lichenstein, *Travels,* II, 244.

51. D. Moodie, *The Record* (Amsterdam, 1969), III, 34, 77ff. For such persons managing loan farms, or farming themselves, see for example *Journal of Brink,* pp. 74—75; Lichtenstein, *Travels,* I, 55, 82; W. Paterson, *A Narrative of Four Journeys into the Country of the Hottentots and Caffraria* (London, 1787), pp. 46, 102—3.

52. See Campbell, *Second Journey,* II, 359ff; and, for eighteenth-century Cape archival references to Adam Kok (sometimes described as a 'Hottentot'), Heese, 'Onderwys', p. 76; R.J. Ross, 'The Griquas of Philippolis and Kokstad, 1826—1879' (Ph.D., University of Cambridge, 1974), p. 21.

53. For origins of the Berends family see Legassick 'Griqua', pp. 112—15; also MacCrone, *Race Attitudes,* p. 80. Heese claims that Klaas Berends married a white woman named Cloete, the same to whom Le Vaillant, *Travels,* II, 150–51, refers as the chief of a Little Nama community (personal communication from Hermann Giliomee).

54. Though there is a certain convergence between the terms 'Bastaard' and 'Oorlam', it should be noted that the first originates in a designation applied within the colonial system of social stratification, becoming 'accepted' by those to whom it applied; 'Oorlam' seems to originate in a designation applied by extra-colonial Khoikhoi to those who had been 'in service', becoming 'accepted' by

those to whom it applied. In Namibia in the nineteenth century there remained a clear distinction between Oorlam communities and the Bastaard communities who emigrated from the south later; in central Transorangia both terms tended to disappear in favour of 'Griqua'.

55. For an example of a Bastaard-led raiding party, see *Journal of Wikar*, p. 47.

56. For subsequent estimates of the date that Bastaards reached (or established cattle-kraals on) the Orange, see Lichtenstein, *Travels*, II, 240, 252; LMS, Anderson, 12 Aug. 1806; Burchell, *Travels*, I, 252; Campbell, *Second Journey*, II, 359—60.

57. For the pre-1800 journey by Cornelius and Hans Luyken (Hans Lucas?) to the Rolong, see Theal, *RCC*, IV, 404; J. Barrow, *Voyage to Cochinchina* (London, 1806).

58. For the growing scarcity of elephants, see Lichtenstein, *Travels*, II, 259; LMS, Anderson, 21 Aug. 1809.

59. Lichtenstein, *Travels*, II, 240, 252, 259. J. Barrow, *An Account of Travels into the Interior of Southern Africa*, II, 305, says that the *official* figures for the ivory trade over four years (probably c. 1795—1798) were 5,981 pounds valued at 6,340 rixdollars. On the profitability and potentialities of the ivory trade see also Neumark, *South African Frontier*, pp. 64—67; S. Bannister, *Humane Policy...* (London, 1829), pp. 110—16.

60. Lichtenstein, *Travels*, II, 259, claimed that 'Individuals among the Bastaard families have sometimes come privately to Cape Town, where they have bought the powder more advantageously; but experience has taught them that it is better to give the higher price, and be spared the fatigue and expense of the journey'. Given the strenuous post-1800 attempts by Bastaards to open up legal access to Cape Town, it would seem more likely that it was other concerns (possibilities of military conscription?) that were hindering them before that time.

61. See Burchell, *Travels*, II, 329, 391; Campbell, *Second Journey*, II, 23, 274; Moffat, *Apprenticeship*, pp. 171, 280; LMS, Melvill, 2 April 1827; Smith, *Diary*, I, 332, 362, 371, 408—9. The institution of trading *maats*, which characterised this trade, involved the sharing of property and of wives.

62. See LMS, Edwards, 27 July 1802; Anderson, 12 Aug. 1806; LMS Journals, Anderson entries 21 April 1806, 11 May 1807; Burchell, *Travels*, I, 253—54; II, 196, 230, 280ff, 368, 379—80, 414; Campbell, *Second Journey*, II, 216; Moffat, *Apprenticeship*, p. 187; Smith, *Diary*, I, 251.

63. Flints, steel knives, European clothing and haberdashery also began to develop a small market. On trade see Barrow, *Cochinchina*, p. 403; *RCC*, IV, 380—86; Lichtenstein, *Travels*, II, 308–10; LMS Journals, Anderson, entry March 1808; see also Legassick, 'Griqua', pp. 254, 273, 535–36.

64. See Burchell, *Travels*, I, 253–54; II, 196, 284, 380; Legassick, 'Griqua', pp. 235—37. The Bastaards at Klaarwater were also able to increase their supply of firearms from about 50 in 1801 to perhaps 500 in 1823.

65. In perhaps only two years of hunting, J.M. Kok netted 3,000 rixdollars, and in 1806 William Edwards made 3,200 rixdollars in two journeys to the Cape. See LMS Journals, Anderson, entry Nov. 1804; Burchell, *Travels*, II, 283; Campbell, *Travels*, p. 317. See also Legassick, 'Griqua', p. 236.

66. These frontiersmen were all previously involved with the Xhosa. See R. Wagner, 'Coenraad de Buys in Transorangia', *Collected Seminar Papers on the Societies of Southern Africa in the Nineteenth and Twentieth Centuries*, IV

(1974), pp. 1–3; Legassick, 'Griqua', pp. 244ff.

67. Legassick, 'Griqua', pp. 353—55. These activities in western Transorangia contest the implication in G.M. Theal, *Basutoland Records* (Cape Town, 1883), II, 424 that the Boers first crossed this part of the Orange River in 1819, but only to hunt.

68. *RCC,* XI, Somerset – Bathurst, 23 Jan. 1817, pp. 252—56. See also *inter alia RCC,* XII, Stockenstrom – C.O., 27 Aug. 1818, pp. 34–36; Smith, *Diary,* I, 357—58; Wagner, 'De Buys', p. 3 and Legassick, 'Griqua', p. 247.

69. Thus, despite desperate efforts directed towards all who visited them, the T'lhaping were unable to evade the Bastaard refusal to sell them firearms until the 1820s; see Legassick, 'Griqua', pp. 259—60, 270, 275—76, 363—64, 368—70.

70. A colonially recognised Nama chief named Wildschut was able to have the claims of his community to the Khamiesberg farm of Leliefontein upheld over the white frontiersman Hermanus Engelbrecht: see Moodie, *The Record,* III, 10—11; Le Vaillant, *Travels,* III, 430—37.

71. In Graaff-Reinet a separate roll of Bastaard landowners existed from 1787 until at least 1822. See Marais, *Cape Coloured People,* p. 12; MacCrone, *Race Attitudes,* p. 121 fn.; J.S. Marais, *Maynier and the First Boer Republic* (Cape Town, 1944), p. 31.

72. Marais, *Cape Coloured People,* p. 12. See also Lichtenstein, *Travels,* II, 185, 241; Campbell, *Travels,* 258—60; Theal, *RCC,* XII, 111—12; XXVII, 382—83.

73. See *Journal of Wikar,* pp. 4, 34 fn.; *Journal of van Reenen,* p. 307; P.J. van der Merwe, *Die Noordwaartse Beweging van die Boere voor die Groot Trek* (The Hague, 1937), pp. 4—5.

74. See the description of the missionary Sass who remarked that in this region people have 'but mats and bushes, for that they have nothing to build with and they must move from one place to another for to find food for the cattle.' LMS, Sass, 10 April 1812.

75. Heese, 'Onderwys', p. 84.

76. The precise meaning of 'burgher rights' is not quite clear. For the legal position see ch. 8, p. 324 fn.

77. See Legassick, 'Griqua', pp. 118, 122, 140–43, 170–71; Heese, 'Onderwys', pp. 76—7.

78. See the (retrospective) statements by Lichtenstein, *Travels,* II, 241—42.

79. See, for example, Moodie, *The Record,* III, 104–5.

80. Moodie, *The Record,* III, 77. The complaint was made by one Van Zyl, almost certainly the person leading an extra-colonial raiding party in 1786; see note 39.

81. LMS, Philip Papers, Anderson – Meynell, 26 March 1814; G. Thompson, *Travels and Adventures in Southern Africa* (London, 1827), p. 301.

82. Quote by Bannister, *Humane Policy,* p. 211.

83. See MacCrone, *Race Attitudes,* pp. 84, 130.

84. LMS, Anderson, 15 Nov. 1814, wrote that 'The restrictions made relative to Hottentots leaving the Colony have been made within a few years, since slavery in the Colony has decreased'. For the interpretation of the codes see Macmillan, *Cape Colour Question,* p. 155; Marais, *Cape Coloured People,* p. 123. See also in this volume chapters 6 and 8.

85. *RCC,* XI, 252—56; XII, 111—12, 242—48; XXVIII, 37. For evidence on this

'desertion' by slaves, dependants and non-white landholders, see Legassick, 'Griqua', pp. 198–200, 247–48, 349–51; Ross, 'Griqua', pp. 26–27; Wangemann, *Geschichte*, II, 2, 97.

86. Legassick, 'Griqua', pp. 136–37.
87. *Ibid.*, pp. 141–48. The relationship of this revolt to that on the Eastern Frontier is suggested not only by their simultaneous existence and comparable recruitment of Khoisan dependants, but by the presence among Afrikaner's following of Xhosa, with whom he maintained connections for a while thereafter.
88. This chapter does not treat the history between 1800 and 1820 of the 'protostate' which Jager Afrikaner, son of Klaas, attempted to establish in southern Namibia (in parallel with the Bastaard attempt at Klaarwater), which was resisted by the dominant 'Bondelswarts' community of the area. Jager died in 1823 and his son, Jonker, resumed raiding activities, subsequently (in the 1830s) moving northwards to the Windhoek area, where his following established a hegemony over both Nama and the Herero: see, for example, Legassick, 'Griqua', pp. 216, 257, 260, 444; Vedder, *South West Africa*, pp. 179–82, 186–89, 196–281.
89. Legassick, 'Griqua', pp. 201, 248–50, 258; Wagner, 'De Buys', pp. 1–3.
90. Wagner, 'De Buys', pp. 1–3; Legassick, 'Griqua', pp. 244–47.
91. See Legassick, 'Griqua', pp. 244–47, 270–72; Wagner, 'De Buys', pp. 3–5, who argues that it was a Griqua commando set in motion by landdrost Andries Stockenstrom in September/October 1818 which was the decisive event encouraging De Buys to sever his trading links with the colony.
92. Moorsom, 'Political Economy of Namibia', p. 34.
93. Smith, *Diary*, I, 215. Compare Burchell, *Travels*, II, 525.
94. The Nama then, and for some time, had come to identify all 'hatwearers' as raiders: see LMS, Albrecht *et al.,* entry 14 Oct. 1805; Albrecht, entries June-September 1806; Moffat, *Missionary Labours*, ch. 8. Both the Kok and the Berends families led commandos against Afrikaner in this period.
95. See Legassick, 'Griqua', pp. 116–17, 146–49, 172–75, 179–80, 253.
96. On government relations with missionaries, see Legassick, 'Griqua', chapters 3, 6, 9. See also in this volume, chapter 6.
97. Before Berends, requests had come from Kora on the Orange, and links had been established with members of the Bastaard (?), Oorlam (?), Balie and Goeyman families: see LMS, Anderson, 12 Aug. 1806; Campbell, *Travels*, p. 228.
98. At about the same time Cornelius Kok persuaded Klaas Afrikaner to allow the establishment of a missionary at his Warmbath headquarters. In the lower Orange area, however, LMS stations never took root, either in Little Namaqualand or across the river in southern Namibia; the extension of missionary activities was the work of other societies at a later time. The Wesleyans established a mission at Leliefontein (Khamiesberg) in 1816. The post-1800 history of the Bastaard communities of Little Namaqualand is not treated in this chapter. For this see Marais, *Cape Coloured People*, ch. 3.
99. There is some debate as to whether Dutch Reformed Church ministers would, by the early nineteenth century, baptise Bastaards: Ross claims there was some discrimination ('Speculations') while Giliomee (personal communication) argues that Bastaard children were usually baptised if they met the requirements.
100. The 1801 expedition was principally concerned with the purchase of cattle from the Tlhaping, and only incidentally with the Klaarwater mission. By 1805 the Batavian regime was concerned about the existence of foreign (i.e., British)

missionaries outside the colony among the 'equivocal and dangerous . . .
Hottentots of the Great River' and this was the reason for sending the
expedition: see particularly Lichtenstein, *Travels,* II, 150—52, 257, 260.

101. LMS Journals, Anderson, entry 3 Feb. 1806; the Bastaards had, according to
Anderson, 'without knowledge' made use of this powder 'for other purposes.'

102. Imperial Blue Book 50 of 1835, *Papers relative to the condition and treatment of
the native inhabitants of South Africa,* Edict of Janssens, 20 Feb. 1805, pp.
163—64.

103. Lichtenstein, *Travels,* II, 260—61. See also LMS Journals, Anderson, entry
June 1805.

104. It was Anderson who had to travel to Cape Town in 1806 and 1809 to try to
procure supplies of powder for the mission; Legassick, 'Griqua', p. 156.

105. See Lichtenstein, *Travels,* II, 150, 240—41.

106. Legassick, 'Griqua', pp. 182—88.

107. Besides post-1813 additions from the colony or middle Orange Khoisan, the
Klaarwater settlement was joined by perhaps 600 of the Kok following, so that
by the early 1820s there may have been some 2,000 to 3,000 in central and
western Transorangia who were called 'Bastaards' or 'Griqua'. On population
figures see Legassick, 'Griqua', pp. 146, 196–200, 380–81. In 1805 H. van de
Graaff and H. Lichtenstein conducted a census at the Klaarwater settlement. It
should be attached to AR, Janssens Collection, H. van de Graaff, 'Dagverhaal der
Rijse van de Drostdye Tulbagh naar de Griquas en terug . . .', but is not. Anyone
who can locate it will have a rich source.

108. P.B. Borchards, *An Autobiographical Memoir* (Cape Town, 1861), p. 118;
LMS, Anderson, 7 Sept. 1802.

109. Burchell, *Travels,* I, 253—54; LMS, Anderson, 12 Aug. 1806; 4 Aug. 1812;
Campbell, *Second Journey,* II, 277—78.

110. Borcherds, *Memoir,* pp. 117—19. Also Kicherer, *LMS Transactions,* II, 1, p.
27; Campbell, *Second Journey,* II, 260, 265—67.

111. Lichtenstein, *Travels,* II, 242, 244—45, 261; Campbell, *Travels,* pp. 227—29;
LMS, Campbell, 26 July 1813; R. Moffat in Imperial Blue Book 50 of 1835, pp.
127–28 and a letter reflecting on his period in the area between 1813 and 1816–
1820; LMS, Read, 6 Feb. 1850. Some 'Bushmen' also seem to have been
landholders.

112. See Legassick, 'Griqua', pp. 202, 214—16.

113. Lichtenstein, *Travels,* I, 47.

114. Certainly Adam Kok II acquired a staff of office in 1809 as kaptyn at Klaarwater.
Campbell, *Second Journey,* II, 359 (who was in a position to know) originated
the story about the grant of a staff of office to Adam Kok I, though Heese can
find no record of this in the Cape Archives (personal communication from
Hermann Giliomee). Although Adam Kok I, according to Campbell, was a
manumitted slave, it is interesting to find that the loan farm was granted to him
as a 'Hottentot', and that in 1806 Albrecht *et al.* (LMS Journals, entry 3 Oct.
1805) were told by Adam Kok II that Cornelius was baptised but 'a Hottentot
born'. In view of the clear association between the Koks and the Chariguriqua, it
may be plausible to assume that the family founder was an *escaped* slave (and this
Khoikhoi community in the seventeenth century was almost the only Cape
Khoikhoi group receptive to such persons: see ch. 1, p. 32 of this volume), who
collected a following of Khoikhoi and at a later date was able to pose as a

'Hottentot'. See also R. Ross, 'Assimilation and Collaboration: The Aspirations and Politics of the Griqua Captaincies of Mid-Nineteenth Century South Africa' (unpublished mimeo, n.d.), p. 3.

115. Borcherds, *Memoir,* pp. 117—18.

116. Lichtenstein, *Travels,* II, 306.

117. LMS Journals, Anderson, entry 16 May 1807; Legassick, 'Griqua', pp. 172, 182. It is unclear to what extent the Berends family saw themselves as autonomous equals of the Koks or subject to their overall authority. There was certainly animosity between Cornelius and the Berends family in 1798—1801: See LMS, Anderson, 12 Aug. 1806. But Berend Berends seems to have been the son of Cornelius Kok's sister (married to Klaas Berends): Waterboer 'A short account'. LMS Journals, Anderson and Jansz, entry Oct. 1807.

118. LMS, Andries Waterboer, 'A short account of some of the most particular and important circumstances attending the Government of the Griqua people' (c. Nov. 1827). This important document, it should be mentioned, was written in a spirit of great antagonism towards the Kok family, and to discredit the character of their rule.

119. See, for example, ch. 9, in this volume, and E.A. Walker, *The Great Trek* (London, 1960).

120. See LMS Journals, C. Sass, entry Aug. 1815; LMS, Read, 29 July 1813. Lambert Jansz, son of the Jansz-Pienaar marriage, later became an important Griquatown figure.

121. LMS Journals, Anderson and Jansz, entry Oct. 1807—Feb. 1808; LMS, Anderson, 31 Aug. 1809; Campbell, *Travels,* p. 239.

122. Legassick, 'Griqua', pp. 186—87, 217.

123. LMS Journals, Anderson and Jansz, entries Oct. 1807, Jan. 1808. For his origins see Legassick, 'Griqua', pp. 107, 186, 211; and Wangemann, *Geschichte,* I, 268: Thompson, *Travels,* p. 79.

124. These events are not recorded in contemporary missionary letters, except for the mention in LMS Journals, Jansz, entry 3 June 1810 of 'two captains'. Kok and Berends were certainly the 'captains' at the time of Burchell's visit. See Legassick, 'Griqua', pp. 170–71, 187–88.

125. Campbell, *Travels,* pp. 235—36.

126. See Legassick, 'Griqua', pp. 194—95, chs. 7 to 12; Ross, 'Griqua'.

127. Burchell, *Travels,* I, 253. He instanced a trial before Adam Kok and 'several of the head people, as his council'.

128. Campbell, *Travels,* pp. 236—39, 244, 282; Campbell, 5 May 1813; LMS, Anderson, 18 Jan. 1816.

129. *RCC,* IX, Campbell — Cradock, 12 Feb. 1814, pp. 353–55. On the 'native agency' see also Campbell, *Travels,* pp. 239—40.

130. LMS, 'Minutes of conference . . . of missionaries, Graaff-Reinet', Aug. 1814; Report of LMS Directors, 1815 (quoted in D. Arnot and F. Orpen, *The Land Question of Griqualand West,* [Cape Town, 1875], p. 156).

131. R. Ross, 'Griqua Government', *African Studies,* XXIII (1974), pp. 25—42.

132. The LMS also established two stations for the 'Bushmen' at and near Colesberg in 1815—16 under Erasmus Smit and a black West Indian named William Corner, who were accompanied by a number of Khoikhoi. See LMS 8/3A, 'Ramah Missionary Station', 'Konnah Missionary Station'; Campbell, *Second Journey,* II, 244, 289—90, 301—3; Helm, 9 Sept. 1822; Corner, 2 Sept. 1816;

LMS, Read, 12 Oct. 1816.

133. See Legassick, 'Griqua', pp. 206, 213—17.

134. LMS, Read, 12 Nov. 1816; Legassick, 'Griqua', pp. 199, 216.

135. See Legassick, 'Griqua', pp. 261—75 *passim*. Read, who was strongly opposed to the degree of political influence exerted by Anderson at Griquatown, was able to win the confidence of the Tlhaping.

136. Apart from those mentioned, these included one Cupido Kakkerlak, who employed revivalist methods of conversion among the Kora, including all-day house-to-house singing parties, which he claimed had been successful at Bethelsdorp. LMS, Anderson, 19 April 1816; Kakkerlak, 29 May 1816.

137. LMS P. Papers, Meynell to Anderson, 3 Jan. 1814.

138. LMS P. Papers, Bird to Anderson, 27 May 1814.

139. *RCC,* IX, 310—12, 318—19, 349—55; Legassick, 'Griqua', p. 197. Until 1813, according to Anderson, there were only three such desertions to Griquatown itself, though desertions to Transorangia in general increased thereafter.

140. See, for example, *RCC,* IX, Cradock to Vicars, 14 Nov. 1812, pp. 7—10.

141. Legassick, 'Griqua', pp. 164, 166—67, 201, 204, 284. Anderson was claiming that the Griqua were *not* colonial subjects, but 'independent of this settlement and its Government'.

142. See Legassick, 'Griqua', pp. 202ff.

143. See Nicholas Kruger, Jan Pienaar, in *Bloemhof Bluebook,* pp. 19—21, 350. See also ch. 9 in this volume.

144. Buys told the rebels that they were a free people who ought not to submit themselves 'to laws made by Englishmen'. Campbell's intention from the beginning was to 'betray them by the Government'; he was 'the cause of the late requisitions for their children by the Government'. The purpose of the registration of births was only 'to betray the number of males to the Government'. (The Griqua refused to register births and deaths until at least 1819.) See LMS Journals, Anderson and Helm, entry 23 June 1815; LMS, Anderson, 18 Jan. 1816; see also Legassick, 'Griqua', pp. 204—5, 244ff; Wagner, 'De Buys', pp. 2—3.

145. The mistrust of the role of missionaries at Griquatown spread to other communities like the Tlhaping. Nevertheless a mission was established among the Tlhaping which soon generated lines of conflict parallel to those at Griquatown, and sowed the seeds of the fragmentation of a much more solid and powerful polity than the Griqua had been. See Legassick, 'Griqua', pp. 261—79, 361—71.

146. These quotations may be found in LMS Journals, Anderson and Helm, entry March 1815 — Dec. 1815; LMS, Anderson, 19 April, 1816.

147. Hartenaar leaders were Hendrick Hendricks and A.N. Kok, probably the same 'Kort Adam' who had been magistrate before 1808: see Legassick, 'Griqua', pp. 182, 208—10. For Hendricks at Philippolis see Ross, 'Griqua'.

148. LMS, Anderson, 17 Sept. 1816; *RCC,* XI, Anderson – Stockenstrom, 25 Nov. 1816, p. 229.

149. Andries Waterboer, in a partisan account of the rebellion, later showed that the kaptyns could exert no effective power. See LMS, Waterboer, 'A short account . . .'; Legassick, 'Griqua', pp. 206, 208.

150. LMS, Waterboer, 'A short account . . .'; Legassick, 'Griqua', pp. 209, 213–15.

151. LMS, Read, 23 May 1817. Also LMS, Read, 15 March 1817; Anderson, 24 Aug. 1820.
152. LMS, Waterboer, 'A short account...'; Legassick, 'Griqua', pp. 219—21, 291.
153. CO 2625/34, Letter of Baird, 21 April 1820.
154. *RCC*, XI, Somerset – Bathurst, 23 Jan. 1817, pp. 252—56.
155. See Legassick, 'Griqua', pp. 159—63, 283—90 and the sources quoted.
156. In the following year, however, some concessions were made to the Griqua. Persons from Griquatown authorised by the missionaries might proceed to the annual fair at Beaufort West in order to trade with the farmers. But although the Griqua acquired wagons, horses, tobacco and brandy, the fair excluded trade in arms and powder. The Griqua were also unable to get cloth, beads and implements for agriculture and carpentry. See *RCC*, XI, 252—56; *RCC* XII, 62—64, 111—12, 242—48. For the fair and other Griquatown/farmer trade see Legassick, 'Griqua', pp. 132—33, 238—40.
157. *RCC*, XII, Somerset – Bathurst, 30 June 1819, pp. 242—48.
158. Stockenstrom, *Autobiography*, I, 177—83. See also the memorial by Philip, *Researches*, II, 72—75. (The original is in CO 120/32 and was received before 26 May 1820.) In this memorial Philip warned that the Griqua might 'disperse themselves in hostile bands among the neighbouring tribes . . . and bring war upon the colony, from the mouth of the Keiskamma to the mouth of the Orange River . . .'
159. For Stockenstrom's visit, and recommendations, see Imperial Blue Book 50 of 1835, Stockenstrom, 13 Sept. 1820, pp. 129—33.
160. This argument was subsequently adopted very vehemently by John Philip. See LMS, Philip, 'A brief view . . .' (c. 1823); Philip in *South African Commercial Advertiser*, 26 Nov. 1825; Legassick, 'Griqua', pp. 449—61.
161. For the Griqua polities and their politics in the 1820s and 1830s see Legassick, 'Griqua', pp. 298—576 *passim*.
162. See S. Trapido, 'The South African Republic: Class Formation and the State, 1850—1900', *Collected Seminar Papers on the Societies of Southern Africa in the Nineteenth and Twentieth Centuries* (London, 1973), III, 53—65; 'Aspects in the Transition from Slavery to Serfdom: The South African Republic, 1842—1902', *ibid*, 24—31; 'The long apprenticeship: captivity in the Transvaal, 1843—1881' (unpublished mimeo, 1976).
163. LMS, Wright, letter of 25 Sept. 1835.
164. Marais, *Cape Coloured People*, pp. 42—47.
165. Macmillan, *Bantu, Boer and Briton*, pp. 68, 70.
166. History has many ironies. If the Griquatown polity had had the economic and political base to survive, and even to extend its authority over the Tlhaping, it might have fared better in the era of diamond discoveries. And, if it had survived that period and become after 1910 a 'Native Reserve', we would now have the spectacle of the new mineral wealth of the Northern Cape being described as a 'new Witwatersrand' or a 'new Copper Belt' (*Financial Mail Supplement*, 1 Oct. 1976) situated within a 'Griquatown'. To whom does that mineral wealth 'belong'? To the 'Bushmen', the Rolong, the Tlhaping, the Griqua, the LMS? All laid claims to the territory under which it rested in the period covered in this chapter. Perhaps the actual contemporary irrelevance of the question might lead us to wonder why we South Africans are burdened with such questions deriving from the system of private property relations imposed by the extension and

stabilisation of 'the frontier'. The wealth belongs to all South Africans, indeed to all humankind.

167. LMS, Thompson – Philip, 25 Dec. 1844, quoted in R. Ross, 'Assimilation and Collaboration: The Aspirations and Politics of the Griqua Captaincies of Mid-Nineteenth Century South Africa', (unpublished mimeo, n.d.), p. 10.

168. See, *inter alia,* T. Kirk, 'Some Notes on the Financial State of the Eastern Cape, 1840—1850, and the Fate of the Kat River Settlement', *Collected Seminar Papers on the Societies of Southern Africa in the Nineteenth and Twentieth Centuries* (London, 1973), III, 13—23; Ross, 'Griqua', chapter 5.

169. D.J.P. Haasbroek, 'The Origin of Apartheid in South Africa', *Historia,* XV (1970—71), pp. 13—23. On the Cape franchise see also S. Trapido, 'Origins of the Cape Franchise Qualifications of 1853', *JAH,* V (1964).

170. *Oxford History of South Africa,* II, 4. Compare C.W. de Kiewiet, *A History of South Africa* (Oxford, 1942), pp. 57, 67, 89.

The Eastern Frontier, 1770—1812*

Hermann Giliomee

At the end of the seventeenth century the limits of European habitation were only 80 km from Cape Town. During the eighteenth century the line moved more than 800 km further as hunters, traders, raiders and, finally, cattle farmers pushed eastward into the interior. During the same period, along the southeastern coast, the limits of Xhosa settlement were slowly moving westward. In about 1770 the vanguards of the two peoples met, and the so-called Eastern Frontier opened. This was to be the most dramatic of all South African frontiers. Here European and black pastoralists dispossessed and finally subjugated the last of the eastern Khoikhoi ('Hottentot') clans. Here, too, began the process of interaction between white and black which has dominated South African history. For four decades *trekboers* and Xhosa, both aided at various times by Khoikhoi, jostled each other, neither succeeding in establishing supremacy, until in 1812 a combined colonist-Khoikhoi force under British military leadership finally pushed the Xhosa over the Fish River.

The Eastern Frontier and its inhabitants

The frontier, as the term is used in this chapter, has two dimensions: social and geographical. In the geographical sense, white historians in the twentieth century have meant by 'the Eastern Frontier' the coastal belt between the Sundays and the Kei Rivers where armed clashes between European and black took place. In this chapter the term will be used in two

* I am indebted to Leonard Thompson for opening new perspectives and providing warm encouragement; to Richard Elphick, a hard and therefore invaluable taskmaster as regards style and structure; to the following scholars who also made incisive and most helpful critical comments on previous drafts: George Fredrickson, John Hopper, Martin Legassick, Shula Marks, Richard Moorsom, Jeffrey Peires and Christopher Saunders; and to Louis Botha and J.A. Heese for advising me on the tricky subjects of Xhosa society and white genealogy respectively. To all *baie dankie*.

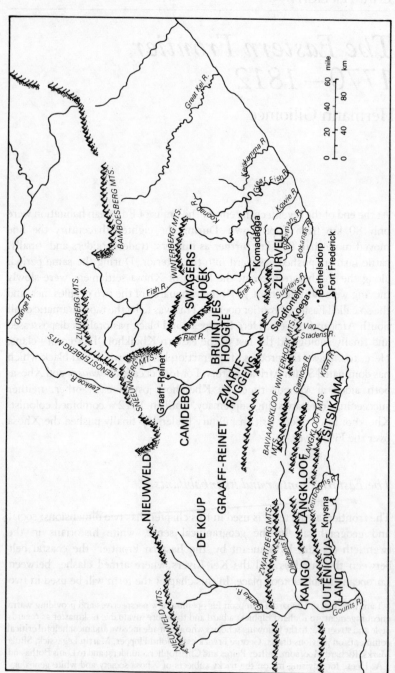

Figure 8.1 The Eastern Frontier, 1803

geographical senses: in the context of colonist-Khoikhoi relations to correspond to the Graaff-Reinet district established in 1786 (see Fig. 8.1), and in the framework of colonist-Xhosa relations to refer to a smaller part of that district, namely the Zuurveld and adjacent divisions.

The Graaff-Reinet district can be divided into three parts. The Zuurveld comprised most of the southeastern quarter of the district. It is bounded by the Zuurberg and Fish River mountain chains in the north, the Fish River in the east, the Sundays River in the west, and the Indian Ocean in the south.† The pastures of the Zuurveld are suitable for both sheep and cattle farming. As the name Zuurveld (sourveld) indicates, its soil is of high acidity; it produces fast-growing vegetation, most of which is harmful, even fatal, to cattle in autumn and winter. As a result, the Zuurveld plains are suitable for pasturage only during certain parts of the year, usually from August/September to December/January. However, the river valleys with their dense, semi-succulent, thorny scrub thickets and sweetveld provide good grazing throughout the year. Thus the early pastoral occupants of the region concentrated themselves in the valleys, using the plains mainly as summer pastures. As the Zuurveld became more densely settled, one of the biggest problems was to achieve the desired rotation of livestock between sourveld in the summer and sweetveld in the winter. Such transhumance often led to territorial disputes between different communities.[1]

The second region is the northeastern part of the Graaff-Reinet district. This includes the well-watered Sneeuwberg and the choice division of Bruintjes Hoogte, and is the best part for stock farming. Large areas are covered by sweet grassveld and shrubs growing on soil with neutral acidity. The veld may therefore be grazed throughout the year.

The third region, i.e., the western half of the district, includes the Nieuwveld, De Koup and Camdebo divisions. Although dry, its shrubs and succulents offer good pasturage for sheep. In the eighteenth century it provided winter grazing for stock raised in the Zuurveld.

During the course of the eighteenth century Khoikhoi clans, some of which had previously lived in the southwestern Cape, retreated in the face of the colonists' expansion until they were east of the Gamtoos River. Xhosa, pushing westward beyond the Kei River, forced other Khoikhoi to withdraw in the direction of the Fish River. In the area between the Fish and the Gamtoos various Khoikhoi clans combined to form chiefdoms, each headed by a chief of limited authority.[2] In the late eighteenth century the most important chiefdoms between the Gamtoos and the Fish were those of the Gona, who had incorporated Xhosa on a large scale, and the Hoengeiqua.

† During the period under discussion contemporaries also referred to the Zuurveld in a more restricted sense as the area between the Boesmans and the Fish Rivers.

This latter group had been formed from Khoikhoi remnants by Ruyter, a Khoikhoi fugitive who had killed a fellow Khoikhoi in the Roggeveld.[3]

The trekboers (European colonists who usually called themselves Christians') reached the Sneeuwberg Mts., Camdebo and Sundays River by the end of the 1760s.‡ They had gradually colonised the interior by acquiring loan farms from the government (the Dutch East India Company). These farms were roughly 6 000 acres (2,420 ha) in size. In densely settled areas the basic social unit was the extended family, which consisted of several related nuclear families living close together under the leadership of the senior male member. On their farms there were often one or two *bijwoners* (Europeans who had no claim to the land but were part of a broader European cultural and kinship network), Khoikhoi servants and their families, and, in the case of wealthy landholders, a slave or two.

By 1770 the Xhosa, a branch of the Nguni-speakers, were organised at three levels: patrilineages, consisting of the descendants of a known common ancestor; patriclans, composed of a number of lineages, all-claiming descent from a putative common ancestor; and chiefdoms which were political units, each occupying a certain area under a chief. Chiefdoms, which were usually spatially separated, enjoyed a great measure of independence from one another.

Two major splits had occurred in Xhosa society in the hundred years before 1770. At the end of the seventeenth century, while the Xhosa were living west of the Mbashe River, several minor chiefs and their followers had hived off from the nuclear political unit under the paramount, and established

‡ The discussion of the causes of trekboer expansion has been dominated by P.J. van der Merwe, who concluded that the trekkers consisted predominantly of the surplus population of the settled areas which was unable to find free or cheap land elsewhere: see especially his *Trek* (Cape Town, 1945), pp. 59—60. Subsequently S.D. Neumark in his *Economic Influences on the South African Frontier* (Stanford, 1957) argued that the major force behind the expansion was the better opportunities provided by stock farming and hunting, and that the marketing of certain products like soap, butter and tallow gave the expansion movement an additional impetus. Neumark's work provides valuable insights into the way in which trekboer society was linked to its Cape Town base, but one must question his attempt to relate frontier expansion to market opportunities rather than to population pressure (see ch. 2, pp. 67—71). Apart from the fact that Neumark is obviously wrong to see the marketing of soap and butter as a factor determining expansion beyond Swellendam, he exaggerates the degree to which stock farming was geared to the market. Stock farmers did not sell the majority of their stock as Neumark asserts. There is, instead, abundant evidence of overstocking and of the farmers owning more cattle than they could market. There were two reasons for this. Firstly, market prices in Cape Town were never high enough for the farmers to sell the majority of their stock at a profit. Secondly, the stock farmers, with their meagre consumer needs, had little reason to convert cattle into money. Far from being mainly marketable commodities, livestock were predominantly capital and consumption goods. See J. Barrow, *Travels,* II, 302, 332; BO 6, Consideratiën noopens ... het Slagtvee, 8 Sept. 1799; GR 1/1, Minutes, 1 Nov. 1790, p. 147; GR 1/4, Minutes, 5 Aug. 1805, pp. 22—23.

separate chiefdoms at a distance. By 1750 these chiefdoms, which included the Ntinde, Gwali, Mbalu, Dange and Gqunukhwebe, were located in the area between the Kei and the Keiskamma Rivers. The westernmost chiefdom, the Gqunukhwebe, was distinct from the others because its members had mixed to a much greater extent with the Gona who, as Khoikhoi, were not initially regarded as equals in Xhosa chiefdoms into which they had been incorporated.[4] It is conceivable that the Gqunukhwebe, although Xhosa in culture, were regarded as inferior by the Xhosa because of their partly Khoikhoi origin. The Gqunukhwebe chief was scorned by his fellow chiefs because he was not of the royal lineage,[5] but there is no evidence that he was politically subordinate to them in the late eighteenth century.[6]

The second major schism occurred in the middle of the eighteenth century when the Xhosa nucleus split into the Gcaleka and Rharhabe sections, with the Rharhabe moving westward in the direction of the Fish River. In the authority crisis which followed, the Rharhabe and Gcaleka chiefs each claimed to be a paramount with some authority over other chiefs in his vicinity.

Some scholars believe that all Xhosa chiefdoms which had been established as a result of fission were independent of one another and of the Gcaleka and Rharhabe 'paramounts'.[7] They argue that chiefs did not have to act in unison in external affairs, nor did they have to pay tribute or provide military aid to the paramount. This may have been the position in the nineteenth century. However, the flux of Xhosa society in the eighteenth century makes such a static model inadequate.

In particular, the relationship of the chiefs in the Ciskei with Rharhabe and his successors was vague and shifting. When Rharhabe moved west of the Kei after c. 1760, he claimed authority over the Ntinde, Gwali, Dange, Mbalu and Gqunukhwebe.[8] It is not clear whether he really considered them as rebellious subjects who should be subjugated by force, or whether he made this claim merely to acquire the colonists' support. In any event, these chiefdoms were unwilling to relinquish the degree of independence they had established since the beginning of the eighteenth century, and rejected Rharhabe's claim whenever they felt themselves to be in a strong enough position to do so.[9] It was not genealogical ranking — that is, the seniority of chiefs — but power which was the main determinant of relationships between the Rharhabe and the Gcaleka chiefs, between the Rharhabe and other Ciskei chiefs, and among these chiefs themselves.[10]

The Xhosa were cattle-herders and hoe-farmers who lived on well-watered lands in dispersed *kraal* settlements, each of which could supply most of the economic needs of its inhabitants. There was a tendency for each chiefdom to occupy a specific river valley. A chief was forced to expand at the expense of his neighbours if a territory could no longer satisfy the needs of his subjects, who otherwise might join another chief.[11] A corresponding phenomenon occurred in colonial society. Here capital was scarce and extensive land use the norm. When an area became densely settled, the European stock farmers did not attempt to increase the carrying capacity of the land, but expanded further, forcing Khoikhoi out. When expansion beyond the colony was no longer possible, 'forcing in' between the loan farms or expansion into Xhosa territory were seen as the only solutions.[12]

Thus at certain stages in the late eighties and early nineties the Zuurveld was a confined space where chiefdoms and European farmers jostled each other in competition for land. This competition was exacerbated by the conflicting views about landholding of the colonists, who considered a certain defined area as belonging exclusively to them, and the Xhosa, who saw land as communal property, the boundaries of which were hardly ever sharply defined. Conflict over livestock was also important, for in both Xhosa and colonial society cattle were a major form of capital and a commonly recognised symbol of wealth. Raids to supplement stock and recoup losses were endemic in the frontier struggle.

The open frontier: Its characteristics

We noted before that the frontier has not only a geographical but also a social dimension.[13] Unlike a boundary, which evokes the image of a line on a map and demarcates spheres of political control, the frontier is an area where colonisation is taking place. Here two or more ethnic communities co-exist with conflicting claims to the land, and no authority is recognised as legitimate by all the parties or is able to exercise undisputed control over the area. Thus the stress is on coercive power, i.e., the ability to forcibly realise aims in the face of opposition from others. In this sense the Cape Eastern Frontier calls to mind W.K. Hancock's reference to the frontier which once existed between England and Scotland: '[It] was not a line but a district where thieving Scot and thieving Englishman had sufficient liberty for roving forays.'[14]

One of the major characteristics of the frontier, then, is that it is a disputed area, claimed at one stage or other by the various peoples settled there. Some time between 1750 and 1780 the Gqunukhwebe penetrated that part of the Zuurveld lying between the Boesmans and Fish Rivers. They were followed by the Mbalu under Langa and his sons Umlawu (also known as Nqeno) and Thole, the Gwali under Tsatsu, the Dange, and the Ntinde. During the 1770s the colonists started occupying the land between the Sundays and the

Fish Rivers. Hemmed in by Xhosa and colonists, the Khoikhoi chiefdoms, whose survival depended on a large territory in which they could hunt and pasture stock, disintegrated.

The Zuurveld became an area where various attempts were made to legitimise conflicting claims to the land. Ruyter's Hoengeiqua chiefdom, now consisting mainly of the Gona, claimed prior occupation; but the Gqunu-khwebe insisted that their chief, Tshaka, had purchased the land between the Fish and the Kowie Rivers from Ruyter. This was denied by Ruyter's grandchildren. The colony's claim was based on the boundary settlement concluded by Governor van Plettenberg in 1778, when he had persuaded some Gwali chiefs to recognise as the boundary of the colony the upper reaches of the Great Fish River and the Boesmans River Mountains. Two years later this claim expanded when the Council of Policy proclaimed the Fish River along its entire length as the boundary.[15] Thus the land between the Boesmans and the Fish was now also regarded as colonial territory. Some Xhosa and Khoikhoi disputed this; however, nobody waited for the disputes to be resolved at a higher level. Europeans, Khoikhoi and Africans settled down close to one another: from the beginning 'kraals and [European] habitations were mixed.'[16]

Another characteristic of a frontier is the lack of a single government to exercise undisputed authority over all individuals in the frontier zone. On the frontier there were of course various authorities exercising some control over their respective communities. But while they were considered legitimate by probably the majority of their subjects, they were often too weak to prevent challenges which ranged from unauthorised action to rebellion.

No Xhosa authority was able to fill this authority vacuum. There was no political leader — not even a paramount — who could make decisions and agreements without the consent of the various Xhosa chiefdoms which would be affected. The colonial officials failed to understand this. From the beginning they attempted to find a supreme chief with whom an agreement could be made which would be binding on Xhosa on both sides of the Fish River. Eventually they attempted to establish peace between the Rharhabe chief, whom they regarded as a paramount, and the Zuurveld chiefs, who claimed that they were at war with him and therefore afraid to return over the Fish.[17]

Secondly, the Zuurveld chiefs, who were indeed recognised as legitimate authorities by their subjects, could only to a limited extent control them or bind them in negotiations. In normal times chiefs were able to punish thieves, but in unsettled frontier conditions they would hardly risk losing their following by punishing a large number of their subjects who had enriched themselves in a raid. The rationale of serving a chief was, after all, the security which he provided for the accumulation of cattle.[18]

Lastly, the colonial government failed to establish itself as an undisputed authority on the frontier. The colonists, of course, originally accepted the Company's authority, but they were mainly concerned with two aspects of Company rule. Firstly, they wanted to be incorporated into the landholding system of the colony. Under this system the Company would recognise their claim to the land in return for their acknowledgement of Company rule and their agreement, at least in theory, to pay rent (*recognitiepenningen*) for their farms. Secondly, the colonists wanted the government to appoint from their ranks a capable person to be field-commandant.[19] This would set in motion the commando system which was fundamental to the security of colonists on the frontier. Under this system the colonists were obliged to serve on commandos against indigenous enemies while the government would provide ammunition for these expeditions.

The Company's authority was further undermined by the inadequacy of its military and police force. The establishment of the Graaff-Reinet district in 1786 only nominally increased its control over the frontier. The *landdrost* of Graaff-Reinet was assisted by only four or five *ordonnantie ruiters* (mounted police).[20] In a situation where colonists had almost free access to guns and ammunition and considered it their right to fire on raiders, the landdrost could not remotely claim to monopolise the use of force. His authority and the colonists' respect for the colonial laws suffered accordingly. Landdrost Woeke of Graaff-Reinet remarked in a letter to the colonial government that unless he was aided by fifty or sixty soldiers 'the rot will continue . . . and if not suppressed will increase to such an extent that everyone will act arbitrarily and do everything at his own sweet will.'[21]

In these circumstances the landdrost was forced to rely on the *veldwacht-meesters* (later field-cornets) to ensure compliance with the laws in their respective divisions. But the field-cornets were dependent on the support of their fellow colonists and often chose to uphold their interests. Thus the key role in the local administration came to be played by men who were often the agents of the colonists rather than of the colonial government.

Company officials on the frontier were unsuccessful in asserting their authority over the Xhosa in the Zuurveld. Awed at first, the chiefs soon sensed that these officials were unable to make good their threats to expel them forcibly. They also exploited the widening rift between the government in Cape Town and the frontier colonists.[22] On the other hand, both the colonial government and the colonists did succeed in establishing their authority over the Khoikhoi, whose political structure had disintegrated under European and Xhosa impact, leaving them no system of authority around which to rally.

In the fragmented political structure of the frontier it was common for various ethnic communities, or rather groups within these communities, to form alliances to obtain specific ends. Thus there was an alliance against the Zuurveld Xhosa consisting of the Rharhabe leaders, who wished to integrate the various Xhosa chiefdoms in the west under their command, and the colonists in the southeastern part of Graaff-Reinet, who desired the removal of these same chiefdoms.[23] To counter this, the Gqunukhwebe increased their power by incorporating Khoikhoi and slaves who had absconded from European farms. The conflicts between the colonists and the colonial government also saw both sides attempting to enlist allies across ethnic lines. In the rebellions on the frontier some colonists solicited the help of Xhosa. And as late as 1803 Governor Janssens would tell Graaff-Reinet colonists that if disorder in the district did not cease 'he would have to adopt such measures as would exterminate those who were the cause of the turbulence, even if it were only possible with the assistance of Kafirs and Hottentots.'[24]

During the period 1770—1812 one can distinguish two phases, overlapping one another in time and space, in the evolution of the frontier. These may be called the open and the closing frontiers. There was a fluidity on the open frontier which contrasted strongly with the increasingly stratified closing frontier. On the open frontier a low population density allowed Khoikhoi labourers to move freely between farm and kraal. It was comparatively easy to desert, and employers were often unable to use coercion effectively. Thus the labourers who had been attracted to their service could be called 'clients' as distinct from the unfree labourers of the closing frontier.

Closely related to this was the complexity of a situation in which the three contending parties (Khoikhoi, Xhosa, and colonists) were each unable to exert coercive power over all inhabitants in the region. Goals were pursued more commonly through negotiations than through violence. There was an uncertainty of status: Europeans were not all masters, non-Europeans were not all servants. This produced the paradox of, on the one hand, a degree of inter-ethnic cooperation and, on the other, bitterness and rivalry as members of different groups attempted to find a footing on which they could base their relationship. In all these respects the open frontier was distinct from the situation which would obtain after the closing of the frontier had progressed significantly.

The open frontier, 1770—1793

Although some Khoikhoi kraals in the 1770s and 1780s were smashed by Xhosa and trekboers, many Khoikhoi were incorporated into these societies peacefully. The Zuurveld was not a safe area. Lions roamed freely[25] and

'Bushman' raiders threatened the security of herding communities. These dangers prompted some Khoikhoi to seek the protection of Xhosa chiefdoms. However, they often found that it was impossible to leave without loss of their cattle. During the first phase of incorporation Khoikhoi were usually simply menial servants.[26]

Khoikhoi who rejected Xhosa domination,[27] but who still desired protection and a chance to build up stock, attached themselves to trekboers, an action facilitated by the existence of a clientship tradition in Khoikhoi society. While there were obviously trekboers who from the beginning used violent methods against Khoikhoi, seizing their cattle and compelling them to stay in their service,[28] there were cases where Khoikhoi and colonists established a symbiotic relationship.[29] In such relationships a Khoikhoi entering a trekboer's service retained his livestock; these were supplemented by payments in kind which he received for tending his master's cattle and accompanying him (or going in his place) on commandos against Xhosa and 'Bushmen'.[30]

The *opgaaf* rolls (census lists taken for tax purposes) show that many Khoikhoi in colonial service owned a considerable number of cattle. An opgaaf taken in 1798 lists between 1,300 and 1,400 Khoikhoi in the Graaff-Reinet district; they owned 140 horses, 7,571 cattle and 30,557 sheep — an average of 5 cattle and 23 sheep per man. However, there were some who owned considerably more. Adriaan, a servant of B.J. Forster, owned 30 cattle and 207 sheep; Adriaan Deerling, in the service of S.J. Burger, owned 58 cattle and 250 sheep; and Clara, in the service of D.P. Liebenberg, owned 33 cattle and 177 sheep. Those Khoikhoi who owned more livestock than average tended to be concentrated on a few farms, a fact which suggests that they were living in a kraal on the farm.[31]

For a Khoikhoi the transition from independent herder to client may not have been traumatic, provided he could retain his stock and also maintain the bonds with his clan or kinsmen, perhaps settling with them on a colonist's farm.[32] In fact, Khoikhoi often succeeded in bringing their kinsmen along to the farm. Explaining why some trekboers had so many Khoikhoi in their service while others had so few, Andries Stockenstrom, landdrost of Graaff-Reinet from 1803 to 1811, remarked that Khoikhoi refused to separate from their families.[33]

Thus the frontier, rather than being a place where new modes of life and institutions originated (as some historians have suggested)[34] was an area in which the disparate groups attempted to maintain conditions and institutions similar to those existing before contact.[35] In adopting this conservative strategy the Khoikhoi, especially in the way in which they retained and supplemented their stock, often obtained better economic terms from the colonists than from the Xhosa, who at times seized their stock. However, their social prospects, in the sense of full integration with the new society, were far better with the Xhosa. Because biological mixing with Xhosa occurred freely, Khoikhoi did not develop into a separate caste; rather their descendants became Xhosa. In colonial society, however, they were rarely baptised, seldom married to colonists, and never granted *burgher* status. Despite the degree of miscegenation which took place, it did not take long before the Khoikhoi came to form an inferior caste in colonial society.

In other ways the open frontier also spelled the decline of the Khoikhoi. As they lost land they lost their political leverage in colonial society. They also inevitably became enmeshed in, and often bore the brunt of, hostilities between the Xhosa and the colonists. Indeed, Khoikhoi were indispensable to the commandos, and Khoikhoi herdsmen were the first to be killed in Xhosa raids.

The colonists and Xhosa had had an uneasy relationship ever since their advance guards had started to mingle in the 1770s. The high value which each attached to cattle, and the opportunities each saw for supplementing stock through raiding and trading, became both bonds and sources of conflict between two peoples who soon found that they could live neither with nor without each other.

Barter was the tie which initially brought colonists and Xhosa together. Many Xhosa were keen to acquire European copper, iron and beads, which they had formerly obtained from Khoikhoi intermediaries. European officials and colonists regarded such trade as an excellent opportunity to acquire cheap livestock. Some tried to barter with the Xhosa, as they had with the Khoikhoi, by cajoling or dragooning them into parting with their cattle. The difference was that the Xhosa could retaliate if duped or dispossessed of their cattle.[36] Collins characterised this process as follows: the Xhosa 'at first gave their cattle and labour without knowing its value; but a little experience having opened their eyes on these points, altercations between them and the farmers were the necessary consequence. These contentions grew into enmities . . .'[37]

It was partly to prevent this that the Company declared it illegal for colonists to barter with Xhosa. Equally important, however, was its desire to secure control of the trade for itself, thereby making the colony less dependent on the colonists for its meat supply.[38] After announcing the Company's plans to barter cattle with the Xhosa, Landdrost Woeke to his dismay discovered that the *heemraden* of Graaff-Reinet were implacably opposed to such a course, arguing that this would spark off hostilities between colonists and Xhosa. Woeke, however, was convinced that the underlying reason for their opposition was the fear that such a trade would depress the price the Company paid the colonists for their cattle. In the mean time the cattle trade between colonists and Xhosa continued illegally. In 1786 Field-Sergeant H.J. van Rensburg of the Boesmans River division reported that many, if not all, of his fellow-colonists were guilty of bartering with the Xhosa.[39]

Labour was a second tie and source of conflict. Khoikhoi were unevenly distributed among the farms, not only because Khoikhoi families were unwilling to split up, but also because they could not always know about better working conditions elsewhere. Thus many farmers were forced to seek Xhosa labour. To Xhosa, especially those who had suffered misfortune, this was an acceptable opportunity to build up their livestock and earn food.[40] But there were various points of friction in the labour situation. When herdsmen lost cattle through negligence, colonists punished their servants. Misunderstandings also arose over payment and colonists withheld wages. As an old coloured man, Brantanje Jantjes, recounted of the early frontier: 'Many of the Caffres served the farmers and there were constant disputes among them. The Caffres when not regularly paid or flogged informed their chief and came and stole cattle from the farmers by way of repaying themselves for the injuries they had sustained.'[41] Both Jantjes and Landdrost Maynier regarded the cycle of maltreatment and reprisals as a cause of the 1793 war.[42]

A third activity in this context was begging — or so colonists regarded it. To the Xhosa this was reciprocal exchange in which a poor man asked for food from someone without offering payment. In traditional Xhosa society this was given unstintingly because the giver saw it as a form of insurance against the day when he himself might experience need.[43] At first the colonists gave food liberally to build up goodwill. Soon, however, this practice became a source of friction. As the Xhosa population in the Zuurveld grew, increasing numbers of Xhosa visited farms to request or even demand food. In some cases it was difficult to distinguish between begging and exacting tribute. Lichtenstein wrote: '. . . in peace the Xhosa expect as a sort of tribute what in war they seize by force. They often come in large bodies, and will stay several days or even weeks . . . Their importunity, their numbers and the fear of quarreling with them . . . commonly secure them good entertainment.'[44]

Thus those Xhosa who had earlier moved into the Zuurveld, mainly as a result of political developments in Xhosa society, were now joined by others seeking pasture and opportunities for barter, labour and begging. Some were fleeing from their home regions after committing a crime or suffering defeat in war. Xhosa moved in groups, bringing along large numbers of cattle. In this way two cultures, which both valued land as a means of production and cattle as a source of wealth and prestige, were brought together in a single area.

Were ethnic or material factors the most important sources of conflict between the colonists and the Xhosa? The colonists carried with them to the frontier a set of attitudes, most important of which was the notion that as 'Christians' they were culturally superior to the 'heathens' whom they often associated with crudeness, conflict and treachery.[45] Although a few individuals went to live among the Xhosa, the colonists were bent on excluding them from their culture and kinship network, and from their political system. As for the Xhosa, eighteenth-century encounters with colonists were such that many distrusted and feared them.[46] However, partly because they were much more numerous, the Xhosa never dreaded that they would be submerged or dominated by Europeans. Indeed, their approach to neighbours was in direct contrast to that of the colonists: Xhosa society was basically an open one which, through intermarriage and other means, incorporated and eventually integrated non-Nguni speakers. There is evidence that Xhosa were inclined to incorporate the colonists in the same way. In this they were unsuccessful, often being rebuffed by the colonists, who misunderstood their approaches. Consequently during this period colonists and Xhosa kept their separate identities. To a large extent one regarded the other as standing outside his moral community. Such an attitude helps to explain wartime atrocities (such as the mutilation of corpses and the colonists' abduction of Xhosa children) which so embittered relations.[47]

Yet, however important ethnic differences were, it is hard to believe that the conflict between the colonists and Xhosa would have occurred on such a large scale had it not been for their opposing material interests. It is difficult to say which was the most important source of conflict, land or cattle. The colonists clearly wished to have the Zuurveld to themselves, most of all because the land could not provide pasture for the cattle of both the colonists and the Zuurveld Xhosa.[48] However, such was the stalemate in the battle to control the Zuurveld that possession of cattle became an alternative of equal or even overriding importance.

This phenomenon is illustrated by the events of the First Frontier War (1779—81). Towards the end of the 1770s the Prinsloos of Agter Bruintjes Hoogte raided cattle east of the Fish and killed some Xhosa. Bands of Xhosa retaliated late in 1779, capturing a large number of cattle (21,000 according to the usually exaggerated estimate of the colonists). This led to commandos in 1780 and 1781 in which the raiding of cattle was the main activity. Summing up the events of those early years, Collins remarked: 'The wars that were at first waged against the Caffres were carried on exclusively by the settlers, who seem, whenever they have been unsuccessful, to have failed in a great degree from their having considered the recovery of stolen cattle as the principal object of hostility.'[49] Campagne, an observer sympathetic to colonists, offered this explanation: while it was not possible to subjugate the Xhosa by force of arms, it was easy to capture cattle.[50]

In the case of the Zuurveld Xhosa there was a parallel tendency to attach prime importance to control over cattle rather than land. When the First Frontier War broke out their main concern was cattle — protecting their own and capturing their enemy's. After a skirmish they were quite prepared to withdraw over the Fish, provided they could keep their booty.[51] The one exception was the Gqunukhwebe. Not of royal lineage, and acknowledging the Gcaleka chief rather than the Rharhabe chief as paramount, the Gqunukhwebe chief, Tshaka, considered his stake in the Zuurveld as crucial and was, of all the Xhosa chiefs, least inclined to retreat. Beyond the Fish, positioned between him and his paramount, was the Rharhabe chief, who might easily capture his cattle and subjugate or even destroy his chiefdom. If Tshaka were to maintain his autonomy, the Zuurveld was definitely the safest place. The fact that the Gqunukhwebe, to a far greater degree than other Xhosa, had entered the service of colonists and had close links with the Khoikhoi in the colony, also explains their determination to stay.

During the course of the First Frontier War the commandos defeated the Ntinde, Gwali, Mbalu and Dange, thus inducing their chiefs to recognise the Fish as the boundary between themselves and the colonists.[52] This left Tshaka of the Gqunukhwebe as the only important chief in the area with whom no boundary settlement had been concluded. The settlement with the other Xhosa did not last long. It was ignored by Xhosa as well as by some colonists; both crossed the Fish to hunt and to barter cattle, or to graze their own. Nevertheless, the frontier remained comparatively quiet for the next five or six years.[53]

In 1786, in response to requests by Adriaan van Jaarsveld and other leading colonists, the Company established the frontier district of Graaff-Reinet. This decision stemmed from the Company's desire to assert greater administrative control over the colony's outlying regions as well as to prevent another clash between the colonists and the Xhosa.[54] Landdrost Woeke was instructed to prevent colonists from trespassing beyond the Fish, to persuade the Xhosa to settle east of the Fish, and to prevent any contact between colonists and Xhosa. When his request for fifty or sixty soldiers was turned down, Woeke attempted to obtain these objectives through negotations. He soon discovered that several smaller issues were negotiable. Xhosa chiefs, especially Tshaka, were prepared to punish cattle thieves on representations from the landdrost or veldwachtmeesters in the Zuurveld. On his side Woeke was ready to redress wrongs which the chiefs reported. Thus a degree of communication and understanding developed between European and black as the two societies became increasingly interlocked.[55]

However, Woeke was soon to be faced with an unnegotiable conflict. From 1786 the numbers of the Xhosa in the Zuurveld progressively increased, and colonists demanded that they be expelled. By 1789 a traveller saw several thousand Xhosa with over 16,000 cattle on a farm at Kariega.[56] In the same year Woeke reported that four Xhosa chiefs were west of the Fish with a multitude of followers.[57] One of them was Langa, who in 1781 had been driven from the Zuurveld and had now returned; another was Tshaka, who had probably never left.

There were two immediate causes of the Xhosa influx into the Zuurveld after 1786. Firstly, there was a severe drought in that year which killed many cattle and almost all game.[58] Many Xhosa came to the Zuurveld for pasture and food and, after the drought had broken, stayed on. Secondly, political disputes in Xhosa society induced many Xhosa to move westward for safety. The death of Rharhabe in c. 1781 brought to the fore an aggressive new leader in the person of his son, Ndlambe. Ndlambe was next in rank to the heir, Mlawu, who had died before his father. Acting as regent while Mlawu's heir, Ngqika, was still a minor, Ndlambe aimed to establish himself as paramount with effective control over both his own chiefdom and the 'rebel' chiefdoms in the west. During the late 1780s and early 1790s Ndlambe, in alliance with Langa, defeated the Gqunukhwebe, who suffered heavy losses and subsequently retreated further westward into the colony. There were now many destitute Xhosa in the Zuurveld, anxious to recoup their losses or simply to find food. It was they who were mainly responsible for cattle thefts in the Zuurveld after 1789; such thefts had rarely occurred during the preceding decade.[59]

It was not only Xhosa numbers and thefts which outraged the colonists; Langa at this time was becoming increasingly self-assertive. Demanding compensation when one of his subjects was killed or injured, he sent word in c. 1788 to Coenraad de Buys that the 'Christians' should not think he was afraid to make war.[60] During this time his people, according to Woeke, roamed the Zuurveld in groups of ten to twenty, 'getting up to all kinds of mischief and troublemaking, raiding cattle and in general refusing to listen to friendly warnings.'[61] 'Mischief' included the looting of houses for copper and iron, destruction of crops, and killing of game on farms.

In response to the colonists' insistence that the Zuurveld Xhosa be driven from the colony, Woeke in 1789 sent out a commando under Captain Kühne to 'goad' the Xhosa over the Fish. This plan failed because the river was in flood and prevented the commando from expelling those Xhosa that it had rounded up.[62]

Later in 1789 Woeke set out at the head of a small negotiating party to urge the Xhosa to withdraw west of the Fish. He was under strict orders from the government to avoid violence but to buy off all Xhosa claims to the land in the Zuurveld.[63] He encountered resistance, especially from the Gqunukhwebe, who claimed that they had bought the land between the Kowie and the Fish, and now refused to renounce their claim.[64] Moreover, some Xhosa had come to see the issue as a clash between irreconcilable claims: they insisted that if they had to leave the land, the colonists would have to do the same.[65] In 1792 another commando also failed in an attempt amicably to persuade the Gqunukhwebe and other Xhosa to leave the Zuurveld. Hereafter both parties increasingly turned to force in order to back up their demands and claims.

At the same time numbers of Khoikhoi were absconding from colonists' farms and allying themselves with the Xhosa, especially the Gqunukhwebe. These Khoikhoi were rebelling against the loss of their land, restrictions on their mobility, and maltreatment at the hands of their masters.[66] They enhanced Xhosa military power, since they often brought guns they had taken from their masters, or at least could handle the firearms which Xhosa had bartered from the colonists for cattle.[67] Unlike the Xhosa, some Khoikhoi were superb horsemen and knew the colonists' strategy. The Zuurveld Xhosa valued these allies, while the Khoikhoi welcomed the opportunity for revenge against the colonists. On occasion when the colonists appealed to Xhosa to release their runaway servants, the Xhosa showed their solidarity with these Khoikhoi by refusing. The colonists were also asked why they did not let their other servants go.[68]

Having lost confidence in the government's peaceful policy towards the Xhosa and in its ability or willingness to protect them, the colonists in the southeastern divisions resolved to expel the Xhosa themselves. As Woeke remarked: 'War was not only inevitable but many inhabitants felt very much inclined to do battle'.[69] Several colonists used violence against individual Xhosa, even against chiefs. Langa, for instance, was locked up by R. Campher and forced to barter cattle; his wife was seized by Coenraad de Buys and used as a concubine. Chungwa was imprisoned in a mill and forced to work it himself. Some of the chiefs' followers were shot by men like De Buys, the Bezuidenhouts and C. Botha.[70] Apart from these individual acts of violence, there is also some evidence of a massive cattle raid by a commando in 1789.[71] This raid, if in fact it did occur, would further explain the increase in cattle raids by the Xhosa after 1789.

Unlike the 1780s, when they were still awed by the colonists' guns and horses, the Xhosa from the early 1790s onwards started to challenge the colonists' position in the Zuurveld. The colonists in general were unable to accept a situation in which 'heathens' were allowed to lord it over 'Christians'.[72] They were convinced that with a sufficient supply of ammunition they could re-establish 'proper relations'. The Zuurveld Xhosa had a different conception of what proper relations were. The points on which colonists felt superior — literacy, different sexual mores and Christian religious beliefs — had, after all, little meaning for the Xhosa.[73] Unlike the Khoikhoi, the Zuurveld Xhosa retained their traditional culture while the various chiefdoms remained intact. This provided them with strength and self-assurance in their resistance to the colonists. Their strength was bolstered by the guns they had acquired since the opening of the frontier and by the support of Khoikhoi marksmen.[74] It is conceivable that they also derived comfort from the compact way in which they were settled compared to the colonists, who were thinly spread over a vast area.

Some Xhosa were now demanding gifts, raiding farms when their owners were absent, and threatening to attack colonists who had particularly aroused their wrath.[75] Even where no actual violence had taken place there was still constant friction over pasture and water. A colonist echoed the feelings of most Europeans near the Boesmans River when he wrote of the 'nuisance caused me by a Kaffir captain Langa on my farm . . . With his people and his stock he lies between me and Zwaanepoel and not only overgrazes the field and consumes the water supply but also ruins the veld by burning.'[76] What had started as an uneasy co-existence turned into an increasingly aggressive battle for pasture and cattle. There were still colonists like Adriaan van Jaarsveld who proposed that 'for the sake of lasting peace with the Xhosa the Zuurveld [meaning the area between the Fish and the Boesmans], which had been their own land, should be handed back to them.'[77] However, on both sides there was a growing feeling that neither negotiations nor concessions, but only force, would resolve disputes.

Thus the period 1770—92 had given rise to the preconditions of the strife and warfare which would engulf the frontier in the two decades after 1793. In summary they were: conflict over land and cattle; the absence of any force which could impose peace and order; maltreatment of Khoikhoi and Xhosa servants; the transfer of allegiance of some Khoikhoi clients of the colonists; the presence in colonial territory of large numbers of Xhosa whom the colonists perceived as a threat to their lives and property; and mutual suspicion and mistrust which, as the result of individual acts of aggression and violence, grew into bitterness and hate. To take only one example: during the hostilities of 1779—81 Adriaan van Jaarsveld tossed out some tobacco to a band of Xhosa, and then, while the Xhosa were scrambling to pick up the tobacco, fired on them, killing many. He later explained that he had feared treachery. According to the Xhosa historian, J.H. Soga,[78] this incident rankled in the minds of the Ntinde even into the twentieth century.¶ In an

¶ A similar event, but with the roles reversed, took place in 1811 when Landdrost Stockenstrom and fourteen of his men were killed by Xhosa. Stockenstrom in good faith had

atmosphere so pervaded with fear and violence the outbreak of armed hostilities was a distinct possibility.

The frontier crisis, 1793—1812

In 1793 a severe drought made the conflict over pasture much more explosive. Wars between Europeans and Africans, however, did not break out simply because tempers snapped.[79] An assault — whether it be of a political or military nature — which threatened to destroy the balance of power or the existing measure of accommodation was also needed for colonists and Xhosa to become embroiled in warfare. On this occasion two events on different sides of the Fish River triggered a war. Firstly, a number of Xhosa engaged in a feud with Ndlambe fled from him into the colony, prompting some colonists to abandon their farms. Secondly, in May 1793 Barend Lindeque, a militia officer in the Zuurveld, who early in 1792 had given public warning of his intention to attack the Zuurveld Xhosa, on his own initiative attempted to push them over the Fish. He had already contacted Ndlambe, who was anxious that all Zuurveld Xhosa be driven back so that he could subjugate these 'rebel' chieftains to his authority.

The Second Frontier War (1793) broke out when Lindeque's commando and Ndlambe's men attacked the Zuurveld Xhosa and captured about 2,000 cattle. Thereupon, as a result of some misunderstanding, the coalition fell apart. The Zuurveld Xhosa, with the Gqunukhwebe in the vanguard, counter-attacked. This sparked off a general panic in which the colonists abandoned the Zuurveld almost completely.[80] In ensuing raids the Xhosa killed forty Khoikhoi servants, burnt twenty homesteads and, according to the colonists' estimate, captured 50 to 60,000 cattle, 11,000 sheep, and 200 horses.

A combined commando from Graaff-Reinet and Swellendam took the field under Landdrosts Maynier and Faure. It had instructions to expel the Xhosa from the Zuurveld and to indemnify the colonists for their losses. Besides capturing 8,000 cattle, the commando forced a considerable number of Xhosa to retreat beyond the Fish, where Ndlambe's forces defeated them, killing Tshaka (the Gqunukhwebe chief) and capturing Langa (the Mbalu chief), who apparently died soon afterwards. The commando found it impossible to

---

tried to persuade these Xhosa to leave the Zuurveld before they would be attacked by armed forces. This event, like the one noted above, only led to greater distrust between colonists and Xhosa. The next generations of course only remembered the 'massacre' that the 'other' had perpetrated.

clear the Zuurveld of all Xhosa, and after the commandos withdrew those beyond the Fish began to return. After the war Maynier, who refused to call out another general commando against the Xhosa, failed to negotiate the withdrawal of the Xhosa in the Zuurveld and the restitution of raided cattle. He limited police action to the apprehension of thieves.[81]

Historians of the war of 1793 have been divided in their sympathies, some siding with the Zuurveld colonists and their demand that the Xhosa be expelled, and others with Maynier and his policy of conciliation. More important than taking sides, however, is an investigation into the power balance of the area. All evidence suggests that the colonists of the Graaff-Reinet southeastern divisions, even with the help of some Swellendam burghers, could not successfully subjugate the Xhosa. Unable to draw on the northern divisions, which were fighting a desperate battle against the 'Bushmen', they were far inferior in numbers to the Xhosa.[82] The advantages provided by their guns and horses were neutralised by the opportunities the Zuurveld offered the Xhosa for concealment in the bush. And they were hampered by dissension, lack of leadership, and the government's control over the flow of ammunition. It was probably because they sensed their weakness that few of the 150 European families who had formerly inhabited the Zuurveld returned after the war. By the beginning of 1798 Landdrost Bresler reported that no colonists lived between the Fish and the Sundays; by September of that year only a third of the Zuurveld families had returned.[83]

After the war new leaders attempted to seize control of their respective communities. Each apparently realised that an unchallenged, single-leadership structure could more effectively negotiate, wage war and perhaps establish a monopoly in trade with other communities.[84] In 1795, the same year in which the British first occupied the Cape,[85] the colonists of the southeastern divisions seized control of Graaff-Reinet and renounced their allegiance to the government in Cape Town (see ch. 9, p. 341). Across the Fish, Ngqika ousted the regent Ndlambe, who had been reluctant to step down, and then tried to extend his own power by various measures,[86] like deposing councillors and bringing their people directly under him, and by claiming the entire estate of deceased commoners.[87] In the Zuurveld, where chiefdoms like the Mbalu, Dange and the Ntinde had suffered almost fatal blows in the war of 1793, the new Gqunukhwebe chief, Chungwa, attempted to extend his authority over his weakened neighbours. He realised that power lay in numbers: in 1797, when two small chiefs started to retreat over the Fish, he confiscated their cattle, declaring that if they left he would be too weak to sustain his claim to the land.[88] By 1799 he was claiming the Sundays River as his western boundary.[89]

None of these three attempts were successful. The Graaff-Reinet rebellion petered out because the government cut off the supply of ammunition. Ngqika's attempt to build up his power failed because some councillors resisted him and led their followers over the Fish. They were followed by Ndlambe shortly afterwards. Finally, Chungwa was unsuccessful since Ndlambe, soon after his arrival in the Zuurveld in 1800, established himself as the most important chief there. Unable to dominate the frontier, the various leaders sought to establish alliances. Ngqika and the colonists enlisted each other's help in their conflict with the Zuurveld Xhosa,[90] while Chungwa did his best to attract Khoikhoi allies to defend himself against a two-pronged attack.

Meanwhile in 1799 another rebellion broke out in Graaff-Reinet (the Van Jaarsveld rebellion), an event which would shortly trigger the Third Frontier War (1799—1802). The British government sent a force of British and Khoikhoi troops under General Vandeleur to suppress the rebellion (see ch. 9, p. 343). This action caused a frontier upheaval in three ways. Firstly, when Khoikhoi saw a partially Khoikhoi force advancing, some raided their masters and then sought the protection of the army. Secondly, Vandeleur unsuccessfully tried to push the Gqunukhwebe, by now the westernmost chiefdom in the Zuurveld, over the Fish, thus arousing their hostility. Thirdly, having failed to resolve the situation, Vandeleur made arrangements to return to Cape Town. It soon became clear that the Khoikhoi who had flocked to his side would be left behind. A number of these Khoikhoi now allied themselves to the Gqunukhwebe and started to raid the entire southern part of Graaff-Reinet, sparking off a large-scale retreat of colonists from these divisions. The colonists tried to regroup; but a Khoikhoi force, consisting of 700 men with horses and 150 guns, together with Gqunukhwebe and other Zuurveld Xhosa, defeated a commando of 300 men, pinned down Vandeleur and 200 regular troops in Algoa Bay, and forced almost all the colonists to evacuate the southern part of Graaff-Reinet and some of the eastern divisions of Swellendam.

In August 1799 British reinforcements under General Francis Dundas left Cape Town for the interior. Accompanied by Maynier, whose influence among the Khoikhoi and Xhosa was highly rated by the British, Dundas desired to establish peace through conciliation. Toward the end of 1799 Maynier succeeded in ending the war by persuading the Khoikhoi to break off their alliance with the Xhosa. A large number went back to the farms in return for a promise of better protection from their employers. The rest stayed with the Xhosa or lived independently under Klaas Stuurman and other chiefs at the Sundays River.

Hostilities broke out again in the second half of 1801 and continued until the end of 1802. Bands of Khoikhoi and Xhosa raided large areas of Graaff-Reinet and Swellendam. By the end of 1802 some 470 farms, fully 35 per cent of the farms registered in the two districts, were estimated to have been laid waste. Peace was concluded early in 1803 on the sole condition that each side retain possession of the cattle it had captured. The colonists' losses, according to their own estimate, were approximately 50,000 cattle, 50,000 sheep and 1,000 horses. A quarter to a third of the European population of the southeastern sector of the colony had fled their farms. As in 1793, European settlement in the east had been rolled back.

The Batavian administration (1803—06) was resolved to maintain the colonial government's claims to the frontier zone and to restore the European-dominated social order.[91] To this end it founded the district of Uitenhage in the Zuurveld and appointed an able man, Ludwig Alberti, as its landdrost. Through persuasion as well as compulsion a large number of colonists were induced to return to their farms in the southeast.[92] The Batavians were also successful in persuading more Khoikhoi to leave the Zuurveld Xhosa and return to the farms. Already during the war the alliance of Khoikhoi and Xhosa raiders had begun to fall apart as the partners began to dispute the division of the booty. Some Xhosa, in fact, killed a Khoikhoi leader, Boezak, although he claimed to have served them loyally.[93] In peace time there was also an irreconcilable conflict between the Zuurveld Xhosa chiefs, who wanted settled conditions in which they could exercise more effective control, and the Khoikhoi chiefs, who wished to continue raiding. Even among the Khoikhoi leaders divisions appeared as some chiefs challenged Klaas Stuurman, who apparently also opposed further raiding and wished to settle down quietly in the Zuurveld. Eventually the government bought off Klaas Stuurman and other Khoikhoi leaders by giving them small plots of land; their followers who had left the Xhosa had no alternative but to return to the farms or join the Cape Regiment (Hottentot Corps; see ch. 6, p. 222).

However, the Batavians failed to dislodge the Zuurveld Xhosa, establish a firm border,[94] or regulate the relationships between colonists and Xhosa. The British, who again occupied the Cape in 1806, made futile attempts through Captain J.G. Cuyler, Alberti's successor as landdrost of Uitenhage, to persuade the Zuurveld Xhosa to retreat beyond the Fish. They were unwilling to provide the military resources necessary for a forcible expulsion, especially not while a major European war was in progress. Government policy was neatly summarised by Governor Caledon's statement that 'it is better to submit to a certain extent of injury than risk a great deal for a prospect of advantage by no means certain.'[95] In these circumstances frontier landdrosts were compelled to erect a makeshift security system which hinged on winning the goodwill of the chiefs and securing their cooperation in apprehending thieves. At the same time the colonists were strictly forbidden to do anything which might provoke hostilities. Patrols commanded by field-cornets were established to follow the spoor of stolen cattle to the thief's kraal. There the patrols were amicably to persuade the chief to hand over the cattle.[96]

These measures greatly handicapped the colonists' ability to maintain their interests effectively, and the government's policy was criticised both by contemporaries and by later historians. Some critics, however, assume that the colonists could have given substance to the claim, expressed by three commandants in 1803, that they were 'strong enough to recover [their] belongings at the point of the sword and to provide a peace that would give quiet and security to . . . Government for years to come'.[97] But was this indeed the case? Even if the colonists were to receive from the government 'a good supply of powder and lead', as the commandants requested, it is doubtful whether, in the absence of generally accepted leaders, they could have totally expelled the Zuurveld Xhosa. Still more questionable was their ability to maintain peace by manning a boundary patrol which would prevent the return of Xhosa to the Zuurveld. The colonists showed no great enthusiasm for participating in these patrols; but they also so distrusted the Khoikhoi that they would have opposed any plan to arm them in this capacity, unless they were commanded by men in whom they had complete confidence.[98] In these circumstances the colonial government assumed that peace could best be maintained by limiting local confrontations.

During the first decade of the nineteenth century the Zuurveld Xhosa, especially Ndlambe, gained in strength as Ngqika's power decreased. In 1800 it had been different. Ngqika had defeated Hintsa, the Gcaleka chief, and then claimed to be paramount of all the Xhosa. He had also established a sound relationship with the colony, born of a common desire to subjugate the Zuurveld Xhosa. On the other hand, Chungwa and Ndlambe, despite their cattle gains in the Third Frontier War (1799—1802), still lacked both confidence and strength. Then in about 1807 Ngqika committed a grave error by ordering the abduction of one of Ndlambe's wives. Capitalising on the general revulsion at this deed, Ndlambe attacked and defeated Ngqika. Although Ngqika subsequently succeeded in recouping some of his losses and honour, it was clear that he had lost the initiative. He realised that his collaboration with the colonists was costing him dearly. In 1809 he lamented that 'the favours [the Christians] had almost exclusively bestowed on him made every Kaffer his enemy.'[99]

In contrast Ndlambe, having returned to the Zuurveld after the battle, steadily gained in power and prestige. Colonial observers were at first sceptical of his claim that he could subdue the other chiefs. In 1805 Alberti reported that if he attempted to do so he would be resisted because each chief wished 'to be his own master.'[100] To some extent Alberti was correct. Not only Chungwa but also some less powerful Xhosa chiefs like Habana and Galata of the Gwali, Nqeno of the Mbalu, and Xasa of the Dange, were still successfully resisting control by Ndlambe, whose interests differed from theirs. For instance, by raiding and generally antagonising the colonists, these four chiefs almost certainly did not meet with Ndlambe's approval. However, Ndlambe's power was steadily increasing, and by 1809, with 3,000 men under his command, he was undoubtedly the most powerful chief in the Zuurveld. Cuyler even thought that he was head of all Xhosa within the colonial boundaries.[101]

Chungwa, whose strength seems to have declined in inverse proportion to Ndlambe's rise, moved further westward during this period. This could have been due both to his desire to escape Ndlambe's control and to the necessities of transhumance. By 1808 there was a kraal of Chungwa's followers at Leeugamka, halfway between the Fish River and Cape Town; Chungwa himself was building a kraal in the Langkloof. He was, however, forced to retreat and became increasingly hemmed in by Ndlambe, who threatened his autonomy, and the colonial authorities. The government scorned his attempt to pay for pasture and his expressions of goodwill, and insisted that he should retreat over the Fish, a move which would end his independence.[102]

For Xhosa the opportunities as well as the scope for small-time raiding gradually decreased in the period between the frontier wars of 1801—02 and the year 1809, as important chiefs in the Zuurveld became more powerful. In times of peace, Chungwa, and even more so Ndlambe, tried to curtail cattle-lifting in order to prevent conflict with the colony. These Xhosa chiefs seem to have favoured an equilibrium on the frontier which would allow them to enjoy the benefits of labour and trade with the colonists. To foster stability they sought to increase their control over chiefdoms in their vicinity. Yet despite Ndlambe's growing strength, he could not control all the minor chiefs, especially those in the mountains, who were primarily responsible for the convulsion on the frontier which started in 1809. In this year the partial accommodation between colonists and Xhosa started to collapse.

The disintegration of the political order manifested itself in various ways. Firstly, Xhosa belonging to minor chiefdoms pushed into Bruintjes Hoogte and as far north as Buffelshoek (the present Cradock), settling among the colonists. They wanted both to pasture their cattle on sweetveld, which had become exhausted in the Zuurveld, and to escape from Ndlambe's control.[103] Secondly, from 1809 minor chiefs like Nqeno, Xasa, Habana and Galata began to raid cattle on a much larger scale than before, causing colonists in the exposed divisions to retreat. Field-cornet reports indicate that in Uitenhage alone more than 2,000 head of cattle were stolen in 1810. It was clear that the pattern of these raids differed from the petty thefts of four or five years before and that an extensive raiding network was in operation. In 1810 Cuyler declared: 'I am convinced that the cause of the intrusion of many of the Kaffir Chiefs so near upon the settlement is to cover or favour the stealing of their people, which booty they more or less share — indeed stealing among the Kaffirs from the inhabitants is become quite a trade. The cattle are stolen and driven to the furthest Kaffirs where they are eagerly exchanged for Kaffir cattle, and the cattle received in exchange are brought back by the thieves.'[104] Stockenstrom believed that these cattle were bartered to the Tembu and other kraals beyond the Kei River.[105]

The aggressiveness of the raiders, and the resulting loss of heart among the frontier colonists, had much to do with the feeling on both sides that the colonial government was intent on avoiding aggressive measures at all costs. In 1810 the government sent 200 regulars and 360 members of the Cape (Hottentot) Regiment to replace the burgher patrols. Executing a repeatedly issued proclamation against the employment of Xhosa, these troops rounded up the colonists' Xhosa servants, numbering 'some thousand', and brought them to the Sundays River to join their chiefs.[106] Many of these servants then joined the raiders. It soon became obvious that the troops, inhibited by their instructions to avoid hostilities, would not stop the raids. At the same time government regulations made it virtually impossible for the colonists to do so either. Cuyler wrote: 'the Caffres already knowing that they cannot be fired at by the Boors except when attempting to kill them, commit their outrages with that degree of confidence and impunity to defy our feeble attempts to take them alive and encourage them to repeat their robberies.[107]

In 1810 and the first half of 1811 Xhosa scoured the country in groups of four or five to demand gifts or to raid cattle, prompting colonists to evacuate large parts of Graaff-Reinet and Uitenhage. A British officer in 1811 reported from Bruintjes Hoogte: 'The country is on every side overrun with Kaffres, and there never was a period when such numerous parties of them were known to have advanced so far in every direction before; the depredations of late committed by them exceed all precedent and . . . unless some decisive and hostile measures are immediately adopted, I solemnly declare I apprehend considerable and most *serious consequences.'* [108] By the middle of 1811 raiders and Xhosa who wandered around to 'beg' were active at the Sundays River, Bruintjes Hoogte and Buffelshoek. Great numbers of Xhosa turned up in Tarka and Sneeuwberg in the northeast of Graaff-Reinet under the pretence of visiting, which usually entailed 'begging'. Along the entire eastern border colonists were preparing to abandon their farms. Hardly any farms were occupied east of the Uitenhage drostdy, and many colonists had left Bruintjes Hoogte and Buffelshoek. The majority of the Bruintjes Hoogte colonists were reportedly ready to quit the district.[109]

Both the colony and Ndlambe attempted to stabilise the situation. At the initiative of Stockenstrom, patrols of burghers and soldiers gradually pushed most of the Xhosa out of his district (Graaff-Reinet). Ndlambe in turn exerted pressure on the minor chiefs who were mainly responsible for the raids. Before the end of 1811 Habana, Xasa, Galata and Nqeno were all compelled to leave the colony. During the second half of 1811 there was indeed a lull on the frontier, but the situation was far from normal and many colonists refused to return to their farms. In Cape Town the dislocation on the Eastern Frontier was viewed with great concern. Sir John Cradock, who became governor in 1811, was warned that Xhosa might penetrate close to Cape Town. Unlike his predecessor, Caledon, the new governor was a military man who saw the Xhosa as an alien threat to British subjects, to the security of the hinterland and to the meat supply of Cape Town. Accordingly he instructed Lieutenant-Colonel John Graham to drive all the Xhosa (Chungwa and Ndlambe included) over the Great Fish River, 'the acknowledged boundary of . . . His Majesty's Settlement.'[110]

With the arrival of efficient military men such as Graham a new element was introduced to the frontier scene. Up till then the European and the Xhosa on the frontier had in some respects resembled a couple in a disastrous forced marriage: they would fear and fight each other, but neither would destroy the other — in fact their constant battle to gain the upper hand or stand up against one another was what made their lives meaningful and morbidly filled their daily thoughts. For the colonists the Xhosa were labourers, trading partners, foes — sometimes all in one. For Graham there was none of this: the Xhosa were simply enemies, 'horrid savages'. Plundering parties should be followed to the kraal and there 'every man Kaffer' that could be found, ' if possible the chief', should be 'destroyed'.[111] In the summer of 1811–12 British officers, heading 900 burgher militia and 700 men of the Cape (Hottentot) Regiment, drove roughly 8,000 Xhosa, women and children included, over the Fish while 500 British troops brought up the rear. During the campaign Chungwa was killed. Afterwards Cradock established twenty-seven military posts near the Fish River to prevent the return of the Xhosa.

Thus ended the first phase of intensive contact between colonists and Xhosa. Ties of trade and labour had bound them together in a system which for a long time could survive the ongoing struggle. In times of war no quick and decisive victory had been possible, because the more numerous Zuurveld Xhosa lacked horses, guns and coordinated leadership while the colonists had guns and horses but insufficient numbers and inadequate leaders. Eventually the colonists prevailed, but only after their disunity and rebelliousness were overcome by the appearance of a strong imperial power around which they could rally. Victory was achieved by European and Khoikhoi cavalry under British leadership, and ultimately by the links with Europe which provided indispensable guns and ammunition.[112]

For much of the period 1770—1812 the frontier remained open to the Xhosa. Attempts to dislodge them from the Zuurveld were unsuccessful and chiefdoms rarely faced shortages of pasture severe enough to create irreconcilable conflicts. The frontier was a place to which commoner clans who resisted subordination could escape, and where the poor and destitute could attempt to improve their position. Peace-time cattle raids were generally the work of small kraals, evidently attempting to build up stock and power.

The closing of the frontier

We noted earlier that two phases in frontier history can be distinguished: the open and the closing frontier. However, one should remember that the closing of the frontier did not start at the same time in all areas: it was always dependent on whether a group could establish its hegemony over others in its immediate vicinity or whether some external power was able to put an end to the relative anarchy of the open frontier. In general one may say that the frontier began to close for the Khoikhoi in the 1780s, gradually for the colonists during the 1790s, and for the Xhosa between 1807 and 1812.

There were three ways in which the closing differed from the open frontier. One vital difference was the gradual disappearance of that measure of liberty which individuals and groups had previously possessed in establishing relations and maintaining their interests. One frontiersman illuminated the essence of the transition when he reminisced that 'in those older times [c. 1780] when colonists were robbed they redressed themselves, but now their hands were tied.'[113] Of course this loss of liberty was closely connected with the emergence of an authority of the kind the British government established over the colonists in the frontier zone. Thus in a sense the frontier rebellions, which are discussed separately in chapter 9, were instances of futile resistance against the closing of the frontier.

Secondly, there was a distinct change in the ratio of population to land. In contrast to the sparsely populated open frontier, the closing frontier was characterised by pressures on the land which were caused by the arrival of several new peoples. During the 1770s it was still quite possible for a young colonist with little or no capital to acquire land and start raising cattle.[114] By

1798, however, only 26 per cent of the colonists owned farms. By 1812 this had shrunk to 18 per cent.[115] (Figures for married men were higher: 39 per cent and 25 per cent respectively.[116]) The Khoikhoi, who during the opening years of the frontier had roamed about freely, were gradually squeezed out of the few remaining unoccupied spaces. In 1797 Barrow reported that there were no independent Khoikhoi kraals in the district of Graaff-Reinet.[117]

Thirdly, the status of non-European labourers deteriorated, and many of them became fixed at the lowest stratum of society. On the open frontier there was some quid pro quo between a master who dealt justly with his clients and protected them, and his client who rendered services in return. On the closing frontier Khoikhoi rapidly lost their land as well as the ability to refuse their labour and exist outside someone's service. One should not, however, think that the status and conditions of labourers changed dramatically. There were various intermediate stages between the master-client relationship at the one extreme and serfdom on the other. The master-client relationship easily evolved into paternalism. This implied that the master had to provide for and dispense justice to his labourers and treat them humanely, while his labourers, who had slowly lost the freedom and status of clients, were bound by the duty to work properly and obey their master's commands.[118] Paternalism again could shade into the more extreme system of labour-repression in which extra-economical devices were employed to ensure an adequate and docile labour force.[119] At the furthest extreme some colonists abducted native children[120] and sold them or kept them in bondage almost like slaves.[121]

The colonists' institution of labour-repressive practices and involuntary servitude was dependent on the establishment of hegemony over the Khoikhoi and on the realisation among Khoikhoi that colonists had the force to smash any resistance. Under this system the master kept his servant on the farm by withholding his wages, impounding his livestock, or preventing his family from leaving the farm with him. Abundant evidence suggests that these practices were widespread. From Swellendam where, with the exception of one or two isolated spots, the frontier had long closed, Landdrost Faure reported that Khoikhoi were constantly complaining to him that their wages were not paid or that they were not permitted to leave when their contracts expired.[122] By 1809 the same conditions prevailed in Graaff-Reinet. Collins, who in general was sympathetic to the colonists, reported: 'A Hottentot can now seldom get away at the expiration of his term. If he should happen not to be in debt to his master . . . he is not allowed to take his children, or he is detained under some frivolous pretence, such as that of cattle having died through his neglect, and he is not permitted to satisfy any demands of this nature otherwise than by personal service.'[123]

Through the landdrost the colonial government attempted to check some of these practices. Especially under Maynier (1793—95 and 1799—1801) colonists were frequently reprimanded or taken to court when they did not pay their servants or release them when the contracted period expired. However, there were limits to the colonial government's commitment to providing Khoikhoi equal protection under the law. In practice its policy was subservient to two needs: the need for 'order' (which also implied the maintenance of the social hierarchy), and the need for labour, both of which were strongly felt by the last decade of the eighteenth century. Firstly, the colonial government desired that Khoikhoi should not be idle but be constantly employed. If they neglected their duties 'the good order', as Fiscal J.A. Truter put it, demanded that they, like 'children, apprentices and slaves', be punished by their superiors.[124] Secondly, Cape Town's demand for meat greatly increased after the coming of the British in 1795,[125] necessitating a docile and regulated work force. The need was especially great after the abolition of the slave trade in 1807 and the expulsion in 1810 of Xhosa servants working on farms in the eastern districts.

For these two reasons the government increasingly supported or institutionalised some of the labour-repressive methods of the colonists. For example, during the last decades of the eighteenth century the indenture system (which had originally compelled the children of Khoikhoi women and slave men to serve the farmer who had indentured them up to their twenty-fifth year) was informally extended by colonists to all Khoikhoi children. The indenture system was abolished by the Batavians, but during the second British occupation was reinstated in law by Cradock.

The indenture system should not be seen as an unqualified evil. Some regarded it as a method of improving the conditions of Khoikhoi labourers by officially recording the farmers' acceptance of responsibility for the Khoikhoi children on their farms. However, it could be widely abused. Stockenstrom observed that a Khoikhoi would rather suffer the worst kind of maltreatment on a farm than abscond and leave his wife, children and cattle behind,[126] with the result that the colonists acquired almost the same control over their Khoikhoi labourers as they had over their slaves, except that they did not own them. In fact it could be argued that the indenture system obviated the need for slavery in order to maintain a subservient non-European labour force. For the British the indenture system posed no particular problem, despite the fact that anti-slavery sentiment was beginning to prevail in Britain. Although they opposed plantation slavery, even Britain's reformers seemed to give their approval to coercive forms of labour which did not involve the ownership of one person by another.[127]

Another curb on Khoikhoi mobility and the search for better opportunities was provided by pass and vagrancy regulations designed to prevent Khoikhoi from absconding to Xhosa kraals or other farms where they received better treatment. In 1794 the central government issued a proclamation permitting colonists to arrest as deserters any armed Khoikhoi who were found idle along the roads or in the fields.[128]

At the end of the eighteenth century the Swellendam and Graaff-Reinet district authorities prohibited Khoikhoi and slaves from moving from one farm to another or from farm to *drostdy* without a pass issued by a colonist or official.[129] In his comprehensive Hottentot Proclamation (1809) Caledon retained these restrictions: he made it compulsory for Khoikhoi to have certificates of residency and passes, issued by their master or the landdrost, when they left their abode. It is true that Caledon's proclamation was issued with ameliorative intent; indeed, the elaboration of labour contract regulations and the definition of the rights of servants was the reason why a reformer such as the younger Stockenstrom saw it as a major advance. However, many of the gains were sacrificed by stipulating that contracts could be signed before field-cornets who, being farmers themselves, were unlikely to inform Khoikhoi of their rights.[130] By assigning these key functions to local officials and colonists, the proclamation could easily be turned into a device for coercing Khoikhoi farm labour.

Thus even a strong central government, deeply concerned about the condition of Khoikhoi labourers, was not prepared to institute any structural changes in their favour. The British, while subscribing to a limited conception of equal justice for all, did not grant Khoikhoi political or social equality with the colonists. And as men of their times they had no intention of removing the vast disparities in wealth and economic opportunity by guaranteeing a minimum wage (Khoikhoi on farms in Graaff-Reinet earned an average of nine to twelve sheep per year), or by supplying them with land. Such was the structure of colonial society that even Ordinance 50 of 1828 failed materially to change the position of the Khoikhoi. As the younger Stockenstrom was to observe in a later period: they were subjected to the same treatment as slaves, except that they could not be sold and were not bound to their master except by contract. Far removed from the magistrate, Stockenstrom went on, they were in a state of moral debasement and physical misery; they were treated even worse than slaves, because a farmer valued his slave more than his Khoikhoi servant, who could not be sold.[131]

Khoikhoi reacted in various ways to the closing frontier. There were those living on farms who internalised their servile and inferior status, seeing themselves, as one expressed it, as 'heathens who must obey the commands of our *baas*.'[132] Others resisted. Roving Khoikhoi bands, some of which declared that they would take back their land,[133] operated in Graaff-Reinet as late as

1809. The supreme effort of the Khoikhoi to liberate themselves had been the great revolt of 1799. However, despite its short-term success, it had taken a heavy toll in Khoikhoi lives[134] and had failed to stop the closing of the frontier.

For one Khoikhoi group, the Gona, there was still a respite as long as the Xhosa remained in the Zuurveld. Both Xhosa and colonists valued the Gona as spies, emissaries and messengers. Moreover, the colonial government made a clear distinction between the Gona living among the Xhosa and the 'Hottentots' who had long been living on farms. Colonists were forbidden to fire on Xhosa or Gona except in self-defense and were instructed to treat all chiefs kindly.[135] Throughout the period of this chapter Xhosa incorporation of Gona continued.

Some Khoikhoi joined Dr J.T. van der Kemp's missionary station at Bethelsdorp (founded in 1803) in an attempt to escape serfdom. Van der Kemp wanted them to be 'perfectly free, upon an equal footing in every respect with the colonists.'[136] However, by offering Khoikhoi a haven, the missionaries blunted the edge of their resistance to conquest and finally induced them to accept their lot as a landless and marginal group in society. In 1812 the missionary James Read wrote that Bethelsdorp had become an asylum for numbers of Khoikhoi 'who otherwise were accustomed to join the Caffers or unite themselves in the woods to seek redress.'[137]

Bethelsdorp, moreover, was unable to provide the Khoikhoi with a viable economic alternative. The station, encompassing an area of twenty-one km², could not provide enough food or work for the 600 to 800 people who congregated there. These Khoikhoi were thus forced to seek employment on neighbouring farms. Furthermore, those who sought to occupy intermediate roles in the economy by hunting, driving wagons, or bartering soap, timber and salt, often found obstacles thrown in their way. They were thwarted by colonists who saw such activities as falling in the category of 'burgher trades.'[138] They were also hampered by the restrictions imposed by Landdrost Cuyler who refused to provide them with passes for hunting and cutting timber.[139]

Although some of Cuyler's restrictions were the result of the unsettled conditions in the Zuurveld, there was also a fundamental issue at stake: the completely different goals the missionaries and colonial authorities envisaged for Bethelsdorp. The authorities insisted that Bethelsdorp should not, as the missionaries desired, provide an alternative to farm labour — a place where the Khoikhoi were on a par with the colonists on their farms. Instead, the government wanted it to be a receptacle for surplus Khoikhoi — the sick and the unemployable — as well as a training station sending industrious Khoikhoi into society. In the government's view Bethelsdorp also had to provide the colony with recruits for the Hottentot Corps (Cape Regiment) and labour for the construction of roads or buildings at the drostdy.

To the missionaries these views were anathema, since they fatally undermined their insistence that Khoikhoi be accorded the same status and rights as colonists.[140] They fought a running battle against Cuyler on this issue. In the end they decided that they could best help the Khoikhoi by advising them of the laws which protected them, and by informing friends in Cape Town and England of all the allegations of Khoikhoi maltreatment which had come to their notice,[141] thereby becoming, as it were, 'Khoikhoi field-cornets'.

In response to the missionaries' campaign the government appointed a circuit court, the controversial Black Circuit (1812), which investigated charges of cruel treatment of Khoikhoi. Some historians have argued that the court's well-known lambasting of the missionaries proved that their charges were unfounded and that the colonists did not illtreat their servants.[142] They overlook the fact that the missionaries reported *all* allegations of atrocities and maltreatment which had come to their notice; the colonial government, however, decided only to prosecute crimes allegedly perpetrated after 1806.[143] Cuyler, an observer sympathetic to the colonists, declared: 'I have no hesitation in believing that some years ago, particularly under the first Dutch government's time and perhaps of later date, barbarous cruelties were committed in the distant districts from the capital.'[144] This is borne out by the records of Graaff-Reinet, which contain approximately twenty cases of unnatural deaths of Khoikhoi between 1786 and 1800. In most of these a *prima facie* case of murder or homicide could be made out against colonists. The documents give the impression that the colonists often covered up evidence against accused fellow colonists, with the result that judicial proceedings were not instituted before the Court of Justice.[145]

The question remains whether the missionaries did more harm than good to the Khoikhoi by the methods they used. On the one hand it may be argued that, instead of winning over enlightened colonists to their cause, the missionaries alienated them. They sent their complaints of Khoikhoi maltreatment directly to London and not to the governor in Cape Town; they also created the erroneous impression that the crimes had been recently perpetrated and laid unfounded charges before the court, which earned them a rebuke from the judges.

But two observations are pertinent here. The missionaries decided to appeal directly to London because complaints laid before the colonial government were bound to be referred to Cuyler, who disagreed fundamentally with them on what constituted proper treatment of Khoikhoi. Secondly, the missionaries' strategy was not designed to win the hearts and minds of the dominating class, but to wage war relentlessly against the structure of domination in which the Khoikhoi were caught. They sought maximum publicity for the plight of the Khoikhoi, anticipating that any decisive intervention on their behalf would come only from the imperial authorities, spurred on to action by a public outcry overseas. In this larger struggle the missionaries made progress by spreading a greater awareness of the position of the Khoikhoi and by inducing the government to a broader commitment to equal justice for all classes.[146]

The closing of the frontier deeply affected not only the Khoikhoi but also the 'Christians', among whom there emerged large disparities of wealth. It has already been pointed out that only 26 per cent of the 972 people listed as 'inhabitants' in the 1798 opgaaf** (all male burghers and landholding widows) held farms. This 26 per cent owned 75.2 per cent of the slaves, 56.6 per cent of the cattle, 55.8 per cent of the sheep and 51.3 per cent of the horses in the district.[147]

Even within the landholding group there were considerable disparities in wealth. The 1798 opgaaf listed 174 inhabitants who held only one farm each, 63 who held two, 14 who held three and 2 who held four farms.[148] Of the group of landholders approximately 44 per cent owned less than 400 livestock units.

Table 8.1 summarises the differences in livestock wealth among the various categories of 'Christians'.

Table 8.1   Livestock units owned by 'Christians': Graaff-Reinet, 1798
(One livestock unit = 1 head of cattle or 6 sheep)

Livestock units	Landholding 'inhabitants'	Landless married 'inhabitants'	Landless unmarried 'inhabitants'	Company servants	Baptised Bastaards
0—11	3	30	109	48	10
12—19	14	118	121	26	22
100—199	25	122	33	6	5
200—399	71	125	13	2	2
400—799	93	33	5	1	—
800—1 199	36	3	—	—	—
1 200+	11	3	—	—	—

The upper stratum of 'Christian' society consisted of landholders, followed by people living on a kinsman's farm, some of whom could look forward to

** Opgaaf lists are defective as indices of absolute wealth, since some colonists underreported to diminish their taxes. However, apart from inventories of estates they are the only indices we have. I have chosen the list of 1798 for these calculations, since that opgaaf was the first one to be performed under oath. Moreover, shortly before, soldiers had for the first time been stationed on the frontier and they could make good the government's threat to punish irregularities.

becoming landholders themselves. Beneath these were the bijwoners, i.e., colonists who lived and farmed on other people's land or eked out an existence as woodcutters. In the face of increasing pressure on the land, the position of the bijwoners, and even of those colonists living with kinsmen, deteriorated rapidly. By 1810 many had of necessity become nomads. Stockenstrom reported from Graaff-Reinet that there were 800 to 900 colonists without farms who roamed about, staying some months on one farm before moving to another.[149] Since opgaaf lists did not clearly distinguish between kinsmen and bijwoners, it is not possible to indicate their respective wealth.

Company servants, although considered as 'Christians', were mentioned separately in the opgaaf lists. They were persons who had been removed from the Dutch East India Company's payroll while being temporarily employed by farmers as itinerant teachers, farm managers or tradesmen.[150] A few became wealthy after marrying the widow or daughter of an affluent farmer — all nine Company servants owning more than a hundred units of livestock were married — but most remained poor. Only one of the eighty-three Company servants on the 1798 opgaaf roll held a farm; seventy-five lived on someone else's farm and eight lived in Graaff-Reinet town.

Another group officially regarded as Christians but also listed separately were the so-called baptised Bastaards. The 1798 opgaaf lists thirty-eight men, sixteen women, twenty-eight boys and thirty-nine girls in this category. Only one of them held a loan farm.

In the more stratified closing frontier, as distinct from the more egalitarian open frontier, the burden of civil duties fell mainly upon the 'poorer class', as Governor Janssens noted. He also remarked that 'people do not respect the field-cornets as they ought, the rich especially.'[151] Janssens was referring to the self-supporting administrative system of Graaff-Reinet, in which field-cornets and other office holders had the right to command colonists to participate in commandos, provide transportation and relays, forward mail, and help erect public buildings. According to an early historian, these levies formed 'a system of impressment which opened a wide door to favouritism on the one hand, and oppression on the other, in many cases an intolerable burden.'[152] The closing frontier was thus stratified politically as well as socially, for rich people were powerful enough to resist the demands the government made upon them. It also suggests that the closing frontier witnessed increasing oppression, not only of masters over servants, but also of rich over poor Europeans and of Europeans over Bastaards, though they all belonged to the *official* category of 'Christians'. Research covering a longer period would be necessary to test this tentative conclusion, but the following passage in the 1802 journal of William Somerville shows how the strong treated the weak in the absence of institutional controls. Commenting on the docility of the Bastaards on the Orange River who fled the colony, Somerville wrote that 'the circumstances they related of the oppression and tyranny of the wagtmasters [field-cornets] are truly shocking. In a matter of 600 sheep one of them under the former Government told a bastaard: You have right to the sheep but your adversary is a Christian and you are but a heathen therefore I can't compel him.'[153]

Despite an increasing racial rigidity, the closing frontier was not stratified solely in terms of Europeans' ethnic and racial perceptions, that is, their attitudes towards different cultures and physical types. Rather it consisted of a number of status groups with varying ranks on the social scale. There were many criteria of status. Race was very important, but there were also other indicators of status, like baptism — regardless of colour, baptised people shared certain privileges[154] — control of land, and possession of livestock. Since almost all independent farmers were European and baptised, these categories largely overlapped. However, outside the group of landholders, their kinsmen and the more affluent bijwoners, there were people who qualified for relatively high status on some grounds but not on others. For example, baptised Bastaards were 'non-white'; however, on the 1798 opgaaf rolls they owned on average more livestock units than the European Company servants (fifty-six against thirty-nine units per person). They were also recognised as practitioners of a burgher craft or occupation, while Company servants still had to apply for burgher status.†† In both these groups people who thought themselves worthy of respect, but were in fact marginal people, strove to be fully accepted as burghers. For instance, when a Company servant named De Jong accused David Willemzen, a baptised Bastaard, of improper conduct and assaulted his wife, Willemzen exclaimed that he was as good 'a burgher man' as De Jong and beat him up.[155]

The 'racial' groups tended to be endogamous. Of the 689 couples listed in the opgaaf as 'inhabitants' only 5 to 6 per cent can be described as 'mixed', in that one of the partners had a grandparent who was not European. Barrow remarked that the Bastaards 'generally marry with each other, or with persons of colour, but seldom with Hottentots.'[156] However, a study of the opgaaf lists shows that the percentage of mixed marriages among the lower status groups was not inconsiderable.[157] Of the seventeen married Company servants on the 1798 opgaaf roll, four had non-European wives; and of the

---

†† It is not quite certain what 'burgher status' meant. People wishing to leave the Dutch East India Company service had to apply for burgher status; children of married burgher couples were automatically considered to be burghers. However, in the eyes of the colonists the crucial question seems not to have been one's nominal status, but whether one actually exercised burgher rights, like practising a burgher craft or occupation, or holding office. See *RCC*, IX, Truter—Bird, 7 Jan. 1816, p. 120.

seventeen baptised Bastaards five had wives who, judged by their immediate ancestry, were European. Some of the children of mixed parentage eventually emerged as European and others as non-European. The children born out of the liaison between Coenraad de Buys and his concubine, the Bastaard Maria van der Ros (or Horst), went into different groups: one son, Coenraad Wilhelm, married a European woman, most of his descendants becoming Europeans; a daughter, Elizabeth, married a European named Sowietsky and had descendants who became Europeans. De Buys's other seven children and their descendants in all probability passed into the non-European fold.[158]

It was partly because racial categories were not yet as rigid as they were to become that some Europeans occasionally sought to overthrow Europeans in power by using non-Europeans as allies. There were, for example, 'skelmbaster kraals' consisting of British deserters, Bastaards and colonists scheming to 'liberate' themselves and conquer part of the colony.[159] And there are indications that in 1795, during the British attack on the Cape, Delport and his Swellendam burghers incited not only the lowly Company servants but also free blacks in Cape Town against Company rule.[160] Lastly, in more remote regions there were always colonists like De Buys and the Bezuidenhouts who had no objection to soliciting the help of non-Europeans in their struggle against the government.[161]

It was not only among the various categories of 'Christians' that there was a distinct measure of stratification. Hunted and hated, the Khoisan hunter-gatherers were considered inferior by the Khoikhoi menial servants,[162] themselves in many respects on a par with slaves and thus despised by Bastaards, who enjoyed greater freedom of movement. All these groups were in turn held in contempt by the socially superior categories of people.[163]

People constantly strove to rise to a higher status group. Khoisan hunter-gatherers became 'tame Hottentots', fugitive slaves tried to pass for Bastaard-Hottentots in order to move about without passes and obtain paid employment,[164] and Khoikhoi and especially Bastaard-Hottentots hoped to enter Christian society through baptism. The converse also occurred: a free Bastaard-Hottentot (the son of a slave father and Khoikhoi mother) might easily be apprehended after having been mistaken for a slave born of a liaison between a female slave and a male Khoikhoi.

However, this analysis should not detract from the key significance of race as an indicator of social and political status. The cross-racial alliances mentioned above were mainly temporary and opportunistic and they disintegrated rapidly. As frontier society evolved, landless European colonists sought the protection of affluent landholders, even though they might have been despised or exploited. As for the lowest strata of society, the formal and informal means of control of the closing frontier compressed 'Bushmen',

Khoikhoi and Bastaard-Hottentots into an undifferentiated servile class, none of whose members were European. True, some still tried to acquire status through baptism and marriage. But only at Bethelsdorp were they allowed to receive these rites, and in any event Europeans did not really value these segregated symbols of status.

The expulsion of the Xhosa in 1811—12 effectively closed the frontier to them. It deprived them not only of extensive grain fields but also of the use of the Zuurveld as an escape hatch. In addition, they had lost a considerable number of cattle, which Graham kept as a guarantee against further Xhosa inroads, and as compensation for European victims of Xhosa raids. By the end of 1812 there was so much hunger among the Xhosa that Graham was compelled to allow some to return to the Zuurveld to reap the harvest.[165] This was a lesson which subsequent administrators would also learn: that to expel the Xhosa was not to rid the colony of its Xhosa 'problem'.

Thus by 1812 the frontier zone was largely closed to members of all three societies. Or to put it differently, the frontier had been colonised. The Xhosa gradually ceased to regard the Zuurveld as a disputed area, one to which their ancestors had once staked a claim.[166] At the same time the colonial government established unquestioned authority in the area. In time it achieved full legitimacy over the Khoikhoi, as an ever increasing proportion of Khoikhoi adults knew no other government. The government did not tolerate some of the colonists' labour-repressive practices. However, through the pass laws it ensured for the farmer a docile work force trapped at the lowest tier of society.

There were still parts west of Graaff-Reinet district, such as the hillier areas of Rivier Zondereind, where officials protected Khoikhoi rights to the land and prevented the frontier from completely closing in on them. However, Xhosa, like the freebooter Danster,[167] Khoikhoi, Bastaards, and burghers such as De Buys were increasingly attracted to the next open frontier of Transorangia in the north, where they could regain their former freedom.[168]

Conclusion

Frontier history between 1770 and 1812 has traditionally been seen as a stark conflict between distinct and hostile 'races'. More recently, some liberal historians have moved away from the 'conflict-between-races' interpretation: instead of emphasising conflict, they have had as their central themes cooperation and peaceful interaction between the frontier peoples, and the failure of the colonial government to limit these processes. Revisionist historians, while continuing to see conflict as primary, have paid increasing attention to the non-conflictual aspects of the frontier, such as cross-racial alliances or the coalescence of classes across racial lines.

These interpretations have deepened our understanding of the frontier. The open frontier, particularly, is incomprehensible if one does not realise that relationships were formed in a system embracing various peoples and held together by the goods and services they exchanged with one another. Different groups found it to be in their interests to establish and maintain a balance of 'no war — no peace' which allowed this system to survive.

However, such cooperation and voluntary interaction did not result in the biological, cultural, political or economic integration of separate peoples.[169] Especially on the closing frontier, the prevailing characteristics were withdrawal, exclusion and strife. Thus, far more important than miscegenation between colonists and Khoikhoi (apart from the De Buys case there is hardly any evidence of Xhosa-colonist miscegenation) was the limited degree to which children born out of interracial liaisons were assimilated into the European community. Though there was considerable acculturation, particularly between Europeans and Khoikhoi (see ch. 4, pp. 157—59) it did not lead to the removal of ethnic distinctions. The colonists resisted efforts to instruct Khoikhoi in the more complex aspects of their culture, such as reading, writing and religion, because this would 'put [them] upon an equal footing with the Christians.'[170] As for European-Xhosa acculturation, each group borrowed only minimally from the other. In the sphere of politics it was not the establishment of colonist-Xhosa political alliances that was significant, but rather that these alliances failed to achieve anything substantial.

One must also qualify the second element of the traditional interpretation, i.e., that the frontier was dominated by *racial* conflict. An analysis of class‡‡ rather than race relations can illuminate important aspects of intergroup contact. In a loose sense one might see the colonists not so much as a race, but as a class clustering around a core of landholders (including the field-cornets, the most important authority outside the drostdy) who controlled an immobile, servile class. The colonists' resistance to government interference in their labour relations may be understood as an expression of specific economic interests. Similarly, colonist-Xhosa conflict may be seen as a struggle between rival classes of cattle-owners with different political systems and differential access to European technology.

‡‡ 'Class' is used here in the sense of most radical historians, i.e., to denote a group of people with a common relationship to the means of production. This is to be contrasted with the concept 'status group' which denotes a group with a social status conferred by members of a society with common values, according to certain criteria such as physical type, baptism, wealth, achievement, etc.

But even if full weight is given to these views, the fact remains that Xhosa and colonists distinguished themselves from others mainly by their perceptions of racial and ethnic differences.[171] They had come to see each other more as racial adversaries than as economic competitors, and conflict occurred mainly along racial lines. This is not to suggest that prejudice and fantasies about race and culture in themselves gave rise to the struggle on the Eastern Frontier. Conflicts arising from the struggle to control land, cattle and labour — or, more simply, class cleavages — greatly reinforced the racial cleavage and made the conflict much more intense and all-embracing.

Although stable relations and various forms of cooperation existed at times between the various peoples, conflict was pervasive. Because it had both a racial and a class dimension, negotiations were less effective in resolving disputes than is often the case in purely economic conflicts. To realise their objectives, men turned increasingly to forceful means, such as labour-repressive devices, exaction of ransom, raiding and war. The ultimate power struggle was, of course, the battle for hegemony on the frontier. This struggle reached its climax in 1812, when the last remnants of peaceful cooperation between colonists and Xhosa in the Zuurveld were destroyed, along with the frontier system which had bound them together in this area.

Chapter Eight Notes

1. J. Barrow, *Travels into the Interior of Southern Africa* (London, 1806), II, 373—76; D.G. van Reenen, *Die Joernaal van Dirk Gysbert van Reenen* (Cape Town, 1937), p. 195; J.P.H. Acocks, *Veld Types of South Africa* (Pretoria, 1953), map I and pp. 76—84, 150, 154.
2. F. Mason, 'An Account of Three Journeys from Cape Town into the Southern parts of Africa', *Philosophical Transactions of the Royal Society,* LXVI (1776), p. 177. See also H. Lichtenstein, *Travels in Southern Africa in the years 1803, 1804, 1805 and 1806* (Cape Town, 1930), II, 319.
3. G. Harinck, 'Interaction between Xhosa and Khoi: emphasis on the period 1620—1750', *African Societies in Southern Africa,* ed. Leonard Thompson (London, 1969), pp. 166—67.
4. C.A. Haupt, 'Joernaal'. *RZA.* III, 310—11. For discussion of Khoikhoi incorporation into Xhosa chiefdoms, see J.B. Peires, 'A History of the Xhosa, c. 1700—1835' (M.A. dissertation, Rhodes University, 1976), pp. 56—60.
5. No eighteenth-century source verifies J. Henderson Soga's statement that the Gqunukhwebe were aliens who never had a place assigned 'within the body of the Xhosa tribe': *The South Eastern Bantu* (Johannesburg, 1930), p. 117.
6. In contrast Hammond-Tooke describes the Gqunukhwebe as a tributary chiefdom. See W.D. Hammond-Tooke, 'Segmentation and Fission in Cape Nguni Political Units', *Africa,* XXXV (1965), p. 146.
7. Anthropologists see segmentation and fission as a regular process in the unstable Cape Nguni political units. Hammond-Tooke in 'Segmentation and Fission', pp.

143–56 and 'The "other side" of frontier history: a model of Cape Nguni political process', *African Societies in Southern Africa*, ed. Leonard Thompson (London, 1969), p. 240 describes a Xhosa chiefdom as structurally unstable since it is divided into a Great House, headed by the Great House wife's eldest son (who is the legal heir), and the Right-Hand House, headed by the eldest son of the Right-Hand wife. The other wives were allocated to either the Great or the Right-Hand Houses. Segmentation and fission frequently occurred along the lines of these two Houses. There was even an expectation of fission: the Right-Hand House had a pre-emptive right to break away. This interpretation has been attacked by a historian, J.B. Peires, who is currently doing primary research on Xhosa history. Peires argues that there was no fission in the Xhosa paramountcy since the overall authority of the paramount remained unquestioned. Subdividing occurred when junior members of the royal lineage dispersed to conquer new lands and independent Khoikhoi, hunters and Nguni. Rather than setting up independent chiefdoms, they expanded the territory, population and authority of the Xhosa chiefdom: J.B. Peires, 'The Rise of the "Right-Hand House" in the history and historiography of the Xhosa', *History in Africa*, II (1975); and 'Xhosa Expansion before 1800', *Collected Seminar Papers on the Societies of Southern Africa* (Institute of Commonwealth Studies, 1976), vol. 6.

For the eighteenth century the Hammond-Tooke theory of independent states cannot be accepted. But there is also insufficient proof for the view that there was one paramount who retained overall authority as the political head of the Xhosa 'nation' and that the Xhosa were a 'state' rather than a 'cluster'. The actual position seems to have fluctuated, according to prevailing power relationships, between the two positions depicted by Hammond-Tooke and Peires. In his M.A. dissertation, written after the articles cited above, Peires is prepared to classify the Xhosa as being organised in a segmentary state in which the centre only excercised limited control over the subordinate authorities on the periphery, provided it is taken into account that there were both centralising and decentralising forces at work. See J.B. Peires, 'A History of the Xhosa, c. 1700–1835' (M.A. dissertation, Rhodes University, 1976), pp. 218–26.

8. Stb. 20/2, Report of Van Jaarsveld—Landdrost of Stellenbosch, 22 June 1780. See also Donald Moodie, *The Record* (Cape Town 1960), III, Extract Letters of Landdrost of Stellenbosch, 10 Oct. 1781, p. 96.

9. Technically they were entitled to do this: if they were subject to anyone it was to Gcaleka rather than Rharhabe. In social and ritual matters, at least, they acknowledged the importance of the Gcaleka chief. Chungwa, in fact, once described him as his king.

10. A sentence in the journal of Collins illustrates this: 'Zlambie having taken a fancy . . . to the lands near the Bosjesmans River, occupied by some of the kraals of Konga [Chungwa], and the latter having refused to resign them on his demand, his people were driven from them by force.' Moodie, *The Record,* V, 14.

11. See the figures in Robin Derricourt, 'Settlement in the Transkei and Ciskei before the Mfecane', *Beyond the Cape Frontier,* ed. C. Saunders and R. Derricourt (Cape Town, 1974), pp. 66–68; Basil Sansom, 'Traditional Rulers and Realms', *The Bantu-Speaking Peoples of Southern Africa,* ed. W.D. Hammond-Tooke (London, 1974), pp. 258–59.

12. *RCC*, VIII, Report of the Commission of Circuit, 28 Feb. 1812, p. 298; 'Journal of Swellengrebel', *Zuid-Afrika,* IX (1932), p. 136.

13. For a suggestive analysis of the frontier concept, see M.C. Legassick, 'The Griqua, the Sotho-Tswana, and the Missionaries, 1780—1840: The Politics of a Frontier Zone' (Ph.D. Thesis, University of California, 1969), pp. 6—19.

14. W.K. Hancock, *Survey of Commonwealth Affairs* (London, 1940), Vol. II, part 1, p. 3. Cf. also the remark of Owen Lattimore in *Inner Asian Frontiers of China* (Clinton, 1940), '. . . the concept of a linear boundary could never be established as an absolute geographical fact. That which was politically conceived as a sharp edge was persistently spread by the ebb and flow of history into a relatively broad and vague margin' (p. 238).

15. P. Cloeten, Journal of Swellengrebel's Journey, 1776, *RZA*, IV, 46—50; Moodie, *The Record*, III, 93, 99.

16. Moodie, *The Record*, Journal of Collins (1809), V, 10. It is not clear whether the Xhosa or the colonists first moved into the territory between the Fish and the Boesmans Rivers. Compare P.J. van der Merwe, *Die Trekboer in die Geskiedenis van die Kaapkolonie* (Cape Town, 1938), p. 266 and J.S. Marais, *Maynier and the First Boer Republic* (Cape Town, 1944), p. 6. In 1794 Adriaan van Jaarsveld declared that the Zuurveld (probably meaning the territory between the Boesmans and Fish Rivers) was formerly the land of the Xhosa. (GR 1/9a, Records of Militia Officers, 1794).

17. BO 27, Diary of Du Plessis and Van Rensburg, 27 Aug. 1797, pp. 255—59. The frontier colonists at times seem to have had doubts about the paramountcy of the Rharhabe chief (see note 71).

18. See Ngqika's remarks in Moodie, *The Record*, V, Journal of Collins, 1809, p. 48.

19. This is illustrated by a letter of some colonists, living illegally beyond Bruintjes Hoogte, who asked the government to extend its authority over them. See Moodie, *The Record*, III, 5, 24; CO 309, Memorial of Willem Prinsloo and Others, 10 Nov. 1774, p. 302.

20. GR 8/1, Sluysken—Maynier, 2 Dec. 1794, no. 118. Sometimes there were even fewer mounted police: (cf. *RCC*, IX, 62).

21. C 470, Woeke—Governor, 16 Nov. 1786, p. 663. (My translation).

22. Cf. Chungwa's remark to Wagener, a Graaff-Reinet official, that the 'Groot Baas' would not begrudge him the Zuurveld; only his adversaries living in the vicinity did so. (GR 1/1, Minutes, 3 Aug. 1789, pp. 109—10.)

23. GR 1/9, Letter from Lucas Meyer, n.d. (c. 1790); GR 1/9a, fragment of letter to militia officers, 22 March 1795; *Transactions of the Missionary Society* (London, 1804), I, 388; Moodie, *The Record*, III, 96.

24. Van Reenen, *Joernaal*, p. 209. Examples of other coalitions or proposed coalitions abound. In 1792 Tshaka proposed to field-cornet Hurter that they should attack Langa together; he said Langa and Ndlambe wished to force him across the Boesmans River. In 1792 Langa was reported to have concluded an alliance with a 'Bushman' band to attack the colonists.

25. For a description of the menace from lions, see VC 753—54, Gordon ms., Journal of Third Journey, 28 Aug. 1778 — 25 Jan. 1779.

26. Moodie, *The Record*, V, Journal of Collins, 1809, p. 12; *RCC* VI, 46; C.A. Haupt, 'Joernaal', *RZA*, III, 310—11; CO 2572, Statement by Graham, 1812.

27. Moodie, *The Record*, V, Journal of Collins, 1809, p. 12.

28. (Oppenheimer) Kitchingman Papers, vol. 406, Statement by Klaas Klopper (n.d.)

29. For a description of the symbiotic relationship, see M. Banton, *Race Relations* (London, 1967), pp. 77—79.

30. A. Sparrman, *A Voyage to the Cape of Good Hope... chiefly into the country of the Hottentots and Caffers from the year 1772 to 1776* (Dublin, 1786), II, 167.

31. J 116, Graaff-Reinet Opgaaf, 1798.

32. For illuminating remarks on this phenomenon, see A.P. Elkin, 'Reaction and Interaction: A Food Gathering People and European Settlement in Australia', *Beyond the Frontier,* ed. P. Bohannen and F. Plog (New York, 1967).

33. GR 16/1, Stockenstrom—Janssens, 7 July 1804.

34. Until a few years ago this was the orthodoxy in South African historiography. Particularly influential has been the work of I.D. MacCrone, 'The Frontier Tradition and Race Attitudes in South Africa', *Race Relations Journal,* XXVII (1961), pp. 19—30, and *Race Attitudes in South Africa* (London, 1937), pp. 98—136. For a critique, see M.C. Legassick, 'The Frontier Tradition in South African Historiography', *Collected Seminar Papers on the Societies of Southern Africa* (Institute of Commonwealth Studies, 1970—71), vol. II.

35. See the remarks by Stanley Lieberson in 'A Societal Theory of Race and Ethnic Relations', *Racial Conflict,* ed. Gary T. Marx (Boston, 1971), p. 122.

36. C 470, Woeke and Heemraden — Governor and Council of Policy, 4 Nov. 1786, p. 707.

37. Moodie, *The Record,* V, 10.

38. In 1786 O.G. de Wet tried to assuage the colonists' fears in this connection. See GR 8/1, De Wet—Woeke, 16 Dec. 1786, p. 236. See also C 470, Woeke—Governor and Council of Policy, 16 Nov. 1786 pp. 659—66.

39. Moodie Afschriften, Woeke—Council of Policy, 8 Dec. 1786.

40. GR 1/9, Journal of Hurter, 26 Feb. 1792.

41. (Oppenheimer) Kitchingman Papers, vol. 4061, statement by Brantanje Jantjes, 29 Dec. 1836. (I altered the spelling of 'Caffres').

42. C 196, Report of Maynier, 9 May 1794, pp. 182—90.

43. Basil Sansom, 'Traditional Economic Systems', *The Bantu-Speaking Peoples of Southern Africa,* ed. W.D. Hammond-Tooke (London, 1974), p. 156.

44. H. Lichtenstein, *Travels in Southern Africa...* (Cape Town, 1928), I, 268—69. See also Moodie, *The Record,* V, Cuyler—Caledon, 10 Aug. 1810, p. 58.

45. MacCrone, *Race Attitudes,* pp. 123—32 cites various pronouncements in this regard.

46. Moodie Afschriften, Journal of H. Muller, 23 March 1783.

47. For a discussion of the openness of Xhosa society, see O.F. Raum, 'A Topological Analysis of Xhosa Society', *Wort und Religion: Kalima Na Dini,* ed. H.J. Greschat and H. Jungraithmayr (Stuttgart, 1969), pp. 321—32 and Peires, 'History of the Xhosa', pp. 81—84, 105—107. For atrocities, see BO 24, Faure—Dundas, 21 November 1802, no. 156. For abduction of children, see sources quoted in note 120.

48. Stb. 20/2, Report of Van Jaarsveld, 22 June 1780.

49. Moodie, *The Record,* V, 17.

50. VC 76, Campagne: Berigt, 1796, pp. 243—45.

51. GR 1/1, Minutes, 12 Aug. 1793, p. 234; Moodie, *The Record,* III, Report of Van Jaarsveld, 20 July 1781, p. 111.

52. The first time this settlement is mentioned in the records is with reference to the Woeke commission, which in 1789 attempted to negotiate the withdrawal of the Gqunukhwebe. The commission claimed that after the conflict of 1779—81 peace was concluded with 'most of the Xhosa' and in particular with 'Marottie' (Mahote of the Dange), 'Dika' (probably Cika, commander of the Ntinde army), Langa of the Mbalu, and 'Koba' (probably Kobe, the Gwali chief). See also Soga, *The South-Eastern Bantu*, pp. 134—35.

53. C 470, Woeke—Governor and Council, Oct. 1786, pp. 680—86.

54. C 79, Resolutiën, Aug. 1786, pp. 601—02.

55. Woeke, for instance, attempted to satisfy Langa's demand for compensation in the case of one of his followers who had been killed by a colonist. A similar dispute sparked off the first hostilities in 1779 (C 470, Woeke—Governor and Council of Policy, 6 Nov. 1786, pp. 683—85.)

56. F(ranz) von W(inkelman), Reisaantekeningen, 1788—89, *RZA*, IV, 74.

57. C 493, Woeke—Governor, 9 Feb. 1789, pp. 39—43.

58. C 470, Woeke—Governor and Council, 6 Nov. 1786, p. 669.

59. Moodie Afschriften, Woeke—Governor and Council of Policy, 8 Dec. 1786, and Lucas Meyer—Woeke, 6 Nov. 1787; P.J. van der Merwe, *Die Trekboer*, p. 317.

60. Moodie Afschriften, C. de Buys—Landdrost and Court of Militia, 6 April 1788.

61. C 473, Woeke—Governor and Council of Policy, 9 Feb. 1789, p. 40 (my translation).

62. C 473, Woeke—Governor, 8 March 1789, pp. 65—67.

63. GR 8/1, Governor and Council of Policy, 20 March 1789, no. 33.

64. Van der Merwe incorrectly states that Wägener, an official who was left behind to continue the negotiations, allowed the Gqunukhwebe to return from east of the Fish River to their kraals (*Trekboer*, pp. 309—10). Wägener, in fact, remarked that despite all his efforts he could not succeed in getting the Xhosa to leave the 'district of the Kowie' (an area west of the border). See C 321, Wägener—Landdrost, 3 Aug. 1789, p. 963.

65. GR 1/1, Minutes, 13 July 1789, p. 99.

66. GR 1/1, Minutes, Report of Wägener, 5 July 1789, pp. 102—03.

67. VC 66, Proclamation of 23 Oct. 1793, pp. 316—23.

68. GR 12/2, Report of C. van Aardt, 2 Oct. 1787.

69. GR 1/1, Minutes, 13 May 1789, p. 94.

70. There are more details, with references, in J.S. Marais, *Maynier and the First Boer Republic* (Cape Town, 1944), pp. 24, 28—31.

71. The Kühne commando in 1789 apparently disobeyed its instructions when it acted against the Xhosa. There is no reference to what the commando actually did, but subsequently the landdrost and heemraden sent gifts to Khawuta, the Gcaleka paramount, assuring him that they desired peace despite the 'wrong conduct' of Kühne and the resulting tumult. In 1825 Maynier testified before the Commission of Inquiry that he had witnessed on Kühne's commando the distribution of 30,000 cattle taken in booty. (*RCC*, XXI, Evidence by Maynier, 25 April 1825, pp. 386—87). The fact that Maynier arrived in Graaff-Reinet after the commando had returned conflicts with this evidence. On the other hand, it is unlikely that Maynier would make such a statement if nothing of the sort had ever occurred.

72. See the remarkable letter of C. de Buys in Moodie Afschriften, C. de

Buys—Landdrost and Militia Officers, 6 April 1788. See also G 1/9, Scheepers—Woeke, 21 Dec. 1789.

73. For a discussion of this in the context of Indian reaction to European settlement in North America, see N.O. Lurie, 'Indian Cultural Adjustments to European Civilization', *Seventeenth Century America,* ed. J.M. Smith (Chapel Hill, 1959), p. 31.

74. In 1792 Chungwa, to whom most of the Khoikhoi had fled, remarked to Hurter than even with 'honden [hundred ?] gewaapende mannen' he would not do him much harm. (GR 1/9, Journal of Hurter, 14 Feb. 1792.) Hurter commanded twenty-five men.

75. Some fifty Xhosa once told the wife of a certain Jordaan that if her husband had been at home they would have cut him from end to end since he was so good at shooting Xhosa. (GR 12/1, Letter of C.J. van Rooyen, 11 Dec. 1796.) See also C 196, Woeke—Rhenius, 9 Feb. 1792, pp. 309—11; GR 1/1, Minutes, Report of Wägener, 5 July 1789.

76. GR 1/9, Scheepers—Woeke, 27 Dec. 1789.

77. GR 1/9a, Combined Meeting of Landdrost, Heemraden and Militia Officers, 26 May 1794.

78. Soga, *The South-Eastern Bantu*, pp. 137—38. G.M. Theal asserts that the Dange were involved *(History of Africa South of the Zambesi from 1505-1795* [London, 1922], III, 279–80.)

79. For a perceptive discussion of the causes of Xhosa—colonist conflict see Peires, 'History of the Xhosa', pp. 101—06.

80. According to J.L. Maray only three farms in the Zuurveld were still occupied by September 1793 (GR 12/2).

81. The most important documents pertaining to the war are C 104, Joint Report of Maynier and Faure, 27 Nov. 1793; VC 68, Journal of Faure, 10 December 1793; C 106, Maynier's report of 31 March 1794; and VC 76, Campagne's Berigt.

82. Before the war there were approximately 150 families of colonists in the Zuurveld and roughly 4,000 colonists (1,000 adult men) in the entire district of Graaff-Reinet. According to one estimate there were 6,000 Xhosa in the Zuurveld (GR 8/1, Council of Policy — Maynier, 12 Aug. 1793, no. 87).

83. Hermann Giliomee, *Die Kaap tydens die Eerste Britse Bewind* (Cape Town, 1975), p. 274.

84. The colonial authorities wanted to negotiate and trade with a single chief representing all Xhosa (*RCC*, VII, Journal of Collins, 1809, p. 75).

85. For a full discussion of the conquest and occupation, see Giliomee, *Eerste Britse Bewind*, chapter 2.

86. For discussion of the concepts 'scope' (degree of authority) and 'location of command', see Sansom, 'Traditional Rulers', pp. 247—48.

87. *RCC*, VII, Journal of Collins, 1809, pp. 54, 78; L. Alberti, *Account of the Tribal Life and Customs of the Xhosa in 1807* (Cape Town, 1968), p. 81; Peires, 'History of the Xhosa', pp. 98—99.

88. BO 27, Statement by Bresler, 3 Dec. 1797, p. 306.

89. *Transactions of the Missionary Society,* Journal of Van der Kemp, pp. 466—67.

90. In 1799 Ngqika offered to the colonists land between the Kacha mountains and the Koonap River (*Transactions,* I, 388). Obviously the colonists would have served as a buffer against his Xhosa enemies.

91. William M. Freund, 'The Eastern Frontier of the Cape Colony during the Batavian Period (1803—1806)', *Journal of African History,* XIII (1972), pp. 631—45.
92. Journal of the Journey of Janssens, 1803, *RZA,* IV, 172.
93. Moodie, *The Record,* V, Journal of Collins, 1809, p. 14. See also *RCC,* III, Vandeleur—Dundas, 22 Aug. 1799, p. 475.
94. The Batavians, in fact, accepted the principle that Xhosa who had been in the service of colonists for more than a year could stay. See Van Reenen, *Joernaal,* pp. 132—33.
95. *RCC,* VII, Caledon—Cradock, 1 July 1811, p. 111.
96. For a discussion, see Giliomee, 'Die Administrasietydperk van Lord Caledon, 1807—1811', *AYB* (1966), no. 2, chapters 10 to 12.
97. Van Reenen, *Joernaal,* p. 119.
98. *RCC,* IV, Provisional Justification of Maynier, April 1802, pp. 326—27; Marais, *Maynier,* pp. 120—21.
99. Moodie, *The Record,* V, Journal of Collins, 1809, p. 48.
100. Quoted by W.M. Freund, 'Society and Government in Dutch South Africa: The Cape and the Batavians, 1803—6' (Ph.D. thesis, Yale University, 1972), p. 320. For an assessment of the various chiefs' strengths, see Moodie, *The Record,* V, 50.
101. CO 2575, Cuyler—Bird, 6 May 1811, no. 23. It was probably in c. 1809 that Ndlame claimed that he had purchased the right to reside in the Zuurveld from a commission consisting of a landdrost and some colonists. For various reports on this, see Moodie, *The Record,* V, Report of Collins, 1809, p. 10; (Cory Library, Grahamstown) Stretch Journal ms., n.p.; A. Stockenstrom, *The Autobiography of the late Sir Andries Stockenstrom* (Cape Town, 1964), I, 50, 52, 58.
102. See Giliomee, 'Lord Caledon', pp. 323—24; Peires, 'History of the Xhosa', pp. 111—12.
103. CO 2572, Stoltz—Cuyler, 23 June 1810. For a further discussion see Peires, 'History of the Xhosa', pp. 6—9, 107—112 and Table 1.
104. CO 2572, Cuyler — Alexander, 18 Dec. 1810, no. 11.
105. CO 2571, Stockenstrom — Caledon, 14 July 1810.
106. CO 2575 Cuyler — Bird, 6 April 1811, no. 23.
107. CO 2566, Cuyler — Colonial Secretary, 4 July 1809, no. 14.
108. CO 2576, Hawkes — Cuyler, 24 June 1811, enclosure to no. 3.
109. CO 2576, Stockenstrom — Bird, 26 July 1811; CO 2577, Stockenstrom — Bird, 7 Aug. 1811.
110. *RCC,* VIII, Cradock — Graham, 6 Oct. 1811, pp. 160—62; *RCC,* IX, Cradock — Bathurst, 18 Nov. 1812, pp. 14—16.
111. CO 2582, Graham — Alexander, 30 Nov. 1812.
112. Graham wrote: 'With the exception of a few artillery and dragoons none of the regular troops are in the field.' (CO 2582, Letter of Graham, 31 Jan. 1812).
113. Quoted by C.F.J. Muller, *Die Oorsprong van die Groot Trek* (Cape Town, 1974), p. 193.
114. Sparrman, *Voyage,* II, 168—69.
115. J 115 and J 138, Graaff-Reinet Opgaaf, 1798 and 1812.
116. Van der Merwe, *Trek,* p. 55.
117. Barrow, *Travels,* I, 93.
118. For an elaboration of the concept of paternalism, see Eugene D. Genovese, *Roll*

Jordan Roll: The World the Slaves Made (London, 1975), pp. 133—49. Genovese, of course, uses the concept in the context of the master-slave relationship.

119. For a discussion of labour-repressive systems, see Barrington Moore, *Social Origins of Dictatorship and Democracy: Lord and Peasant in the Making of the Modern World* (Boston, 1966), pp. 433—35.

120. RCC, XXI, Evidence of Maynier, 25 April 1825, pp. 387—88; Lichtenstein, *Travels*, I, 409; BO 24, Faure—Dundas, 21 Nov. 1802. These sources suggest that the abduction of Xhosa children was not uncommon.

121. P.J. van der Merwe, *Die Noordwaartse Beweging van die Boere voor die Groot Trek, 1770—1842* (The Hague, 1937), cites various sources pertaining to traffic in hunter children and concludes that it could only have occurred in exceptional cases (pp. 168—75). The evidence regarding a traffic in indentured Khoikhoi children is ambiguous, but there is a case of a Khoikhoi woman complaining that a colonist had sold five of her children for 176 rixdollars: see BO 53, Barnard—Faure, 28 Feb. 1800, no. 264; W.B.E. Paravicini di Capelli, *Reize in de Binnenlanden van Zuid-Afrika* (Cape Town, 1965), who travelled in the interior at the time of the Batavian administration, wrote that many farmers preferred that the Khoikhoi be forced to serve them like slaves (p. 9).

122. Swm 1/3, Minutes, 4 Dec. 1797, p. 330.

123. Moodie, *The Record*, V, Report of Collins, 1809, p. 22.

124. GR 9/10, J.A. Truter — Stockenstrom, 7 April 1810.

125. Giliomee, *Eerste Britse Bewind*, pp. 157—58.

126. GR 16/1 Stockenstrom — Janssens, 7 July 1804; Freund, 'The Eastern Frontier', p. 640.

127. See D.B. Davis, *The Problem of Slavery in the Age of Revolution, 1770—1823* (Ithaca, 1975), especially pp. 453—68, and a review of it by G.M. Fredrickson, 'The Use of Antislavery', *The New York Review of Books,* 16 Oct. 1975. For a discussion of the 'unfreedom' of workers in England and the views of the English ruling class toward them by the turn of the century, see E.P. Thompson, *The Making of the English Working Class* (London, 1968), especially chapter 6.

128. VC 66, Proclamation of 23 Oct. 1793, p. 330.

129. Swm 1/3, Minutes, 4 Dec. 1797, p. 330; GR 1/2, Minutes, 2 Jan. 1798, p. 174.

130. This is pointed out in GR 9/10, J.A. Truter — Stockenstrom, 7 April 1810.

131. Imperial Bluebook no. 50 (1836), Aborigines Committee Report, question 2310. For an incisive discussion of the significance of Ordinance 50, see Leslie Clement Duly, 'A Revisit with the Cape's Hottentot Ordinance of 1828', *Studies in Economics and Economic History*, ed. Marcelle Kooy (London, 1972), pp. 26—56.

132. GR 3/18, Deposition of J.H. Otto, 9 Aug. 1784, no. 67.

133. GR 3/19, Depositions of Schutte, Koegelman and Streso, 16 Dec. 1809, 5 Jan. 1810.

134. GR 16/1, Stockenstrom — Commission on Stockbreeding, 13 Jan. 1806.

135. RCC, VI, Collins—Cuyler, 6 April 1809, pp. 484—88.

136. *Transactions*, I, 490—91, 494.

137. CO 2582, Read — Cradock, 23 Jan. 1812.

138. CO 2582, Memorandum by Read, n.d.

139. CO 2582, Graham—Bird, 1 Sept. 1812.

140. Stockenstrom recounted the heated disputes between Cuyler and Van der Kemp

over the question of equal justice for all (*Autobiography*, I, 84). See also the remarks quoted by Freund, 'The Eastern Frontier', pp. 634, 641–42.

141. CO 2582, Graham—Bird, 1 Aug. 1812.

142. See for instance C.R. Kotzé, "n Nuwe Bewind, 1806–1834', *Vyfhonderd Jaar Suid-Afrikaanse Geskiedenis*, ed. C.F.J. Muller (Pretoria, 1968), p. 113.

143. *RCC*, VIII, Truter — Cradock, 15 June 1812, pp. 439–41.

144. *RCC*, VII, Cuyler — Caledon, 25 Oct. 1810, p. 399. See also Alberti, *Account of the Xhosa*, p. 101.

145. GR 3/16 and GR 3/18.

146. *RCC*, IX, Report of the Commission of Circuit, 18 Jan. 1813, p. 56.

147. J 115, Opgaaf Graaff-Reinet, 1798.

148. By 1798 there were 492 registered loan farms in Graaff-Reinet (Barrow, *Travels*, II, 185). When this opgaaf was taken, almost two-thirds of the Zuurveld colonists had not yet returned to the farms which they had abandoned in the war of 1793.

149. GR 16/1, Stockenstrom — Bird, 20 Sept. 1810.

150. Although after 1795 these people were no longer in the employ of the VOC, they were still being described as Company servants in 1798. The 1798 opgaaf lists 43 knechts in Graaff-Reinet. Most of the knechts were Company servants. Sometimes a burgher who lost all his cattle became a knecht. One of them was Andries van der Heyden who in 1798 earned a 'knecht's wage' of 170 rixdollars from one employer and 72 rixdollars from another.

151. LM 37, Janssens — Landdrosts, 26 May 1805, no. 243.

152. G.A. Watermeyer, 'The Rise and Early History of Graaff-Reinet', *The Graaff-Reinet Herald*, 27 July 1861.

153. MS. Journal of William Somerville, entry of 11 March, 1802 (Dr Frank Bradlow kindly gave permission to consult his photocopy of this journal).

154. W.J. Burchell, *Travels into the Interior of Southern Africa* (London, 1953), II, wrote of a certain baptised Bastaard, Cornelis Goeïman, that he 'was by his baptism entitled to the same privileges as the Dutch colonists.' Because Goeïman drank too much, the minister and the landdrost prohibited the sale of brandy to him without their permission. When Goeïman discovered this, he indignantly asked 'what right anyone had to restrain him as if he were a Hottentot; was he not a Christian?' It is clear that the theoretical rights of baptised Bastaards could not always be enforced in practice, and there was much room for misconceptions on the one hand and discriminatory practices on the other.

155. GR 3/18, Depositions of Janssens and Nieuwenhuizen, 2 July 1795, no. 74.

156. Barrow, *Travels*, I, 97. When Bastaard children were baptised, other Bastaards usually acted as witnesses.

157. In an important article Robert Ross has recently argued that it was the poorer and less well-connected male members of the Christian community who 'paired off' with the non-whites ('The "White" Population of South Africa in the Eighteenth Century', *Population Studies*, XXIX, 230).

158. Except where otherwise indicated this paragraph is based on J.A. Heese, *Die Herkoms van die Afrikaner* (Cape Town 1971), and personal communications by him with respect to the relevant opgaaf rolls.

159. BO 27, Deposition of Du Plessis, 2 April 1798, p. 31.

160. VC 65, Report of Sluysken, p. 201.

161. *RCC*, III, Report of Maynier, 14 Aug. 1800, and Criminal Claim, 14 Aug. 1800, pp. 212—43; BO 27, Vandeleur — Van Rensburg, 24 May 1799, pp. 223—25.
162. On seeing his children tied by their necks to a tree, a Khoikhoi protested to his master that they were not 'Bushman' children. GR 3/16, Deposition of Jacob, 10 Jan. 1791, no. 162.
163. Burchell, *Travels*, I, 128; II, 170, 203—04, 324, 330. See also *RCC*, IX, Bathurst — Cradock, 9 Oct. 1813. Here the defence in a murder trial referred to the prevailing notion that to kill a debased Khoikhoi was less reprehensible than to kill another man.
164. Moodie Afschriften, Extract Dagregister, Landdrost and Heemraden of Stellenbosch, 7 Aug. 1780. Armed Bastaard-Hottentots played a leading role as resisters. See for instance GR 14/1, Extract Resolutie. 13 July 1792.
165. CO 2582, Graham—Alexander, 16 Aug. 1812 and 5 Sept. 1812; *RCC*, VIII, Cradock — Liverpool, 23 Jan. 1812 and 7 March 1812, pp. 254, 354.
166. Like the eastern Ndlambe of today, for instance (personal communication of Mr Louis Botha, who has done extensive fieldwork among them): the fact that Chungwa's grave is in Alexandria district (in the Zuurveld) may serve to keep alive among the Gqunukhwebe the memory of their Zuurveld background and claims.
167. For Danster, see Peires, 'History of the Xhosa', p. 116.
168. For a discussion of this particularly interesting frontier, see Legassick, 'Griqua, Sotho-Tswana and Missionaries'.
169. For illuminating theoretical discussions of the relationship between different ethnic communities, see *Ethnic Groups and Boundaries: the Social Organisation of Cultural Difference*, ed. Fredrik Barth (Boston, 1969), introduction, and William J. Foltz, 'Ethnicity, Status and Conflict', *Ethnicity and Nation Building*, ed. Wendell Bell and Walter E. Freeman (Beverley Hills, 1974), pp. 103—16.
170. *Transactions*, I (Van der Kemp's Journal), pp. 480—83.
171. For a further discussion, see Heribert Adam and Hermann Giliomee, *Ethnic Power Mobilized: Can South Africa Change?* (New Haven, 1979).

The burgher rebellions on the Eastern Frontier, 1795—1815[*]

Hermann Giliomee

Chapter 8 described how European cattle-farmers settled the district of Graaff-Reinet. One of the most important parts of this district was Bruintjes Hoogte/Zuurveld. It was from here that the colonists issued a series of challenges to the government, almost from the time of their first arrival in the area, but especially in the rebellions of 1795, 1799, 1801 and 1815. This chapter will discuss the causes and nature of these rebellions and will try to resolve some of the historiographical controversies which surround them. The degree to which Enlightenment ideas influenced political opposition in the Cape Colony has been analysed in chapter 5 (pp. 201—02).[1] This chapter will concentrate on the place of these rebellions in the political and intellectual development of European South Africa — particularly on their alleged contribution to the first blossoming of democracy and nationalism among Afrikaners.[2]

The 'Patriotic movement' in Graaff-Reinet, 1795—1799

From the earliest days of European settlement in the future Graaff-Reinet district, the southeastern region enjoyed little governmental or social control. Rather it was the scene of illegal trading and uncontrolled raiding. In 1777 an officer in the *burgher* militia commented that 'there are many who live without God in the world, for were the fear of the Lord in them, they would also fear the earthly magistrate; but now many are living according to their own fancy.'[3] In the early 1780s Adriaan van Jaarsveld, the senior militia officer for the eastern divisions of the colony, was involved in a bitter feud with the Prinsloos of Agter Bruintjes Hoogte. The Prinsloos opposed Van Jaarsveld's policy of peace toward the Xhosa, interfered with the appointment

---

* I am indebted to Leonard Thompson and Richard Elphick for incisive criticism of a previous draft and to J.A. Heese and Johan de Villiers for helpful advice on some details.

of minor militia officers, and refused to participate in commandos against 'Bushman' raiders in the north.[4] Van Jaarsveld not only had to contend with this 'band of rebels' (as he called the Prinsloos) but with burgher officers like *veldwachtmeester* C. Botma, who scorned the laws and disobeyed his commands. Fearing that Botma would incite the colonists to a rebellion like that of Barbier (ch. 5, pp. 196—98), Van Jaarsveld had him dismissed by the Stellenbosch district authorities. Van Jaarsveld also feared that Botma and the Prinsloos would provoke a war with the Xhosa. He therefore urged the Stellenbosch authorities to remove them from the frontier, but failed.

Dispirited, Van Jaarsveld asked the central government to appoint a *landdrost* for the new district, expressing the hope that the 'discords and disputes . . ., licentiousness and disobedience' would cease in the presence of government officials.[5] But with its customary lack of interest in the interior the government waited some years before acting on this request. It was not until 1786 that M.H.O. Woeke arrived in the district as the first landdrost. He immediately succeeded in reconciling Van Jaarsveld (who was now living in the central part of the Graaff-Reinet district) with the Prinsloos.[6] This achievement, however, did little to establish order, for Woeke had inadvertently created an alliance which would soon be turned against the central government.

During the 1780s the Cape Patriot movement rose and fell in the southwestern Cape. It had little direct impact on the Eastern Frontier. In its intellectual approach, economic concerns, and political strategy the Patriotic movement was quite different from the insurrectionary movement which would arise in Graaff-Reinet and take over its name and several of its slogans. But common to both was a general dissatisfaction with Company rule. In its single-minded concern with profits, the Company had alternately exploited the colonists and neglected them. While exploitation meant that the stock farmers of Graaff-Reinet received exceedingly low prices for their products, neglect enabled them to avoid paying rent (*recognitiepenningen*) to the government on their loan farms. From 1792, however, the central government, in a desperate attempt to increase revenue, vigorously stepped up the collection of rent, a step which led to widespread dissatisfaction.[7]

In addition, the southeastern divisions of Graaff-Reinet nourished a sectional grievance. In the 1793 war with the Xhosa the colonists there had suffered severe losses in land and cattle. They were bitter that the commandos had failed to recapture their cattle or force the Xhosa to withdraw from the Zuurveld. They blamed this failure on H.C.D. Maynier, Woeke's successor as landdrost, who had led the commando in the war.[8] To add to their discontent, the post-war defence policy of Graaff-Reinet favoured the northern divisions, the so-called Sneeuwberg area. While aggression against the Xhosa was strictly prohibited, the military efforts of the district were concentrated on the desperate battle against 'Bushman' raiders, who had forced the colonists to evacuate several divisions along the Northern Frontier.[9] As a result the Graaff-Reinet colonists split on sectional lines, with the Sneeuwberg supporting the official defence policy while Bruintjes Hoogte/ Zuurveld ignored calls to enlist for expeditions against the 'Bushmen' and demanded an attack on the Zuurveld Xhosa.

Personal factors also contributed to the outbreak of rebellion. In contrast to strong frontier landdrosts like the Stockenstroms, Maynier was apparently unable to assert his authority. He had a knack of estranging influential colonists without scoring any gains in terms of reforming the existing order. Unlike Woeke, Maynier commonly interfered in the colonists' relations with their servants. If a Khoikhoi complained that he had not been paid or had not been released from service on the expiry of his contract, Maynier would summon the master to the *drostdy*. This was simply the policy of the government, but one without much power at its command. The colonists regarded Maynier's attempts as a threat to their position as a class entitled to privileged treatment by the government.

With neither a police nor a military force at his command, Maynier alienated his only basis of support by issuing peremptory summonses to veldwachtmeesters and other prominent colonists, and by threatening them with dire consequences if they failed to obey. At no time does he seem to have assessed his ability to give substance to his commands. In December 1794 he ordered Marthinus and Willem Prinsloo and other leading colonists in Bruintjes Hoogte to appear before him without delay.[10] In January 1795 his secretary wrote to C.J. Tregardt, a militia officer who had failed to bring one of the Khoikhoi families in his service to the drostdy: 'You are ordered for the last time to send them here so that the landdrost is not forced to employ adequate means to restrain your excessive obstinacy and recall you to your duty of proper subservience.'[11]

To add to Maynier's problems, the influential Adriaan van Jaarsveld, once a stalwart of government policy, was on a collision course with the authorities. For unknown reasons the central government had from 1790 refused to appoint Van Jaarsveld as *heemraad*, even though he had been nominated by the Board of Heemraden. Van Jaarsveld became increasingly disaffected and undermined Maynier's authority on several occasions. At the same time his material fortunes were declining as a result of 'Bushman' raids on his lands. In December 1794 Maynier ordered him to produce, within fourteen days, two guarantors for the sum of about 4,000 rixdollars which he had borrowed from the Orphan Chamber: otherwise 'unpleasant proceedings would be instituted.'[12]

About two months later the rebellion began. In the first week of February 1795 a party of rebels appeared outside the town of Graaff-Reinet. With Adriaan van Jaarsveld and C.J. and J.G. Tregardt acting as intermediaries, the rebels demanded that the landdrost call a meeting of heemraden, former heemraden and militia officers. When this meeting took place on 6 February, Marthinus Prinsloo emerged as leader of the rebels — or Patriots, as they styled themselves. They ordered Maynier to leave the district immediately. They also removed from their posts some officers who had supported Maynier's peace policy towards the Xhosa, and threatened other militia officers with a similar fate if they did not 'take up the sword again' and recover the cattle captured by the Xhosa in 1793.[13]

Maynier withdrew to Cape Town. Shortly after his arrival there the government cut off further supplies of ammunition to Graaff-Reinet and sent out a commission of enquiry under O.G. de Wet. It soon became clear that De Wet, like Maynier before him, would not countenance the expulsion of the Xhosa from the Zuurveld. Accusing the commission of siding with the Khoikhoi and Xhosa against the colonists, a party of 200 armed rebels, led by Marthinus Prinsloo and C.J. Tregardt, expelled it from Graaff-Reinet. They also publicly renounced Company rule.[14]

A month later the rebels sent selfstyled *representanten des volks* (representatives of the people) to attend meetings of the Board of Heemraden. These 'representanten' played an increasingly important role in subsequent meetings in which they, together with heemraden, ex-heemraden and militia officers, participated. They overruled recommendations from the heemraden and militia officers and, according to one source, became the real legislative power in the district government.[15]

Where did these representanten come from? Altogether fourteen names of representanten appear in the minutes of these meetings. Of these, ten hailed from the southeastern divisions; the others cannot be located. How were they appointed? The sources simply state that the *volkstem* (voice of the people) 'approved' their appointment or 'chose' them to safeguard the rights and interests of the burghers.[16] But what was the volkstem? It seems, on close analysis, that the rebel leaders used the terms 'volk' and 'volkstem' in a loose and confused way, sometimes even requesting that they themselves be recognised as the volkstem.[17] They often made statements in the name of the volk or the volkstem without apparently canvassing burgher opinion in any way. At least one observer thought that the volk remained in the dark about everything done in its name.[18]

Though they now controlled the district authority, the Bruintjes Hoogte/Zuurveld rebels still needed military leaders, allies and renewed supplies of ammunition before they could wage war against the Xhosa. After some vacillation the experienced Xhosa fighter Van Jaarsveld decided to throw in his lot with the rebels and assumed the position of 'president of military affairs'. Probably in an attempt to gain the support of Sneeuwberg, the rebels appointed C.D. Gerotz and Jan Booysen, both from that region, as provisional landdrost and president of the heemraden respectively. Now supported by some non-rebel colonists, they asked the British government (which had taken over at the Cape in September 1795) to appoint proper magistrates. However, along with this conciliatory gesture toward the government the rebels continued to insist that the representanten would always sit in the local government, thus ensuring a voice to sectional interests.[19]

Early in 1796 General Craig, the acting governor, sent Frans Bresler to Graaff-Reinet as the new landdrost. When they discovered that a former servant of the Dutch East India Company had been appointed, the rebels decided not to concede power to him: they were convinced that the old policy of conciliating the Xhosa was to be continued. After his arrival in Graaff-Reinet, Bresler refused to recognise the representanten, only to be told that the 'volk' would not allow any meeting without them. Shortly afterwards he learnt that Marthinus Prinsloo, styling himself 'Protector of the Volkstem', had prohibited Graaff-Reinetters from swearing loyalty to the British Sovereign; Prinsloo had threatened to appear at Graaff-Reinet on 22 March and punish all those who had taken the oath, with the help of the people of Langkloof (where most of the colonists of the Zuurveld had retreated after the 1793 war) and Bruintjes Hoogte.

On 22 March a large crowd in front of the drostdy refused to take the oath or recognise Bresler as landdrost. Bresler was convinced that the burghers were intimidated by C. J. Tregardt and the representanten. The representanten then handed Bresler a petition in which they requested that in future the landdrost be appointed by the burghers, and that the office of representant be recognised by the government.[20] Bresler returned to Cape Town, leaving the rebels in control.

With no supply of ammunition, the rebels had acquired only the shadow of power. In order to force the government to release ammunition, they had tried to organise a meat boycott of Cape Town. By the middle of 1796 it became clear that this attempt had failed. The shortage of ammunition had become critical in Sneeuwberg, forcing farmers there to abandon the fight against 'Bushman' raiders. Whereas the Sneeuwbergers had before this time allowed Bruintjes Hoogte/Zuurveld to dictate affairs in Graaff-Reinet, they now decided that it was no longer in their interest to do so. At a meeting in August 1796 the northern and western divisions resolved to inform Craig that they accepted British authority.

The Bruintjes Hoogte/Zuurveld burghers were now isolated. They attempted to salvage something of the rebellion by offering to submit to British authority provided the government would allow them to recapture cattle from the Xhosa, occupy lands east of the Fish River, and choose their own heemraden from then on. Governor Craig, however, declared that no ammunition would be issued before an unconditional surrender. Early in 1797 the burghers of Bruintjes Hoogte/Zuurveld wrote to Craig promising to be loyal to the government.[21]

However, dissatisfaction continued in Bruintjes Hoogte/Zuurveld throughout 1797, partly because many Xhosa were migrating into the Zuurveld. In addition, the government was strictly enforcing the payment of land rent and district taxes, and was instructing all European refugees from the Zuurveld to return to their farms on pain of losing them. Toward the end of 1798 the 'Patriots' decided to renew their struggle. Some rebel leaders may have been motivated by the desire to expand over the Fish River into the land between Kacha Mountain and the Koonap. Their enthusiasm for rebellion was intensified by the news that the strength of the garrison in Cape Town had been greatly reduced.

The new outbreak of rebellion was precipitated by Van Jaarsveld's arrest in January 1799 on a charge of fraud regarding the money he had borrowed from the Orphan Chamber. While being taken to Cape Town, Van Jaarsveld was liberated by a party of rebels led by Marthinus Prinsloo. These rebels subsequently attempted to mobilise support among the colonists by appealing to their patriotism and by proclaiming the slogans of liberty, equality and fraternity. It soon became clear that Bruintjes Hoogte/Zuurveld was intent on re-establishing control of the district.[22] Its leaders, however, received no support from Sneeuwberg.

The British government sent out a force to crush the rebellion. On 6 April 1799 it made contact in Bruintjes Hoogte with Marthinus Prinsloo and 150 rebels who, having offered no resistance, laid down their arms. This was the end of the Patriotic movement. The Court of Justice condemned Prinsloo and Van Jaarsveld to death and sentenced several rebel leaders to imprisonment. The death sentences were later commuted to life imprisonment. Van Jaarsveld died in prison; Prinsloo and the other rebels were released in 1803 by the Batavian regime.

The 1801 rebellions and their aftermath[23]

The rebellions of 1801, like the Patriotic movement, originated in the southeastern divisions, but they were led by men who either had been pro-government before or had stayed neutral. The most important leader was

H.J. van Rensburg, who had suffered severe losses in the 1793 war while living on his farm at the Boesmans River in the Zuurveld. Considering the Zuurveld too unsafe, Van Rensburg subsequently moved to Bruintjes Hoogte. In the rebellion of 1799 he was active as a commandant on the government side.

The rebellions of 1801 should be viewed against the background of the Frontier War of 1799 and Maynier's subsequent peace policy. Since the Eastern Frontier had opened in the 1770s the colonists had endured no more traumatic a year than 1799, when many of their Khoikhoi servants rebelled and, in alliance with Zuurveld Xhosa, captured vast numbers of cattle, defeated a burgher commando, and forced the colonists to evacuate virtually the entire southeastern part of the colony. At the end of 1799, when Maynier arrived in Graaff-Reinet as 'Commissary of the Frontier Districts', the colonists had not yet returned to the land between the Sundays and the Fish Rivers. The Zuurveld was still controlled by some Xhosa chiefs and by Klaas Stuurman, the leader of the Khoikhoi revolt, who had now established a *kraal* on the bank of the Sundays River.

Maynier's peace policy consisted of the following measures. Firstly, he tried to induce colonists to return to their abandoned farms. Secondly, he instituted a system of labour contracts, registered at the drostdy, to provide for proper treatment of those Khoikhoi who had re-entered the service of the colonists. He acted immediately when he learnt that the conditions of service, as specified in these contracts, were violated or when he learnt of Khoikhoi being maltreated. The third point of his policy was his patrol system. Maynier argued that thefts committed by a few vagrant thieves did not justify calling out a general commando, which would attack Xhosa and Khoikhoi indiscriminately in order to recapture cattle and drive the Zuurveld Xhosa over the Fish. Maynier's patrols, which initially consisted of young colonists, were instructed to follow the spoor of stolen cattle and, if necessary, to shoot the thieves. Later Maynier reinforced these patrols with armed Khoikhoi. Finally, though he attempted to negotiate the evacuation of Xhosa and Khoikhoi kraals from the Zuurveld, Maynier was prepared to accept their presence for the time being.

The root cause of the 1801 rebellions was not Maynier's policy — though all his measures were unpopular among various groups of colonists — but his inability either to gain the trust of the colonists or to make them fear him. That he was not trusted was a heritage of his Khoikhoi and Xhosa policies of 1793—95. That he was not feared, except as some kind of bogeyman during the 1801 rebellion, was the result of his strange assurance that he could make peace singlehanded. This overconfidence led him to refuse an offer of a thousand troops; he decided to carry on without any significant garrison in

Graaff-Reinet. Under these conditions it was comparatively easy for his enemies to overthrow him.

Three events jointly precipitated the rebellion against Maynier. Firstly, from the middle of 1800 marauding Khoikhoi and Xhosa started to commit petty thefts in the southeastern part of the district. These thefts by themselves may not have been enough justification for a revolt against Maynier.[24] But they should be viewed in their context — the 1799 war and the colonists' fear that that nightmarish event might be repeated. In this perspective the thefts were indeed cause for alarm.

Secondly, Maynier's Khoikhoi policy collapsed. Maynier had in 1799 succeeded in persuading most of the rebel Khoikhoi to re-enter the service of the colonists. A considerable number, however, had joined Stuurman's kraal in the Zuurveld. Despite the central government's exhortations, Maynier had failed to find land elsewhere where they could settle. When Van der Kemp and Read started missionary work in Graaff-Reinet in the first half of 1801, these Khoikhoi, as well as others from all parts of the district, flocked to the town. The colonists particularly distrusted Maynier when he was surrounded by so many Khoikhoi. Many believed that he had assembled the Khoikhoi to kill the colonists and seize their wives in order to distribute them among Khoikhoi. His use of armed Khoikhoi patrols fed these suspicions. Moreover, his decision to allow Khoikhoi to worship in the church in Graaff-Reinet was considered sacrilegious by the colonists. Maynier did not believe in the concept of the noble savage; nor did he, like Van der Kemp, desire social equality between Khoikhoi and colonists. But he did scorn the prejudices of the colonists and their fear of another Khoikhoi uprising. In doing so he lost much of his remaining support.

The rebellion was finally triggered by rumours circulating in the district. Rumours, which flourish in crisis situations when norms and interests are challenged and when danger threatens,[25] were common on the Eastern Frontier. But in 1801 for the first time substantial numbers of people believed and acted upon them. Hearing that the colonists wanted to exterminate them, more Khoikhoi fled to the drostdy. Rumours spread among the Europeans that Maynier had inspired a joint Khoikhoi-Xhosa attack on the colonists and that the British planned to induct colonists into their armed forces; perhaps the colonists thought the British had inherited the VOC's right to force recalcitrant burghers into naval service (see ch. 5, p. 178). In response to these rumours the inhabitants of the southeastern divisions fled to Tarka in the northeast. The last two rumours had almost certainly been deliberately propagated by Van Rensburg and others. Their aim was to remove Maynier as the main obstacle to an aggressive policy against the Xhosa and Khoikhoi of the Zuurveld. They hoped that through an attack they would recapture cattle and relieve the land-pressure in Bruintjes Hoogte, which had been caused by the influx of colonists from the Zuurveld and other unsafe parts. In Tarka, rebels from Bruintjes Hoogte/Zuurveld persuaded influential men in the northern divisions to combine with them in an attack on the district authorities. On 6 July, 200 colonists, led by Van Rensburg and Commandant J.P. van der Walt of Tarka, appeared on the outskirts of Graaff-Reinet town. They warned that they intended to raze the drostdy and stop the authorities from 'favouring' Khoikhoi and Xhosa.

With twenty-two British regulars, nineteen Khoikhoi troops, another ninety armed Khoikhoi and some burghers, Maynier prepared to defend the town. The rebels did not attack but sent out negotiators. Complaining that the Khoikhoi 'were instructed by [the missionaries] in reading, writing and religion and thereby put upon an equal footing with the Christians',[26] they demanded that the mission congregation be barred from using the church. They also requested that field-cornets and commandants, rather than Maynier, register Khoikhoi labourers and settle disputes between them and their masters.[27] The two leaders from Bruintjes Hoogte asked for an adequate supply of ammunition and for permission to attack the Xhosa. Maynier agreed to close the church to the Khoikhoi, but flatly refused to grant permission to attack the Xhosa, and made an ambiguous promise that the rebels would receive more ammunition.

The rebels withdrew, but not to their farms. Some 400 of them assembled in the northeast just beyond the district border. In Graaff-Reinet town, Maynier retreated into a world of fantasy. He still believed that he could persuade the colonists to return quietly to their farms and that all his troubles would disappear. Consequently he peremptorily refused to allow the commander of the British troops to construct a blockhouse or to send for adequate reinforcements. He declared that he wished to avoid civil war and preferred amicable measures to force.[28]

Order now quickly disintegrated. Before the end of 1801 nearly a thousand Khoikhoi sought refuge in Graaff-Reinet town from colonists who they believed intended to kill them. Panic-stricken about rumours that Khoikhoi, with the approval of Maynier, were plotting to murder them and have black children by their wives, more colonists fled to Tarka and the Bamboesberg Mountains in the northeast. Maynier was virtually isolated from all colonist support after the inhabitants of the northern divisions, now also convinced that he was favouring the Khoikhoi, petitioned the government for a commission of inquiry. Even the British troops in Graaff-Reinet turned against him. In October 1801 the colonists assembled in the northeast and advanced on Graaff-Reinet. Having encircled the town, they fired a few shots and kept it besieged, waiting for reinforcements. The episode ended in November 1801 when a division of 300 troops arrived from Cape Town. This force ended the rebellion and handed Maynier orders for his recall. The colonists had achieved a mixed success in their rebellion. They had got rid of Maynier but had failed to establish control over the district. Moreover, the Khoikhoi, in alliance with Xhosa marauders, embarked on a series of raids in late 1801 which were even more devastating than those of the 1799 Khoikhoi uprising.

For a decade after 1801 the colonists on the Eastern Frontier issued no challenge to the authorities. There were several reasons for their quiescence. Firstly, the threat from Khoikhoi had now subsided: Khoikhoi leadership disintegrated during the 1801—02 hostilities and the rank and file were effectively subjugated as labourers. At the same time there was a growing coalescence between the view of the government and the farmers on the position of the Khoikhoi in colonial society.[29] Secondly, the Zuurveld Xhosa remained relatively peaceful until 1809. When in 1809—11 Xhosa bands embarked on a new wave of raids and 'begging', the colonists' defences were so strained that they could not give any serious thought to revolt. Thirdly, the failure of the rebellions of 1795 and 1799, and the establishment in 1799 of a strong garrison at Fort Frederick (modern Port Elizabeth), had convinced most colonists that factiousness, disorder and rebellion gained them nothing and fatally undermined their struggle to maintain themselves against the Xhosa. They now realised that only in alliance with the colonial government could they expel the Xhosa and at the same time win respite from the pressure on the land.

Thus, when discussing possible links between the 1795 and 1799 rebellions and the Great Trek of the 1830s, it is important to stress that there was no continuity in the colonists' resistance to the British. Indeed, by 1811 the most important political development among the frontier colonists was their evolution towards full cooperation with the colonial government, especially with regard to policy toward the Xhosa.[30]

Yet there was a limit to the colonists' loyalty to the government. By 1810, when bands of Xhosa were overrunning large parts of Graaff-Reinet and Uitenhage, a British officer on the frontier warned: 'The suffering of the unfortunate Boers is really great . . . many talk of quitting the country entirely and with what little they have left seek a place . . . where they can rest in peace.'[31] The implementation of this 'Great Trek strategy' would lie dormant for two more decades. But in the mean time, in 1815, the Slachtersnek rebellion broke out, in which one of the schemes of the rebels was to barter land from the Xhosa and establish their independence.

The Slachtersnek rebellion of 1815[32]

In April 1813 a Khoikhoi labourer named Booy brought a complaint to the young deputy-landdrost, Andries Stockenstrom. He claimed that Cornelis Frederik (Freek) Bezuidenhout, a farmer in the isolated division of Baviaans River, withheld his wages (in cattle) after his term of service had ended. However, Bezuidenhout, in letters to Stockenstrom, alleged that Booy had caused him much damage: he would dispense with Booy's services and release his cattle only after receiving adequate indemnification. In May 1814 Booy tried to recover his cattle from Bezuidenhout, who then allegedly assaulted him. Bezuidenhout ignored repeated summonses to appear in court. Eventually the Circuit Court sentenced him in absentia to one month's imprisonment for contempt of court. On 10 October 1815 a detachment of fourteen men, consisting of two drostdy officials as well as two officers and twelve Khoikhoi troops (*pandours*) of the border posts, arrived on Bezuidenhout's farm to arrest him. Bezuidenhout resisted, aided by a young European man and by his Bastaard concubine and son (who, interestingly enough, addressed him as 'Baas' [Boss]). In a gunfight Bezuidenhout was killed by a pandour.

At the funeral Johannes Jurgen (Hans) Bezuidenhout, a brother of Freek, swore vengeance on Stockenstrom and the soldiers responsible for his brother's death. Supported by H.F. Prinsloo (the son of the Patriot leader Marthinus Prinsloo), who claimed to have the support of the whole of Bruintjes Hoogte, Zuurveld and Tarka, Hans Bezuidenhout and his brother-in-law, Cornelis Faber, tried to mount a rebellion.

The rebels failed in an attempt to enlist the help of the Xhosa chieftain Ngqika; nor did they whip up any substantial support among colonists in the eastern divisions. On 18 November sixty rebels surrendered at Slachtersnek to a government force. They had not fired a shot. Hans Bezuidenhout attempted to escape but was killed. Subsequently the government hanged five rebel leaders and a central theme was born in the Afrikaner nationalist indictment of British imperialism.

Slachtersnek occurred because some colonists had not faced the fact that the days of the open frontier (ch. 8, pp. 296—308) had passed. Freek Bezuidenhout meted out his own justice at a time when the visible authority of the colonial government and the advent of the Circuit Court had encouraged Khoikhoi to have recourse to the law. To compound his error, Bezuidenhout thought it was still possible to ignore the injunctions of the authorities. In fact, the British force stationed on the frontier now enabled the landdrost to act quickly and decisively against recalcitrant subjects. For instance, the rebels received a fatal blow when a key figure, H.F. Prinsloo, was swiftly removed and kept in safe custody in a military post. Stockenstrom clearly saw the issue at stake: 'a choice between order[33] and civilization on the one hand, and a return to the days of Woeke and Maynier, Bresler, Van der Poel and Gerotz on the other.'[34]

The causes of the rebellion should be sought in the conditions of a frontier which had largely closed. The rebels were men lashing out against restrictions imposed on them by changed circumstances. In their deep frustration, a personal grievance such as Hans Bezuidenhout's grudge about the killing of his brother could escalate into rebellion.[35] For the rebels the closing of the frontier had manifested itself firstly in a land crisis. In 1802 the Bezuidenhouts and several other rebels had been driven by the Xhosa from the Zuurveld. With the increase of population it was difficult for them to trek from one place to the other as before. On the Eastern Frontier many families were forced to live together on one farm. The land shortage was most serious in the Tarka and Baviaans River divisions, and it was from there that most of the Slachtersnek rebels came. In Tarka only sixteen of the ninety-one European families (total population 542) held registered farms, and in Baviaans River only five of the fifty families.[36] The perpetual quitrent system, which was introduced in 1813, made land even harder to acquire. Referring to this new system, Cornelis Faber complained that the English had made the farms too small,† and when farmers pointed out that the cattle '[ate] one another dead the English only answered "sell the cattle and make them fewer." '[37] When asked why he wanted to drive the English out of the country, H.F. Prinsloo, a rebel leader, pointed to the heavy burden of the quitrent.[38]

To deal with the land shortage, the rebels planned to expand over the border. One of them declared that the strategy was 'to maintain a certain understanding with the Kafirs, which would enable them . . . to cross over the proclaimed boundaries, and settle down in one or other portion of Kafirland . . . to take possession of the territory at the Gonap [Koonap] in the form of an independent Union.'[39]

The closing frontier also impinged on the rebels in the form of increasing government intervention. Caledon's Hottentot Proclamation of 1809 encroached upon the great measure of power colonists had previously had over their labourers. The Circuit Courts served notice that the government was serious in protecting Khoikhoi against maltreatment and in preventing arbitrary conduct. In 1813 a Circuit Court tried thirty-three cases against Graaff-Reinet colonists. Several of the men of Slachtersnek had had recent

---

† In contrast to the loan farm system, which only vaguely defined a farm and resulted in open space between the circular farms, the perpetual quitrent system demanded that land newly applied for must be carefully surveyed. The rent was higher, although the land a farmer could use was sometimes considerably smaller.

brushes with the law or were related to others who had had similar experiences.[40]

Apart from land and law, other preconditions of the rebellion should be considered. Firstly, the racial factor. There is no conclusive evidence that the rebellion was provoked by the use of Khoikhoi (non-European) troops in apprehending a white man.[41] It is, however, clear that there was a widespread feeling, intensified by the 'Black Circuit' (Circuit Court of 1812), that the government was favouring non-Europeans. As Stockenstrom wrote in 1816, 'the people were talking that the "Black nation was protected and not the Christians." '[42] H.F. Prinsloo incited men to rise against the government because 'Hottentots [were] preferred to the Burghers.'[43]

The rebellion was also marked by some quasi-nationalistic appeals. Rebel leaders called on their men to extirpate the English, whom they depicted as tyrants and villians.[44] The fact that the government was English rather than Dutch naturally added an additional element to the colonists' sense of their 'oppression' on the closing frontier. Yet the rebellion was hardly nationalistic in any strict sense of the word. Its appeal was purely sectional: it won little support in the rebels' own district, much less from the colonists as a whole. In addition, any attempt to regard Slachtersnek as a direct link between the rebellion of 1795 and the Great Trek is misleading. It has recently been shown that many families who were rebels in 1795 joined the side of the government or were neutral in 1815. Moreover, the descendants of government supporters rather than those of the Slachtersnek rebels were the ones that participated in the Great Trek.[45]

There is also tentative evidence that the rebellion can be analysed in class terms. The rebels were mostly poor and landless men. Fewer than ten owned farms. Many owned only a horse and a few sheep or cattle. Hardly any had more than a hundred units of stock. In contrast, the people who supported the government or stayed neutral were comparatively wealthy landholders.[46] The judges who tried the rebels remarked 'that the persons implicated in this rebellion, or the chief participators in the same, were no owners of land, but either resided with others, or without a fixed residence wandered about with their cattle.' In contrast, the judges declared, the well-to-do farmers were 'animated with a good spirit' and confident that their 'real interests [were] objects of care with the government.'[47]

Thus the rebellion showed how the landless colonists emerged as a class dangerous to the established order. The Bezuidenhout brothers were known to be violent men who used or threatened force in land disputes with their neighbours.[48] They and Faber were considered by Stockenstrom as 'men of the most depraved morals'[49] because they often lived with the Xhosa across the border. In 1815, when it became clear that the rebels had no substantial support, they threatened to seek Xhosa allies. Those who refused to join the rebellion would be killed and their families and property given over to Xhosa. In return for this assistance the rebels would be prepared to give the Zuurveld back to the Xhosa.[50] Clearly this growing class of poverty-stricken frontiersmen was a threat to wealthy landholders, who consequently gave the government much more enthusiastic support than they had during the previous rebellions.

The nature of the rebellions

During the nineteenth century, Afrikaner political and cultural leaders seldom mentioned the 1795 and 1801 rebellions. But by 1868 the nationalists resurrected Slachtersnek, and until deep into the twentieth century continued to hold it up as an example of the wrongs of British imperialism. Recently an interesting reversal has taken place. During the past two decades the need for white unity in South Africa has encouraged the memory of Slachtersnek to fade away. At the same time the 1795 rebellion has come to the fore. Some historians see 1795 as an important date in the emergence of a national consciousness among Afrikaners. Others regard it as a milestone in the Afrikaner democratic revolution, which started in the last quarter of the eighteenth century and was consummated when Great Britain recognised the Voortrekker states in the 1850s.[51]

Before discussing the ideological importance of these rebellions, it is necessary to recall who the rebels were. In all the rebellions the overwhelming majority of the rebels identified with one section of the district. In 1795 and again in 1801 almost all of them came from Bruintjes Hoogte and the Zuurveld. In 1815 they were mostly men from Baviaans River, a division along the Xhosa border to the north of Bruintjes Hoogte. The rebellions were thus almost exclusively planned and carried out by colonists living close to the Xhosa. Except in 1801, the rebels failed to gain support from outside their own divisions.

The Patriots of 1795—96 were comparatively wealthy land-owners intent on increasing their hold over land, cattle and servants.[52] The 1801 rebellions were also led by comparatively wealthy men of the southeast and north, who succeeded in winning widespread support. The men of Slachtersnek, as has been noted, were mostly poor and landless and were resisted by well-to-do landholders, alarmed by the possibility of cooperation between the lower class Europeans and the Xhosa. This difference in class may in part explain the difference in the rebels' methods. The Patriots of 1795—96 and the 1801 rebels removed unpopular administrators and took over the district government. The Slachtersnek rebels were less interested in power than in revenge and land. They planned to attack the military posts on the border, kill officers or officials whom they held responsible for Freek Bezuidenhout's death, and settle in a part of 'Kaffirland'.

The rebels were almost all Europeans. Of the 317 people who in 1795 signed petitions against Maynier (43 signed the *Te Samenstemming* of 29 January and 276 the petition of 16 April) only three had a non-European grandmother; all the others had even less non-European ancestry.[53] No baptised Bastaards signed the petition, nor any Khoikhoi. Whenever they asserted their rights, the rebels referred to themselves as 'burghers'. In their view, if not that of the government, the concept 'burgher' had become virtually synonymous with 'European'.

In all three cases the rebels desired to gain greater control over their relationships with the Xhosa and the Khoikhoi. Regarding the Xhosa, a major objective (especially in 1795 and 1801) was to recoup cattle losses and regain the Zuurveld for the Europeans. As for the Khoikhoi, the persistent theme was the rebels' opposition to *gelykstelling* (levelling) or, as they put it, the 'favouring' of Khoikhoi. They opposed interference by the colonial authorities in master-servant relationships, missionary work among Khoikhoi (which provided Khoikhoi with the symbols of superior status) and the arming of Khoikhoi as an auxiliary police and military force.[54] A crucial question in the minds of the frontiersmen was whether the government could be trusted to use force in their favour. They did not know that in this they could rest assured. There is evidence of a growing sympathy on the side of the government with the colonists' views toward the non-Europeans. In 1815 the colonial governor even considered withdrawing the Cape (Hottentot) Regiment from the eastern districts 'on account of the prejudices of the people.'[55]

Against this background the alleged nationalistic and democratic spirit of the rebellions can be discussed. The essence of these rebellions was their local character and the sectional interests they tried to promote. This does not mean that they had no connection whatever with nationalism: indeed, the Great Trek, which fed Afrikaner nationalism, largely emanated from these southeastern divisions. As the American historian, David Potter, has remarked about the history of the American South: 'Nationalism, in fact, may be the terminal result of a full development of strong sectional forces, while sectionalism may be an emergent nationalism which has not yet matured.'[56]

However, if one is open to the nationalistic potential of sectionalism reflected by the Bruintjes Hoogte/Zuurveld rebellions, one should also consider that conflicting sectionalisms could thwart the development of nationalism. And if one accepts that the Bruintjes Hoogte/Zuurveld rebellions may have been a step toward the formation of a new national character, one should also recognise the real differences between these sectionalist rebellions and the Afrikaner nationalist movement of later years. The rebels showed no apparent interest in the cultural aspects of nationalism. They were not even consistently anti-imperialist or anti-British. The first rebellion occurred under the Dutch East India Company when the rebels desired, not independence, but direct rule by the States-General in the Netherlands. When Frans Bresler, a colonial-born ex-Company servant, was sent out in 1796 as landdrost of Graaff-Reinet, the rebels rejected him, demanding that an Englishman should be appointed in his place.

The assertion that the rebellions were democratic also bristles with difficulties. The rebels themselves could hardly be described as democratic. They acquired and exercised control over the district authorities by force and intimidation. The representanten of 1795—96 chose themselves, or were chosen by a small faction, and invested themselves with the power to rule. They made no attempt to regularise the participation of the volkstem in district affairs. Moreover, the intimidation of opposition in 1799 and 1815 suggests that the rebels, had their movements succeeded, would have been unlikely to forge a Graaff-Reinet consensus by encouraging free debate. Apart from a few phrases used by the Cape Patriots and later by the French revolutionaries, the Graaff-Reinet rebels had no democratic ideology. By their actions they clearly showed what democracy is not.

But it may still be asked whether the Graaff-Reinet rebellion embodied immature seeds of democracy which would only later develop and bear fruit. The rebellions reflected elements both of anarchy, which negates democracy, and of individualism, which is its prerequisite. A potential for anarchy was seen in the way the various sections of Graaff-Reinet opposed and nearly fought one another. In the 1840s and 1850s there would be a similar phenomenon in the fissiparous Voortrekker society north of the Vaal River, where sectionalism and conflicting leadership led to clashes and the creation of several distinct 'republics'. There is clearly a wide gap between the rhetoric of democracy and the concrete institutionalisation of a democratic system of government.

However, to say that democratic theory was not maturely developed or that frontier politics had an anarchic side is not to deny that the rebellions may have been a manifestation of developing sentiments of individual liberty and self-rule which would later develop into a democratic ideology. For how else would one understand the political institutions of the Voortrekkers and the establishment of viable democracies (be it only for Europeans) in Natal, the Orange Free State and later in the Transvaal? Thus, perhaps, the individualism of the Eastern Frontier rebels, their notions of self-determination and their desire to control their relationships with non-Europeans, made them the spiritual precursors of the Voortrekkers and, arguably, of the European electorate of the modern Republic of South Africa.

Chapter Nine   Notes

1. For a brief but perceptive discussion on the Graaff-Reinet rebellion of 1795 within the context of the French and other Western revolutions, see R.R. Palmer, *The Age of the Democratic Revolution* (Princeton, 1964), I, 204—07. The Swellendam rebellion of 1795 is not discussed in this chapter. I have dealt with it in my *Die Kaap tydens die Eerste Britse Bewind 1795—1803* (Cape Town, 1975), pp. 35—36 and in the essay referred to in note 17 below.

2. Compare the views of F.A. van Jaarsveld, *Van Van Riebeeck tot Verwoerd* (Johannesburg, 1971), p. 58 with those of L.M. Thompson, 'Afrikaner Nationalist Historiography and the Policy of Apartheid', *Journal of African History*, III (1962), p. 130.

3. Donald Moodie, *The Record* (Amsterdam, 1960), General Report of Commandant Opperman, 1 April 1777, III, 67.

4. See the various reports by Van Jaarsveld in Stb 13/3 and Stb 10/162.

5. Quoted by J.S. Marais in *Maynier and the First Boer Republic* (Cape Town, 1944), p. 13.

6. GR 3/32, Deposition of D.S. van der Merwe and others, 7 Aug. 1787, no. 4.

7. For a further discussion, see Giliomee, *Eerste Britse Bewind*, pp. 31—32, 41—42.

8. For conflicting interpretations of Maynier's role, see J.S. Marais, *Maynier and the First Boer Republic* (Cape Town, 1944), and P.J. van der Merwe, *Die Kafferoorlog van 1793* (Cape Town, 1940).

9. GR 1/1, Minutes, 11 Jan. 1794, p. 243.

10. The Fiscal had instructed Maynier to take down statements by them. It is not stated in what connection. See GR 16/1, Maynier — W. and M. Prinsloo *et al.*, 5 Aug. 1794; and the letter of 3 Dec. 1794 in the same volume.

11. GR 16/1, Maynier — Tregardt, 24 Dec. 1794.

12. GR 16/1, Maynier — Van Jaarsveld, 3 Dec. 1794.

13. VC 68, Te Samenstemming, 29 Jan. 1975, pp. 183—86.

14. VC 68, Minutes of J.A. Truter of events of 16 June 1795, pp. 138—51.

15. BO 26, Bresler—Craig, 26 May 1796, p. 33; GR 1/2, Minutes, pp. 22—31, 46—48.

16. BO 47, Burghers of Graaff-Reinet — Craig, 29 Oct. 1795, p. 5; GR 1/2, Minutes, 14 June 1796, p. 76.

17. For a fuller discussion, see Hermann Giliomee, 'Democracy and the Frontier', *South African Historical Journal,* VI (1974), pp. 38—39, 43—44.

18. BO 26, Bresler—Craig, 2 March 1796, 22 March 1796 and 26 May 1796, pp. 19—30, 38—54. Bresler's letters are the only eye-witness accounts of these events. He was, of course, an interested party and his evidence has to be treated with circumspection. In his other letters during the period 1796–1802 (especially his testimony in 1802 to the Commission of Enquiry on Maynier's

administration where his evidence could be corroborated with those of other witnesses) he conveys the impression of a dependable observer. Most of his letters are in BO 26—28. His testimony is found in PRO, WO 1/338, Correspondence-In-Letters, Cape of Good Hope, 1795—1812.

19. *RCC*, I, Letter to Craig, 29 Oct. 1795, pp. 209—10.

20. BO 26, 'Propositie' to Bresler, 22 March 1796, pp. 59—64.

21. *RCC*, I, 478—81, 497—500; BO 27, pp. 111—13.

22. For a discussion of this, see Giliomee, 'Democracy and the Frontier', p. 42 and Giliomee, *Eerste Britse Bewind*, pp. 70—73.

23. This section is based on Giliomee, *Eerste Britse Bewind*, pp. 300—11. For a different interpretation, see Marais, *Maynier*, pp. 113—29.

24. Cf. the view of Marais, *Maynier*, p. 123.

25. Tamotsu Shibutani, *Improvised News: a Sociological Study of Rumor* (Indianapolis, 1966).

26. *Transactions of the Missionary Society* (London, 1804), I, 480.

27. For a discussion of another demand, i.e., that some Khoikhoi suspected of murdering a colonist be delivered up to them, see Giliomee, *Eerste Britse Bewind*, pp. 307, 311.

28. It is possible that Maynier hoped to establish an armed corps of 400 Khoikhoi to defend the frontier and use against disaffected colonists. See Giliomee, *Eerste Britse Bewind*, pp. 304, 312.

29. The frontier colonists were at first afraid that the Hottentot Proclamation of 1809 meant a serious curtailment of their control over their servants. This fear quickly subsided. See the letter of Fiscal J.A. Truter to Landdrost Stockenstrom, in which he assured him that the proclamation did not confer any new freedoms on the Khoikhoi (GR 9/10, Truter — Stockenstrom, 7 April 1810). See also the comments of a commission of enquiry on the severe restrictions under which the Khoikhoi lived two decades after the proclamation had been issued (*RCC*, Report of Bigge, Colebrooke and Blair, 10 May 1828, pp. 147—49).

30. See the statements in *RCC*, VIII, 241, 355, 486.

31. CO 2572, Evatt — Cuyler, 20 April 1810, enclosure to no. 18.

32. For a recent detailed study of the rebellion, see J.A. Heese, *Slagtersnek en sy mense* (Cape Town, 1973). This study is especially valuable in the genealogical perspective it uses to explain the actions of leading figures. See also J. de Villiers, 'Die Kaapse Regiment 1806—1817', *South African Historical Journal*, VII (1975), pp. 26—32.

33. In his journal Stockenstrom wrote that the chief conspirators would use any favourable opportunity to 'free themselves from the constraint of laws to which they had never submitted except with the greatest reluctance, if they could bring any ground of objection to them.' Quoted by H.A. Reyburn, 'Studies in Cape Frontier History: Stockenstrom and Slagters Nek', *The Critic,* III, (1935), p. 151.

34. A. Stockenstrom, *Autobiography of Sir Andries Stockenstrom*, ed. C.W. Hutton (Cape Town, 1887), p. 91. The men mentioned served as landdrost or provisional landdrost in Graaff-Reinet prior to the appointment of Stockenstrom's father in 1803.

35. For a discussion of personal grievances as a factor in the rebellion, see Heese, *Slagtersnek*, pp. 13—14, 67.

36. H. Reyburn, 'Studies in Cape Frontier History: Land, Labour and Law', *The Critic,* III (1934), pp. 41—42.

37. H.C.V. Leibbrandt, *De Rebellie van 1815 algemeen bekend als Slachtersnek* (Cape Town, 1903), pp. 53, 776.
38. Leibbrandt, *Rebellie*, p. 237.
39. H.C.V. Leibbrandt, *The Rebellion of 1815 generally known as Slachters Nek* (Cape Town, 1902), p. 867. See also Leibbrandt, *Rebellie*, p. 893.
40. Heese, *Slagtersnek*, p. 67.
41. At the trial of the rebels, the accused or witnesses never mentioned the use of Coloured troops against white men as a grievance. It is, however, pertinent that Governor Lord Charles Somerset wrote to London that it was customary to consider the Hottentot as an inferior species. Not only the rebels, 'who have committed themselves in the present business, in consequence of the death of Bezuidenhout by the hand of a Hottentot', but the colonists in general were extremely impatient of the restraint the British regulations had put upon them, and considered it 'obnoxious to have the Hottentot Regiment among them to enforce those regulations': *RCC*, XI, 5. It is not clear from the above whether Somerset was discussing the causes of the rebellion or only relating the circumstances in which it took place. See also the discussion of Heese, *Slagtersnek*, pp. 49—50, 59—60.
42. GR 16/5, Stockenstrom — Cuyler, 5 Jan. 1816, no. 179.
43. Leibbrandt, *Rebellie*, p. 237.
44. *Ibid.*, pp. 49, 51, 59, 99—100.
45. Heese, *Slagtersnek*, pp. 88, 181.
46. J 73—77, Cradock, 1814—15. More research needs to be done on this topic.
47. Leibbrandt, *Rebellie*, pp. 888—89.
48. See Marais, *Maynier*, p. 29; Heese, *Slagtersnek*, pp. 2—3.
49. Leibbrandt, *Rebellie*, p. 144.
50. *Ibid.*, p. 143.
51. This is discussed in Giliomee, 'Democracy and the Frontier', pp. 43–51.
52. Giliomee, *Eerste Britse Bewind*, p. 72.
53. Four signatories married or lived with full 'non-whites'. I wish to thank Dr J.A. Heese for his invaluable help in this research.
54. See Giliomee, *Eerste Britse Bewind*, p. 252.
55. *RCC*, Somerset—Bathurst, 11 Dec. 1815, p. 5.
56. David M. Potter, *The South and Sectional Conflict* (Baton Rouge, 1968), p. 47.

PART IV

An overview

The structure of European domination at the Cape, 1652—1820*

Hermann Giliomee and Richard Elphick

This chapter deals with social stratification in the Cape Colony between 1652 and 1820. It addresses a question of growing interest: to what extent was the colony's social structure formed by the prejudices, values and institutions of the Netherlands prior to the settlement of the Cape, and to what extent by conditions arising in the colony after 1652? This chapter is based on our own research and on material in previous chapters, but we alone are responsible for its conclusions.

Throughout our period colonial society was dominated by a group whose members variously described themselves as 'colonists', 'inhabitants', 'Afrikaners', 'Christians', 'whites' or 'Europeans'.† This group was larger than an ethnic group as usually defined, for it embraced people of different languages (Dutch, German, French, etc.), different religious denominations (Dutch

* A draft of this chapter was presented on 5 October 1977 to the Southern African Research Program, Yale University. We wish to thank the following scholars who on this occasion offered valuable criticism: Leonard Thompson, William Foltz, Stanley Greenberg, Newell Stultz, Heribert Adam and Richard Ralston. We are also grateful to those scholars who commented on earlier drafts: Jeffrey Butler, Harvey Feinberg, Leonard Guelke, J.A. Heese, Dian Joubert, Martin Legassick, Shula Marks, David Robinson, Robert Ross, Christopher Saunders, Robert Shell and Marcia Wright. We are especially indebted to Robert Shell for suggesting the theme of the second section.

† We need a detailed study of this group's terms for itself. Our impression is that group identity rested on three characteristics: (1) common physical traits like 'white' skin which made members of the group, in almost all cases, instantly recognisable; (2) common origin or ancestry in Europe (although Cape-born Europeans sometimes called themselves 'Afrikaners' to distinguish themselves from those born in Europe); (3) common European culture, of which national cultures were variants and of which Christianity formed the core. The term 'white', rarely used in the early decades of settlement, referred to physical type. The term 'colonist' denoted an origin overseas. So, too, did 'Christian', which affirmed not merely that one adhered to a particular creed and ritual, but also that one's origins were in Christendom (i.e., Europe or European civilisation) and that one's culture derived from there: baptised Khoikhoi and slaves, despite their religious profession, were not normally called Christians, except by the government. Unlike these terms, the word 'European' seems to have embraced all three criteria — appearance, origin and culture. Thus this is the term we shall use.

Reformed, Lutheran, etc.), and different cultures. Despite its diversity the European group remained distinct from other groups in the colony (blacks, Khoikhoi and Bastaards). We saw in chapter 4 (pp. 128—29) that there was a comparatively favourable sex ratio among the European population; thus a rather small number of Cape marriages were mixed and children of extra-marital miscegenation were not usually regarded as European. Of a sample of 1,063 children baptised in 1807 in the Reformed and Lutheran churches at the Cape, only about 5 per cent had a grandparent whom genealogists designate 'non-white' (in our terms, non-European).[1]

This high rate of endogamy confirms the impression we have gained from the documents that the European group was decidedly aware of its identity and distinctiveness from other groups. It retained this identity throughout our period, adding to its members chiefly from further European immigration and internal generation, and much less from admitting outsiders through intermarriage and extra-marital miscegenation. We call the European group a 'race' because membership of it was almost always determined by birth rather than choice, because it embraced many European nationalities, and because physical appearance (which entailed more than mere skin colour) was an important badge of group membership. Table 10.1 furnishes a rough breakdown of the colonial population between 1670 and 1820:[2] the Company's employees and slaves are omitted for the period before 1795.

Table 10.1 Population of the Cape Colony, 1670—1820

Year	European freeburghers	Free blacks	Burghers' slaves	Khoikhoi and Bastaards
1670	125	13	52	not enumerated until 1798
1690	788	48	381	,,
1711	1,693	63	1,771	,,
1730	2,540	221	4,037	,,
1750	4,511	349	5,327	,,
1770	7,736	352	8,220	,,
1798	c. 20,000	c. 1,700	25,754	14,447
1820	42,975	1,932	31,779	26,975

Historians have offered several explanations for the emergence of a social order dominated by Europeans, and for the 'racism' which surfaced or intensified at the Cape in the late eighteenth and early nineteenth centuries. Perhaps most influential is I.D. MacCrone's theory that the fundamental cleavage was originally between Christians and non-Christians. According to MacCrone, conflict on the 'frontier' (*trekboer* regions) transformed this religious cleavage into a racial cleavage and gave rise to a more aggressive colour prejudice which eventually permeated the entire society.³ A second explanation attaches great significance to the belief system of the Afrikaner, particularly his 'primitive Calvinism.'⁴ Recently some scholars have begun to formulate a third view, namely that Cape social structure was determined not by beliefs or myths, but by economic and demographic conditions arising after the founding of the settlement.⁵ In this chapter we emphasise, on the one hand, institutions, ideas and attitudes (mostly inherited from the period before settlement) and, on the other, economic and demographic conditions prevailing in the colony.

The European heritage and the social structure

Most Europeans who settled in South Africa in the seventeenth century were Dutchmen. Like all colonising peoples of the period, they were convinced of the superiority of their culture and religion. Cultural chauvinism was an important component of racism, a feature of all European colonies. But some scholars of comparative race relations have concluded that racism was more intense in colonies of the English and Dutch than in those of the French, Portuguese or Spanish. This was so, they claim, because the English and Dutch came from societies which were moving beyond the spiritual unity of medieval Catholicism and the ordered hierarchy of feudalism, into the ferment of early capitalism. In England and the United Netherlands men were more individualistic and mobile, institutions more egalitarian and democratic, than on the Iberian peninsula. Society consisted not of a complex hierarchy of social ranks, but mainly of two classes: the respectable burghers and the despicable poor who had to be forced to work.⁶ In the colonial setting, it is claimed, this bifurcation of society was easily transformed into a rigid two-tiered society where Europeans dominated non-Europeans.

For the Cape Colony this analysis can be accepted only with modifications. Schutte points out (ch. 5, p. 176) that the Netherlands itself was far from democratic. Moreover, the Cape *freeburghers* enjoyed none of the liberties or representative institutions found in some Anglo-American colonies of the time. But on the other hand, the Company was one of the most advanced commercial enterprises of the age, and as both Guelke and Schutte emphasise, (ch. 2, p. 43 and ch. 5, p. 184) it offered opportunities for individual advancement that were rare in Europe. Thus it is not so much the democratic quality of the Netherlands that is important in analysing social stratification at the Cape as the commercial nature of the Cape government — its tendency to attract upwardly mobile, individualistic employees and colonists, more inclined perhaps than their Iberian counterparts to adopt the two-tier model of society.

Again, like other colonists the Dutch arrived at the Cape with a 'somatic norm image' in their minds, a complex of physical characteristics which formed their norm and ideal of human appearance. In his investigation of New World societies, Harmannus Hoetink has found that certain persons of mixed ancestry were accepted as European by Spanish and Portuguese colonists, who were themselves swarthy and had a long history of mixing with the Moors in Europe, but not by the English and Dutch, who were among the whitest of Europeans and whose ideal physical type was far removed from black.[7] Moreover, David Brion Davis has argued that the European colonists in Latin America were inclined to believe that mulattos, by intermixing with Europeans, would eventually be 'bleached'. By contrast, the Dutch in the New World stigmatised any person with the slightest trace of Negro ancestry and denied mulattos the prospect of gradually progressing towards the status of 'whites'.[8]

Somatic preferences probably played some part in early Cape society. Sailors in Van Riebeeck's time called Khoikhoi 'black stinking dogs'.[9] Colonists preferred blacks‡ over Khoikhoi as sexual partners and chose marriage partners roughly in this order of preference: Europeans, mixed-bloods, Asians, negro Africans and Khoikhoi (ch. 4, pp. 129—31). In these cases, however, it is hard to separate attitudes to physical type from feelings about culture: for example, the dress and skin-grease of Khoikhoi were powerful deterrents against miscegenation between European men and Khoikhoi women. Somatic preferences may also have influenced patterns of manumission, but here again cultural, and even more, economic considerations were also at work (ch. 4, pp. 138—39). Thus the Europeans' social evaluation of physical type had some influence on the social opportunities of non-Europeans, even in the seventeenth century, but the available evidence does not allow us to compute this influence precisely.

Modern historians tend to be uncomfortable with psychological interpretations of social stratification. Yet in the case of the Cape they have been curiously eager to embrace a theological explanation. Charles Boxer, a student of Dutch and Portuguese maritime empires, observed that the 'Portuguese, Spaniards, Dutch, English and French were nearly all convinced that a Christian European was *ipso facto* superior to members of any other race . . . [This view] was inevitably strongest among Calvinists, who, consciously or subconsciously, were bound to believe that they were the Elect of the Lord and

‡ By 'black' we mean persons of African, Madagascan or Asian origin; in practice most blacks were slaves or were wholly or partly descended from slaves. This was the usage in the Company period. Freed slaves were called 'free blacks' even if they were mulattos. Xhosa were seldom called 'blacks' until the late eighteenth century. The same was generally true of the Khoikhoi, despite the unusual quotation from the early colony just cited.

the salt of the earth.'[10] In her study of free blacks at the Cape, Sheila Patterson concluded that 'it would seem that primitive Calvinism, as modified by nearly two centuries of increasing isolation and dispersion, and the imported and increasingly ingrained habit of slave-owning, played a particularly important part in the ordering of attitudes and relationships . . . and in fostering the development of a biracial, white/non-white society instead of the more flexible, pluralistic one imported from the Far East.'[11] Calvinism's role in structuring Cape society has been emphasised not only by scholars who consider its impact harmful, but also by those who think it beneficial.[12]

There are serious problems with this argument. Firstly, it is not yet clear exactly how the Calvinist creed was more exclusivist than Roman Catholicism *vis-à-vis* non-Europeans. Calvinist clergy at the Cape, like their Catholic counterparts in Latin America,[13] certainly did not ban or discourage intermarriage, nor did they put less emphasis on the equality of all men before God. Secondly, the adjectives 'primitive', 'fanatic', and 'fundamentalist', often attached to Calvinism at the Cape, have not been defined: the argument for Calvinist influence cannot be sustained until scholars abandon simplistic stereotypes and attempt a subtle analysis of Calvinist thought, both in Europe and at the Cape. Thirdly, no one has yet shown what aspects of Calvinist doctrine permeated what regions and classes at the Cape, in what forms, and in what eras. It has not even been shown that Calvinism was influential at all. One would naturally expect a high level of Calvinist influence in the pious seventeenth century, when most immigrants to the Cape were either Dutchmen or Huguenots fleeing France to preserve their religion. Yet in 1714 the well-travelled Rev. François Valentyn attended Holy Communion in Cape Town and reported:

> I found that the church members totalled 40 men and 48 women only, including those in the return-fleet, of whom there were a number, and it was entirely surprising that among those who approached the Table there was no Member of the Council of Policy [the ruling body], and apparently also none of them was a church member.
> Inland it may not be expected to be one-half so good.
> From this it can be seen, how little so many Preachers have gained in all these years by their toil among these [European] inhabitants, due in no wise to faltering of their zeal, but to the stupidity and insolence of the Burghers. I perceived also, that there are many Lutherans among the [Company] Servants.[14]

With the decline of religious commitment in eighteenth-century Europe, the increase of non-Dutch (hence non-Calvinist) immigration to the Cape, and the increase in the ratio of clergy to people, one would expect — in the absence of a close study of the documents — the influence of Calvinism to decline even further, at least until Evangelical influences arrived at the end of the century. The Cape, after all, was notoriously lacking in schools, churches and vigorous intellectual life. However, this is not to assert that Calvinist doctrine had no influence on social stratification at the Cape, only that the argument for such influence has yet to be made.

We are on surer ground when we look not at what Calvinism achieved, but at what it did not. Calvinism in general lacked missionary zeal and at the Cape did not create a sizeable Christian community transcending lines of colour and culture. In contrast to the Catholic Church in Iberian America,[15] the Reformed Church at the Cape did not campaign on behalf of slaves for looser manumission regulations, milder treatment, or the right to marry. This inactivity was due in part to the church's organisational structure and the context in which it operated. In Iberian colonies the clergy were guided and supported by the church in Europe, which was powerful enough to condemn the slave trade at an early stage and to dispatch religious orders, particularly the Jesuits, to the colonies to convert Indians. By contrast, the church at the Cape was decentralised. The *classis* of Amsterdam exercised only a nominal influence over it and the Company would not allow the various congregations at the Cape to form their own classis (or presbytery).[16] Moreover, the Cape church was weak: contrary to Calvinist doctrine and practice in parts of Europe, it was dominated by the state. The Reformed clergy were employees of the *VOC*, which anticipated no profit in the evangelisation of the Khoikhoi and had no intention of allowing its servants to challenge its regulations on manumission or to intercede on behalf of the slaves. In his study of the entire VOC empire, Charles Boxer found only one case of a church council attacking government policy, and that show of independence — in Batavia in 1653 — was quickly suppressed.[17]

It was not Calvinism's distinction between the elect and reprobate, but the Company's distinctions among legal status groups, which initially structured Cape society. These distinctions were mainly inherited from colonies established before 1652, although their subsequent development was naturally influenced by local conditions and by the Company policies. The four main groups, both in law and in practice, were Company servants, freeburghers, slaves and indigenous 'aliens'. The legal cleavage between Company servants and freeburghers was familiar in Dutch-controlled Asia and came into effect at the Cape when the first freeburghers were granted land in 1657 (ch. 5, pp. 179—81). The cleavage between both free groups on the one hand, and slaves on the other, was also imported from the East along with regulations and practices necessary to sustain it (ch. 3, pp. 75—76); so, too, were the mechanisms by which slaves could become free and the tradition that, as free blacks, they would suffer few legal disabilities (ch. 4, pp. 145—46). Finally, the distinction in law between all three groups in colonial society and the natives outside it was an automatic consequence of planting a colony over-seas. The Khoikhoi were gradually incorporated into the Cape Colony as their status changed from indigenous aliens to subjects of the Company, but throughout our period they remained legally distinct from freeburghers, Company servants and slaves.

Colonial officials and colonial courts discriminated among the four status groups in many areas of daily life — domicile, marriage, right of movement, taxation, land ownership, and so on. In the official view one's legal status — more than one's race, religion, origin, culture or colour — limited one's opportunities for advancement: only Company servants and freeburghers could hold land or gain political power in the official hierarchy of the colony. But since the Company recruited its servants and free immigrants in Europe and brought few Asian or Eurasian employees and settlers to the Cape, it created the precedent of a political and economic elite which was almost exclusively European. By importing slaves, none of whom were European, it intensified the correlation between legal status and race. And by regarding Khoikhoi initially as aliens and later as subjects who were not freeburghers, it effectively precluded them from political and economic advancement in colonial society.

In short, then, the structure of the early colony was heavily influenced by attitudes and institutions inherited from earlier Dutch experience in Europe and the Indies. Some of these, like cultural chauvinism and feelings of religious superiority, were common to all European colonisers and contribute little to understanding the peculiarities of Cape history. Features more specific to Dutch colonies, like the politically weak Reformed Church, a tendency toward individualism and social mobility, and a specific somatic norm, had some influence on social structure over the long run. But most important, the Company's system of legal cleavages, its control of access to power and wealth, its recruitment and immigration policies, all guaranteed a head start to Europeans in the competition for benefits in the new society.

A society in formation, 1652—c. 1720

Though the structure of seventeenth-century Cape society was fairly simple, it was by no means as rigid or stable as it later became. Before c. 1720 there were many unresolved conflicts and ambiguities regarding the shape of future society. The very economic basis of the colony was in dispute. At first the Company wished to create, not an expanding colony, but merely a refreshment station to victual passing ships with fruit and vegetables from its modest garden and with meat bartered from Khoikhoi. When it subsequently decided to entrust part of the settlement's food production to the freeburghers, it was not a foregone conclusion that all these burghers would be Europeans. Three of the most influential figures of the early colony — Van Riebeeck, Van Reede and Simon van der Stel — proposed that agricultural production be partly or even totally turned over to free blacks (ch. 4, p. 145). The Company also stumbled through various systems of landholding (ch. 2, pp. 44—53) and long refused to reconcile itself to new forms of extensive pastoralism developing on the colony's borders. It was not until 1707 that it made the freeburghers the sole suppliers of food to Cape Town and the passing ships; in doing so it tightly circumscribed the opportunity of its own employees to become an entrepreneurial class competing with the free-burghers.

Even more vital was the indecision about the colony's labour force. As late as 1716 the Company was vacillating between two conflicting models of colonial development: assisted immigration of European artisans, agricultural labourers and farmers who would work their own lands, or the continued importation of slave labour. The future of at least the western part of the colony depended on the resolution of this issue. A decision in favour of European labour would make the Western Cape a more self-sufficient European settlement with a large internal market. If the Company opted for slave labour, unskilled and some skilled jobs would become closed to the colonists, leaving service occupations in Cape Town and farming in the rural areas as their only opportunities.

Moreover, there were crucial ambiguities regarding the place of the Khoikhoi in the social structure of the seventeenth-century Cape. For most of this period the Khoikhoi were in transition from being independent aliens to being a labouring class in the colony. Their ambiguous position was reinforced by the policies of the Company, which asserted that the Khoikhoi were a free and independent people but which, as early as 1672, established its authority to try some Khoikhoi under Dutch law. By the turn of the century even relatively strong rulers had been subordinated by the Company and were subject to interference in their daily lives.[18] The legal status of Khoikhoi was now novel. They were no longer independent aliens; nor were they slaves or freeburghers holding land from the Company.

The transitional and ambiguous status of the Khoikhoi was reflected in confusion about their position in the ideal model of society. Individual clergymen and officials held out the hope that Khoikhoi would yet adopt European culture and convert to Christianity, and some tried to treat select Khoikhoi (like Eva, see ch. 4, p. 118) as members of European society. Only gradually were Europeans beginning to perceive them as a labouring class.

True, there were freeburghers who, by the turn of the century, spoke of Khoikhoi in the same breath as slaves, and by 1713 perhaps the majority of the Western Cape Khoikhoi were already on European farms. Yet the Khoikhoi themselves still asserted that they were free men and distanced themselves from slaves: some even re-established themselves as independent herders beyond the colony's borders.

There were also uncertainties with respect to slaves and free blacks. The conditions for manumission were less clear than they would be after 1708 when government approval was needed. The official doctrine of the church was that baptised slaves were entitled to their freedom — as were slave children of European fathers, according to the influential commissioner Van Reede. But most baptised slaves (including those with European fathers) were not in fact freed (ch. 4, pp. 121—22). There was a similar variance between the frequent regulations against miscegenation between Europeans and slaves, and the practice. Moreover, the future position of free blacks in Cape society was still uncertain. Most were poor, but others appeared to be on the way to becoming successful agriculturalists, while the shortage of European women enabled free black women to marry Europeans and acquire wealth and status. However, the legal status of free blacks, unlike their social position, was quite clear: they were in law the equals of European burghers, and there is no evidence of official discrimination against them in the seventeenth century.[19]

Race attitudes were not systematically expressed. Although Europeans frequently expressed disgust at the appearance of Khoikhoi and (less frequently) of slaves (see ch. 3, p. 83), there was no question of lumping all non-Europeans together and castigating them as different and inferior. Moreover, it was often changeable customs rather than biologically determined physical features which drew the Europeans' scorn: most observers were horrified by the 'brutish' smell, apparel and customs of Khoikhoi but not negatively affected by their brown colour.[20] Finally, there was no need for a systematic racial ideology — had one been available — to support the social order. Khoikhoi were 'heathen' and alien. Slaves were slaves. No further justification was needed to rule and exploit them.

In short, the seventeenth-century Cape was a European-dominated society on which the European heritage and the Dutch administrative experience had an important impact. But it was a society in the making. Inherited attitudes and structures could not, without further debate and development, deal with all exigencies of the Cape situation. There were doubts about the future forms of European domination and — should the government opt for massive manumissions or importation of free blacks — even about European domination itself.

Cape society, c. 1720—c. 1820: Underlying forces

By 1720 most of the major conflicts and contradictions had been resolved. In 1717 the government had decided that there would be no more assisted immigration of European families. The labour needs of the Cape were to be met by the continued importation of slaves. The economic base of the colony was to be agriculture. Intensive cultivation had been replaced by extensive arable and stock farming, and almost all farming was in the hands of European burghers. The free blacks had left agriculture and were back in Cape Town. The smallpox epidemic of 1713 had completed the transformation of the sovereign Western Cape Khoikhoi into subordinated colonial 'Hottentots'. The government had tightened up manumission regulations and few blacks were being freed. The Christianization of slaves and Khoikhoi continued to be very slow.

In the eighteenth century certain forces, some of which had been incipient during the seventeenth century, became stronger and stabilised the European-dominated social structure. Particularly important were the economic forces. The Cape economy lacked a staple which could effectively compete on world markets, and the local market was small and controlled by the Company, which compelled colonists to sell most of their produce at artificially low prices. But the productive capacity of the colony was greatly increased by slave imports and by the rapid growth of the European population (largely by internal generation). Moreover, prior to the 1770s the trekboers expanded the land base of the colony more or less steadily, encountering little resistance from the Khoisan, whom they absorbed into their labour force. As the land and labour base grew, so did agriculture; consequently in the eighteenth century the colony constantly faced overproduction (ch. 5, pp. 204—05).

The comparatively steady and easy growth of the colony was one reason for the extreme simplicity of its economy. There was no internal stimulus for diversification in an economy which continued to expand without it. Another reason was that the Company, guided by its mercantilist assumptions, did not encourage industry in the colony. The freeburghers in Cape Town engaged in commerce (including smuggling) and the provision of services (mostly accommodation). But outside Cape Town there was little commerce, little building, no mining, and no professional military establishment. In the interior almost all freeburghers farmed, either as independent landholders, or as dependants or tenants of landholders (ch. 2, p. 62). There were few intermediate positions in the economy — work not suitable for either Europeans or slaves — apart from hauling or farm overseeing. The skilled trades — tasks which in other colonies were often performed by free people of colour — were at the Cape performed by slaves.

The nature of the economy largely determined the labour system. In Cape Town the economy was volatile. Demands for labour ebbed and flowed, slaves were speculative commodities, and manumissions were higher than in the rest of the colony. The agricultural regions, by contrast, required a stable labour supply and, particularly after the drastic decline of the Western Cape Khoikhoi, slaves were in demand. However, the small market inhibited the rise of capitalist farming and the employment of large numbers of slaves on expanded units: roughly a third of the owners of arable farms possessed one to five adult male slaves, a third had six to ten, and another third more than ten (ch. 2, p. 56 and ch. 3, p. 97). In the interior the rapid expansion from c. 1700 to c. 1770 of relatively few trekboers — an expansion which pushed the limits of European settlement 800 km eastward and 400 km northward — made it possible for European families to use land extensively, with unimproved pasture as the basic resource. The large extent of the farms, the low level of technology, and the Europeans' disdain for manual labour in the service of others, created the need for many shepherds and graziers. Here slaves were too expensive for most employers, and Khoikhoi were hired.

Thus the economy outside Cape Town was overwhelmingly agricultural, expanding, undiversified, and labour-intensive. Such economies have often appeared in colonial history. What distinguished the Cape economy was that it developed in the hinterland of a single port controlled by a giant mercantile concern with clear goals and tough methods. More interested in the sea and the ships upon it than in the interior of the Cape, the government intervened only when its narrowly defined interests were threatened. Yet it profoundly affected the stratification of Cape society in terms of its own priorities. As Schutte (ch. 5, p. 175) remarks, these priorities were the logical outcome of the VOC's commercial character. It was interested in empire only as a means to profit and was free to pursue its commercial goals unsupervised by the home government: the Dutch Republic, unlike Iberian powers, lacked a strong central executive.

The Company shaped the Cape population by determining who entered the colony. For example, Cape Town's importance in the Company's global strategy made it the host for countless sailors and soldiers, who fathered many of the town's mixed-bloods. The Company's large employment roster, and its willingness to contract it periodically, caused a constant trickle of poor Europeans to enter the colonial population. It was the Company's regular shipping which made possible the arrival of European immigrants at the Cape, including significant numbers of women; but it was also its lack of support for immigration in the eighteenth century that kept the European population fairly low and with an imbalance between the sexes. It was the Company which discouraged (or failed to encourage) the arrival of free blacks from the East, and thus helped create a society unlike that in its stronghold at Batavia.

Moreover, despite its official policy that legal cleavages were fundamental, the government failed to promote the advancement of non-Europeans, and thereby facilitated the rise of a racial order. It promulgated tough manumission regulations and had no objection to (or perhaps even favoured) a situation in which many more slaves were baptised than were freed. It upheld its traditional policy that Khoikhoi were free men who on no account could be enslaved, but did not defend their property or grant them land in loan from the Company. In fact, it all but abandoned the interior to the colonists by turning over the vast interior districts — both Stellenbosch and Graaff-Reinet were larger than Portugal of today — to *landdrosts* who were assisted by only four or five mounted police, and thus it had to rely on burgher officers *(veldwachtmeesters)* to ensure compliance with its laws. It was not that the government always favoured the colonists: Khoikhoi had access to the courts (ch. 1, p. 18), as did the slaves. Their evidence and complaints against their masters in court were sometimes upheld since the VOC wished to impose its authority on the burghers. Generally, however, the government sided with the owners to control the slaves, and maintained the social hierarchy with officials and freemen at the top, Khoikhoi and slaves at the bottom.[21]

The blurring of racial lines through miscegenation was condemned though not suppressed. In 1786 the Company considered expulsion from the colony as a punishment for 'bad men' who had sexual relations with Khoikhoi and slaves.[22] Despite such racial attitudes among its officials, the Company did not contemplate the construction of a racial order. But it materially contributed to it by the way it determined the composition of the population, maintained the social hierarchy, and failed to erect an administrative framework which could uphold the legal equality of non-Europeans with Europeans. Moreover, it did not diversify the economy in ways which might have given opportunities to free blacks. This non-diversification was not of course entirely due to Company policies, but also to the colony's lack of exportable staples and its location far from potential markets.

As an institutional force the state was much more important than the church, whose social role in the eighteenth century continued to be significant mainly in terms of what it did not accomplish. The church was not an avenue for blacks to reach positions of wealth or prestige; nor was it a countervailing force against the government or the slave-owners. As late as 1790 there were still fewer than ten Reformed ministers, all working for the Company, mainly among the colonists. Members of the church did little mission work in the eighteenth century. A visitor to Cape Town in the 1750s noted: 'The inhabitants have no care for the education of their slaves. No one ever speaks to them of religion, and those born in this country have no idea of it.'[23] The church did not want missionary societies to perform the task it neglected, arguing that independent proselytization would lead to religious schism. But even the missionaries who led evangelisation campaigns in the 1790s, apart from some 'radicals' like Van der Kemp and Read, had no intention of breaking down the racial order:[24] their task was to save souls, thereby providing a spiritual haven in which slaves and Khoikhoi could escape from the hardship and humiliations of everyday life.[25] Thus neither missionaries nor official clergy overrode the impact on social structure of the simple, labour-intensive economy and the commercial concerns of the Cape government.

Cape society, c. 1720—c. 1820: The stabilisation of European dominance

The forces we have described in the previous two sections affected the social structure in many interrelated ways. We will concentrate on three: (1) the continuing predominance of Europeans over non-Europeans, (2) the failure of the middle ranks of society — free blacks and Bastaards — to break down the racial order and (3) the failure of poor Europeans to coalesce with free blacks and Bastaards.

Europeans were numerous enough throughout the eighteenth century to occupy all the key positions in the colony's political, economic and social structure. In the interior the veldwachtmeesters (later field-cornets), who represented the colonists as much as the government, settled the day-to-day disputes between them and their servants, and mobilised commandos. The businessmen, traders and slave-owners in Cape Town, like the landholders and producers in the interior, were, with the exception of the Bastaards on or beyond the colonial borders, almost all European (ch. 8, pp. 322—23). The dominant position of Europeans confirmed and intensified feelings of European superiority. As the daughter of a European man and a Khoikhoi woman told a traveller in the 1780s: 'You know the profound contempt which the whites entertain for the blacks, and even for those of a mixed breed like myself. To settle among them was to expose myself to daily disgrace and affronts.'[26]

But we are faced with a second phenomenon, namely that no non-European group emerged, like the free blacks in nineteenth-century Brazil, who became numerous and powerful enough to break down the simple pattern of European over non-European.[27] We shall consider three such groups: free blacks, i.e., black slaves who through manumission became freemen, chiefly in the southwestern Cape (ch. 4); colonial 'Hottentots', i.e., Khoikhoi who were subject to colonial laws (ch. 1); and baptised Bastaards, i.e., offspring of European fathers and Khoikhoi mothers who, mainly in the trekboer regions, were members of the Christian church and enjoyed most of the privileges of Europeans (chs. 7 and 8).

Let us first consider the free blacks of Cape Town and the southwestern Cape. Two features of their position suggest — at first glance — that Cape society was rather more like nineteenth-century Brazil with its fluid racial pattern than, say, the rigid caste system of the American South. These features were the rather high incidence of miscegenation in Cape Town, and the free blacks' considerable freedom from official discrimination before the mid-eighteenth century. In Brazil, however, a high rate of miscegenation was accompanied by a relatively high incidence of manumission. As a result, the boundary between black and European ceased to correspond exactly to the boundary between slave and free, and in any event lines between races became blurred by the emergence of many intermediate shades. Even though Europeans in Brazil were strongly prejudiced against the colour and culture of blacks, it became possible for mulattos to rise in society and for criteria other than race (especially wealth) to determine status.

In Cape Town, by contrast, the fairly high rates of miscegenation were coupled with rather low rates of manumission. This meant that there were few free blacks. Hence most interracial sex involved *slave* women. The mixed children of such unions inherited the status of their mothers and remained slaves. Furthermore, since at the Cape the fathers of these children were mainly in transit or poor, there was less likelihood of their freeing these children after birth than was frequently the case in other parts of the world. At the same time the free European community was also being 'darkened' through miscegenation — but only very slightly. This happened mainly through interracial *marriages,* which involved *free* black women, since slaves did not, and probably could not, marry.[28] But, as we saw in chapter 4 (p. 130) such marriages were fairly rare.

Thus as long as the majority of blacks were slaves, the legal boundaries of slavery allowed Europeans to propagate a mixed race beneath the line while keeping their own race relatively 'pure'. In effect, miscegenation was largely irrelevant to stratification in South African society.

The second seemingly flexible feature of Cape society — the colour-blind nature of legislation affecting freeburghers — was also insufficient to make the free black community a major economic or political force at the Cape. This failure can be explained in four stages.

(1) Very few members of the community were free when they came to the Cape. Though the Company often discussed importing free black labour, it

never did so to any significant extent. The ready supply of Madagascan slaves made such an effort unnecessary, and in any case the Company may have feared creating a subversive alien population like the Chinese on Java. Hence it did not reproduce the social patterns of Batavia, where the many varieties of free persons of colour (many of whom were not ex-slaves), along with widespread miscegenation, gave rise to a spectrum of racial 'classes', in some respects like that of Brazil.

(2) Consequently almost all recruitment to the free black population had come from the limited ranks of the convicts and from the slave force. Yet, for reasons we will consider shortly, comparatively few slaves were freed. The free black group numbered only 7.4 per cent of the free population in 1670, and only 4.4 per cent in 1770 although it was, of course, more significant than this in Cape Town itself. Of those who were freed, few were children with prominent European fathers who could give them a good education or find them lucrative or prestigious positions.

(3) The small community of free blacks increased more slowly than the European and slave communities, and hence declined as a percentage of the total population.

(4) The free black population briefly expanded into Stellenbosch in the period of the 'open frontier' in the southwestern Cape. But as the frontier 'closed' they retreated to Cape Town, separating themselves from the growing agricultural sector of South African society and sinking, in most cases, into poverty. As a result the small trickle of slaves into the free black community, and the full legal rights accorded them, did little to break down the pattern of European over black, and that only in Cape Town.

The most important of the foregoing points is the second, namely the low rate of manumission. This was due in part to the simple economy of the Cape which, especially in rural areas, created few intermediate positions between landholders and unskilled labourers. It was positions such as these, particularly in handicrafts, transportation and farm overseeing, which were filled by free blacks elsewhere in the world. Furthermore, the Cape did not face such great dangers from other European powers that it needed to free slaves to augment its European militia. Nor was the slave population large enough in relation to Europeans, or sufficiently concentrated in any one place, to threaten a rising *en masse*: thus Europeans were not compelled, as in Brazil, to create a free black force to help them keep control.

The Company knew, then, that there were few positions for freed slaves and feared that easy manumission would lead to a large population of unemployed, destitute free blacks. This was the main reason why it progressively tightened manumission regulations for privately owned slaves, and one reason (along with its needs for labour) why it was reluctant to free its own. As for the freeburghers of the southwestern Cape, we have seen that they, too, needed large numbers of slaves (among whom mortality rates were high) and thus rarely freed them (ch. 4, p. 136). There were other economic disincentives to manumission. For example, the total absence of banks at the Cape until 1793 meant that slaves were a major form of investment: a master was unlikely to sell a slave for Cape rixdollars, whose value declined rapidly during the last two decades of the eighteenth century.

But the low manumission rates, like the low rate of mixed marriages, cannot be explained in economic or demographic terms alone. The values and attitudes of Cape society also played a role. For instance, the Cape church, unlike its Latin American counterpart, did not promote manumission by commending it to the laity as a noble act. Moreover, although there were some Cape colonists who wished to manumit their non-European mistresses and children,[29] few did so. This was perhaps because Cape women, unlike their Brazilian counterparts,[30] enjoyed a strong social role and could evidently prevent their husbands from legitimising the offspring of their extra-marital affairs. This was especially the case in the settled southwestern Cape, where the general prejudices against interracial sex (reflected even in official proclamations in the seventeenth century), combined with favourable European sex ratios, worked against the respectability of concubinage. Thus the keepers of concubines were either wealthy married men who, even if they wished, dared not 'free their mistresses and children, or poorer transitory Europeans who could not afford to do so. From the remarks of the traveller Percival, who visited the Cape at the end of the eighteenth century, one can deduce that many a poor European would have manumitted and married an attractive slave but for the impossible price of 800 to 1,000 rixdollars.[31] For instance, in 1810 William Klomphaan was charged 950 rixdollars — a price equivalent to a farm in Graaff-Reinet — for his slave mistress and their twins. He died after having paid only 600 rixdollars.[32]

We must now discuss a second non-European group in the colony, the 'colonial Hottentots'. After Khoikhoi had become subordinated to colonial rule they were no longer aliens, but neither had they become freeburghers or slaves. Most crucially, they were excluded from the landholding system of the colony. Since they did not own the means of production, and since the government exercised little control in the trekboer regions, Khoikhoi were gradually reduced to a position not far removed from that of slaves. Various devices for keeping Khoikhoi on the farms were informally instituted long before their more formal counterparts (e.g., the pass system and indentureship) were entered into the law books (ch. 1, p. 29, ch. 8, p. 317). Though Khoikhoi were not normally bought or sold like slaves, it was the direction of change that was crucial. Khoikhoi constantly moved downward in status toward the slaves, not upward toward the burghers. As a result the structure of trekboer society was roughly similar to that of the agrarian southwestern Cape: in both cases Europeans were free and most non-Europeans totally or partially unfree.

In trekboer areas, especially in the northwestern Cape, there was considerable miscegenation. Sexual intercourse between Khoikhoi men and slave women seems to have been uncommon; when it did occur the children would of course remain slaves. More important were the so-called Bastaards, most of whom were children of European males and Khoikhoi females, and a few of whom were children of European males and slave females. These were not only free, but also tended to identify vigorously with Dutch culture and considered themselves far superior to the Khoikhoi. Apparently those who had been baptised in a Dutch Reformed (rather than a mission) church were regarded by the government, though perhaps not by many Europeans, as freeburghers. They had Dutch surnames, and sometimes appeared along with Europeans as taxpayers on the *opgaaf* rolls. A few of them held loan farms from the Company and sometimes kept other Bastaards as tenants. A few others moved into intermediate occupations in the economy, as supervisors on European farms or as wagon drivers.

The baptised Bastaards, like the free blacks, failed to break down the pattern of European domination over non-Europeans. The reasons in each case were roughly the same. Firstly, the Bastaards were too small a group to cause a major breakdown in the traditional cleavage between European and non-European. In 1798 there were only 136 baptised Bastaards on the Graaff-Reinet rolls compared to 4,262 Europeans, 8,947 Khoikhoi and 964 slaves. Some Graaff-Reinet Bastaards owned considerable livestock but in general held no land. Secondly, the economy provided relatively few intermediate jobs for them to fill. And thirdly, the degree of upward mobility offered by the 'open' frontier was soon lost as the frontier began to close: a shortage of land restricted opportunities for all groups, but chiefly for the Bastaards who found themselves squeezed out into new regions where the frontier was still open. Their outward trek was analogous to the retreat of free blacks from Stellenbosch to Cape Town almost a century earlier: it was not the first — or the last — time in South African history that non-Europeans were pushed out of a growing sector of the economy.

Thus the free blacks of the Western Cape and the baptised Bastaards in trekboer regions found themselves ambiguously positioned between the Europeans in the top tier of society and the slaves and Khoikhoi in the lowest tier. Both groups in the middle category were small and localised. Their members were, with few exceptions, poor, and their social position tended to decline during the course of the eighteenth century. However, in all regions there were many Europeans who were just as poor and powerless. In 1732 Governor de la Fontaine listed fifty-five 'poor, indigent, decrepit' European freeburghers and fifty-four free blacks in the Cape district (ch. 5, p. 189). In Cape Town sailors, soldiers, artisans and labourers, free blacks and some slaves frequented the same lower-class taverns.[33] In trekboer regions there was, in terms of landholding and wealth, little difference between the poor European *knechts* and ex-Company servants on the one hand, and the baptised Bastaards on the other. In certain periods the Company bracketed free blacks and white knechts together on its rolls.

Against this background we must discuss the third phenomenon: that despite their similar legal and economic positions, poor Europeans, free blacks and Bastaards did not coalesce into a selfconscious class. Let us look at this problem first from the perspective of the poorer whites. Since slaves were well distributed among the colonists — by 1750 almost half the free male population had at least one slave (ch. 3, p. 98) — the effects of slavery permeated deeply. Moreover, the status even of a European too poor to own a slave was bolstered by a proclamation that 'no slave might jostle or otherwise behave in an ill-disposed way [qualyk te bejeegenen] towards a European even if he was of the meanest rank.'[34] In 1743 Van Imhoff remarked:

[Having] imported slaves every common or ordinary European becomes a gentleman and prefers to be served than to serve . . . The majority of the farmers in this Colony are not farmers in the real sense of the word . . . and many of them consider it a shame to work with their own hands.[35]

Furthermore, poor Europeans, free blacks and Bastaards competed for the same jobs, and in this competition the advantage of being European seems to have been crucial. In both psychological and material terms a racial order was beneficial to the poor Europeans.

On their side, too, wealthier Europeans apparently favoured the stratification of society along the lines of race rather than class. For example, in choosing marriage partners and social equals they clearly preferred landless Europeans to Bastaards, free blacks or Khoikhoi. They made a similar decision in choosing tenant farmers, even though non-Europeans would almost certainly be more docile than Europeans. Underpinning this trend were the racial attitudes of the slave- and landholding Europeans, which had been intensified by generations of oppression. Boxer has observed in the context of Brazilian slavery: 'One race cannot systematically enslave members of another race for over three centuries without acquiring a conscious or unconscious feeling of racial superiority.[36]

But the prejudices of the wealthy also had another dimension: the threat the poor might pose to their interests. Wealthy burghers dreaded the rise of an armed and rebellious class of poor freemen of mixed racial origin, who could threaten their very existence. This attitude was expressed as early as 1706 by leading farmers of Stellenbosch when they informed the *Heren XVII* that they feared the

> Kaffirs, Mulattoes, Mestiços, Castiços, and all that black brood living among us, who have been bred from marriages and other forms of mingling with European and African Christians [i.e., colonists born in Europe and at the Cape]. To our amazement they have so grown in power, numbers and arrogance, and have been allowed to handle arms and participate with Christians in . . . military exercises, that they now tell us that they could and would trample on us . . . For there is no trusting the blood of Ham, especially as the black people are constantly being favoured and pushed forward.[37]

It was in the interest of the wealthy to forestall any alliance of blacks and poor Europeans, though it is not yet clear that this consideration consciously affected their actions.

The racial feelings of the wealthy manifested themselves in a disapproval of miscegenation, especially in the intense repugnance which 'respectable people' felt for those colonists who lived like, and with, Khoikhoi and Xhosa (ch. 4, p. 157; ch. 9, p. 350). In the 1780s some leading Western Cape farmers referred to 'those who miscegenate with Hottentots and Kaffirs' and warned of 'a bastardisation of morals' and the 'rise of a completely degenerate Nation which might become just as dangerous for the colony as the Bushmen-Hottentots are.'[38]

However, it would not have been so easy to establish a racial coalescence and norms against miscegenation if the eighteenth century had not offered Europeans great social and economic mobility. In the Western Cape there was a small elite consisting of top government officials, merchants and large farmers who employed European foremen and owned many slaves; but no true aristocracy developed. Moreover, the rapid extension of the limits of the settlement from 1700 to 1770 brought into being a trekboer society which remained egalitarian as long as land was cheap and the market for produce poor. Only after the frontier had started to close late in the eighteenth century (ch. 8, p. 322) did considerable inequalities of wealth appear among trekboers. And even in circumstances in which every European male could not possibly have his own farm, the landless still seem to have believed that they could acquire farms beyond the colonial borders and rise socially and economically. All this made for European solidarity and egalitarianism.¶ Whereas at the beginning of the eighteenth century top

¶ The egalitarian, family-centred European society of the Cape has been explained by viewing the Cape colonists as a 'fragment' of the seventeenth-century Dutch bourgeoisie which had become immobilised because of its isolation from the European whole. See Louis Hartz, *The*

Company servants and freeburghers were intensely conscious of status gradations in the European community (ch. 5, pp. 191–92), the opportunities created by Company land policy and the expanding frontier gradually produced an acceptance of the fundamental social equality of Europeans despite some gradations of wealth. Thus W.S. van Ryneveld, a high government official, remarked in 1805, 'Among the true [eigenlijke] inhabitants of this colony there is no real distinction of ranks among the white population.'[39] During the 1820s the traveller George Thompson observed that there was little or no gradation among the Europeans: 'Every man is a burgher by rank, and a farmer by occupation.'[40]

In short, then, the simplicity of the Cape economy, the rapid expansion of the colony between 1700 and 1770, and the tradition of social mobility among settlers, combined to make Europeans see other Europeans as their equals and non-Europeans as their inferiors.

The colony in crisis, c. 1770–1820

The trends discussed so far operated over the long term. But between 1770 and 1820 many of them were intensified by a crisis in the colony in which the racial order of domination was first challenged, then reaffirmed and rigidified. The crisis sprang from accelerated economic development and a new shortage of both labour and land.

From the late 1770s the Cape economy gradually shed its fetters and became freer and more vigorous. Wars in North America and Europe brought ships and garrisons to the strategic outpost, stimulating investment and agricultural production. Wheat crops increased by more than 50 per cent between 1798 and 1820,[41] while wine production doubled between 1795 and 1804.[42] The British conquests of 1795 and 1806 incorporated the Cape into the British imperial system which, as Freund remarks, was much larger and more dynamic than that of the VOC. Exports rose from 180,000 rixdollars in 1807 to 1,320,000 rixdollars in 1815 (ch. 6, p. 216).

Farmers faced a shortage of slave labour. No slaves were imported between

---

Founding of New Societies (New York, 1964). This theory has recently been challenged by R. Cole Harris and Leonard Guelke, who have shown that colonial society both in New France and at the Cape, despite being very different fragments from different European heritages, remained unstratified and egalitarian as long as land was cheap and the market for produce poor. Only when the frontier 'closed' did society become diversified and controls by the government and the wealthy become effective. See R. Cole Harris and Leonard Guelke, 'Land and Society in early Canada and South Africa', *Journal of Historical Geography,* III (1977), pp. 135–53.

1787 and 1795, and slaves entering the colony between 1795 and 1808 were mostly bought by Capetonians to be hired out as tradesmen. As a result of the dwindling supply, the price of slaves quadrupled between 1784 and 1804.[43] In 1808 the slave trade to the Cape was abolished and owners increasingly feared for the security of their property. The assault on slave labour made landholders realise that Khoikhoi and Xhosa labour had to be harnessed more effectively.

In the interior there was a crisis not only in labour, but also in land. From 1700 to 1779 land resources in the colony had been virtually unlimited. This period ended in about 1780 when expansion was halted in the northeast by 'Bushman' hunters and in the southeast by Xhosa. For the next two decades no significant expansion occurred, and by 1800 no suitable land remained for new farms within the limits of the colony.[44] Thus Europeans sought out open spots between existing farms and pushed Khoikhoi and Bastaards out. Lichtenstein described this process during the first decade of the nineteenth century:

> Many Hottentot families . . . had established themselves in the Lower Bokkeveld, when the increasing population of the colony occasioned new researches to be made after lands capable of cultivation, and the white children of the colonists did not hesitate to make use of the right of the strongest, and to drive their half yellow relations out of the places where they had fixed their abodes. These Bastaard Hottentots were then obliged to seek an asylum in more remote parts.[45]

By the end of the eighteenth century many Bastaards, *Oorlams* and Khoikhoi, who had been forced off the land and compelled to work and fight for Europeans, trekked from Little Namaqualand to the Middle Orange (ch. 7, p. 260). But some resisted. Trekboer expansion was stalled in the 1780s not only by 'Bushman' hunters and Xhosa, but also by persons fully or partially of Khoikhoi descent who had formerly worked in the colony.

Even Khoikhoi labourers and slaves in the colony were increasingly insubordinate. In the western part of the colony rumours circulated that the Khoikhoi were conspiring to murder all colonists. Bastaards of Khoikhoi-black descent were in the vanguard of this resistance. As an official remarked: 'The true Hottentots are still governable whereas those who have interbred with slaves call the tune and pay no heed to any authority and even less to any kind of order.'[46]

As the century closed, the eastern part of the colony was also experiencing a crisis in master-servant relationships. Some Khoikhoi, finding themselves hemmed in between the Xhosa and the trekboers, tried to escape the constraints of colonial society. They found a leader in Klaas Stuurman who vowed to end their 'enslavement'. Trekboers of Sneeuwberg and Bruintjes Hoogte had to coax or cajole servants of other colonists to settle on their farms and protect their cattle against roving 'Bushmen' and Xhosa.

Meanwhile in the southwestern Cape, where the ratio of male slaves to male freeburghers had risen sharply, slave-owners were sure that the slaves hated them and were preparing for an insurrection. At this time the institution of slavery was under fire both in conservative Britain and on the revolutionary Continent. Talk of emancipation inspired some slaves at the Cape to hold meetings 'to decide upon the fate of the free and independent burghers, when the happy days of their own emancipation should arrive.'[47]

After 1795 the British government, stronger than its VOC predecessor, added to the colonists' anxieties by asserting that the Khoikhoi were a free people entitled to equal protection from the courts. The 1790s also saw the arrival of the radical LMS missionaries Van der Kemp and Read, who insisted that 'the Hottentots should be perfectly free, upon an equal footing in every respect with the Colonists, and by no sort of compulsion brought under a necessity to enter into their service.'[48]

These threats to the racial order and to the labour supply intensified sentiments, present in the colony from the beginning, that blacks, Khoikhoi and Xhosa were intrinsically inferior to the colonists. After returning from a visit to the interior in 1780, Governor van Plettenberg remarked that 'it would take more than human efforts to induce the colonists at large to accept Caffres as their fellow Christians, fellow men and brethren; the word heathen seems to be the device with which men in an unrestrained way like to give rein to their thirst for revenge and greed.'[49] Some twenty years later Governor Janssens observed on a visit to the frontier that the colonists called 'themselves men and Christians, and the Kafirs and Hottentots heathens, and on the strength of this consider[ed] themselves entitled to anything.'[50] In the southwestern Cape one traveller encountered the opinion that the Khoikhoi 'in understanding and the powers of the mind . . . scarcely deserve to be ranked with human creatures; and are but little above the level of the brute creation.'[51] Another commented on the prevailing notion in Cape Town that nature had drawn a fixed line between white and black and had destined the latter to be subservient for all time.[52]

Europeans reacted in a similar way when confronted with the government's policy of legal protection for the Khoikhoi. Landdrost Alberti of Graaff-Reinet reported in 1803 that it was impossible to persuade the colonists that a judge could draw no distinction between them and Khoikhoi since, in their view, 'a heathen was not actually human, although he could not be classified with the animals either.'[53] In 1797 the *landdrost* and *heemraden* of Stellenbosch objected when a Khoikhoi summoned his European employer before them. They doubted whether he had the legal right to do so and pointed out that 'such practice would create the impression that a Hottentot was the equal of a burgher.'[54]

In this period we also find the traditional hostility to miscegenation. But now it seemed more rampant and was more often extended to interracial marriages and to mixed offspring born from wedlock. Cape Town, it is true, remained more casual in its attitudes; but even here Lady Anne Barnard recorded that Cape Town Europeans snubbed Catherina van den Berg, the wife of an English officer, because her grandmother was a slave.[55] In rural areas the prejudice was more severe. In the 1770s Sparrman noted that 'a great many of the whites have so much pride, as to hinder, as far as lies in their power, the blacks or their offspring from mixing with their blood.'[56] The missionary Campbell encountered a European man at the Orange River who had fled the colony, ostracised for seeking to marry a black. A field-cornet reportedly 'lost caste from associating with his own children by a Hottentot woman.'[57] And in 1809 an officer of the South African Missionary Society, concerned about the interracial marriages of Van der Kemp and other missionaries, commented that to take a 'black Hottentot is a great scandal among the people here and even the coloured people themselves.'[58]

Increasing tension between Europeans and persons of mixed blood was evident in disputes concerning the militia. In 1780 two burghers of Swellendam refused to let their sons do commando duty since they were considered 'Bastaards' and discriminated against while performing their military duties.[59] During a drill at Stellenbosch in 1788 some burghers refused to serve under their newly appointed corporal, Johannes Hartogh, because 'he was of a blackish colour and of heathen descent.'[60] In the previous year the so-called Free Corps had been formed in the Cape district as a separate unit for 'bastaards and mistiches' (i.e., mixed bloods).[61] It was intended for non-Europeans who were illegitimate but free as well as for children of manumitted slaves. The Free Corps ranked below the regular burgher companies, but above service in the fire brigade and in public works which were compulsory for free blacks. In 1790 Jan Smook, the husband of a manumitted slave, was ordered by a militia officer to enrol his son in the Free Corps. He refused, claiming that his son did not belong to the category for whom the corps had been instituted. He was especially indignant because other young men with black blood — Van Oudtshoorn, Oppel and Voges — were admitted to the (European) militia companies.[62]

There is also evidence of increasing discrimination in the church. As early as 1761 the Zwartland Church had a separate section of the baptismal records for Bastaards and Khoikhoi; and after 1770 the Cape Town church had the same for slaves. The evangelisation campaign of the 1790s, while actively supported by some colonists in the west, encountered stiff resistance from Europeans elsewhere who feared that the mission stations would draw Khoikhoi from the farms and imbue the slaves with notions of equality and rebellion.[63] There was an uproar in Graaff-Reinet when Van der Kemp allowed Khoikhoi into the Reformed Church. He noted that the Graaff-Reinet rebels complained that the 'government protected the Hottentots and Caffres . . . [and] that they were instructed by us in reading, writing and religion, and thereby put upon an equal footing with the Christians.'[64]

Finally, in this period the colonial government, which up to this time had maintained the theoretical equality of all persons except slaves, introduced restrictions on the freedom of Khoikhoi and free blacks. Though it continued to regard the Khoikhoi as freemen who could not be enslaved, the government's chief concerns were to maintain order and encourage production. To attain these goals it controlled the movements of Khoikhoi and forced them to work, thus ensuring full employment and eliminating thefts. In 1787 it decreed that vagrant Khoikhoi 'or bastards of these natives' in and about Cape Town be committed to the slave lodge and set to work for two months alongside slaves in government projects.[65] In the same period it connived in the gradual decline of colonial Khoikhoi to a status close to that of slaves. Through an informal extension of the indenture system (ch. 1, p. 29), Khoikhoi children were generally compelled until their twenty-fifth year to serve the master who had apprenticed them; this prompted Lady Anne Barnard to express the hope that the government would 'shorten the time of slavery to these oppressed creatures.'[66]

In 1797 and 1798 local authorities in Swellendam and Graaff-Reinet decided that Khoikhoi, like slaves, had to carry passes when travelling so that burghers and officials could determine that they were not deserters.[67] The practice was confirmed by the colonial government in Caledon's Hottentot Proclamation of 1809. In 1811 W.J. Burchell remarked that 'every slave, or even Hottentot, who is found at a distance from home without a pasbrief, or passport signed by his master or some responsible person is liable to be taken into custody as a runaway or vagabond . . . It seems hardly fair to place a freeman, as the Hottentot is said to be, under the same restraint [as slaves].'[68] Another observer commented that the Khoikhoi were not treated as favourably as the meanest of slaves.[69]

The first legislative discrimination against free blacks appears to have been in minor proclamations of 1765 and 1771 (ch. 4, p. 146). The documents of subsequent years yield evidence of more serious restrictions. In 1801 the government gave notice in Cape Town that, on account of recent robberies, the military guards and police officers 'have strict orders to apprehend and to commit to prison agreeable to the existing regulations of this Colony all slaves or people of colour who shall be found in any of the streets after nine o'clock at night, without having lighted lanthorns.'[70] In 1816 Governor Lord Charles Somerset found it necessary to make the registration of slaves compulsory in order to prevent manumitted slaves, prize Negroes and their offspring from 'merging into a state of slavery, or being confounded with the domestic or other slaves.'[71] The second clause of Ordinance 50, which in 1828 made Khoikhoi and free blacks equal with Europeans before the law, explained that by 'usage and custom of this Colony, Hottentots and other free persons of colour have been subjected to certain restraints as to their residence, mode of life, and employment, and to certain compulsory services to which others of His Majesty's subjects are not liable.'[72]

These views and discriminatory acts reflect, on the one hand, the material interests of the dominant class. On the other hand, they represent a consciousness of racial and cultural differences which helped to shape and support the social structure. Some of the statements we have listed relate merely to the status distinctions between freemen and slaves; others stress the cultural inferiority of 'heathens'; still others simply emphasise colour. There are also indications of a new scheme of racial thinking which — going beyond mere aversion to culture or physical type — focused on the inferior ancestry of non-European peoples. Thus the Court of Justice, opposing the abolition of judicial torture of slaves, argued in 1796 that many of the slaves 'are descended from wild and rude nations, who hardly consider the privation of life as a punishment, unless accompanied by such cruel circumstances as [would] greatly aggravate their sufferings.'[73] As George Fredrickson has noted of the development of slavery in Virginia: 'The concept of heathen ancestry was a giant step toward making racial differences the foundation of servitude.'[74]

Racial prejudice and official discrimination against non-Europeans undoubtedly increased during the eighteenth century. However, we cannot agree with MacCrone's theory that the frontier, particularly the Eastern Frontier, was primarily responsible. MacCrone failed to explain how those in the economically and culturally backward parts of the colony could export their prejudices and practices to the dominant core. Moreover, our evidence of these phenomena comes almost equally from the pastoral regions on the frontier and from the southwestern Cape.

This does not mean that there were no regional differences. Cape Town had a relatively high incidence of miscegenation. The settled southwestern Cape, with few transients and a comparatively low sexual imbalance in its European population, appears to have been more rigid in its racial views and disapproval of concubinage. In the trekboer regions one finds fluidity on the open frontier, as Europeans sometimes had to cloak their prejudices in order to establish military alliances and patron-client relationships across racial lines. On the closing frontier, by contrast, an increasingly rigid racial order emerged. However, despite these differences, Europeans in the colony generally shared certain views about a proper social order. Rooted in the European heritage, these views had been reinforced and strengthened by the economic, demographic and institutional forces operating in the colony since its founding.

Conclusion

In the first decade of the Cape Colony's history almost all positions of power and wealth in colonial society had been held by persons who were both European and free; all the unfree were non-European. At that time race and legal status coincided and reinforced each other. But by 1820 race and legal status no longer coincided exactly because of the emergence of the free blacks and baptised Bastaards, who were free but non-European. There was now no confusion about which of the two criteria was more important for socio-economic advance. To enjoy status, wealth and power in colonial society one had to be European; to be free was not enough.

At the pinnacle of society were those Europeans who controlled land and labour and held political power. At the bottom were the servile, unfree people — including by now Khoikhoi as well as slaves — who were wholly or partly non-European. Between these two was a third category of Europeans and non-Europeans who were free but generally poor. This category was sharply split along racial lines. Europeans, especially the tenant farmers in the interior, identified strongly with the dominant Europeans against non-Europeans. On the other hand, the non-Europeans of this category generally failed to obtain land, progressively lost their freedom and dignity or, as in the case of some Bastaards and Khoikhoi (ch. 7, p. 257), left the colony.

It has recently been argued that pre-industrial colonial society was not primarily based on racial distinctions; that the line between European and black was vaguely drawn and was frequently crossed through intermarriage; and that, while racial lines seemed most blurred at the outer edges of the colony, the urban environment of Cape Town also favoured social fluidity: 'Above all, money whitened.'[75] This interpretation is a useful reminder that in 1820 Cape society was not as rigid, nor were its members as systematically categorised, as in modern apartheid society. Europeans and non-Europeans lived in close contact, especially in Cape Town. Some 8 per cent of the pupils who in 1779 attended the (integrated) Cape Town public schools were slave children. Also in Cape Town, marriage or stable liaisons between European men (particularly demobilised soldiers) and non-European women were not exceptional; and 'passing for white' on an individual level was possible for some fair-skinned girls of mixed ancestry. Moreover, it is doubtful if even in the interior colonists considered all categories of non-Europeans as black and therefore racially inferior. There were too many different status groups among those who were not European to consider them as one racial block (ch. 8, pp. 323—25). Indeed, it would take quite some time before a rigid division between European ('white') and non-European ('black') came about and the concept of race in its modern sense was generally imposed and accepted.[76]

But this interpretation should not be taken so far as to ignore the evidence for increasing official and unofficial racial discrimination which we have presented. The prevailing trend among Europeans was to stigmatise people born out of mixed liaisons as black and to oppose their rare nomination to office. This happened even in the case of J.A. Vermaak who, genealogically speaking, was a quarter non-European and prominent enough to be nominated by the Batavians to the *Raad der Gemeente* (the former Burgher Senate).[77] European fathers were generally unable or unwilling to ensure that their mixed children were accepted in European society. Neither baptism, marriage nor wealth could by themselves negate the unfavourable social evaluation of race which, as we noted in the beginning, consisted of perceptions of all of origin, culture and physical type. This is illustrated by the Bastaards who, despite their partly European culture and appearance and their modest wealth, were rejected by Europeans as social structures hardened on the closing frontier. The same fate would overtake their descendants and successors, the Griqua — a richer and more Christianized group — when their frontier closed in the 1850s. According to Robert Ross, colonial opinion towards the Griqua was correctly described by a British military officer who noted that although the Griqua ' is just as white in many cases as the darker Boer and quite as much civilized, yet he must be classed among the blacks and have no right to the land.'[78]

Emerging racial attitudes and stratification on racial lines were shaped both by the European heritage and the economic, demographic and institutional forces operating in the colony. No single 'factor' can be isolated as most important. For instance, without the European's chauvinism toward different physical types and cultures there would not have been the relatively low rates of mixed marriages; but without favourable sex ratios the European community would not have been able to maintain its fairly rigid endogamy while replacing itself and growing in each generation.

Between 1652 and 1820 the colonists had sufficient power to impose and maintain a racial order which differed from the Company's initial commitment to structure society along lines of slave and free. The colonists' access to superior European technology, their control over capital and land, their constantly growing numbers, their security as producers protected by the central government, their favoured access to political power in the interior — all these constituted their power. However, they did not generate their own labour force or command enough power to control or sweep away their first formidable adversaries, the Xhosa (ch. 8, pp. 308–16). In these two respects they remained vulnerable.

A crucial development was the coming of the British. The new rulers, though they were more concerned about legal inequality and injustice to non-Europeans, propped up the racial order more effectively than the weak old Company could ever have done. They provided leadership and support to the commandos which in 1812 forced the Xhosa to retreat beyond the colonial boundary. They were also much more efficient than the Company in policing the free labourers and slaves. In doing this the British wished not only to uphold the existing social order, but also to guarantee sufficient labour to sustain the accelerated economic development of the Cape, begun in the 1780s.

Thus between 1652 and 1820 there developed in South Africa a racial structure of domination and shared convictions among Europeans of the 'proper order' of society. These were crucial developments. The Voortrekkers would take these institutions and convictions with them and would try to use them in structuring their relations with the Bantu-speaking peoples of Natal, the Orange Free State and the Transvaal. And although the subsequent industrialisation of South Africa would bring forms of labour which were more systematic, formal and impersonal, these were adapted to a racial order which had been shaped during the first 170 years of European settlement.

Chapter Ten   Notes

1. For approximately a further 5 per cent, one of the grandparents was of unknown (but not necessarily non-European) descent. The sample of 1,063 consisted of children whose descendants can be traced to the present and are now designated as white. In the baptismal records there are a total of 1,128 names of children with both parents' names recorded. These children, together with their parents, represented roughly 15 per cent of the 'Christian' population of 1807: G.F.C. de Bruyn, 'Die Samestelling van die Afrikaner', *Tydskrif vir Geesteswetenskappe*, XVI (1976), and personal communication on subsequent research; J.A. Heese, *Die Herkoms van die Afrikaner, 1652–1867* (Cape Town, 1971).
2. Figures for the Company period are based on the annual opgaafs. The number of free blacks has been subtracted from the total figures for freeburghers. On identifying free blacks, see chapter 4, pp. 148 & 167 *n* 100. For 1798 the figure

for the first column was calculated by subtracting from Barrow's totals for 'free people of colour and servants'. The figure for the second column is only a rough indication: probably as much as half of the exact total of 1767 were European servants. Much more accurate census-taking in 1798 is mainly responsible for the sharp rise in the totals since 1770. The heading of column one in the 1820 census reads only 'Christians' and probably includes all freemen other than free blacks, who are listed separately. See J. Barrow, *Travels into the Interior of South Africa* (London, 1806), II, 23, 67, 73, 82—83; *RCC,* XII, 354.

3. I.D. MacCrone, *Race Attitudes in South Africa* (London, 1937), pp. 1—136. MacCrone also published a popular version of his theory in 'The Frontier Tradition and Race Attitudes', *Race Relations Journal,* XXVIII (1961), pp. 19—30.

4. For a recent statement of this position, see Sheila Patterson, 'Some Speculations on the Status and Role of the Free People of Colour in the Western Cape', *Studies in African Social Anthropology,* ed. M. Fortes and S. Patterson (London, 1975), pp. 160—205.

5. For interpretations which stress material factors, see Martin Legassick, 'The Frontier Tradition in South African Historiography', *Collected Seminar Papers on the Societies of Southern Africa* (Institute of Commonwealth Studies, 1976), II, 1—32; W.M. Freund, 'Race in the Social Structure of South Africa, 1652-1836', *Race and Class,* XVIII (1976), pp. 53–67.

6. Winthrop D. Jordan, *White over Black: American Attitudes toward the Negro, 1550—1812* (Chapel Hill, 1968), pp. 40—43; George P. Rawick *The American Slave: A Composite Autobiography* (Westport, 1972), I, 125—53. Eugene D. Genovese, *The World the Slaveholders Made* (New York, 1971), pp. 103—13; George M. Fredrickson, 'Toward a Social Interpretation of the Development of American Racism', *Key Issues in the Afro-American Experience,* ed. Nathan G. Huggins *et al.* (New York, 1971), I, 249—51.

7. H. Hoetink, *Caribbean Race Relations: A Study of Two Variants* (Oxford, 1967), and H. Hoetink, *Slavery and Race Relations in the Americas* (New York, 1973).

8. D.B. Davies, *The Problem of Slavery in Western Culture* (Ithaca, 1966), pp. 275—78.

9. Donald Moodie, *The Record* (Cape Town and Amsterdam, 1960), p. 250.

10. C.R. Boxer, *The Dutch Seaborne Empire* (London, 1965), p. 233.

11. Patterson, 'Free People of Colour', p. 199. See also J.J. Loubser, 'Calvinism, Equality and Inclusion: The Case of Afrikaner Calvinism', *The Protestant Ethic and Modernisation,* ed. S.N. Eisenstadt (London, 1969), pp. 367—83.

12. F.A. van Jaarsveld, *From Van Riebeeck to Vorster, 1652—1974* (Johannesburg, 1975), pp. 37—38.

13. See for instance the comparative observations of Hoetink, *Caribbean Race Relations,* pp. 21, 49, 173—74.

14. François Valentyn, *Description of the Cape of Good Hope . . .* (Cape Town, 1973), II, 259.

15. Eugene D. Genovese, *Roll, Jordan, Roll: The World the Slaves Made* (London, 1975), p. 179; Frank Tannenbaum, *Slave and Citizen: The Negro in the Americas* (New York, 1946), pp. 62—65. For a brief summary of the debate on Tannenbaum's argument that the institutions of Latin America account for the differences between slavery in North and South America, see Carl N. Degler,

Neither Black nor White: Slavery and Race Relations in Brazil and the United States (New York, 1971), pp. 19—21.

16. George McCall Theal, *History of South Africa under the Administration of the Dutch East India Company [1652 to 1795]* (London, 1897), I, 421.

17. Boxer, *Dutch Seaborne Empire*, pp. 137—38.

18. Richard Elphick, *Kraal and Castle: Khoikhoi and the Founding of White South Africa* (New Haven and London, 1977), pp. 188—92.

19. For a fuller discussion, see A.J. Böeseken, 'Die Verhouding tussen Blank en Nie-Blank in Suid-Afrika aan die hand van die vroegste dokumente', *South African Historical Journal*, II (1970), pp. 3—18.

20. Elphick, *Kraal and Castle*, pp. 196—97.

21. Robert Ross, 'The Rule of Law at the Cape of Good Hope in the Eighteenth Century' (unpublished paper, 1977).

22. C 79, Res 19 April 1786, pp. 424—26.

23. N.L. de la Caille, *Travels at the Cape, 1751—1753* (Cape Town, 1976), p. 35.

24. Some Khoikhoi, however, expected equalisation to result from conversion: a Khoikhoi was excluded from the congregation at Baviaanskloof because she boasted, while under the influence of liquor, that her baptism had made her an equal of the colonists. See Bernhard Krüger, *The Pear Tree Blossoms* (Genadendal, 1966), p. 59.

25. The Rev. M.C. Vos consoled himself with the thought that, although the slaves were excluded from Communion, they would one day sit in the Kingdom of Heaven: M.C. Vos, *Merkwaardig Verhaal aangaande het Leven en de Lotgevallen van Michiel Christiaan Vos* (Cape Town, 1911), p. 138.

26. F. le Vaillant, *New Travels into the Interior Parts of Africa by way of the Cape of Good Hope in the Years 1783, 1784, and 1785* (London, 1976), II, 49—50.

27. In Brazil by 1800 the free coloured accounted for roughly a quarter to a third of the total 'coloured' population, by 1850 for a half, and by 1872 for three-quarters: Herbert S. Klein, 'Nineteenth Century Brazil', *Neither Slave Nor Free: The Freedman of American Descent in the Slave Societies of the New World*, ed. David W. Cohen and Jack P. Greene (Baltimore, 1972), pp. 312—16. In 1798 and 1820 free blacks at the Cape accounted for little more than 5 per cent of the total free black and slave population. In the U.S.A. it was 11 per cent in 1860. See also Davies, *Problem of Slavery*, pp. 283—84. Davies adds that some internal pressure was supplemented in the late eighteenth century by enlightened reforms of the Portuguese crown.

28. Robert Ross, 'Sexuality and Slavery at the Cape in the Eighteenth Century', *Collected Seminar Papers on the Societies of Southern Africa* (Institute of Commonwealth Studies, 1977), VIII, p. 22 and fn. 12.

29. J. Hoge, 'Miscegenation in South Africa in the Seventeenth and Eighteenth Centuries', *New Light on Afrikaans and 'Malayo-Portuguese'*, ed. Marius F. Valkhoff (Louvain, 1972), pp. 99—118.

30. Degler, *Neither Black nor White*, pp. 232—39.

31. R. Percival, *An Account of the Cape of Good Hope* (London, 1804), pp. 286—92.

32. CJ 2558, Supplication of Led, 14 April 1814, pp. 444—46.

33. O.F. Mentzel, *A Geographical and Topographical Description of the Cape of Good Hope* (Cape Town, 1925), II, 86.

34. *KP*, IV, Proclamation, 20 Aug. 1794, p. 249.

35. *The Reports of Chavonnes and his Council, and of Van Imhoff on the Cape* (Cape Town, 1918), p. 137.
36. C.R. Boxer, *Race Relations in the Portuguese Colonial Empire* (Oxford, 1963), p. 56.
37. KA 4035, Adam Tas *et al.* — XVII, n.d., p. 1035v.
38. C 316, Memorial of J.M. Cruywagen and 14 other inhabitants — Governor and Council of Policy, 17 Feb. 1784.
39. W.S. van Ryneveld, 'Schets van den Staat der Kolonie in 1805', *Het Nederduitsch Zuid-Afrikaansch Tydschrift*, VIII (1831), p. 124.
40. George Thompson, *Travels and Adventures in Southern Africa* (London, 1827), p. 324. See also W. von Meyer, who stated that there were no other distinctions or ranks in Cape society but those indicated by the colour of the skin: *Reisen in Süd-Afrika während der Jahren 1840 und 1841* (Hamburg, 1843), p. 82.
41. D.J. van Zyl, 'Die Geskiedenis van Graanbou aan die Kaap, 1795—1826', *AYB*, (1968), I, 178.
42. D.J. van Zyl, *Kaapse Wyn en Brandewyn, 1795—1860* (Cape Town, 1975), p. 10.
43. Van Ryneveld, 'Schets', p. 196.
44. P.J. van der Merwe, *Trek* (Cape Town, 1945), p. 86.
45. H. Lichtenstein, *Travels in Southern Africa in the Years 1803, 1804, 1805 and 1806* (Cape Town, 1930), II, 303—04. For a succinct analysis of the processes by which the European ruling class established their dominance in South Africa over non-Europeans, see Robert Ross, *Adam Kok's Griquas* (Cambridge, 1976), pp. 1—11, 134—38.
46. Hermann Giliomee, *Die Kaap tydens die Eerste Britse Bewind 1795—1803* (Cape Town, 1975), p. 21.
47. Barrow, *Travels*, II, 163.
48. *Transactions of the Missionary Society* (London, 1804), I, 494.
49. AR, Swellengrebel Archives, Van Plettenberg—Swellengrebel, 12 May 1770.
50. *Belangrijke Historische Dokumenten over Zuid-Afrika*, ed. George McCall Theal (Cape Town, 1911), III, 219.
51. Percival, *Account*, p. 92.
52. Cited by Michael Streak, *The Afrikaner as viewed by the English* (Cape Town, 1974), p. 20.
53. BR 68, Alberti—Janssens, 12 June 1805, pp. 280—81.
54. BO 50, Landdrost and Heemraden – Craig, 5 Feb. 1797, no. 33.
55. *The Letters of Lady Anne Barnard to Henry Dundas*, ed. A.M. Lewin Robinson (Cape Town, 1973), p. 174.
56. Anders Sparrman, *A Voyage to the Cape of Good Hope . . . from the Years 1772—1776* (Cape Town, 1975), I, 264.
57. Cited by Freund, 'Race in the Social Structure', p. 60.
58. LMS papers on South Africa, Box 4, Pacalt—Hardcastle, 18 Sept. 1809.
59. Moodie Afschriften: Extract Dagregister of Landdrost and Heemraden and Militia Officers, Swellendam, 16 June 1780. Significantly only Zeelie was ordered by the district authorities to enroll his son.
60. MacCrone, *Race Attitudes*, p. 133.
61. *RCC*, I, 249.
62. Requesten or Memorials, 1787: Smook's petition, 19 Nov. 1792; C 93, Report of the Burgher Military Council; MacCrone, *Race Attitudes*, pp. 133—45.

63. In Roodezand the Rev. M.C. Vos was asked: why, if missionary work among slaves were necessary, did no minister advocate it before? The predecessors of Vos had not even instructed their own slaves in the Christian religion. (Vos, *Merkwaardig Verhaal*, p. 119.)

64. *Transactions*, I, 481—82.

65. *KP*, IV, 8—9.

66. *The Letters of Lady Anne Barnard*, p. 140.

67. Giliomee, *Eerste Britse Bewind*, p. 259.

68. W.J. Burchell, *Travels into the Interior of Southern Africa* (London, 1953), I, 29.

69. Barrow, *Travels*, I, 373.

70. *KP*, V, 255.

71. *RCC*, XI, 102.

72. G.W. Eybers, *Select Constitutional Documents illustrating South African History* (London, 1918), p. 26.

73. *RCC*, I, Court of Justice — Craig, 14 Jan. 1796. p. 304.

74. George Fredrickson, 'The rise of racial slavery in the American South and the Cape of Good Hope', unpublished paper, p. 38.

75. Freund, 'Race in the Social Structure', pp. 58—62. The quotation from the Council of Justice is on p. 58.

76. This argument is developed further in Ross, *Adam Kok's Griquas*, pp. 3—11.

77. Giliomee, *Eerste Britse Bewind*, p. 22.

78. Cited by Robert Ross, 'Griqua Power and Wealth: An Analysis of the Paradoxes of their Interrelationship', *Collected Seminar Papers on the Societies of Southern Africa* (Institute of Commonwealth Studies, 1974), IV, 15.

Glossary of foreign and technical terms

assegai	spear used by Khoikhoi and Bantu-speakers
Bastaard	in the Cape district, a person born out of wedlock; in trekboer and frontier regions, a person of mixed Khoikhoi-European or, less frequently, slave-European descent; any person accepted as a member of a Bastaard community
bandiet	'convict'; i.e., person convicted of a crime, generally non-political, by the VOC in the East and sentenced to hard labour at the Cape
bijwoner	tenant farmer
burgher	See *freeburgher*
dagga	marijuana
drostdy	administrative building of district government
freeburgher	*(vrijburger)*; person not employed by the VOC and free to own or rent land, practice certain trades and hold office.
heemraad	(pl. *heemraden*); member of the board of heemraden aiding the landdrost in the administration of a district
Heren XVII	'the Lords Seventeen'; the central board of directors of the VOC
imam	Muslim religious leader
kaptyn	Dutch term for Khoikhoi chiefs; Griqua term for chief
karos	animal skin
knecht	released company servant or more rarely a free black in the service of a freeburgher; on farms, often an overseer of Khoikhoi and slave labour
kraal	circular camp of huts; a livestock enclosure
landdrost	chief administrator and magistrate of a district
Mardijker	free black from the VOC's Eastern territories
muid	dry measure roughly equivalent to one hectolitre
Oorlam	on the Northern Frontier, a person usually of Khoikhoi descent, previously in colonial service
opgaaf	enumeration of freeburghers, free blacks and their property for tax purposes
opstal	fixed improvements on a farm

pacht	trading rights in certain commodities; monopoly rented by VOC to *pachters* in return for *pachtgeld* (lit., 'monopoly money')
plakkaat	proclamation with the force of law
predikant	minister of the Dutch Reformed Church
representant	representative
request	petition to the Council of Policy for burgher rights, manumissions, monopoly rights, etc.
transport	deed of transfer
trekboer	semi-nomadic livestock farmer
veldwachtmeester	freeburgher militia officer in rural areas; also responsible for some civil administrative duties in the division to which he was appointed
VOC	(*Verenigde Oost-Indische Compagnie*); the Dutch East India Company
volkstem	voice of the people

Index